ASSESSING
ORGANIZATIONAL
CHANGE

Wiley Series On
ORGANIZATIONAL ASSESSMENT AND CHANGE

Series Editors:
Edward E. Lawler III and
Stanley E. Seashore

ASSESSING ORGANIZATIONAL CHANGE

A Guide to Methods, Measures, and Practices

Edited by

STANLEY E. SEASHORE
Institute for Social Research
University of Michigan

EDWARD E. LAWLER III
Center for Effective Organizations
University of Southern California

PHILIP H. MIRVIS
School of Management
Boston University

CORTLANDT CAMMANN
Institute for Social Research
University of Michigan

A WILEY-INTERSCIENCE PUBLICATION

JOHN WILEY & SONS

New York · Chichester · Brisbane · Toronto · Singapore

Library of Congress Cataloging in Publication Data:

Main entry under title: 658.406
                                           A846
Assessing organizational change.

   (Wiley series on organizational assessment and change,
ISSN 0194-0120)
      Companion vol. to: Organizational assessment. c1980.
      "A Wiley-Interscience publication."
      Includes indexes.
      1. Organizational change—Evaluation—Addresses,
essays, lectures.   2. Organizational effectiveness—
Addresses, essays, lectures.   3. Organizational behavior
—Evaluation—Addresses, essays, lectures.   I. Seashore,
Stanley E. (Stanley Emanuel), 1915-   . II. Series.
HD58.8.A85   1983   658.4'06   82-24762

L.C. call no.   Dewey classification no.   L.C. card no.
ISBN 0-471-89484-2

Printed in the United States of America

10 9 8 7 6 5 4 3 2 1

Contributors

R. J. BULLOCK
Department of Psychology
University of Houston

EDWARD J. CONLON
College of Industrial Management
Georgia Institute of Technology

ROBERT A. COOKE
Northbrook, Illinois

DENNIS EPPLE
Graduate School of Industrial
  Administration
Carnegie-Mellon University

JOHN N. FEATHER
Department of Sociology
State University of New York
  at Buffalo

MARK FICHMAN
Graduate School of Industrial
  Administration
Carnegie-Mellon University

EDUARD FIDLER
Faculty of Commerce
University of British Columbia

DALE FITZGIBBONS
College of Commerce and
  Business Administration
University of Illinois at Urbana-
  Champaign

PAUL S. GOODMAN
Graduate School of Industrial
  Administration
Carnegie-Mellon University

WALTON M. HANCOCK
Department of Industrial
  and Operations Engineering
University of Michigan

MARTIN HANLON
Department of Urban Studies
Queens College–City University
  of New York

G. DOUGLAS JENKINS, JR.
College of Business
  Administration
University of Texas-Austin

JOHN R. KLESH
Strategic Personnel Research
  Studies
IBM

BARRY A. MACY
College of Business
  Administration
Texas Tech University

MICHAEL MOCH
School of Management
University of Texas at Dallas

DAVID A. NADLER
Organizational Research and
  Consultation, Inc.
New York, New York

DENNIS N. T. PERKINS
School of Organization
  and Management
Yale University

MARK F. PETERSON
Department of General Business
University of Miami

SUSAN PETERSON
Miami, Florida

DENISE M. ROUSSEAU
Department of Organizational
  Behavior
Northwestern University

Series Preface

The ORGANIZATIONAL ASSESSMENT AND CHANGE SERIES is concerned with informing and furthering contemporary debate on the effectiveness of work organizations and the quality of life they provide for their members. Of particular relevance is the adaptation of work organizations to changing social aspirations and economic constraints. There has been a phenomenal growth of interest in the quality of work life and productivity in recent years. Issues that not long ago were the quiet concern of a few academics and a few leaders in unions and management have become issues of broader public interest. They have intruded upon broadcast media prime time, lead newspaper and magazine columns, the houses of Congress, and the board rooms of both firms and unions.

A thorough discussion of what organizations should be like and how they can be improved must comprehend many issues. Some are concerned with basic moral and ethical questions—What is the responsibility of an organization to its employees?—What, after all, is a "good job"?—How should it be decided that some might benefit from and others pay for gains in the quality of work life?—Should there be a public policy on the matter? Yet others are concerned with the strategies and tactics of bringing about changes in organizational life, the advocates of alternative approaches being numerous, vocal, and controversial; and still others are concerned with the task of measurement and assessment on grounds that the choices to be made by leaders, the assessment of consequences, and the bargaining of equities must be informed by reliable, comprehensive, and relevant information of kinds not now readily available.

The WILEY SERIES ON ORGANIZATIONAL ASSESSMENT AND CHANGE is concerned with all aspects of the debate on how organizations should be managed, changed, and controlled. It includes books on organizational effectiveness, and the study of organizational changes that represent new approaches to organization design and process. The volumes in the series have in common a concern with work organizations, a focus on change and the dynamics of change, an assumption that diverse social and personal interests need to be taken into account in discussions of organizational effectiveness, and a view that concrete cases and quantitative data are essential ingredients in a lucid debate. As such, these books consider a broad but integrated set of issues and ideas.

They are intended to be read by managers, union officials, researchers, consultants, policy makers, students, and others seriously concerned with organizational assessment and change.

EDWARD E. LAWLER III
STANLEY E. SEASHORE

Los Angeles, California
Ann Arbor, Michigan
April, 1983

Preface

This book is about assessing organizational change. It is a progress report on the results of a multiyear large-scale effort to develop measures, methods, and practices to measure change. To a significant degree it is a how-to book that contains a wide range of measurement instruments, observation techniques, and analytical methods. It is complementary to an earlier book in this series, *Organizational Assessment: Perspectives on the Measurement of Organizational Behavior and Quality of Working Life,* which treats the strategic decisions that need to be made in organizational assessment.

The book is for people who are seriously interested in the study of organizations and organizational change. It is intended to be a contribution to the scientific literature, but the material covered is relevant to people—both inside and outside of organizations—who are concerned with implementing and evaluating planned change efforts. Thus scholars and researchers from many different persuasions and disciplines should find it of value. In addition, professionals in organizations who are concerned with gathering information for diagnostic change or assessment purposes should find it useful.

The material in this book reflects the history of our interest in writing it. It is a product of the Quality of Work Program of the Institute for Social Research, University of Michigan. This program is concerned with assessing planned change projects in organizations. All four of us were involved in the creation of that program. From our initial need to evaluate certain change projects, we began to attend more generally to issues of organizational assessment and measurement.

When the program began, in the early 1970s, we turned to the literature for instruments and procedures that would help us assess a complex series of planned change efforts in organizations. We found, along with some useful guidelines and tested procedures, many voids and deficiencies. The examples found tended, with very few exceptions, to rest upon single methods and on limited or unsuitable models of organizational behavior and effectiveness. In addition, they failed to consider the measurement of change over time and seldom mentioned the issues of field practice in obtaining the data. We wanted to measure change, with multiple methods, with some degree of conceptual integration, and under conditions involving extensive collaboration by people in the organizations. We set out to accumulate and assess our experiences, document our procedures, and make them available to others.

In attempting to design our own assessment approach, we quickly realized that the range of activities, methods, and issues we needed to consider was far beyond our own knowledge. We therefore turned to others for ideas and inputs. This book, like the program itself, is the product of many individuals from diverse disciplines and orientations. It is to their credit they were willing to come together and set aside many of the disciplinary blinders in order to develop the measures reported in this volume. Their behavior is testimony to the view that the effective study of organizations is a venture that can attract outstanding scholars from many disciplines. It also highlights the point that complex organizational problems require inputs from multiple disciplines. Special thanks to the many individuals who aided us with the development of these measures and whose work forms the basis for this volume.

A number of institutions and funding agencies have provided critical support for the work. Primary support for the Quality of Work Program at the University of Michigan has come from the Ford Foundation and the Economic Development Administration of the U.S. Department of Commerce. Special thanks go to Basil Whiting and Louis Phillips for their support. The support of the Institute for Social Research is also gratefully acknowledged; it is one of the few places in the world where this activity could have been carried out on this scale. Thanks go to the research support staff at the Institute, and especially to Gary Herline, Sherry Nelson, Sue Macher, and Carole Barnett.

STANLEY E. SEASHORE
EDWARD E. LAWLER III
PHILIP H. MIRVIS
CORTLANDT CAMMANN

Ann Arbor, Michigan
Los Angeles, California
Boston, Massachusetts
Ann Arbor, Michigan
April 1983

Contents

PART ONE

BACKGROUND AND APPROACH

The three chapters in this section give a strategic perspective on an approach for assessing organizations and organizational change. Most of the later chapters deal with specifics of conception, field practice, and interpretive procedures that relate to different facets of organizational change. For these to be properly appreciated with respect to their roles in a broader assessment plan and to their strengths and limitations, the reader needs to know about the broader plan, the context from which it arose, and the approach to fitting the plan to a particular organizational context.

Chapter 1 begins by linking the research program with its historical context—the quality of work life movement and the thrust toward societal experimentation. Then it reports the aims and purposes of the program as it was originally delineated to funding sources and sponsors, as it was represented to participating organizations and unions, and as it was aspired to by the many contributors to this volume. Some guidelines follow for choosing measures and for interpreting them for the purposes of documenting the results of change programs, tracking realms of organizational theory, research, and practice. A roster of field studies where the measures and methods have been used up to the present time is provided, with comments on some of the practical dilemmas encountered in their application. The chapter concludes by highlighting the meta-theoretical and methodological issues in assessing organizational change: questions regarding universality and uniqueness of organizational phenomena, the feasibility of detecting causality in change efforts, and the capacity to model and measure quality of work life and the effectiveness of work organizations. Readers are left with an appreciation of the Promethean aspirations and Procrustean concerns of the overall research program.

Chapter 2 provides a global map of the research program and expresses its aims in terms of theory, measurement, evaluation, and the researcher's role. It is asserted that assessments should be based upon some encompassing theoretical model or models of organizational behavior and change. The chapter reviews two "small-scale" models used to guide the research program. One links criteria of quality of work life and organizational effectiveness to the characteristics and behavior of individuals, groups, and the work organization—representing organizational behavior as multilevel and multivariate. That model also incorporates features of the organization's environment—including affiliated unions—and acknowledges systemic connectedness among the variables represented. The other model links changes in an organization's behavior to phases in a change program. These phases include start-up of the program, implementation and adoption of interventions, institutionalization of the change, and its diffusion.

The authors contend that assessments "should rest upon information obtained in some describable and replicable way" and call for assessments based upon multiple measures of organizational phenomena through multiple measurement methods. They then describe the array of instruments and procedures used in the research program, considerations in their selection for use, and means for establishing their validity. The authors review criteria of internal and external validity for evaluations of organizational change programs and the rationale for development of an adaptive experimental design that features longitudinal measurement, post hoc comparison units, and multivariate statistical analyses in an effort to increase the validity of conclusions drawn about the results of a program. The chapter concludes with a review of the strengths and limitations of independent assessment in organizational change programs.

The final chapter in this section continues the discussion of the research role and describes its implementation at a research site. The authors argue against the arbitrary imposition of the researcher's own behavioral norms and assert that the effective and ethical fulfillment of the research role is "realized by the purposeful and public creation of roles and role relations that serve to emphasize mutual dependencies and control." They review the diverse roles and interests of participants in a study and the sources of role ambiguity and conflict that can confound role relationships. Next, they describe the steps taken to create and clarify the assessment role, to build role relations and codify responsibilities, and to manage role conflicts as they emerge.

CHAPTER ONE

Issues in Assessing Organizational Change

STANLEY E. SEASHORE

The research enterprise initiated in 1972 known as the Michigan Quality of Work Program (MQWP) has had two facets. One is concerned with the assessment of a set of demonstration projects aimed toward the improvement of the quality of work life (QWL) and of the economic performance of work organizations. These projects thus far have included a number of joint union–management QWL efforts aimed toward system-wide improvements and also a number of change projects of a more focused nature—for example, focused upon new plant start-ups, compensation, communication, and information management—initiated by a management in collaboration with the employees. Results of some of these cases have been reported in books and journal articles, and other reports are in preparation. The second facet of the program—the subject matter of this book—has been the development and testing of methods that may be employed in describing the structure and functioning of organizations and for detecting and documenting changes that occur over time.

The assessment side of this program reflects the environment in which the program came into being. It has not been an autonomous intellectual exercise in theory building, although some contributions of that kind have emerged. It has not been directed toward the invention or perfection of novel methods for measurement, although a few side benefits of that type have accrued. Instead, the work aims to extract maximum knowledge and learning from complex social experiments and to provide credi-

This chapter draws extensively from "The Michigan Quality of Work Program: Issues in Measurement, Assessment, and Outcome Evaluation," in *Perspectives on Organization Design and Behavior,* eds. A. Van de Ven and W. A. Joyce (New York: Wiley—Interscience, 1981).

3

ble information of sufficiently inclusive scope for the evaluation of their costs and benefits.

There are key words and phrases in the foregoing sentences. By *complex social experiments,* we direct attention to multifaceted efforts for purposeful change in real-life settings, unprotected from the vagaries of environmental conditions. By *learning,* we refer not to intellectual mastery or discovery on the part of the researcher, but to behavioral, attitudinal, and value changes on the part of individual actors and to systemic changes on the part of organizations that tend toward maximizing benefits and minimizing costs for all concerned. Campbell captures this theme in "Reforms as Experiments," as does Lawler in "Adaptive Experiments: An Approach to Organizational Behavior Research"[1,2] By the words *credible information,* we invoke aspirations to adduce information of such scope, cogency, and reliability so as to command the attention of the disbeliever, the hostile critic, and the initially inattentive. The actual achievements, of course, are less grand than such aspirations suggest, but progress can be reported in learning how to assess organizational change. In this chapter we will discuss the background of the program and introduce some general themes that guided the assessment work and that provide a needed context for understanding the chapters that consider specific measurement approaches.

A HISTORICAL NOTE

The Michigan program arose in the context of the quality of work life movement that was beginning to assert itself in the United States in the late 1960s. Some signal events occurred. A report issued by the U.S. Department of Health, Education and Welfare depicted a variety of ills associated with suboptimum working conditions, and it generated much controversy and gained public attention.[3] In 1971 a conference called New Directions in the World of Work was held, which was stimulated by the Upjohn Institute and largely underwritten by the Ford foundation. This brought together about 40 influential representatives of management, labor, government, and academia to debate the feasibility and means for achieving significant changes in the prevailing quality of work life. The International Conference on the Quality of Working Life followed, which was again supported by the Ford Foundation and organized by Louis Davis of the University of California at Los Angeles and Albert Cherns of Loughbrough University. Aside from the influential two-volume report of the proceedings, this conference led to the formation of an international network of people concerned with the topic and the determination by the Ford Foundation and U.S. Department of Commerce to stimulate some demonstration experiments of significant scale, high visibility, and ample assessment. The Institute for Social Research (ISR) was asked to assume a leading role in planning the entire project and to address itself to the task of developing and applying assessment procedures. Our original proposal to the supporting agencies set forth the following objectives:

> We conceive of the overall objectives to be the public trial and demonstration of a variety of ways through which management and labor unions may apply social science knowledge to accomplish significant improvement in the conditions of work within an organization.* To meet this objective, the changes need to be evaluated against the broadest possible range of considerations reflecting the interests of the employees, of the firm's management, of the employees' union, and of the public. We conceive of the more specific objectives of the evaluation phase of the program as follows:
>
> 1. To describe the sites and their initial states and contexts in terms that are necessary for later interpretation of the changes that may occur and for evaluating factors contributing to or inhibiting changes of various kinds.
> 2. To describe the nature of the interventions undertaken and the course of their development at each site.
> 3. To measure as best as possible the kinds and degrees of changes that occur, or do not occur, at each site with special reference to:
>
> Changes of an economic or operational nature concerning the firm—for example, changes relating to productivity, cost performance, quality of product or service, maintenance of facilities and effective staff, process innovation rates, and the like.
>
> Changes in the attitudes, beliefs, and motivations of members of the firm (at all levels) as these may bear upon the effectiveness of the firm as an economic unit and its effectiveness in meeting the interests, needs, and preferences of its members—for example, satisfactions, willingness to remain with the enterprise, opportunities for career fulfillment, effectiveness of communications and coordination of activity, maintenance of health and safety, and the like.
>
> Changes in the features of the relationship between management and the labor union that bear upon the effective resolution of issues concerning the union and its members.
>
> Changes in any other features of the site organization, or its members, or its context that may in a particular case appear to be important, and feasible of measurement, as part of the intent to be inclusive in assessment. Examples of such "special" topics of measurement are: community relations, health and safety of members, rates of innovation and adaptation, problem-solving capabilities, communication effectiveness, and the like.
>
> 4. To endeavor to understand the manner and degree to which the various changes arise from the activities of the intervention program.

---

*For a description of the "variety of ways," see Drexler and Lawler,[4] Goodman,[5] and Macy[6] in regard to joint labor–management efforts; see Lawler,[7,8] Nadler, Mirvis, and Cammann,[9] and Lawler, Mirvis, Clarkson, and Randall[10] with respect to some other change efforts studied in the program.

5. To endeavor to draw conclusions and suggested courses of action for those who may later wish to emulate one or another of the observed program plans.

6. To assess in the context of these field trials the adequacy of concepts, procedures, and instruments used in evaluation and to suggest ways to make the instruments efficiently and effectively usable by others.

7. To produce the basic data from these field trials in a form suitable for use by us or others who may need to pursue inquiries of a theoretical, methodological, or operational sort lying beyond the limits of this proposal; that is, to preserve and make usable the information from the trials.

8. To produce data and materials from these projects that will help nonprofessionals understand the results of the projects and that will facilitate work place improvements elsewhere.

FRAMEWORK FOR CHOOSING MEASURES

In the foregoing, the reader will not discern any commitment to a particular conceptual framework or theoretical approach. There is good reason for this. The task was defined by us with practical reference, not conceptual neatness. The value framework, while generally humanistic and oriented ultimately to the welfare of individuals, embraces the interests of workers, managers, union officers, the public, and others; the individual interests of these groups are often divergent. The substantive orientation emphasizes topical breadth and inclusiveness rather than focus; the current roster of variables has over 1000 entries ranging alphabetically from the *a*'s (attitudes, accident rates) through the *g*'s and *h*'s (groups and grievances, holidays, and hand tools) through the *p*'s (profit margins, piece rates) to the *t*'s, *v*'s, and *y*'s (technological changes, volume of output, yields), although there are no *z*'s yet. The entities for assessment span the hierarchy from individuals to groups, to larger functional segments of organizations, to entire organizations, and to surrounding communities.

The choice of concepts and operational variables for inclusion has not been random. Four principal guidelines have been employed in roughly the following order or priority:

1. Preference for concepts representing results, that is, states or directions of change that are thought to be valued for their intrinsic worth by some segment of the interested parties.

2. Inclusion of concepts and operational variables judged to be potentially relevant to the inducement of, or understanding of, such results.

3. Preference for concepts and variables that exploit contemporary theoretical and empirical resources that might aid in understanding the results, their causation, and the contingencies associated with variance in them.

4. Preference for concepts and operational variables thought to allow comparisons among the organizations studied and within each organization over time.

These four guidelines will be elaborated in the paragraphs that follow, but before we do that we need to mention some lesser considerations that will not be elaborated on here. For example, preferance was given to concepts that can be measured in ways that are seen as valid by a wide range of observers. In addition, some measures have been included simply because they are familiar to and are expected by potential users of the resulting data. Some were included because we attempted to invent an improved measurement method or test a novel hypothesis; some, because the data could be collected without cost or risk and might prove useful to some analyst; and some, because they were requested by an interested party—perhaps the consultant-intervenor at a site. Also, numerous concepts of importance have been omitted simply because we knew no way to obtain the information while still staying within bounds of ethics, validity, reliability, and cost.

The original proposal to the sponsor specified some of the gross categories of possible results, or outcomes, of interest that might follow from a program of organizational change. Some are primarily relevant at the individual level of analysis, such as security, health, or satisfaction. Others, however, are primarily relevant at the level of organizational or institutional analysis, for example, systemic adaptability or economic viability. A "valued outcome," of course, and the priorities among such results are a matter of opinion. The relevant opinion is, first, that of some organizational actor, and second, that of some analyst or interpreter. Thus, in a given organizational setting, a reduced rate of absences for reasons of illness might be regarded by some as an important, intrinsically valued outcome. It might be regarded by others as an indicator of, or causal contributor to, organizational viability, or perhaps it might be regarded as merely a side effect of some technological change. Some results are positively valued by one segment of the organizational population and negatively by another. A rise in individual productivity may be valued by the management but not by employees if it is obtained at the cost of additional strain.

There was, therefore, a broad mandate to identify and measure concepts relevant to individuals, groups, subunits of the organization, the organization as a whole, and the involved union or unions. Those of prime importance represent the effectiveness of the organization and the quality of work life of employed personnel.[11–13] These include abstract concepts, such as adaptability and flexibility, conflict and cooperation, welfare and well-being, and specifiable states, including grievance rates, productivity, and satisfaction levels. Given the diverse preferences of groups and individuals for one or another of these outcome conditions, our strategy was to measure primarily those likely to have an effect on or be affected by a change project, to make public our measurement operations and findings, and to invite comment from all concerned as to their interpretation and value.

Explanatory Variables

Explanatory and causal variables associated with outcome variables enter into the assessment plan for a particular organization on theoretical or empirical grounds, or on grounds of some plausible, atheoretical, common-sense rationale. For example, the degree of change in work-group cohesiveness might be assessed for any one of several reasons. For example, there might be an effort to increase group cohesiveness in the expectation that specified desirable results will then follow; or an intended outcome may be considered contingent upon the presence of group cohesiveness so that measures of low cohesiveness would help explain a failure to achieve the desired result; or an increment in group cohesiveness might be regarded by some as an intrinsically valued condition. Similarly, a prevalent view exists among production supervisors and managers that gains of some sort, for example, increased productivity, are often accompanied by offsetting costs or losses of some other kind, for example, in materials wastage or product quality. In such an instance, the measurement of potential collateral conditions and changes may be undertaken in order to allow evaluation of the set of interdependent changes.

Theoretical Input

The measurement program described here is not dominated by any single theoretical system, but it does incorporate—eclectically—a number of contemporary theories of proven or probable validity. The list of such incorporated ideas is quite extensive, including theories at the individual level relating to perceptions of equity, the role of expectations in motivation theory, the existence of a need hierarchy, the effects of participation, the differential effects of alternative forms of control, and so on. At the group level, theories are employed relating to cohesiveness, boundaries, size, and normative integration. Concepts at the level of complex organizational units include the traditional concepts arising from Weberian theory concerning intergroup relations and the fit of formal structure to technological constraints. In these ways the approach to organizational assessment is richly imbued with theoretical orientations, but it is not intentionally constrained by any one. Some other theories employed are the Hackman and Oldham theory of optimal job design,[14] the French's theory concerning the sources of stress in work environments,[15] and the theory of Tannenbaum concerning the distribution of control in hierarchical systems.[16]

Comparisons across Sites

Comparability as a consideration in the choice of concepts and measures arises from two factors: first, the intended longitudinal and change orientation, which requires preference for measures that are likely to remain comparable over time; and second, preference for measures that are not unique to a given organization but that allow comparison of states and changes among organizations. The first consideration is not as self-evident as it may at first seem, for many commonly used measures of organizational characteristics are vulnerable to recalibration with changing circumstances, or are so embedded in a set of associated interacting variables that the meaning of any one may in time be altered or even reversed in its interpretive implication.[17] The second consideration rests upon a belief that comparison among cases is just as important as is understanding the uniqueness of a given case when searching for valid generalizations about organizational change and the suitability of alternative strategies and tactics for inducing desired changes.

There are, of course, severe limits to comparability among organizations. We conceived of a hierarchy of generality of concepts associated with a scale of comparability. The volume of shoes produced by one firm is hardly comparable to the volume of research reports produced by another. But more general concepts—for example, rate of change or direction of change in volume—may well be comparable. Similarly, an index of "direct participation in day-to-day decisions" may well be comparable among organizations even though any single component of such an index may not be directly comparable. Different organizations may elect alternative means for achieving the same degree of member participation. The assessment of the comparability of organizations is viewed as a matter that can be approached empirically. By attempting to achieve and validate comparability, we hope to contribute to some enhanced understanding of the degree and means through which interorganizational comparisons may be made.

ANALYTIC AND INTERPRETATIVE STRATEGIES

Analytic and interpretive strategies of various kinds are implied by the foregoing description of the guidelines for inclusion of concepts and their operational variations. The main considerations are the "level" of the analyses and the analytic role assigned to variables.

We have assumed that different purposes will require analyses at different levels. To understand the impact of some intervention upon individuals, analyses of individual-level data (treating each person as a "case") is highly desirable, even though valuable and valid clues or confirming evidence may be found in aggregated population statistics or in cross-comparisons among work groups. Similarly, to ascertain whether a change in system productive output arises from system properties (e.g., increased rate of capital investment or reduction in the available market), the analyses should be primarily at the level of the sociotechnical system as a whole, even though clues and confirming evidence may be sought at the levels of specific subunits (e.g., where the investments were concentrated) or at the level of individuals (e.g., individual work motivations). Ideally, the data should be obtained in such a form that analyses may be multilevel in character without predetermining the level about which interpretations are to be made.

Similarly, we have avoided the constraints of relying upon any single conceptual model in which a variable is assigned some fixed role in analysis or interpretation. The discussion of "group cohesiveness," for example, affirms that the same variable may be treated, in different contexts, as an independent variable, a dependent variable, or in a contingent or moderating relationship to other variables. The analytic use of a variable is assumed to be independent of any inherent quality of the construct itself; indeed, preference has been given to variables known or believed to have utility in several analytic roles.

Critiques of Approach

Controversy has been elicited by the preceding approach to the assessment of organizations—for valid reasons. One set of objections concerns the basic theoretical assumptions of this approach, with some critics challenging the pluralism of the theories, others the predominance of "traditional" theoretical streams. Still others question the focus on "outcome explanation"; others question the elaboration of complex, contingent, causal schemes. Our attempt to steer a "middle course" can thus be viewed as either prudent or ill conceived. Another set of objections centers on our aspirations for comparability in assessment, with some arguing we are too "grounded" in the assessment of the change program to develop generalizable conclusions. Others argue that we are too "abstracted" from the situation to assess the meaning of events in a particular case. A related objection is that we do too much (or too little) theory testing versus theory building. In this position, we might be viewed as either "balanced" or "fence straddlers."

A final set of objections focuses on both the epistemology and practicality of our analytic and interpretive strategies. Some vocal critics have correctly noted that the approach is at odds with the contemporary thrust toward less reductionist, more "organic" and "molar" conceptions of organization life. Others have correctly noted that it lacks the "rigor" of classical scientific experimentation. Some have observed that it is impractical to "assess everything that is relevant." Some have stated that the approach involves factors of complexity, cost, and intrusiveness that are not supportable in the general practice of organizational and change assessment. Still others have argued that we do not do "enough." The next chapter of this volume details the theoretical assumptions, comparative methods, and analytic and interpretive strategies employed in this approach. The bulk of the text examines them in detail. Suffice it to say here that a close reading of these chapters reveals our preferences and biases. Our hope is that improved theory and practice may emerge from the criticism, debate, and controversy over their contents.

APPLICATIONS OF THE APPROACH

The assessment portion of the Michigan Quality of Work Program was conceived and designed expressly for the purpose of aiding the evaluation of several specific sets of demonstration projects. From the beginning, it was thought that the largest number of change projects would involve union–management QWL change efforts. Much of the initial funding and interest was in this type of project. The assessment program has, in fact, been applied to eight joint union–management quality of work life projects (see Table 1-1).* The organizations studied varied considerably in their sizes, sectors, and technologies. In size, the range is from organizational units of less than 50 people to those with over 1000. The technologies range widely and include coal mining, metal fabrication, postsurgical health care, engineering design, wood fabrication, public transport, and others. Organizations are in the governmental, profit-making, and private, nonprofit sectors. Not all of these projects received the same assessment, however, as some were in progress while the assessment plan and instruments were in development, and others required omission or modification of some parts of the overall assessment plan.

In addition to these eight instances of application, various components of the assessment program have been employed in other situations—by us and by others. Our other applications, which are listed in Table 1-2, include a tool and die factory, a metropolitan bank system, a ball-bearing plant, a furniture factory, a pharmaceutical factory, and others. French- and Spanish-language versions of some instruments have been used by others in foreign countries.

Issues in Application

Some observations from our experiences in applying the assessment methods that are described in this book need to be stated before we

---

* Principal support for these projects has come from the organizations studied, the Ford Foundation, and the following federal agencies: U.S. Department of Commerce, U.S. Department of Labor, National Institute of Mental Health, and the National Center for Productivity and Quality of Work Life (see Table 1-1).

Table 1-1 Joint Labor–Management QWL Projects

Organization Name or Function	Union(s)	Start Year	Study Team	Assessment Funding Source(s)
1. Rushton Coal Mine	United Mine Workers of America	1973	P. Goodman[a] E. Lawler C. Cammann	NCPQOW; The Ford Foundation
2. Bolivar (Beatrice Foods; Harman Int'l. Indust.)	United Auto Workers	1973	B. Macy[a] G. Ledford P. Mirvis	The Ford Foundation; U.S. DOC
3. Tennessee Valley Authority	TVA Engineering Association (TVAEA) and Office and Professional Employees International Union (OPIEU)	1974	B. Macy[a] A. Nurick M. Moch	The Ford Foundation; U.S. DOC
4. Food company	International Bakery, Confectionery, and Tobacco Workers Union	1974	E. Lawler[a] M. Moch[a]	The Company
5. Hospital	New York State Nurses Assn. (SNA), and National Union of Hospital and Health Care Employees	1975	E. Lawler[a] D. Nadler[a]	NIMH
6. Wood fabrication	International Woodworkers of America	1976	E. Lawler[a] J. Drexler[a]	The Company
7. Public Transportation Authority	Transportation Employees Union	1976	C. Cammann[a] D. Berg L. Laughlin J. LaPointe	NIMH
8. Municipal government	American Federation of State, County, and Municipal Employees	1977	E. Lawler[a] J. Walsh* D. Tracey	U.S. DOL

[a] Site coordinators.

Table 1-2   Other Change Projects

Organization	Type of Change	Start Year	Study Team	Funding Source(s)
1. Tool & Die Company	New compensation system	1973	G. Jenkins[a] E. Lawler	U.S. DOL; Company
2. National Bank	New information system	1974	C. Cammann[a] D. Nadler[a]	U.S. DOL; U.S. DOC
3. A pet food company	New plant design	1974	E. Lawler[a] G. Jenkins P. Mirvis	Company
4. A ball-bearing firm	New compensation system	1974	E. Lawler[a] G. Jenkins	U.S. DOL
5. Printing company	New information system	1975	P. Mirvis[a] E. Lawler[a] J. Kane M. Marks	U.S. DOL; Company
6. Pharmaceutical company	New plant design	1975	D. Perkins[a] R. Nieva[a] E. Lawler	U.S. DOL
7. Appliance manufacturing company	New plant design	1976	R. Bullock[a] E. Lawler	Company
8. Furniture manufacturing company	New compensation system	1977	R. Bullock[a] C. Cammann E. Lawler	Company
9. Manufacturing company	New compensation system	1977	R. Bullock[a] E. Lawler	Company

[a]Site coordinator(s).

present the methods. These points are made to set the context for reading later chapters; we will return to them in the concluding chapter.

First, to assess the results of a change effort and intervening and causal factors contributing to those results requires an assessment of considerable scope, cost, and intrusion. In fact, the full array of field procedures has been applied in only one project, which was characterized by ample funding, compliant and interested organization members, tolerance for observations at work and in meetings, and ready consent for access to organizational records and information about identified individuals. Because of the magnitude of a "full assessment," the general practice has been to make selective use of a limited number of program components, with an eye to their relevance for assessing the change program, their applicability to local conditions, and their value in a cost-benefit calculus.

Second, assessment requires a very hospitable research site. Such sites are not born. They are developed by considerable preparatory work on the part of the researchers who need to educate local personnel to the aims and intentions of the assessment effort and to establish guidelines for the ethical conduct of the research. Considerable "legwork" is also involved in working at the sites to establish or improve upon ongoing measurement operations of, say, productivity and quality indicators. In practice, this has proved feasible at all sites. It has even been locally beneficial at some sites where the firm has needed better ongoing measurement of key factors and has become educated to their uses.

Nonetheless, there have been instances in which sites objected to the scope and intrusiveness of the assessment plan and exercised their rights in the research contract to veto the use of certain measures. In other instances, consultants objected to some measurement plans. Resolution of all such conflicts of interest have been amicable, constructive, and public, though not without points of tension.[18] In other cases, however, it has proven infeasible to use aspects of the measurement program for logistical reasons. For instance, in the assessment of the surgical ward of a hospital, it was discovered that personnel were drawn from many functional departments and were frequently scheduled to work in other parts of the hospital. Under these conditions a questionnaire assessment of "members" of the unit was inappropriate, and the researchers instead relied on direct observations.

Third, assessment requires the collection and synthesis of diverse kinds of data from diverse sources. We have found that multiple measures and alternative information sources frequently prove their worth, sometimes by allowing strong interpretations of otherwise dubious data or by preventing overinterpretation of the data at hand. Another practice has been to collect objective, subjective, and phenomenological data ranging from "hard" data to participants' somewhat discrepant reports about "objective" conditions and events, to data intended to capture the unique "reality" experienced by each participant or class of participants. Such data serve distinct analytic and interpretive purposes, and thus are complementary rather than competitive. In practice, however, assessors have often ended up concentrating on a single type of data. Thus, we have frequently had to rely on assessment teams that bring together persons with different methodological perspectives and substantive skills within an expansive assessment role.

Fourth, assessment also invites longitudinal measurement and the use—where feasible—of comparison units. In practice, however, we have studied projects of differing durations and with uncertain beginnings and undefinable ends that make the meaning of preintervention and postintervention assessments less clear. In addition, we have been unable and unwilling to impose controls for extraexperimental events, such as the introduction of new personnel, work technologies, or organizational and union policies. Finally, in only a few of the projects have we been able to make effective use of an external "control" group for comparative purposes.

BASIC ISSUES IN ORGANIZATIONAL ASSESSMENT

The preceding issues in application are of an operational sort. There are other issues relating to conception, methodology, and the like that will be examined in subsequent chapters. There are also broader features of the task of assessing and evaluating organization change—implicit in our conceptual and theoretical framework but common to all such approaches—that need to be mentioned here so that the reader can keep this in mind while considering the specific measurement approaches.

Three basic issues have been highlighted by our experience in attempting the assessment of organizations over periods of change. These concern the validity of the comparative method, the explication of causes, and the models of the effectiveness to be employed.

The method of comparison is fundamental to the traditional canons of research on organizations. To understand the state of an organization, one must compare it with other organizations. To understand change, one must compare prior states with later states. To understand causation, one must compare potential causal factors and their links to different outcomes. This image or paradigm of organizational research is being challenged on grounds that each organization is unique in its input of energy, information, and purpose and therefore correspondingly unique in its internal processes and outcomes. Such uniqueness can arise either from sheer complexity, meaning that combinations of inputs are so numerous as to preclude replication, or from conceptions of biological aberration, meaning that small variations in inputs may, in accommodating environments, be sustained rather than suppressed. The statistical view is not the same as the biological view. The approach of the Michigan Organizational Assessment Program is based on the assumption that organizations are fundamentally the same as to identifiable and quantifiable inputs, organizational processes, and consequential outcomes. This is of course an hypothesis, not an immutable fact. The opposed view emphasizes the emergent new forms of organizational input, process, and outcome rather than the mere statistical range of variation that provides a semblance of uniqueness. Miller has addressed the issue of identity (as compared with analogy) of the structure and processes of living systems.[19] Herbst has attempted to show that uniqueness in living systems may occur.[20] Contributors too numerous to mention argue that an individual's purpose may intrude upon organizational processes and become an integral part of an organization.

The net result of this is that the method of comparison in organizational studies is challenged, and nowhere is the challenge more evident than in the reductionist and decomposing strategy that has been emphasized, although not exclusively, in the assessment approach described in this book. Our choice is not a matter of dogma or philosophical belief, but it is, rather, a matter of pressing to the limit the notion that understanding measureable components of organizational behavior will serve to explicate both the uniformities and the uniqueness of organizational phenomena.

The explication of causes and the potential for influencing results that may accompany such explications is surely the justification for efforts to describe, assess, and evaluate organizations as they change. The complexity of organizations makes it unlikely that significant insights into causal processes will occur from casual, unguided observations. There is a need for some model or theory of change processes. Some conception of organizational effectiveness is needed that can be regarded as defining the results desired from change. The approach to these matters exemplified by the Michigan Organizational Assessment Program has two significant aspects both matters of choice in the presence of attractive alternatives.

As to causation—a slippery concept at best—the choice is to work with a large number of causal systems, each of manageable and therefore limited scope. The hope and expectation is that small theories, empirically validated, will in time become additive and connected. The imagery includes a network of variables hierarchically arranged so that each variable regarded as an outcome is supplied with multiple chains of potential causation; much of the outcome variance—but never all of it—can be predicted from a limited roster of prior descriptive variables. This is, of course, a linear model, and it is one that assumes some degree of indeterminacy. It is also a mechanistic model in the sense that there is no allowance for the possibility that "new" causal variables may come into being or that unprecedented, unique causal systems may emerge.[21] There are alternative kinds of models of causation. It is likely that others will display, as ours does, features of dubious assumption, logical fallacy, and operational difficulty.

As to a model of effectiveness, we have chosen scope over clarity. The valuing of results is left in the public domain, with each interested party entitled, even obligated, to choose the results of importance from his or her frame of reference and to weigh the results in their combinations. The domain of results is defined by three overlapping but distinguishable areas: (1) exportable outputs of the work system, including such factors as the volume, quality, timeliness, and cost of the goods or services; (2) systemic integrity of the organization with reference to its capacity to regulate its internal processes through the allocation of resources provision of coordination, strain management, and the like; and (3) adaptive capacities of the organization as represented primarily in its means for information management and problem solving. An effective organization, in this view, is one that sustains its environment, maintains its own operational capacities, and regulates the relationships of the organization with its changing environment. Plainly, this is a model of effectiveness that is appallingly complex. Other models exist that also serve the aims of understanding organizational states and changes.

Our guiding ideas about "quality of work life" have been similarly complex. Among the factors considered have been those relating immediately to the employees' mental and physical well-being at work, but consideration is given also to the following: (1) well-being off the job, in the context of family and community life, recreation, and the like, as these are affected by the conditions of employment, and (2) well-being over the employees' life span, with consideration for the likely delayed effects of present employment upon self-development, career enhancement, and upon future health and well-being. While QWL is thus defined by the outcome or consequences of employment, the causal factors of interest are within the work setting—for example, organizational characteristics and policies, job and technology characteristics, experienced physical and social factors, rewards and protective benefits, and the like.

REFERENCES

1. Campbell, D. T. Reforms as experiments. *American Psychologist,* 1969, **24,** 3, 409–429.
2. Lawler, E. E. III. Adaptive experiments: An approach to organizational behavior research. *Academy of Management Review,* 1977, **2**(10), 576–585.
3. O'Toole, J. (Ed.). *Work in America.* Cambridge: MIT Press.
4. Drexler, J. A., & Lawler, E. E. III. A union–management cooperative project to improve the quality of work life. *Journal of Applied Behavioral Science,* 1977, **13,** 3, 373–387.
5. Goodman, P. S. *Assessing organizational change: The Rushton experiment.* New York: Wiley-Interscience, 1979.
6. Macy, B. A. Progress report on the Bolivar quality of work experiment. *Personnel Journal,* 1979, **20,** 8, 527–559.
7. Lawler, E. E. The new plant revolution. *Organizational Dynamics,* 1978, **6,** 3–12.
8. Lawler, E. E. *Pay and organization development.* Reading, MA: Addison-Wesley, 1979.
9. Nadler, D. A., Mirvis, P. H., & Cammann, C. The ongoing feedback system. *Organizational Dynamics,* 1976, **20,** 63–80.
10. Lawler, E. E., Mirvis, P. H., Clarkson, W. & Randall, L. Measuring the quality of work life in Graphic Controls. *Management Review,* in press.
11. Biasatti, L. L., & Martin, J. E. A measure of the quality of union–management relations. *Journal of Applied Psychology,* 1979, **64,** 4, 387–408.
12. Glich, W., Mirvis, P. H., & Harder, D. Union satisfaction and participation. *Industrial Relations,* 1977, **16,** 2, 145–151.
13. Seashore, S. E. Assessing the quality of working life: The U.S. experience. *Labour and Society,* 1976, **1,** 2, 69–79.
14. Hackman, J. R., & Oldham, G. *Work redesign.* Reading: Addison-Wesley, 1980.
15. French, J. R. P. The social environment and mental health. *Journal of Social Issues,* 1963, **19,** 4, 39–56.
16. Tannenbaum, A. S. *Control in organizations.* New York: McGraw-Hill, 1968.

17. Golembiewsky, R. T., Billingsly, K., & Yenger, S. Measuring change and persistence in human affairs: Types of change generated by OD design. *Journal of Applied Behavioral Science,* 1975, **12,** 3, 133–157.

18. Mirvis, P. H., & Seashore, S. E. Being ethical in organizational research. *American Psychologist,* 1979, **35,** 9, 766–780.

19. Miller, J. G. *Living systems.* New York: McGraw-Hill, 1978.

20. Mitchell, T. R. Organizational behavior. In M. R. Rosenzweig & L. W. Porter (Eds.), *Annual review of psychology.* Palo Alto, CA: Annual Reviews, 1979.

21. Herbst, P. G. *Behavioural worlds: The study of single cases.* London: Tavistock Publications, 1970.

CHAPTER TWO

Organizational Change and the Conduct of Assessment Research

EDWARD E. LAWLER III, DAVID A. NADLER, AND PHILIP H. MIRVIS

Available literature and lore suggest many ways in which organizations can be purposefully changed with a view toward increasing their effectiveness and to better the quality of work life of the members. Among these ways are the enrichment of jobs, formation of autonomous work groups, introduction of improved incentive payment plans, introduction of participative decision-making processes, formation of quality control circles, and the like. Some ways involve creating a new initiating structure—for example, joint union–management committees—without specifying the forms of change activity that might follow. All of these approaches to change have their advocates and all are supported by some favorable evidence, as well as enthusiastic opinions. All are known, also, to fail in some instances or to produce results of disappointing scope and significance. Not enough is known about why and how such well-conceived and well-meaning change efforts may fail or succeed.[1]

The Michigan Quality of Work Program (MQWP), as one of its several goals, has sought to assess a number of organizational-change intervention efforts and to attempt the improvement of the art and science of such assessments. In some cases, we have attempted to play the roles of independent evaluators, examining change programs designed and conducted by others. In other cases, we have attempted to employ improved assessmen procedures proactively to guide the development of change programs in which we had a hand in the implementation. This chapter will discuss some of the broad strategic issues in the design and conduct of assessment research. Later chapters will deal in more detail with various facets of an assessment program.

The purpose of program- and policy-assessment research is to provide valid and comprehensive information about the impact of the change initiatives upon the organization and upon the members. Past evaluation studies have been properly criticized on several grounds—for inadequate descriptions of the change program and activity, for failing to employ a suitable theory to guide the choice of evaluation criteria, for relying on data of unknown and unexamined reliability and validity, for employing designs that invite many alternative explanations of the findings, and for omitting reference to the unique initial states and environments of the organizations studied.[2,3] Such criticisms must be taken seriously, and efforts made to do a better job. In our attempts to do so, we have been guided by three general propositions:

1.   When feasible, assessment should be based not upon ad hoc choice of outcome criteria and control variables, but upon some encompassing theoretical model of organizational behavior and change. Such a theory or model, however tentative and inadequate, serves the function of directing attention to the full array of variables and conditions that might have a role in the understanding of the evaluation outcomes. Further, such a model is likely to emphasize that organizational behavior is not only multivariate but also multilevel, with necessary attention to individual and group, as well as to organizational states, processes, and outcomes. Such a model is likely to help identify the features of the change program itself that need to be described and measured, and to which the choice of evaluation variables must be linked.

2.   To the extent feasible, an assessment program should rest upon information obtained in a describable and replicable way, so that its nature and quality may be independently judged. This suggests an emphasis upon quantification and upon operational specification.

3.   The design of the assessment program should be such, to the extent feasible, that it allows the elimination of plausible but invalid interpretations of the findings. This implies anticipating an array of interpretational schemata and potential sources of invalidation of the findings, and incorporating information and design features that take them into account.

THEORETICAL MODELS IN ASSESSMENT RESEARCH

In the course of devising theories of organizational behavior suited to our aims, two distinct strategies were employed. One was the drafting of detailed, theory-based maps, each displaying with specificity a segment of the conceptual domain to be represented by data. Thus there were speculative models as to the impact of pay, work groups, supervisors, and the like on the behavior of organization members. Such maps also displayed the likely influence of organizational structures and policies, as well as those of the larger economy and the practices of other firms, on the variables of interest. The other strategy was the employment of more global maps intended to represent gross categories of variables. One such map was our model of the determinants of organizational effectiveness and QWL.

A Model for Assessing Organizational Behavior

Figure 2-1 depicts the global map used for identifying main classes of determinants of organizational effectiveness and QWL. It shows organizational effectiveness and QWL to be a product of the work-related behaviors of individuals and groups, with these in turn partially determined by the prevailing attitudes, beliefs, and expectations of individuals and of individuals clustered in work groups. Prior "causes" in this global model include the attributes of individuals imported into the organization, as well as the attributes of jobs and work subsystems and their surrounding organization characteristics. The external environment of the organization, including attributes of union(s), is also portrayed as influencing the attitudes and behaviors of organization members as well as the characteristics of the organization. This model suggests six broad classes of variables that should be included in organizational assessments. They will be briefly reviewed next.

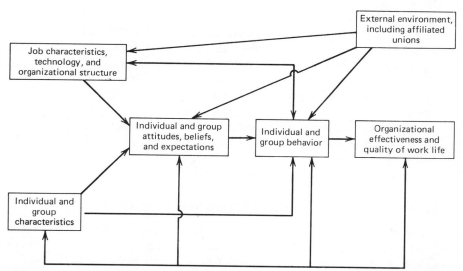

Figure 2-1   Relevant classes of variables in assessment of organization behavior.

Effectiveness Outcomes

A broad range of variables can represent the effectiveness of an organization and the QWL of its members. For example, effectiveness may be represented in an organization's productive output. In goods-producing firms, this includes the rate, cost, and quality of production, downtime, waste, and the like. In service firms it includes such factors as cost, timeliness, and quality of service. Other aspects of effectiveness are reflected in an organization's allocation of resources, coordination of functions, resolution of conflicts, innovativeness, and responsiveness to change in its environment. In turn, QWL in an organization may be reflected in the material and psychological well-being of its members.[4] This includes, for example, satisfaction of "basic" needs, such as job security, adequate pay and benefits, and safe working conditions, as well as needs for social relations, self-expression, and personal development.

In many instances, variables representing effectiveness and QWL are complementary. For example, satisfaction is often associated with lower rates of absenteeism and turnover that, in turn, contribute to higher productivity and lower costs.[5] But in other instances they can be opposed. Increments in productivity, for example, might be accompanied by an increase in accidents or job-related tensions. Lower turnover might reflect greater job insecurity. The model therefore distinguishes between outcomes representing effectiveness and QWL.

Individual and Group Behavior

Although many aspects of individual and group behaviors, such as productivity and identification with the organization, are represented as outcome variables, of equal importance are behaviors not necessarily reflected in the end results. These include individual effort, problem-solving methods, supervisory relations, intragroup teamwork, intergroup conflict resolution, and the like. Such behaviors are often the focus of human-relations training workshops, team-building efforts, quality-circle innovations, and intergroup conflict laboratories, in the expectation that such interventions will produce measurable end results.[6,7] The model shows this linkage but also notes it may be modified by individual attitudes and expectations and by the organization's structure and control systems that coordinate members' behavior.

Individual and Group Attitudes and Beliefs

The behavior of persons and groups is influenced, in part, by attitudes, perceptions, and expectations. If, for example, individuals like their work and find membership in the organization rewarding, they are likely to remain members of their organizations. Similarly, if they expect that satisfaction and recognition will follow from improvements in their work performance, they are likely to strive to improve it.[8] Shared beliefs and social norms influence these attitudes and can support or weaken these intentions.[9] Nonetheless, as the model shows, because of personal or situational factors, these intentions may or may not be expressed in productive or satisfying work behaviors.

Job Characteristics, Technology, and Organization Structure

The attributes of jobs, including their variety, autonomy, and significance, influence how organization members feel about their work and whether they find it interesting and rewarding.[10] In the context of a work group, such attributes can promote cooperation and capitalize on members' joint expertise or, alternatively, frustrate individual initiative. Enriching jobs or combining them in autonomous work groups—both prominent job redesign approaches—aim directly at influencing individual and group attitudes and behaviors by altering job characteristics.

The organization's work technology also has an important influence on its effectiveness and functioning. The type of capital equipment used by the organization, its modernity, the way the machinery is serviced, the appropriateness of the work flow, the existence of buffers (such as inventories), the use of professionalized services, and the ease of information flows in the organization—all affect the way organization members approach their work, the way they relate to each other, and their ability to work productively.

An organization's structure also influences member beliefs and behaviors and, ultimately, the outcome variables. Too many or too few rules, too many or too few support-staff personnel, too much or too little coordination, and too much or too little control, in the context of an organization's technology, can be important determinants of effectiveness. Moreover, an organization with a structure that is ill fitted to its technology is also likely to place more stress on members.[11] Structural change is the focus of many organizational redesign efforts, as in the aim to tighten up the structure by adding a new reporting level or to loosen it up through the creation of a matrix. However, unless such changes are accompanied by supportive changes in information, reward, and motivation systems, they may limit effectiveness and may strain the capacities of personnel.[12]

In sum, the model shows that the work environment can influence the outcome variables in two ways. First, it influences the attitudes and expectations of employees and work groups. Second, it directly affects work behavior. Even an intrinsically motivating job, for example, cannot be performed effectively unless needed resources are available and in good order and unless the next department is prepared to receive the output.

Individual and Group Characteristics

The results achieved by an organization are also influenced by the characteristics of the individuals and groups employed within it. Persons from different backgrounds, of different sexes, races, or levels of education, and with different job preferences and abilities react differently to their work environments and perform their jobs in different ways.[13] As the model shows, the existing composition of a work force can be a bane or boon to a change program: a work-place change that some find motivating, others resist; and a new policy that some favor, others oppose. Hence it is important to consider the nature of individuals and groups when planning or assessing change efforts.

External Environment

A number of aspects of the environment of an organization influence its effectiveness. It is known, for example, that the effectiveness of various organizational designs may be contingent on their "fit" with the environment.[14] Market factors, such as stability, degree of competition, and the like have been found to be related to effectiveness of various structures and technologies, for example, and the labor market exerts a strong influence on the ways employees react to employment conditions.

The presence of a union and a collective-bargaining agreement also can have a decisive influence on the kinds of changes that can be initiated and their likelihood of success. It is especially important to consider the character of union–management relationships in assessing joint labor–management change projects as it is quite possible that prior collaboration will strongly affect the outcomes.

Connectedness in Organizations

So far, the model of organizational behavior described here has identified six broad domains of variables that have relevance for understanding the impact of an organizational change program. One other characteristic of the model needs to be mentioned. Organizations are viewed as connected, holistic systems. This is represented in the model by the several lines connecting the components. The model is intended to suggest that an organization is more than a collection of parts, and that the outcomes of interest—effectiveness and QWL—are, in part, influenced by global systemic properties of the organization.[15]

This view has distinct implications for organizational assessment. First, it implies that behavior in the organization is multiply determined, and, by extension, it has multiple consequences. Thus, although a targeted intervention might produce a change in one organizational variable (or class of variables), some other focus of intervention may also produce such a change. Other organizational changes are likely to be induced as well, even though they are not intended. When an organizational variable is "overdetermined," that is, fixed by a number of factors of overlapping effect, then the expected consequences of a change in a single targeted variable may be forestalled or modified. This necessitates the measurement of the full range of independent and dependent variables pictured in Figure 2-1. Second, it implies that it is not sufficient to look only at sets of variables: The relationships between sets of variables must be looked at as well. Of interest to assessment, then, is change within sets of variables and also in the relationships among the sets. Third, it implies that organizations need to be thought of in dynamic, rather than in static terms. Organizations change over time and are characterized by cycles of events. Thus, the classification of variables as independent and dependent, although necessary in formulating a model of organization behavior, has no enduring status over time. Variables treated as determinants of others at one point in time may be reversely determined, or irrelevant, in a causal sequence at another point in time.

This view also implies that the system needs to be considered "as a whole." Since the different parts of the system are, by definition, interdependent, any one part examined in isolation may provide a limited or distorted picture of its function, determinants, or consequences. In particular, the system view means that assessing the impact of change on the congruence of system elements is frequently more important than its impact on single sets of variables.

A Model for Assessing Change Projects

The assessment of an organizational change program and its results poses special problems that arise from the fact that no single independent variable is changed and no single dependent variable is affected. Moreover, rather than a single event, the program must be conceived of as a set of events, ordered into phases over time. Thus an assessment task is to identify the many components of a change project and to trace their phased implementation into, and its effects upon, an organization and its members.

Two strategies were used in developing models of such a phased process of organizational change. Delimited theoretical maps were devised for the assessment of specific interventions—changes in pay and information systems, jobs and work subsystems, and so forth—that traced their likely direct impact on relevant variables. A more general map of the stages of the change process, beginning with start-up and concluding with institutionalization of the change, was also prepared.[16]

Figure 2-2 shows a model of the phases that a change process might go through and that need to be anticipated in the design of an assessment program. Not all change programs progress through the entire cycle: Some are rejected or subverted at an early stage; some become encapsu-

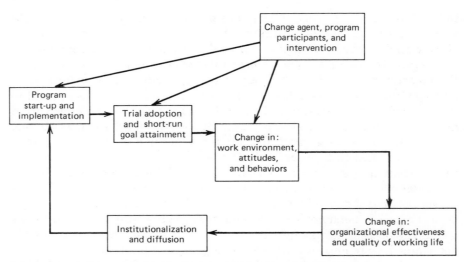

Figure 2-2   Phases in organization change programs.

lated within a limited part of the organization; and some lead to a reversion to something like the original state.

The first stage in the process consists of the start-up of the program and the implementation of interventions into the organization. This is followed by the trial adoption of changes by experimental or pilot units and, over time, by the attainment of immediate objectives. These are reflected, in turn, in changes in the work environment, in attitudes and behaviors, and in individual and organizational outcomes. The final stage of the process consists of the institutionalization of the program and its diffusion to other parts of the organization. This process is influenced by the change agent and the individuals and groups participating in the program, and, of course, by the nature of the interventions themselves. The external environment of the organization as well as its unions also has effects on the course of a change program and its impact.

In applying this model to union–management QWL projects, for example, the start-up involves preliminary negotiations with the union and management and the formation of the joint union–management committee. Implementation entails the committee's efforts, often with the assistance afforded them by a consultant, to diagnose problems and introduce changes into the organization. The change program itself may be comprised of several interventions, some of which are more effectively conceived and introduced than others. They may be more or less enthusiastically received by experimental units, and they may not all occur at the same time. Hence there is need to identify these change-program components and assess their implementation into, and their adoption by, the organization. In the laboratory such a "manipulation check" is made to determine whether the intervention "takes." In the field setting, it is an assessment of short-run program impact, and it avoids the extended appraisal of "nonevents."[17] Analysis of institutionalization and diffusion is needed to assess the durability of the change program and the procedures established to extend it to other parts or other functions of the organization. Many successful pilot programs have withered or been narrowly encapsulated when managements, unions, and consultants have been unable to effect their diffusion.[18,19]

Program Start-Up and Implementation

Lawler and Drexler have identified some conditions—favorable and unfavorable—to the start-up of experimental programs involving union and management cooperation.[20] A key to effective start-ups, they contend, lies in reducing the forces initially impeding cooperation (e.g., reducing threats) rather than increasing favorable forces (e.g., introducing incentives). Much of the initial effort of third parties when negotiating with labor and management and forming the joint committe involves reducing opposition to the program and arranging mutually protective agreements. Later work focuses on cultivating cooperation and developing mutual working relationships.

The implementation of a change program follows the diagnosis of problems and formulation of action plans. In union–management programs, as in most change efforts, the quality of the diagnosis and planning depends upon the effectiveness of the parties in gathering complete and valid information, fully digesting and openly evaluating its implications, and identifying appropriate and feasible solutions. For instance, a committee dominated by one party or another may be unable to gather unbiased data or agree upon solutions to problems. Implementation, in turn, depends upon communicating ideas to experimental units and involving them in the design of specific initiatives. Even a harmonious committee may have difficulty implementing plans if it lacks acceptance or influence in the organization. The successful implementation of a change program also depends upon the quality of technical advice and facilitation offered by a consultant, the clarity of goals and responsibilities, and the time and resources available and expended in the implementation itself.[21] All of these need to be measured in a full evaluation.

Trial Adoption and Goal Attainment

The adoption of change programs is influenced by both personal and environmental factors that need to be assessed.[22] Beginning with the start-up and continuing through implementation, individuals and groups in experimental units form attitudes about the overall program and expectations regarding the risks, costs, and benefits of adopting specific interventions. These, in turn, are affected by their knowledge of the program and their participation in the design and implementation of the components that are of relevance to them. The successful adoption of the change also depends upon the unit members finding the time and acquiring the technical and interpersonal skills required to achieve program objectives.[23]

Goal attainment depends partly upon the adoption of the program by experimental units. If the unit members give the program a full and vigorous trial, they test its merits; if they only half-heartedly adopt it, or pay lip service to its demands, they doom it from the outset. The success of their first experiences in adopting the program determines, in large measure, its continued adoption and goal attainment. Measurement of goal attainment, however, assesses only the intended effects of the program. Of equal interest are the unintended consequences. A program to increase the decision making of hourly personnel, as an example, may deprive first-line supervisors or management of valued power and influence.[24] Accordingly, it is important to assess not only what is supposed to happen following program adoption, but also what else occurs.

Organization Behaviors and Outcomes

As the program reaches its objectives, changes are expected in the work environment, in attitudes and behavior, and, ultimately, in individual and organizational outcomes. Specific components of the program, however, are expected to produce targeted effects. Some interventions, such as job enrichment and organizational redesign, are directed toward the work environment and should have a measurable impact on job attributes and the coordination of responsibilities, respectively. Others, such as team building, are directed toward attitudes, beliefs, and relationships in the organization, and they should have a measurable effect on cooperation, provided, of course, that the programs are effectively implemented. A few interventions, particularly in organizations hiring employees and forming new work groups, address the characteristics of the work force.[25] Finally, some interventions, such as the formation of autonomous work groups, should have measurable effects on jobs, people, and working relationships. Tracing these expected effects tests the theory behind the intervention and helps to determine how and why it succeeded or failed.

This evaluation can be applied to the overall change program and to its specific components. The advantage of the "microanalysis" is that it can be used to determine which components of the change program were and were not effective.[26] The advantage of the "macroanalysis" is that it can be used to identify the unintended consequences of the interventions and, over time, their secondary and tertiary effects. It becomes, in effect, a goal-free evaluation.[27]

Institutionalization and Diffusion

Institutionalization of a change program refers to the organization's continued reliance on the change and to the durability of its effects. Its continuity depends, in large part, upon its sustained support by management and the employees, generally in the face of changing economic and social conditions, and its legitimation by members of the organization at all levels. At that point, the pilot program matures into standard operating procedures and norms. Diffusion refers to the spread of the process to other parts of the organization. Often, however, there is great confusion over what is to be diffused.[18] If only the theory behind the change is diffused, other units may be unable to translate the concepts into action; if only the specific change components are diffused, other units may see them as irrelevant to their situation. Successful diffusion depends upon exporting both theory and practices and overcoming opposition and bureaucratic barriers to change. This involves new negotiations and a new start-up, guided by the lessons derived from the initial endeavor.

As Figure 2-2 suggests, merely introducing change into an organization does not automatically lead to changes in its effectiveness or in its quality of working life. A program may succeed or fail because of its implementation and adoption or because it did or did not produce the anticipated and desired outcomes. This distinction is important for assessment.[28] Assessing start-up, implementation, and adoption reflects upon the effectiveness of the change program and the underlying theory; assessing changes in the work environment, attitudes, behaviors, and outcomes reflects upon the adequacy of the theory of organizational behavior that underlies the change. This has two implications. First, it is clear that both a valid theory and an effective change program are essential if successful results are to be achieved. Second, an assessment of the program requires an evaluation of both the theory (e.g., assumptions, hypotheses, and hopes) behind the change program and its implementation into, and adoption by, the organization. This assessment can have a profound effect upon the diffusion of change programs to other settings. Among those who lament the declining interest in job enrichment, some have attributed its demise to its ineffective implementation, not to the soundness of the theory relating job design to job behavior.[29] The assessment model pictured in the figure provides for an assessment of both the process of change and the theory underlying it as well as its intended and unintended effects.

This again brings to mind the systemic character of organizations and thus the systemic character of organization change. Change programs can be thought of not only as distinct interventions or sets of them, but also as a coherent set of related interventions. Seashore and Bowers speculate, for example, that introducing coordinated changes in the pay plan, the work flows, the information system, and job assignments contributed to the durability of the effects of the participative management program in the Weldon plant.[30] Their cumulative effect, they argued, was greater than would be expected from introducing only some of the changes or implementing them separately. This perspective also requires recognition of the holistic character of organization change. In this view, understanding the change program requires not just an awareness of its components but also their interrelation and the context in which they are introduced.

MEASUREMENT IN ASSESSMENT RESEARCH

The model presented previously includes a broad array of concepts whose assessment requires a broad array of measures. Social, behavioral, and administrative scientists, engineers, and accountants all contributed to the measurement package. The result of this effort is a variety of instruments and procedures from which one may choose appropriate measures for a particular assessment effort.

Instruments and Procedures

At the present time there are 11 distinguishable instruments or field procedures for collection of information. They will be briefly described here and then presented in more detail in the remainder of the book. These vary as to the source of information, the methods of collection, and the degree to which they are structured as to method and substantive content. Some are relatively complete as to development and field testing, whereas others are still in preliminary form. They are enumerated below with brief descriptions.

1. *Michigan Organizational Assessment Questionnaire (MOAQ)*. This instrument is designed for use with organization members to obtain descriptive information on the respondent's job and work environment as well as the respondent's attitudes and perceptions in several domains. The instrument is composed of modules, each relating to a different area of topical content. The modules presently in general use are the following: demographics, a "general-attitudes" module, job rewards and reward contingencies, task and role characteristics, work-group functioning, supervision, and compensation administration. Each module provides a number of discrete scales so that the full instrument yields 67 multi-item indexes plus the demographic data. Many scales have both short and long versions, the shorter being used when reduced reliability is acceptable, given constraints on organizational and respondent time. The modular arrangement allows the preparation of a questionnaire tailored to the organization under study by selective omission of modules, scales, or

items. New items of special local interest may be added. The MOAQ is a "living" instrument, with additional items occasionally added and with additional modules under consideration.

2. *Interview: Organizational Structure and Environment.* A set of semistructured interview schedules is used to collect data about key aspects of organizational structure and environment. The interviews are used with both line and staff personnel, and they serve also as a guide to the collection of relevant documents and data from archival sources.

3. *Technology and Technological Change.* Data about jobs and tasks are obtained primarily through questionnaires and direct observation. The detection, description, and assessment of change in larger technological systems has been resistant to measurement through standardized methods. Observational and questionnaire methods have been used to examine dimensions of work processes, including material and informational flows, and technological adaptations and adjustments. These have been ad hoc instruments and procedures adapted to each site.

4. *Observations of Task Characteristics.* An instrument has been designed and field tested to guide the direct observation of jobs and reporting of aspects of task activities and job environment. Emphasis is upon job and task characteristics having psychological and behavioral implications. There are provisions for observer training and for scheduling of observation periods on a time-sampling basis.

5. *Union–Management Relations.* Semistructured interviews with key union and management informants are supplemented with questionnaire measures from union members. The main themes are concerned with union organization and activities, member involvement, and attitudes regarding union–management relationships.

6. *Behavioral-Financial Measures.* Standardized reporting forms and methods are provided for data collection or for abstracting information from archival sources, as well as for the analysis of such information. The focus is upon specific employee behaviors in the work setting, such as absences, lateness, turnover, nonproductive behavior, accidents, and the like. The methods are oriented toward assessing the costs associated with such behavior, in addition to their rates of occurrence.

7. *Productivity Measures.* Semistandardized procedures and analytical guidelines are employed to measure output volumes, material utilization, machine-time utilization, output quality, and the like. Measurements are sought, where feasible, at the individual, work-group, departmental, and organizational levels.

8. *Intervention Observations.* Standardized recording forms and observer guidelines are used for assessing joint union–management committee meetings and similar meetings, and for reporting implementation efforts in the target organization. These data can be used descriptively for producing narrative accounts of the course of events, or they can be quan-

tified for purposes of documenting group interactions or the substantive content of discussions.

9. *Change Implementation and Goal-Attainment Questionnaire.* A questionnaire is employed, perhaps on more than one occasion, to obtain employee views about the implementation of changes and about their impact. Topics include the activities of the joint labor–management committee, the effectiveness of actions taken, the clarity of the change program, receptivity to the program, and allied matters. Goal-attainment measures assess the extent to which employees perceive improvements or other changes in their jobs, their rewards, their access to information, and other characteristics of their work environment that result from the change program.

10. *Intervention Costs and Benefits.* Standardized reporting and analysis guides are used for the collection of data about the costs of the change project, the benefits obtained that can be quantified, and the selective impact of costs and benefits in different parts or segments of the organization. The costs in question include, for example, the direct costs of consultants' time and expenses, lost productivity, or productive time associated with the program, gains associated with productivity and "costly behaviors," and the like.

11. *Naturalistic Observation.* A log of events and on-site observations is maintained, together with tentative interpretations of their significance. An interpretive history of the change program is derived from such records and the recollections of the site observers.

Of these 11 procedures, the first 7 are used in operationalizing the model of organization behavior, and the next 3 are used in directly assessing the change program. The last "instrument" is, of course, the assessors themselves. It represents their insights, impressions, and interpretations about the change program and its effect on the organization. These judgments derive from spending time in the setting, communicating and empathizing with the participants, and soliciting their views. The benefits of this kind of observation are twofold. On the one hand, it provides a rich, although potentially biased and prejudiced, description of aspects of the intervention, some of which can be verified through subsequent questionnaire and interview methods. On the other hand, it helps the evaluators to take a holistic view of the intervention, immersing themselves in the experience of the organization in change. It provides an understanding of the flow of events that can be obtained neither from questionnaire and other cross-sectional data-collection methods nor from longitudinal data on a few predetermined topics. Still, firsthand observation of the intervention prevents a fragmented analysis of the change. More structured data-gathering methods, in turn, provide a check against the biases that may arise from exclusive use of clinical methods.

Considerations in the Choice of Variables and Methods

A number of choices and dilemmas are encountered when planning a program for the assessment of organizations and of organizational change. Among the considerations that we feel are particularly important in designing a measurement package are the following:

1. *Confirmatory Data.* Certain variables are judged to be key variables. Where feasible, an attempt should be made to provide multiple measures of such variables, using different methods. For example, an indicator of job variety can be obtained by means of questionnaires or interviews with individual workers and also by direct observation by trained staff members.

2. *Adaptability to Different Site Conditions.* For many variables, optimum measurement in the context of one organization may be incompatible with optimization in another, and it may indeed be irrelevant or impossible in another. This calls for standardized methods for some variables and for adaptive alternative methods for others. The decision may rest upon judgments of the feasibility of alternative methods and upon estimates of the range of conditions that may be encountered in different organizations.

3. *An Open-Ended Measurement Plan.* The preceding paragraph relates to the adaptability of the measurement plan to local opportunities and constraints at each site. A related consideration in the development of the plan is to allow adaptation to emergent ideas about additional variables that merit attention. None of the instruments and procedures employed so far precludes the addition of new material as the change project develops. Thus, for example, if changes in the pay system are undertaken, more questions about pay and benefits can be employed, and a close watch can be kept on earnings, inflation, and payroll costs.

4. *Measurement of Change over Time.* Since an aim of assessment is the detection and documentation of changes, considerable emphasis needs to be given to the measurement of variables that lend themselves to repeated or continuous measurement and thus to time-series analysis. The aim of detecting change also forces comprehensiveness of topical coverage, as the nature of the changes cannot be known in advance.

5. *System Tolerance/Overload.* What can be done from an assessment point of view is often limited.

Instrument Validation

Determining the adequacy of measures involves comparing the description of the organization they afford with the "true" state of the organization. In actuality, no such comparison can be made. Nevertheless, some standards of instrument and data quality need to be kept in mind and tested where it is feasible to do so. These criteria include the following:

1. *Instrument Sensitivity.*   The extent to which the measurement instrument is able to discriminate among objects or states that are expected to be different. Operationally, this means the extent to which the instrument produces predictable variability when used in a range of different situations.

2. *Instrument Reliability.*   The extent to which the measurement instrument produces measurements that remain constant when repeated under conditions taken to be constant. Operationally, this means the extent to which functionally equivalent measures taken at the same point in time correlate with each other or, alternatively, the extent to which the measurement results taken at one time and place correlate with those taken in a similar situation at another time and place.

3. *Convergent Validity.*   The extent to which different measurement instruments designed to measure the same construct produce similar results when they are used in the same situation.[31] Convergent validity is generally assessed from the correlations between different measures taken in the same set of situations.

4. *Discriminant Validity.*   The extent to which measurement instruments designed to measure different constructs produce different results in situations taken to be different.[31] Discriminant validity is assessed by the correlations of measures of different variables taken in the same set of situations, and it generally includes a test of the possibility that differences may be due to differences in method (such as between interviews and questionnaires), rather than to differences in the construct measured.

The information collection instruments described here and in later chapters have been statistically analyzed to test the quality of the information collected. In the case of frequently used structured data-collection methods such as questionnaires, standardized interviews, and structured observations, this involved using standard statistical tests of reliability and validity, and these data will be presented. In the case of other forms of data collection, tests are less refined, but they have been attempted nonetheless. If, for example, the assessors rely on their unquantified impressions as data, they can compare their impressions to see if they share a common view, and they can compare them with data from other sources to test for convergent and discriminant validation.

One final implication of the concern over instrument validity is that assessors use multiple methods of data collection whenever possible. All methods of data collection have limitations in their validity. Using multiple methods allows researchers to identify convergence between assessment methods. When applied to a single concept, convergence between multiple methods and measures is evidence of *construct validity*. When applied to two or more concepts in hypothesized causal relationship, convergence across time periods is evidence of *predictive validity*.

EVALUATION IN ASSESSMENT RESEARCH

In drawing conclusions about the impact of a change program upon an organization, assessors need to interpret the effects and test the causal connections between the program and the outcome. This requires careful thought about research design and statistical analysis of the data. The aim is to describe how and why the program "worked" and to generalize the results to other situations. Two criteria need to be used to establish the validity of conclusions and generalizations drawn from semiexperimental studies:

1. *Internal Validity*.   The level of confidence that is justified in holding that the program produced the measured results. Operationally, this means examining the extent to which other factors, such as changes in the composition of the work force or events other than the change program, were responsible for the results.

2. *External Validity*.   The level of confidence that the causal relationship between the program and its results can be generalized to other situations. Operationally, this means examining the likelihood that the change program would produce comparable results if implemented in the same way in another organization.

Experimental designs maximize the internal validity of research studies by limiting the number of variables to be considered, bounding them in time, and by controlling for extraneous factors that can effect the observed results.[32] In many organizational studies, however, the assessors are neither able nor willing to conduct true experiments, since the methodological requirements fail to mesh with the realities of life in organizations and with ethical constraints. A true experimental design requires, among other things, a limited, carefully defined change program, control over variables that might confound the experiment, random assignment of the participants to experimental conditions, and use of control or comparison groups. These conditions are difficult, if not impossible, to establish in change efforts under field conditions.

The introduction of any change into an ongoing organizational setting is a very complex process—so complex that it is often difficult to define in advance, or later, just how and when the change components are introduced. To a substantial degree, the process of implementation of a change is modified as it evolves, which means that it can be described only after it has occurred. Thus the idea of a carefully predefined intervention within a definite introduction process is usually unrealistic in organizational assessment research.

The situation is further complicated by the fact that organizational environments are always changing, and organizations change in order to cope with them. Thus, unlike the laboratory where other factors can be controlled, it is difficult in a field setting to study a single change or even a group of changes in isolation. Instead, the researchers are faced with a series of changes that have an impact on the organization, some of which are part of the intervention while others are not.

Random assignment is difficult to attain for several reasons. Employees, as well as those acting for organizations, want to have a say in how they are to be treated, and, indeed, they should have a say. This is both an ethical issue of informed consent and a practical issue of what people are willing to accept. In most situations, in any case, there are too few organizational units available to allow randomization, and the people involved are likely to have their own compelling reasons for defining the "experimental" units purposefully and selectively rather than randomly. Finally, when randomization is desired, it is often unclear whether it is individuals or organizational units that should be randomly assigned.

Control or comparison groups are also difficult to obtain within organizations because very few have units that are comparable in all relevant ways. Different parts of the same organization and different organizations in the same environment may differ in important ways even when they share the same general structure and purpose. It may, of course, be possible in some instances to impose comparability just for the purpose of having a control group that differs from an experimental group only with respect to participation in the program. However, this would represent an intrusion into an organization that is difficult to justify. Moreover, even if such a control group could be established, it is unlikely that it could be maintained as such throughout the program. Control units are often contaminated by knowledge of the events in the experimental group. Although Campbell has offered several strategies justifying the establishment and maintenance of control groups in assessment studies, the experience to date indicates that their use in a field setting is precarious and problematic.[33]

Given these impediments to evaluating change programs, the only alternative is to acknowledge the realities of the field situation and still seek to incorporate the feasible attributes of experimentation in the design of the evaluation. A term useful in describing such research is *adaptive experiments,* where adaptive means that the final form of the evaluation is likely to be known only after the change program has been completed and much of the data collected.[34] Adaptive experiments are not as robust as one would wish in countering threats to internal and external validity. They are, however, a definite improvement over studies wholly lacking in experimental features. They allow researchers to rule out many of the alternative explanations for the findings that weaken the conclusions drawn from the typical case of nonexperimental action research. Adaptive designs fit what Campbell and Stanley call a non-equivalent control-group design. This involves the selection of participating units and nonparticipating comparison units, nonrandom assignment of participants, and at a minimum, before and after measurement in the groups. It is classified as a quasi-experimental design.

In some ways this is a preferred design in field settings because the conclusions can have greater generalizability than those derived from true experiments. With respect to internal validity, it controls for the effects of history, maturation, and mortality. Because of the presence of the comparison group, all of these can be dismissed as causes of changes in the results.

Nevertheless, because it lacks random assignment, an adaptive experiment cannot address all the threats to internal validity. The possibility cannot be ruled out that the results of the program are attributable to characteristics of the particular unit or situation in which it took place. A change in the employment market, for example, might have a differential effect on turnover in groups of different age and ethnic compositions. This possibility can be confronted, to some extent, if it can be demonstrated that the experimental and control groups are comparable in such areas as age, education, organizational performance and if an accounting can be made of nonexperimental events that might interact with unique unit characteristics.

Addressing the threats to external validity in adaptive experiments is also difficult. First, there is simply no way to control for the fact that the organizations that sponsor change programs are not representative. Second, the publicity that often accompanies change programs and the excitement that is sometimes evident in the organization can produce artificial conditions. Too brief an evaluation runs the risk, therefore, of assessing temporary euphoria. Moreover, given the complexity in implementing changes in an organization and the sizable time lag between formal implementation and effective change in the organization itself, this can lead also to a premature conclusion that the program had no effect.

The key to enhancing the validity of an adaptive experiment lies in the skillful application of a broad-coverage measurement package and the careful adaptation of design, measurement, and analysis plans throughout the course of the experiment. Three features of such a plan are of particular importance: (1) the longitudinal measurement of the change program; (2) the use of a nonrandomly selected control group or of a post hoc comparison group; and (3) the statistical analysis of program results.

Longitudinal Measurement

The modest amount of longitudinal research that has been done in organizations suggests that the effects of change efforts may appear long after the introduction of the change program.[35] Changes directed toward improving the quality of work life may first affect the work environment, employee satisfaction, and motivation. These factors in turn may affect such intermediate factors as absenteeism, skill development, or work quality, which in turn may influence organizational cost performance. But often the causal linkage is not immediate or direct, and the impact on costs and therefore on profits can be delayed.[36]

As an example, changes in job design seem to affect job satisfaction and absenteeism almost immediately. However, the impact on turnover may not appear for six or more months, and the impact on operating costs may not appear for a year or even longer. This time lag occurs because savings from absenteeism come mainly from being able to reduce the size of the "extra" work force through attrition or from commensurately increasing output and lowering unit costs. The situation is further complicated because the time lag between the actual change and changes in the measures of organizational effectiveness and QWL may not be the same for all the change components or for all of the outcome measures.

The only way to "capture" the change program and its effects is to assess the program before, during, and after the intervention. Figure 2-3 shows a time deployment of the measures described earlier. The record-

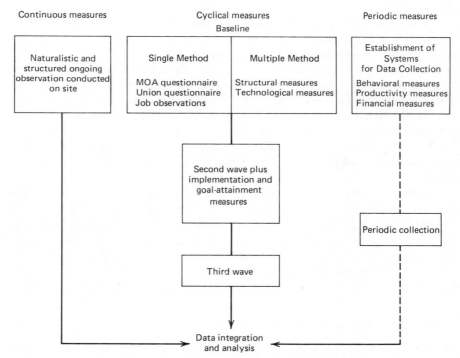

Figure 2-3 Illustrative measurement schedule.

collecting systems for organizational performance are established before the program begins, and they are used to collect baseline data (a year before the change program begins), periodic data (monthly or quarterly throughout the program), and postintervention data (for a year or more). Measures of the variables in the model of organization behavior presented earlier are taken before, during, and after the program. Implementation and goal-attainment measures are taken in the second and third waves. Finally, the structured and naturalistic observations of the change and its effects on the organization are undertaken continuously through the study period. They are needed to document the history of the program and to guide the selection of evaluation measures in the second and third waves of data collection.

The importance of these on-site observations for the integration and analysis of the data can hardly be overstated. The assessments involve the collection and analysis of large amounts of data, and help is needed in generating hypotheses when the data are analyzed. In addition, the components of the change programs cannot be specified until they are introduced. They may go undetected unless an observer is present to record them and suggest how they may affect other measures. In an extreme case, the "expected" impact can only be specified post hoc—after the experiment is over. Nevertheless, it is critical that observations identify specific interventions so that their consequences might be, at best, predicted, or else retrospectively interpreted.

Comparison Unit

It is always desirable to compare changes in the experimental situation with those in another situation where no such change has been attempted. Since random selection is often impractical in assessment studies, the use of a comparable unit, or "matching group," helps the evaluator to assess whether improvements or problems in the participating units were due to the change effort. In some instances, however, this is impossible since comparable units or situations in an organization are not available. In such cases, comparisons can sometimes be made between units after the intervention. For example, in one case a program intended to promote cooperation and problem solving was adopted by one department but rejected by another.[26] Comparisons could be made between the results in the two units since the group that rejected the program served as a comparison group. In another project, observation and implementation measures showed that a new information system was in fact adopted by some units but not by others.[23] In this case comparisons were made between the high users, the comparison units, and the low users. Researchers have also successfully used still another approach in establishing a post hoc comparison group.[37] In a job redesign experiment, the employees alternated their jobs during an extended study period, allowing the researchers to compare attitudes between the two different jobs with the participants acting as their own controls.

Analysis

Given the methodological limitations of adaptive experiments, statistical procedures are needed in the analysis of the data to help counter the remaining threats to internal validity and generalizability. Along with a comparison group and longitudinal measurement, quasi-experimental designs depend upon several analytic strategies that can help to prove, or to disprove, that the change recorded by the outcome measures is attributable to the intervention.

Given the use of a nonrandomly selected control group or of a post hoc comparison group, four sources of invalidity affect the assessor's confidence that the program is responsible for the observed results of an adaptive experiment.

The first is that changes in the measured variable may be due not to the program's direct impact but rather to changes in the meaning of the instruments to the respondents. This is a common concern in evaluating the results of questionnaire measures, but it may apply as well to interview and observation data. The concern is whether the change reflects an increase or decrease in the "true" level of the measured variable, the respondent's recalibration of the intervals of measurement of the variable, or the respondent's redefinition of the variable itself. Golembiewski, Billingsley, and Yeager refer to these respectively as alpha, beta, and gamma changes.[38] There are, at present, no means to distinguish between alpha and beta changes. However, steps may be taken at the outset to use behaviorally anchored questionnaire measures that minimize the respondent's recalibrations of the meaning and, at the end of the study, to debrief them as to their interpretation of the intervals of measurement. To assess gamma change, say, in measures of participation, a statistical test may be used to determine whether there is congruence between measures of the variable across time. If there is congruence between the measures, it can be assumed that respondents are viewing participation through the same frame of reference across time.

A second threat to internal validity—statistical regression—has to do with the change in measured results over time that is attributable to deviant scores on the initial measurement. Because organizational units are not randomly chosen to be participating or comparison units, they may score significantly higher or lower than one another on baseline measures. In the second and third waves of data collection, there is a tendency for extremely high-scoring groups to have relatively lower scores, and for extremely low-scoring groups to have relatively higher ones. In situations where regression effects are suspected, steps can be taken to remove the variance solely attributable to status on the first measurement in assessing change in the measured variables.

A third threat to internal validity concerns change in the measured results that is attributable to unique characteristics of organizational units that may interact with their own histories or growth processes to affect the measured results of a change program. In such cases, relationships between group membership and preintervention and postintervention measures can be examined through an analysis of covariance or other modified regression techniques.[39] In such analyses, factors other than group membership (e.g., job level, tenure) might be shown to interact with the program in producing the results, and thus they are explanatory factors themselves.

A final threat to internal validity is that turnover, or the introduction of new members into the comparison and participating groups, may affect the results. To control for this, comparisons can be made for "veterans only," that is, individuals who remain in their units throughout the program.

There are three remaining threats to the external validity or generalizability of the findings that need mention. First, the results can be confounded by the participating unit's composition: At best, this effect can be documented through the analysis of covariance, or generalization can be limited to units of comparable composition. A second threat to generalizability is the participants' reactivity to the change program and the resultant short-term increase or decrease in their measured outcome variables. Time-series analysis can test the durability of the program's effect, as can analyses based upon moving averages or periodicity.[40] Simply plotting the scores can highlight initial euphoria and its decline if the change is not sustained.

A final threat to the generalizability of the findings resides in the complexity of the change program. A change project might involve job design in one unit, interpersonal consultation in another, and no activities in still another. In such cases, comparisons can be made between the results in the units, distinguishing the relative effectiveness of each intervention versus doing nothing at all.

The primary purpose of statistical analysis is to complement the measurement and design features of the experiment by controlling for remaining threats to the validity of conclusions drawn about the relative success or failure of the program. In addition, it is also used to further validate the theory upon which the change program is based. In order to assess program impact, correlations between measures of components of the program (e.g., measures of the committee, the consultants, the program's implementation) and the measures of impact (e.g., goal-attainment measures) can be computed. A positive relationship between these program-component and impact measures, coupled with significant change in measures of the organizational characteristics themselves, provides supportive evidence of an experimental program's overall effect and helps to distinguish the unique effects of particular interventions.

In order to trace these effects on attitudes, behavior, and outcomes in the organization and thus test the causal model that underlies it, cross-lag correlations can be computed.[41,42] With these statistics, correlations between two measures collected at two different points in time are calculated and compared against correlations, across the time period, of the variables with one another. As an example, in one site the correlation between the first measure of communication and the second measure of satisfaction was larger than the first measure of satisfaction and second measure of communication. The size of this difference, when analyzed in a formula that takes account of the relationships between the variables within the time periods, documented the causal effect of organizational communication on work satisfaction within the site.[23] With three waves of data collection, this provides an even more stringent test of the theory behind the change. This test can show the repeated causal effect of variables throughout a sequence of time periods. It can also show the dynamic nature of social systems so that a variable identified analytically as a determinant of another in the first phase of a change program may show a reversed causation in a later phase.

Adaptive experiments featuring the measurement, design, and analytic strategies described here conform to Seashore's criteria of a field experiment: "(1) Definable and measurable change in organizational environment, situation, or process; (2) Some means for quantification of variables; and, (3) Some provision for testing of causal hypotheses through the method of difference" (p. 164).[43] Nevertheless, there are methodological limitations in the measures, methods, and analytic strategies that are used. Moreover, causality in any experiment, whether in the laboratory or the field, can never be certainly established to the exclusion of other causal factors.

On the one hand it is comforting, as Blalock suggests, to assume "as if" all alternative explanations for the findings can be eliminated and all extraneous factors can be controlled.[44] The realities of organization life, however, force the researchers to put that assumption into quotations. The validity of the conclusions drawn about a change program depend upon a correspondence between many sources of information about the program—information gathered from different people and situations using different methods. In this light, information gathered through naturalistic observation takes on special importance. These data, specifically the insights and clinical judgments of the assessors, along with the opinions of the consultants and participating organization members, can confirm, augment, and extend the quantitative data. They can also pose alternative explanations for the results that require further investigation.

Of course, the final aspect of evaluation is the "valuation" of the results. The intent of the analysis is to provide some implicit criteria for valuation, as in, say, the comparison of financial costs and benefits and reported changes in levels of cooperation, satisfaction, and other factors of social worth. Beyond this, the explicit intention from the beginning of the Michigan program has been to encourage evaluation of the results from multiple value perspectives since changes and results that are valued highly by some might be devalued or given small note by others. This includes, of course, the value-laden opinions of assessors.

A FINAL ASSESSMENT ISSUE

An assessor may fill one of two roles in organizational-change research. One emphasizes the independent assessment of change projects; the other stresses the involvement of researchers as both actors and researchers. There are strengths and weaknesses in fulfilling either an "independent-evaluation" or "action-research" role in the study of organizational change. Careful consideration needs to be given to these before the "assessment role" is designed. The study of organizational change by a group that is not an active part of the change program offers a number of advantages over a study done by the person actively involved in the process of change. First, there is always a credibility problem when the person responsible for the change reports on the effectiveness of his or her own change effort. Particularly in the case of a publicized success, the public is suspicious of reports of grandiose achievement, and there are data that suggest that this suspicion has a basis in reality. A recent review of evaluation research projects (not concerned with organizational problems) found that significantly more successes are reported when "affiliated" researchers (the change agent or a colleague at the same institution) do evaluations than when they are done by a third party whose main interest is in doing the research well rather than in the success or failure of the change effort.[3]

Second, when a person is engaged in both change and measurement, there is often a conflict between what is good for research and what is good for the change. This can take the form of competing demands for time and energy, or it can take the form of problems about whether particular measures should be collected. Thus it would seem that having an independent assessor should improve the quality of evaluation research through reduction of such role conflicts. Gordon and Morse, in their review of evaluation research, present data that support this point. They found that evaluations done by third parties are typically better methodologically than those done by affiliated researchers.[3]

Third, the research on innovative organization practices and designs is often criticized because failures are underreported. The reasons for this are complex, but one is obvious: The disappointed change agent has little reason to report a failure even though others might learn from it. Having another party involved might help to stimulate the analysis and reporting of more failures. Presumably, the assessor would be interested in reporting failures because professional credit would come to him or her as long as the assessment was done well. Finally, having a third party involved means that a different—perhaps more objective—description of what has gone on will be attained. Organizational change efforts are often properly criticized because they are not described in a way that allows an outsider to understand and replicate what has taken place. One reason for this is that the effort is usually reported by the persons doing the change. As an involved party to the change, they often are in a poor position to judge what a naive outsider needs to know about the effort.

There are counterarguments to each of these points. On the problem of the participant's bias toward a favorable assessment, it might be argued that independent assessors derive their kudos from successfully documenting a failure and pontificating on the theories and strategies they would have employed. Thus they might be *too* motivated toward finding fault. As to the point of competing time pressures, it might be argued that action researchers would be more sensitive to timely and relevant data and more motivated to collect it, thus insuring a more accurate, if not as methodologically elegant, an assessment. Regarding the point of underreporting failures, it is notable that there are also few accounts of the ineffective implementation of assessments. And, with respect to the point about the need to communicate to naive observers, it might be argued that insiders would have the more accurate picture of events but that in either case it would be informative to hear from both perspectives.

Beyond this defensive posture, there are also clear advantages to the action-research role. These include familiarity with on-site personnel, which eases entry into data-rich events and opens communication channels closed to less intimate assessors, and an in situ sensitivity to the meaning and import of change within an organization. Much has been made of this latter point in Argyris' review of organic and rigorous research, in Alderfer's distinctions between clinical and nonclinical assessments, and in Seashore's valuation of the action-research versus the independent assessment roles. There is no need here to repeat these arguments.[45–47]

Given these strengths and weaknesses, our position is that the separation of intervention and assessment responsibilities is feasible and of significant value, but it is not without risks and costs that are difficult to evaluate. It is not timely to recommend the practice for general application. Certainly there should be further exploration of ways to do it with minimal strain, cost, and disturbing intrusion. The end to be sought is the development of professional norms that promote adequate and unbiased assessment practices that are selectively invoked to fit the purposes and requirements of the parties at interest. Research and development need not always be the priority purpose.

REFERENCES

1. Mirvis, P. H., & Berg, D. N. *Failures in organization development and change: Cases and essays for learning.* New York: Wiley-Interscience, 1977.
2. Cummings, T. G., Molloy, E. S., & Glen, R. A methodological critique of fifty-eight selected work experiments. *Human Relations,* 1977, **30**, 675–708.
3. Gordon, G., & Morse, E. U. Evaluation research: A critical review. *The Annual Review of Sociology,* 1975, **1**, 339–361.
4. Lawler, E. E. III. Measuring the psychological quality of working life: The how and why of it. In L. E. Davis & A. B. Cherns (Eds.), *The quality of working life.* New York: Free Press, 1975.
5. Macy, B. A., & Mirvis, P. H. A methodology for assessment of quality of work life and organizational effectiveness in behavioral-economic terms. *Administrative Science Quarterly,* 1976, **21**, 212–226.
6. Maier, N. R. F. *Psychology in industrial organizations,* 4th ed. Boston: Houghton Mifflin, 1973.
7. Dyer, W. G. *Team building: Issues and alternatives.* Reading, MA: Addison-Wesley, 1977.
8. Lawler, E. E. III. *Motivation in work organizations.* Monterey: Brooks/Cole, 1973.
9. Hill, J. M., & Trist, E. L. *Industrial accidents, sickness, and other absences.* Pamphlet no. 4. London: Tavistock Institute of Human Relations, 1962.
10. Hackman, J. R., & Lawler, E. E. III. Employee reactions to job characteristics. *Journal of Applied Psychology,* 1971, **55**, 259–286.
11. Kahn, R. L. Conflict, ambiguity, and overload: Three elements of job stress. *Occupational Mental Health,* 1973, **3**, 2–9.
12. Lawler, E. E. III. Reward systems. In J. R. Hackman & J. L. Suttles (Eds.), *Improving life at work.* Santa Monica: Goodyear, 1977.
13. Ghiselli, E. E. *The validity of occupational aptitude tests.* New York: Wiley, 1966.
14. Lawrence, P. R., & Lorsch, J. W. *Organization and environment.* Boston: Division of Research, Graduate School of Business Administration, Harvard University, 1967.
15. Katz, D., & Kahn, R. L. *The social psychology of organization,* rev. ed. New York: Wiley, 1978.
16. Nadler, D. A., & Tushman, M. L. A diagnostic model for organizational behavior. In J. R. Hackman, E. E. Lawler III, & L. W. Porter (Eds.), *Perspectives on behavior in organizations.* New York: McGraw-Hill, 1977.
17. Charter, W. E., & Jones, J. E. On the risk of appraising non-events in program evaluation. *Evaluation Researcher,* 1973, **11**, 5–7.
18. Walton, R. E. The diffusion of new work structures: Explaining why success didn't take. *Organizational Dynamics,* Winter 1974, 3–21.
19. Goodman, P. *Assessing organizational change: the Rushton quality of work life experiment.* New York: Wiley-Interscience, 1979.
20. Lawler, E. E. III, & Drexler, J. A., Jr. Dynamics of establishing cooperative quality-of-worklife projects. *Monthly Labor Review,* March 1978, 23–28.
21. Nadler, D. A., Hanlon, M., & Lawler, E. E. III. Factors influencing the success of

labor–management quality of work life projects. *Journal of Occupational Behavior,* 1980, **1**, 53–67.

22. Zaltman, G., & Duncan, R. *Strategies for planned change.* New York: Wiley-Interscience, 1977.

23. Nadler, D. A., Mirvis, P. H., & Cammann, C. The ongoing feedback system: Experimenting with a new managerial tool. *Organizational Dynamics,* 1976, **4**, 63–80.

24. Nadler, D. A., & Pecorella, P. A. Differential effects of multiple interventions in an organization. *Journal of Applied Behavioral Science,* 1975, **11**, 348–366.

25. Lawler, E. E. III. The new plant revolution. *Organizational Dynamics,* 1978, **6**, 3–12.

26. Nieva, F. F., Perkins, D. N. T., & Lawler, E. E. III. Improving the quality of life at work: Assessment of a collaborative selection process. *Journal of Occupational Behavior,* 1980, **1**, 43–52.

27. Scriven, M. Pros and cons about goal free evaluation. *The Journal of Educational Evaluation.* Los Angeles: Center for the Study of Evaluation, University of California, 1972, **3**, 1–5.

28. Weiss, C. H. *Evaluation research: Methods for assessing program effectiveness.* Englewood Cliffs: Prentice-Hall, 1972.

29. Hackman, J. R. Work redesign. In J. R. Hackman & J. L. Suttles (Eds.), *Improving life at work.* Santa Monica: Goodyear, 1977.

30. Seashore, S. E., & Bowers, D. G. Durability of organizational change. *American Psychologist,* 1970, **25**, 227–233.

31. Campbell, D. T., & Fiske, D. W. Convergent and discriminant validation by the multitrait–multimethod matrix. *Psychological Bulletin,* 1959, **56**, 81–105.

32. Campbell, D. T., & Stanley, J. C. *Experimental and quasi-experimental designs for research.* Chicago: Rand-McNally, 1966.

33. Campbell, D. T. Reforms as experiments. *American Psychologist,* 1969, **24**, 409–429.

34. Lawler, E. E. III. Adaptive experiments: An approach to organizational behavior research. *Academy of Management Review,* 1977, **2**, 576–585.

35. Likert, R. *New patterns of management.* New York: McGraw-Hill, 1961.

36. Mirvis, P. H., & Lawler, E. E. III. Measuring the financial impact of employee attitudes. *Journal of Applied Psychology,* 1977, **62**, 1–8.

37. Lawler, E. E. III, Hackman, J. R., & Kaufman, S. Effects of job redesign: A field experiment. *Journal of Applied Psychology,* 1973, **3**, 49–62.

38. Golembiewsky, R. T., Billingsley, K., & Yeager, S. Measuring change and persistence in human affairs: Types of change generated by OD design. *Journal of Applied Behavioral Science,* 1975, **12**, 133–157.

39. Kenny, D. A. A quasi-experimental approach to assessing treatment effects in the nonequivalent control group design. *Psychological Bulletin,* 1973, **82**, 345–362.

40. Box, G. E. P., & Jenkins, G. M. *Time-series analysis: Forecasting and control.* San Francisco: Holden-Day, 1970.

41. Campbell, D. T. From description to experimentation: Interpreting trends as quasi-experiments. In C. W. Harris (Ed.), *Problems in measuring change.* Madison: University of Wisconsin Press, 1963.

42. Pelz, D. C., & Andrews, F. M. Detecting causal priorities in panel study data. *American Sociological Review,* 1964, **29**, 836–848.

43. Seashore, S. E. Field experiments with formal organizations. *Human Organization,* 1964, **23**, 1964–1970.

44. Blalock, H. M. *Causal inference in nonexperimental research*. New York: Norton, 1972.

45. Alderfer, C. P., & Brown, L. D. *Learning from changing: Organizational diagnosis and development*. Beverly Hills: Sage, 1975.

46. Argyris, C. *Intervention theory and method*. Reading, MA: Addison-Wesley, 1970.

47. Seashore, S. The design of action research. In A. W. Clark (Ed.), *Experimenting with organizational life: The action research approach*. New York: Plenum Press, 1975.

CHAPTER THREE

Doing Independent Assessment Research

STANLEY E. SEASHORE AND PHILIP H. MIRVIS

Although assessors of an organizational change program may aspire to independence, autonomy, and the single-minded pursuit of research objectives, in actual practice they are faced with threats to their independence, limits to their autonomy, and diversionary demands posed by persons and events. From the start they depend on others to achieve their purposes, and these others also depend on them. There are legitimate and unavoidable reciprocal claims. Thus to achieve a degree of independence and autonomy, assessors must work within a framework of interdependence and reciprocity. While this diverts precious energy from their assessments, it is necessary to the formation of a viable role for doing assessment research.

It is the theme of this chapter that independence and autonomy are realized neither by distancing the assessor from the host organization and change agent nor by interposing barriers against influence. Rather, they are realized by the purposeful and public creation of roles and role relationships that serve to emphasize mutual dependencies and control. First, we will analyze the parties at interest in an assessment and the role-forming and relationship-building tasks that face assessors working with these parties at different stages of the effort. Second, we will report on some strategies that have helped in implementing the assessment role and on some hazards that have accompanied its fulfillment. Our verbal tools will be the language of role theory and our conceptual framework that of dynamic role systems.[1] First, who are the parties at interest?

THE PARTIES AT INTEREST

The Participants

It should be recognized at the outset that rather than dealing with individual participants at the site, assessment researchers are working with a social system. This system is composed of people who have positions in an hierarchy and who, in their collective identity as an organization, also have relationships with supporters, consumers, competitors, governments, unions, and other organized entities. In addition, they have working ties with other "outsiders" who are connected with the change program or connected with the evaluation. The participants in an assessment are all those who contribute time, resources, or information to the assessment as well as those affected by the research process or its results. Taken together, these are the clients of the assessors, including sponsors, the organization that hosts them, and various stakeholders who can benefit from, or are vulnerable to, the consequences of the research itself.

In the assessment studies described in this volume, the roster of relevant parties at the time of the assessment is impressive if not sometimes appalling. First, in most organizations there was a committee composed of representatives from management and from the employees or their union. The committee's charge was to review problems and change opportunities, set priorities, create a climate that fosters collaborative problem solving, and help initiate actions and solutions. Second, the committee members had the aid of an external consultant—often a team—of their own choosing. Third, in some cases, representatives of the American Center for the Quality of Working Life served as agents to locate promising sites, to help negotiate initial agreements among the parties, and to serve as external intermediaries should problems arise. Fourth, an Institute for Social Research (ISR) assessment team was authorized to observe events over the course of the study, to obtain such data and measurements as the team saw fit, and to make a public report describing and evaluating the change effort. Finally, in some instances the direct costs of the assessment, or some part of them, were borne by external funding agencies. All of these individuals and groups contributed time, resources, and information to the assessment and accepted some obligations and risks.

Others who fit within these criteria of participation are the employees, the organization itself, and the affiliated unions. Also, all employees, organizations, and unions who are part of a comparison site are participants in the research activity. Finally, assessors also have ties to their own scientific communities, depending on their theoretical, methodological, and substantive products. They—like the researchers' home institutions—are also parties to the study since they are affected by the research results.

When engaging such an array of disparate participants, assessors are denied the possibility of working with each of them, or each class of them, separately. Each party is linked in a network in which each has rights and responsibilities as regards some—perhaps all—of the others. Thus the assessors engage the participants' roles that are embedded in the complex role system that regulates behavior among them. Moreover, they bring to the engagement their own roles and role relations and become—with the participants and consultants—part of a new and enlarged role system. Although assessors may have established ways for dealing with, say, individual research subjects, professional colleagues, isolated informants, or fiscal sponsors, these practices have to be modified and adapted to fit a situation in which multiple participants have overlapping interests that are, to varying degrees, in conflict. Furthermore, ethical, as compared to efficacious, practices must also be tailored to the demands of this complex system, for assessors cannot single-handedly manage the ethical dilemmas that arise over the course of the study. Assessors are but a weak force in a field of powerful ones, with only limited means for insuring the ethical behavior of others and for redressing ethical lapses. In sum, to conduct their research in a productive and ethical way, assessors need explicitly to consider their relationship not only with participants as persons as semi-isolated circumstances but also with their roles in role systems and with the disturbances that occur when independently established role systems intersect for the first time.[2]

Role Novelty, Ambiguity, and Conflict

The intersection of existing role systems in organizational change programs is new to most participants, but the enlarged role system is constructed largely of old and familiar parts. All cultures whether a large society or a small work group, provide standard role models that can be invoked and modified to fit new situations. Thus the process of role formation relating to the change effort is greatly aided (or impeded) by the past experiences of the parties with outside consultants and by the mutuality of their role expectations. Quite a different situation exists with assessors. Few work organizations have any established role models that fit, or come near fitting, the case of independent assessment researchers. During the first meetings, assessors are likely to encounter a bewildering diversity of role expectations from others. They are also likely to send messages about their own intended roles that are interpreted in different ways. Their initial role is inevitably ambiguous. Moreover, as role defining and testing exchanges occur, it is inevitable that some—perhaps many—of the role expectations they encounter will prove to be incompatible. Some incompatibilities are superficial or transient and pose no threat to the research, but others are rooted in the different interests of the participants. To varying degrees, these twin problems of role ambiguity and role conflict are present in all assessment efforts. They are not to be resolved by role taking but, instead, by proactive and collaborative role making.[3,4]

The approaches for addressing these actual or potential role-relation issues should have three features. First, a conscious and persistent effort should be made from the start to clarify research roles, anticipate role conflicts, and respond to them through research policies. Also, plans can be committed to writing in the form of contracts or letters of agreement. Second, since role systems embody, and must be compatible with, shared normative standards, the values that lie at their bases can be articulated and affirmed. Asserting the values of informed consent, voluntarism, personal privacy, equity, reciprocity, and the like can ease role-making processes in assessment and serve to maintain roles in the face of competing expectations. Third, the assessors should work closely with the other parties to maintain the integrity of the independent assessment role and to fulfill their mutual responsibilities to insure that the research is conducted effectively. An effective assessment is not simply a product of the assessors. It must be a joint achievement that results from the creation of roles that are mutually compatible and the establishment of norms that protect the welfare of all the parties involved.

Steps in Doing Assessment Research

Organizational assessment follows a course of action parallel to that of the change effort. In the ISR projects described in Chapter 1, after the site is selected and negotiations are underway to start the project, the assessors take baseline measures of the organizational records, administer a preexperimental survey, conduct interviews, and begin on-site observations. Then, as pilot programs are implemented in the organization and initial goals are achieved, the assessors continue observing at the site, monitoring records, and administer a mid-experiment attitude survey or surveys. When the project nears its end and plans are made for institutionalizaton of the changes and their diffusion to other areas in the firm, the assessors complete their observations, administer a final survey, close the books, and begin preparing a public report of the program events and results.

To perform the assessment tasks, a series of steps must also be taken by the researchers to create, establish, and maintain their assessment role. Among the objectives are self-protecting ones such as gaining access to the participants and insuring the candor of their information and opinions; moderating "evaluation apprehensions"; thwarting attempts at cooptation; and avoiding identification with one party or another in conflicts that may arise. There are also more altruistic objectives, such as insuring against misuse of information, asserting the public and scientific interests in the data, assuring consideration of all legitimate perspectives in the planning, and conduct of the assessment work.

The general strategy employed by ISR assessors to implement their role has involved the following:

1. Initial efforts to create and clarify assessment roles.
2. Early attempts to build role relations and to reach agreements in writing and defining role responsibilities and the norms governing role behavior.
3. Ongoing efforts to formulate policies and decision-making procedures to respond to instances where roles are ambiguous or in conflict.
4. Continuing attempts to cope with role pressures by reviewing relationships, affirming norms, renegotiating agreements and providing, as is possible, for the continued legitimation of the assessment function by consent of all involved.

The following description of the steps taken by assessors to implement their roles will serve to indicate how these matters are proposed, negotiated, committed to formal agreement, tested in application, and adapted to changing circumstances.

IMPLEMENTING THE ASSESSMENT ROLE

When an organizational change program is to be assessed by an independent and autonomous third party, it is highly desirable, perhaps essential, that the assessors be a party to the early negotiations. The reasons are obvious. First, the provision for an external evaluation apart from the action consultation is rare, although not unprecedented, in organizations. Second, the commitment to a public analysis and report is not commonly a condition in change programs, and the implications are not commonly understood. The presence of an assessment team is not a trivial factor, and all parties involved must consider its implications. These negotiations enable the participants to meet the assessors, appraise their competencies and values, acquaint themselves with their aims and purposes, and decide whether to accept the assessment as part of the program. In turn, the assessors can meet the participants, determine their interests and expectations regarding the assessment, familiarize themselves with the plans for the change program, and decide whether to assume the assessment role. In addition, observation of the process of early negotiations is significant since these negotiations influence the course of both the change effort and the assessment, and they set the stage for the creation of the assessment role at the site.

Creating Roles in a Quality of Work Life Program

In the ISR change programs involving unions, the preliminary negotiations usually involved the top management of the host organization and of the union(s) as well as representatives of the American Center for the Quality of Working Life. The negotiations commonly extended over a year or more and ended with the preparation of a letter of agreement authorizing the program, the identification of a consenting demonstration site, and the formation of a local, joint management–union committee to oversee the change effort. The roles of committee members, change agents, and assessors were then negotiated at the local site. The assessors' crucial early role negotiations at the site usually involved the newly established joint labor–management committee, key union and management officials who were not members of that committee, and (somewhat later) the external consultant chosen to assist the committee at sites. In sites where no union existed, a cross-sectional committee was typically created to oversee the change effort.

The assessors worked to define themselves as neutral observers and—through policy and practice—sought to maintain impartiality. They also asked for permission to attend all committee meetings, take notes, and review pertinent documents. In addition, they requested access to members of the organization and to the operating and fiscal records of management and the union, with provisions that the voluntary and informed consent of the informants would be obtained and with assurance that rules of privacy, confidentiality, and anonymity would be maintained.

The assertion of such an assessment role, however, is not sufficient to insure its effective implementation at a site, for the assessment work cannot be accomplished without substantial voluntary local understandings, acceptance, and practical help. During the first meetings of the assessors with the joint committee and the change agents, therefore, there were significant exchanges of role communications. From the committee's perspective, these first contacts provide an initial look at a new and unfamiliar role. Their initial impressions of the assessors' role may rest upon their dress, demeanor, or other personal attributes, or upon impersonal attributes, such as their presumed identification with the employer, the union, or the sponsor of the study. In addition, committee members may generalize from past experiences or from local folklore. Recently, a team of researcher from ISR administered an assessment survey to employees in a division of a large service organization. Ten years previously another survey had been conducted, but with inadequate provision for feedback of the data by management throughout the division. As a belated consequence, some employees initially refused to cooperate with the new group of "rip-off artists." Even after a decade, the role definition derived from this earlier study, which was remembered by some and transmitted to others, rose to haunt the researchers in their efforts to define their role.

The committee members' first impressions can sometimes lead to a stereotyped view of the assessor's role. It is commonplace, for example, for a researcher who enters a site through management to be perceived as their agent. Although in all unionized locations the ISR assessors entered through the auspices of both labor and management officials, their role definition was still a source of misunderstanding and uncertainty. At one site, for instance, local management objected to the purposefully casual attire of a researcher, claiming that no one should "represent management dressed like a slob." After the repercussions of this matter reached the corporate and union brass and returned to the committee with a reaffirmation of the original understanding, the evaluator's independence was symbolically, if somewhat comically, affirmed, He thereafter appeared more clearly as a representative of ISR, not of the management nor the union, often *sans cravat*.

In this light, the first task of the researchers is to communicate clearly, explicitly, and by behavioral example their intended role definitions. This not only helps assessors to clarify their own roles, but it also helps to clarify the coordinate role responsibilities of the key local participants. They, too, need to determine whether they are to be uninvolved in the assessment, passive observers, or active participants. Field studies, just as those in the laboratory, have their demand characteristics: Key participants often have to "guess" at the researchers' intentions and define their own roles accordingly, as subservients, colleagues, accomplices, or saboteurs.[5] It is incumbent upon the assessors to reduce the guesswork by working closely with the participants to define their respective roles and to arrive at mutually understood role definitions.

Building Role Relations

The initial letter of agreement becomes part of the framework within which the assessors' role at the site can be both elaborated and constrained. Such an agreement usually authorizes the assessment effort, defines the broad parameters, and is subject to affirmation and proposed amendments by the local committee and the local key people. For example, the agreement asserts the principle of voluntarism for all local participants in the program, including the assessment activities. Voluntarism aids the assessors in resisting coercive efforts that may be directed toward their informants, and, on the other hand, it puts upon the assessors the burden of eliciting voluntary contributions to the assessment work. The agreement includes a provision that either management or union may unilaterally terminate the program on short notice for any reason. This understanding implies that any unduly offensive, intrusive, or potentially threatening actions by the assessors may be countered by suspension of the project. The agreement usually provides that committee meetings will be held during working hours and that no members shall "lose pay or benefits for attendance at such meetings," a provision that entitles the assessment team to request and obtain committee time and effort for review and direction of the assessment work. The agreement specifies that the local committee is the agency through which all assessment activities are monitored, thus precluding any "end-around" plays that might otherwise seem convenient or attractive to the assessors. In short, the formal preliminary agreement lays out the main protective role features for all parties.

To address their week-to-week work relations with the committee members, the assessors also negotiate more informal role contracts with them that detail their respective rights, duties, and responsibilities in the study and that affirm norms of privacy, informed consent, honesty, equity, and impartiality with respect to the assessment in the organization. In addition, the contracts establish the additional norm that conflicts of interest over the collection and use of assessment data be confronted openly and fully by the assessors and the members of the committee. This norm legitimates the airing of differences and asserts that conflicts should be settled by reason and reciprocity, rather than by the preemptive use of power or the selfish reliance on personal whim.

As part of their responsibility to the committee, the assessors agree to review in detail their instruments, work procedures, and evaluation plans with the members in return for having access to organizational records, the employees, and the committee meetings themselves. One intent is to further insure the continuing informed consent of the key participants and to familiarize them with the aims of the research. When practiced, however, it also enhances the quality of the research, since the committee members often suggest new and relevant sources of information and better ways of phrasing questions or gathering data. The committee members are also consulted about, and contribute to, the ongoing evaluation effort. As a result, a climate of mutual trust is encouraged.

Building role relations with the consultant is particularly problematic for assessors. An independent evaluation of one professional's work by another means that appraisals of the implementation of the change program and, by implication, of the skills and expertise of the consultants will have the weight of expert opinion. In addition, the provision for a public report means that the results will be broadly communicated, and with a measure of credibility. The consultant may reasonably ask himself or herself whether the assessment will rest upon criteria that he or she values, upon data that he or she considers pertinent, and upon interpretive perspectives that fit his or her professional intentions as a consultant.

Several steps can be taken to ease this inherently threatening role relationship. In some instances, steps have been taken by assessors to agree upon criteria for the evaluation and to establish practices regarding the collection and use of assessment information. In addition, efforts can be made to insure that it is primarily the change program—not the work of the consultants themselves—that is the subject of the evaluation. At one site, the consultants and the evaluators openly shared their mutual expectations and apprehensions and agreed to a periodic review and examination of their relationship.

Broadening Role Relationships

When the time comes to establish direct contacts and work relationships with others in the organization, the assessors have further role-defining and norm-setting tasks. In the projects monitored by ISR, this extension of role relationships is commonly initiated through formal and public communications, which are accommodated to the past practices of the site. There is likely to be a story in the house organ—if one exists—air time by means of public address system, or staff and union membership meetings—if such are available. Whatever the medium, as much information as feasible is transmitted; the legitimacy of the assessment program is displayed with respect to management and union sponsorship. The assessors informally interview as many people as time allows—both management and union, and at all ranks—to allow response to queries about the assessment aspect of the program, and to learn about potential problems or misunderstandings that need attention.

Many assessors see the collection of data in organizations as relatively routine and benign. However, it may seem quite incredible to some participants that anyone would collect data solely for scientific purposes, without intent to employ the data in trade or in a self-serving action. Thus it is quite common for organization members to question the motives of academics in collecting data from them or to suspect collusion between the academics and top officials. These suspicions can also carry over to assessment instruments. Employees may fear they are being asked "trick" questions or are being deceived about the aims of observers. To counter these suspicions, ISR researchers have sought to clarify the aims and intent of the research to the participants and to establish their role responsibilities toward them. At most sites, public announcements that describe the research have been posted. Letters from the joint committee have been issued from time to time regarding evaluation plans. Public question-and-answer sessions are held to clarify intentions. Finally, instruments have been scrutinized to eliminate ambiguous questions and insure that the data sought has high face validity for the assessment purposes.

Role contracting and norm setting have been more formalized with the participants directly involved in the data gathering. As an example, survey administrations among the work force are preceded by presentations that outline the purpose of the measurement and solicit the voluntary consent of the respondents. A cover letter on the questionnaire assures the participants of the confidentiality of their individual responses, and it outlines ISR procedures to protect anonymity. A sample cover letter with these assurances can be found in Appendix 4-1.

Despite efforts of these sorts, organization members have a backlog of experiences regarding the collection and use of information in their organization that can be a source of concern to them. Their only experience of direct visual observation, for example, may have been in a motion-and-time study. Their only experience in having their records examined may have been during a performance appraisal. Quite naturally, then, they may see small benefit and much potential harm to be derived from cooperating with evaluators. The relationship between the assessors and the participants, therefore, must also be characterized by reciprocity.

A norm of reciprocity in exchange infuses most social relations, and in a research effort this norm is central to the role contracts and subsequent role relations. The task of the assessment researchers is not simply to define their own research role and invoke its attendant norms, but rather it is to create a close working relationship with the parties in the research project so that mutually acceptable roles can be designed and maintained.

Role Relations in Information Use: Policies and Procedures

Considering that evaluation researchers deal with complex information of significant and novel kinds, it is not surprising that role misunderstandings and tensions can arise over information management. The assessors' role responsibilities relating to information may be ambiguous in a given situation; they may be clear but incompatible and thus confront the assessor with a dilemma. A site committee may propose substantial additions or alterations to a "standard" research instrument, with a consequent need to balance the assessors' commitment to standard and economical procedures against the commitment to accommodation and role reciprocity. A prior general agreement that the assessors are not to intervene actively in program decisions at the site does not always serve to moderate committee resentment when the observing assessor withholds professional opinion about a subject under discussion. The agreed intention to avoid intrusion into the "normal" course of a change program is, at least in part, incompatible with interviewing and questionnaire surveys that inevitably have impact upon employees' perceptions and expectations.

Certain matters of information use and management can be treated by explicit, recorded, general agreements. An example is the issuance, at most of the sites monitored by ISR, of a "statement of intent regarding the return of research information to [the site]." The statements varied somewhat but included a number of common features. Data returned would be factual, without ISR interpretation or opinion. The data would be available equally to management, union(s), and consultants. Data would be provided only to the site committee, and the committee would then control its further distribution and use. Data would be returned only upon specific request from the committee with the concurrence of the consultant(s). No data would be returned that risked violation of ISR's obligations to persons regarding confidentiality or which exceeded budgetary provisions; only such data would be returned that could, in principle, be gathered by the committee itself if it chose to do so. An example of such a statement of intent is provided in Appendix 3-1.

A similar statement of intent has been used in connection with the external release of information from or about the program site. Such agreements covered potentially conflictful issues, such as ISR's ultimate right to publication after clearance with the site committee (and its designates) regarding matters of confidentiality and factual correctness but not regarding matters of interpretation; the right of on-site people to make whatever public release of information they wished; and affirmation of the local committee's full "ownership," responsibility, and credit for the conduct of their experiment or program. The intent of such statements is to protect the integrity of the program plan, avoid compromise of ISR's ultimate evaluative opinions through premature public release of information, and to discourage false impressions about the role of ISR in the activities at the site. A sample statement appears as Appendix 3-2.

A third area of potential role conflict concerns access to the assessment data by persons other than the ISR research team. Some external fiscal sponsors press for arrangements that will insure maximum use of the research data for scientific and public-information purposes—a view shared by ISR as a general principle. The site people have a legitimate concern about the release of information to users who are not bound by undertakings concerning confidentiality and proprietary interests and who are not accessible for monitoring of released data. Anticipating such issues, ISR prepared a statement concerning the guidelines and conditions for release of research data to other researchers (Appendix 3-3 shows a current version).

Such agreements seem excessively legalistic and rigid when abstracted from their contexts. Each of the provisions negotiated in agreements at the start and throughout the projects affirms ethical norms for the protection of clients *and* researchers—norms such as those pertaining to privacy and informed consent, the protection of the participants' welfare, preservation of scientific interests, avoidance of coercion, minimization of risk, and the like. It is significant that under such terms, the achievement of ethical solutions to operational problems is plainly a matter of concern to all the parties, and is not only a matter of the researchers' judgments. In all instances, the provisions were elaborated through discussions or through the precedent of earlier specific actions. In many cases, the original specifications were altered by informal agreement to meet the necessities of unanticipated conditions. Such role contracts have been applied not as inflexible credos but as reminders of original intentions to conduct research effectively and ethically.

Coping with Problems in Implementation

The reader should not assume that all this attention and effort has resulted in unqualified success in implementing the assessment role. The approach has been successful so far, in the sense that the assessment requirements have been met and the assessors' role has been tolerated in all places, even honored in some, despite the stresses that accompany organizational change programs. Nevertheless, if mention was made of all ethical and role dilemmas encountered and painfully resolved or tolerated in some fashion, it would form a long list. For example, in one situation the "impartial" and "nonintervening" ISR researchers, under great pressure from the site committee and the fiscal sponsors, consented to join in a strategy to replace an ineffective team of consultants. In another situation, the research team consented to a data-feedback activity wherein indicators of the role performance of certain middle-level managers were reported to peers and superiors in the absence of unanimous consent by the managers, some of whom were "volunteered" for this exposure by their peers. In yet another case, the consultants and committee members felt so threatened by the evaluators that they formed a coalition to thwart the evaluation effort. Then the researchers, intent upon their duties but cut off from data from these parties, increased their authorized collateral surveillance and sought out new sources of information. There emerged an unhealthy cycle of threat and deception that was spurred in part by the conflict engendered by the evaluation role. Neither policy nor contingency planning could break this cycle, although an uneasy, workable truce was achieved.

In most sites, the researchers worked with the consultants and committee members to achieve a positive commitment to the assessment role and to maintain it in the face of competing pressures. The early specification of agreed ground rules minimizes power imbalances that could rupture trust or inhibit dialogue. Then, throughout the period of study role definitions are continuously redefined and responsibilities renegotiated, for the fluid nature of the field situation generates a number of unforeseeable events, which make necessary the continuous renegotiations and reshaping of initial agreements.

ASSESSING THE ASSESSMENTS

Just as change programs need to be assessed, assessors too need to be assessed. It is essential therefore that each report from sites where the assessment is completed include information about the assessors' role at that site and the events that signal operational difficulties or limitations on assessment accomplishments. To this end also, variations in practice at different sites can be undertaken with an explicit intention to make comparative analyses. These variations in role definition or role emergence can include the following: (1) supplementing the "core" data-collection plan with additional material and methods of local interest or promise; (2) provision of relatively open and prompt return of concurrent assessment data for possible "formative" use in program development by the site committees; and (3) providing for the ISR team the dual functions of assessment *and also* action and process consultation to the local committee. These variations are all departures from the "ideal" of providing an independent, autonomous, nonintrusive assessment role—departures in the direction of engagement, accommodation, and active intrusion. They, however, make it possible to learn about the value of different approaches to assessment.

For the prescriptions we suggest to be relevant to assessment, they must be useful in action. We believe they can be useful, and although they cannot be prescriptive with respect to the role to be formed and with respect to the relations to be asserted with the consultant and site committee, they can be prescriptive *with respect to the processes that can lead to the implementation of a mutually agreeable assessment role* and to the continued legitimation of the role by the consensus of all the parties involved. This view does not lessen the researchers' responsibilities to complete the data gathering, analysis, and interpretation tasks in the assessment. On the contrary, it adds the additional task that assessors create and maintain an acceptable public role when conducting the assessment—or else leave the scene.

REFERENCES

1. Katz, D., & Kahn, R. L. *The social psychology of organizations,* 2nd ed. New York: Wiley, 1978.
2. Mirvis, P. H. & Seashore, S. E. Creating ethical relationships in organizational research. In J. Sieber (Ed.), *The ethics of social research: surveys and experiments.* New York: Springer-Verlag, 1982.
3. Graen, G. Role making processes in organizations. In M. D. Dunnette (Ed.), *Handbook of industrial and organizational psychology.* Chicago: Rand-McNally, 1976.
4. Klein, L. *A social scientist in industry.* Essex: Gower Press, 1976.
5. Orne, M. T. On the social psychology of the psychological experiment with particular reference to demand characteristics and their implications. *American Psychologist,* 1962, **17,** 776–783.

APPENDIX 3-1 STATEMENT OF INTENT: RETURN OF RESEARCH INFORMATION TO (SITE)

We regard the experimental programs introduced by [the committee] and the site assessment information collected by ISR as two separate although related activities. To the extent possible, the experimental change plans are not to be influenced or distorted by the measurement program, and the measurement activity is not to be diverted or distorted by incorporation in the experimental programs.

At the same time, it is recognized that some information collected for project assessment purposes will have interest and possible value for those engaged directly in the experiments. We therefore need to keep open the possibility that the ISR research data may be made available. In making decisions about providing data, we will be guided by the following general considerations:

1.   ISR may provide research data to people at the site during the course of the experimental program in response to a specific request from the (local committee) that has the consent of their outside consultant.

2.   Research data may be provided only under the condition that its local distribution and use is to be controlled by (the committee) and that it is to be accessible equally to the management, the union, and the outside consultant.

3.   Data will be provided in as factual and objective a manner as is feasible, avoiding any representation of ISR opinions, evaluations, or recommendations. ISR, however, will endeavor to make clear the technical characteristics and limitations of the information.

4.   The data will be limited to those kinds that, in principle, could be obtained by (the committee) itself if it chose to do so. Information uniquely obtainable from the ISR research team is excluded. Data in forms that might violate ISR assurances of individual confidentiality or anonymity are also excluded.

5.   Since ISR is limited by its main priorities of purpose, by manpower limits, and by tight budgets, research data will be provided only if the added work, time, and costs are supportable within budget, or if supplemental resources are provided for the extra costs incurred.

The view expressed by these guidelines is that ISR desires to be helpful to the experimental site activities within the limits of (1) protecting the integrity of the experimental plan, (2) observing assurances of confidentiality and anonymity, and (3) available manpower and fiscal resources.

APPENDIX 3-2   STATEMENT OF INTENT: PUBLIC RELEASE AND USE OF INFORMATION

Information concerning the plans, activities, and outcomes of the Quality of Work Life experiment are the property and responsibility of [the committee]. At the same time, the purpose of supporting sponsors and of the Institute for Social Research require that information be employed promptly and vigorously to promote public understanding of QWL efforts, to engage further public interest in QWL efforts, and to diffuse scientific and technical information about QWL efforts. Thus, all parties agree to free public access and use of information, subject only to limitations arising from the need to protect the experimental plan and the need to honor commitments as to the confidential nature of proprietary information and anonymity of individual participants. In making decisions about the public use of information regarding such experiments, we will be guided by the following policies:

1.   In public representations of information about the Quality of Work experiment, the experiment is to be represented as having been conducted by the site organization and union, not by ISR.

2.   Information once made public by the company or the union is in the public domain, and its use by ISR is not restricted except by considerations of goodwill and professional ethics.

3.   Public documents and presentations by ISR and its subcontractors that are derived from proprietary or confidential information will be in a form that effectively prevents disclosure that may be harmful to the company's or union's interests. For example, scientific articles in technical and professional journals may use such information only if the interests of the company and the union are protected by the modification of the data or the concealment of the data's source or both. When doubt exists, the material to be made public is subject to prior review and consent by the company and the union with respect to the release of previously confidential information.

4.   The [joint committee] will be the agency for review and consent, as well as the responsible source of consultation with ISR, regarding the release of confidential information bearing upon their experiment. It is noted that the committee is to have both management and labor representation, each with veto power regarding the release of information deemed confidential in relation to their respective interests. On matters of both public and internal release of previously confidential information that exceed the authority of that committee, it is expected that management and labor representatives will seek advice and authorization as they deem necessary.

5.   It is understood that this agreement pertains solely to ISR and its subcontractor(s).

Because the experimental period is a particularly sensitive time during which the intervention may need to be protected, the following special policies will hold only during that period:

1.   It is proper for ISR or funding sponsors to encourage early and full publicity about experimental plans and activities to the extent that this does not jeopardize the experimental conditions or plans. For example, ISR might arrange new releases, conferences, films, publications, and the like through which responsible (site) representatives, if they so choose, may make public representations of their activities, plans, and results.

2.   When making public representations of information that is identified as being from (the site), ISR will endeavor to be objective and factual, avoiding any expression or implication of their own opinion or judgment that may prejudice the course of the experimental plan or that may prejudice their own later conclusions regarding the experiment.

3.   During the experimental period, ISR will not present to the public any information that has not been previously made public by the company or union unless its release is approved by [the committee] or it is presented in a manner that maintains the anonymity of the site and the individuals at the site.

Because the need to protect the experimental intervention is expected to diminish in importance after the experimental period ends, it is appropriate that the following less-restrictive policy replace the preceding policies after the experimental period ends:

1.   It is accepted that the scientific objectives of ISR and its sponsoring agencies require public description of the events and publication of the final results of the experiment as well as interpretations of their significance. [The committee] has the right to review such material in advance of release as to the correctness of factual information and as to consent for release of previously confidential information but not as to interpretations, opinions, and evaluations by ISR staff. Such public releases by ISR staff will be identified as expressing the views of the author(s) and not necessarily expressing the views of [the company or the union].

The view expressed by these guidelines is that ISR desires and has an obligation to promote early, full, public information and evaluation concerning Quality of Work Life Program experiments, but only within practices that (1) insure full credit for accomplishments to those who undertake the experiments, (2) protect the integrity of the experimental plan and process during the action phases, and (3) do not compromise the ultimate scientific, professional, and public-policy interpretations that must ultimately be formed and made public by ISR staff members.

APPENDIX 3-3   GUIDELINES FOR ACCESS TO QUALITY OF WORK LIFE PROGRAM DATA BANK

General

The QWL data bank is viewed as a common resource to be shared freely with qualified researchers for purposes compatible with the QWL program objectives, but with constraints arising from considerations of cost,

ISR staff resources, and protection of the interests of individuals and organizations participating in the program.

Constraints

1.   Eligible recipients are persons who are qualified to conduct complex statistical analyses of social-science data and who are located in an institutional setting that offers a reasonable likelihood for effective use of the data and continuing responsibility for their protection. Students requesting data will be sponsored by a qualified faculty member who accepts primary responsibility for the use and care of the data.

2.   Information that allows ready identification of individual participants, or of the organizational source, will not ordinarily be released.

3.   Data regarding a particular site or population ordinarily will become available immediately after the expiration of the period of active participation in the QWL program.

4.   Release of data may be deferred by ISR if, in its judgement, the dataset is not yet sufficiently clean and sufficiently well documented to allow effective use by others who lack access to the original sources for verification or correction.

5.   No data will be released that are protected by ISR commitments regarding confidential or proprietary information.

Procedures and Administration

1.   All costs of preparing the data for transmission and of ISR consultation regarding their use will be borne by the recipient on an actual-cost, nonprofit basis.

2.   The data may be provided in any feasible form—tapes, cards, or printout—as requested.

3.   Requests for data will be in writing, with specification of the population (data sources/referents) and the measures or classes of data required. The request will ordinarily be prepared with ISR staff consultation and assistance to insure optimum exploitation of the data resources and avoidance of unnecessary costs.

4.   Publications and oral presentations based upon these data will include a suitable credit notice for provision of the data and a suitable disclaimer of ISR responsibility for the analyses and interpretations.

5.   When data have been provided of a nature that puts participants at risk as to anonymity or confidentiality, any proposed publication will be provided to ISR for review prior to publication. These reviews will be solely with regard to the protection of the data sources; ISR reserves the right to proscribe or alter the material if, in its judgment, the interests of data sources are put at risk.

6.   Requestors will be required to provide a statement of provisions for the disposition of the data after use and as to their continuing protection from unauthorized use.

7.   Interpretations, exceptions, and amendments to the foregoing guidelines rest exclusively with ISR's QWL staff during the period while maximum, safe utilization of the data-bank is being explored.

PART TWO

MEASUREMENT PRACTICES

This section is concerned with measurement practices. Measurement is conceived broadly to include a variety of feasible methods and sources for getting information that might aid the assessment of the state of an organization and its change. There are treatments of interview and questionnaire procedures, observation of events, abstraction of data from an organization's records, and the use of analytical methods to codify complex data and to test its quality.

Chapter 4 describes the *Michigan Organizational Assessment Questionnaire (MOAQ)*, a survey instrument designed to get information directly from and about individual members of an organization. The information obtained is partly an "objective" reporting of events and conditions as they are directly observed by people. It also includes highly "subjective" reporting of the respondent's own opinions and evaluations. Topics covered include the work environment, the respondent's own job and role relationships, work-group characteristics, supervision received, reward systems (pay, benefits, etc.), and working conditions. The chapter describes the conceptual sources employed in designing the questionnaire, the statistical pedigree of each derived scale, and the available evidence concerning the validity of the measures obtained.

Chapter 5, like Chapter 4, is focused upon data from and about individuals, with an emphasis upon measurable or recorded behaviors that can be aggregated to estimate the rates and costs of such behaviors for work groups, departments, or the whole of an organization. This approach assumes that individual choices about being productive, being absent, quitting, becoming ill, having an accident, and the like are in some significant way determined by the social and technological properties of the organization. Organizational changes may thus have a direct and intentional impact upon the rates of occurrence of such costly behaviors, or the effect may be indirect, as an unintended result of changes. A distinction is made between behaviors representing presence and participation in the organization and those representing the individual's quality of role performance. Criteria for choosing, defining, and costing the behaviors are provided, along with an example of their application in one organization during a change program.

Chapters 6 and 7 treat methods for measuring aspects of the structure of organizations—aspects that are complementary to those represented in formal organizational plans and charts. Chapter 6 is concerned with the distribution of influence among organizational units or across hierarchical levels. A distinction is made between influence over personnel decisions, coordination decisions, and decisions about the work itself. Chapter 7 views organizational structure in terms of linkages (networks) that cluster and connect individuals, or work groups, by ties of friendship or of work interdependency. Illustrations are provided of measurement methods, analytical procedures, and the use of the resulting data in tracing the effect of organizational change programs. Such effects may increase or decrease the amount of structuring that is present, and they may alter the compatibility of the informal structure with the work flow and technology.

Chapters 8, 9 and 10 concern the assessment of an organization's technological systems and of change in such systems. Chapter 8 summarizes our efforts to find and adopt, or to invent, a conceptual basis for describing and comparing technologies. An approach is proposed that differentiates five facets of an organization's work-flow system and allows application at three levels of description and analysis. "Technology" is viewed as the process for transforming inputs of information and physical resources into outputs and regulating the component processes. While uniqueness in each technological system is acknowledged, the proposed framework can guide a researcher in decisions about what to measure and how to link the "levels" in the analysis of nested technologies. Chapter 9 displays an approach to the assessment of technologies with data from expert observations, questionnaires, and interviews. An example of application addresses the problem of estimating the extent to which the intrinsic properties of a work system are optimally utilized in practice, as well as the use of the information in correcting faults of sociotechnical compatibility. Chapter 10 concerns the description of individual jobs and job-performance contexts, using both questionnaire and observational methods. The chapter reports the convergence and points of nonconvergence between the job occupant's ratings and those of the trained observer. The instruments and procedures are described in operational detail.

Chapters 11 and 12 form a pair that are concerned with the practice of naturalistic observation of organizational functioning and of the activities undertaken in organizational change programs. The procedures described in Chapter 11 assume access to the organization for continuous or episodic observation by individuals whose main function is to record, codify, and interpret the flow of events and the character of critical or representative episodes. Suggestions are offered to guide the field practices of observers and to systematize the use of observational and documentary data. A coding scheme is presented that allows the cataloging of events and observations, the in-process recording of tentative interpretations, and, if desired, the quantitative analysis of sequences and trends of events. Chapter 12 reports a procedure for the observation and reporting of scheduled meetings. Such meetings are commonly prominent in planned change programs in which groups are formed to plan, activate, and/or evaluate the change program. A method of approach is displayed for the initial recording of the process and content of the discussion in meetings and the coding of episodes as to content and process characteristics. Examples are provided of the application of these procedures in a particular case.

The final chapter of this section—Chapter 13—treats unions and union–management relations. The authors report on the use of interview, documentary, and questionnaire procedures to establish the structure of the union organization and of union–management relations, the union members' description and evaluation of their unions, and changes that may occur in these domains. Included in this chapter are structured interview and questionnaire guides for use in obtaining participant views of the functioning of joint union–management organizational change programs.

CHAPTER FOUR

Assessing the Attitudes and Perceptions of Organizational Members

CORTLANDT CAMMANN, MARK FICHMAN, G. DOUGLAS JENKINS, JR., AND JOHN R. KLESH

The Michigan Organizational Assessment Questionnaire (MOAQ) is designed to provide information about the perceptions of organizational members. The information ranges from the "objective" reporting of events and conditions as they are directly observed by the employees, to wholly "subjective" reports of the respondents' own opinions and evaluative judgments. As participant-observers, the members are uniquely qualified to describe the work, work environments, and organizational activities in their respective areas of the organization. As active members, they are uniquely qualified to report their own personal beliefs, opinions, expectations, and affective responses that may, in aggregation, reveal important attributes of the organization.

In this chapter we will describe the rationale and methods employed in the development of the questionnaire instrument, together with summary statistics bearing upon the reliability, validity, and discriminating power of the various component measures. This report is the third in a series of progress reports, and it includes all refinements, simplifications, and content extensions in the measure since its development by Edward Lawler, Cortlandt Cammann, David Nadler, and Douglas Jenkins in 1975.[1] Since the developmental process is continuous, this should also be considered a "progress report" subject to later updating and amendment.

Before describing the questionnaire itself, it may be worthwhile to describe our rationale for developing a questionnaire at all. Our reasoning involves two aspects: a sense that a complete organizational assessment needs to include information reflecting the views of individual organization members, and a belief that a questionnaire represents one of the most cost-efficient ways of collecting this type of information.

The need for collecting individual-level information stems from two parts of our view of organizational assessment. The first involves evaluation. As we have argued previously, a complete assessment of an organization's existing state or of an organizational change program requires an evaluation that reflects the criteria of all interested parties. Since organization members almost always qualify as relevant interested parties, it is essential that assessors have some method to describe the way organization members view and react to aspects of organizational functioning that are of interest. It seems to us that the most straightforward way to find out the views of these people is to ask them.

The second reason for collecting individual-level information is based on our view of organizations. Organizations are very complex human systems, and no individual ever has complete information about all of the things that take place within them. The meaning of organizational events and the description of organizational states tend to vary, depending on the perspective of the observer who is describing them. Any overall description of the organization must, of necessity, ignore a great deal of information. One method for capturing this complexity is to collect information from all organization members or some adequate random sample. This provides the assessor with access to information that can only be meaningfully collected at the individual level (such as the degree of challenge individual employees experience on their jobs) as well as to information that reflects variations in states that exist within the organization (e.g., variation in the trust of top management across groups or variations in the styles of supervision in different departments). Of course, once the information is collected, the assessor faces the problem of summarizing the complexity for use in the assessment, but the summary at least can be based on a decision about what is most important to describe, and the information does exist to allow other summaries if at some future date these should prove appropriate.

Our decision to use a questionnaire to collect information about individual perceptions was based on the relative advantages and defects of this methodology. The defects are well known: Valid responses depend upon the clarity of the questions and the linguistic competence of the respondents. The questionnaire method—even when modified by the use of open-ended response opportunities—imposes upon the respondent a predefined array of topics and response categories that may not fit the "real" situation of the respondent well. Finally, responses may be inadvertently biased or knowingly distorted.

Offsetting these hazards are a number of advantages—the most compelling being efficiency in data gathering. The questionnaire survey process allows one, with relatively modest time and money costs, to get information about a broad range of topics from a large number of respondents, and to do so with relatively little disturbance of the normal activities of an organization. "Relatively" refers to the comparable costs and disturbance of an interview or observation process, or the institution of new systems for reports and records. Further, questionnaires provide data in a quantitative or codable form, and often they can do so in a highly standardized, precoded format. This feature of questionnaire data, along with the availability of many data sources (respondents), allows the institution of quality-control procedures and the assessment of the reliabilities and validities of the data. It is also easy to assure anonymity. Finally, the data may be aggregated in multiple ways for a variety of modes of analysis, display, and interpretation. Given these advantages and defects, the relative ease of standardization and the relative efficiency of questionnaires dictated that we use this method as our primary technique for collecting information about individual perceptions and attitudes.

QUESTIONNAIRE DESIGN AND DEVELOPMENT

Four main goals were identified for the questionnaire design and development effort:

1. To provide a survey with topical coverage suited to the intended assessment and interpretive uses.
2. To assure that the questionnaire is suitable for use in a variety of organizational contexts with respondents of diverse situations and characteristics.
3. To achieve a satisfactory level of scale reliability and validity in use.
4. To ascertain the utility of the instrument in "practical" use—that is, its meaningfulness to nonprofessional data interpreters in feedback and to analysis in theoretical inquiries.

Measurement Domains

A major initial strategic choice in selecting topical domains for an assessment questionnaire lies in the ground rules for inclusion. One possible guideline is to formulate a coherent theoretical framework and then to concentrate the measurement effort on the essential conceptual components of that theory. This approach has the advantage of providing an explicit rationale and theoretical basis for inclusions and exclusions. It has the disadvantages of omitting measures deemed theoretically important by others, imposing a restriction on content that limits its usefulness among members of the organizations studied, and tying the questionnaire to a theory of limited scope that is destined to be supplanted in time with a better one. An alternative guideline is to adopt the prevailing language, operative constructs, and implicit theories of organizational members, and then aim to conform the questionnaire to this set of data users. A third possible guideline is to scan the existing literature in search of constructs and questionnaire measurement operations that have some established evidence of empirical reliability, validity, and utility, giving little regard for their places in some coherent theoretical framework.

The choice we made was to use all three guidelines to a limited extent. The questionnaire is based on a theoretical framework that is adapted from Hackman and Oldham.[2] It assumes that the reactions of individuals to their work settings can be described in terms of (1) *descriptors* of critical aspects of the work environment, (2) *psychological states* that are presumed to be influenced by the work environment, (3) *individual-level outcomes* commonly valued by organizational members, and (4) *individual differences* (demography, preferences, "personality") that may moderate or condition the response of individuals to their environments. Thus questionnaire construction has concentrated on developing measures in each of these areas.

It seemed likely, however, that there would be variations between organizations in the meaning of words and in the relevance of different aspects of the work environment. For example, first-level managers may be called foremen, supervisors, or group leaders, depending on the context, and in some settings there is no single person who performs the role at all. Similarly, work groups are entities meaningful in some work settings, but they do not really exist in others. As a consequence, we designed the questionnaire in a *modular* fashion, with sets of questions that reflected various issues that seemed to be of some general importance. In each case, we designed the questions so that the referents could be changed to reflect the context (e.g., the person that a respondent reports to may be called a supervisor, a foreman, or whatever designation is appropriate) and so that the modules could be used, dropped, or shortened as appropriate. (If respondents do not report to a single person in any meaningful sense, the questions referring to the supervisor can be dropped.) This strategy allows us to adapt our questionnaire to the language and circumstances of any particular organization without losing comparability across organizations where the same issues are important.

Finally, within any particular domain of measurement, we have attempted to use constructs and measurement operations that are reasonably similar to existing approaches that have worked in the past and to test empirically the utility of the measures we have developed. In general, we have attempted to keep our scales as short and as specific as possible because we have found that respondents object to answering many questions that they perceive to be similar, and because our assessments usually require that we collect information about a wide range of issues. Since we have found that organizations often resist having ques-

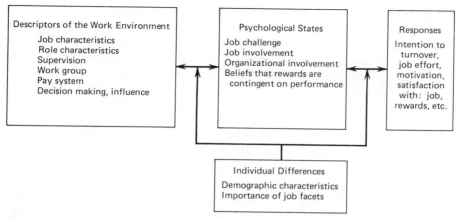

Figure 4-1   *Some topical areas currently covered by scales in the* Michigan Organizational Assessment Questionnaire.

tionnaires that take much over an hour to administer, we have tried to keep our scales brief.

An overview of the topical content of the questionnaire is displayed in Figure 4-1. The core questionnaire appears in Appendix 4-1 in its entirety. Most of the scales have survived successive tests for field utility and for satisfactory statistical properties, and they are thus relatively "final." A few are included on a tentative basis, subject to further improvement. A number of scales previously intended for inclusion do not appear at all (e.g., measures of the perception that awards and penalties are contingent on attendance) because, in successive trials, we have not been able to find or to devise scales that met our minimum standards of conciseness, internal consistency, and differentiation from other scales.

Certain supplemental modules are in various stages of development, and may later be incorporated in the MOAQ. One domain of measurement that is regrettably omitted from the core MOAQ is that of "personality." There exist established scales for measuring individual differences as to, for example, self-esteem, work-related stress reactions, need for achievement, internal-external control, and the like. These are known to be useful in organizational assessments. We do not use them because they require more time and questionnaire space to administer than we feel we can justify in most cases, and because respondents sometimes object to the questions as "intrusive."

Scales and Items

The selection of scales and of component questionnaire items has been carried forward in successive stages. First, a preliminary roster was prepared of constructs (scales) thought to be relevant to the assessment purposes and thought to be measurable through questionnaire items or sets of related items. The starting list was quite long, containing constructs drawn from both theoretical and empirical sources, and including elements likely to prove redundant or mutually inconsistent. For each such conceptual construct questionnaire items were prepared, or they were borrowed from existing sources. An effort was made to use items that were unambiguous, cognitively simple, and phrased in colloquial language.

Over 2000 such items were generated. They were then given a preliminary screening for clarity and construct relevance. This was done by having qualified persons, not members of the questionnaire-development staff, review the items offered for a given module, note or edit any that seemed ambiguous or too complex, and sort the items to the a priori constructs. A number of items were discarded on grounds of ambiguity, complexity, or inconsistent matching to constructs. The remaining items were then incorporated in questionnaires administered in various organizations to which we had access and, after accumulation of sufficient data, they were subjected to item-analysis procedures, as follows:

1. The respondents were split into two random-half samples.

2. The underlying relationships among the items were examined in one of the samples using both a nonmetric multidimensional scaling routine,[3-6] and a principal-axis factor analysis[6,7] with a varimax rotation on the factors selected using Kaiser's criterion. This was done independently for each of the intended modules.

3. The results of these analyses were examined, and items were retained that clustered with other items that were a priori intended to measure the same construct. In some instances, an item was allocated to another construct and retained, a construct was split, or two constructs merged, as a result of these analyses.

4. The resulting pool of items was refactored, and the new factor structure compared[6,8] to that of the second random-half sample. Generally, the two factor solutions showed high convergence. In one case (measures of organizational climate), they did not, and the entire domain was dropped, with two stable scales being retained for a placement in other modules.

5. The items belonging to each of the revised scales were identified, and internal-consistency estimates (Cronbach's a)[9] were calculated for each scale.

These analyses resulted in revised modules, with reduced numbers of items. In cases where the revision resulted in scales with two few items for reliable measurement or in too few scales to adequately assess the domain, new items were prepared and the entire analytic procedure was repeated. The modules described in this chapter, with one exception, have been through this developmental cycle at least twice. The module containing demographic questions was exempted from item-analysis procedures.

FIELD ADMINISTRATION PRACTICES

The field practices may vary in adaption to local conditions, but in some fashion they must provide for the following: (1) adaption of the questionnaire to local requirements; (2) reaching agreement regarding the use of the survey data; (3) providing facilities and supervision for the distribution and return of questionnaires; (4) assurances of anonymity and confidentiality; and (5) assurances of voluntary participation. The need for some flexibility in such matters may arise from any of several conditions. For example, the organization may already have established and tested conditions and procedures for member surveys, or there may be an established committee or work group appropriate for review and coordination. There may be prior agreement for use of a standard questionnaire without local adaptations. If survey practices are new to the organization and the levels of distrust very high, exceptional steps may be needed to reassure and protect respondents or to ascertain whether a survey should be conducted at all.

As a general rule, it is desirable to find or form a liaison group (occasionally more than one) of diverse members of the organization to have general responsibility for the planning and conduct of the survey.[10] The first task of such a group is to consider the purposes of the survey, the general nature of the information to be obtained, and the intended uses of the resulting data. A number of issues are likely to be raised that need to be confronted. These issues may concern, for example, the survey content, the populations included or excluded, the format and detail of data reports to be supplied, expected internal uses and disposition of the information, and the consequences that might reasonably be expected.

Such a liaison group can also aid in the task of adapting the questionnaire to local conditions. This may involve selection of modules, getting advice on language usages, and the formulation of any supplemental questionnaire modules that treat unique local topics. The group may wish to have their recommended version of the questionnaire reviewed independently by certain management or union groups.

The liaison group can also be of significant help in soliciting voluntary cooperation from the intended respondents. While the local arrangements vary, it is commonly preferred that information about the survey be widely dispersed throughout the organization to forestall erroneous rumors, and that the survey be presented with whatever legitimation is valid. It is common, for example, for a letter to go to each intended participant explaining the survey purposes and conditions, requesting cooperation, and indicating the support or consent of both top management and top union officials. A "hot line" or some similar arrangement may be made for informed responses to any questions that arise.

The actual administration of the questionnaires may pose unexpected problems that need to be worked out. Practices can range from a mail-back procedure with questionnaires filled out at home to the scheduling of group-administration sessions at the workplace during working time. The group-administration procedure has great advantages that offset the cost of paid time and scheduling of people and locations. A representative of the survey team can be present to offer explanations and respond to questions. In addition, the group setting provides encouragement for the indifferent or reluctant responder, and the paid time indicates a seriousness of purpose.

The creditable assurance of confidentiality is often crucial, especially in organizations without a reassuring history of surveys or where distrust is high. Aside from verbal assurances and explanations of protective procedures, it often helps to provide visible reminders of the concern for confidentiality, such as sealed envelopes, collection boxes resembling ballot boxes in which questionnaires are pooled, personal collection by an outsider representing the research team, or mail-back to a distant address.

However, in many instances, "confidentiality" is not the same as "anonymity," for the survey data are to be linked with data from other sources (e.g., personnel records, payroll records) or with responses to a subsequent survey questionnaire. For ethical reasons, this intent must be known to and accepted by the respondents. To assure confidentiality without loss of identity, the following procedure has been found efficacious. The questionnaire is delivered to the respondent in an envelope bearing his or her name. A randomly assigned identification number appears on the questionnaire only, with a master list of names and assigned numbers under safeguard at a distant location and accessible only to the survey team. Respondents remove their names and have the option—should they wish to use it—of removing the number.

MODULES AND SCALES

The sections that follow describe in succession the modules and their component scales. In each case, with the exception of the module on demographics, discussion is provided about the theoretical and statistical bases for the inclusion of scales, comments are given about the present and prospective status of the module, and the statistical information needed to guide scale usage and interpretations is also supplied.

The data base for the statistical information is not uniform across all scales and modules. Successive questionnaires were used in field sites as the modules were being continuously revised over a four-year period of questionnaire development. The data shown, however, unless specifically noted otherwise, are based upon an N of respondents greater than 400, drawn from not less than three different organizations. Thus, where product-moment correlations are shown, the .05, .01, and .001 levels of statistical significance (p values) are attained with, at most, correlations of .09, .13, and .15, respectively.

The data sources used for the analyses presented in the following pages were included for reasons of accessibility, convenience, and variety of populations and jobs. While the MOAQ instruments have been employed in other organizations as well, the data in this chapter are from 11 of the sites listed in Chapter 1.*

These organizations are located in all major regions of the United States, and together they provide a very diverse population of respondents as to age, sex, race, job type, hierarchical status, and educational attainment.

MODULE O: DEMOGRAPHICS

Data on the demographic characteristics of respondents are needed to allow analyses relating to differential work experiences among members and differential responses to them. For example, age, educational attainment, sex, and number of dependents are known to have important effects upon employee perceptions and behavioral responses. Aside from the utility of identifying such demographically unlike groups for program planning, policy formulation, and outcome assessment, such characteristics can also be used speculatively as proxies for psychological attributes. For example, one might assume that employees in early mid-life, with many dependents, might well be more concerned about income and economic fringe benefits than employees with other demographic patterns.

Listed later are the demographic questions most commonly asked and most often used in various analyses. They are designed to provide information about the individual respondent's background (education, urban or rural upbringing), demographic identity (age, race, sex), current life situation (marital status, number of dependents, income, employment tenure), and job situation (job classification, hours worked per week). Other areas, such as religious preferences, were considered, but they were rejected because they seemed less directly relevant to the job situation and might be seen as too great an intrusion on the respondent's privacy.

Reliability data are not provided. However, in several organizations, comparisons have been made between the distributions of responses to

---

* 1. tool and die company, $N = 85$; 2. metropolitan bank, $N = 278$; 3. ball-bearing factory, $N = 136$; 4. engineering division, public utility, $N = 365$; 5. pharmaceutical plant, $N = 80$; 6. wood-processing firm, $N = 326$; 7. urban transportation authority, $N = 195$; 8. furniture factory #1, $N = 759$; 9. furniture factory #2, $N = 85$; 10. urban solid-waste disposal department, $N = 550$; and 11. baked foods factory, $N = 522$.

the questionnaire and distributions obtained from firm records. These comparisons reveal a close correspondence, with little evidence of systematic response bias.

1. Are you? (female or male)
2. What is your education level? [indicate by last completed; alternatives are: some elementary school (grades 1–7), completed elementary (8 grades), some high school (9–11 years), graduated from high school or G.E.D., some college or technical training beyond high school (1–3 years), graduated from college (B.A., B.S., or other bachelor's degree), some graduate school, graduate degree (master's, Ph.D., M.D., etc.)]
3. What is your marital status? (married, widowed, separated, divorced, never married)
4. Are you? (black, oriental, American Indian, Spanish surnamed, white, other)
5. How old were you on your last birthday?
6. What was the size of the community in which you spent the largest portion of your life up to the time you were 16 years old?
7. Is your income the primary source of financial support for your family?
8. How many dependents do you have (others who depend on you for their financial support)?
9. How many hours do you usually work per week?
10. When did you first come to work for [this organization]?
11. When did you start working in your current job at [this organization]?
12. Current income from job (response categories vary in each site)
13. Current job classification (question varies in each site)

MODULE 1: GENERAL ATTITUDES

The general-attitudes module contains scales measuring outcomes and psychological states that are considered relevant to QWL issues in most work settings. The outcome measures include the following:

1. *Overall Job Satisfaction.* To provide an indication of the organization members' overall affective responses to their jobs.
2. *Intention to Turnover.* To assess the individual's intention to continue to be an organization member.
3. *Internal Turnover Desire.* To assess the individual's desire to move to another job in the same organization.
4. *Self-Report of Effort.* To find out how much energy organization members put into their jobs.

The psychological state measures include the following:

1. *Internal Work Motivation* The extent to which doing the job is itself rewarding.
2. *Overall Task Quality Index.* The extent to which the tasks within the job provide challenge, meaning, and responsibility (a composite index from the task and role characteristics module).
3. *Pay Attitude Summary Index.* The extent to which respondents view their pay as satisfactory in amount, equitable, and properly administered (a composite index derived from various items in the pay module).
4. *Job Involvement.* The extent to which individuals personally identify with their work.
5. *Organizational Involvement.* The extent to which individuals personally identify with the organization.
6. *Locking In.* The respondents' perception of their ability to leave the job situation should they wish to do so.

The choice of general attitude measures was not based on some particular theoretical scheme. Rather, the concepts are our distillation from the large brew of ideas in organizational behavior. The choices were based on our understanding of the needs of organizational scientists, policy makers, and organization members involved in QWL activities. The outcome measures reflect our interest in job satisfaction and its possible consequences (turnover intentions, both internal and external), which are expected to be affected by QWL activities. The underlying theoretical viewpoint is an expectancy theory, arguing that one consequence of participative QWL activities may be more strongly perceived linkages between job activities and valued outcomes. Consequently, effort, satisfaction, and turnover should be affected by changes in perceived performance–outcome contingencies.

The psychological state measures also reflect this orientation. *Internal work motivation* and *task quality* have been viewed as primary intervening variables in generic QWL-type activities, in the work on two-factor theory,[11] need theory,[12,13] expectancy theory,[14,15] job design,[2,16] and in much of the theorizing about participation in decision making.[17] Involvement (both with the job and organization) has been proposed as a central concept in understanding QWL activities when ideal organizations are conceptualized as high-involvement systems.[18] Rabinowitz and Hall[19] have presented reasonable support for the hypothesis that involvement is often related to QWL-type activities and their outcomes.

Our interest in pay is derived from an expectancy-theory orientation.[18,20] which argues for the powerful effect pay can have in QWL activities. Further support for this is presented in Deci's[21] work on intrinsic motivation, where he indicates that pay can, under certain circumstances (i.e., pay as a feedback mechanism), enhance intrinsic motivation.

The concept of locking in has been developed by Quinn and Jenkins in response to their recognition that people's decisions about whether to remain in an organization or leave are constrained by the alternatives available to them. The Porter and Steers[22] review of turnover supports the idea that certain factors (e.g., age) may constrain behavioral freedom to turnover. Since we view turnover as an important individual and organization outcome, it is essential to consider turnover intentions in light of the perceived constraints on turnover.

Table 4-1 shows the correlations among the scales included in the general-attitudes module and the scale reliability (internal consistency). Table 4-2 shows the individual items and the results of a factor analysis of the items. The measures in the general-attitudes module are intended for use as dependent variables in relational analyses. These scales will be used in the descriptions of later modules to illustrate their relational characteristics and those of the scales in the other modules.

The general-attitudes module appears to be fairly fixed as to the scales and indices presented here, except for two important points. To supplement the single-item measure of effort as an assessment of the energy employees put into their jobs, we are currently testing additional items such as these:

1. I get upset when I fall behind in my work.
2. I generally produce high-quality work on my job.
3. I put in extra effort on the job when I get behind schedule.

We are also testing a *trust of organization* scale to assess the employees' overall feeling about the management of the organizations they are in. The items included are the following:

1. When the management of this company says something you can really believe that it is true.
2. People in this organization will do things behind your back.
3. This organization cares more about money and machines than people.
4. People here feel that you cannot trust this organization.
5. This company will take advantage of you if you give it a chance.

MODULE 2: JOB FACETS

The job-facets module contains scales that ask respondents their attitudes about a variety of potential job rewards. The contents of this module derive most explicitly from an expectancy-theory perspective, although other contributions have an influence as well.[14,15,23] The module is

Table 4-1 Intercorrelations Among Scales for the General Attitudes Module

Scale	[1]	[2]	[3]	[4]	[5]	[6]	[7]	[8]	[9]	[10]	[11]	Number of Items
[1] Job satisfaction	(.77)											3
[2] Job involvement	.35	(.62)										3
[3] Intention to turnover	-.58	-.27	(.83)									3
[4] Internal turnover desire	-.32	-.12	.36	*								1
[5] Internal work motivation	.32	.21	-.24	-.06	(.60)							3
[6] Self-report of effort	.26	.28	-.12	-.10	.33	*						1
[7] Overall task[a] quality index	.43	.36	-.32	-.19	.33	.25	(.62)					3
[8] Organizational involvement	.44	.32	-.41	-.12	.41	.31	.33	(.68)				2
[9] Pay attitude[a] summary index	.30	.10	-.27	-.13	.09	-.00	.11	.17	(.74)			4
[10] Pay-based-on performance belief	.24	.36	-.18	-.00	.14	.16	.30	.19	.18	*		1
[11] Locking-in	.08	.07	-.23	-.07	-.08	-.12	-.05	.01	.29	.06	(.67)	4

Note. Parenthesized values on the diagonal are internal consistency reliability estimates for the scales. $N > 400$; $r = .13$, $p < .01$. Asterisks denote missing data arising from single-item scales.

[a] The Task Quality Index and the Pay Attitude Summary are included in other modules as part of other scales.

83

Table 4-2   Factor Analysis for General Attitudes Module

Attitude	Factor						
	I	II	III	IV	V	VI	VII
Job satisfaction							
All in all, I am satisfied with my job.						.50	
In general, I don't like my job. (reversed scoring)						.66	
In general, I like working here.	.43					.47	
Job involvement							
I am very much personally involved in my work.	.56				.48		
I live, eat, and breathe my job.					.54		
The most important things which happen to me involve my job.					.58		
Intention to turnover							
How likely is it that you will actively look for a new job in the next year?				.79			
I often think about quitting.				.41		.49	
I will probably look for a new job in the next year.				.75			
Internal turnover desire							
If I had the chance I would take a different job within this organization.				(.26)			(.25)
Internal work motivation							
I feel bad when I do a poor job.	.40						
I get a feeling of personal satisfaction from doing my job well.	.65						
Doing my job well gives me a good feeling.	.66						
Self-report of effort							
I work hard on my job.	.48						
Overall task quality index							
My job is very challenging.	.38				.36		−.36
The work I do on my job is meaningful to me.	.51					.37	
I feel personally responsible for the work I do on my job.	.51						
Organizational involvement							
What happens to this organization is really important to me.	.53						
I don't care what happens to this organization so long as I get a pay check. (reversed scoring)	.37						
Pay attitude summary index							
I am very dissatisfied with my pay. (reversed scoring)		.49					

Table 4-2   (*Continued*)

Attitude	I	II	III	IV	V	VI	VII
My pay is fair considering what other people in this organization are paid.		.61					
My pay is fair considering what other places in this area pay.		.66					
I am very content with the way management handles pay.		.69					
Pay based on performance belief							
How much pay I receive depends almost entirely on how well I perform my job.					.39		
Locking-in							
How likely is it that you could find a job with another employer with about the same pay and benefits you have now?			.52				
It would be very hard for me to leave my job *even* if I wanted to.			.57				
I dread the thought of what might happen if I quit my job without another one lined up.			.59				
I have too much at stake in my job to change jobs now.			.55				

based on the assumption that a variety of outcomes are available to employees at work; that these outcomes are differentially important to people; that people will try to perform well when important outcomes are contingent on good performance. In addition, it is assumed that satisfaction with the amount of specific outcomes received will be indicative of feelings toward those aspects of the organization that provide the outcomes, and that these feelings are predictive of attitudes toward the organization overall. Thus the module includes measures of the *importance* of a series of potential rewards, the extent to which the rewards are perceived to be *contingent on good performance,* and the degree of satisfaction with the amount of rewards provided.

Certain problems were expected and, indeed, encountered. To have a compact, standard, and generally usable questionnaire, the identification of key job facets can not be very specific. This led to a strategy of searching for clusters of more specific facets (e.g., pay, fringe benefits, security) that reasonably could be subsumed under a more general rubric (e.g., extrinsic facets). Also, it was known that measures-of-reward valences (importance) are likely to become less discriminating as the rewards of reference become less specific, and that demonstrated empirical utility of "importance" measures is dubious.[24,25] Nevertheless, whether used in the

context of expectancy theory/job-satisfaction theory or not, the component questionnaire items deal with topics of great concern in work organizations, they lend themselves to alternative interpretive approaches,
and they are thus worth asking.

Initially, the development steps distinguished between extrinsic and
intrinsic rewards. Later steps added a distinction between those intrinsic
rewards that are self-administered (internally mediated) and those that
require some type of organizational actions or conditions in order for the
individual to reward himself or herself.[21] Social rewards[12] and the rewards associated with influence[17] were also distinguished on both theoretical and empirical grounds as well as on their "face validity" to people
in work organizations.

The choice of these four domains (e.g., social, intrinsic, extrinsic, and
influence rewards) was based on our reading of the literature in the area
of job satisfaction, when considered in the context of QWL activities. The
extrinsic and intrinsic reward categories have shown their value in most
job-satisfaction research,[26] and this is one of the most widely applied
distinctions in motivation research. Furthermore, much work in QWL
efforts addresses intrinsic rewards.

Social rewards are of interest since work groups often constrain and
differentially reinforce work behavior.[27] Influence rewards have been
shown to pertain to satisfaction, motivation, and performance in the literature on control and participation.[17,28] Additionally, influence rewards
are variables that are often critical to the operation of QWL efforts.

Developmental item analyses and scaling were conducted separately
for the contingency, importance, and satisfaction questionnaire items.
Table 4-3 shows the intercorrelations among all three classes of scales,
with internal-consistency reliability estimates, as well. Table 4-4
presents the factorial structure of the items in the 11 scales that constitute the final scaling solution. Table 4-5 provides illustrative relational
data showing the correlations of the job-facet scales with measures of job
satisfaction, job involvement, job effort and intention to turnover. These
results illustrate that the facets measured do have predictable relationships with other job attitude and response measures that, according to
theory and other research studies, they should be related to. Additional
regression analyses cast doubt on the general utility of importance ratings. Our analyses indicate that facet satisfaction by facet-importance
interaction terms adds no significant predictive power over and above
facet-satisfaction ratings in predicting overall job satisfaction.

The job-facet module is stable at this time. The measures appear to
serve their intended purposes. The leading possibility for enlargement of
this module would be the inclusion of a set of questionnaire items relating to an additional reward facet, namely, career enhancement (e.g.,
promotion) and the reward contingencies in relation to good job performance. One domain of items that failed to survive developmental tests

Table 4-3 Intercorrelations Among Scale Means for Module 2: Job Facets and Good Performance Contingencies

Scale	[1]	[2]	[3]	[4]	[5]	[6]	[7]	[8]	[9]	[10]	[11]	Number of Items
Good performance contingencies												
[1] Externally mediated intrinsic reward contingency	(.80)											2
[2] Internally mediated intrinsic reward contingency	.56	(.75)										2
[3] Extrinsic reward contingency	.56	.24	(.75)									2
Facet importances												
[4] Social rewards	.23	.29	.15	(.79)								3
[5] Intrinsic rewards	.32	.39	.18	.50	(.80)							3
[6] Influence rewards	.14	.19	.14	.52	.56	(.51)						2
[7] Extrinsic rewards	−.05	.04	−.03	.35	.28	.28	(.71)					3
Facet satisfactions												
[8] Social rewards	.34	.22	.20	.18	.10	.03	−.00	(.87)				3
[9] Intrinsic rewards	.57	.42	.29	.14	.09	−.01	−.04	.41	(.87)			3
[10] Influence rewards	.46	.32	.30	.06	.05	−.02	−.03	.52	.70	(.63)		2
[11] Extrinsic rewards	.25	.15	.23	.02	.01	−.01	−.13	.30	.36	.43	(.63)	3

Note. Parenthesized values on the diagonal are internal consistency reliability estimates for the scales. $N > 400$; $r = .13$, $p < .01$.

Table 4-4 Factor Loadings for Module 2: Job Facets and Good Performance Contingencies

Scale	I	II	III	IV	V	VI	VII
Externally mediated intrinsic reward good performance contingency							
If you performed your job especially well, how likely is it that you will have the opportunity to develop your skills and abilities?			−.50		.43		
If you performed your job especially well, how likely is it that you will be given chances to learn new things?			−.55		.43		
Internally mediated intrinsic reward good performance contingency							
If you performed your job especially well, how likely is it that you will feel better about yourself as a person?					.36		.47
If you performed your job especially well, how likely is it that you will get a feeling that you've accomplished something worthwhile?					.43		.53
Extrinsic reward good performance contingency							
If you performed your job especially well, how likely is it that you will be promoted or get a better job?			−.71				
If you performed your job especially well, how likely is it that you will get a bonus or a pay increase?			−.63				
Social reward importance							
How important is the way you are treated by the people you work with?		.70					
How important to you is the respect you receive from the people you work with?		.67					
How important to you is the friendliness of the people you work with?		.68					
Intrinsic reward importance							
How important to you are the chances you have to learn new things?		.41					.53
How important to you are the chances you have to accomplish something worthwhile?		.45					.56
How important to you are the chances you have to do something that makes you feel good about yourself?		.52					.47
Influence importance							
How important to you are the chances you have to take part in making decisions?		.41					
How important to you is the amount of freedom you have on the job?		.42					

Table 4-4　(*Continued*)

Scale	Factor						
	I	II	III	IV	V	VI	VII
Extrinsic reward importance							
How important to you is the amount of pay you get?				.59			
How important to you are the fringe benefits you receive?				.63			
How important to you is your job security?				.60			
Social reward satisfaction							
How satisfied are you with the way you are treated by the people you work with?	.76						
How satisfied are you with the respect you receive from the people you work with?	.76						
How satisfied are you with the friendliness of the people you work with?	.73						
Intrinsic reward satisfaction							
How satisfied are you with the chances you have to learn new things?					.73		
How satisfied are you with the chances you have to accomplish something worthwhile?					.77		
How satisfied are you with the chances you have to do something that makes you feel good about yourself as a person?					.78		
Influence satisfaction							
How satisfied are you with the chances you have to take part in making decisions?	(.22)				.54	(.32)	
How satisfied are you with the amount of freedom you have on your job?	(.34)				.49	(.28)	
Extrinsic reward satisfaction							
How satisfied are you with the amount of pay you get?						.53	
How satisfied are you with the fringe benefits you receive?						.61	
How satisfied are you with the amount of job security you have?						.44	

concerns the opposite of "reward," i.e., punishments, or negative rewards, that may be contingent upon performance. These items have been dropped because in most of our test populations the occurrence of punishment for poor performance or absence was reported to be too rare or too improbable for statistical treatment; such items, however, may well be useful in selected organizational sites.

Table 4-5 Correlations of Job Facet Measures with Some General Attitude Measures

			General Attitude Measures			
Job Facet Measures	Internal Turnover Desire	Self-Report of Effort	Job Satisfaction	Job Involvement	Intention to Turnover
[1] Externally mediated intrinsic reward contingency	−.12	.08	.40	.39	−.29
[2] Internally mediated intrinsic reward contingency	−.15	.23	.37	.22	−.29
[3] Extrinsic reward contingency	−.01	.09	.23	.21	−.16
[4] Social rewards importance	−.02	.13	.12	.09	−.05
[5] Intrinsic rewards importance	.03	.16	.04	.09	.02
[6] Influence importance	.07	.08	−.03	.09	.07
[7] Extrinsic rewards importance	.05	.09	−.01	−.03	.00
[8] Social rewards satisfaction	−.14	.11	.40	.18	−.24
[9] Intrinsic rewards satisfaction	−.36	.21	.62	.38	−.45
[10] Influence satisfaction	−.18	.01	.52	.26	−.33
[11] Extrinsic rewards satisfaction	−.13	−.00	.33	.14	−.28

Note. $N > 400$; $r = .13$, $p < .01$; $r = .09$, $p < .05$.

MODULE 3: TASK, JOB, AND ROLE CHARACTERISTICS

Module 3 contains scales of three types. There are nine scales that allow respondents to describe key characteristics of the tasks they perform. Three scales describe job characteristics, viewing the job broadly as a role within the organization. Finally, four scales measure psychological states that are presumed to arise, in part, from the individual's particular mix of task and role characteristics. The focus in this module is upon the work to be done, rather than upon the surrounding conditions (e.g., rewards, work-group functioning, and so on) that are treated in other modules.

The justification for inclusion of such a module has two sources. First, there is an extensive literature, both theoretical and empirical that indicates causal connections between task characteristics and role characteristics, on the one hand, and the job occupants' psychological states, affective reactions, and observable job-related behaviors, on the other hand. The 1976 report by Hackman and Oldham is an example of this type of literature.[2] Second, in the context of work effectiveness and QWL, the design or redesign of tasks and work roles has been one of the most frequently chosen targets for direct intervention.[29,30] The scales in this module, accordingly, have potential use in assessment as directly interpretable indicators of job qualities and deficiencies, as mediating factors that help to explain affective states of members of work organizations, or as indicators of the achievement of intended job and role changes.

Task Characteristics

The starting point in developing measures of task characteristics was the approach initiated by Hackman and Lawler[16] and elaborated upon by Hackman and Oldham.[2] They proposed five main task characteristics that are general enough to be relevant to the characterization of all jobs: variety, task identity, task significance, autonomy, and task-performance feedback. However, in the course of module development, deviations from this schema arose from both empirical and theoretical sources. For example, the questionnaire items intended to represent task identity failed in repeated tests to generate satisfactory internal consistency. The solution was to divide task identity into two distinguishable variables: task completeness (the extent to which the job allows the completion of an entire unit of product or service) and task impact (the extent to which task performance makes a significant difference in the final product or service). Another deviation concerns the term *autonomy,* which is not familiar to all respondents and for which the term *freedom* was substituted. Also, given the importance attributed to work pace in some prior studies, a scale called "pace control" was introduced that is distinguished from, although it is related to, the scale representing general freedom in task performance.

In addition, two complementary scales were developed and incorporated in this module: One is a scale representing the skill requirements of the job, and the other is a scale representing the degree to which these requirements match the training and experience opportunities of the respondent (training adequacy). These are regarded as elaborations upon the general theme of job challenge and fit of tasks to the occupants' abilities.

Roles and Psychological States

Following the Hackman and Oldham schema, this module includes scales representing certain psychological states thought to be associated with the task and role characteristics of jobs. These scales are job meaningfulness (reported in terms of the respondent's own sense of "meaning"), responsibility (for how well the work gets done), and knowledge of results (knowing whether or not the job has been done well). To these a scale of job challenge was added, which was thought to be an umbrella state and which appears to perform empirically in that manner. It incorporates the three scales proposed by Hackman and Oldham.

The three scales introduced to represent certain characteristics of the job as an organizational role were taken from the prior work of Kahn and associates,[31] Caplan and associates,[32] and the more recent work of Rousseau.[33] The scales refer to role clarity, role (work) overload, and role conflict.

Scale Analyses

Intercorrelations and internal-consistency reliabilities of the 16 scales mentioned previously are displayed in Table 4-6. The factorial structures were determined separately for each of the three classes of scales; the results appear in Tables 4-7 (task characteristics), 4-8 (psychological states), and 4-9 (role characteristics).

The domain of task characteristics appears to be described with scales of usable to high reliability and of differentiating power. It will be noted in both Tables 4-6 and 4-7 that the separation of "task identity" into two scales of task completeness and task impact resulted in factorially distinguished scales. The addition of a scale of pace control, to complement the scale of freedom, leaves the two scales differentiable but of common factorial identity. The scales for feedback, impact, and significance also share a common factorial identity, and they are not very clearly differentiated. They also perform similarly in relational tests with other measures, and it appears that for some purposes they might well be subsumed as components of a more inclusively defined task descriptor.

With respect to the "psychological-states" scales, two observations are warranted (see Table 4-8). First, the knowledge-of-results scale, com-

Table 4-6 Intercorrelations Among Scales for Task and Role Characteristics Module

Scale	[1]	[2]	[3]	[4]	[5]	[6]	[7]	[8]	[9]	[10]	[11]	[12]	[13]	[14]	[15]	[16]	Number of Items
[1] Variety	(.81)																3
[2] Freedom	.44	(.75)															3
[3] Task feedback	.23	.37	(.54)														2
[4] Task completeness	.23	.37	.28	(.58)													2
[5] Task impact	.24	.26	.48	.41	(.46)												2
[6] Task significance	.20	.21	.46	.22	.45	(.45)											2
[7] Pace control	.30	.59	.30	.25	.18	.16	(.83)										3
[8] Required skill	.39	.29	.22	.18	.14	.18	.16	(.71)									3
[9] Training adequacy	-.06	.03	.11	.01	.05	.08	.04	-.03	(.59)								3
[10] Challenge	.57	.49	.37	.36	.41	.33	.29	.45	-.07	(.81)							4
[11] Meaningfulness	.33	.36	.33	.18	.29	.30	.24	.41	-.01	.51	(.50)						2
[12] Responsibility	.22	.42	.31	.22	.27	.29	.27	.28	.14	.35	.40	(.41)					2
[13] Knowledge of results	.12	.11	.37	.07	.28	.53	.05	.13	.08	.18	.31	.16	(.31)				2
[14] Role clarity	.02	-.01	.23	.18	.13	.33	.18	-.06	.21	.04	.07	.16	.25	(.53)			3
[15] Role overload	.09	-.14	-.04	.10	.01	-.11	-.19	.19	-.12	.05	-.16	-.06	-.11	-.19	(.65)		3
[16] Role conflict	.02	-.05	-.07	.01	.04	.02	-.07	.07	-.03	.03	-.26	-.06	-.04	-.13	.32	(.58)	2

Note. Parenthesized values on the diagonal are internal consistency reliability estimates for the scales. $N > 400$; $r = .09$, $p < .05$; $r = .13$, $p < .01$; $r = .15$, $p < .001$.

Table 4-7   Factor Loadings for the Measures of Task Characteristics

Characteristic	I	II	III	IV	V	VI
Freedom						
How much freedom do you have on your job? That is, how much do you decide on your own what you do on your job?	.57		.36			
I have the freedom to decide what I do on my job.	.59					
It is basically my own responsibility to decide how my job gets done.	.56					
Variety						
How much variety is there in your job?			.40			.51
I get to do a number of different things on my job.						.51
My job requires that I do the same thing over and over. (reversed scoring)						.37
Task feedback						
As you do your job, can you tell how well you're performing?		.52				
Just doing the work required by my job gives me many chances to figure out how well I am doing.	.39	.55				
Task completeness						
How much does your job involve your producing an entire product or an entire service?				−.50		
On my job I produce a whole product or perform a complete service.				−.50		
Task impact						
How much does the work you do on your job make a visible impact on a product or service?		.54			−.37	
I can see the results of my own work.		.53				
Task significance						
A lot of people can be affected by how well I do my work.		.53				
In general, how *significant* or *important* is your job; that is, are the results of your work likely to significantly affect the lives or well-being of other people?		.45				
Required skills						
My job is so simple that virtually anybody could handle it with little or no initial training. (reversed scoring)			.67			
It takes a long time to learn the skills required to do my job well.			.52			
What is the level of education you feel is needed by a person in your job?			.59			
Training adequacy						
I do not have enough training to do my job well. (reversed scoring)				.43		

Table 4-7 *(Continued)*

Characteristic	I	II	III	IV	V	VI
				Factor		
I have all the skills I need in order to do my job.				.62		
I have more than enough training and skills to do my job well.				.61		
Pace control						
How much control do you have in setting the pace of your work?	.75					
My job allows me to control my own work pace.	.75					
I determine the speed at which I work.	.74					

Table 4-8 Factor Loadings for the Measures of Psychological States

Psychological State	I	II	III
		Factor	
Challenge			
How much challenge is there on your job?	.79		
On my job, I seldom get a chance to use my special skills and abilities. (reversed scoring)	.66		
To be successful on my job requires all my skill and ability.	.65		
My job is very challenging.	.66		
Meaning			
The work I do on my job is meaningful to me.	.63		
I feel that most of the things I do on my job are meaningless. (reversed scoring)	.43	.42	
Responsibility			
I feel personally responsible for the work I do on my job.	.49		
I deserve credit or blame for how well my work gets done.			.38
Knowledge of results			
I seldom know whether I'm doing my job well or poorly. (reversed scoring)		.38	
I usually know whether or not my work is satisfactory on this job.	(.32)		

Table 4-9   Factor Loadings for the Measures of Role Characteristics

Role Characteristic	Factor	
	I	II
Role conflict		
On my job, I can't satisfy everybody at the same time.	.52	(.03)
To satisfy some people on my job, I have to upset others.	.52	(−.09)
Role clarity		
Most of the time I know what I have to do on my job.		.44
On my job I know exactly what is expected of me.		.55
On my job, most of my tasks are clearly defined.		.47
Role overload		
I never seem to have enough time to get everything done.	.57	(−.20)
I have too much work to do to do everything well.	.63	(−.15)
The amount of work I am asked to do is fair. (reversed scoring)	.39	(−.30)

posed of two questionnaire items, shows unsatisfactory internal consistency for the test population as a whole, and it should be used cautiously—if at all. Second, the remaining three scales are quite highly intercorrelated, and all tend to load on a common factor. This suggests that for most purposes they could be merged as an overall indicator of job challenge. This is the rationale for the task-quality index employed in Module 1.

The three role-characteristics scales are differentiated in measurement (relatively low intercorrelations), but the conflict and overload scales tend to load on a common factor, differentiated from role clarity (see Table 4-9).

The understanding of these several scales and their potential uses can be aided by examination of their correlations with selected variables from other modules of the MOAQ. Table 4-10 is provided to illustrate this kind of analysis and to suggest some conclusions. First, reference to Table 4-6 shows that the task-characteristics scales generally correlate more strongly with the challenge scale than with the other two "psychological-state" scales—meaningfulness and responsibility. Also (see Table 4-10), the challenge scale correlates more strongly with the selected scales from other modules than do the scales of meaningfulness and responsibility. This set of observations gives support to the idea that the three psychological-state measures (ignoring the fourth scale, of low reliability) can well be viewed as alternative measures of a common construct that is best labeled "challange."

Second, inspection of Tables 4-6 and 4-10 shows that the job-characteristic scales correlate more strongly with the challenge scale than they do (with one exception) with the scales from other modules, while the chal-

Table 4-10   Correlations of Task Characteristics and Job Related
Psychological States with Selected General Attitude Scales

Scale	Overall Job Satisfaction	Job Involvement	Intrinsic Motivation	Intrinsic Satisfaction	Intrinsic P → O (outside)	Intrinsic P → O (self)
Task characteristics						
Freedom	.25	.24	.19	.33	.29	.19
Variety	.26	.15	.24	.32	.35	.20
Feedback	.37	.28	.27	.37	.29	.31
Completeness	.24	.23	.13	.24	.25	.15
Impact	.31	.22	.30	.24	.26	.34
Significance	.01	.02	.00	.04	.07	.01
Required skills	.22	.10	.20	.21	.23	.17
Pace control	.26	.25	.07	.24	.26	.09
Psychological states						
Challenge	.51	.46	.34	.56	.48	.32
Meaning	.40	.18	.32	.25	.23	.33
Responsibility	.24	.20	.22	.18	.13	.18

Note. $N > 400$; $r = .09$, $p < .05$; $r = .13$, $p < .01$; $r = .15$, $p < .001$. The training adequacy scale is omitted; data available from too few sites. See Module 2 for a description of the P—O (reward contingency) scales.

lenge scale correlates more strongly with these same other scales than do the task-characteristic scales. This combination of observations suggests that the psychological-state scale called "challenge" (and others that might be discovered) serves as a mediating construct between the task characteristics and such remote outcomes as job involvement, intrinsic motivation, and other similar variables of interest.

The nature of the relationships between job characteristics and such remote outcomes was explored further to see whether the several job characteristics might operate interactively and whether they are more discriminating if moderated by the respondents' ratings of the importance of the job factors. The answer to both issues appears to be negative. In the population considered here, an interactive model proved no more predictive of "challenge" than a simple weighted linear model. The predictive-power addition from importance weighting proved to be negligible. While these negative outcomes may arise from multicollinearity among the measures, they do not encourage any treatment more complex than unadjusted linear aggregation.

Another analysis, among several conducted to assess the qualities of the data produced by Module 3, is shown in Table 4-11. The intent was to

Table 4-11   Correlations Between Role Characteristics and
Selected Task Characteristics and Affective Reactions to the
Job

Scale	Conflict	Clarity	Overload
Task characteristics			
Freedom	−.05	.01	−.14
Variety	.02	.02	.09
Feedback	−.07	.23	−.04
Completeness	.01	.04	.10
Impact	.04	−.13	.01
Pace control	−.07	.18	−.19
Affective reactions			
Overall job satisfaction	−.04	.17	−.13
Intrinsic satisfaction	−.04	.15	−.20
Extrinsic satisfaction	−.17	.20	−.30

Note. $N > 400$; $r = .09$, $p < .05$; $r = .13$, $p < .01$; $r = .15$, $p < .011$. The
omitted task characteristics have no significant correlations with the role
characteristic scales.

see whether the task characteristics (assuming causality) had an impact
upon role characteristics and whether the role characteristics, in turn,
are related to outcome variables such as satisfaction. The table shows the
correlations between selected task characteristics and the three role
scales. They are generally weak, but 8 out of 18 are statistically significant, and the significant relationships show a plausible pattern as to role
clarity and role overload (none for role conflict). The lower portion of the
table establishes that job satisfaction—both intrinsic and extrinsic—is
associated with the role characteristics. The relationships are similar to
those reported by Rousseau.[33]

Status and Outlook for Module 3

Module 3 is regarded as being stable in its current state, except for two
possible additions to the task-characteristics set. If the scale for knowledge of results (a task characteristic) cannot be made more reliable by the
addition or substitution of questionnaire items, it will be dropped, or it
will be recommended for use only in instances where these two items are
judged to be of special significance. It is expected, for most uses, that the
job-challenge scale may be used alone, omitting the three other scales
now in the "psychological-states" category.

One of the intended additions refers to the degree of unpredictability
inherent in the respondent's job. The tentative questionnaire items are as
follows:

1. How much uncertainty is there in your job?
2. On my job, I often have to handle surprising or unpredictable situations.
3. I often have to deal with new problems in my job.

The second prospective addition refers to the extent to which the respondent's job can be performed alone or, instead, involves interdependency with others. The tentative questionnaire items are the following:

1. How much do you have to cooperate directly with other people in this organization in order to do your job?
2. How often does your job require that you meet with or check with other people in this organization?

Preliminary results suggest that these scales will prove to be sufficiently reliable and discriminative for use and that they will prove to be associated with other measures in a meaningful way. The scales for role conflict, role clarity, and role overload, for example, correlate with the task-predictability scale (r's of $-.28$, $.44$, and $-.28$) and the interdependence scale (r's of $.22$, $-.23$, and $.18$).

MODULE 4: WORK GROUP FUNCTIONING

In many organizations work groups are very prominent features of the work environment, and they are very important to the understanding of workplace phenomena. Work groups commonly comprise a set of people who share the same or adjoining work places, report to the same supervisor, and engage in tasks that are similar or related. When work groups exist, and particularly when they remain stable over an extended period of time, they can have a strong effect on an organization member's job experiences and on his or her behavior. The people in the group become an important part of the individual's social and work environment and can have a significant effect on one's feelings about, and performance in, the workplace. The significance of group phenomena in organizational functioning and in the individual's reactions to the workplace have been amply documented. This is a central theme in some organizational theories.[28,34,35]

To assess such work groups, measures are provided on five aspects of the work group. *Homogeneity,* measured by a two-item scale, is included because the similarity of group members as to backgrounds and job competencies has long been recognized as an important determinant of their attraction for each other. The social characteristics of the group—measured by two scales, one assessing *cohesiveness* and the other the *clarity of the group's work goals*—are included because the cohesion and goal orientation of the group as a social and work unit is often a critical determinant of the group's effects on organization members. Internal group processes are measured by two scales: one assessing the *openness of communication and influence* in the group and the other the interpersonal friction or *internal fragmentation* of the group.

Table 4-12 shows the work-group scales that have been developed. Table 4-13 provides a factor analysis of the items. The data indicate satisfactory scale reliability and differentiation among the scales.

To illustrate the relational characteristics of these scales, their correlations were calculated with a selected, varied set of measures from Modules 1, 2, and 3. These are shown in Table 4-14. They demonstrate that the group measures correlate generally and significantly to a variety of individual-level variables of interest.

Examination of Table 4-14 shows a set of relationships supporting the validity of the group measures. Open group process is associated with higher levels of satisfaction, involvement, social-reward satisfaction, and job challenge, and with lower levels of role conflict and intention to turnover. This fits with the idea that open communication processes in groups clarify roles and outcomes, in addition to being valued outcomes in and of themselves. The internal fragmentation scale, which measures conflicts in groups, leads to the opposite set of outcomes, as would be expected. Furthermore, internal fragmentation has a more powerful effect on role conflict and satisfaction, while having a lesser effect on job involvement and challenge. This fits the concept of fragmentation, which is primarily about interpersonal relations rather than job-content effects.

Group cohesiveness, which is measuring how attractive the group is to the individual, works as expected, since more cohesive groups are seen as more rewarding by respondents ($r = .58$). Group goal clarity, which speaks to people's knowledge of group goals, also shows the expected positive associations (clear goals being associated with higher satisfaction) and negative associations (i.e., lack of clear goals is related to higher levels of role conflict).

Table 4-12 Intercorrelations Among Scales for the Work Group Module

Scale	[1]	[2]	[3]	[4]	[5]	Number of Items
[1] Group homogeneity	(.62)					2
[2] Group goal clarity	.04	(.61)				2
[3] Group cohesiveness	.06	.41	(.64)			2
[4] Open group process	.08	.42	.55	(.72)		4
[5] Group fragmentation	.10	−.30	−.37	−.58	(.79)	4

Note. Parenthesized values on the diagonal are internal consistency reliability estimates for the scales. $N > 400$; $r = .09$, $p < .05$; $r = .13$, $p < .01$; $r = .15$, $p < .001$.

Table 4-13   Factor Loadings for the Work Group Module

Scale	I	II	III
Group homogeneity			
Members of my work group vary widely in their skills and abilities.			−.56
My work group contains members with widely varying backgrounds.			−.61
Group goal clarity			
My work group knows exactly what things it has to get done.	.54		
Each member of my work group has a clear idea of the group's goals.	.56		
Group cohesiveness			
I feel I'm really a part of my work group.	.58		
I look forward to being with the members of my work group each day.	.57		
Open group process			
We tell each other the way we are feeling.	.50	(−.32)	
My coworkers are afraid to express their real views. (reversed scoring)	.39	−.47	
In my work group everyone's opinions get listened to.	.47	−.49	
If we have a decision to make, everyone is involved in making it.	.43	(−.33)	
Internal fragmentation			
There are feelings among members of my work group which tend to pull the group apart.		−.71	
Some of the people I work with have no respect for others.		−.63	
There is constant bickering in my work group.		−.73	
People who offer new ideas in my work group are likely to get "clobbered."		−.52	

In sum, the work-group scales do seem to fit our theoretical expectations insofar as their impact on individual responses to their work environment is concerned.

Administration

Using the work-group module can pose significant problems in some organizations. The user must find some method to specify the referent of the

Table 4-14 Correlation Between Work Group Scales and Selected Response Scales from Other Modules

Response	Job Satisfaction	Job Involvement	Intention to Turnover	Social Reward Satisfaction	Job Challenge	Role Conflict
Group homogeneity	.13	.12	-.06	.03	.11	.23
Group goal clarity	.37	.22	-.23	.31	.15	-.28
Group cohesiveness	.48	.31	-.31	.58	.27	-.11
Open group process	.43	.24	-.31	.47	.33	-.14
Internal fragmentation	-.37	-.11	.29	-.56	-.18	.31

Note. For the first four columns of figures, $N > 400$; $r = .09$, $p < .05$; $r = .13$, $p < .01$; $r = .15$, $p < .001$. For the last two columns, the N's are approximately 210 cases, with a slight increment in the r's required to reach significance levels.

term *work group*. One approach is to define the work group as the people with whom the respondent usually works on a day-to-day basis. This has the advantage of allowing the respondent to define the psychologically significant group, but it has the disadvantage of not revealing the identity of the group. If one is interested only in the effects of the work group on individuals, this method for defining a work group seems satisfactory, but it does not allow the aggregation of data for the comparison of work groups.

A second approach is to define work groups in formal organizational terms, for example, all the people who report to the same supervisor. This method provides an explicit referent, and it allows aggregation of data to the group level. However, it runs the risk that some respondents will rate groups that are not psychologically and behaviorally significant. A third approach is to have the respondents name the members of the group that they are rating. This approach insures that the referent—a work group— is psychologically significant, but it causes an analytical difficulty because respondents can and will rate groups that are not consistently defined as to membership.

Each of these approaches has its own strengths and weaknesses; the assessor must choose the method for defining the group referent that seems to fit the situation best. Whatever method is chosen, the referent used must be clearly communicated to the respondents so that the assessor can take account of the nature of the groups that are being described.

Current Status and Outlook for Module 4

The group-functioning module appears to suit its purposes with satisfactory statistical credentials. Additional scales would be required for an in-depth assessment of work-group functioning, but no further development in this area is planned at this time.

MODULE 5: SUPERVISION

In most organizations, a member's immediate supervisor is singularly important in determining the subordinate's QWL, and under some circumstances can have a significant impact upon work performance. The effect of leadership has been studied extensively from many different perspectives.[36-39] Our own approach has followed the relatively traditional one of asking descriptive questions about a supervisor's style for the purposes of describing him/her as an aspect of the respondent's environment. The supervisor commonly influences the nature of the tasks to be performed and who will do them, helps to form goals, mediates rewards, controls resources, provides a linkage between the individual subordinate and the organizational system, and serves as an agent in policy and information transmission. This situation arises in conjunction with the traditional pyramidal authority structure that is commonly employed by organizations to insure coordination and control.

Module 5 of MOAQ has been designed to describe and assess supervisory behavior as it is experienced by subordinates. It is applicable at all levels of organizations—as subordinates may themselves also be supervisors. The module is intended to serve two distinct functions.

One purpose is to describe supervisory behavior as a significant feature of the subordinate's work environment. Scales such as those for describing the supervisor's degree of work facilitation, personal consideration for subordinates, and encouragement of subordinate participation, for example, can help in the understanding of subordinates' attitudes and behaviors. They can serve also as indicators of goal achievement in instances where such features of the work environment are themselves the targets for organizational-improvement programs.

A second purpose is to provide information about the way decision making, coordination, and control activities are carried out in the organization. For this use, the subordinates are considered to be informants whose descriptive reports, upon aggregation, represent useful information about the way control activities are carried out.

Two caveats are important here. The first is that this module is intended to provide information about these activities—it is not to be the sole grounds for an assessment of them. The supervisory behaviors measured by the module do not cover all the activities of supervisors relevant to decision making, coordination, and control, but they focus only on those activities that involve subordinates. Second, the module itself is to be used only in organizations where members typically have a single primary supervisor, as in most pyramidal organizational structures. It should not be used where there are multiple supervisors and ambiguous lines of authority; in these situations, other methods must be devised to examine decision making, coordination, and control issues.

The theoretical perspective adopted in developing scales for assessing leadership style was similar to that described by Bowers and Seashore.[38] The scales actually developed were defined somewhat less broadly in order to facilitate their use in providing feedback to supervisors in organizations and in order to give more potential for discovering changes as a result of interventions designed to increase supervisory participation. The scales that were developed include the following aspects:

1. *Production Orientation.* The extent to which the supervisor stresses performance outcomes in dealing with subordinates.

2. *Control of Work.* The extent to which the supervisor maintains control of work that is being done by knowing the state of projects, planning work flows, and making sure the work is being done correctly.

3. *Work Facilitation—Goal Setting.* The extent to which the supervisor helps the subordinates to have clear and integrated goals so that they can know what they should be doing.

4. *Work Facilitation—Problem Solving.* The extent to which the supervisor helps the subordinates solve work-related problems.

5. *Work Facilitation—Subordinate Relations.* The extent to which the supervisor maintains good communication and helpful, equitable relations with subordinates.

6. *Bias.* The extent to which the supervisor is biased by race or sex in dealing with subordinates.

7. *Consideration.* The extent to which the supervisor relates to and helps subordinates as individuals.

8. *Participation.* The extent to which the supervisor encourages subordinates to participate in decisions.

9. *Decision Centralization.* The extent to which the supervisor makes important decisions without involving subordinates.

10. *Competence.* Overall supervisory competence (a single item).

The reliability of the supervisory scales, the correlations among the scales, and sample items are shown in Table 4-15. The items for the scales and the full sample factor analysis are shown in Table 4-16. As can be seen from both the scale intercorrelations and the factor analysis, there is a significant amount of shared variance among these items and scales. This implies that the length of this module could be reduced considerably without much loss of information. While we expect that short forms of this module (e.g., sampling items from the work-facilitation scales) will be used in many situations, the current larger set of scales is preserved because of its usefulness in providing concrete descriptions of perceived supervisory behaviors.

To illustrate the relational characteristics of these scales, they were correlated with a number of psychological-state and individual-outcome measures from Modules 1 and 2. These correlations are shown in Table 4-17.

Previous research[40] has demonstrated that the effects of supervisory behaviors can vary, depending on the nature of an individual's job and growth needs. The relationships between some of the supervisory scales and the measures of job satisfaction, job effort, and experienced job challenge were examined for different levels of experienced role overload and reported importance of intrinsic rewards. The results are shown in Table 4-18. They illustrate that the expected pattern appears, using the MOAQ measures. Production orientation appears to be more strongly related to job satisfaction and job challenge when overload is low and intrinsic-reward importance is high. Work control appears to relate more strongly

Table 4-15 Intercorrelations Among Scales for the Supervision Module

Scale	[1]	[2]	[3]	[4]	[5]	[6]	[7]	[8]	[9]	Number of Items
[1] Production orientation	(.86)									3
[2] Control of work	.34	(.87)								5
[3] Work facilitation—goal setting	.38	.75	(.82)							3
[4] Work facilitation—problem solving	.24	.71	.65	(.83)						2
[5] Work facilitation—subordinate relations	.27	.79	.76	.73	(.93)					7
[6] Bias	-.12	-.34	-.31	-.30	-.41	(.77)				2
[7] Consideration	.24	.64	.69	.69	.84	-.45	(.89)			3
[8] Participation	.24	.61	.61	.61	.81	-.41	.69	(.76)		2
[9] Decision centralization	-.02	-.34	-.31	-.38	-.48	.26	-.41	-.56	(.81)	2

Note. Parenthesized values on the diagonal are internal consistency reliability estimates for the scales. $N > 400$; $r = .09$, $p < .05$; $r = .13$, $p < .01$; $r = .15$, $p < .001$.

Table 4-16 Factor Loadings for the Supervision Module

Scale[a]	Factor				
	I	II	III	IV	V
Production orientation					
demands that people give their best effort.		.81			
insists that subordinates work hard.		.77			
demands that subordinates do high quality work.		.76			
Control of work					
keeps informed about work which is being done.	.70				
plans out work in advance.	.65				
handles the administrative parts of his or her job extremely well.	.71				
maintains high standards of performance.	.68				
knows the technical parts of his or her job extremely well.	.66				
Work facilitation—goal setting					
makes sure subordinates have clear goals to achieve.	.52				.49
makes sure subordinates know what has to be done.	.61				.38
makes it clear how I should do my job.	.52				.33
Work facilitation—problem solving					
helps me solve work-related problems.	.55				.44
helps me discover problems before they get too bad.	.59				.43
Work facilitation—subordinate relations					
keeps informed about the way subordinates think and feel about things.	.50				.57
keeps subordinates informed.	.57				.48
helps subordinates develop their skills.	.52				.55
has the respect of subordinates	.57				.48
deals with subordinates well.	.56				.52
is always fair with subordinates.	.47				.56
tends to play favorites. (reversed scoring)	.36				.42
Bias					
is biased on the basis of race. (reversed scoring)				.67	
is biased on the basis of sex. (reversed scoring)				.69	
Consideration					
helps subordinates with their personal problems.	.35				.58
is concerned about me as a person.	.36				.73
feels each subordinate is important as an individual.	.36				.74

Table 4-16   (*Continued*)

Scale[a]	Factor				
	I	II	III	IV	V
Participation					
encourages subordinates to participate in making important decisions.	(.31)		.52		.49
encourages people to speak up when they disagree with a decision.	.39		.41		.44
Decision centralization					
makes most decisions without asking subordinates their opinions.			.72		
makes important decisions without involving subordinates.			.73		
Global competence					
is competent.	.73			.35	

[a] Each item is preceded by "My supervisor. . . ."

to job challenge and job effort when overload is low, while consideration seems to relate equally to the individual responses measured under all conditions. Participation does not appear to have stronger relationships under varying conditions of overload, but it does relate more strongly to the general attitude measures when the employee's needs for intrinsic rewards are high than when they are low. These relationships are generally in accord with previous research, and they provide some evidence that these scales have construct validity.

Current Status and Outlook

Two additional scales are currently being developed for the supervision module: *interpersonal competence* and use of *contingent-reward* allocation. The items for these scales are shown later. Otherwise, the module is reasonably complete as it is now. Due to the high correlations among many of these scales, it is suggested that only parts of this module be used in certain work sites where it is desirable to shorten this part of the *MOAQ*. The whole module would be used in situations where supervision is a particularly important domain.

Use of Contingent Reward Allocation

1. (My supervisor) rewards me for good performance.
2. (My supervisor) praises good work.
3. (My supervisor) treats me better if I do a good job.

Table 4-17 Correlations of Supervisory Scales with Measures of Psychological States and Individual Outcomes

Scale	Job Satisfaction	Job Involvement	Effort	Challenge	Intrinsic Reward Satisfaction	Extrinsic Reward Satisfaction
Production orientation	.11	.15	.22	.13	.14	.01
Control of work	.39	.20	.14	.34	.38	.23
Work facilitation—goal setting	.36	.23	.11	.28	.38	.27
Work facilitation—problem solving	.39	.19	.08	.32	.38	.30
Work facilitation—subordinate relations	.46	.25	.13	.45	.43	.28
Bias	-.24	-.06	-.12	-.22	-.23	-.04
Consideration	.39	.28	.08	.43	.45	.39
Participation	.36	.28	.10	.44	.44	.30
Decision centralization	-.13	-.08	-.01	-.24	-.22	-.17

Note. N > 400; *r* = .09, *p* < .05; *r* = .13, *p* < .01; *r* = .15, *p* < .001.

Table 4-18   Correlations of Selected Leadership Scales with Job
Satisfaction, Effort, and Challenge for Different Levels of Role Overload and
Intrinsic Reward Importance

Scale	Production Orientation	Work Control	Consideration	Participation
Job satisfaction				
Low overload	.21	.37	.44	.38
Medium overload	.13	.40	.35	.36
High overload	.08	.39	.31	.32
Low intrinsic reward importance	−.05	.27	.36	.26
Medium intrinsic reward importance	.13	.44	.37	.34
High intrinsic reward importance	.22	.43	.45	.45
Job effort				
Low overload	.27	.23	.11	.11
Medium overload	.19	.14	.07	.10
High overload	.20	.10	.07	.10
Low intrinsic reward importance	.22	.13	.02	.05
Medium intrinsic reward importance	.23	.12	.06	.08
High intrinsic reward importance	.21	.17	.14	.13
Job challenge				
Low overload	.22	.46	.49	.47
Medium overload	.11	.31	.32	.40
High overload	.01	.25	.45	.41
Low intrinsic reward importance	.06	.30	.38	.35
Medium intrinsic reward importance	.11	.25	.37	.40
High intrinsic reward importance	.20	.45	.52	.53

Note. $N > 400$; $r = .09$, $p < .05$; $r = .13$, $p < .01$; $r = .15$, $p < .001$.

4. (My supervisor) criticizes people who perform poorly.
5. (My supervisor) keeps poor performers from getting rewarded.

Interpersonal Competence

1. (My supervisor) cannot stand being criticized.
2. (My supervisor) looks for one of us to blame when things go wrong.

3. (My supervisor) does not realize how he or she makes subordinates feel.
4. (My supervisor) is someone I can trust.

MODULE 6: PAY

The pay module was designed to measure certain psychological aspects of pay administration that have been identified by Adams,[41] Opsahl and Dunnette,[42] and Lawler.[20] The primary source for the current set of measures is the work of Porter and Lawler[20,43] and some recent research by Jenkins.[44] On the basis of these studies, a set of constructs was identified that should relate to satisfaction with pay and to the effectiveness of pay for motivating effort and performance. These measures are drawn primarily from Lawler's models of pay motivation and pay satisfaction, which drew on expectancy and equity concepts. Several multiple-item scales have been tested that were designed to measure constructs in two domains—pay administration and determinants of the amount of pay.

Pay Administration

1. *External Equity*   The degree to which the respondent's pay is equitable in comparison to the pay of people in other organizations.
2. *Internal Equity*   The degree to which the respondent's pay is equitable in comparison to the pay of others in the organization.
3. *Personal Equity*   The degree to which the respondent's pay is equitable given his/her own inputs on the job.
4. *Expectancy Constructs—Pay Importance*   The degree to which pay is important to the respondent.
5. *Performance-Pay Contingency*   The degree to which the respondent perceives that pay is contingent on his/her level of performance on the job.
6. *Outcomes—Pay Administration Satisfaction.* The degree to which the respondent is satisfied with how pay is administered in the organization.
7. *Pay Satisfaction.*   The degree to which the respondent is satisfied with the amount of his/her pay.

To assess whether variance in the responses is due to flaws in the pay system itself or to inadequate knowledge about the pay system, one item is included to measure the extent of knowledge of how the pay system operates. For example, low confidence in performance-to-pay contingencies may be due to either inadequate knowledge about the pay system or problems in the structure of the pay system itself.

Pay Determinants

A second set of measures, originally reported by Porter and Lawler,[43] is employed to measure performance-to-pay contingency relationships. These items, which ask respondents to rate the importance of 11 factors in determining the respondent's pay, originally had no expected scaling solution. An item analysis was performed, which indicated the following item groupings.

1. *Tenure.* The importance of organization tenure in determining pay.
2. *Responsibility and Background.* The importance of job responsibility and personal-background qualifications in determining pay.
3. *Performance* (two subscales):
   a. *Individual performance.* The importance of individual performance in determining pay.
   b. *Group performance.* The importance of group performance in determining pay.
4. *Organizational performance.* The importance of organizational performance in determining pay.

A scale was also constructed to measure respondent's degree of support for openness (nonsecrecy) regarding pay. Lawler[20] has presented evidence that pay secrecy may have a negative effect upon organizational effectiveness. The use of this scale is optional. If an organization considers an intervention involving alteration of the existing degree of pay openness, consideration can be given to the use of this scale to assess members' views on the matter. Since this scale is not detailed in the tables that follow, the component items are shown here. The item intercorrelations range from .43 to .57, and the internal-consistency reliability (Cronbach's a) is .74.

5. *Pay-rate openness:*
   a. I believe annual salaries (pay) should be kept secret.
   b. I think all base-pay rates should be made public.
   c. I have no objections to other people in this company knowing my annual salary (pay).

The intercorrelations among these scales are shown in Table 4-19. It is evident from inspection that the three equity and two satisfaction scales are not very well differentiated by the respondents. The factorial structure of the pay-administration items (Table 4-20) lead to the same observation. The set of pay-determinant scales are more clearly differentiated by respondents (Table 4-19), but they have a simple two-factor structure (Table 4-21).

Table 4-19 Intercorrelations Among Pay Module Scales

Scale	[1]	[2]	[3]	[4]	[5]	[6]	[7]	[8]	[9]	[10]	[11]	[12]	[13]
Pay administration													
[1] Performance-pay contingency	(.74)												
[2] Internal equity	.33	(.85)											
[3] Pay importance	-.14	-.17	(.47)										
[4] Pay administration satisfaction	.42	.58	-.22	(.81)									
[5] Personal equity	.31	.63	-.24	.68	(.86)								
[6] External equity	.14	.35	-.15	.46	.66	(.76)							
[7] Pay satisfaction	.36	.60	-.27	.68	.88	.59	(.89)						
Pay determinants													
[8] Tenure	.13	.08	.08	.12	.07	.03	.07	*					
[9] Responsibility and background	.39	.21	-.05	.22	.18	.07	.21	.40	(.73)				
[10] Individual performance	.36	.16	.03	.17	.11	.02	.14	.33	.63	(.88)			
[11] Group performance	.27	.14	.01	.17	.13	.08	.16	.23	.44	.69	(.87)		
[12] Organizational performance	.13	.13	.11	.09	.08	.08	.09	.20	.23	.42	.55	(.86)	
[13] Pay rate openness	-.27	.01	.04	-.12	-.07	-.07	-.12	-.06	-.16	-.14	-.10	-.03	(.74)

Note. Parenthesized values on the diagonal are internal consistency reliability estimates for the scales. Asterisks indicate the scale has only one item. $N > 400$; $r = .09$, $p < .05$; $r = .13$, $p < .01$; $r = .15$, $p < .001$. Data are from two sites.

Table 4-20 Factor Analysis of Pay Administration Items

		Factors		
Scale	**I**	**II**	**III**	**IV**
Performance-pay contingency				
How much pay I receive depends almost entirely on how well I perform my job.		−.61		
Pay raises around here depend on how well you perform.		−.63		
My pay level is determined by my individual job performance.		−.70		
Internal equity				
My pay is fair given what my coworkers make.	(.32)		.63	
My pay is fair compared to the pay of others in this company.	(.28)		.74	
My pay is fair considering what other people in this organization are paid.	(.33)		.71	
Pay importance				
How important is pay to you?				.49
How important is the amount of pay you get?				.49
Pay administration satisfaction				
All in all, pay is administered very well in this organization.	.46	(−.38)	(.37)	
I feel the pay system should be kept as it is.	.43	(−.37)	(.31)	−.24
I am very content with the way management handles pay.	.52	(−.34)	(.32)	
Personal equity				
All in all, my pay is about what it ought to be.	.71		(.31)	
My pay is fair.	.74		(.36)	
Considering my skills and effort, I make a fair wage.	.71		(.31)	
I don't make the kind of money I should for the job I do. (reversed scoring)	.61			
External equity				
Other companies in this area pay better than this one does.	.66			
My pay is fair considering what other places in this area pay.	.77			
Pay satisfaction				
I am very happy with the amount of money I make.	.70		(.27)	(−.25)
Considering my skills and the effort I put into my work, I am very satisfied with my pay.	.70		(.31)	(−.24)
How satisfied are you with the amount of pay you get?	.71		(.33)	(−.22)

Table 4-21   Factor Analysis of Pay-Determinant Items

Scale	Factors	
	I	II
Responsibility and background		
How important to this company is your education, training, and experience?	.64	
How important to this company is the amount of responsibility and pressure on your job?	.68	
Individual performance		
How important to this company is the quality of your job performance?	.82	
How important to this company is your productivity?	.74	
How important to this company is the amount of effort you expend on the job?	.75	
Group performance		
How important to this company is the quality of your work group's performance?	.64	.48
How important to this company is the productivity of your work group?	.56	.55
Organizational performance		
How important to this company is the overall performance of the company?		.70
How important to this company are the total labor costs?		.85
How important to this company are the costs for material usage?		.80
Tenure[a]		
How important to this company is your length of service?		

[a] This item is currently being retained, for future testing, although it did not show adequate scaling characteristics in the pay-determinant analysis.

The correlations of the pay-module items with a set of items from the general-attitudes and job-facet modules show an expected pattern of correlations (Table 4-22), although pay fairness and pay satisfaction do not appear to have discriminant validity and will probably have to be combined in the next iteration.

Examination of the correlations with outside measures of pay satisfaction, internal, personal, and external equity show virtually indistinguishable patterns of correlations for all four measures. Given this obser-

Table 4-22 Correlations of Pay Module Scales with Selected General and Facet Module Scales

Scale	Pay Administration								Pay Determinants				
	Performance-pay Contingency	Internal Equity	Pay Importance	Pay Administration Satisfaction	Personal Equity	External Equity	Pay Satisfaction	Tenure	Responsibility and Background	Individual Performance	Group Performance	Organizational Performance	Pay Rate Openness
General attitudes													
[1] Job satisfaction	.26	.27	-.06	.38	.36	.32	.38	.07	.26	.23	.24	.14	-.00
[2] Job involvement	.22	.10	-.00	.20	.09	.12	.15	.08	.18	.18	.23	.17	-.05
[3] Intention to turnover	-.20	-.25	.10	-.31	-.37	-.37	-.35	-.06	-.18	-.17	-.19	-.14	.00
[4] Internal turnover desire	-.11	-.14	.01	-.17	-.17	-.10	-.18	.07	-.13	-.12	-.12	-.09	-.06
[5] Internal work motivation	.17	.09	.01	.14	.17	.20	.18	.04	.21	.21	.21	.12	.00
[6] Organizational involvement	.23	.19	-.05	.28	.29	.29	.30	.04	.23	.21	.24	.17	-.06
[7] Self-report of effort	.07	-.06	.05	.04	-.00	.05	.03	.01	.07	.14	.15	.04	-.06
Good performance contingencies													
[8] Extrinsic contingency	.46	.20	-.13	.32	.28	.13	.31	.12	.31	.30	.25	.09	-.13
[9] Externally mediated intrinsic contingency	.40	.23	-.11	.29	.26	.10	.28	.11	.37	.35	.30	.14	-.08
Facet satisfaction													
[10] Extrinsic facet satisfaction	.39	.51	-.25	.56	.63	.42	.72	.12	.27	.20	.20	.13	.00
[11] Intrinsic facet satisfaction	.34	.28	-.13	.36	.32	.21	.38	.13	.31	.29	.27	.17	-.05

Note. $N > 400$; $r = .09$, $p < .05$; $r = .13$, $p < .01$; $r = .15$, $p < .001$. Data are from two sites.

vation and the high intercorrelations among the four measures (Table 4-19), it seems inadvisable to continue using all these measures without more indication of some discrimination among these scales.

Current State and Outlook

The pay module has been used in a number of sites, but it has been subjected to item and scale analyses procedures only once, with data from two sites. Since the items and scales have a long history of successful prior use, it is not expected that major changes or additions will be required in the future. It is likely that a second round of scaling analyses will result in some simplification of the scales, representing equity and satisfaction, but they can be used in their present form.

CONCLUDING NOTE

This chapter has presented a questionnaire of modular design intended for use in the assessment of organizations and of organizational change where the perspectives and observations of members are deemed to be important. For each module, there has been provided some explanation of the theoretical and/or empirical bases for content inclusion together with statistical information regarding scale reliability and factorial structures. Also presented are examples of the kinds of evidence of construct validity that can be derived from examination of scale intercorrelations across unlike domains of information. The MOAQ is considered to be sufficiently well along in its development to allow general use, and, in fact, it is currently being used in numerous organizations in the United States and Canada.

In our view, the MOAQ should be considered a "living" instrument. It is adapted each time it is used to fit the particular circumstances involved, and there is no one final form. Modules have been added and will continue to be as circumstances dictate their necessity, and items or scales are dropped from particular administrations and from the instrument itself as experience shows they are not useful. The questionnaire could more appropriately be described as a useful repository of tested items, along with some general scales and procedures for guiding its use.

At this point in time, the modules and items described here have all been tested in the field, and the results generally show acceptable empirical utility. The information generated by the questionnaire has been used in conducting a range of assessments and activities. The results have proven satisfactory for our purposes[44-48] and may be useful for others. We would stress, however, that each researcher needs to examine the empirical and theoretical validity of our measures in the context of his or her own projects and adapt the instruments appropriately if the best results are to be achieved.

REFERENCES

1. Nadler, D. A., Jenkins, G. D., Jr., Cammann, C., & Lawler, E. E. III. *The Michigan organizational assessment package: Progress report* II. Ann Arbor: Institute for Social Research, University of Michigan, 1975.

2. Hackman, J. R., & Oldham, G. Motivation through the design of work: Test of a theory. *Organizational Behavior and Human Performance,* 1976, **16**(2), 250–279.

3. Shepard, R. N. The analysis of proximities: Multidimensional scaling with an unknown distance function. I, II. *Psychometrika,* 1962, **27**, 125–140, 219–246.

4. Kruskal, J. B. Multidimensional scaling: A numerical method. *Psychometrika,* 1964, **29**, 1–27.

5. Kruskal, J. B. Multidimensional scaling by optimizing goodness of fit to a nonmetric hypothesis. *Psychometrika,* 1964, **29**, 115–129.

6. *OSIRIS III, Volume I: System and program design.* Ann Arbor: Institute for Social Research, University of Michigan, 1973, 599–625.

7. Harman, H. H. *Modern factor analysis,* 2nd ed. Chicago: University of Chicago Press, 1967.

8. Factor comparison. In *OSIRIS III, Volume I: System and program design.* Ann Arbor: Institute for Social Research, University of Michigan, 1973, 627–636.

9. Nunnally, J. *Psychometric methods.* New York: McGraw-Hill, 1967.

10. Lawler, E. E. III, Nadler, D. A., & Cammann, C. *Organizational assessment.* New York: Wiley-Interscience, 1980.

11. Herzberg, F., Mausner, B., & Snyderman, B. *The motivation to work.* New York: Wiley, 1959.

12. Alderfer, C. P. *Existence, relatedness and growth: Human needs in organizational settings.* New York: Free Press, 1972.

13. Maslow, A. H. A theory of human motivation. *Psychological Review,* 1943, **50**, 370–396.

14. Lawler, E. E. III. *Motivation in work organizations.* Monterey, CA: Brooks/Cole, 1973.

15. Vroom, V. *Work and motivation.* New York: Wiley, 1964.

16. Hackman, J. R., & Lawler, E. E. Employee reactions to job characteristics. *Journal of Applied Psychology,* 1971, **55**, 259–286.

17. Tannenbaum, A. *Control in organizations.* New York: McGraw-Hill, 1968.

18. Lawler, E. E. III. *Pay and organizational development.* Reading, MA: Addison-Wesley, 1981.

19. Rabinowitz, S., & Hall, D. T. Organizational research on job involvement. *Psychological Bulletin,* 1977, **84**(2), 265–288.

20. Lawler, E. E. III. *Pay and organizational effectiveness: A psychological view.* New York: McGraw-Hill, 1971.

21. Deci, E. *Intrinsic motivation.* New York: Plenum, 1975.

22. Porter, L. W., & Steers, R. M. Organizational work and personal factors in employee turnover and absenteeism. *Psychological Bulletin,* 1973, **80**, 151–176.

23. Mitchell, T. R. Expectancy models of job satisfaction, occupational preference, and effort: A theoretical, methodological and empirical appraisal. *Psychological Bulletin,* 1974, **81**, 1053–1077.

24. Wanous, J. P., & Lawler, E. E. III. Measurement and meaning of job satisfaction. *Journal of Applied Psychology,* 1972, **56**, 95–105.

25. Quinn, R. P., & Mangione, T. W. Evaluating weighted models of measuring job satisfaction. *Organizational Behavior and Human Performance,* 1973, **10**, 1–23.

26. Smith, P., Kendall, L., & Hulin, C. L. *The measurement of satisfaction in work and retirement.* Chicago: Rand-McNally, 1969.

27. Porter, L. W., Lawler, E. E. III, & Hackman J. R. *Behavior in organizations.* New York: Wiley, 1975.

28. Likert, R. *New patterns of management.* New York: McGraw-Hill, 1961.

29. *Work in America.* Report of a special task force to the Secretary of Health, Education, and Welfare. Cambridge: MIT Press, 1971.

30. Cummings, T. G., & Molloy, E. S. *Improving productivity and the quality of work life.* New York: Praeger, 1977.

31. Kahn, R. L., Wolfe, D. M., Quinn, R. P., Snoek, J. D., & Rosenthal, R. A. *Organizational stress: Studies in role conflict and ambiguity.* New York: Wiley, 1964.

32. Caplan, R. D., Cobb, S., French, J. R. P., Jr., Harrison, R. V., & Pinneau, S. R. *Job demands and worker health.* Washington, D.C.: U.S. Government Printing Office, 1975.

33. Rousseau, D. M. Technological differences in job characteristics, employee satisfaction and motivation: A synthesis of job design research and sociotechnical systems theory. *Organizational Behavior and Human Performance,* 1977, **19,** 18–42.

34. Porter, L. W., & Lawler, E. E. III. Properties of organization structure in relation to job attitudes and job behavior. *Psychological Bulletin,* 1965, **64,** 23–51.

35. Hackman, J. R., & Morris, C. G. Group tasks, group interaction process and group performance effectiveness. In L. Berkowitz (Ed.), *Advances in experimental social psychology (Vol. 7).* New York: Academic Press, 1975.

36. Stogdill, R. M. *Handbook of leadership.* New York: Free Press, 1974.

37. Feidler, F. E. *A theory of leadership effectiveness.* New York: McGraw-Hill, 1967.

38. Bowers, D., & Seashore, S. E. Predicting organizational effectiveness with a four factor theory of leadership. *Administrative Science Quarterly,* 1966 11(1), 238–263.

39. Mintzberg, H. *The nature of managerial work.* New York: Harper & Row, 1973.

40. House, R. J., Filley, A. C., & Kerr, S. Relation of leader consideration and initiating structure to R and D subordinates' satisfaction. *Administrative Science Quarterly,* 1971, **16,** 19–31.

41. Adams, J. S. Injustice in social exchange. In L. Berkowitz (Ed.), *Advances in experimental social psychology (Vol. 2).* New York: Academic Press, 1965, 267–299.

42. Opsahl, R. L., & Dunnette, M. D. The role of financial compensation in industrial motivation. *Psychological Bulletin,* 1966, **66**(2), 94–118.

43. Porter, L. W., & Lawler, E. E. III. *Managerial attitudes and performance.* Homewood, IL: Irwin-Dorsey, 1968.

44. Jenkins, G. D., Jr. *The impact of employee participation in the development and implementation of a base pay and a performance bonus plan.* Unpublished doctoral dissertation, University of Michigan, 1977.

45. Mirvis, P. H., & Lawler, E. E. III. Measuring the financial impact of employee attitudes. *Journal of Applied Psychology,* 1977, **62**(1), 1–8.

46. Ledford, G. E., Jr., Lawler, E. E. III, & Macy, B. A. *The Bolivar project: The quality of work life experiment at Harman International Industries.* Book in preparation; to be published by Wiley-Interscience.

47. Nadler, D. A., Mirvis, P. H., & Cammann, C. The ongoing feedback system. *Organizational Dynamics,* 1976, 4(4), 63–80.

48. Perkins, D. N. T., Nieva, V. F., & Lawler, E. E. III. Managing creation: The challenge of building a new organization. New York: Wiley-Interscience, forthcoming.

APPENDIX 4-1   QUALITY OF WORK COMMITTEE QUESTIONNAIRE

QUALITY OF WORK COMMITTEE QUESTIONNAIRE

Dear National Production Employee:

This questionnaire is designed to find out how you and others feel about the National Production Company as a place to work. These data will provide the Quality of Work Committee with some of the information they will need to better understand how people feel about the quality of working life in the factory. This questionnaire will also provide a basis for understanding the changes which occur here over the next three years.

If this questionnaire is to be useful, it is important that you answer each question frankly and honestly. There are no right or wrong answers to these questions, since we are interested in what you think and feel about your life at the factory.

Your answers to these questions are completely confidential. All questionnaires will be taken to the Institute for Social Research at the University of Michigan for analysis and safekeeping. No one at National Production will ever have access to your individual answers.

To see if things have changed here, we may ask you to fill out another questionnaire some time next year, and we need some way to identify individual responses to compare them over time. As a result, we have put a number on this questionnaire (on the following page) which can be matched with your name on a list to be kept at the Institute for Social Research. We would appreciate it if you would leave this number intact.

After you complete the questionnaire, please place the questionnaire back in its envelope, remove your name from the envelope, and place it in the box in the back of the room.

Thank you in advance for your cooperation and assistance. We hope you find the questionnaire interesting and thought provoking.

QUALITY OF WORK PROJECT ASSESSMENT TEAM

GENERAL INSTRUCTIONS

Most of the questions ask that you check one of several numbers that appear on a scale to the right of the item. You are to choose the one number that best matches the description of how you feel about the item. For example, if you were asked how much you agree with the statement, "I enjoy the weather in this area," and you feel that you do agree, you would check the number under "Agree" like this:

I enjoy the weather in this area. .... [1] [2] [3] [4] [5] [6] [7]

Note that the scale descriptions may be different in different parts of the questionnaire. For example, they may ask not whether you agree or disagree but perhaps whether you are satisfied or dissatisfied, or whether you think something to be likely or not likely to happen, etc.

So, be sure to read the special instructions that appear in the boxes on each page. Be sure to read the scale descriptions before choosing your answers.

When you have finished, please place the questionnaire in the envelope, remove your name from the outside, and return the envelope to the designated place or person.

* * * * * * * * *

This is your Michigan identification number:

Label: 1:1—7

These codes are for Michigan use only:

Deck: 1:08

MODULE 0 — DEMOGRAPHICS

The following information is needed to help us with the statistical analyses of the data. This information will allow comparisons among different groups of employees and comparisons with similar employees in other organizations.

All of your responses are strictly confidential; individual responses will not be seen by anyone within this organization. We appreciate your help in providing this important information.

PLEASE ANSWER EACH OF THE QUESTIONS BELOW BY MARKING THE NUMBER NEXT TO THE DESCRIPTION WHICH BEST FITS YOU OR BY WRITING IN THE CORRECT INFORMATION.

---

1. Are you — (check one)   1:09

   [1] Female

   [2] Male

2. What is your education level (indicate highest completed)?   1:10

   [1] Some elementary school (grades 1—7)

   [2] Completed elementary school (8 grades)

   [3] Some high school (grades 9—11)

   [4] Graduated from high school or G.E.D.

   [5] Some college or technical training beyond high school (1—3 years)

   [6] Graduated from college (B.A., B.S., or other Bachelor's degree)

   [7] Some graduate school

   [8] Graduate degree (Masters, Ph.D., M.D., etc.)

3. What is your marital status?   1:11

   [1] Married

   [2] Widowed

   [3] Separated

   [4] Divorced

   [5] Never married

4. Are you — (check one)   1:12

   [1] Black

   [2] Oriental

   [3] American Indian

   [4] Spanish surnamed American

   [5] White

   [6] None of the above

5. How old were you on your last birthday?   1:13—14

   _____ years

6. What was the size of the community in which you spent the largest portion of your life up to the time you finished high school?   1:15

   [1] On a farm or ranch

   [2] In a rural area, not on a farm or ranch

   [3] A suburban town near a city

   [4] A small city (less than 100,000)

   [5] A large city (more than 100,000)

7. Is your income the primary source of financial support for your immediate family?   1:16

   [1] Yes
   [2] No

8. How many dependents do you have
    (others who depend on your income
    for their financial support)?   1:17—18

    _____ dependents

9. When did you first come to work
    for National Production (please use
    a number for the month, for
    example, 6 for June or 12 for
    December)?   1:19—22

    _____, 19____
    month   year

10. When did you start your present job
    in this factory (please use a number
    for the month)?   1:23—26

    ___ __, 19____
    month   year

11. Which of the following salary ranges is
    nearest to your total income from your
    job last year?   1:27

    [1] Under $4,000
    [2] $4,000 — 5,999
    [3] $6,000 — 7,999
    [4] $8,000 — 9,999
    [5] $10,000 — 12,999
    [6] $13,000 — 15,999
    [7] $16,000 — 19,999
    [8] $20,000 — 24,999
    [9] $25,000 or more

MODULE 1 — GENERAL ATTITUDES

The next questions are about you and your job. When answering, keep in mind the kind of work you do and the experiences you have had working here. Follow the directions given in the boxes at the beginning of each set of questions.

---

1. HERE ARE SOME STATEMENTS ABOUT YOU AND YOUR JOB. HOW MUCH DO YOU AGREE OR DISAGREE WITH EACH?

Strongly Disagree — Disagree — Slightly Disagree — Neither Agree nor Disagree — Slightly Agree — Agree — Strongly Agree

a.	I get a feeling of personal satisfaction from doing my job well.	[1] [2] [3] [4] [5] [6] [7] 2:09
b.	It would be very hard for me to leave my job even if I wanted to.	[1] [2] [3] [4] [5] [6] [7] 2:10
c.	I am very much personally involved in my work.	[1] [2] [3] [4] [5] [6] [7] 2:11
d.	I work hard on my job.	[1] [2] [3] [4] [5] [6] [7] 2:12
e.	If I had the chance, I would take a different job within this organization.	[1] [2] [3] [4] [5] [6] [7] 2:13
f.	I dread the thought of what might happen if I quit my job without having another one lined up.	[1] [2] [3] [4] [5] [6] [7] 2:14
g.	All in all, I am satisfied with my job.	[1] [2] [3] [4] [5] [6] [7] 2:15
h.	I will probably look for a new job in the next year.	[1] [2] [3] [4] [5] [6] [7] 2:16
i.	In general, I don't like my job.	[1] [2] [3] [4] [5] [6] [7] 2:17
j.	What happens to this organization is really important to me.	[1] [2] [3] [4] [5] [6] [7] 2:18
k.	Doing my job well gives me a good feeling.	[1] [2] [3] [4] [5] [6] [7] 2:19
l.	I often think about quitting.	[1] [2] [3] [4] [5] [6] [7] 2:20
m.	I don't care what happens to this organization as long as I get my paycheck.	[1] [2] [3] [4] [5] [6] [7] 2:21
n.	I feel personally responsible for the work I do on my job.	[1] [2] [3] [4] [5] [6] [7] 2:22
o.	In general, I like working here.	[1] [2] [3] [4] [5] [6] [7] 2:23
p.	I feel bad when I do a poor job.	[1] [2] [3] [4] [5] [6] [7] 2:24
q.	I live, eat, and breathe my job.	[1] [2] [3] [4] [5] [6] [7] 2:25
r.	The most important things which happen to me involve my job.	[1] [2] [3] [4] [5] [6] [7] 2:26
s.	I have too much at stake in my job to change jobs now.	[1] [2] [3] [4] [5] [6] [7] 2:27

---

2. PLEASE ANSWER THE FOLLOWING QUESTIONS.

Not At All Likely — Somewhat Likely — Quite Likely — Extremely Likely

a.	How likely is it that you could find a job with another employer with about the same pay and benefits you now have?	[1] [2] [3] [4] [5] [6] [7] 2:28
b.	How likely is it that you will actively look for a new job in the next year?	[1] [2] [3] [4] [5] [6] [7] 2:29

MODULE 2 — JOB FACETS

So far you have been asked questions about your job. This next section asks how you think and feel about certain specific parts of your work.

---

1. DIFFERENT PEOPLE WANT DIFFERENT THINGS FROM THEIR WORK. HERE IS A LIST OF THINGS A PERSON COULD HAVE ON HIS OR HER JOB. HOW IMPORTANT IS EACH OF THE FOLLOW— ING TO YOU?

HOW IMPORTANT IS . . .

	Moderately Important or Less				Quite Important		Extremely Important	
a. . . . the fringe benefits you receive.	[3]	[4]	[5]	[6]	[7]	[8]	[9]	3:09
b. . . . the friendliness of the people you work with.	[3]	[4]	[5]	[6]	[7]	[8]	[9]	3:10
c. . . . the amount of freedom you have on your job.	[3]	[4]	[5]	[6]	[7]	[8]	[9]	3:11
d. . . . the chances you have to learn new things.	[3]	[4]	[5]	[6]	[7]	[8]	[9]	3:12
e. . . . the respect you receive from the people you work with.	[3]	[4]	[5]	[6]	[7]	[8]	[9]	3:13

HOW IMPORTANT IS . . .

f. . . . the chances you have to accomplish something worthwhile.	[3]	[4]	[5]	[6]	[7]	[8]	[9]	3:14
g. . . . the amount of pay you get.	[3]	[4]	[5]	[6]	[7]	[8]	[9]	3:15
h. . . . the chances you have to do something that makes you feel good about yourself as a person.	[3]	[4]	[5]	[6]	[7]	[8]	[9]	3:16
i. . . . the way you are treated by the people you work with.	[3]	[4]	[5]	[6]	[7]	[8]	[9]	3:17
j. . . . the chances you have to take part in making decisions.	[3]	[4]	[5]	[6]	[7]	[8]	[9]	3:18
k. . . . the amount of job security you have.	[3]	[4]	[5]	[6]	[7]	[8]	[9]	3:19

2. IN THE QUESTION YOU JUST ANSWERED
    YOU RATED THE IMPORTANCE OF DIF—
    FERENT ASPECTS OF YOUR WORK.

    HERE YOU ARE BEING ASKED SOMETHING
    DIFFERENT. IN THIS QUESTION, PLEASE
    INDICATE HOW SATISFIED YOU ARE WITH
    EACH OF THE FOLLOWING ASPECTS OF
    YOUR JOB.

HOW SATISFIED ARE YOU WITH . . .

		Very Dissatisfied	Dissatisfied	Slightly Dissatisfied	Neither Satisfied nor Dissatisfied	Slightly Satisfied	Satisfied	Very Satisfied	
a.	. . . the fringe benefits you receive.	[1]	[2]	[3]	[4]	[5]	[6]	[7]	3:20
b.	. . . the friendliness of the people you work with.	[1]	[2]	[3]	[4]	[5]	[6]	[7]	3:21
c.	. . . the amount of freedom you have on your job.	[1]	[2]	[3]	[4]	[5]	[6]	[7]	3:22
d.	. . . the chances you have to learn new things.	[1]	[2]	[3]	[4]	[5]	[6]	[7]	3:23
e.	. . . the respect you receive from the people you work with.	[1]	[2]	[3]	[4]	[5]	[6]	[7]	3:24

HOW SATISFIED ARE YOU WITH . . .

f.	. . . the chances you have to accomplish something worthwhile.	[1]	[2]	[3]	[4]	[5]	[6]	[7]	3:25
g.	. . . the amount of pay you get.	[1]	[2]	[3]	[4]	[5]	[6]	[7]	3:26
h.	. . . the chances you have to do something that makes you feel good about your- self as a person.	[1]	[2]	[3]	[4]	[5]	[6]	[7]	3:27
i.	. . . the way you are treated by the people you work with.	[1]	[2]	[3]	[4]	[5]	[6]	[7]	3:28
j.	. . . the chances you have to take part in making decisions.	[1]	[2]	[3]	[4]	[5]	[6]	[7]	3:29
k.	. . . the amount of job security you have.	[1]	[2]	[3]	[4]	[5]	[6]	[7]	3:30

3. HERE ARE SOME THINGS THAT COULD
    HAPPEN TO PEOPLE WHEN THEY DO
    THEIR JOBS ESPECIALLY WELL. HOW
    LIKELY IS IT THAT EACH OF THESE
    THINGS WOULD HAPPEN IF YOU PER—
    FORMED YOUR JOB ESPECIALLY WELL?

		Not At All Likely		Somewhat Likely		Quite Likely		Extremely Likely	
a.	You will get a bonus or pay increase.	[1]	[2]	[3]	[4]	[5]	[6]	[7]	3:31
b.	You will feel better about yourself as a person.	[1]	[2]	[3]	[4]	[5]	[6]	[7]	3:32
c.	You will have an opportunity to develop your skills and abilities.	[1]	[2]	[3]	[4]	[5]	[6]	[7]	3:33

HOW LIKELY IS IT . . .

		Not At All Likely		Somewhat Likely		Quite Likely		Extremely Likely	
d.	You will be given chances to learn new things.	[1]	[2]	[3]	[4]	[5]	[6]	[7]	3:34
e.	You will be promoted or get a better job.	[1]	[2]	[3]	[4]	[5]	[6]	[7]	3:35
f.	You will get a feeling that you've accomplished something worthwhile.	[1]	[2]	[3]	[4]	[5]	[6]	[7]	3:36

MODULE 3 — TASK AND ROLE CHARACTERISTICS

The next questions are about you and your job. When answering, please keep in mind the kind of work you do and the experiences you have had working here. Follow the directions given in the boxes at the beginning of each set of questions.

1. HERE ARE SOME STATEMENTS WHICH DESCRIBE JOBS. HOW MUCH DO YOU AGREE OR DISAGREE WITH EACH STATEMENT AS A DESCRIPTION OF YOUR JOB?

Strongly Disagree / Disagree / Slightly Disagree / Neither Agree or Disagree / Slightly Agree / Agree / Strongly Agree

a. I often have to deal with new problems on my job. .... [1] [2] [3] [4] [5] [6] [7]   4:09

b. A lot of people can be affected by how well I do my work. .... [1] [2] [3] [4] [5] [6] [7]   4:10

c. I can see the results of my own work. .... [1] [2] [3] [4] [5] [6] [7]   4:11

d. My job allows me to control my own work pace. .... [1] [2] [3] [4] [5] [6] [7]   4:12

e. Just doing the work required by my job gives me many chances to figure out how well I am doing. .... [1] [2] [3] [4] [5] [6] [7]   4:13

f. On my job, I produce a whole product or perform a complete service. .... [1] [2] [3] [4] [5] [6] [7]   4:14

g. It takes a long time to learn the skills required to do my job well. .... [1] [2] [3] [4] [5] [6] [7]   4:15

2. What is the level of education you feel is needed by a person in your job?   4:16

[1] Some elementary school (grades 1—7)

[2] Completed elementary school (8 grades)

[3] Some high school (9—11 years)

[4] Graduated from high school or G.E.D.

[5] Some college or technical training beyond high school (1—3 years)

[6] Graduated from college (B.A., B.S., or other bachelors degree)

[7] Some graduate school

[8] Graduate degree (Masters, Ph.D., M.D., etc.)

3.   HERE ARE SOME STATEMENTS WHICH DESCRIBE JOBS. HOW MUCH DO YOU AGREE OR DISAGREE WITH EACH STATEMENT AS A DESCRIPTION OF YOUR JOB?

		Strongly Disagree	Disagree	Slightly Disagree	Neither Agree nor Disagree	Slightly Agree	Agree	Strongly Agree	
a.	I do not have enough training to do my job well.	[1]	[2]	[3]	[4]	[5]	[6]	[7]	4:17
b.	On my job, I often have to handle surprising or unpredictable situations.	[1]	[2]	[3]	[4]	[5]	[6]	[7]	4:18
c.	On my job, most of my tasks are clearly defined.	[1]	[2]	[3]	[4]	[5]	[6]	[7]	4:19
d.	I get to do a number of different things on my job.	[1]	[2]	[3]	[4]	[5]	[6]	[7]	4:20
e.	I determine the speed at which I work.	[1]	[2]	[3]	[4]	[5]	[6]	[7]	4:21
f.	I have more than enough training and skills to do my job well.	[1]	[2]	[3]	[4]	[5]	[6]	[7]	4:22
g.	My job requires that I do the same things over and over.	[1]	[2]	[3]	[4]	[5]	[6]	[7]	4:23
h.	My job is so simple that virtually anybody could handle it with little or no initial training.	[1]	[2]	[3]	[4]	[5]	[6]	[7]	4:24
i.	I usually know whether or not my work is satisfactory on this job.	[1]	[2]	[3]	[4]	[5]	[6]	[7]	4:25

The next questions ask you to describe the JOB ON WHICH YOU WORK. Please do not try to show how much you like or dislike your job; just try to be as accurate and factually correct as possible.

First, read the descriptions at each end of the scale, under [1] and [7] and in the middle under [4]. Then check one of these boxes -- or one in between -- that best describes what your job is like.

4.   How much <u>variety</u> is there in your job?   4:26

[1]   [2]   [3]   [4]   [5]   [6]   [7]

Very little; I do pretty much the same things over and over, using the same equipment and procedures almost all the time.

Moderate variety

Very much; I do many things, using a variety of equipment and procedures.

5. How much does the work you do on your job make a <u>visible impact</u> on a product or service?

4:27

[1]   [2]   [3]   [4]   [5]   [6]   [7]

None at all; it is
hard to tell what
impact my work
makes on the pro-
duct or service.

A moderate amount;
the impact of my
job is visible along
with that of others.

A great amount;
my work is clearly
visible; it makes a
noticeable difference
in the final product
or service.

6. How much <u>freedom</u> do you have on your job? That is, how much do you decide on your own what you do on your job?

4:28

[1]   [2]   [3]   [4]   [5]   [6]   [7]

Very little; there
are few decisions
about my job which
I can make by my-
self.

A moderate amount;
I have responsibility
for deciding some of
the things I do, but
not others.

Very much; there
are many decisions
about my job which
I can make by my-
self.

7. How often does your job <u>require that you meet or check with other people</u> in this organization?

4:29

[1]   [2]   [3]   [4]   [5]   [6]   [7]

Not at all; I never
have to meet or
check with others.

I sometimes need
to meet or check
with others.

Very often; I must
constantly meet or
check with others.

8. How much <u>challenge</u> is there on your job?

4:30

[1]   [2]   [3]   [4]   [5]   [6]   [7]

There is very little
challenge on my
job; I don't get a
chance to use any
special skills and
abilities and I never
have jobs which
require all my
abilities to complete
them successfully.

Moderate challenge

There is a great
deal of challenge
on my job; I get
a chance to use
my special skills
and abilities and
often have jobs
which require all
my abilities to
complete successfully.

9. As you do your job, <u>can you tell how well</u> you're performing?

4:31

[1]   [2]   [3]   [4]   [5]   [6]   [7]

Not at all; I could
work on my job
indefinitely without
ever finding out
how well I am doing
unless somebody tells
me.

Moderately; some-
times by just doing
the job I can find
out how well I'm
performing, some-
times I can't.

A great deal; I can
almost always tell
how well I'm per-
forming just by
doing my job.

10. In general, how <u>significant</u> or <u>important</u> is your job. That is, are the results of your work likely to significantly affect the lives or well-being of other people?   4:32

      [1]   [2]   [3]   [4]   [5]   [6]   [7]

| Not very significant the outcomes of my work are not likely to have important affects on other people. | | | Moderately significant | | | Highly significant; the outcomes of my work can affect other people in very important ways. |

11. How much <u>uncertainty</u> is there in your job?   4:33

      [1]   [2]   [3]   [4]   [5]   [6]   [7]

| Very little; I almost always know what to expect and am never surprised by something happening unexpectedly on my job. | | | Moderate uncertainty | | | A great deal; I almost never am sure what is going to happen, and unexpected things frequently happen. |

12. How much <u>control</u> do you have in setting the pace of your work?   4:34

      [1]   [2]   [3]   [4]   [5]   [6]   [7]

| Very little; pace is predetermined and I must work at a strict pace set by someone or something else. | | | Moderate control of work pace. | | | A great deal; I determine my own work pace. |

13. How much do you have to <u>cooperate</u> directly with other people in this organization in order to do your job?   4:35

      [1]   [2]   [3]   [4]   [5]   [6]   [7]

| Very little; I can do almost all my work by myself. | | | A moderate amount; some of my work requires cooperating with others. | | | Very much; all my work requires cooperating with others. |

14. How much does your job involve your producing an <u>entire product</u> or an <u>entire service</u>?   4:36

      [1]   [2]   [3]   [4]   [5]   [6]   [7]

| My job involves doing only a small part of the entire product or service; it is also worked on by others or by automatic equipment and I may not see or be aware of much of the work which is done on the product or service. | | | My job involves doing a moderate sized 'chunk' of work; while others are involved as well, my own contribution is significant. | | | My job involves producing the entire product or service from start to finish, the final outcome of the work is clearly the results of my work. |

15.   THE FOLLOWING STATEMENTS DESCRIBE HOW YOU MIGHT FEEL ABOUT YOUR JOB. HOW MUCH DO YOU AGREE OR DISAGREE WITH EACH STATEMENT?

Strongly Disagree / Disagree / Slightly Disagree / Neither Agree nor Disagree / Slightly Agree / Agree / Strongly Agree

a.   The work I do on my job is meaningful to me. [1] [2] [3] [4] [5] [6] [7]   4:37

b.   It is basically my own responsibility to decide how my job gets done. [1] [2] [3] [4] [5] [6] [7]   4:38

c.   To be successful on my job requires all my skill and ability. [1] [2] [3] [4] [5] [6] [7]   4:39

d.   I have too much work to do to do everything well. [1] [2] [3] [4] [5] [6] [7]   4:40

e.   I have all the skills I need in order to do my job. [1] [2] [3] [4] [5] [6] [7]   4:41

f.   To satisfy some people on my job, I have to upset others. [1] [2] [3] [4] [5] [6] [7]   4:42

g.   I have the freedom to decide what I do on my job. [1] [2] [3] [4] [5] [6] [7]   4:43

h.   I feel that most of the things I do on my job are meaningless. [1] [2] [3] [4] [5] [6] [7]   4:44

i.   On my job, I can't satisfy everybody at the same time. [1] [2] [3] [4] [5] [6] [7]   4:45

HOW YOU FEEL ABOUT YOUR JOB — AGREE OR DISAGREE . . .

j.   The amount of work I am asked to do is fair. [1] [2] [3] [4] [5] [6] [7]   4:46

k.   I feel personally responsible for the work I do on my job. [1] [2] [3] [4] [5] [6] [7]   4:47

l.   Most of the time I know what I have to do on my job. [1] [2] [3] [4] [5] [6] [7]   4:48

m.   On my job, I seldom get a chance to use my special skills and abilities. [1] [2] [3] [4] [5] [6] [7]   4:49

n.   I never seem to have enough time to get everything done. [1] [2] [3] [4] [5] [6] [7]   4:50

o.   My job is very challenging. [1] [2] [3] [4] [5] [6] [7]   4:51

p.   I deserve credit or blame for how well my work gets done. [1] [2] [3] [4] [5] [6] [7]   4:52

q.   I seldom know whether I'm doing my job well or poorly. [1] [2] [3] [4] [5] [6] [7]   4:53

r.   On my job, I know exactly what is expected of me. [1] [2] [3] [4] [5] [6] [7]   4:54

MODULE 4 — WORK GROUP FUNCTIONING

The next set of questions is concerned with groups in this organization. For this questionnaire, please think of your "work group" as the set of people with whom you work most closely on a day-to-day basis.

If you are a member of only one work group, the questions are easy to answer. If you are a member of two or more work groups, you will need to decide which one group to think about when answering the questions.

For this part of the questionnaire, keep this one group in mind.

1. THE FOLLOWING ARE STATEMENTS THAT MAY OR MAY NOT DESCRIBE YOUR WORK GROUP. HOW MUCH DO YOU AGREE OR DISAGREE WITH EACH STATEMENT?

		Strongly Disagree	Disagree	Slightly Disagree	Neither Agree nor Disagree	Slightly Agree	Agree	Strongly Agree	
a.	I feel I am really part of my work group.	[1]	[2]	[3]	[4]	[5]	[6]	[7]	5:09
b.	My work group knows exactly what things it has to get done.	[1]	[2]	[3]	[4]	[5]	[6]	[7]	5:10
c.	People who offer new ideas in my work group are likely to get "clobbered."	[1]	[2]	[3]	[4]	[5]	[6]	[7]	5:11
d.	Members of my work group vary widely in their skills and abilities.	[1]	[2]	[3]	[4]	[5]	[6]	[7]	5:12
e.	My co-workers are afraid to express their real views.	[1]	[2]	[3]	[4]	[5]	[6]	[7]	5:13
f.	Each member of my work group has a clear idea of the group's goals.	[1]	[2]	[3]	[4]	[5]	[6]	[7]	5:14
g.	If we have a decision to make, everyone is involved in making it.	[1]	[2]	[3]	[4]	[5]	[6]	[7]	5:15
h.	My work group contains members with widely varying backgrounds.	[1]	[2]	[3]	[4]	[5]	[6]	[7]	5:16
i.	We tell each other the way we are feeling.	[1]	[2]	[3]	[4]	[5]	[6]	[7]	5:17
j.	Some of the people I work with have no respect for others.	[1]	[2]	[3]	[4]	[5]	[6]	[7]	5:18
k.	I look forward to being with the members of my work group each day.	[1]	[2]	[3]	[4]	[5]	[6]	[7]	5:19
l.	There are feelings among members of my work group which tend to pull the group apart.	[1]	[2]	[3]	[4]	[5]	[6]	[7]	5:20
m.	In my work group, everyone's opinion gets listened to.	[1]	[2]	[3]	[4]	[5]	[6]	[7]	5:21
n.	There is constant bickering in my work group.	[1]	[2]	[3]	[4]	[5]	[6]	[7]	5:22

MODULE 5 — SUPERVISORY BEHAVIOR

This part asks about your immediate supervisor in this organization. Your supervisor is the individual that you report to directly. He or she may also evaluate your work, give you assignments, etc.

---

1. THE FOLLOWING STATEMENTS DESCRIBE THE WAY A SUPERVISOR MIGHT PERFORM HIS OR HER JOB. PLEASE INDICATE WHETHER YOU AGREE OR DISAGREE WITH EACH OF THE STATEMENTS AS DESCRIPTIONS OF YOUR DIRECT SUPERVISOR.

MY SUPERVISOR . . .

		Strongly Disagree	Disagree	Slightly Disagree	Neither Agree nor Disagree	Slightly Agree	Agree	Strongly Agree	
a.	. . . encourages subordinates to participate in important decisions.	[1]	[2]	[3]	[4]	[5]	[6]	[7]	6:09
b.	. . . plans out work in advance.	[1]	[2]	[3]	[4]	[5]	[6]	[7]	6:10
c.	. . . keeps subordinates informed.	[1]	[2]	[3]	[4]	[5]	[6]	[7]	6:11
d.	. . . is always fair with subordinates.	[1]	[2]	[3]	[4]	[5]	[6]	[7]	6:12
e.	. . . encourages people to speak up when they disagree with a decision.	[1]	[2]	[3]	[4]	[5]	[6]	[7]	6:13
f.	. . . makes sure subordinates have clear goals to achieve.	[1]	[2]	[3]	[4]	[5]	[6]	[7]	6:14
g.	. . . demands that people give their best effort.	[1]	[2]	[3]	[4]	[5]	[6]	[7]	6:15
h.	. . . handles the administrative parts of his or her job extremely well.	[1]	[2]	[3]	[4]	[5]	[6]	[7]	6:16
i.	. . . keeps informed about the work which is being done.	[1]	[2]	[3]	[4]	[5]	[6]	[7]	6:17

MY SUPERVISOR . . .

j.	. . . makes it clear how I should do my job.	[1]	[2]	[3]	[4]	[5]	[6]	[7]	6:18
k.	. . . demands that subordinates do high quality work.	[1]	[2]	[3]	[4]	[5]	[6]	[7]	6:19
l.	. . . helps me solve work related problems.	[1]	[2]	[3]	[4]	[5]	[6]	[7]	6:20
m.	. . . makes sure subordinates know what has to be done.	[1]	[2]	[3]	[4]	[5]	[6]	[7]	6:21
n.	. . . is concerned about me as a person.	[1]	[2]	[3]	[4]	[5]	[6]	[7]	6:22
o.	. . . helps me discover problems before they get too bad.	[1]	[2]	[3]	[4]	[5]	[6]	[7]	6:23

MY SUPERVISOR . . .

		Strongly Disagree	Disagree	Slightly Disagree	Neither Agree nor Disagree	Slightly Agree	Agree	Strongly Agree	
p.	. . . keeps informed about the way subordinates think and feel about things.	[1]	[2]	[3]	[4]	[5]	[6]	[7]	6:24
q.	. . . helps subordinates develop their skills.	[1]	[2]	[3]	[4]	[5]	[6]	[7]	6:25
r.	. . . feels each subordinate is important as an individual.	[1]	[2]	[3]	[4]	[5]	[6]	[7]	6:26
s.	. . . makes most decisions without asking subordinates for their opinions.	[1]	[2]	[3]	[4]	[5]	[6]	[7]	6:27
t.	. . . has the respect of subordinates.	[1]	[2]	[3]	[4]	[5]	[6]	[7]	6:28
u.	. . . is biased on the basis of race.	[1]	[2]	[3]	[4]	[5]	[6]	[7]	6:29
v.	. . . makes important decisions without involving subordinates.	[1]	[2]	[3]	[4]	[5]	[6]	[7]	6:30
w.	. . . deals with subordinates well.	[1]	[2]	[3]	[4]	[5]	[6]	[7]	6:31
x.	. . . maintains high standards of performance.	[1]	[2]	[3]	[4]	[5]	[6]	[7]	6:32
y.	. . . helps subordinates with their personal problems.	[1]	[2]	[3]	[4]	[5]	[6]	[7]	6:33
z.	. . . insists that subordinates work hard.	[1]	[2]	[3]	[4]	[5]	[6]	[7]	6:34
aa.	. . . knows the technical parts of his or her job extremely well.	[1]	[2]	[3]	[4]	[5]	[6]	[7]	6:35
bb.	. . . tends to play favorites.	[1]	[2]	[3]	[4]	[5]	[6]	[7]	6:36
cc.	. . . is competent.	[1]	[2]	[3]	[4]	[5]	[6]	[7]	6:37
dd.	. . . is biased on the basis of sex.	[1]	[2]	[3]	[4]	[5]	[6]	[7]	6:38

MODULE 6 — PAY

The next section of this questionnaire contains a number of questions and statements about you, your job, and related issues at National Production. Please answer the following questions keeping in mind the kind of work you do and the experiences that you have had working here. Follow the directions that are given in the boxes at the beginning of the list of questions.

---

1. IN THE SECTION BELOW ARE LISTED NUMBERS OF THINGS THAT ARE OFTEN USED TO DETERMINE AN INDIVIDUAL'S PAY. FOR EACH THING, YOU ARE ASKED TO INDICATE HOW IMPORTANT NATIONAL PRODUCTION FEELS THAT THING IS FOR DETERMINING AN INDIVIDUAL'S PAY.

   PLEASE CHECK THE NUMBER ON THE SCALE THAT REPRESENTS THE IMPORTANCE OF THE THING BEING RATED. FOR THIS PART OF THE QUESTIONNAIRE, LOW NUMBERS REPRESENT UNIMPORTANT THINGS. IF YOU THINK A GIVEN THING IS UNIMPORTANT IN DETERMINING YOUR PAY, YOU WOULD CHECK THE NUMBER [1]. IF YOU THINK IT IS 'JUST A LITTLE IMPORTANT,' YOU WOULD CHECK A NUMBER TO THE RIGHT.

   FOR EACH ITEM, CHECK ONLY ONE NUMBER AND PLEASE DO NOT LEAVE OUT ANY ITEMS.

For the purpose of determining your pay, how important to National Production is . . .

		Very Unimportant			Important			Very Important	
a.	. . . your education, training, and experience	[1]	[2]	[3]	[4]	[5]	[6]	[7]	7:09
b.	. . . the amount of responsibility and pressure on your job.	[1]	[2]	[3]	[4]	[5]	[6]	[7]	7:10
c.	. . . the quality of your job performance.	[1]	[2]	[3]	[4]	[5]	[6]	[7]	7:11
d.	. . . your productivity.	[1]	[2]	[3]	[4]	[5]	[6]	[7]	7:12
e.	. . . the amount of effort you expend on the job.	[1]	[2]	[3]	[4]	[5]	[6]	[7]	7:13
f.	. . . the quality of your work group's performance.	[1]	[2]	[3]	[4]	[5]	[6]	[7]	7:14
g.	. . . the productivity of your work group.	[1]	[2]	[3]	[4]	[5]	[6]	[7]	7:15
h.	. . . the overall performance of the company.	[1]	[2]	[3]	[4]	[5]	[6]	[7]	7:16
i.	. . . the total labor costs.	[1]	[2]	[3]	[4]	[5]	[6]	[7]	7:17
j.	. . . the costs for material usage.	[1]	[2]	[3]	[4]	[5]	[6]	[7]	7:18

> **2.** HERE ARE SOME STATEMENTS ABOUT YOU AND YOUR JOB. HOW MUCH DO YOU AGREE OR DISAGREE WITH EACH OF THE FOLLOWING STATEMENTS?

		Strongly Disagree	Disagree	Slightly Disagree	Neither Agree nor Disagree	Slightly Agree	Agree	Strongly Agree	
a.	I am very happy with the amount of money I make.	[1]	[2]	[3]	[4]	[5]	[6]	[7]	7:19
b.	How much pay I receive depends almost entirely on how well I perform my job.	[1]	[2]	[3]	[4]	[5]	[6]	[7]	7:20
c.	Other companies in this area pay better than this one does.	[1]	[2]	[3]	[4]	[5]	[6]	[7]	7:21
d.	I believe annual salaries should be kept secret.	[1]	[2]	[3]	[4]	[5]	[6]	[7]	7:22
e.	I don't make the kind of money I should for the job I do.	[1]	[2]	[3]	[4]	[5]	[6]	[7]	7:23
f.	I have a real understanding of how the pay system works at National Production.	[1]	[2]	[3]	[4]	[5]	[6]	[7]	7:24
g.	All in all, my pay is about what it ought to be.	[1]	[2]	[3]	[4]	[5]	[6]	[7]	7:25
h.	Considering my skills and the effort I put into my work, I am very satisfied with my pay.	[1]	[2]	[3]	[4]	[5]	[6]	[7]	7:26
i.	Considering my skills and effort, I make a fair wage.	[1]	[2]	[3]	[4]	[5]	[6]	[7]	7:27
j.	My pay is fair given what my co-workers make.	[1]	[2]	[3]	[4]	[5]	[6]	[7]	7:28
k.	I think all base pay rates should be made public.	[1]	[2]	[3]	[4]	[5]	[6]	[7]	7:29
l.	All in all, pay is administered very well in this organization.	[1]	[2]	[3]	[4]	[5]	[6]	[7]	7:30
m.	Pay raises around here depend on how well you perform.	[1]	[2]	[3]	[4]	[5]	[6]	[7]	7:31
n.	My pay is fair compared to the pay of others in this company.	[1]	[2]	[3]	[4]	[5]	[6]	[7]	7:32
o.	I feel the pay system should be kept as it is.	[1]	[2]	[3]	[4]	[5]	[6]	[7]	7:33
p.	My pay level is determined by my individual job performance.	[1]	[2]	[3]	[4]	[5]	[6]	[7]	7:34
q.	I am very content with the way management handles pay.	[1]	[2]	[3]	[4]	[5]	[6]	[7]	7:35
r.	My pay is fair considering what other places in this area pay.	[1]	[2]	[3]	[4]	[5]	[6]	[7]	7:36
s.	My pay is fair.	[1]	[2]	[3]	[4]	[5]	[6]	[7]	7:37
t.	I have no objections to other people in this company knowing my annual salary.	[1]	[2]	[3]	[4]	[5]	[6]	[7]	7:38
u.	My pay is fair considering what other people in this organization are paid.	[1]	[2]	[3]	[4]	[5]	[6]	[7]	7:39

3. PLEASE ANSWER THE FOLLOWING QUESTIONS.

a. How much pay is there for your job at present?   7:40

   [1]   [2]   [3]   [4]   [5]   [6]   [7]

   A minimum amount   A maximum amount

b. How much pay should there be for your job at present?   7:41

   [1]   [2]   [3]   [4]   [5]   [6]   [7]

   A minimum amount   A maximum amount

c. How important is pay to you?   7:42

   [1]   [2]   [3]   [4]   [5]   [6]   [7]

   Unimportant   Important

THIS COMPLETES THE QUESTIONNAIRE. COULD YOU PLEASE ANSWER THESE FINAL THREE QUESTIONS?

1.   What did you think about the length of this questionnaire?   7:43

    [1]   Much too long
    [2]   Somewhat too long
    [3]   Just about right
    [4]   Somewhat too short
    [5]   Much too short

2.   How seriously did you answer the questions?   7:44

    [1]   Not at all seriously
    [2]   A little seriously
    [3]   Somewhat seriously
    [4]   Quite seriously
    [5]   Very seriously

3.   How much did you enjoy taking this questionnaire?   7:45

    [1]   Not at all pleasant, enjoyable or fun
    [2]   A little enjoyable
    [3]   Somewhat enjoyable
    [4]   Quite enjoyable
    [5]   Extremely pleasant, enjoyable and fun

    We appreciate your cooperation in spending time to answer our questions. If you have any comments on this study or other issues here in this organization, please feel free to use the space below for that purpose.

    Once again, thank you.

COMMENTS:

CHAPTER FIVE

Assessing Rates and Costs of Individual Work Behaviors

BARRY A. MACY AND PHILIP H. MIRVIS

The measurement and assessment of work organizations often focus on productive and financial outcomes. Variables used to represent effectiveness commonly include the volume of goods and services produced, their cost, their quality, and the like. For administrative and research purposes, however, such gross measures are not sufficient to appraise the performance of organization members or the overall effectiveness of an organization. A broader view of effectiveness must include absenteeism, turnover, work disruptions, and other nonproductive behaviors as important elements in assessing organizational effectiveness.[1] Indeed, researchers are beginning to use these criteria to assess individual and organizational performance. As an example, Cummings and Molloy employ data on costs, productivity, quality, and employees' absences and turnover, along with data on attitudes, to evaluate efforts to improve effectiveness and the quality of work life in organizations.[2]

This chapter describes the development of a standardized approach for identifying, defining, and measuring indicators of work behavior and performance, and for expressing these indicators in financial terms. The indicators of interest are derived by the aggregation of individual-level behaviors that have cost implications. The purpose is to complement the usual gross financial and performance measures with reliable, stable, and valid measures that are pertinent to the longitudinal assessment of organizations and organization change.

The need for standardized assessment methods has become more pronounced with the expansion of work-improvement programs and the growth of commercial and governmental interest in the quality of work life and productivity. Many have argued that such programs can enhance the work lives of employees and also provide a financial benefit to the firm.[3] Unfortunately, few such programs have been evaluated with the behavioral and financial criteria necessary to test this appealing proposition.[4] An illustration is the 1972 *Work in America* report that attempted to make a persuasive case for the economic significance of improvements in the quality of work life.[5] The findings in that book have been challenged on grounds of the adequacy of the data and the validity of the underlying assumptions. In the 34 case studies cited, absenteeism was measured in only 5 sites, turnover in only 3, and the financial results, when cited at all, were not comparable in their definition, breadth of coverage, or measurement.

In addition to describing the development and implementation of a behavioral and financial assessment methodology, this chapter illustrates its use in evaluating a quality of work life experiment. A 5-phase 56-month assessment of a collaborative labor–management change program in a manufacturing and assembly facility is reported.

DEVELOPMENT OF THE METHOD

This methodology is based on concepts from the field of behavioral economics which emphasize the economic activity is influenced by individual attitudes, choices, and behaviors. As applied here, this approach begins with the assumption that employees' behavior at work results from choices they make about being available to work and performing within their role on the job.[6,7] It posits that employees are more likely to come to work and remain in the organization if they are satisfied with their jobs and that they are more likely to work effectively if they expect to be rewarded for their efforts and performance.

Employees' satisfactions and reward expectations, in turn, are assumed to be influenced by their work environment and the extent to which it affords them valued rewards. Implicit in this view is the idea that work behaviors—whether by intention or not—are products of the social and technical environment in the organization. Thus innovations and experiments that alter organizational characteristics and employees' reward expectations should affect their job-related behavior because they affect the choices employees make.[8-10] These choices are, of course, also influenced by the external labor and production markets, technological constraints, and individual differences.

Selecting, Defining, and Measuring the Behaviors

Although there are some precedents for assessing organization change in behavioral terms, a standardized approach to measurement does not exist. Reviews by Price and by Campbell and associates underscore the importance of developing standardized methods that provide for a systematic reporting of behavioral outcomes in order to evaluate and compare the effects of change programs.[11,12] Herrick, recognizing this need, proposed a group of behavioral variables likely to be influenced by work experiments, and together with us developed the operational methods reported here.[13,14]

He proposed the use of three criteria for the inclusion of a behavior in the methodology:

1. Definable, so that incidents that could be significantly affected by the work environment are distinguished from those unaffected.
2. Measurable, in terms that allow representation as significant costs to the organization.
3. The several categories of measures and costs of the behaviors have to be mutually exclusive.

Using these criteria, 11 behavioral and performance variables are distinguished and grouped into two broad categories: (1) participation and membership (i.e., absences and leaves, tardiness, turnover, internal employment stability, strikes, and work stoppages), and (2) job performance (i.e., productivity, quality, grievances, accidents and illnesses, unscheduled machine downtime and repair, material and supply overuse, and inventory shrinkage). Behavioral definitions were devised to be consistent with the three criteria. For example, absences because of funerals, jury duty, or maternity leave, which are presumed to be unrelated to the work environment, are distinguished from absences that might in part be caused by the work environment. Drug and alcohol consumption on the job are omitted, even though they are possibly related to working conditions since they manifest themselves in the more easily measured costly behaviors, such as absenteeism and poor product quality. Appendix 5-1 presents the definitions and recording categories for the selected behaviors. These are generic categories that can be adapted to apply to any industrial or service organization.

Computation rules were then devised for each of the behaviors. Most are reported as rates, which have been adjusted for the number of employees in the organization and the possible incidents of behavior. As an example, the absence rate reflects the number of absences in a month divided by an exposure factor that is the average monthly work-force size multiplied by the number of possible working days. The monthly rates for absences are then averaged over a longer period to arrive at a base absence rate. Appendix 5-2 lists measures of the behaviors and the computational formulas that reflect these exposure factors.

Absenteeism, Leaves, and Tardiness. In measuring absenteeism, the distinct psychological and organizational implications of absences arising from different causes need to be distinguished. Involuntary absences (for example, long-term illness) are less likely to reflect intentional or unconscious withdrawal from participation in the organization than voluntary absences (for example, absence for personal reasons). Indeed, other studies have found these two broad categories of absence measures to correlate differently with various organizational characteristics.[15] Therefore, voluntary and involuntary absences are distinguished and reported separately. However, since each might be influenced by work experimentation and potentially have a financial effect on the organization, both are included for assessment purposes.

Another problem is centered on the measurement of absenteeism. There is contradictory evidence in the literature about whether absenteeism is best represented in terms of lost work time, the number of incidents per employee, regardless of their duration, or an absence rate.[16,17] Latham and Pursell note that Huse and Taylor found low intercorrelations between different measures of absenteeism; as an alternative, they recommend computation of an attendance rate.[18,19] In the measurement system reported here, an absenteeism rate is used: total work-force person days of absence adjusted with an exposure factor of total possible work-force days. This computation can be converted to reflect an attendance rate.

Leaves are distinguished from other forms of voluntary and involuntary absences and are included since they might be influenced by work-improvement programs and have significant costs. Indeed, in many organizations, rates of absence days and leave days are quite similar in their implications. Five categories of leaves are distinguished—medical, military, maternal, personal, and others (such as jury duty). Of these, personal leaves are treated as voluntary; medical, maternal, military, and others, not likely to be affected by work-place changes, as involuntary. Leaves are measured in the same way as absences. Tardiness—defined as an absence of less than four hours—is categorized and also measured like absenteeism.

Turnover and Internal Employment Stability. A turnover is defined as a permanent movement beyond the boundary of an organization, thus distinguishing it from promotions and transfers, which represent internal movements, and from temporary layoffs and rehires. Price notes that most measures of turnover reflect a "crude separation index" that is not amenable to assessment.[11] Therefore, in the method reported here, voluntary and involuntary turnovers are distinguished, predicated on whether or not the employee initiated the action. There is some precedent for categorizing turnover in this way for evaluation. Rice, Hill, and Trist found differences between the incidence rates of employee- and company-controlled turnovers following a change program.[20]

The turnover measure used here is a turnover rate: total work-force turnovers divided by the average work-force size.[21,22] It is computed like absenteeism—on a monthly basis in order to highlight seasonality and significant work-force additions and membership changes due to the employment market and the economy. An alternative to this turnover measure is a regeneration rate, or rate of employment.[23] The turnover measure can easily be translated into an acquisition rate.

Movements within the organization (promotions, transfers, and promotions with transfer) and movements into and out of the organization (new hires and rehires after layoff) are used in assessing the internal employment stability of an organization. Measured separately, these behaviors can be used to express rates of hiring, promotion, transfer, and layoff in an organization. When summed, they represent the internal instability of job occupancy and, with turnover, the overall employment stability.

Strikes and Work Stoppages.   Strikes and work stoppages vary across organizations in both their occurrence and economic impact. Although there are no standard definitions for identifying strikes related to working conditions, Hyman, Imberman, and the Department of Labor (Bureau of Labor Statistics) provide criteria for distinguishing sanctioned work stoppages and indicate that strikes or work stoppages are very costly.[24-26] The measure presented here compares the number of strike or work-stoppage days with the total available working days per month.

Accidents and Illnesses.   Accidents and work-related illnesses are widely regarded as significant indicators of the quality of working life, not only for the obvious reason of harm to employees and costs to both employees and employer, but also because their occurrence may reflect environmental stresses and hazards. Hill and Trist, for example, treated accidents as alternative forms of withdrawal, that are distinct from simple absenteeism but arise from similar causes.[8] To obtain an accident or illness rate, the number of incidents reported for a work group can be divided by the number of group members within a given period of time. Standard reporting categories and definitions for common classes of accidents and illnesses have been devised by the Department of Labor, Occupational Safety and Health Administration (OSHA). These are adopted for use in this methodology.[27]

Firms differ in the detail with which they record minor accidents and illnesses. If feasible, the number of medical visits and revisits to the firms' first-aid facilities and the kinds of accident injuries and illnesses that were treated should be assessed. The rates are computed by recording the number of accidents and illnesses per category, dividing them by the total monthly hours worked and multiplying this figure by 200,000 (base work-year hours per 100 workers)—the standard OSHA procedure.

Grievances.   Records of grievances tend to be unique to an organization and are not comparable among organizations. Indeed, labor–man-

agement contracts often specifically and uniquely define allowable grievance issues, the procedures for their resolution, and the steps involved.[28]
In the method proposed here, grievances are reported as the ratio of
distinct recorded grievances to the average work-force size for a given
period of time. In the case of group grievances, provisions are made for
identifying the employees involved and computing a rate based upon the
number of aggrieved individuals. Grievances are recorded and measured
only once—at their highest resolved level or stage—to avoid double
counting.

Performance Measures.   Measurement of performance presents an
extraordinary problem arising from the uniqueness of the required performances in each organization and the idiosyncrasies of definition, categorization, and measurement. Nevertheless, since the volume of work
performance, the quality of goods and services, and the costs involved are
so central to the assessment of work organizations, a major effort was
undertaken to incorporate performance measurement into this methodology.

Productivity is best regarded as a family of measures comparing a set
of work outputs with a set of work inputs along with intervening process
indicators or activity measures.[29,30] We define this family of measures in
the following ways. The amount of output is defined as the quantity of
goods or services produced. This may be regarded as a measure of productivity when compared against inputs such as man hours or labor costs. It
becomes a measure of efficiency when compared against an engineered
standard, a budgeted standard, or a budgeted variance from the standard.
It becomes a measure of output per employee when compared against the
size of the work force. The inputs and outputs may be expressed in terms
of units of actual measurement, such as the number of units produced and
the man hours involved, or in valuation units, such as dollars. Such
dollar valuations can be reported as labor dollars, total dollar costs, or
sales dollars, which are adjustable as needed to control for payroll, raw-
material, and price increases. The quality of output is defined to include
errors, delays in service, product rejects, customer returns or complaints,
product rework time, and scrap.[31-33] Again, these can be expressed in
units of actual measurement or dollars and adjusted accordingly. The
number of units and costs of poor-quality work can also be compared with
an engineered standard, a budgeted standard, or a budgeted variance
from standard and measured on a per-employee basis in comparison to
the average work-force size. Recoveries and resold goods are treated as
adjustments to quality measures. Intervening process or activity measures may include unscheduled machine downtime and repair and unex-
plained material, supply, and inventory variations.

The central problem in developing an array of performance measures
is finding a common metric: Greenberg's "principle of equivalents" is
commonly used.[34] The principle states that if one output can be valued in,

say, dollars, then dollars can be used to value all other outputs in relative terms. The same applies to inputs and activity measures. Using this principle, diverse performance measures, including productivity, quality, and the intervening processes can be brought to a value equivalence and merged in a common index. In the case described later, there are four general performance factors that are identified and valued—productivity, product quality, machine downtime and repair, and material, supply, and inventory variations. The specific variables used in that case will not apply in all organizations.

Determining the Costs of the Behaviors

The expression of job-related behavior in financial terms is not a novel idea. A classic article by Brogden and Taylor in 1950 addressed the potential for developing on-the-job performance criteria in cost-accounting terms.[35] Predating that was the work of Heinrich determining the costs of industrial accidents.[36] However, it is a relatively new undertaking to systematically quantify a set of behavioral and performance variables in a common dollar metric.

Traditional cost-accounting methods can be used to express productivity measures in financial terms. Following the introduction of human-resources accounting guidelines, however, the other behaviors could also be measured in dollar terms.[37,38] To accomplish this, human-resource accounting *asset* models had to be distinguished from *expense* models.[39] Asset models are used to reflect the organization's investment in employees and their depreciation over time. In contrast, expense models are oriented toward measuring the economic effects of employee behavior. As such, an expense model is used here to measure changes in employees' behavior in financial terms.

To measure the financial effects of employee behaviors, the cost components associated with each behavior have to be identified and their separate and mutually exclusive dollar values computed. The costs can be conceptualized in two ways. One distinguishes outlay costs (e.g., materials used in training new employees) from time costs, such as the supervisor's time allocated to orienting the new staff member.[40] A second distinction is drawn between variable costs, fixed costs, and opportunity costs. An example of a variable cost would be the overtime expense incurred because of an absence; a fixed cost would be the normal salary and fringe-benefit costs for personnel involved in replacing the absent worker; and an opportunity cost would be the profit lost during the replacement process. These distinctions are important because only variable costs are incurred regardless of behavioral variations, and opportunity costs are recorded only if the employees involved could have put their lost time to productive use.

Each behavior has distinct costs to an organization. Included in the costs of absenteeism, for example, are the expenses of fringe benefits, lost efficiency, replacement employees, and overtime. To measure these costs for a particular behavior, however, they have to be separated from their respective expense accounts. Appendix 5-3 illustrates the decision rules used in measuring the costs of one class of absenteeism. Costing procedures and decision rules similar to those illustrated in the appendix have been developed for each of the behaviors treated in this chapter.

To be comprehensive, all of the behavioral costs are measured, but special care is taken not to report a cost component under more than one rubric. For example, if production losses associated with absenteeism are found, they are reported as absenteeism costs and are excluded from the production-cost figures.

Finally, in longitudinal assessment, the costing procedure must control for inflation. The costs of absenteeism, productivity, and the other behavioral and performance variables may increase not because of behavioral changes but because of salary increases or price increases. In the example presented later, the actual contemporary dollar value of the behavior and performance of employees is reported. In a chapter on assessing the costs and benefits of change programs found later in this volume, procedures for discounting such costs are discussed.

Implementing the Methods

The foregoing description of suggested standard methods should not suggest that implementation is simple or easy. In any specific instance of application, it is likely that some proposed measures are not feasible or are irrelevant, that some additional or modified measures appear to be desirable, and that the cost of getting some information is insupportable. In addition, certain reference standards—whether engineered, budgeted, or historically derived—may not exist. Certain units—say, of objects or services produced—may seem too different to be counted in aggregation. These are valid limitations but only rarely, if ever, do they apply so broadly as to preclude useful assessment of behavioral choices and the costs. In implementing the methods, it is necessary to allow for some selection and adaptation of the measures to be used. The more closely the definitions, recording guidelines, and computational rules can be observed, the more useful are the data for interorganizational comparisons and for equivalence of conceptual meaning in interpretations.

Application of the methods in a specific organization begins with a survey of existing data sources and opportunities. This entails interviews with people knowledgeable about local data-collection practices and about the conditions in the organization that might bear upon the quality and meaning of the recorded data. Procedural and policy documents, if such exist, are searched for details of definitional and recording categories for each class of data that might be of interest. For many types of data, there is a physical examination of the forms and records that trace information from its origin(s) to central and summary-record depositories. In all but the smallest of organizations, such a survey is likely to involve several different staff units and several different professional specialties—operations engineers, physicians, personnel administrators, accountants, payroll managers, and the like. The accounting system requires special attention to appraise the cost categories that are employed, the organizational units for aggregation, and the feasibility of disaggregating costs where this is needed for compatibility with costing procedures.

Records of employee absences, leaves, tardiness, and turnover or new hires are commonly maintained in a personnel department or a payroll office, including specification of individual employees and the dates of occurrence of individual incidents. These data can be coded (e.g., voluntary versus involuntary) as needed, summarized by time periods (e.g., months), and aggregated by organizational units (e.g., work groups, departments).

Records of accidents and illnesses are likely to be found in medical, personnel, or safety departments, usually in sufficient detail about each incident to allow recoding or quality verification. These data are likely to be unique to the firm, suitable only for internal comparisons of rate or cost changes over time. The OSHA accident and illness data, however, are collected in standard ways in most firms, and they can be compared with national or industry averages.

Data on strikes, work stoppages, and grievances are usually maintained in personnel or industrial-relations departments, although superior records are sometimes found in union offices. The grievance data are not likely to be comparable across organizations because of variations in both grievance procedures and incident definitions. Person days lost by strikes and work stoppages, however, can be compared with public reports of gross industry averages and trends.

Performance data by individual employees or organizational units are usually available in an accounting department. In some cases, the information is recorded in natural units, such as labor hours or units of output—products, services, clients, and so forth. In all cases these data can be expressed in the common metric of dollars. Quality data, if available at all, are often maintained separately in, say, a quality-control department. But an assessment of quality may also entail examination of records relating to customer or client complaints and rework and reject records, or work group performance records. The data may be judged to be incomparable between organizations even though they are suitable for comparison of trend and change estimates over time.

In summary, after a preliminary study of the production-accounting, personnel, and allied functions of the firm, a search is made to determine the specific behaviors and behavioral definitions that might be measured. This process involves an effort to include all classes of behaviors judged to be of cost significance and to institute certain changes in the way such behaviors are classified and recorded. Those judged to be duplicative or redundant as to cost implications are to be omitted, along with those that are unreliable, invariant, and trivial.

An important part of this work is the exploration of possible ways to improve or extend the organization's record systems relating to the management of rates and costs of behaviors. For example, the definitions of reasons for absence may be brought to closer compatibility with prevalent standard systems. Also, redundancies in the recording or record-keeping practices may be discovered and moderated. Quite often, supplemental data systems can be introduced that not only improve the short-run assessment of performance but provide additional information useful for day-to-day control of work processes to management and employees. An example of the latter is an instance in which it was found feasible and useful to initiate the recording of incidents of rework along with the causes and costs of such incidents. Thus, a by-product of a survey of record systems may well be a permanent improvement in the cost, quality, and utility of the organization's records.

AN ILLUSTRATIVE APPLICATION OF THE METHODS

The following discussion provides an example of the application to a specific case of the methods that have been described. The illustrative case represents the compilation of data concerning the rates of occurrence of the behaviors of interest, their estimated costs, and their trends of change over an extended period of time. The incidents and rates of behavior and performance were measured for 55 continuous months during which organizational change interventions occurred. The average number of hourly employees ranged from 537 to 893 over this period. Substantial changes occurred in wage rates, fringe-benefit costs, and material-supply costs. All of these changes were accounted for by the methodology.

The intervention program was directed by a joint committee composed of union and management representatives who worked with a three-person external consulting team to analyze problems, review opportunities for change, and introduce new programs. A number of actions were taken. For example, a job-rotation plan was introduced in one area and production planning meetings in another. An education program offering courses in language, reading and literature, and the arts was begun as was a community day-care center. One significant activity involved the creation of a "paid-personal-time" program for the hourly work force in which employees, upon reaching their production standard for the day, could use the remaining part of the day for personal time. They could remain working and earn a performance bonus.

The objective of the measurement here described was to complement with "hard" data other kinds of information that might be used in assessing the progress and outcomes of the organizational change program. For analysis purposes, the time span of measurement was divided into five time periods that, by design, also matched distinguishable phases of the change program. The first period, a baseline period before the change program started, encompassed the 11 months of preliminary negotiating and planning that preceded the formation of the joint labor–management committee that was set up to initiate and carry out the program. Thus behavioral and financial data were collected prior to, as well as throughout, the program. Based upon the change program, these data were divided into the following phases.

Phase 1:   May 1972–March 1973 (baseline period)
Phase 2:   April 1973–February 1974 (study period)
Phase 3:   March 1974–January 1975 (experimental period)
Phase 4:   February 1975–December 1975 (plant-wide change)
Phase 5:   January 1976–December 1976 (continuation of change)

Data were available at the site for absences, leaves, tardiness, turnover, accidents and illnesses, grievances, productivity, product quality, machine downtime, and manufacturing supply usage. The work-performance measures were recorded in terms of standard direct-labor dollars, the evaluation by the firm of output, scrap, rework, downtime, and so on, and then adjusted into current dollar values. The main performance measures used were understandard production, product rejects, machine downtime, and the variance between actual and budgeted supply use. Derivative performance measures included output per hourly employee (inflation-adjusted dollars), understandard production as a ratio to budgeted variance, and product rejects as a percentage of finished goods.

Thus there resulted a roster of seven broad classes of measurable behaviors, each including subclassifications of varying number—absences, turnover, accidents and illnesses, grievances, product rejects, production output relative to standard, and those manufacturing costs influenced by employee behavior. The first four of these provide primary data at the individual level (for example, each absence and each accident referred to a particular incident and person). The last three classes were measurable only at the level of the work group or work unit. All classes allowed aggregation for sets of persons (e.g., work groups) and time periods.

Although most of these data were initially recorded in natural units, such as man-hours or units of product, the common metric for equating and costing was the dollar. Subsidiary data, therefore, were employed to calculate or, in some instances, to estimate the required measures and, as necessary, to reduce the current dollar data to a common, inflation-adjusted value.

The costs of the work-time and job-performance behaviors were calculated by reviewing variable and fixed expense accounts and allocating the costs among the relevant behaviors. The costing method was designed to measure the cost per incident of behavior. This involved some averaging, even though the cost per incident at a lower incidence rate may not be the same at a higher incidence rate. In total, the average sample size consisted of 847 incidents of individual behavior aggregated to the level of analysis of the organization. Together with performance data from 19 work groups summed to reflect performance of the organization, these represented 46,575 data points over the five periods.

Number of Incidents and Their Rates

The number of incidents and their rates for each of the variables for the five phases is reported in Table 5-1. Total absenteeism as a percentage of potential absenteeism decreased over the course of the program from 4.7% to 3.1%. Voluntary and involuntary turnover, minor accidents, and dispensary revisits decreased after Phase 2. OSHA accidents decreased after Phase 1. Minor illness in the plant showed a substantial increase, then a slight decline. Grievances fluctuated over the course of the study, and the rate showed no trend of change.

In interpreting such data, consideration must be given to the economy, the employment market, the composition of the work force, and of course, the change program itself. As an example, the declining turnover rate may be attributable partly to the economic recession during Phases 3 and 4. In addition, although the "paid-personal-time" program may have contributed to the reduced absence rates (employees could acquire time away from the job by increasing their rate of output), it also may have contributed to the increase in minor illnesses, for in order to earn their time off, employees had to work more quickly. Indeed, collateral data showed an increase in somatic complaints by employees participating in the program.

The performance data presented in the table also show improvement over the period. What is striking is that both product rejects and understandard production were reduced. A further indication of performance improvement is found in the increase in value of output (adjusted for inflation) per hourly employee from $131 to $161 per day, and in the decrease in net scrap as a percentage of finished goods. Not all of the performance indicators improved, however, as supply use and downtime showed slight increases. The paid personal time program may have contributed to these trends, as one way to work more quickly is to use more supplies and take less care of machinery. Also, since downtime was subtracted from the performance standards, an employee could earn more time off by scrupulously reporting every incident of machine downtime.

Table 5-2 reports the estimated actual cost per incident, as well as the total costs for the behavioral and performance variables measured at the

Table 5-1 Incidents and Rates of Behavior and Performance at Quality of Work Life Site: 1972–1976[a]

Behaviors and Performance[c]	Phase 1 5/72–3/73		Phase 2 4/73–2/74		Phase 3 3/74–1/75		Phase 4 2/75–12/75		Phase 5[b] 1/76–12/76	
	Number of Incidents	Rate	Number of Incidents	Rate	Number of Incidents	Rate	Number of Incidents	Rate	Number of Incidents	Rate
Absenteeism										
Total absences	5,580	.047	7,423	.043	6,684	.040	4,950	.033	5,772	.031
Turnover										
Voluntary	108	.222	204	.291	102	.143	27	.042	49	.063
Involuntary	91	.184	148	.214	82	.111	6	.010	62	.080
Accidents and illnesses										
Minor accidents	2,602	.469	4,947	.664	4,641	.593	3,309	.459	3,305	.374
Minor illnesses	1,890	.344	4,773	.630	5,312	.681	3,734	.515	4,317	.488
Minor revisits	1,491	.278	2,056	.273	1,933	.251	1,543	.214	1,524	.172
OSHA accidents	231	.043	261	.035	185	.024	153	.022	152	.017
Grievances	52	.115	19	.026	33	.052	72	.115	42	.056
Net product rejects		.410		.353		.285		.255		.250
Production under standard		.119		.156		.119		.099		.114
Manufacturing costs										
Supply variance		.020		.020		.025		.036		.007
Machine downtime		.052		.055		.045		.050		.057

[a] Incidents are actual counts of behavior: Rates are reported as mean monthly rates (i.e., the average of the monthly rates of incidents of each employee behavior or plant performance divided by the months in the analysis phase). The term rate refers to the number of incidents of each exposure (see Table 5-2) to the risk of such incidences during the analysis time interval. Rates are for hourly work force only.
[b] Phase 5 incidents have been multiplied by $\frac{12}{11}$ to make them comparable to other phases.
[c] Definitions of variables appear in Appendixes 5-1 and 5-2.

151

Table 5-2 Actual Dollar Value of Behavior and Performance at Quality of Work Life Site: 1972–1976[a]

Behaviors and Performance[c]	Phase 1 5/72–3/73		Phase 2 4/73–2/74		Phase 3 3/74–1/75		Phase 4 2/75–12/75		Phase 5 1/76–12/76[b]	
	Estimated Cost per Incident	Estimated Total Cost	Estimated Cost per Incident	Estimated Total Cost	Estimated Cost per Incident	Estimated Total Cost	Estimated Cost per Incident	Estimated Total Cost	Estimated Cost per Incident	Estimated Total Cost
Absenteeism										
Total absences	$ 50.24	$ 280,339	$ 53.15	$ 394,533	$ 62.49	$ 417,683	$ 73.63	$ 364,469	$ 80.06	$ 462,126
Turnover										
Voluntary	109.63	11,840	131.68	30,741	150.69	15,370	157.59	4,255	160.65	7,805
Involuntary	109.63	9,976	131.68	22,302	150.69	12,357	157.59	946	160.65	10,014
Accidents and illnesses										
Minor accidents	6.04	15,716	5.71	28,247	6.45	29,934	8.67	28,689	9.15	30,237
Minor illnesses	6.04	11,416	5.71	27,254	6.45	34,264	8.67	32,374	9.15	39,496
Minor revisits	6.04	9,006	5.71	11,740	6.45	12,468	8.67	13,378	9.15	13,948
OSHA accidents	661.26	152,751	698.31	182,259	1,106.52	204,706	1,855.15	283,838	1,256.86	191,252
Grievances	29.53	1,536	34.44	654	56.10	1,851	61.98	4,463	54.52	2,299
Product rejects		563,619		661,668		525,758		461,226		619,974
Production under standard		208,222		339,442		631,268		218,360		433,683
Manufacturing costs										
Supply variance		27,493		37,329		45,800		65,050		16,308
Machine downtime		75,347		101,301		82,619		89,939		141,459
Total costs		$1,367,261		$1,837,470		$2,014,078		$1,566,987		$1,968,601
Costs per hourly employee		$2,546		$2,377		$2,678		$2,261		$2,346

[a] Actual dollar values are estimated costs of the behavior in each phase.
[b] Phase 5 costs have been multiplied by 1½ to make them comparable to other phases.
[c] Definitions of variables appear in Appendixes 5-1 and 5-2.

152

site. The major cost factors included lost productivity, downtime, salaries and benefits paid, costs of a replacement work force, and other expenses associated with hiring and training new personnel. For example, the cost-per-incident of absenteeism in Phase 1 ($50.24) was as follows: downtime ($9.11), fringe benefits paid to the missing worker ($4.72), replacement work-force costs ($5.77), and underabsorbed fixed costs ($30.64). The productivity measures were reported in actual dollars, and they were computed by adding a constant to the firm's valuation in standard labor dollars. As would be expected, the costs per incident of the behaviors and the total costs of the performance measures increased over the periods, primarily due to inflation and to increase in the size of the work force. Thus, even though the absence rate declined over the phases, the costs-per-absence increased from $50.24 to $80.06, and the number of incidents from 5580 and 5772. In assessing trends in the costs of the variables, then, it is important to use base-year dollars. In Chapter 17, we report these data in base-year dollars and show substantial reductions in the costs of absenteeism, turnover, accidents, understandard production, and product rejects over the course of the program. In addition, it is important to consider these data in light of the size of the work force. As the table shows, even in current dollars, the costs of nonproductive behavior and performance choices at the site decreased from $2546 to $2346 per employee. Finally, these costs can be compared with total business volume. At this site, the costs were 8.7% of sales in Phase 1 and 6.7% in Phase 5. Thus, although the current costs show an increase across the five periods, the discounted costs, the costs per employee, the costs as compared with sales, all show the favorable trend evidenced in the rates.

These data attest to the feasibility of defining, measuring, and "costing out" the behavioral and financial outcomes of experiments to improve the quality of working life and the effectiveness of organization. Moreover, these data show that such programs can indeed be associated with a financial benefit to a firm. Nevertheless, one problem in using the methodology is its dependence on the quality of the measurement, information and accounting, and other control systems at a site. Limitations in some of these systems at this illustrative site preclude the precise allocation of fixed costs across the behaviors, necessitating some estimation of their relative shares of expense. Further, the costs associated with salaried personnel were not entirely accountable; the data presented in Tables 5-1 and 5-2 pertain only to the hourly work force in the organization. Finally, the profit contribution figures for the firm are deemed proprietary, so no estimates of opportunity costs are reported. The costs reported in Table 5-2 combine some fixed and most variable expenses, but, because of the absence of some of the baseline data, they are conservatively estimated.

The data presented illustrate the feasibility of obtaining them, the ease of detecting differences among the measured variables, and assessing their differential changes over time. The diagnostic and assessment uses of such information is self-evident. However, the interpretations to be made must rest, in part, upon appraisals of the quality of the data—that is, the reliability and stability of the variables, the validity of the measures employed, and the statistical significance of changes over time. We turn now to these topics.

Reliability and Stability

It is difficult to assess the reliability of behavioral and financial data. The sheer number of behavioral recordings, the duration of the assessment, and the extensive use of complex financial data suggest that some mistakes in entering, gathering, coding, and analyzing the data are inevitable. In addition, actual incidents of behavior at any site are not always accurately represented in the record. In the classic example, production workers may underreport or overreport their daily output in order to make it seem constant while allowing them to work strenuously or leisurely on any given day. Also, it is an occasional if not common practice for organizations to advance or delay the recording of transactions for a period of time in order to control the cash flow or smooth the performance figures.

Nevertheless, some steps can be taken to assess the reliability of the data. In the case reported here, on-site sampling procedures were used to check the accuracy of individual behavior data. Time cards were examined periodically and cooperative ventures at the plant were undertaken with union and management officials to insure that the true production rates were eventually being entered into company records. Extreme variations from past trends and norms were discussed with site personnel to determine whether data were misrecorded, and some corrections were made.

Special procedures need to be implemented to verify the accuracy of accident and illness records, for in industrial settings beset with safety concerns and inspections it is not unusual to find OSHA accidents unrecorded or reported as minor accidents and lost-time cases treated as routine absences. In this case, an independent recording of OSHA accidents was instituted; the correlation between the independent assessor's measurement and the OSHA accidents measured by the firm was .94. The only discrepancies between the assessor's recording and the recording by the firm occurred in Phases 4 and 5 and were due to the new assignment of untrained clerical staff members.

The reliability of cost computations is more difficult to assess. Financial data are inherently unreliable in the sense that the "true cost" of a behavior, action, or event can never be determined.[41] In assessing financial data, auditors rely upon examination of the operation and functioning of the data-collecting and reporting procedures. These systems were audited in this case. Another problem in assessing the reliability of cost data is that any given type of employee action can have multiple and variable cost effects. It seems reasonable, therefore, to measure only the recurring behavioral costs, assuming that the occasional extreme effects would be neither representative nor of interest. All costs should be estimated using generally accepted accounting procedures. When dollar components are based upon estimates of time, such as the amount of paid time needed in replacing an absent worker, the judgments of informed supervisors and hourly workers should be pooled.

Direct measures of reliability cannot be applied generally to behavioral and performance data, but estimates of reliability can be computed by correlating the measures across time periods. Ideally, these correlations are computed using individual data, as the incidents themselves reflect individual behavior. They may also be computed using group- or organizational-level aggregated data. As an example, the correlations between mean monthly measures of voluntary turnover at the site in the first three phases were $r_1^2 = .56$, $r_2^3 = .61$, $r_1^3 = .16$. Estimates of the stability of these measures across time can also be computed. The stability of voluntary turnover during these phases was $s_1^2 = .25$, $s_2^3 = .26$, $s_1^3 = .06$. These stability coefficients show that the rates of incidence of the behaviors change over time, as would be expected if a change program was effecting improvement in turnover. Thus, although over relatively short periods of time the measures can be fairly stable, over longer periods they are likely to change in interpretable ways. It is important in assessment, therefore, that the analyst not only detect changes in the rates of performances or behaviors, but also identify the kinds of persons or units that change, and in the context of the research design—*why* their behaviors and performances changed.

Validity

The validity of participation-membership and performance measures can be assessed by convergence among alternative measurement methods, and by their performance in predictive relationships. Flamholtz, for example, has reported finding convergent and discriminant validity between measures of turnover costs, performance, and compensation. Taylor and Bowers, and Pecorella and colleagues have assessed the validity of attitudes in predicting employee's attendance and performance, and Hopwood has presented examples of such predictive validation using financial data.[38,43-45] These forms of validity have been examined for the illustrative membership and performance data described in preceding pages.

The intercorrelations among different turnover reasons over the course of the study, based upon mean monthly rates plant wide, are shown in Table 5-3. The first four measures in this table represent reasons employees give for voluntary turnover; the last three are recorded

Table 5-3 Intercorrelations among Measures of Reasons for Turnover (N = 45 months)

Reason for Turnover	Another Job	Moving	Continue Education	Home and Family	Poor Performance	Poor Attendance	Violation of Rules
Another job	1.00						
Moving	.13	1.00					
Continue education	.03	.33*	1.00				
Home and family	.43**	.35*	.03	1.00			
Poor performance	-.30*	-.29*	-.15	-.24	1.00		
Poor attendance	-.07	-.05	-.08	-.12	.24	1.00	
Violation of rules	-.11	-.25	-.13	-.20	.29*	.55**	1.00

* p = .05; ** p = .01

reasons for involuntary terminations. The table shows convergence within the two groupings and divergence between them. This attests to the convergent and discriminant validity of the two subclasses of turn-over measures. Some instances of leaving the organization could not be assigned to either category. As an example, a termination for no known reason, or ambiguous reasons, could be either voluntary departure or forced resignation. Similarly, probationary employees might have left without declared reasons because they did not want to stay in the organization or because the organization did not want them to stay. These rates of unclassified departures showed low correlations with both voluntary and involuntary turnover rates.

Measures of absenteeism, accidents and illnesses, and product quality also showed convergence among components within each reporting category. Intercorrelations of four measures of voluntary absences and three measures of involuntary absences showing convergence within the set of seven measures, but not much divergence, are shown in Table 5-4. The correlations between voluntary and involuntary absences at the site averaged about .49. Measures of minor and OSHA accidents also showed convergence ($r = .44$), as did quality measures of total plant scrap, customer returns, rework, and recoveries (median $r = .38$).

There is also some evidence of convergent and discriminant validity in the participation-membership and job-performance measures. Table 5-5 shows the intercorrelations within and between these sets of measures. Minor and OSHA accident rates correlate positively with the turnover and absence measures, but negatively with most performance measures. As expected, all three productivity measures correlate negatively and at least moderately with absences, turnover, accidents and illness, machine downtime, and quality indicators.

Table 5-6 shows individual-level correlations between selected attitudes and perceptions about jobs and work environments on the one hand, and absenteeism on the other, with absenteeism represented as rates for three consecutive monthly periods. The correlations are low, but they seem to have a lagged effect in predicted directions. Job satisfaction is associated more strongly with voluntary absences than with involuntary absences. Employees who feel their jobs are secure tend to have more absences, perhaps because they are older or because absence is less risky for such employees. Job-specific attitudes relate more strongly to voluntary absenteeism than does a more general measure of organizational climate. The correlations are low for two reasons. First, absence rates for individuals typically are of relatively low reliability for a period of a single month. Second, absences can arise from many different causes so that attitudes are expected to be contributory in a limited degree. Under these conditions, the presence of significant correlations is fairly strong evidence for the validity of both attitudinal and absenteeism data.

Table 5-4 Intercorrelation of Absence Measures (N = 45 months)

Reason for Absence	Short-term Illness	Short-term Personal Absence	Short-term Family Illness	Short-term Personal Absence (unexcused)	Long-term Illness	Long-term Personal Absence	Long-term Out-of-plant Accident/ Absence
Short-term illness	1.00						
Short-term personal absence	.34*	1.00					
Short-term family illness	.63**	.34*	1.00				
Short-term personal absence (unexcused)	.54**	.29*	.16	1.00			
Long-term illness	.53**	.09	.36*	.29*	1.00		
Long-term personal absence	.25	.21	.22	.30*	.30*	1.00	
Long-term out-of-plant accident/absence	.47**	.24	.48**	.42**	.55**	.30*	1.00

* p = .05; ** p = .01

Table 5-5 Intercorrelation of Behavioral and Performance Measures at Quality of Work Life Site: 1972–1976 ($N = 55$ months)

Measures	1	2	3	4	5	6	7	8	9	10	11	12	13	14	15	16	17	18	19	20
1. Voluntary absenteeism	1.00																			
2. Involuntary absenteeism	.49	1.00																		
3. Voluntary turnover	.55	.51	1.00																	
4. Involuntary turnover	.18	.22	.37	1.00																
5. Grievances	-.07	-.36	-.13	-.07	1.00															
6. Minor accidents	.61	.37	.52	.06	-.26	1.00														
7. Minor illnesses	.55	.26	.03	-.14	-.24	.55	1.00													
8. OSHA accidents	.59	.37	.62	.30	.15	.44	-.11	1.00												
9. Medical revisits	.35	.07	.48	.17	.04	.60	.23	.68	1.00											
10. Supply use	-.34	-.35	-.57	-.19	.30	-.59	-.40	-.49	-.41	1.00										
11. Machine downtime	-.11	-.16	.11	.09	-.22	-.33	-.32	-.11	-.33	.17	1.00									
12. Net product rejects	.11	.39	.22	.15	-.07	-.13	-.38	.20	-.09	.28	.52	1.00								
13. Net product rejects as a % of sales	.37	.51	.48	.18	-.04	.05	-.34	.37	.11	.00	.51	.88	1.00							
14. Understandard production	-.28	-.55	-.56	-.27	.22	-.30	-.03	-.28	.02	.35	-.36	-.35	-.37	1.00						
15. Understandard production versus budgeted variance	-.28	-.57	-.54	-.23	.20	-.34	-.08	-.29	-.04	.34	-.31	-.33	-.33	.97	1.00					
16. Adjusted output per employee	-.58	-.42	-.65	-.29	.15	-.52	-.09	-.56	-.39	.39	-.10	-.25	-.49	.48	.42	1.00				
17. Education	-.33	.04	-.14	-.01	-.08	-.22	-.07	-.22	-.24	-.11	.05	-.14	-.13	-.03	-.10	.29	1.00			
18. Age	-.40	-.41	-.78	-.44	.31	-.72	-.47	-.59	-.56	.71	.22	.07	-.16	.54	.55	.65	-.03	1.00		
19. Organization tenure	-.47	-.40	-.77	-.44	.28	-.73	-.49	-.63	-.59	.65	.26	.02	-.19	.51	.50	.73	.18	.97	1.00	
20. Average hourly employment	-.11	.07	-.19	-.07	-.44	.16	.52	-.49	-.25	-.24	.14	-.32	-.34	-.07	-.07	.22	.63	-.14	.03	1.00

Note. All correlations in this table are based on data aggregated plant-wide for monthly periods. Variables 1 through 9 and 17 through 19 are derived from individual-level data; others from work-group or departmental original data. Correlations of .29 and .38 are significant, respectively, at the .05 and .01 levels of confidence.

Table 5-6   Correlations between Selected Attitude Measures and Individual Absenteeism for Each of Three Consecutive Months ($N = 180$ employees)

Measure	Voluntary Absenteeism			Involuntary Absenteeism		
	M_1	M_2	M_3	M_1	M_2	M_3
Job satisfaction	.03	−.11	−.20**	.02	−.01	−.04
Job security	.01	.10	.22**	.21**	−.04	.01
Working conditions	−.18*	−.07	−.02	.03	−.04	.02
Job facilitates growth	−.04	−.11	−.20**	−.10	.05	−.02
Organizational climate index	.02	−.06	−.02	−.04	.01	−.02

* $p < .05$; ** $p < .01$

Note. The attitude measures were obtained in month 1.

A problem in validation stems from a characteristic of the performance and behavioral measures themselves. The behavior incidence distributions in many cases are skewed sharply. Sometimes, the performance measure changes are nonlinear and have to be tested by complex time-series designs. In addition, while the variance range of the performance measures is often very broad, the range of infrequent events such as absences, accidents, and grievances is quite restricted. In some instances, these analytic problems can be allayed by a log transformation of the measures. A related problem is the autoregressive error in serial measures of performance or behavior where the measurement error in a given time period is dependent upon the error in the previous period. This too can be accommodated in some respects by statistical techniques.[46–49] Nevertheless, even with statistical corrections, the relationships between attitudes and behaviors are often unstable.

The final problem in validation rests upon ambiguities in the theories underlying predictions. The causal relationships between individual attitudes and behaviors in organizations and the time lag of effects have been much debated but with little resolution.[50–53] Critiques of past studies have focused on the level of analysis, the definition of the variables in question, the statistical properties of the measures, and so forth. These questions, as well questions of theory, merit fuller discussion in any interpretation of findings from an organizational change program.

Significance of Trends

Figures 5-1 through 5-4 depict graphically the trends in these data over the five periods. Figure 5-1 shows the general decline in turnover over the first four phases and a slight increase in Phase 5. Figure 5-2 depicts the decline in voluntary and involuntary absenteeism. Figure 5-3 illustrates the early increase and then decline in absences and illnesses. Figure 5-4

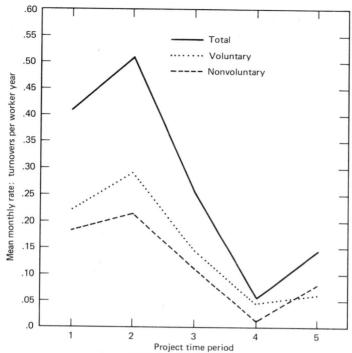

Figure 5-1   Behavioral trends: turnover.

shows the increase in adjusted output per employee, despite the addition of inexperienced new workers to the organization.

The behavioral and performance data collected at the site were subjected to an analysis of variance in order to determine the significance of such trends over the five phases. Of concern when using these analyses are time-series problems in the data that are caused by seasonal variations and by autocorrelations in the residual statistics used in the analysis of variance.[46–47] The use of the ordinary least squares estimation with these types of data is inappropriate if there is confounding by autoregressive errors and, indeed, if the autocorrelation and partial autocorrelation functions of many of the residuals in the behavioral and performance data contain some serially dependent errors.* A simple analysis of variance, assuming independence in the data over time, most likely would be misleading.

* Such evidence makes equivocal a conclusion of the ANOVA test of equality of means because the usual ratio between and within mean squares has an F distribution with $K-1$ and $N-K$ degrees of freedom (K is the number of periods and N is the number of months) and depends upon the assumption that the random errors in the model are distributed independently. Strongly autocorrelated residuals, indicating a dependence of error at time T upon the errors at previous time points, are a violation of this assumption.

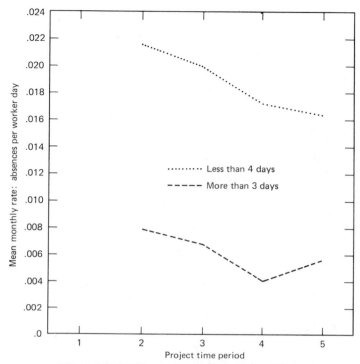

Figure 5-2   Behavioral trends: absence.

The analysis strategy used for resolving this problem was to identify, using the estimated autocorrelation functions of the residuals, the specific type of autocorrelation error, transform the data statistically to remove this error, and then reapply the analysis of variance test to the transformed data.* The participation-membership behavioral measure and the measures of accidents and illnesses, grievances, supply use, and downtime showed simple linear autocorrelated errors.† Accordingly, these measures were transformed and again tested by analysis of variance utilizing Durbin's method of estimated r (i.e., the method of "first differences").[48] As shown in Table 5-7, the transformed results indicated a reduced F-statistic in most cases. However, the improvements in voluntary and total absenteeism, voluntary and total turnover, OSHA and minor accidents and illnesses, and the measures of productivity, quality, and costs were still shown to be statistically significant.

The productivity and product-quality data, however, showed a more complicated autoregressive pattern, possibly due to seasonal variations.

---

* These analytic steps, amounting to a special application of the "generalized least squares" analysis, are then compared to the results obtained from the untransformed data.)
† This is shown as an AR (1)-type autocorrelation error.[48]

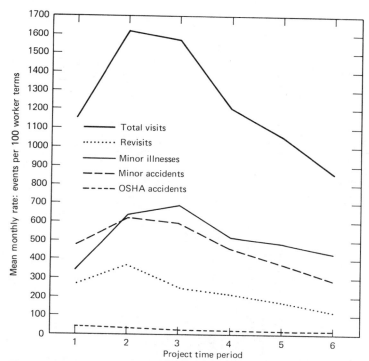

Figure 5-3 *Behavioral trends: medical department visits.*

To investigate the significance of trends in these measures, they were submitted to a least square regression using three distinct time-series designs involving (1) all 55 months, (2) all five phases, and (3) dividing the phases into two groups—before (Phases 1, 2, and 3) and after (Phases 4 and 5) the plant-wide implementation of the change program. Two hypotheses were tested: that productivity and quality improved over time and that the implementation of the program did not influence the relationship between productivity and quality. The former was tested through a regression analysis that took into account lead and lag relationships between the productivity and quality measures; the latter was tested by a simple regression that used cross-correlations between the two measures. This approach tests the statistical likelihood of a relationship (i.e., a nonzero coefficient) between the two variables by t-statistic. The results, presented in Table 5-8, indicate that productivity and quality improved significantly. Specifically, the phase time-series results demonstrated that quality increased during Phases 2 through 4, while productivity declined in Phase 2 but increased thereafter. It appears that a lead–lag relationship was operating between these two variables—a conclusion that is supported by their low cross-correlation, the negative time coefficient, and by the low R^2 values.

Table 5-7   Test of the Significance of Trends in Aggregated Behavioral and Performance Outcomes of the Change Program[a]

Variable	Number of Months (N)	Mean Monthly Rate					Transformed ANOVA F-Statistic
		Phase 1	Phase 2	Phase 3	Phase 4	Phase 5	
Behavioral data							
Absenteeism[b]							
Voluntary	45	NA[c]	.022	.020	.017	.016	2.82*
Involuntary	45	NA	.008	.007	.004	.006	1.84
Total	55	.047	.043	.040	.033	.031	12.18***
Turnover							
Voluntary	55	.222	.291	.143	.042	.063	10.83***
Involuntary	55	.184	.214	.111	.010	.080	2.45
Total	55	.406	.505	.254	.052	.143	17.68***
Accidents and illnesses							
OSHA accidents	55	43	35	24	22	17	8.50***
Minor accidents	55	469	664	593	459	374	5.89***
Minor illnesses	55	344	630	681	515	488	6.54***
Grievances							
Total	55	.115	.026	.052	.115	.056	1.25

Performance data

Productivity

Production under standard	55	.881	.884	.881	.901	.886	4.20***
Production under standard versus budgeted variance	55	.877	.843	.878	.900	.885	4.10**
Output per hourly employee (Adjusted for inflation)	55	131.37	117.96	138.88	153.44	160.67	8.74***
Product quality							
Net product rejects	55	.410	.353	.285	.255	.250	4.23***
Net product rejects as a percentage of sales	55	.668	.579	.417	.432	.443	2.55*
Manufacturing cost control							
Supply use (actual to budget)	45	NA	.426	.488	.534	.518	4.01*
Machine downtime	55	.052	.055	.045	.050	.057	3.92*

* $p = .05$; ** $p = .01$; *** $p = .001$

[a] All measures are transformed using Durbin's estimated r. The turnover and grievance rates shown are annualized; all other rates are means for monthly periods.

[b] Absences attributable to prescheduled personal leave and to lack of available work are excluded from the absence data.

[c] NA means "not ascertained."

Table 5-8 Comparison of Three Time-Series Analysis Designs with Four Selected Performance Indicators

Job Performance Measures[b]	Periods: 55 Months					Periods: 5 Intervention Phases						Two Periods: Before/After				
	R^2	T-Statistic	Signifi-cance Level	Time Coeffi-cient	Signifi-cance Level	R^2	T-Statistic	Signifi-cance Level	Phases	Time Coeffi-cient	Signifi-cance Level	R^2	T-Statistic	Signifi-cance Level	Time Coeffi-cient	Signifi-cance Level
Product rejects as % of sales	.22	14.14	.0000	+.006	.0002	.41	11.72	.0000	II	−.023	.7618	.19	18.25	.0000	−.171	.0007
									III	−.205	.0033					
									IV	−.103	.1126					
									V	+.093	.1281					
Production below standard versus budgeted variance	.09	101.74	.0000	.000	.0200	.35	86.40	.0000	II	−.039	.0043	.18	162.82	.0000	+.028	.0010
									III	+.020	.0930					
									IV	+.032	.0060					
									V	−.007	.4832					
Output per hourly employee adjusted for inflation	.47	28.71	.0000	−.861	.0000	.69	29.71	.0000	II	−12.25	.0381	.54	50.66	.0000	+29.83	.0000
									III	+2.21	.6657					
									IV	+31.55	.0000					
									V	+5.05	.2754					
Productivity/quality	.39	25.83	.0000	−64.88	.0000	—	—	—		—	—	—	—	—	—	—

[a] In the central columns (five-phase design), Period I is used as a constant. Increases and decreases are shown by the symbols + and −.

[b] Three key assumptions should be noted: (a) that the firm's MTS standards are comparable over the 56-month period; (b) that changes in daily production expressed in standard direct labor dollars closely approximate changes in total plant productivity; and (c) that losses of customer goodwill for quality reasons are trivial during the period.

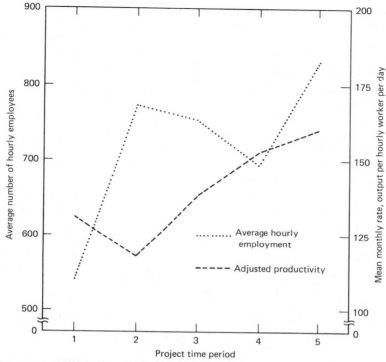

Figure 5-4 Behavioral trends: productivity and number of employees.

If the significance of trends remains in doubt after analyses such as these, it is possible to make further tests with a nonlinear model that uses moving averages over the time period. This was not done in this case because of uncertainty concerning the direction of the trends.[54-58]

Taken together, these graphs, the measures of stability, reliability, and convergent and discriminant validity of the data, the transformed statistical analysis of variance, the regression findings—all attest to the significance of the trends found in these data.

CONCLUSION

The methods displayed here do not exhaust the subject either as to the substantive information to be sought through assessment of behavioral variables or as to the technology for doing so. As to the technology, this volume contains examples of behavioral assessments that are comple-mentary to or that go beyond the methods described here. Chapter 17 employs this methodology, and behavioral measures, such as those de-scribed, are used in conjunction with related data to assess the net benefits or losses and costs associated with an organizational improvement program. Chapter 16 shows how the assessment of changes in productivity can be undertaken with greatly improved precision by taking into account a wider array of factors known to enhance or inhibit the productive outcomes of employee effort. As to the substantive coverage in the present chapter, attention has been limited to certain behaviors that were judged important in the context of a particular illustrative organization and feasible to measure in that organization. Another organization attempting similar behavioral assessments will add variables of particular pertinence to the work technology, economy, and environment of that organization, and will omit measures that are unimportant or inaccessible for measurement at reasonable cost.

To some, the "costing out" of behaviors may seem incompatible with the aims of certain organizational improvement programs in which the economy of the firm is explicitly subordinated to the improvement of the quality of working life for the members. We suggest, however, that the behaviors of interest have important implications for an organization's members—quite apart from their dollar valuation—and that the process of dollar valuation helps in the task of nonmonetary valuation. Examples are the productivity of employees when their pay is tied directly to productivity, or the significance to employees of involuntary absences arising from ill health, since the absence may represent a reduction of quality of life for the worker as well as a cost to the employer.

The intended utility of the methods described, of course, is in the context of the introduction of organizational programs that extend or renew efforts toward the improvement of organizations. Many union leaders and managers are hesitant to undertake such efforts because the social and economic consequences are not always predictable and are not presently well accounted for in most organizations. In our view, the justification for such efforts should include a confident evaluation of the relative financial and social gains and losses to the parties.

For research purposes, we have used these indicators to estimate the cost savings predictable from improvements in employee motivation, satisfaction, and involvement in their organizations. Mirvis and Lawler showed there were such savings following attitudinal improvements among bank employees.[59] We have also found them to be credible "social indicators" of the performances of organizations. Lawler and Mirvis used these behavioral measures along with attitude indicators in the preparation of an independent audit of the quality of work life of an American corporation.[60] Stockholders and financial analysts who evaluated the report understood the measurements and reported an increased understanding of the firm.

Beyond our own experiences, there are broader applications of this methodology. Five contemporary trends make this point evident:

1. Traditional "human-resource accounting," while not yet living up to the promise of its early enthusiastic proponents, continues a quiet course of expanded use and improvements in method and theory. The assessment of changes in rates of costly behaviors is an essential aspect of such accounting.[37,38,44]

2. The exploration of corporate social accounting continues to progress, and it is in part dependent upon the assessment of variables that have both fiscal and employee quality-of-life implications.[60,61]

3. Economists increasingly express a need to differentiate the costs and output contributions of labor from the costs and output contributions of capital and work technology.

4. Increasingly, managers are becoming aware of the utility of behavioral assessments in the ongoing methods for monitoring both the incidence and the costs of such events as accidents, illnesses, absences, and turnovers.

5. The spread of gain-sharing wage plans, such as Scanlon plans, requires the accounting of gains and savings achieved through means that are in addition to direct improvements in the gross-productivity and quality-of-cost centers.

All of these applications, however, are predicated on the further refinement of the methods. Research is needed to confirm the distinctions between voluntary and involuntary absences and between employee-controlled versus management-controlled behaviors. Studies using alternative, multiple measures of a behavior—say, both an absenteeism and attendance rate or a turnover and employment rate—are needed to determine which serves best to assess the work environment in an organization. Attention should also be given to determining optimal rates of absenteeism and turnover and the trade-offs between quality and quantity, since either too little or too much can be harmful to employees or costly to the organization. While this is a broad mandate for research and application, in our view, the methods are ready for such extension.

REFERENCES

1. Katzell, R. A., & Yankelovich, D. *Work, productivity, and job satisfaction: An evaluation of policy-related research.* New York: Psychological Corporation, 1975.
2. Cummings, T. G., & Molloy, E. S. *Improving productivity and the quality of work life.* New York: Praeger, 1977.
3. Mills, T. Human resources—Why the new concern? *Harvard Business Review,* 1975, **53**(2), 120–134.
4. Katzell, R. S., Brenstock, P., & Faerstein, P. H. *A guide to worker productivity experiments in the United States.* New York: New York University Press, 1977.
5. *Work in America.* United States Department of Health, Education and Welfare: Report to a Special Task Force to the Secretary, 1972.

6. March, J. O., & Simon, H. A. *Organizations*. New York: Wiley, 1958.

7. Lawler, E. E. III. *Motivation in work organizations*. Monterey, CA: Brooks/Cole, 1973.

8. Hill, J. M., & Trist, E. L. *Industrial accidents, sickness, and other absences*. Pamphlet No. 4. London: Tavistock Institute of Human Relations, 1962.

9. Rice, A. K. Productivity and social organization in an Indian weaving shed: An examination of some aspects of the sociotechnical system of an experimental automatic loom shed. *Human Relations,* 1953, **6**, 297–329.

10. Marrow, A. J., Bowers, D. G., & Seashore, S. E. (Eds.). *Management by participation*. New York: Harper & Row, 1967.

11. Price, J. L. *Handbook of organizational measurement*. Lexington: D. C. Heath, 1972.

12. Campbell, J. R., Bownas, D., Peterson, N. G., & Dunnette, M. D. *The measurement of organizational effectiveness: A review of relevant research and opinion*. Final Technical Report No. TR 75-1. Minneapolis: University of Minnesota, 1974.

13. Herrick, N. Q. *The quality of work and its outcomes: Estimating potential increases in labor productivity*. Columbus: Academy of Contemporary Problems, 1975.

14. Macy, B. A., & Mirvis, P. H. A methodology for assessment of quality of work life and organizational effectiveness in behavioral-economic terms. *Administrative Science Quarterly,* 1976, **21**, 212–226.

15. Lyons, T. F. Turnover and absenteeism: A review of relationships and shared correlates. *Journal of Applied Psychology,* 1972, **25**, 271–281.

16. Heneman, H. G., Jr., Comaford, C., Jasmin, J., & Nelson, R. J. Standardized absence rate: A first step toward comparability. *Personnel Journal,* July-August 1961, 114–115, 127.

17. Muchinsky, P. M. Employee absenteeism: A review of the literature. *Journal of Vocational Behavior,* 1977, **10**, 316–340.

18. Latham, G. P., & Pursell, E. D. Measuring absenteeism from the opposite side of the coin. *Journal of Applied Psychology,* 1975, **60**, 369–371.

19. Huse, E. F., & Taylor, E. K. The reliability of absence measures. *Journal of Applied Psychology,* 1962, **46**, 159–160.

20. Rice, A. K., Hill, J. M., & Trist, E. L. The representations of labour turnover as a social process. *Human Relations,* 1950, **3**, 349–372.

21. Levine, E., & Wright, S. New ways to measure personnel turnover in hospitals. *Hospitals,* 1957, **31**, 38–42.

22. Price, J. L. *The study of turnover*. Ames: Iowa University Press, 1977.

23. McNeil, K., & Thompson, J. D. The regeneration of social organizations. *American Sociological Review,* 1971, **36**, 624–637.

24. Hyman, R. *Strikes*. London: Fontana/Collins, 1972.

25. Imberman, W. Strikes cost more than you think. *Harvard Business Review,* 1979, **57**(3), 133–138.

26. United States Department of Labor, Bureau of Labor Statistics. *Work stoppage—Selected periods*. Washington, D.C.: U.S. Government Printing Office, January 1971.

27. United States Department of Labor, Occupational Safety and Health Administration. *Recordkeeping requirements: Form 100*. Washington, D.C.: U.S. Government Printing Office, 1972.

28. Kaplan, A. *Making grievance procedures work*. Los Angeles: Institute of Industrial Relations, University of California, 1950.

29. Stein, H. *The meaning of productivity.* Bulletin No. 1714. Washington, D.C.: U.S. Department of Labor, 1971.

30. United States Department of Labor, Bureau of Labor Statistics. *Industrial productivity measurement in the U.S. Office of Productivity, Technology, and Growth.* Washington, D.C.: U.S. Government Printing Office, 1970.

31. Steiner, P. O., & Goldner, W. *Productivity.* Los Angeles: Institute of Industrial Relations, University of California, 1952.

32. Beek, H. G. The influence of assembly line organization on input, quality, and morale. *Occupational Psychology,* 1964, **38**, 161–172.

33. Likert, R., & Bowers, D. G. Organizational theory and human resource accounting. *American Psychologist,* 1969, **24**, 585–592.

34. Greenberg, L. *A practical guide to productivity measurement.* Washington, D.C.: U.S. Bureau of National Affairs, Inc., 1973.

35. Brogden, H. E., & Taylor, E. The dollar criterion—Applying the cost accounting concept to criterion construction. *Personnel Psychology,* 1959, **3**, 133–154.

36. Heinrich, H. W. *Industrial accident prevention.* New York: McGraw-Hill, 1941.

37. Brummet, R. L., Flamholtz, E. G., & Pyle, W. C. Human resource measurement—A challenge for accountants. *The Accounting Review,* 1968, 217–224.

38. Flamholtz, E. G. *Human resource accounting.* Encino: Dickenson, 1974.

39. Mirvis, P. H., & Macy, B. A. Human resource accounting: A measurement perspective. *Academy of Management Review,* 1976, **1**, 74–83.

40. Alexander, M. O. Investments in people. *Canadian Chartered Accountant,* 1971, 1–8.

41. Committee on Nonprofit Organizations, American Accounting Association. Report of the committee on nonprofit organizations. *The Accounting Review,* 1975, Supplement to Vol. XLX, 3–39.

42. Heise, D. R. Separating reliability and stability in test–retest correlations. *American Sociological Review,* 1969, **34**, 93–101.

43. Taylor, J. C., & Bowers, D. G. *Survey of organizations.* Ann Arbor: Institute for Social Research, University of Michigan, 1972.

44. Pecorella, P. A., Bowers, D. G., Davenport, A. S., & Lapointe, J. B. *Forecasting performance in organizations: An application of current value human resource accounting.* Final report, NR 156-051. Ann Arbor: Institute for Social Research, University of Michigan, 1978.

45. Hopwood, A. G. An empirical study of the role of accounting data in performance evaluation. In *Empirical research in accounting: Selected studies,* Supplement to Vol. X. *Journal of Accounting Research,* 1972.

46. Campbell, D. T. Keeping the data honest in the experimenting society. In H. Melton & D. Watson (Eds.), *Interdisciplinary dimensions of accounting for social goals and social organizations.* Columbus: Grid, 1977. See also Campbell, D. T. Reforms as experiments. *American Psychologist,* 1969, **24**, 409–429.

47. Johnston, J. *Econometric methods,* 2nd ed. New York: McGraw-Hill, 1972.

48. Durbin, J. Estimation of parameters in time-series regression models. *Journal of the Royal Statistical Society,* Series B, 1960, **22**(1).

49. Glass, G., Willson, V., & Gottman, J. *Design and analysis of time-series experiments.* Boulder, Colorado: Associated University Press, 1975.

50. Porter, L. W., & Steers, R. M. Organizational, work and personal factors in employee turnover and absenteeism. *Psychological Bulletin,* 1973, **80**(3), 151–176.

51. Mervielde, I. Methodological problems of research about attitude-behavior consistency. *Quality and Quantity,* 1977, **11,** 259–281.

52. Fishbein, M. Attitudes and the prediction of behavior. In M. Fishbein (Ed.), *Readings in attitude theory and measurement.* New York: Wiley, 1967.

53. Aizen, T., & Fishbein, M. Attitude-behavior relations: A theoretical analysis and review of empirical research. *Psychological Bulletin,* 1977, **84,** 888–918.

54. Macwhinney, T. C., & Pack, D. G. Statistical analysis of interrupted time-series experiments: Some problems and recommended solutions. *Working Papers.* Bloomington: Indiana University, Graduate School of Business, 1979.

55. Bagshaw, M., & Johnson, R. A. Segmental procedures for detecting parameter changes in time-series models. *Journal of American Statistical Association,* 1977, **72,** 593–597.

56. Box, G., & Jenkins, G. *Time-series analysis: Forecasting and control.* San Francisco: Holden Day, 1970.

57. Box, G., & Tiao, G. Intervention analysis with applications to economic and environmental problems. *Journal of American Statistical Association,* 1975, **70,** 70–79.

58. Caporase, J. A. Quasi-experimental designs. In J. A. Caporase & L. L. Roos, Jr. (Eds.), *Quasi-experimental approaches, testing theory and evaluating policy.* Evanston: Northwestern University Press, 1973.

59. Mirvis, P. H., & Lawler, E. E. III. Measuring the financial impact of employee attitudes. *Journal of Applied Psychology,* 1977, **62,** 1–8.

60. Lawler, E. E., & Mirvis, P. H. How Graphic Controls assesses the human side of the corporation. *Management Review,* October 1981, 54–63.

61. Dierkes, M., & Bauer, R. G. *Corporate social accounting.* New York: Praeger, 1973.

APPENDIX 5-1   BEHAVIORAL DEFINITIONS AND RECORDING CATEGORIES

Behavioral Definitions	Recording Categories
Absenteeism: each absence or illness over four hours	Voluntary: short-term illness (less than three consecutive days), personal business, family illness
	Involuntary: long-term illness (more than three consecutive days), funerals, out-of-plant accidents, lack of work (temporary layoff), presanctioned days off
	Leaves: medical, personal, maternity, military, and other (e.g., jury duty)
Tardiness: each absence or illness under four hours	Voluntary: same as absenteeism
	Involuntary: same as absenteeism
Turnover: each movement beyond organizational boundary	Voluntary: resignation
	Involuntary: termination, disqualification, requested resignation, per-

Behavioral Definitions	Recording Categories
	manent layoff, retirement, disability, death
Internal employment stability: each movement within organizational boundary	Internal movement: transfer, promotion, promotion with transfer
	Internal stability: new hires, layoffs, rehires
Strikes and work stoppages: each day lost due to strike or work stoppage	Sanctioned: union-authorized strike, company-authorized lockout
	Unsanctioned: work slowdown, walkout, sitdown
Accidents and work-related illness: each recordable injury, illness or death from a work related accident or from exposure to the work environment	Major: OSHA accident, illness, or death which results in medical treatment by a physician or registered professional person under standing orders from a physician
	Minor: non-OSHA accident or illness which results in one-time treatment and subsequent observation not requiring professional care
	Revisits: OSHA and non-OSHA accident or illness which requires subsequent treatment and observation
Grievance: written grievance in accordance with labor–management contract	Stage: recorded by step (first arbitration)
Productivity: resources used in production of acceptable outputs (comparison of inputs with outputs)*	Output: product or service quantity (units or dollars)
	Input: direct and/or indirect (labor in hours or dollars)
Production quality: resources used in production of unacceptable output	Resource utilized: scrap (unacceptable in-plant products in units or dollars); customer returns (unacceptable out-of-plant products in units or dollars); recoveries (salvageable products in units or dollars), rework (additional direct and/or indirect labor in hours or dollars)

* Reports only labor inputs.

Downtime: unscheduled breakdown of machinery	Downtime: duration of breakdown (hours or dollars)
	Machine repair: nonpreventative maintenance (dollars)
Inventory, material, and supply variance: unscheduled resource utilization	Variance: over- or underutilization of supplies, materials, inventory (due to theft, inefficiency, and so on)

APPENDIX 5-2   BEHAVIORAL MEASURES AND COMPUTATIONAL FORMULAS

Behavioral Measures*	Computational Formula
Absenteeism rate (monthly)†	$\dfrac{\Sigma \text{ absence days}}{\text{average work-force size} \times \text{working days}}$
Tardiness rate (monthly)†	$\dfrac{\Sigma \text{ tardiness incidents}}{\text{average work-force size} \times \text{working days}}$
Turnover rate (monthly)	$\dfrac{\Sigma \text{ turnover incidents}}{\text{average work-force size}}$
Internal stability rate (monthly)	$\dfrac{\Sigma \text{ internal movement incidents}}{\text{average work-force size}}$
Strike rate (yearly)	$\dfrac{\Sigma \text{ striking workers} \times \Sigma \text{ strike days}}{\text{average work-force size} \times \text{working days}}$
Accident rate (yearly)	$\dfrac{\Sigma \text{ of accidents, illnesses}}{\text{total yearly hours worked}} \times 200,000‡$
Grievance rate (yearly)	Plant: $\dfrac{\Sigma \text{ grievance incidents}}{\text{average work-force size}}$ Individual: $\dfrac{\Sigma \text{ aggrieved individuals}}{\text{average work-force size}}$

* All measures reflect the number of incidents divided by an exposure factor that represents the number of employees in the organization and the possible incidents of behavior (e.g., for absenteeism, the average work force size × the number of working days). Mean monthly rates (i.e., absences per work day) are computed and averaged for absenteeism, leaves, and tardiness for a yearly figure and summed for turnover, grievances, and internal employment stability for a yearly figure. The term *rate* refers to the number of incidents per unit of employee exposure to the risk of such incidences during the analysis interval.
† Sometimes combined as number of hours missing/average work-force size × working days.
‡ Base for 100 full-time equivalent workers (400 hours × 50 weeks).

Behavioral Measures*	Computational Formula
Productivity§	
Total	$$\frac{\text{output of goods or services (units or \$)}}{\text{direct and/or indirect labor (hours or \$)}}$$
Below standard	Actual versus engineered standard
Below budget	Actual versus budgeted standard
Variance	Actual versus budgeted variance
Per employee	Output/average work force size
Quality§	
Total	scrap + customer returns + rework − recoveries ($, units, or hours)
Below standard	Actual versus engineered standard
Below budget	Actual versus budgeted standard
Variance	Actual versus budgeted variance
Per employee	Total/average work force size
Downtime	labor ($) + repair costs or dollar value of replaced equipment ($)
Inventory, supply, and material usage	variance (actual versus standard utilization) ($)

§ Monetary valuations can be expressed in labor dollars, actual dollar costs, sales dollars; overtime dollar valuations can be adjusted to base year dollars to control for salary, raw material, and price increases.

APPENDIX 5-3 EXAMPLE OF DECISION RULES FOR MEASURING COST OF ABSENTEEISM

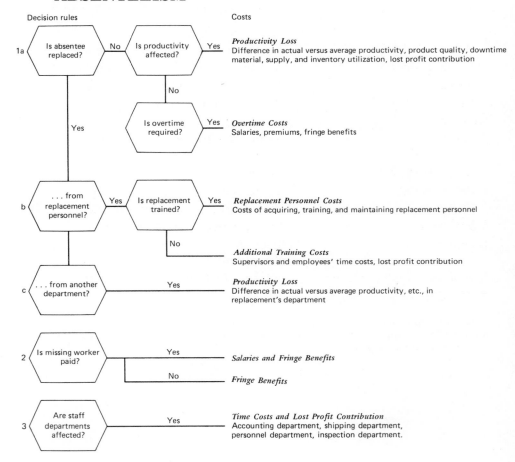

CHAPTER SIX

Organizational Structure: Measuring the Distribution of Influence

MICHAEL MOCH, CORTLANDT CAMMANN, AND ROBERT A. COOKE

Planned change in organizations frequently involves altering patterns of decision making. This is particularly true when the change attempts to establish explicit mechanisms for labor–management cooperation or to increase employment involvement. Alterations in patterns of decision making also can be unintended outcomes of planned change. Change directed by survey-feedback techniques, for example, can make management more aware of employee opinions and views. Whether intended or unintended, change programs can affect the ways decisions get made and, therefore, how influence is distributed among members. Thus, it is important that attempts to assess organizational change should include measures of the distribution of influence.

Established measures of influence, unfortunately, show limited internal consistency and low divergence from some measures of other organizational properties.[1-3] One reason for these shortcomings may be the failure to specify properly the organizational construct involved.

The distribution of influence often is treated as variance between rather than within organizations. This view is implied whenever global measures of influence are employed.[4,5] However, the distribution of influence may vary not only across organizational systems but also across subsystems within organizations. This type of variation is suggested by the report of Lawrence and Lorsch that organizational subsystems responsible for different activities may exhibit distinctive decision-making structures.[6] It is also suggested by Duncan's finding that an effective organizational subunit may exhibit different levels of participation and hierarchy when dealing with different types of decisions.[7] Similarly, Bachrach and Aiken have found that different factors contribute to the influence of members of different status groups and that these groups experience different amounts of influence over work as compared with policy decisions.[8] To the extent that this sort of variation occurs, measures that aggregate across subsystems or decision types will contain errors attributable to subsystem or intertype differences. This has an obvious deleterious effect on measurement precision and on the interpretability of results.

This chapter explores the desirability of distinguishing among subsystems and decision types when measuring influence in organizations. A set of decisional domains is identified, and measures of influence are developed that do not imply aggregation across subsystems. These measures are then tested for their fit with the proposed influence domains, and estimates of their convergent and discriminant validity are made. In addition, the influence exercised by organizational members in various positions is examined to determine whether these positions are characterized by different configurations of influence. Differences in configurations—that is, in the relative amounts of influence over the various domains exercised by members in different roles—are of particular interest. Such differences would indicate that the hypothesized domains do not represent uniform examples of a single, broader, influence construct.

SUBSYSTEMS AND THE DISTRIBUTION OF INFLUENCE IN ORGANIZATIONS

In many studies of control in organizations, influence is measured by asking members to report on the amount of control that various groups have over "what goes on in your organization."[9] While members often agree about the amounts of influence exercised by different groups, they do not always see things the same way. Inconsistencies may arise because some members may respond to the questions in terms of global influence and others may answer in terms of the influence domain that is most immediately important to them—that is, their own work. Work influence may be exercised by—and thus may be salient to—members at all levels of the organizational hierarchy. Top executives have considerable control over their work, and in many organizations middle-level managers also have a considerable amount of influence in this area. Lower-level employees also may determine many of their own work activities; even the worker whose activities are specified in advance can exercise influence by deciding the sequence, pacing, or quality standards for different activities to be carried out.

While work activities may be a highly visible domain over which many organizational members exercise influence, it is not necessarily the only domain nor the one which is most salient to all members. In organizations, many decisions are made and many problems are solved which go beyond the work activities of individual members. For example, the work efforts of different organizational members must be coordinated and resources must be allocated for the performance of this work.[11–14] The solving of these problems implies that at least these two other domains should be considered when measuring influence. It cannot be assumed that these domains are equally important to members in different organizational positions or that influence over these domains is distributed in the same way as work influence.

Coordination by its very nature requires that employees suspend their judgment over at least some of their own activities so that their work may be coordinated with that of others. Furthermore, certain types of work tasks can be coordinated in advance (e.g., by scheduling), and this coordination can often be accomplished by persons other than those who are directly involved in carrying out the work.[12] Influence over the allocation of organizational resources may be even more restricted than influence over coordination decisions. Spending significant amounts of money, allocating new equipment to organizational departments, or making more than routine alterations in staff membership may involve top executives or even board members. While the resource allocation and coordination influence of higher-level members may be as great as their work influence, members at lower levels are likely to feel they have less influence over these domains than they have over their own work. Furthermore, these domains may be less important to lower-level members than to those at the top of the organizational hierarchy.

This line of reasoning suggests that influence over work, resource allocation, and coordination of activities may be distributed in different ways. The subsystem perspective advocated by Becker and Gordon, Parsons, and Katz and Kahn provides some theoretical support for this argument.[14–16] Becker and Gordon view work activities, resource allocation, and coordination as relatively independent areas of responsibility in organizations. Parsons makes an analogous distinction between technical and managerial activities. Technical activities correspond to Becker's and Gordon's work activities, and managerial activities are similar to their coordination and resource-allocation activities. Elsewhere, Parsons distinguishes between allocation and coordination activities.[17] Similarly, Katz and Kahn place coordination and at least some resource-allocation activities within two different subsystems—the managerial and maintenance substructures, respectively.

Previous theoretical work therefore suggests that organizations are characterized by at least three distinct influence domains, which are called subsystems here. Measures of influence should reflect at least these three domains: *work activities, coordination activities,* and *resource-allocation activities.* While these domains are not exhaustive and do not represent the only ways of viewing organizational subsystems, they provide a theoretically adequate set of decisional areas for assessing the appropriateness of a subsystem measurement approach.

The Data

Multiple measures of influence over work, personnel resource-allocation, and coordination activities were applied in each of five organizations. Measures of influence over the allocation of material resources were applied in one organization, but they showed such poor consistency that they were dropped from the questionnaire for subsequent applications. Two of these organizations are engineering divisions of a public utility. Two others are plants belonging to a pharmaceutical company—one located in the Southwest and the other in the West. The fifth is a service organization in the Midwest. Employees in each organization filled out standard questionnaires. In addition, unit supervisors of 55 departments in two divisions of the public utility were interviewed. The primary purpose of this effort was to identify influence domains that would vary systematically across hierarchical levels and also among organizational subunits.

Questionnaire measures of influence over work, coordination, and resource-allocation activities applied in the five sites are identified in the left-hand column of Table 6-1. At least one measure of each domain was applied in each site, but certain measures were not used in all sites. The items included in the interviews with unit supervisors in the engineering organizations can be found in Table 6-4. Identical interviews were conducted with 33 supervisors in engineering division 1 and with 22 supervisors in engineering division 2. Questionnaire respondents were asked to report the amount of influence they exercised over various activities. In the interviews, supervisors were asked to report the amount of influence people at different levels exercised over different activities carried out in their work units.

Method of Analysis

Two procedures were used to assess the appropriateness of distinguishing among the influence domains under consideration. First, the data were examined to determine whether the survey items produced reliable measures of the three influence constructs and whether these constructs, as measured, were discriminable from one another. Second, mean levels of influence over the various domains were examined for organizational members in different positions to identify any differences in their reported amounts and configurations of influence.

Table 6-1 Path Coefficients Linking Concepts and Measures for Eleven Influence Measures in Each of Five Sites[a]

	Organization				
Measures: How much say do you actually have in making decisions . . .	Engineering Division 1 (N = 331)	Engineering Division 2 (N = 327)	Southwest Pharmaceutical Firm (N = 80)	Western Pharmaceutical Firm (N = 98)	Midwest Service Organization (N = 199)
Influence over work activities					
1. about how you do your own work?	.78	.73	.77	.76	.79
2. about changing how you do your work?	.92	.78	.87	.78	.74
3. about how work-related problems are solved?	.82	—	—	—	—
4. about what you do day to day?	—	.82	—	—	—
Influence over personnel activities					
5. about hiring people?	.87	.79	—	—	.92
6. about pay raises?	—	—	.68	.51	—
7. about promoting people?	.91	.86	.94	.84	.87
8. about firing people?	.87	.77	.92	.79	.94
Influence over coordination activities					
9. about how to settle disagreements between people in your work group?	.85	.76	.65	.78	.65
10. about what to do when someone you depend on does not do their job?	—	.73	.75	.73	.72
11. about how work gets divided up among people?	.82	.78	.78	.68	.71

[a] Numbers in the table are path coefficients reflecting the impact of the unmeasured domain on the measure designed to tap it.

RESULTS

Convergence and Discrimination

The convergent and discriminant validity of the questionnaire items were tested through the use of confirmatory factor analysis.[18-20] This technique produces three types of information: (1) estimates of the strength of association between the items and the constructs they are intended to measure; (2) estimates of the strength of association between the constructs; and (3) residual matrices for each analysis. These matrices allow an examination of the extent to which the proposed model explains all of the relationships actually observed among the items used to operationalize the constructs. Confirmatory factor analysis generates estimates of these parameters simultaneously with estimates of measurement error. It implicitly corrects for attenuation due to measurement error, and therefore the measures of item-construct and interconstruct association are estimates of true association.

Table 6-1 shows the estimates of the strength of association between the items and the constructs that they are intended to measure for each of the five organizations. These estimates can be interpreted in a manner similar to the interpretation of factor loadings in a factor analysis. The data generated by this confirmatory model indicate that the questionnaire items are strongly associated with the constructs they are intended to measure.

Table 6-2 provides estimates of the true correlations among the influence constructs for each organization. With the exception of the southwestern pharmaceutical plant, these correlations indicate that the measures only marginally discriminate between resource and coordination

Table 6-2   Correlations among Unmeasured Influence Variables for Each of the Five Organizations

Organization	Work Influence and Influence over Personnel Resources	Influence over Personnel Resources and Coordination Influence	Coordination Influence and Work Influence
Engineering Division 1	.67	.87	.84
Engineering Division 2	.59	.86	.82
Southwest pharmaceutical firm	.33	.76	.52
Western pharmaceutical firm	.65	.88	.89
Midwest service organization	.52	.78	.89

influence and between coordination and work influence. Shared variance between these sets of measures across firms ranges from 79% ($r = .89$) to 27% ($r = .52$). Measures of work and resource influence appear to discriminate somewhat more adequately, as the shared variance between these constructs ranges from 45% to 11%.

For all comparisons, greatest discrimination occurs in the southwestern pharmaceutical plant. This organization is the only one in the sample with a mass-batch technology; it also is considerably newer than the western pharmaceutical plant and the other three organizations. It is possible that influence domains can be more clearly distinguished when mass-production techniques are employed and coordination can be accomplished by plan, as suggested by Thompson.[12] Age and attendant traditions may also blur clear distinctions between positions initially created to exercise influence primarily within different domains. Whatever the reason, the discrimination among domains seen in the southwestern pharmaceutical plant provides evidence that the domains are distinguishable. The high correlations among domains for the other organizations, however, raises doubt about the utility of making such distinctions under all circumstances. Overall, Table 6-2 provides only mixed support for the domain approach to influence.

The residual matrices (see Table 6-3) show the correlations among the items after subtracting the correlations predicted by the confirmatory model. These predicted correlations are calculated in the manner of path analysis by multiplying the path coefficients and the interconstruct correlation that connects each pair of measures. Ideally, all these correlations would be .00, indicating that the model fits the observed data perfectly. Inspection of Table 6-3 reveals that the criterion of similarity between expected and observed correlations is largely met. Ninety-five percent of the differences are less than ±.10. Only one difference out of 148 exceeds ±.12. It seems clear that correlations among these influence measures can be adequately explained by distinguishing among work, coordination, and resource influence in the proposed manner.

The convergence and discrimination patterns in the interview data were examined in an analogous manner. Confirmatory factor analysis was not used because of the small number of cases involved; instead, scales were formed by averaging the component items and then the correlations between the items, and the scales were calculated. These correlations provide an estimate of the strength of the relationships of the items and the constructs. The correlations among the scales were then calculated in order to assess the relationships among the constructs themselves.

The correlations between the scales and their component items are presented in Table 6-4. It should be remembered that the items and the scales being correlated measure unit leaders' perceptions of the influence of personnel at different organizational levels in the two engineering

Table 6-3 Goodness of Fit of Measurement Model to Observed Correlations among Measures (Observed Minus Expected Correlations)

Engineering Division 2

1		.03	.00	.04	.00	−.08	−.02	−.03	−.04	1
2	.00		−.03	.02	−.02	−.06	.04	.02	−.04	2
3	.03	−.02		.05	.05	−.01	.02	−.02	.06	4
5	−.03	.03	.02		−.02	.03	−.02	.02	.00	5
7	−.02	.00	−.04	−.03		.00	−.02	.01	.06	7
8	−.07	.02	−.04	.02	.00		−.04	.00	−.02	8
9	−.04	−.01	.00	.03	.04	−.02		.04	.00	9
11	−.01	.05	.00	−.06	.06	−.05	.00		−.03	10 11

Engineering Division 1

Southwest pharmaceutical firm

1		.00	.03	.05	−.03	.11	−.02	−.05	1
2	.00		−.10	.02	−.03	.08	.03	−.07	2
6	.00	.08		−.03	.01	.18	.08	.11	6
7	.02	−.02	.00		.00	−.01	−.04	.06	7
8	−.01	−.01	−.02	.01		−.03	−.05	−.02	8
9	.00	−.03	.04	.01	−.01		.01	−.04	9
10	−.04	−.01	.12	.02	.01	.02		.02	10
11	.03	.07	−.11	−.05	.01	.01	−.04		11

Western pharmaceutical firm

1							
2	.00						
5	.04	−.02					
7	.01	−.05	.00				
8	.00	.01	.00	.00			
9	.08	.10	−.10	−.12	−.12		
10	−.08	−.02	.08	.05	.07	.00	
11	.00	−.07	.08	−.01	.04	.03	−.03

Midwest service organization

Table 6-4 Correlations Between Measures and Constructs for Influence Measures (Interview) in Both Engineering Divisions

Rating (how much *direct influence* each of these types of individuals has over these different types of decisions)	Engineering Division 1 (N = 33) Level					Engineering Division 2 (N = 22) Level					
	A (top)	B	C	D	E (bottom)	A (top)	B	C	D	E	F (bottom)
Influence over work activities											
How work-related problems are solved in the unit.	.85	.90	.71	.88	.93	.84	.66	.69	.58	.89	.73
What people in the unit do day to day.	.45	.74	.63	.59	.88	.80	.73	.69	.73	.78	.78
Changing how people do their work in the unit.	.90	.85	.77	.84	.81	.79	.69	.60	.81	.79	.59
Influence over resource allocation											
Hiring new people for the unit.	.79	.66	.85	.75	.96	.87	.63	.85	.89	.91	*
Pay raises for unit personnel.	.65	.89	.82	.87	*	.94	.78	.50	.84	.76	*
Firing people in the unit.	.77	.87	.61	.78	.97	.68	.21	.75	.89	.86	.99
Who to promote in the unit.	.60	.86	.71	.85	.96	.86	.66	.76	.73	.87	.99
Influence over coordination activities											
What to do when someone in the unit is not doing his or her job.	.78	.87	.85	.91	.88	.91	.86	.83	.64	.85	.75
How work will be divided up among people in the unit.	.15	.85	.71	.77	.86	.81	.74	.87	.80	.83	.64
What should be done when people do not get what they need to do their work.	.98	.85	.74	.64	.82	.72	.77	.75	.64	.81	.90

* Insufficient variance to compute correlation.

Table 6-5 Correlations Among Influence Scales by Level and by Domain—Engineering Division 1 ($N = 33$)

Scale	Level	Influence Over Work Activities					Influence Over Personnel Resource-Allocation Activities					Influence Over Coordination Activities				
		1	2	3	4	5	1	2	3	4	5	1	2	3	4	5
Influence over work activities	1															
	2	.52														
	3	.39	.55													
	4	.01	-.02	-.06												
	5	.11	-.13	-.45	-.11											
Influence over personnel re-source-allocation activities	1	.49	.67	.43	-.31	-.27										
	2	.00	.48	.20	-.30	.08	.64									
	3	.42	-.12	-.05	.09	.45	.19	-.30								
	4	.22	-.01	.25	.46	-.28	-.01	-.40	.35							
	5	.21	-.31	-.52	-.33	.64	-.16	-.21	.50	.16						
Influence over coordination activities	1	.65	.54	.34	.15	-.30	.53	.11	.18	.37	.08					
	2	.39	.84	.29	.06	-.15	.59	.34	-.15	-.05	-.29	.55				
	3	.14	.13	.55	.06	-.07	.24	.33	.08	-.04	-.53	-.12	-.08			
	4	.12	.25	.14	.50	.26	.04	.06	-.06	.91	-.46	.13	-.02	.07		
	5	.29	-.08	-.51	-.23	.77	.02	.18	.51	-.13	.82	-.02	-.09	-.30	-.22	
Level		1	2	3	4	5	1	2	3	4	5	1	2	3	4	5

divisions. Only two of the correlations in this table fail to meet generally acceptable levels of reliability, and these do not seem to indicate any consistent problem with the reliability of the measures.

Tables 6-5 and 6-6 show the correlations among the influence scales for engineering divisions 1 and 2, respectively. These correlations indicate reasonable discrimination in perceptions of influence across different domains (outlined main diagonals), especially for the influence exercised by people at middle levels (i.e., levels 2, 3, and 4). They also indicate that considerable discrimination in influence across domains is greatest for resource and work influence and for resource and coordination influence. The measures did not discriminate as well between work and coordination influence exercised by employees at the same level.

Overall, these analyses provide evidence that both the questionnaire and the interview measures of influence show convergence within each measurement domain and at least some divergence between these domains. High interdomain correlations, especially between work and coordination influence, however, suggest that, under some conditions, distinctions among domains may be only marginally useful to the extent that analyses are restricted to covariance structures. When mean differences are observed, however, a different picture emerges.

Configurations of Influence by Job Classification

Figure 6-1 illustrates the mean levels of influence reported by respondents in different job classifications in four of the five organizations. Data are not presented for the Midwest service organization because the relevant classification information was not available. In all four organizations, top management reported havng more influence over each domain than did their lower-level counterparts ($p \leq .05$). In the engineering divisions, professional personnel reported having more work and coordination influence than did technical personnel ($p \leq .05$). The difference across these levels for resource influence was significant beyond the .05 level only for respondents in engineering division 2. In the pharmaceutical plants, differences across the various lower-level positions (i.e., operator, clerk, quality-control technician) were not very pronounced. This was not unexpected, since the design of these plants did not call for a differential distribution of influence across these positions.

Patterns of influence across domains were at least as interesting as those across positions. In all four organizations, respondents at all levels felt they exercised more influence over their own work activities than over resource-allocation decisions ($p \leq .05$). Respondents at middle level or lower levels reported exercising significantly more work than coordination influence ($p \leq .05$).

While there are differences in the patterns of influence among the lower-level positions, these differences are not as striking as those be-

Table 6-6 Correlations Among Influence Scales by Level and by Domain (Interview Data)—Engineering Division 2 (N = 22)

Scale	Level	Influence Over Work Activities						Influence Over Personnel Resource-Allocation Activities						Influence Over Coordination Activities					
		1	2	3	4	5	6	1	2	3	4	5	6	1	2	3	4	5	6
Influence over work activities	1																		
	2	.66																	
	3	.32	.53																
	4	.27	.34	.34															
	5	-.27	-.18	-.35	.00														
	6	-.03	-.01	-.08	-.12	-.62													
Influence over personnel resource-allocation activities	1	.57	.33	.19	.05	-.24	-.14												
	2	.43	.50	.35	.40	.03	-.08	.04											
	3	.08	.05	-.02	.45	.32	.32	.19	.57										
	4	.24	.17	.14	.23	.10	.28	.16	.11	.29									
	5	-.16	-.04	-.04	.12	.39	.06	.35	.12	.33	.70								
	6	-.16	.46	.04	.12	.39	.26	-.18	-.07	.15	-.31	-.14							
Influence over coordination activities	1	.80	.55	.20	.30	-.14	.07	.61	.29	.52	.10	.18	-.15						
	2	.63	.59	.36	.37	-.08	-.09	.55	.52	.51	.39	.41	.17	.77					
	3	.50	.58	.67	.30	-.09	-.12	.43	.51	.39	.25	.09	.01	.42	.75				
	4	.13	.14	.17	-.48	.45	.04	.09	.17	.19	.25	.42	-.18	.36	.43	.28			
	5	-.28	-.09	-.28	-.13	.68	.33	-.27	.19	.01	.42	-.16	.31	-.27	-.36	-.32	.35		
	6	.20	.37	.02	.00	.38	.66	.01	.23	.52	.43	-.16	.58	.16	.02	.11	-.02	-.02	
Level		1	2	3	4	5	6	1	2	3	4	5	6	1	2	3	4	5	6

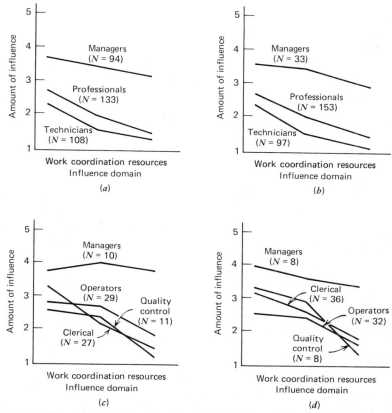

Figure 6-1 *Control graphs by influence domain (aggregated perceptions: (a) engineering division 1; (b) engineering division 2; (c) southwestern pharmaceutical firm (d) western pharmaceutical firm.*

tween the lower levels and the managerial level. To explore whether there are differences among managers at different levels, the interview data from the engineering divisions were arrayed to illustrate the influence that supervisors felt people at various levels exercise. As before, influence over work, over coordination, and over personnel resource-allocation activities were distinguished. The results are presented in Figure 6-2.

The two graphs in this figure represent the average supervisor response by organization. They provide additional evidence that the distribution of work and coordination influence is distinct from that of personnel resource-allocation influence. Resource-allocation activities are perceived to be controlled at higher points in both engineering organizations. Interestingly, however, even these decisions are not seen as being

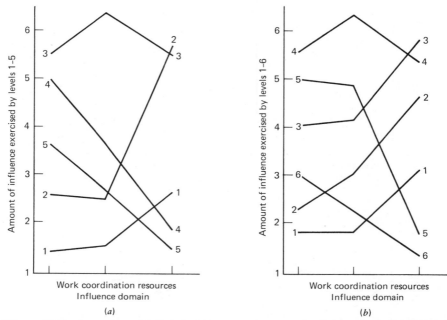

Figure 6-2   Amount of influence over work unit, by domain and by level, level 1 being the highest managerial level. (a) Engineering division 1; (b) engineering division 2.

controlled at the very top of the organization. In engineering division 2, which had one more hierarchical level than division 1, they are controlled mostly at the third level. In division 1, these activities are the responsibility of second-level personnel and their immediate subordinates.

Coordination and work influence are perceived by supervisors to peak at the third level in engineering division 1 and at the fourth level in engineering division 2. These domains, in effect, seem to be more decentralized than the resource domain. The data also suggest that work influence is perceived as more decentralized than coordination influence. Moreover, the rank ordering of perceived influence over different domains is a function of hierarchical position. Top executives are viewed as having greater influence over personnel resource-allocation than work influence. This ordering is reversed for individuals located lower in the hierarchy. They are perceived to have more influence over work than over coordination activities and more influence over coordination than over resource allocation.

Overall, these data demonstrate that both the average amount of influence and the configuration of influence appear to vary by organizational rank. There are striking differences between managers and other employees, as well as some potentially interesting differences among nonmanagers and across organizations. Furthermore, supervisors clearly perceive differences in the influence exercised by managers at different levels, indicating that different managerial positions may be characterized by distinct configurations of influence.

USING THE INFLUENCE MEASURES TO ASSESS CHANGE OVER TIME

To determine the extent to which the influence measures could be used to detect changes in the distribution of influence over time, they were applied twice over the course of a quality of work life experiment in a medium-sized food products factory. The two applications were separated by one year, during which a plant-wide program was initiated to increase employee involvement in decision making. A joint labor–management committee was established, and the committee met regularly to try to translate employee preferences into concrete recommendations. During the course of the experiment, production demands on the factory increased, efficiency declined, and management became increasingly resistant to implementing the committee's recommendations. Several committee members, for their part, felt constrained and frustrated by management's resistance. In addition, their fellow workers began to question the usefulness of the committee and management's support of employee participation in general. Accordingly, we did not expect perceptions of influence to increase during the one-year period. If anything, a decline in perceived influence was anticipated, since the experiment may have drawn attention to the relatively low levels of worker influence in the plant. It was thought that, since the experiment constrained managerial influence during the year, personal influence may have declined even among supervisors.

Measure Convergence and Discrimination

Three measures of work influence and three measures of coordination influence were used at both points in time. Since few meaningful resource-allocation decisions were made at the plant level, this dimension was not included in the study. Correlations of measures within each dimension at both time periods produced evidence of congruence. Correlations of measures across time and across dimensions provide evidence of discriminability. These correlations are presented in Table 6-7. Average within-category correlations are presented above the diagonal. These indicate greater within-construct, within-time association than is evidenced either within construct across time or across construct within time. The measures, therefore, exhibit both convergent and divergent validity.

Table 6-7 Convergence and Discrimination of Measures of Work and Coordination Influences across Influence Types and over Time (N = 289; time interval one year)

Reported Influence over Decisions about. . . .	(1)	(2)	(3)	(4)	(5)	(6)	(7)	(8)	(9)	(10)	(11)
Work Decisions (t₁)											
(1) . . . how you do your work			X̄ = .57					X̄ = .45			X̄ = .36
(2) . . . changing how you do your work	.58				X̄ = .51						
(3) . . . what you do day-to-day	.55	.59									
Coordinating decisions (t₁)											
(4) . . . how to settle disagreements among people in your work group	.42	.62	.54			X̄ = .61		X̄ = .38			
(5) . . . what to do when someone you depend on doesn't do their job	.43	.52	.55	.57						X̄ .45	
(6) . . . how work will be divided up among people	.37	.52	.64	.63	.62						
Work decisions (t₂)											
(7) . . . how you do your work	.57	.38	.41	.31	.29	.30			X̄ = .57	X̄ = .52	
(8) . . . changing how you do your work	.48	.49	.47	.47	.40	.44	.61				
(9) . . . what you do day-to-day	.37	.38	.53	.38	.41	.45	.52	.59			
Coordination decisions (t₂)											
(10) . . . how to settle disagreements among people in your work group	.37	.42	.37	.51	.39	.45	.54	.67	.52		X̄ = .54
(11) . . . what to do when someone you depend on doesn't do their job	.28	.29	.31	.33	.46	.36	.36	.49	.50	.52	
(12) . . . how work will be divided up among people	.37	.41	.40	.49	.43	.60	.42	.59	.58	.59	.52

Measuring Change over Time

Means and standard deviations for both types of influence measures are presented in Table 6-8. Separate statistics are presented for labor and management and for all employees versus those who were present and responded to the questionnaire at both times. Mean differences among the measures indicate a consistent decline in perceived work influence and in perceived coordination among union employees' over time. The average decline in work influence (.36 for all respondents and .15 for those responding at both time periods) was greater than the average decline in coordination influence (.16 for all respondents and .12 for those responding at both time periods). This decline was not consistently exhibited for managers. While the overall pattern suggests a decline, a slight increase is evidenced in three of the comparisons.

Influence scales were constructed for both coordination and work influence through a linear combination of those respective measures. Statisti-

Table 6-8 Means and Standard Deviations for Measures of Work and Coordination Influence for Union and Management Employees at Two Points in Time[a]

Employee's Perceived Influences over Decisions About. . . .	All Respondents				Those Responding at Both Time Periods			
	Union		Management		Union		Management	
	t_1	t_2	t_1	t_2	t_1	t_2	t_1	t_2
Work								
How you do your own work	3.23 (1.75)	2.97 (1.62)	4.88 (1.04)	4.63 (1.26)	3.11 (1.74)	3.04 (1.63)	4.83 (1.01)	4.77 (1.14)
Changing how you do your work	2.68 (1.66)	2.34 (1.44)	4.33 (1.46)	4.46 (1.44)	2.66 (1.71)	2.37 (1.46)	4.33 (1.30)	4.53 (1.38)
What to do day-to-day	(2.20) (1.66)	2.02 (1.54)	4.52 (1.53)	4.25 (1.59)	2.14 (1.64)	2.04 (1.57)	4.17 (1.53)	4.26 (1.57)
Coordination								
How to settle disagreements among people in your work group	(2.46) (1.62)	2.26 (1.51)	4.58 (1.57)	4.62 (1.67)	2.44 (1.65)	2.40 (1.58)	4.73 (1.31)	4.59 (1.72)
What to do if someone you depend on doesn't do their job	2.37 (1.65)	2.18 (1.48)	4.57 (1.53)	4.17 (1.64)	2.37 (1.67)	2.22 (1.51)	4.90 (1.26)	4.13 (1.66)
How work will be divided up among people	1.84 (1.53)	1.74 (1.36)	4.46 (1.77)	4.31 (1.76)	1.88 (1.57)	1.72 (1.35)	4.57 (1.70)	4.33 (1.71)
N (min)	425	448	47	34	276	276	29	29

[a] Figures in parentheses are standard deviations

cal tests comparing scale scores across time provided some evidence that union employees who responded to both questionnaires perceived, as expected, less work influence at time 2 than at time 1 ($p = .05$, one-tailed test). There was no corresponding difference for coordination influence. Supervisors who took the questionnaire at both times registered no statistically significant difference in either influence type over time.

DISCUSSION

In general, the data presented suggest that the subsystem approach to the measurement of influence is feasible and potentially useful. Measures of influence in work, coordination, and personnel-resource domains demonstrate at least some degree of convergent and discriminant validity in both interviews and questionnaires. Measurement discrimination, however, is greater between certain domains than between others, and domains appear to be more distinctively differentiated in some organizations than in others. There also is greater discrimination in some organizations than in others. In addition, there is greater discrimination of domains when the influence of middle-level personnel is considered than when that of either higher- or lower-level personnel is investigated.

Despite sometimes marginal discrimination through covariance techniques, there appear to be differences in both the level and configuration of influence associated with different organizational positions. This finding indicates that people in organizations distinguish influence in one domain from influence in another, and apparently they do not see the influence measures as different reflections of the same basic phenomenon. Measuring influence in terms of the different domains therefore can provide additional information about the way people perceive influence. The utility of this additional information, however, may depend on the type of research being conducted. On the one hand, this information may be very useful when absolute influence levels (e.g., mean scores) are of primary concern. Researchers conducting covariance analysis, on the other hand, could employ measures of work and coordination influence more interchangeably, since they often are highly correlated despite showing significant mean differences.

Assuming that the subsystem approach is basically viable, there remain a number of important questions concerning the measurement of influence in multiple domains. The first concerns the domains that should be measured. The three domains considered in the present study were identified on the basis of one particular theoretical approach to the problem. Other researchers[14,21,22] have distinguished other subsystems that might be useful as well. Considerable work is needed to identify the most appropriate methods of distinguishing among domains and the conditions that moderate the utility of different methods.

Second, while this research suggests that the influence measures in each domain are not different operational measures of the same phenomenon, it is still likely that a single, general-influence measure may be, at least for certain purposes, appropriate. This would be the case, for example, if one unit of work influence was found to be equal to one unit of resource influence in terms of giving organizational members the perception of being "influential in general." If this was true, the subsystem approach would not necessarily be superior to the global approach in its ability to understand and predict responses and attitudes that are a function of global perceptions of influence. One alternative hypothesis is that the configuration of influence that is most appropriate (and thus produces the greatest feeling of being influential) may vary by position or task, and that global measures are therefore inappropriate. This question needs to be explored in more detail before the value of single-influence measures can be properly assessed.

Third, our analyses do not fully explore the experienced influence levels and influence configurations associated with different managerial positions. Although the interview results make it clear that union supervisors perceive differences across managerial positions, their data do not represent the influence actually experienced by managers at the various levels. More detailed research is needed to determine whether different types of managerial positions are, in fact, characterized by different influence profiles.

A related question concerns the influence of organization members at the top of the hierarchy. Data provided by the supervisors in the engineering divisions indicate that the managers at the top are not necessarily seen to be those with the greatest amounts of resource allocation and coordination influence. Unless these top managers really do have very limited influence, they must exercise control over other unmeasured domains. For example, their influence may be institutional—pertaining to the overall goals and policies of the organization in the context of the larger social system.[14,23] Similarly, they may occupy boundary-spanning roles and exercise control over the organization's relations with other groups and organizations.[12,16] Alternatively, their influence may be integrative; that is, these top managers may be responsible for articulating decisions made in the coordination and resource-allocation domains.[24]

A final issue pertains to the methods that are most appropriate for measuring influence in different domains or subsystems. Though survey techniques are used in most studies, it is possible that other methods (such as observational techniques) may be more useful in certain situations. Even if it is assumed that interviews and questionnaires represent the best approach to the measurement of influence, questions remain about the wording of the survey items. The questionnaires presented in Appendixes 6-1 and 6-2 measure work influence by asking respondents to report on their influence over their "own work." However, managers may see their own day-to-day work as including coordination and resource-allocation activities. It is possible that these activities would be less dominant in their responses if the question focused on "the work of the organization"; if this was the case, a higher level of divergence among the constructs might be achieved.

Implications for Assessing Organizational Change

Data obtained at the food-products firm suggest that work and coordination can be distinguished and that their respective measures can detect different patterns of variation over time. If, as the early analyses indicated, influence over these domains and resource-allocation decisions is distributed differently among organizational members, measures of each of the domains will allow researchers to address a number of issues that are important for the assessment of change. For example, as has often been noted by those who have conducted research on the topic, influence may be fixed or variable in amount. There may be only so much influence to "go around," or influence may be more like an "expanding pie." In this case, increasing influence for one type of employee may not imply decreasing influence for others.

The correlations in Tables 6-5 and 6-6 suggest that the total amount of influence may be fixed in some cases and expandable in others. Influence over work and coordination activities by top-level managers, for example, does not appear to preclude influence over these activities by other personnel (which indicates a possible expansion). The amount of work influence exercised by top managers, for example, is relatively independent of the amount of work influence exercised by bottom-level employees ($r = .11$ in division 1 and $r = .03$ in division 2). The correlations between the exercising of coordination influence by top-level personnel and the exercise of coordination influence by bottom-level personnel are $r = -.02$ (division 1) and $r = .16$ (division 2). However, influence by middle-level managers in these domains appears to be associated with reduced influence on the part of lower-level employees, which indicates that influence is fixed at these levels. The correlations for work influence exercised by middle-level managers and fifth-level employees are $r = -.45$ (division 1) and $r = -.35$ (division 2). The corresponding correlations for coordination influence are $r = -.30$ (division 1) and $r = -.32$ (division 2). Similarly, top-level influence over the allocation of personnel resources may reduce the influence of lower-level members, while influence of this type on the part of middle managers appears to be associated with greater influence by lower-level employees.

These results suggest that total control, as defined by Tannenbaum, may be expanded by allocating influence over different domains to different groups in the organization. Change attempts that result in greater middle-level control over work or coordination decisions may lead to lessened work or coordination influence perceived by lower-level employees. Likewise, change that gives middle-level managers greater control over resources might lead to greater influence perceived by lower-level employees. By discriminating among domains and among levels, assessors may be able more precisely to identify tensions and tradeoffs that characterize the decision-making process and thereby more finely pinpoint the impact of change programs.

A second issue relevant to the assessment of change concerns influence configurations and the extent to which different types of influence are important for organization members in different positions. Resource influence possibly is more central for upper-level managers, coordination influence for personnel at the middle levels, and work influence for members at the lower levels. It also is possible that the importance of influence over the different domains may depend on the levels of uncertainty, interdependence, and skill associated with the particular job or position. If the centrality of different influence domains does vary by job level and job characteristics, then different influence configurations could produce variations in individual satisfaction and performance as well as in organizational effectiveness.[24,25] Distinguishing among influence domains therefore could be important for assessing changes directed toward the employees' quality of work life as well as toward their levels of performance.

Finally, the data in Tables 6-4 and 6-5 raise another interesting issue for change evaluation. The finding that some domains of influence seem to be more fixed than others suggests that the political dynamics and pressures surrounding decisions in these domains may be quite different and further, that the processes might be different at different levels. For example, the correlations of influence over work and coordination by middle-level managers (level 3 in Table 6-4; level 4 in Table 6-5) with the work and coordination influence exercised by bottom-level personnel are negative $(-.45, -.12, -.30, -.02)$, while the corresponding correlations for influence over personnel resources allocation are positive $(.50, .33)$. This suggests that middle-level managers, at least in the organizations studied here, either centralize or decentralize decision making in areas related to work, but use participative styles for making personnel decisions when they have discretion over this domain. The dynamics underlying these processes and their implications for organizational change are interesting areas that call for further research. It may be, for example, that changes in the area of resource distribution will have different but still systematic consequences, as compared with changes in the area of work assignment or coordination and control.

In general, the subsystem perspective leads to a series of research questions about the dynamics of influence that could have important implications for understanding the elaboration of structure within organizations and the implications of this elaboration for both the process and the outcomes of planned change. If systematically applied across a broad variety of change attempts, the subsystem perspective and its associated measures may give us considerable information on the antecedents and consequences of different change strategies. They also may offer insight into the conditions that are conducive to successful change efforts and that, therefore, suggest adoption of one or another of several alternative approaches.

REFERENCES

1. Azumi, K., & McMillan, C. *Subjective and objective measures of organization structure: A preliminary analysis.* Paper presented at the annual meetings of the American Sociological Association, New York, 1973.

2. Dewar, R., Whetten, D., & Boje, D. *On the measurement of structural variables: An examination of the Hall-Hage and Aiken studies.* Unpublished manuscript. Northwestern University, Evanston, IL.

3. Pennings, J. M. Measures of organizational structure: A methodological note. *American Journal of Sociology,* 1973, **79,** 686–704.

4. Hage, J., & Aiken, M. Relationship of centralization to other structural properties. *Administrative Science Quarterly,* 1967, **12,** 72–92.

5. Pugh, D. S., Hickson, D. J., & Turner, C. Dimensions of organization structure. *Administrative Science Quarterly,* 1968, **13,** 65–105.

6. Lawrence, P., & Lorsch, J. *Organization and environment.* Cambridge: Graduate School of Business Administration, Harvard University, 1967.

7. Duncan, R. B. *The effects of perceived environmental uncertainty on organizational decision unit structure: A cybernetic model.* Unpublished doctoral dissertation, Yale University, 1971.

8. Bacharach, S., & Aiken, M. Structural and process constraints on influence in organizations. *Administrative Science Quarterly,* 1976, **21,** 623–642.

9. Tannenbaum, A. S. (Ed.). *Control in organizations.* New York: Wiley, 1968.

10. Tannenbaum, A. S., & Cooke, R. A. Control and participation. *Journal of Contemporary Business,* Autumn 1974, 35–46.

11. March, J. D., & Simon, H. *Organizations.* New York: Wiley, 1958.

12. Thompson, J. *Organizations in action.* New York: McGraw-Hill, 1968.

13. Georgopoulos, B. S. The hospital as an organization and problem solving system. In B. S. Georgopoulos (Ed.), *Organization research on health institutions.* Ann Arbor: Institute for Social Research, 1972.

14. Parsons, T. *Structure and process in modern society.* Glencoe, IL: Free Press, 1960.

15. Becker, S., & Gordon, C. An entrepreneurial theory of formal organizations. *Administrative Science Quarterly,* 1966, **2,** 315–344.

16. Katz, D., & Kahn, R. L. *The social psychology of organizations,* 2nd ed. New York: Wiley, 1978.

17. Parsons, T. Suggestion for a sociological approach to the theory of organizations. *Administrative Science Quarterly,* 1955, **1,** 63–85.

18. Alwin, D. An analytic comparison of four approaches to the interpretation of relationships in the multi-trait multi-method matrix. In H. Costner (Ed.), *Sociological methodology, 1973–74.* San Francisco: Jossey-Bass, 1974.

19. Joreskog, K., Gruvaeus, G., and Thillo, M. van. *ANOVA: A general computer program for analysis of covariance structures.* Princeton: Educational Testing Service, 1979. (Mimeographed)

20. Kalleberg, A. L., & Kluegel, J. R. Analysis of the multitrait–multimethod matrix: Some limitations and an alternative. *Journal of Applied Psychology,* 1975, **60**, 1–9.

21. Anthony, R. M. Framework for analysis. *Management Sciences,* 1964, **1**, 18–24.

22. Rossmeier, J. G. *An exploratory study of relationships between control and authority patterns and organizational responsiveness in urban multiunit community college systems.* Unpublished doctoral dissertation, University of Michigan, 1973.

23. Thompson, J. D., & McEwen, A. Organizational goals and environment: Goal-setting as an interaction process. *American Sociological Review,* 1958, **23**, 23–31.

24. Mohrman, A., Cooke, R. A., & Mohrman, S. Participation in decision-making: A multidimensional perspective. *Educational Administration Quarterly,* 1978, **14**(1).

25. Feather, J. S., & Moch, M. K. *Interdependence, influence, and employee responses in work organizations.* Paper presented at the annual meeting of the American Sociological Association, New York, 1976.

APPENDIX 6-1 QUESTIONNAIRE ITEMS FOR ASSESSING INFLUENCE OVER WORK, COORDINATION, AND PERSONNEL RESOURCE-ALLOCATION ACTIVITIES

13. Here is a list of decisions that get made at work. For each of the following decisions, please indicate how much say you actually have in making these decisions.

Influence over work activities

		No say at all	Some say		A good deal of say		A very great deal of say
a.	Decisions about how you do your own work	[1]	[2]	[3]	[4]	[5]	[6]	[7]
b.	Decisions about changing how you do your work	[1]	[2]	[3]	[4]	[5]	[6]	[7]
c.	Decisions about how work related problems are solved	[1]	[2]	[3]	[4]	[5]	[6]	[7]
d.	Decisions about what you do day to day	[1]	[2]	[3]	[4]	[5]	[6]	[7]

Influence over personnel resource-allocation activities:

a.	Decisions about hiring people	[1]	[2]	[3]	[4]	[5]	[6]	[7]

	No say at all		Some say		A good deal of say	A very great deal of say

b. Decisions about pay raises   [1]   [2]   [3]   [4]   [5]   [6]   [7]

c. Decisions about promoting people   [1]   [2]   [3]   [4]   [5]   [6]   [7]

d. Decisions about firing people   [1]   [2]   [3]   [4]   [5]   [6]   [7]

Influence over coordination activities:

a. Decisions about how to settle disagreements between people in your work group   [1]   [2]   [3]   [4]   [5]   [6]   [7]

b. Decisions about what to do when someone you depend on does not do his or her job   [1]   [2]   [3]   [4]   [5]   [6]   [7]

c. Decisions about how work gets divided up among people   [1]   [2]   [3]   [4]   [5]   [6]   [7]

APPENDIX 6-2   INTERVIEW QUESTIONS FOR ASSESSING INFLUENCE OVER WORK, COORDINATION, AND PERSONNEL RESOURCE-ALLOCATION ACTIVITIES BY HIERARCHICAL LEVEL

"Now, I'd like to talk with you about various decisions that get made in (respondent's organizational unit). Depending upon what is being decided, some people have influence and others do not. I want you to rate how much direct influence each of several kinds of staff people have over each of several kinds of decisions. This card shows how you can answer—just call out the number."

Interviewer hands respondent a card bearing a response scale ranging from 1 (very little influence) to 7 (a great deal of influence), 8 (don't know) and 9 (inapplicable).

"For example, decisions about changing how people in your unit do their work. How much influence is had by

a. *The division director and his/her immediate assistants?*
b. *The branch chief and/or his/her assistant?*
c. *The group head?*
d. *The section supervisor?*
e. *The SD3's and SD4's?*
f. *The SD1's and SD2's?"*

The units a through f are hierarchical levels in the organization with names and number of levels adapted to the particular organization. After obtaining six responses (in this illustrated case), the interviewer covers in succession the remaining kinds of decisions:

Decisions about *how* work-related problems are solved in (your unit)

Decisions about what people in (your unit) do day to day

Decisions about what should be done when people in (your unit) don't get what they need to do their work

Decisions about *how* work will be divided up among the people in (your unit)

Decisions about what to do when someone in (this unit) isn't doing his/her job

Decisions about hiring new people for (your unit)

Decisions about pay raises for personnel in (your unit)

Decisions about firing people in (your unit)

Decisions about who to promote in (your unit)

CHAPTER SEVEN

Conceptualizing and Measuring the Relational Structure in Organizations

MICHAEL MOCH, JOHN N. FEATHER, AND DALE FITZGIBBONS

Many measures of organizational structure, such as formalization, standardization, centralization, span of control, and administrative ratio, have been derived from principles of scientific management[1] and Weberian sociology.[2] They are concerned with the organizational level of analysis and are not intended to facilitate understanding of individuals and individual responses at work or planned organizational change. Nevertheless, they often have been used to do just that.[3,4] Reviews of research relating these structural attributes of organizations to individual responses consistently have lamented the lack of explanation for *why* associations are observed.[5-7] Unfortunately, there is little detailed theory explaining how and why attributes of structure should be related to variables at the individual level and why structure change might have consequences for individuals.

Weber viewed organizational structure as a function of broad-based historical trends. Taylor was concerned almost exclusively with the effect of structure on organizational effectiveness and efficiency. It is small wonder, therefore, that the structural dimensions upon which they focused have only tenuous theoretical ties to individual attitudes and behavior and to assessing the effects of planned change. One goal of the present volume is to present measures that will allow researchers to

The authors received valuable assistance from Jean Bartunek, Cortlandt Cammann, Sandy and Tom Leung, and Barry A. Macy.

assess the effects of planned change. A second goal is to present measures that will allow researchers to assess the impact of organizational change programs on individuals' effectiveness and on the quality of work life. In order to accomplish this, a theoretical reconceptualization of organization structure, one which incorporates—but goes significantly beyond—the traditional set of variables is needed as is a corresponding set of measurement operations.

STRUCTURE AS A RELATIONAL CONCEPT

What seems to be missing in the literature relating structure to individual responses is a middle level of analysis that can bridge the theoretical gap between individuals and organizations and between the global characteristics of organizations and measures of individual attitudes and behavior. Lazarsfeld and Menzel have appropriately labeled variables that span this gulf as "structural."[8] They are characteristics of *relationships* among elements of a larger social system.

There is much sociological literature to support structure as being relational at root. Many authors consider social structure to consist of *relationships* among elements.[9-13] Mullins recently has argued that those who focus their attention primarily upon networks of relationships among elements are beginning to constitute a distinct school of sociological thought.[14] Relational analyses also have been proliferating in social anthropology,[15-17] and they have a long tradition in social psychology.[18-25] Even early studies of formal organizations considered relationships to be central to understanding behavior at work.[26-34] With a few exceptions, however, recent studies of formal organizations have ignored relational variables.[35-43]

The essential distinction between more traditional structural variables and relational structure variables is that the former are measured by assessing attributes of elements, while the later are measured by assessing attributes of relationships among elements. In the case of the traditional structure, elements are arrayed at points in space defined by their individual characteristics. In the case of the relational structure, elements are arrayed at points in space defined by their relationships to the other elements in the space. The position of any element in relational structure, however, is a direct function of the positions of every other element.

It is not always easy to make a clear distinction between traditional and relational variables, especially at the conceptual level. The distinction, however, usually becomes clear at the operational level. For example, Emerson has argued that influence is a characteristic of relationships.[44] Yet it generally is operationalized as a characteristic of individuals.[45,46] A relational measure would assess the *relative* influence or centrality of elements in a network of influence relations.

A second potential source of confusion between traditional and relational variables involves a possible difference between the level of analysis and the unit of observation. For example, the percentage of those with whom one communicates in a group is a relational variable to the extent that communication scores are a function of interactions initiated by both parties. Here the unit of observation is the individual. Aggregating to the group level of analysis, however, the average or the total proportion of communication links would be a measure of interaction or communication density.[47] This would, by our definition, be a traditional variable, since it would be a characteristic of an element rather than of a relationship. Aggregated relational variables, therefore, are likely to be traditional variables at a higher level of analysis. If such variables then are disaggregated—individuals within groups are given group-level scores— they would revert to being relational variables, since the data upon which they were originally based were relational rather than traditional.

Several of the distinctions made so far are considered simultaneously in Figure 7-1. Relational and traditional concepts have been applied to help understand individual, group, and organizational behavior. It is not always the case, however, that studies concerned with either of these aspects of organizations use measures in which the unit of observation corresponds to the level of analysis. Some studies take individuals as the units of observation and aggregate individual responses to the group or organizational level for analysis.[48] Almost all of these, however, involve traditional structural variables. Studies of relationships among individuals in organizations as they affect individual, group, and organizational behaviors are in short supply. Recently, Tichy, Tushman, and Fombrun have attempted to develop several measures of relational variables.[49] We

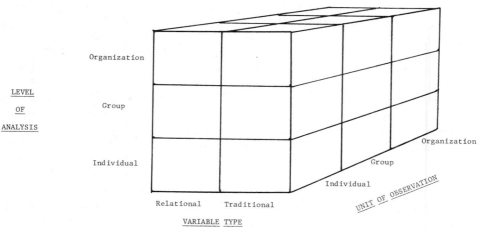

LEVEL OF ANALYSIS

Organization

Group

Individual

Relational   Traditional

VARIABLE TYPE

Organization

Group

Individual

UNIT OF OBSERVATION

Figure 7-1

believe the development of such measures is a necessary first step toward integrating individual and organizational levels of analysis.

MEASURES OF THE RELATIONAL STRUCTURE

Several variables, often overlooked, locate individuals with respect to one another. They include whether one is an isolate, a member of a distinct cluster, a liaison among clusters, or a member who has some links outside the cluster, and so on. Variables such as these were first identified by Moreno, and they have an extensive history in the social-psychology literature.[24,50]

Social anthropologists have been moving away from these simpler but perhaps less generalizable concepts.[15] Barnes, for example, argues that network analysis begins only when the researcher goes beyond simply counting links.[47] In their search for "morphological" characteristics of networks, these researchers tend to employ individuals as the unit of observation and analysis, and their measures are "ego centered."[15,17] For example, the relative centrality of individuals in a communications network (e.g., the number of links exhibited by an individual divided by the number of possible links) is ego centered. Other ego-centered measures include such things as integrativeness, reach, range, compatibility, and choice-rejection status.[51-53]

Simple nominal assignments of individuals to positions in social networks (e.g., isolate, group member, liaison, boundary spanner, and the like) and ordinal or interval measures of individuals' relationships (e.g., centrality, integrativeness, and the like) assume that structure is unitary. However, as Mears, Cherry, and others have pointed out, there are multiple structures that can be overlaid to describe the complex or polythetic nature of social relations.[54-57] Guetzkow has identified five such structures—conceptually independent networks—composed of authority relations, relations characterized by information exchange, or the exchange of expertise, friendship, and status.[58] There may be as many nominal, ordinal, or interval measures of ego positions, therefore, as there are distinct social networks. Also, those who are central to an authority network may be isolates in a friendship network. Those with low degrees of integration into a friendship net may have a high degree of integration into the communication or interaction networks. One's position in one network, therefore, may not correspond to one's position in another. Moreover, the degree of correspondence or lack of correspondence may vary, depending on the measures used as well as on the networks compared.

This complex array of dimensions and networks presents the researcher with a bewildering array of measurement possibilities. We have dealt with this by choosing to develop and test only a few concepts and a limited number of networks. To date, measures of individual location (isolate, group member, liaison), whether an individual is or is not a boundary spanner across groups, and individual integrativeness, mutuality, range, reach, and centrality have been developed and tested for each of three types of networks. The networks selected involve friendship, interaction, and work-groups links. In addition, measures of relative centrality in the network of work-flow interdependencies have been developed and tested. In this case, however, the measures are not ego centered. They are based upon interdependencies among work groups but could easily be applied using individuals as the units of observation.

FRIENDSHIP AND INTERACTION RELATIONS—NOMINAL MEASURES OF POSITION IN NETWORKS OF WORK

Methods for identifying individuals' positions in networks of social relations have been limited by data-processing constraints associated with mapping links among a large number of individuals. With the development of electronic data processing, choice matrices can be efficiently manipulated, and recent developments have made such analyses practical and even convenient.[28,51,59-66] These approaches, however, have not solved the problem of identifying discrete clusters of elements. Early approaches required that all possible intragroup choices be made as a criterion of clique identification.[67] Luce relaxed this criterion, but the problem has continued to hamper sociometric research.[68] Richards classifies an element as a group member if at least half of the links established are within-group choices.[51] In addition, no group can fail to have each member connected to every other member by a path lying completely within the group, and there can be no single path or element that, if eliminated, would cause the group to fail to meet any of the other criteria.

In Richards' approach, isolates are elements with one or fewer connections or with connections only to elements that have only this link. Liaisons have at least 50% of their choices with group members, but they cannot have 50% or more of their choices to be with members of the same group. Richards' criteria for cluster identification, while somewhat arbitrary, are quite conservative. His approach also is appealing to those with primary interest in formal organizations because his software can process more than 4000 elements simultaneously. The Richards' algorithm therefore was adopted to provide at least a first approximation to assessing relational structure in organizations.*

The data upon which this initial assessment is based consist of lists of individuals with whom each employee works, interacts, and whom each employee considers to be his/her friend. These were obtained from 522

---

* We are indebted to Richard Farace and Timothy Mabee for their assistance in making Richards' software available.

employees in a southern assembly and packaging plant. In this organization, many employees had relatives also working in the plant. Data on family ties, therefore, were also obtained and processed using Richards' technique. The specific questions used to obtain these data are presented in Appendix 7-1. Richards' procedure allows the researcher to include intensity weightings for each relationship. Time and space limitations precluded our securing these from respondents. Instead, they were inferred from the ordering of the names on the list. This procedure resulted in a more differentiated structure—more clustering and cluster members—than was the case when equal weights were applied.

The organization studied assembles and packages nondurable goods. It is divided into several departments: assembly, packaging, supplies, sanitation, maintenance, and office. These departments are located at different places in the plant, so little clustering across departments was expected.

The results of the sociometric analyses for work, friendship, and interaction relations are presented in Figures 7-2, 7-3, and 7-4. Departments

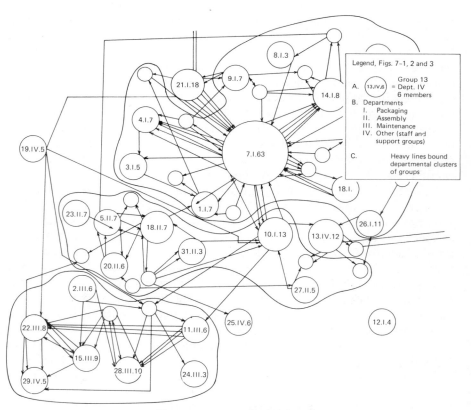

Figure 7-2 Work groups.

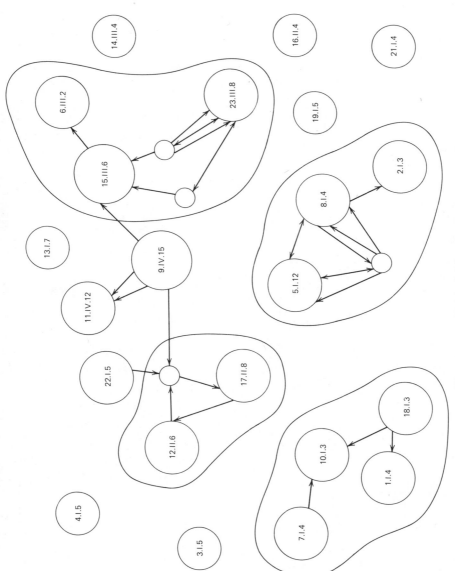

Figure 7-3 Friendship groups.

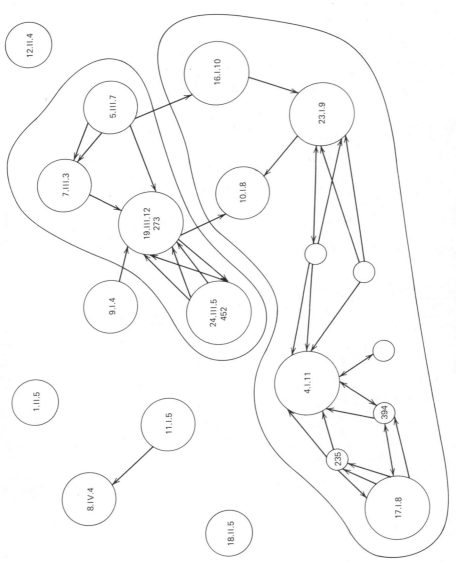

Figure 7-4 Interaction groups.

are distinguished in these figures. Each circle in the figures represents a cluster; connections between groups are made through intervening liaisons or boundary spanners. Individuals 235 and 394 in Figure 7-4, for example, are liaison persons connecting clusters 4 and 17 in the packaging department. Individuals 452 and 273 are boundary spanners linking groups 24 and 19 in the maintenance department. Individual group members who are isolates or who are neither liaisons nor boundary spanners are not shown in the diagram. Of 522 employees responding to the questionnaire, there were 248 members of work groups, 54 work-group isolates, 18 liaisons, and 75 others. One hundred and four employees were associated with distinct friendship clusters. There were 28 friendship isolates, 4 liaisons, and 215 others. The interaction network was somewhat less finely differentiated. Here, there were 80 group members, 4 liaisons, 12 isolates, and 297 others.

Identification of family ties revealed that over 35% of the employees had at least one relative working in the plant. The family-network diagram, however, identified only two family clusters. It also showed many nonmembers who were linked to a cluster through only one or two others. It was as though there were many second cousins but few nuclear families. Yet such loose ties may be extremely important; like a letter from an infrequent correspondent, they may carry much information that otherwise would not be available.[69] Accordingly, after Luce and Perry, a family cluster was defined as a set of three or more completely linked elements.[67] By this definition, there were 13 family clusters in the plant. However, these clusters had connections with individuals who did not choose and/or were not chosen by all members of the cluster. Accordingly, after Luce, individuals were allowed to enter a cluster as long as they were connected to it by a series of N steps.[68] A method was devised to allow the researcher to choose the value of N up to a maximum of 5. This method provides the flexibility required to assign individuals to groups under both strong and weak assumptions.

FRIENDSHIP AND INTERACTION RELATIONS—MEASURES OF INDIVIDUALS' POSITIONS WITHIN CLUSTERS OF WORK

Measures of several of the relational concepts mentioned previously were developed and applied to each of the three types of networks in the assembly and packaging plant. These concepts refer to individuals' relationships with others within and between groups. With the exception of integrativeness, they apply only to employees who are members of distinct groups. These concepts and their respective measures are as follows:

Centrality. The number of links an individual has (incoming or outgoing) divided by the number of possible links in the group.

Integrativeness. The number of links among those with whom an individual is directly connected divided by the number of such possible links.

Mutuality. The number of reciprocated choices for group members.

Incoming Range. The number individuals choosing ego.

Outgoing Range. The number of individuals chosen by ego.

Reach. The average number of steps ego must traverse to reach the other members of her/his group.

Boundary Spanning. A dichotomous variable reflecting whether or not the individual is linked to a member of another group (1 = no; 2 = yes).

Separate correlation matrices were generated for each network type to assess the degree to which the measures discriminate. They are presented in Tables 7-1, 7-2, and 7-3. These tables indicate that only measures of reach and centrality fail to discriminate among individuals. The more central an individual, the smaller his or her range for each of the three networks. The magnitude of these correlations suggests that these measures should be combined to form an overall centrality scale.

Other correlations in Tables 7-1, 7-2, and 7-3 are not so high as to preclude discrimination, and several patterns lend a measure of support about construct validity. In all three networks, individuals with greater incoming range are likely to have lessened outgoing range. Those who are listed by many others, themselves tend to list relatively few people. Those with greater outgoing range also tend to be less integrated. Those with whom they have direct links are themselves less densely connected. Those who have more outgoing links also are more likely to be boundary spanners and to have links to members of other groups. Boundary-span-

Table 7-1 Correlations among Measures of Individual Position in Interaction Groups ($N = 80$)

		1	2	3	4	5	6
1.	Centrality						
2.	Reach	−.73*					
3.	Integrativeness	.11	.09				
4.	Boundary-spanners	.11	−.11	−.21*			
5.	Mutuality	.00	−.16	−.12	.07		
6.	Range-incoming	−.17	.24*	−.09	.03	−.21*	
7.	Range-outgoing	−.03	−.24*	−.37*	.23*	.27*	−.36*

* $p \leq .05$

Table 7-2   Correlations among Measures of Individual Position in Work Groups (*N* = 248)

	1	2	3	4	5	6
1. Centrality						
2. Reach	−.83*					
3. Integrativeness	.29*	−.17*				
4. Boundary-spanners	−.01	−.10	−.33*			
5. Mutuality	.20*	−.25*	.30*	−.03		
6. Range-incoming	−.18*	.06	.02	.33*	−.09	
7. Range-outgoing	−.10	.09	−.27*	.32*	.13	−.31*

* *p* ≤ .05

ning links are associated with incoming ties only in the work-group network. Boundary spanners also are less well integrated than are non-boundary spanners in all three networks. Employees with more incoming links in the interaction and friendship networks tend to have fewer mutual or reciprocated links. In the interaction network, outgoing range is positively associated with the number of mutual links.

There are other patterns in the data. Reach is positively correlated with incoming range and negatively associated with outgoing range for the friendship and interaction networks. Incoming links appear to come from those who are further removed from ego. In the work-group and friendship networks, reach is negatively associated with the number of mutual links. In the work-group network, centrality is positively associated with the number of mutual links. Individuals who are central to work groups are more likely to have their choices reciprocated.

Table 7-3   Correlations among Measures of Individual Position in Friendship Groups (*N* = 104)

	1	2	3	4	5	6
1. Centrality						
2. Reach	−.75*					
3. Integrativeness	.21*	−.22*				
4. Boundary-spanners	−.02	.00	−.18*			
5. Mutuality	.00	−.19	.09	.09		
6. Ranging-incoming	−.08	.10	.08	.07	−.29*	
7. Range-outgoing	−.09	−.23*	−.28*	.22*	.11	−.31*

* *p* ≤ .05

These patterns of relationships lend themselves to several interpretations. The relationships between centrality and reach is understandable, since those who have direct links to a higher proportion of others in their groups can be expected to be able to reach group members in fewer steps. It is also understandable that boundary spanners are less integrated; those with whom they are directly linked often are in different groups and therefore are less likely to be connected themselves. People who choose many others select among people who are themselves relatively loosely connected. Finally, reach and centrality identify focal individuals; it should not be surprising that the choices these people make are more likely to be reciprocated than are those of their less-central counterparts.

WORK-FLOW INTERDEPENDENCIES— MEASURES OF WORK-GROUP POSITION IN THE NETWORK

Interdependence is one of the most common denominators of formal organizations. Yet there have been few concerted attempts to develop interdependence measures. Van de Ven and colleagues, after Thompson, measured the extent to which work units could be characterized by sequential, reciprocal, and team interdependence.[70,71] There is no assurance, however, that these adequately reflect the variety of work-flow interdependencies. An approach was sought, therefore, that allows for the possibility of many forms of interdependence as well as one that would have direct application at the individual as well as the work-unit level.

The measures of work-flow interdependence were developed using data from two divisions of a large public utility. Interviews were held with the supervisors of 51 work units, and employees within each of these groups completed a detailed questionnaire. The supervisors were asked to rate the intensity of their interdependencies with every other branch in the division. Separate ratings were obtained for the extent to which the focal unit depended upon every other unit and branch, and for the extent to which every other unit and branch depended upon the focal unit (see Appendix 7-2). The ratings were taken on a 7-point Likert-type scale.

Interdependence links were considered significant when both respondents from linked work units were in agreement and when at least moderate levels of intensity (three or greater) were reported. Once these links had been established, work-flow diagrams were drawn and intensity scores attached to each link. These scores were calculated by averaging the intensity ratings provided by both supervisors from the linked units.

An example of one diagram for intrabranch interdependence relations is presented in Figure 7-5. Space limitations preclude presentation of the diagrams for interdependencies within other units and between work units and divisions other than their own.

The interdependence networks, such as the one displayed in Figure 7-5, were validated through comparisons with qualitative data supplied by directors, division chiefs, senior engineers, and unit supervisors. While qualitative descriptions exist of the work-flow activities that underlie each of the links in Figure 7-5, it is not possible to summarize them here. Suffice it to say that with few exceptions, the work-flow interdependence diagrams mirror descriptions of the work flow obtained from other sources.

Measures of work-flow centrality for each work unit were generated by scoring units for (1) the number of incoming and outgoing links divided by the number of possible links and (2) the average intensity of incoming and outgoing links. These measures were calculated for intradivision and for interdivision interdependencies. Intercorrelations among these measures are presented in Table 7-4.

The correlations in Table 7-4 indicate that measures of intradivision work-flow centrality and measures of interdivision work-flow centrality

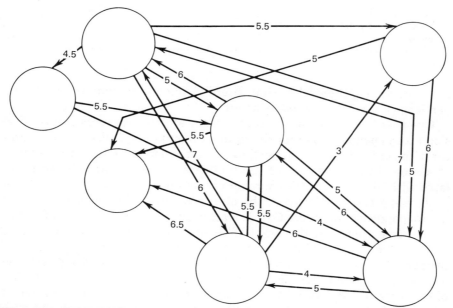

Figure 7-5 **Example of a network diagram for intrabranch interdependencies.**

Table 7-4   Correlations Among Measures of Work Flow Interdependence

Measure	1	2	3	4	5	6	7
Intradivision Interdependence							
1. Number of other units dependent upon focal unit/number of sections in branch −1.							
2. Number of other units depended on by focal unit/number of sections in branch −1.	.61						
3. Average intensity of links representing other units' dependence on focal unit.	.49	.32					
4. Average intensity of links representing focal unit's dependence on other units.	.37	.58	.55				
Interdivision Interdependence							
5. Number of other divisions dependent on focal unit/number of other divisions −1.	.33	.18	.12	.16			
6. Number of other divisions depended on by focal unit/number of other divisions −1.	.17	.22	.00	.28	.72		
7. Average intensity of links representing other division's dependence on focal unit.	.08	.21	.03	.18	.48	.53	
8. Average intensity of links representing focal unit's dependence on other divisions.	.12	.22	.13	.28	.37	.55	.72

converge among themselves, but interdivision and intradivision interdependence are relatively independent.

One possible reason for the convergence among measures of intradivision interdependence is that the number of outgoing links and the number of incoming links are divided by the same denominator—the number of sections in the division −1. Both of these measures are highly correlated with division size (the number of sections in the division, −.59 and −.50, respectively). However, the observed correlation between the two interdependence measures (.61) is significantly greater than what would be expected solely on the basis of their common association with size (−.59 × −.50 = .30). The same holds for the corresponding measures of interdivision interdependence, which are associated with group size (the number of divisions in the groups, $r = -.30$ and $-.37$, respectively). Moreover, the average intensity scores are not artifactually associated with size. Yet they are significantly associated with each other and with the number of incoming and outgoing links.

The groups of the public utility under study design complex buildings—power generators, substations, and conveyances. A specification set by one unit must be adjusted to fit specifications made by other units and vice versa. Units that are depended upon by other units can be expected to be dependent in return. Table 7-4 indicates that this is so for units that are central to the work flow within their own branches and for units that have links across divisions. Moreover, those units that have a high frequency of interdependence links also tend to have links of higher average intensity. This holds true for both intradivision and interdivision links.

The extent to which units are central to the work flow in or across divisions is likely to affect managers' perceptions of the extent to which they themselves are dependent upon and/or are depended upon by people outside their own units. Such an association would constitute criterion validity for the measures of unit interdependence. To test for this association, an index of unit work-flow centrality was constructed by multiplying the number of incoming and outgoing links by their respective average intensities and then multiplying the resulting products. This index assesses the extent to which each unit is simultaneously dependent upon and is depended upon by other units.

Separate indices were constructed for intradivision and interdivision relationships. Analogous indexes were constructed from questionnaire responses provided by managers (unit supervisors, assistant supervisors, and squad leaders in the units). Managers were asked to rate the extent of their dependence on others outside their units but in their divisions and on others outside their divisions. They also were asked to rate these others' dependencies upon them (see Appendix 7-3). Indices of reciprocal interdependence were constructed by multiplying the two ratings of intradivision interdependence and the two ratings of interdivision interdependence. The resulting measures tap the extent to which managers felt they were simultaneously dependent upon and depended upon by people outside their units but in their divisions and outside their divisions. These scores were averaged across managers in each unit, and the unit averages were correlated with the work-flow centrality measures constructed from the interview data. Intradivision work-flow centrality correlated with average-manager intradivision reciprocal interdependence ($r = .44$). Interdivision work-flow centrality correlated with average manager interdivision reciprocal interdependence ($r = .30$). Both of these correlations are statistically significant ($p \leq .05$), and they provide evidence for the validity of the measures of unit work-flow interdependence.

DISCUSSION

It has been argued that traditional structural variables have been over-emphasized in organizational research. In addition, there is little concise theory explaining why they should be associated with employee attitudes and perceptions. This chapter has attempted to define the structure of organizations in relational terms and to generate measures of relational variables. By using such mid-range concepts, it is hoped that individual and organizational levels of analysis can be more readily integrated— empirically and theoretically.

Two types of relational variables were identified and measured in a southern assembly and packaging plant. Each measure was applied for each of three network types: friendship, interaction, and work group. In addition, measures of work-flow interdependence relations were developed and applied in two groups of a large public utility. The two types of variables measured in the southern plant were (1) nominal measures of network location (isolate, liaison, group member, and other) and (2) nominal and interval measures of employee position within groups (centrality, reach, integrativeness, mutuality, range incoming, range outgoing, and boundary spanning). Measures of work-flow interdependence relations obtained from the public utility distinguished between units' interdependence with other units in the same division and with other divisions. These measures were combined into indices of intradivision and interdivision work-flow centrality.

Sociometric measures of organizational structure, such as those described here, are likely to be of use in a variety of research contexts. They are particularly likely to be useful, however, for the assessment of planned change. First, change attempts may be directed toward altering established patterns of formal or informal relations at work. Attempts to alter supervisory style often are directed toward increasing upward communications at work. Likewise, sociotechnical interventions often are directed toward matching social relations with work-flow interdependencies. Relational analyses of work, friendship, interaction, and other types of relationships could be of considerable utility in establishing the extent to which such change programs achieve their desired effect. They also could be of use in establishing the consequences of such interventions. For example, it has been shown that integration into networks of friendship relations is associated with employee satisfaction, and that integration into networks of work relationships is associated with employee involvement and internal motivation.[72,73] To the extent that relational factors account for changes in outcome variables such as these, interventions directed toward altering employees' relationships with others would be credited with being responsible for change in outcomes.

Relational analyses may be important in the evaluation of change attempts for another reason. They are likley to mediate the effects of change. Groups of friends, interaction partners, and co-workers may be important loci for the establishment of social reality.[74] Social comparison processes, shared information, or shared experiences at work may serve to lead different groups to have different interpretations of events.[75] Even when they share interpretations, members of different groups may differ in the meanings given to these events. In a change effort where different groups have either positive or negative attitudes toward one another, we would expect that group members would be inclined to feel positively or negatively about proposed changes, depending on their perceptions of how members of the other groups feel.[18] Establishing employee membership in various groups, therefore, may allow researchers to explain some of the variance in employee attitudes toward the changes being introduced.

Identifying patterns of relationships among employees also may be important for understanding the diffusion of the proposed changes or the diffusion of attitudes toward the changes. It has long been known that information about innovations does not travel randomly throughout a social system. Rather, such information travels through established channels of relationships.[76–78] Information about proposed organizational changes is likely to show similar patterns. More important, perhaps, the channels through which proposed changes are introduced to employees are likely to be significant determinants of employee responses. These channels could be identified and plotted, using the relational perspective described here.

Finally, relational variables may be useful as controls. It was noted before that patterns of employee clustering might be associated with differential interpretations of events. Partialing out employee location in social or work networks, therefore, allows researchers to assess employee attitudes or attitude change while controlling for the effects of relational location. Since much of the cluster effect is likely to involve general affect directed toward others (e.g., management, fellow workers), controlling for network position might also be a useful way to control for general response bias. Such controls also may be useful in avoiding spurious results. For example, position in the network of work interdependencies has been found to be associated with experienced role stress[79] and with employee satisfaction.[33] Researchers might wish to assess the impact of a change attempt on the extent to which experienced role stress leads to employee satisfaction. If the intervention is not directed toward altering the pattern of work relationships among employees, controlling for such relationships may allow researchers to determine more precisely the success or failure of the intervention by controlling for at least one potential source of spuriousness.

Relational variables, reliably measured, should document relationships between employees' structural lcoation and several variables that have been the objects of change efforts, such as employee motivation and satisfaction. These relationships were hypothesized by even the earliest human relationists,[80] but little direct empirical investigation has been carried out. As mentioned, initial work indicates that these relationships exist.[72,73] If a causal link between integration and positive employee responses can be documented, it could influence the design of change efforts. For example, integration into the network of work-based relations may increase employee involvement and reduce absenteeism. Integration into networks of friendship relations may not have the same effect. Change strategies, therefore, may be more successful if they are directed toward altering work-based relations rather than purely social relations. Before relational variables can be used to direct change, however, reliable and valid measures of relational constructs must be developed.

Much more work must be done before the full potential of relational measures can be realized. Several alternative analytic procedures are available, each with their respective costs and benefits.[81] These must be evaluated and compared before intelligent choices can be made among them. Concepts depicting individual locations in social networks need to be refined and linked theoretically to problems associated with organization change. Currently, relational concepts seem to be selected in part on the basis of whether available software provides adequate indices. Once relational concepts and their measures have been developed, work must be done to assess measurement reliability and validity. There is no information at present that concerns the reliability of relational measures used in organizations.

REFERENCES

1. Taylor, F. W. *The principles of scientific management.* New York: Norton, 1947.
2. Gerth, H. H., & Mills, S. W. *From Max Weber: Essays in sociology.* New York: Oxford University Press, 1946.
3. Blauner, R. *Alienation and freedom.* Chicago: University of Chicago Press, 1964.
4. Fullan, M. Industrial technology and worker integration in the organization. *American Sociological Review,* 1970, **35**(6), 1028–1039.
5. Porter, L. W., & Lawler, E. E. III. Properties of organizational structure in relation to job attitudes and job behavior. *Psychological Bulletin,* 1965, **64**, 23–51.
6. James, L. R., & Jones, A. P. Organizational structure: A review of structural dimensions and their conceptual relationships with individual attitudes and behaviors. *Organizational Behavior and Human Performance,* 1976, **16**, 74–113.
7. Berger, C. J., & Cummings, L. L. Organizational structure, attitudes, and behaviors. In B. Stan (Ed.), *Research in organizational behavior, Vol. 1.* Greenwich, CT: JAI Press, 1978.
8. Lazarsfeld, P. F., & Menzel, H. On the relation between individual and collective properties. In A. Etzioni (Ed.), *A sociological reader on complex organizations.* New York: Holt, Rinehart and Winston, 1961.
9. Coleman, J. S. Social structure and a theory of action. In P. Blau (Ed.), *Approaches to the study of social structure.* New York: Free Press, 1975.
10. Good, W. J. Homan's and Merton's structural approach. In P. Blau (Ed.), *Approaches to the study of social structure.* New York: Free Press, 1975.
11. Blau, P. Parameters of social structure. *American Sociological Review,* 1974, **39**(5), 615–635.
12. Laumann, E. O. *Bonds of pluralism: The form and substance of urban social networks.* New York: Wiley, 1973.

13. Laumann, E. O., & Pappi, F. *Networks of collective action: A perspective on community influence systems.* New York: Academic Press, 1976.
14. Mullins, N. C. *Theories and theory groups in contemporary American sociology.* New York: Harper & Row, 1973.
15. Mitchell, J. C. *Social networks in urban situations.* Manchester: Manchester University Press, 1969.
16. Barnes, J. A. *Social networks.* Addison-Wesley Module in Anthropology 26, 1972. Reading: Addison-Wesley.
17. Whitten, N. E., & Wolfe, A. Network analysis. In J. J. Honigman (Ed.), *Handbook of social and cultural anthropology.* Chicago: Rand-McNally, 1973.
18. Festinger, L., Schacter, S., & Back, K. *Social pressures in informal groups: A study of human factors in housing.* New York: Harper, 1950.
19. Heider, F. *The psychology of interpersonal relations.* New York: Wiley, 1958.
20. Newcomb, T. M. The prediction of interpersonal attraction. *American Psychologist,* 1956, **11**, 575–586.
21. Newcomb, T. M. *The acquaintance process.* New York: Holt, Rinehart and Winston, 1961.
22. Byrne, D. E. *The attraction paradigm.* New York: Academic Press, 1971.
23. Byrne, D., & Griffitt, W. B. Interpersonal attraction. In *Annual review of psychology.* Palo Alto: Annual Reviews, Inc., 1973.
24. Lindzey, G., & Byrne, D. Measurement of social choice and interpersonal attractiveness. In G. Lindzey & E. Aronson (Eds.), *The handbook of social psychology, Vol. II.* Reading, MA: Addison-Wesley, 1968.
25. Harary, F., Norman, F. Z., & Cartwright, D. *Structural models.* New York: Wiley, 1965.
26. Blau, P. *The dynamics of bureaucracy: A study of interpersonal relations in two government agencies.* Chicago: University of Chicago Press, 1955.
27. Blau, P. Critical remarks on Weber's theory of authority. *American Political Science Review,* 1963, **57**, 305–316.
28. Weiss, R. S., & Jacobson, E. A method for the analysis of the structure of complex organizations. *American Sociological Review,* 1956, **20**, 661–668.
29. Jacobson, E., & Seashore, S. E. Communication practices in complex organizations. *Journal of Social Issues,* 1951, **7**, 74–113.
30. Gouldner, A. W. *Patterns of industrial bureaucracy.* New York: Free Press, 1954.
31. Melville, D. *Men who manage.* New York: Wiley, 1959.
32. Homans, G. C. *The human group.* New York: Harcourt, Brace and World, 1950.
33. Massarik, F., Tannenbaum, R., Kahane, M., & Weschler, I. Sociometric choice and organizational effectiveness. *Sociometry,* 1953, **16**, 211–238.
34. Whyte, W. F. *Human relations in the restaurant industry.* New York: McGraw-Hill, 1948.
35. Schwartz, D. F., & Jacobson, E. Organizational communication network analysis: The liaison communication role. *Organizational Behavior and Human Performance,* 1977, **18**, 158–174.
36. Evans, P. Multiple hierarchies and control. *Administrative Science Quarterly,* 1975, **20**, 250–259.
37. Payne, R. L., & Pheysey, D. Organization structure and sociometric nominations amongst line managers in three contrasted organizations. *European Journal of Social Psychology,* 1971, **1**, 261–284.
38. Friedel, M. F. Organizations as semi-lattices. *American Sociological Review,* 1967, **32**, 45–64.

39. Tichy, N. M. An analysis of clique formation and structure in organizations. *Administrative Science Quarterly,* 1973, **18,** 194–208.

40. Tichy, N. M. *Prescribed and emergent structures in organizations.* Unpublished manuscript, Graduate School of Business, Columbia University, 1977.

41. Brass, D. J. Structural relationships, job characteristics, and worker satisfaction and performance. *Administrative Science Quarterly,* 1981, **26,** 331–348.

42. Lincoln, J. R., & Miller, J. Work and friendship ties in organizations: A comparative analysis of relational networks. *Administrative Science Quarterly,* 1979, **24,** 181–199.

43. Rice, L., & Mitchell, T. R. Structural determinants of individual behavior in organizations. *Administrative Science Quarterly,* 1973, **18,** 56–70.

44. Emerson, R. Power-dependence relations. *American Sociological Review,* 1972, **27,** 31–41.

45. Tannenbaum, A. S. (Ed.). *Control in organizations.* New York: McGraw-Hill, 1968.

46. Bacharach, S. B., & Aiken, M. Structural and process constraints on influence in organizations: A level-specific analysis. *Administrative Science Quarterly,* 1976, **21,** 623–642.

47. Barnes. J. A. *Network analysis: Orienting notion, rigorous technique of substantive field of study?* Paper presented at Mathematical Social Science Board, Advanced Research Symposium on Social Networks, Hanover, NH, 1975.

48. Hage, J., & Aiken, M. Relationship of centralization to other structural properties. *Administrative Science Quarterly,* 1967, **12,** 72–92.

49. Tichy, N. M., Tushman, M. L., Fombrun, C. A network approach to organizational assessment. In E. E. Lawler III, D. A. Nadler, & C. Cammann (Eds.), *Organizational assessment: Perspectives on the measurement of organizational behavior and the quality of working life.* New York: Wiley-Interscience, 1980.

50. Moreno, J. L. *Who shall survive?* Washington, D.C.: Nervous and Mental Disease Publishing House, 1934.

51. Richards, W. D. *A manual for network analysis.* Stanford: Stanford University, 1975, mimeographed.

52. McKinney, J. C. An educational application of a two-dimensional sociometric test. *Sociometry,* 1948, **11,** 356–367.

53. Proctor, C. H., & Loomis, C. Analysis of sociometric data. In M. Jahoda, M. Deutsch, & S. Cook (Eds.), *Research methods in social relations.* New York: Dryden Press, 1951.

54. Mears, P. Structuring communications in a working group. *Journal of Communication,* 1974, **24,** 71–79.

55. Cherry, C. *On human communication: A review, a survey and a criticism.* Cambridge: MIT Press, 1957.

56. Gluckman, M. (Ed.). *Essays on the ritual of social relations.* Manchester: Manchester University Press, 1962.

57. Farace, R., & Mabee, T. Communication network analysis methods. In P. Monge & D. Capelia (Eds.), *Multivariate techniques in communication research.* New York: Academic Press, in press.

58. Guetzkow, H. Communication in organizations. In J. G. March (Ed.), *Handbook of organizations.* Chicago: Rand-McNally, 1965.

59. Forsyth, E., & Katz, L. A matrix approach to the analysis of sociometric data: Preliminary report. *Sociometry,* 1947, **9,** 340–349.

60. Festinger, L. The analysis of sociograms using matrix algebra. *Human Relations,* 1949, **2,** 153–158.

61. Beum, C. O., & Brundage, E. G. A method for analyzing the sociomatrix. *Sociometry,* 1950, **13,** 141–145.

62. Coleman, J. S., & MacRae, D., Jr. Electronic processing of sociometric data for groups up to 1,000 in size. *American Sociological Review,* 1960, **25,** 722–727.

63. Borgatta, E. F., & Stolz, W. A note on a computer program for rearrangement of matrices. *Sociometry,* 1963, **26,** 391–392.

64. Holland, P. W., & Leinhardt, S. Local structure in social networks. In D. Heise (Ed.), *Sociological methodology.* San Francisco: Jossey-Bass, 1976.

65. White, H. C., Boorman, S., & Breiger, R. Social structure from multiple networks I. Blockmodels of roles and positions. *American Journal of Sociology,* 1975, **81,** 730–780.

66. Alba, R. D. A graph-theoretic definition of a sociometric clique. *Journal of Mathematical Sociology,* 1972, **3,** 113–126.

67. Luce, R. D., & Perry, A. D. A method of matrix analysis of group structure. *Psychometrika,* 1949, **14,** 95–116.

68. Luce, R. D. Connectivity and genealogical cliques in sociometric group structure. *Psychometrika,* 1950, **15,** 169–190.

69. Granovetter, M. The strength of weak ties. *American Journal of Sociology,* 1973, **78,** 1360–1380.

70. Van de Ven, A. H., Delbecq, A. L., & Koenig, R. Determinants of coordination modes within organizations. *American Sociological Review,* 1976, **41,** 322–338.

71. Thompson, J. C. *Organizations in action.* New York: McGraw-Hill, 1967.

72. Moch, M. K. *Racial differences in job satisfaction: Testing four common explanations.* College of Commerce Working Paper 533. Urbana: University of Illinois, 1980.

73. Moch, M. K. *Job involvement, internal motivation, and employees' integration into networks of work relationships.* College of Commerce Working Paper 542. Urbana: University of Illinois, 1981.

74. Berger, P., & Luckmann, T. *The social construction of reality: A treatise on the sociology of knowledge.* New York: Doubleday, 1966.

75. Festinger, L. A theory of social comparison processes. *Human Relations,* 1954, **7,** 117–140.

76. Coleman, J. S., Katz, E., & Menzel, H. *Medical innovation: A diffusion study.* Chicago: Bobbs-Merrill, 1966.

77. Rogers, E. M., & Shoemaker, F. F. *Communication of innovations.* New York: Free Press, 1971.

78. Weick, K. E. *The social psychology of organizing.* Reading, MA: Addison-Wesley, 1969.

79. Moch, M. K., Bartunek, J., & Brass, D. *Workflow centrality and organizational stress.* Unpublished manuscript, Department of Business Administration, University of Illinois, Urbana, 1978.

80. Mayo, E. *The social problems of an industrial civilization.* Cambridge: Harvard University Press.

81. Burt, R. S. Cohesion versus structural equivalence as a basis for network subgroups. *Sociological Methods and Research,* 1978, **7.**

APPENDIX 7-1   MEASURES OF THE RELATIONAL STRUCTURE IN ORGANIZATIONS: QUESTIONNAIRE ITEMS

The following questions will help us determine who talks to whom at _____. Like the questions you filled out in Part 1, your answers to these questions will help us with statistical analyses of the data.

For each question below, please list the first and last names of *no more than seven* individuals (please print).

1.   Who are the people you talk with most frequently in the plant?

    a. _____

    b. _____

    c. _____

    d. _____

    e. _____

    f. _____

    g. _____

2.   Who do you consider to be your closest friends in the plant?

    a. _____

    b. _____

    c. _____

    d. _____

    e. _____

    f. _____

    g. _____

3.   Please list any relatives that you have working in the plant.

    a. _____

    b. _____

    c. _____

    d. _____

    e. _____

    f. _____

    g. _____

4. Earlier in the questionnaire, we asked you questions about your work group. We asked you to think of your work group as the set of people you work most closely with day to day. Please list the names of the people in your work group. (Again, please list *no more than seven.*)

a. _____

b. _____

c. _____

d. _____

e. _____

f. _____

g. _____

APPENDIX 7-2   MEASURES OF INTERDEPENDENCE: INTERVIEW OR QUESTIONNAIRE

1. Please rate the extent to which your unit is directly dependent upon every other unit in order to get your work done.
   a. Unit 1 (Named)*
      1. Not at all dependent
      2.
      3.
      4. Moderately dependent
      5.
      6.
      7. Very dependent
      8. DK
      9. NA
   b. Unit 2 (Named)
      .
      .
      .
   n. Unit n (Named)
2. I'd like you to rate the extent to which these other units are *directly* dependent upon *your* unit.
   a. Unit 1 (Named)*
      1. Not at all dependent
      2.
      3.

* Use same code for Questions **b–n.**

    4. Moderately dependent
    5.
    6.
    7. Very dependent
    8. DK
    9. NA
 b. Unit 2 (Named)

  ·
  ·
  ·

 n. Unit n (Named)
3. Please rate the extent to which your unit is directly dependent upon every other division in order to get your work done.
  a. Division 1 (Named)*
    1. Not at all dependent
    2.
    3.
    4. Moderately dependent
    5.
    6.
    7. Very dependent
    8. DK
    9. NA
  b. Division 2 (Named)

  ·
  ·
  ·

  n. Division n (Named)
4. I'd like you to rate the extent to which these other divisions are *directly* dependent upon *your* division.
  a. Division 1 (Named)*
    1. Not at all dependent
    2.
    3.
    4. Moderately dependent
    5.
    6.
    7. Very dependent
    8. DK
    9. NA
  b. Division 2 (Named)

  ·
  ·
  ·

  n. Division n (Named)

APPENDIX 7-3 QUESTIONNAIRE MEASURES OF INTRAUNIT, INTERUNIT, INTRADIVISION, AND INTERDIVISION INTERDEPENDENCE*

The following questions refer to different ways in which you may depend on others. For each question, think of what you need in order to do your job well, and indicate to what degree you may depend on others in the way mentioned.

1. To what degree do you need assistance in doing your work from each of the following?

	Not at all		To some degree			To a large degree	To a very great degree
   a. Other people in your unit | [1] | [2] | [3] | [4] | [5] | [6] | [7]
   b. People in other units of your division | [1] | [2] | [3] | [4] | [5] | [6] | [7]
   c. Employees of other divisions or groups | [1] | [2] | [3] | [4] | [5] | [6] | [7]

2. To what degree do you need information or *advice* from each of the following?

   a. Other people in your unit | [1] | [2] | [3] | [4] | [5] | [6] | [7]
   b. People in other units of your division | [1] | [2] | [3] | [4] | [5] | [6] | [7]
   c. Employees of other divisions or groups | [1] | [2] | [3] | [4] | [5] | [6] | [7]

3. To what degree to you depend on the work performed by each of the following to provide the *materials* you need?

   a. Other people in your unit | [1] | [2] | [3] | [4] | [5] | [6] | [7]
   b. People in other units of your division | [1] | [2] | [3] | [4] | [5] | [6] | [7]
   c. Employees of other divisions or groups | [1] | [2] | [3] | [4] | [5] | [6] | [7]

* Given the nature of the technology applied in the organization, the critical resource was considered to be assistance rather than information/advice or materials. Accordingly, the item emphasizing assistance was used in the present analysis. Because this analysis concerns only interunit and interdivision interdependencies, questions concerning intraunit interdependencies (*a*'s) also were not included in the index construction. All measures are presented, however, in the interest of completeness.

These questions refer to different ways in which *others* may depend on *you* in order to do their jobs well.

		Not at all		To some degree		To a large degree	To a very great degree	

1. To what degree do each of the following need your assistance in doing their work?

   a. Other people in your unit
   [1] [2] [3] [4] [5] [6] [7]

   b. People in other units of your division
   [1] [2] [3] [4] [5] [6] [7]

   c. Employees of other divisions or groups
   [1] [2] [3] [4] [5] [6] [7]

2. To what degree do each of the following need *information* or *advice* from you?

   a. Other people in your unit
   [1] [2] [3] [4] [5] [6] [7]

   b. People in other units of your division
   [1] [2] [3] [4] [5] [6] [7]

   c. Employees of other divisions or groups
   [1] [2] [3] [4] [5] [6] [7]

3. To what degree do each of the following depend on the work you perform to provide the materials they need?

   a. Other people in your unit
   [1] [2] [3] [4] [5] [6] [7]

   b. People in other units of your division
   [1] [2] [3] [4] [5] [6] [7]

   c. Employees of other divisions or groups
   [1] [2] [3] [4] [5] [6] [7]

CHAPTER EIGHT

Technology in Organizations: A Constructive Review and Analytic Framework

DENISE M. ROUSSEAU

This chapter reviews theory and research on technology in organizations from a behavioral-science point of view with an emphasis on conceptualization and assessment. It integrates that diverse literature into a framework to guide future research and measurement. A technology is defined here as a process for transforming physical and information inputs into outputs. This review finds that research on technology in organizations treats technology according to five phases of the transformation process: input characteristics, input control, conversion, output control, and output characteristics. Further, three levels of analysis are employed in research on technology: organizational, subunit, and individual. These levels of analysis not only influence the aspects of technology studied in organizational research but, also, the type of organizations chosen for study and the results obtained. A framework for assessing technology is proposed that reflects the multiple phases of technology as well as the multiple levels of activity it encompasses. The goals of this chapter are to assess the theoretical and operational underpinnings of the construct and to provide a framework for assessing technology in organizational research.

The term *technology* comes from *techne,* the Greek word for art, and it signifies the knowledge, capacity, or skill an individual uses to produce a product or artifact. As used in the modern world, technology refers to the application of knowledge for human purposes.[1] Computers are said to represent high technology because of their physical complexity. Nationalized health care is a form of social technology in which knowledge with regard to social rules as well as healing techniques are combined. An assembly line is a kind of organizational technology in which knowledge regarding production processes shapes organizational activities. Physical, social, and organizational technologies each represent the application of knowledge to perform work. Each provides an example of the widespread use of the term *technology* to characterize different sorts of processes.

We hear a clamour for definitions of technology from organizational scientists, historians, and philosophers.[2-4] However, the difficulty of finding an appropriately general yet clear definition suggests that the problem of what is technology has not yet been solved. Probably, the most intensive discussions regarding the nature of technology are to be found in the literature on organizational behavior and theory. Technology is a central concept in the organizational sciences. It has been viewed as a determinant or as an explanation of organizational structure,[5,6] employee well-being,[7] social interaction,[8] and attitudes.[9,10] However, numerous organizational scientists have documented the confused and often contradictory nature of the construct of technology in organizational research and theory.[2,11-13] This confusion reflects the richness of the construct and the processes it subsumes as well as the uncertainty regarding its meaning.

THE CONCEPT OF TECHNOLOGY IN ORGANIZATIONS

Organizational scientists use the term *technology* to refer to anything from job routineness[14] to the hardness of raw materials.[15] There is disagreement as to whether technology is an object, such as an assembly line or a computer, or a process, such as the flow of throughput within the organization. Scott has argued that to study the technology of an organization it is necessary to view it as a mechanism for transforming input into output.[16] This view is compatible both with an open-systems model[17] and with the traditional model of work employed by industrial engineers (see Chapter 9). The basic phases of this process are input (material and information are brought into the work place), conversion (material and information to be worked on is transformed through the capacities of both operators and equipment), and output (products, services, or information is provided to the environment).

Descriptions of both the input and output phases can be divided into two distinct components: characteristics and control functions. Characteristics of inputs are attributes of the materials, ideas, and other resources brought into the organization. Input control functions are mechanisms that influence the availability and distribution of inputs in preparation for conversion. Input characteristics, such as hardness of materials, can be distinguished from input control functions, such as stockpiling. In a similar manner, output has two aspects. Output characteristics are qualities of output following completion of the conversion process, such as the diversity or number of different products or services provided. Output control refers to mechanisms used in influencing the quality or quantity of output released to the environment, such as quality-control systems and stockpiling. Any change in the conversion process or how input or output is handled is a technological change.

These five dimensions can be used to describe the transformation of input into output that is accomplished by the implementation of technology in organizations. Virtually all organizational research and theory that addresses technology is based on definitions of technology derived from one or more of these dimensions. However, most conceptualizations of technology emphasize the conversion process and ignore its connection with input and output activities. The predominance of attention given to the conversion process in research on technology stems from the emphasis given it in theoretical descriptions of technology.

THEORETICAL MODELS AND DESCRIPTORS OF TECHNOLOGY

The organizational sciences are rich in theoretical models and descriptors of "organizational technology." Four schemes are commonly used, each varying in the specificity, generalizability, and conceptual elaboration involved: the classification schemes developed by Woodward,[5,6] Thompson,[18] and Perrow,[19,20] and the scales developed by Hickson, Pugh, and Pheysey.[21]

Woodward's is the first major study explicitly using technology as an analytical variable. It initiated consideration of the technological imperative: the thesis that technology determines organizational structure. Because Woodward was interested in the relationship of technology to organizational structure, she examined the typical technology employed by the organizations she studied. Woodward focused only on the predominate conversion process of these organizations and did not address input functions. However, she did address output characteristics by grouping conversion processes on the basis of their products: integral or manufactured products (such as tools or machines) and dimensional or process products (such as aspirin tablets). Although Woodward herself focused on both conversion and output characteristics, researchers who base assessments of technology on her classification scheme tend to focus solely on the conversion process (see Peterson, for example.)[22]

Woodward's approach was designed for industrial organizations and may not be appropriate for studying technologies for nonindustrial firms. This limitation is particularly true of her output measures, which are not applicable to service organizations. To allow technology to be studied in a variety of complex organizations, Thompson proposed a classification scheme based on the interdependence of human operators and the amount of discretion they exercise.[18] Thompson's three-part classification scheme (long-linked, mediating, and intensive technologies) reflects the degree of control, or technical rationality, the work system manifests over the responses of its members and the inputs and outputs of that system. Because of the high degree of control possible in "long-linked" assembly-line and continuous-process operations, Thompson says that these are more nearly perfect than are other forms of technology. Underlying his scheme is the notion that control and routinization are the ultimate ends served by technology in organizations.

Although Thompson distinguished between input, technological (generally restricted to conversion processes), and output activities in describing organizations, he suggests that these activities are interdependent and hence must be geared to each other. Thus, the stockpiling of supplies (a form of input control) and the stockpiling of output (a form of output control) affect the degree of variability in the conversion process. It would seem consistent to expect that different types of input and output control activities would be associated with Thompson's three conversion processes—a conclusion supported by his discussion of organizational rationality. From this discussion, we can conclude that input and output phases are influenced by the work-system attempts to exert control and thus are as much a part of the organization's technology in Thompson's view as are conversion processes.

The view of technology advanced by Perrow explicitly addresses two dimensions underlying routineness: task variability and task uncertainty.[20] Perrow suggests that the effectiveness of various organizational structures is contingent on the types of technologies employed. Unlike Thompson, Perrow makes no judgment that any type of technology is more desirable than another. Like Thompson, however, Perrow's technological dimensions are applicable to diverse types of organizations. Further, his dimensions of technology reflect different phases of the organization's technology. Task uncertainty reflects the knowledge operators bring with them to the conversion process, while task variability reflects the diversity of inputs. Perrow's classification scheme has probably contributed to more diverse forms of technology assessment than any other model, since research based on his model employs both classification systems as well as multidimensional scales (e.g., Lynch[12] and Grimes and Klein[23]).

The Aston group's concept of work-flow integration is another model frequently used to conceptualize technology in organizations.[21] Work-flow integration is defined as the degree of automated, fixed-sequence operations in the work flow and is assessed by an index composed of four intercorrelated measures: (1) work-flow automation, the extent to which energy and information are provided by machines rather than people; (2) work-flow rigidity, the extent to which the process is nonadaptable and invariable in sequence; (3) work-flow interdependence, the extent to which segments of the work flow are sequentially interdependent; and (4) work-flow evaluation specificity, the extent to which quality of output may be specified by standards in advance.

The conceptualization of technology as work-flow integration effectively differentiates between manufacturing and service organizations, with manufacturing organizations scoring higher on the index. Since work-flow integration has been used primarily to explore differences in manufacturing organizations, its utility as a descriptor of technological differences within samples of service organizations is unknown. However, as service organizations become increasingly mechanized (e.g., through increased use of computers) work-flow integration may differentiate among types of technologies within samples of service organizations. Although its primary emphasis is on characteristics of the conversion process, work-flow integration also addresses one aspect of output control—work-flow evaluation specificity.

Although these four approaches are the most frequently cited conceptualizations of technology, many studies employ unique concepts and measurement operations and thus make integration of research on technology difficult. We shall now examine how divergencies in conceptualization are related to the nature and results of research on technology in organizations.

RESEARCH ON TECHNOLOGY

The empirical studies of technology reviewed here (see Table 8-1) are representative of the research conducted by those organizational scientists interested in technology. To summarize these studies, two definitions of technology have been extracted from each report: a theoretical definition and an operational one. Theoretical definitions represent either the explicit definition of technology used by the researcher or the label given to the facet of technology measured in the study when no explicit definition is reported. Operational definitions represent what is actually measured by the researcher. Each study has also been classified according to the *phases of technology* assessed, such as input control or conversion processes. This classification is based on the phases reflected in each author's operational definition of technology since the theoretical definition is often more global than its operationalization. The theorist attributed to each study reflects the theoretical model from which technology measures are derived. Further, each study is classified according to the *level* at which technology is measured. In most cases, technology is measured at one of three levels: organizational, subunit (e.g., departmental), or individual (job). There are two exceptions: Rushing[15] derives a

Table 8-1 Summary of Empirical Studies of Technology

Study	Technology Definition	Dimensions[a]	Theorist[b]	Level of Technology Measurement	Methods of Technology Measurement	Setting	Findings
Woodward	Theoretical: technical complexity Operational: classification into unit, mass, or continuous production processes	CON	W	Organization	Records and interviews with managers	Manufacturing firms (N = 100)	Technology is related to structure, particularly in effective organizations
Bell	Theoretical: job complexity Operational: predictability of work demands, number of difficult tasks, amount of discretion, and extent of responsibility	CON	O	Individual	Interviews and questionnaires administered to full-time day staff (N = 171)	Departments in one community hospital (N = 30)	Supervisor span of control is negatively related to subordinate and supervisor job complexity
Harvey	Theoretical: mechanisms or processes by which an organization turns out its product or service Operational: technical diffuseness—number of product changes in last 10 years, average number of different kinds of products offered during last 10 years	OCH	O	Organization	Production records	Manufacturing firms (N = 43)	Technical diffuseness is negatively related to number of specialized subunits, levels of authority, and program specification
Rushing	Theoretical: hardness of material Operational: ease with which a substance is pierced, penetrated, or broken	ICH	O	Industry	Classification of manufacturing industries by 16 sociologists using census data	Manufacturing industries (N = 44)	Hardness of material is positively related to the division of labor
Hage & Aiken	Theoretical: routineness of work Operational: overall routineness	CON	P	Individual	Structured interviews of professional staff; scores were aggregated at the organization level	Social welfare and health agencies (N = 16)	Routine work is positively related to centralization and formalization; it is negatively related to professional training

Author	Definition	Code		Level	Method	Sample	Findings
Hickson, Pugh, & Pheysey	Theoretical: techniques organization uses in its work flow. Operational: automation of equipment, rigidity of work-flow sequences, interdependence of workflow segments, and specificity of output evaluation, production continuity	CON, OCO	A, W	Organization	Interviews with chief executives and department heads	Manufacturing firms ($N = 31$) and service organizations ($N = 15$)	Technological variables are related to structural variables impinged on by workflow
Fullan	Theoretical: manual and machine operations performed on an object. Operational: classification of firms according to production system: craft, mass production, or continuous process	CON	O	Organization	Author classified firms	Manufacturing firms ($N = 12$)	Employees in continuous process firms have more opportunity for promotion and social integrations than those in other technologies
Inkson, Pugh, & Hickson	Theoretical: workflow integration, the degree of automated, continuous, fixed sequence operations. Operational: automation of equipment and specificity of output evaluation	CON, OCO	A	Organization	Interviews with chief executives	Manufacturing firms ($N = 24$) and service organizations ($N = 16$)	Technology is less highly related to structuring of activities than is size
Zwerman	Theoretical: technical complexity. Operational: classification of firms according to Woodward's scheme	CON	W	Organization	Interviews with managers	Manufacturing firms ($N = 55$)	Technology is related to structure, particularly in effective organizations
Mohr	Theoretical: manageability of tasks and materials. Operational: uniformity, complexity, analyzability of material, routineness of tasks, task interdependence, noise level	ICH, CON	O	Subunit	Author assigned work groups to eight categories based on level of routineness; experts rated work groups on basis of written task descriptions; questionnaires were completed by supervisors	Work groups in 13 local hospitals ($N = 144$)	Task interdependence was positively related to participativeness and negatively related to manageability; education of supervisor and subordinate were both negatively related to manageability
Taylor	Theoretical: sophistication of input, throughput, and output. Operational: standardization of materials, automation of throughput, and performance feedback	CON, OCO, ICO	O	Subunit	Questionnaire responses from in-plant judges	Nonsupervisory work groups at petroleum refinery ($N = 140$)	Technological sophistication facilitates social change

Table 8-1 (*Continued*)

Study	Technology Definition	Dimensions[a]	Theorist[b]	Level of Technology Measurement	Methods of Technology Measurement	Setting	Findings
Child & Mansfield	Theoretical: work-flow integration and production continuity Operational: work-flow integration—automation of equipment, rigidity of work-flow sequences, interdependence of work-flow segments, and specificity of evaluation; production continuity—classification of firms into 10 categories based on Woodward (1958)	CON, OCO	A	Organization	Interviews with chief executives	Manufacturing and service firms ($N = 82$)	Structural variables such as specialization are related to work-flow integration independently of size, although relationship of structure to technology appears to be greater in smaller firms. Dimensions of workflow integration are only slightly correlated
Form	Theoretical: technical complexity Operational: types of equipment, routines required to operate machines, and work-flow design	CON	O	Organization	Author ranked organization on technical complexity	Automobile plants ($N = 4$) in four countries	Skills and interaction opportunities differ across technologies
Freeman	Theoretical: mechanization of production systems Operational: type of substance produced (integral or dimensional), use of production lines, and extent of automation	CON, OCH	O, W	Organization	Interviews with managers	Manufacturing firms ($N = 41$)	Automation is positively related to administrative intensity; administrative intensity differs according to type of product

	Definition			Level	Method	Sample	Findings
Grimes & Klein	Theoretical: role specificity and task variability Operational: classification according to routine, engineering, or craft technologies	P	CON, ICH	Subunit	Authors classified departments based on first level manager responses on questionnaires; an additional classification was based on company job codes for first and second level managers across work groups	Plants in a manufacturing organization each divided into direct and indirect labor groups (N = 25); department managers formed task units (N = 828)	No strong relationship between technology and structure for subunits grouped by task or by modal technology; relationship of technology to autonomy is greater at task level than at modal level
Hrebiniak	Theoretical: technological level, task predictability, task interdependence, and task manageability Operational: job descriptions were classified into levels reflecting complexity, uniformity, analyzability, and discretion; employee descriptions of job uniformity and routineness, dependence on others, understanding, and complexity	O	CON, ICH	Individual	Expert ratings and questionnaires completed by supervisors (N = 36) and subordinates (N = 174); analyzed at individual and aggregate levels	General hospital (N = 1)	Job technology and structure are unrelated at the individual, but are related at the aggregate level when supervision effects are partialled out
Khandwalla	Theoretical: mass output orientation Operational: classification of firms into custom, small-batch, large-batch technology, mass production, and continuous process technology	O	CON	Organization	Company president completed a questionnaire	Manufacturing firms (N = 79)	Mass-output orientation is related to vertical integration but not related to use of sophisticated controls
Lynch	Theoretical: actions an individual performs on an object with or without aid of tools or mechanical devices in order to make some change in that object (Perrow, 1967) Operational: predictability of events, routineness of operations, insufficient knowledge, overall routineness, and task interdependence	P	CON, ICO	Individual	Questionnaires administered to full-time library staff (N = 384); responses were aggregated to department level	Departments in three university libraries (N = 15)	Technology scores vary according to the individual for whom the data are aggregated: scores differentiate among departments

Table 8-1 (*Continued*)

Study	Technology Definition	Dimensions[a]	Theorist[b]	Level of Technology Measurement	Methods of Technology Measurement	Setting	Findings
Mahoney & Frost	Theoretical: nature of discretion permitted Operational: classification as long-linked, mediating, or intensive technologies	CON	T	Subunit	Authors classified units according to employees' levels of discretion	Units in 17 manufacturing and service firms (N = 386)	Technologies differ in criteria of effectiveness employed by managers
Van de Ven & Delbecq	Theoretical: kind of work performed by organizational unit Operational: task difficulty and variability	CON, ICH	P	Individual	Questionnaire was completed by all unit members; data were aggregated to work group level with equal weight given to supervisory staff and average nonsupervisory scores	Work units in local offices of government security agencies (N = 120)	Task variability and difficulty vary across different structural units
Morrisey & Gillespie	Theoretical: manner in which relevant variables are manipulated given a desired outcome and state of knowledge (Thompson, 1967) Operational: classification as long-linked, mediating, or intensive	CON	T	Organization	Authors classified firms	Manufacturing firms (N = 2) and service organizations (N = 16)	Relationship of professionalism to bureaucracy varies according to technology
Peterson	Theoretical: production process or technological core Operational: classification of organization into small batch, large batch/mass and process categories	CON	W	Organization	Key officials in each firm indicated appropriate category on a questionnaire	1023 employees in Norwegian firms (N = 15)	Climate dimensions such as intrinsic and extrinsic motivation are higher in small batch and process firms than in mass production firms

Study	Definition			Level	Method	Sample	Findings
Blau, Falbe, McKinley, & Tracy	Theoretical: substitution of mechanical equipment for human labor. Operational: amount of automation, technical complexity, and use of computers	CON	O, W	Organization	Structural questionnaire completed by senior managers	Manufacturing plants ($N = 110$)	Size is more highly related to structural variables than are automation or technical complexity; computer use is related to structural variables
Billings, Klimoski, & Breaugh	Theoretical: techniques used to transform inputs into outputs. Operational: large batch vs. mass production, routineness, work-flow rigidity, automation, and long-linked classification	CON	O, W, T, P, A	Subunit	Authors describe change in technology in terms of the operational concepts of technology	Hospital dietary department ($N = 1$)	Perceived job characteristics change in group closest to change in technology
Comstock & Scott	Theoretical: technological predictability at task and work-flow levels. Operational: type of care (work flow), need for nursing judgment, standardization of care, and number of choice alternatives (task)	CON	O	Subunit	Authors ranked wards according to predictability of type of care (work flow); expert ratings of predictability of surgical operations (task) were computed for each ward	Patient care wards in 16 hospitals ($N = 142$)	Technology is a more powerful predictor of subunit structure than is size
Overton, Schneck, & Hazlett	Theoretical: raw materials, techniques, and task interdependence. Operational: raw materials—number of patients requiring frequent observation, frequency of emergency, variety of health problems, patient age groups, predictability of hospital stay, and length of health history required; techniques—use of technical equipment, specification of patient goals, differences in nursing care, use of problem solving, and sociopsychological care; task interdependence—within-unit reliance on other nurses, dependence upon patient feedback, communication with physicians, and other units	ICH, ICO, CON	O	Individual	Questionnaire responses from full-time nursing staff ($N = 339$); responses were aggregated to the subunit level	Subunits in 8 hospitals ($N = 71$)	Factor analysis suggests that raw materials, techniques, and task interdependence are not independent dimensions of technology; each is related to three independent factors of uncertainty, instability, and variability

Table 8-1 (*Continued*)

Study	Technology Definition	Dimensions[a]	Theorist[b]	Level of Technology Measurement	Methods of Technology Measurement	Setting	Findings
Randolph & Finch	Theoretical: collection of plants, machines, tools, and procedures available for execution of a task and the rationale and knowledge underlying their use. Operational: classification of units as routine, mediating, and nonroutine technologies	CON	P	Subunit	Authors classified units	Departments in a veterans home	Patterns and frequencies of communication differ across technologies
Reimann	Theoretical: techniques and processes by which the focal organization transforms inputs into outputs. Operational: proportion of firm's output in each of a series of ordered classes was multiplied by weights and summed; rate of industrywide productivity change	CON, OCH	O	Organization	Interviews with executives, observation, and consulting documents	Manufacturing firms ($N = 19$)	Technological variables are less highly related to structural variables than are size and dependence
Rousseau	Theoretical: process of transforming input into output. Operational: classification as long-linked, mediating, or intensive	CON	T	Subunit	Experts classified units	Production units in 13 manufacturing and service firms ($N = 19$)	Intensive and mediating technologies are higher on job satisfaction and motivation and have higher job autonomy and variety than long-linked ones

Author	Definition			Level	Operationalization	Sample	Results
Rousseau	Theoretical: process of transforming informational and material inputs into outputs Operational: classification as long-linked, mediating, or intensive, and perceived job characteristics	CON	T, O	Subunit and individual	Experts classified units according to Thompson's (1967) scheme; employees rated job characteristics; ratings were examined at job level and also were aggregated to the subunit level	Production units in 13 manufacturing and service firms ($N = 19$)	Individual level job characteristics were the best predictors of employee attitudes; technological classification was the poorest predictor; aggregation did not alter pattern of relationships between job characteristics and attitudes
Rousseau	Theoretical: process of transforming raw materials into output Operational: classification of units into long-linked, mediating, and intensive; level of mechanization	CON	T, A	Subunit	Experts classified units according to Thompson's classification; department managers indicated types of equipment used during structured interviews	Departments in one manufacturing and one service organization ($N = 19$)	Classifications are better predictors of employee attitudes, behaviors, and job perceptions than is level of mechanization; technology and structure influence employee responses through their effects on job characteristics

[a] ICH = input characteristics; ICO = input control; CON = conversion; OCH = output characteristics; OCO = output control.
[b] W = Woodward; T = Thompson; P = Perrow; A = Aston; O = other or mixed.

technology measure at the industry level, while Rousseau[9] assessed technology at both departmental and individual-job levels.

The scheme employed here for summarizing technology is derived from an earlier review by Lynch.[12] However, the present review attempts to specify more clearly the meaning of classification and the origins of theoretical and operational definitions. It also attempts to present a general framework for interpreting research on technology.

Definitions of Technology

The definitions of technology vary greatly in the 31 studies reviewed. Technology is most commonly defined as technical complexity, the transformation of input into output, or the operations performed on an object. Operational definitions often are represented by classifications, according to the types of technologies specified by Woodward, Thompson, or Perrow (e.g., Grimes and Klein,[23] Mahoney and Frost,[24] Morrissey and Gillespie,[25] and Randolph and Finch[26]). However, citing the same theorist does not ensure comparability of either theoretical or operational definitions. For example, Grimes and Klein and Lynch both derive their definitions of technology from Perrow. Grimes and Klein define technology as role specification and task variability, while Lynch cites Perrow's[19] definition of "actions an individual performs on an object." The operationalization of technology also differs in these two studies. Grimes and Klein used a three-category classification scheme; Lynch assessed departments on five separate dimensions. In addition, these two studies reflect differences in levels of analysis, with Grimes and Klein studying technology at two subunit levels and Lynch studying it at the individual level. Such lack of conceptual and operational comparability seems to typify the research on technology.

Level of Analysis

Three levels of analysis are commonly treated in research on organizational technology: the organization, subunit, and individual. Rushing's industry-level assessment is an exception. The majority of studies reviewed here (14) involve assessment of technology at the organization level, while the fewest studies (6) assess technology at the individual level. Only 1 study assesses technology at more than one level, employing both subunit and individual-level measurement.[9] Comstock and Scott addressed the conceptual distinction between subunit and job-level technology (with the latter referred to as "task technology"); however, both forms of technology were measured at the departmental or subunit level.[27]

The level at which technological characteristics are measured has important implications for its conceptualization. When technology is assessed at the organizational level through interviews or questionnaires completed by higher-level management or through observation and expert classification, the focus is on the modal or most typical processes used to perform work. Most studies using organizational-level assessment of technology are investigations of the relationship of technological variables to dimensions of organizational structure. When modal measures of technology are used, relations between technology and structure may vary as a function of size. Although Aldrich[28] has called the findings of Hickson and associates[21] into question, technological variables have been found by Child and Mansfield to be more highly related to structure in smaller organizations than in larger ones.[29] These findings may be due to the amount of heterogeneity in types of technology found in any given organization. A large organization is more likely to employ more types of technical processes and people with more diverse knowledge and skills than is a smaller firm. Thus, the modal technology of a large organization may be less descriptive of the processes used in that organization than is the modal technology of a small firm.

Implicit in the concept of modal technology is an assumption that one technology is predominant in the organization. Although most researchers acknowledge that organizations may have numerous technologies or means to perform work—perhaps as many technologies as there are departments and positions in the organization—research is seldom done to assess the amount of variation in the technologies used within an organization. Inconsistent results regarding the relationship of structure to technology may be attributed to some extent to differences in the heterogeneity of an organization's technologies. Investigations of the relationship of core conversion-process technologies (those that directly yield a product or service) to support technologies (those technologies that aid the core) could provide insight into the complex nature of modal technologies. Support technologies include, among other activities, input and output control functions (e.g., supply and quality assurances). Assessment of these may provide important information on such mechanisms as leveling, buffering, and uncertainty reduction that organizations employ to exert control over the work flow.

Technological characteristics of the work flow of departments or subunits of an organization are often referred to as characteristics of unit technologies. Nine technology studies employ measures of technology assessed at the subunit level. The majority of these studies investigate the relationship of structure to technology (e.g., Comstock and Scott,[27] Grimes and Klein,[23] and Mohr[30]), although only Comstock and Scott find a strong relationship between the two.

In addition to the nine subunit-level studies of technology, three of the six individual-level studies involved aggregation of technology measures to the subunit or departmental level. Individuals' descriptions of their jobs were combined in some way to form aggregate measures of technology. All scores of individuals within a department can be averaged at the departmental level,[12,31] or supervisory staff scores can be averaged independently of nonsupervisory scores and the averages for the two groups combined to give both groups equal weight.[32]

The aggregation of technology scores measured at the individual level presumes that a combination of individual perceptions results in a more objective measure than is obtainable from any one individual. It also presumes that there is some consensus regarding the technology of the unit. This assumption may be tested by comparing within-group variance to between-group variance. As yet, however, no study of technology has done this. Aggregation of individual-level perceptions to higher levels of analysis also assumes that these averages reflect something other than descriptions of jobs—a questionable and untested assumption.[33] Lynch found that technology scores vary, depending on how data are aggregated.[12] At present, little is known about the impact of aggregation on our measures of technology. We do know that aggregation may alter our results,[33,34] often spuriously increasing the correlations between variables.

In research on technology, aggregation of individual-level data to the subunit or organizational level typically represents the form of aggregation Blalock[34] termed "grouping by proximity." Here, averages are computed for all individuals in the same organizational unit. This grouping may produce aggregation bias in the form of a spurious correlation at the aggregate level between dimensions of technology and structure. For example, such a correlation may result from conditions experienced by all members of an organizational unit that affect both technology and structure (i.e., a common cause), although no causal relationship may exist between the two. Environmental characteristics, such as market conditions or the nature of the labor force, are possible sources of spurious correlations.

Taking the studies involving aggregation of technology measures together with those studies assessing technology at the subunit or organizational level, only two studies were found to attribute technology to the individual level consistently. Both these studies characterize aspects of technologies assessed as job-level variables. Bell conceptualizes technology as job complexity,[35] while Hrebiniak refers to it as job technology.[11] Interestingly, both studies parallel most subunit and organizational-level studies by assessing the relationship of technology to structure. This focus reflects the assumption that isomorphism exists in the concepts and functional relations of technology and structure across organizational levels.

There appear to be technological differences in the types of organizations studied at the organizational, subunit, and individual levels of analysis. Most studies in which organizational-level assessments of technology were derived were conducted in manufacturing organizations, although four sampled both manufacturing and service organizations.

Subunit-level studies represent a mix of organizational types: four used service organizations, two manufacturing, and three a mixture of service and manufacturing firms. At the individual level, all studies were conducted in such service organizations as hospitals. The lack of comparability in organizations across levels of analysis makes it difficult to describe relationships among technological dimensions across levels of analysis. Thus, for example, we may find that certain types of organizational-level technologies are associated with employee alienation,[36] as are types of subunit technologies.[37] However, we cannot infer from such studies that organizational-level technology influences alienation through its effect on subunit technology. The types of technology assessments used in manufacturing organizations and those used in studies of manufacturing and service firms are not comparable.

Phases of Technology

Virtually all the technology studies reviewed here assess technology as a conversion process. Descriptions of conversion processes generally have taken two forms: classification on the basis of gross characteristics of production processes such as the use of mass production techniques[12,38] or measures of the level of automation.[21,39] Classification schemes tend to rely on expert ratings, usually by authors, and often they do not clearly specify the phases on which classification is made. Classifications, often treated as "objective" (nonperceptual) measures, reflect categorizations according to ideal or pure types to which the units are most similar. Conversion-process classifications generally reflect the role equipment plays in conceptions of technology. Thus they tap only one aspect of the conversion process and ignore the role of the human operator's knowledge and skills.

Because measures of automation often do not address the role of the human operator, they may be inappropriate for characterizing service organizations, and thus they may not facilitate comparative studies of technology in a broad range of organizations. Not all technological factors are physical. Certain social and psychological conditions also may represent the application of knowledge. It may be useful for assessments of conversion to view it as a sociotechnical system, where work is a product of the interaction between equipment and work-flow sequences, on the one hand, and human discretion and knowledge, on the other. Both social and physical components must be assessed for accurate description of the conversion process.

Despite the strong emphasis given to the conversion process, research on technology also generally involves assessment of the input and output phases. Half of the studies reviewed here assess aspects of input and output in addition to the conversion process. The most commonly studied dimensions following conversion are input characteristics such as variability,[32] uniformity,[23] and frequency of emergencies.[31] Though Thompson's propositions regarding technical rationality provide a basis for evaluating the input-characteristics conversion-process connection, little organizational research has been done regarding this critical interdependency. Research on organizational inputs and their impact on the conversion process is scant despite its relevance to human service organizations and other work systems where properties of inputs may greatly affect the core of conversion operations (see Chase[40] for an exception).

Input control has been assessed in three studies through measurement of predictability of length of hospital stay,[31] predictability of events,[12] and standardization of materials.[41] Predictability of patient stay or events is particularly important in shaping allocation of inputs to treatment (e.g., by influencing the scheduling of staffing). It is noteworthy that those studies addressing input characteristics and input control dimensions of technology have generally been conducted in service organizations, such as hospitals and government service organizations, where the use of human inputs (e.g., clients) makes input dimensions particularly important to organizational researchers. Since the proportion of service organizations is increasing, input characteristics may become more important in the research on technology.

Technological dimensions related to output have been less widely studied than input dimensions. Studies assessing output characteristics measure technology at the organizational level. For example, Freeman[39] assessed the type of substance produced, and Reimann[13] measured the rates of product change. These studies investigated the relationship of technology variables to structural dimensions. Freeman found a correlation between administrative intensity and product type, although Reimann discovered little relationship between product change and such structural dimensions as specialization, centralization, and formalization.

Output control was assessed in five studies, three of which used organizational-level assessments. The Aston group's index of work-flow integration includes specificity of output evaluation—an output control variable that is related to the level of automation.[21,42] Highly automated work processes are expected to be able to use exact standards for the evaluation of output, while less automated systems are expected to rely on the personal judgment of output quality. At the subunit level, output control was assessed by Taylor through four factors measuring performance feedback: the absence of feedback from supervisor, the degree to which the supervisor provides feedback on request, speed of feedback, and the primary source of feedback.[41] It represents the most thorough conceptualization of output control to date.

The lack of emphasis on output-oriented variables in technological research may stem from the conceptual overlap between the concepts of output and outcome. While such variables as rate of product change have been treated as output characteristics, or as dimensions of technology, such indicators may also reflect organizational adaptiveness. Adaptiveness, in the natural-systems view, is a dimension of organizational effectiveness—an outcome of organizational activity. To avoid confusing dimensions of technology with those of effectiveness, it would perhaps be best if technologically oriented output characteristics represented states or qualities of output (e.g., its diversity or complexity) and effectiveness-oriented outcomes reflected evaluations of these outputs by the organization's constituencies (e.g., customer sales). From this perspective, rate of product change would clearly be an output characteristic, while the market share these product changes activated would be an indication of effectiveness.

Models Underlying Technology Assessment

When the theories or models underlying operationalizations of technology are examined, the most striking observation is that half of these studies use original measures of technology that are not derived from the theories discussed before or from any previous research. This means that for a large number of studies, unique measures are employed that make cross-study comparisons difficult, if not impossible. In those studies using assessments derived from a prior model of technology, Perrow and Woodward are the most favored sources.

Characteristic of those studies employing original measures of technology is the equating of a single dimension or variable with the concept of technology. For example, Bell[32] conceptualizes technology as job complexity, while Rushing[15] focuses solely on the hardness of the materials processed. Piecemeal conceptualization of technology may be the root of the ambiguity surrounding the nature of technology in organizations. Part of the problem may reside in the failure to conceptualize technology's many dimensions, and part of the problem is the absence of cross-level treatment of the concept. These oversights represent neglect of what one may term the "content," or dimensionality of the technology concept, and the "composition," or hierarchical connection among its dimensions. The notions of content and composition models employed here are derived from Hannan.[33]

A Content Model of Technology

Dimensionality of the technology construct may vary from one context to another. In organizations, technology plays a special role; the application of knowledge that technology reflects is directed toward processing inputs into outputs through the organization's work flow. Research on organizational technology suggests that it reflects multiple aspects of this work flow or process, which can be characterized by five dimensions. "Input characteristics," such as the availability of raw materials, shape "input control" processes that buffer the conversion process from uncertainty and variability in the environment. "Conversion processes" add value to the raw material or throughput. "Output control" attempts to reduce the variability in the product through its influence on output quality and quantity and thus influences "output characteristics" before the output is introduced into the environment. These five dimensions, or phases, form the *content* of one concept of technology.

The significance of these phases for organizational structure and employee behavior depends on the nature of the organization. For example, effective human-service organizations (e.g., hospitals) may require more elaborate input control mechanisms because of client demands than do effective manufacturing organizations. Elaborateness of input control processes is a function of the diversity of those input characteristics that affect conversion (e.g., patients' diagnoses). Conversion processes are a function of existing technical knowledge, the distribution of work and responsibility among individuals, and the social system in which work is performed. Output control functions are determined to a large extent by the predictability of conversion processes and environmental demands for product quality.

Disaggregation of the technology concept is necessary to understand the nature of these phases, their interrelations, and their impact on organizational structuring and individual responses. To disaggregate our conceptions of technology, the technology construct can be divided into the phases of the transformation process described before. Such a disaggregation reflects the nature of the flow of work within the organization, and it may facilitate development of theories reflecting the interdependence among technological characteristics. These technological phases are likely to be related to different variables. For example, input characteristics and input control may be more highly related to such environmental characteristics as homogeneity and turbulence than are conversion characteristics. However, conversion characteristics may be more highly related to such structural characteristics as staffing ratios. Much ambiguity in technology research could be eliminated if the technological phase associated with operationalizations was specified.

Toward a Composition Model

The multiple phases of technology are reflected in multiple levels of activity at the organizational, subunit, and individual job levels. This cross-level nature of technology necessitates consideration of the hierarchical relations among its dimensions. How does job complexity (a presumed dimension of technology) affect subunit work-flow complexity? Do they correlate similarly with measures of structure? Such issues are the subject of theories of composition.

Theories of composition are hypothesized relations among constructs derived from different levels of analysis.[33] For example, in a department characterized by a high degree of variability in its work flow, many individuals may experience great variety in the skills they use and in the tasks they perform. Variability in subunit technology may translate into variety at the individual level or vice versa. Composition theories specify the relations among concepts measured at different levels. Most conceptualizations of technology derive from content theories describing the relationship of technology to dimensions of structure, communication, or effectiveness measured at the same level of analysis. Research on technology in organizations reflects three levels of analysis, but there are as yet no theories of composition to allow integration of conceptualizations or conclusions across these levels.

At present, there is scant empirical evidence on which to base theories of composition. One study has explored the connection between subunit and individual-level technology.[9] It suggests that individual-level technology, as measured through employee job perceptions, mediates the relationship of subunit technology to individual attitudes and behavior. Another study found a relationship between type of organizational technology and employee perceptions of opportunities for promotion and social integration.[36] Thus a relationship of organization- and subunit-level technologies to individual job experiences and responses is evinced in research on technology. However, research is needed to provide more detailed descriptions of the mechanisms whereby individual-, subunit-, and organization-level technologies interact and influence organizational processes. This research should include assessments of technology involving common constructs operationalized independently at different levels.

A composition model of technology would also assist the researcher who must decide whether aggregation is appropriate in the assessment of unit-level technology. Models specify the assumptions made and guide the choice of measurement strategies. If, for example, subunit work-flow complexity is assessed using mean individual-level job complexity, the assumption made is that work-flow complexity is simply the level of complexity typifying the work done by individual members of the subunit. No interaction between jobs or effects from mixing jobs requiring different skills are considered. If such an assumption is inconsistent with the model, the averaging of individual-level data is an unacceptable means of assessing work-flow complexity. A composition model can indicate if aggregation is theoretically sound.

Assessing Technology in Organizations

To portray accurately the process of converting inputs into output, which is the role of technology in organizations, it is necessary to assess multiple levels of activity across multiple phases of that process. Taken as a whole, the five phases of technology and three levels of analysis form the building blocks of a view of technology that may be used to develop both content and composition theories.

In the framework presented in Figure 8-1, levels of activity are embedded in one another. Individual or job-level technology is subsumed by subunit or department-level technology. Subunit technology is subsumed by organizational technology. Individual jobs are nested in subunits, and subunits are composed of individual jobs much in the same way that groups are composed of individual members. Groups may be qualitatively different from their individual members because of the interactions among members. Subunit technology may be qualitatively different from the individual jobs each department contains. It is not simply the aggregation of individual jobs, but it reflects both characteristics of these jobs and the interactions among jobs. The same relationship is expected to hold between subunit and organizational technology where the subunits or departments within an organization interact to create an organizational technology.

In this framework, core and support technologies reflect variability in functions at the subunit level. Since organizations may have multiple cores, assessments of organizational technology should give attention to differences in subunit characteristics. As organizations become increasingly differentiated, assessments of modal technology become less representative of the organization's technology. Measures of the distribution of core and support functions in the organization and assessments of characteristics of its various subunits may provide better assessments of technology at the organization level than do measures of modal technology.

Dimensions

Levels	Input Characteristics	Input Control	Conversion	Output Control	Output Characteristics
Organizations					
Subunit					
Individual					

Figure 8-1   Framework for assessment of organizational technology.

Although all five aspects of technology are reflected in the three levels of analysis, the extent to which individual-, subunit-, and organization-level characteristics of technology represent similar constructs is an empirical question. For example, the amount of control exercised over the work place by an individual may parallel the extent of mechanization at the subunit or organization level, or each may reflect different constructs having dissimilar relationships to other variables. Isomorphism from one level of analysis to another cannot be assumed.

Technological Change

In the study of planned organizational change, technological factors can serve three roles: as independent variables, conditions that are changed as part of an intervention; as dependent variables, the results of other changes or interventions; and as moderators, conditions across which changes have different effects. The last condition is seldom encountered in research on change since studies of interventions across units differing in technology seldom address those differences.

Many planned interventions are direct manipulations of technological factors, and thus they employ technology as an independent variable. Whenever we alter the type or amount of knowledge individuals apply to do work, we change the technology for that job, work unit, or organization whose base of knowledge is manipulated. Interventions where job redesign or job enrichment is involved, or where training programs are implemented that lead to utilization of new skills, each represent technological changes. However, the technological nature of these changes is frequently downplayed or ignored.

Job design programs, which are traditionally aimed at the individual, and sociotechnical systems changes, addressing intact groups or work units, frequently alter the variety of skills utilized and the amount of discretion and problem solving organization members demonstrate.[37] Typically, such programs alter individual-level conversion activities. However, by increasing employee skill utilization and discretion, such programs may also affect the nature of employee input and output control activities. Higher levels of skills may be accompanied by greater amounts of performance feedback and the expansion of the quality assurance or output control activities employees engage in. Greater discretion and problem solving afforded by job enrichment and sociotechnical changes give employees a larger repertoire of behaviors in which they may engage to do their work. This expanded repertoire may mean that employees have more control over the amount and variety of inputs such as the clients, patients, or problems they process (expanded input control-related activities). Since sociotechnical interventions have an impact on the distribution of work across several job holders and may alter their interdependence (e.g., through the creation of teams), changes in the technology of the work unit are even more likely in sociotechnical interventions than in individually oriented job design programs.

Any change in the level of employee discretion or problem solving associated with training programs or sociotechnical and job design interventions may alter the technology characterizing the work unit. Increased employee discretion can, for example, change a long-linked technology to an intensive one, according to Thompson's scheme.[18] These changes imply major adjustments in organizational design and can have an impact on how the organization, its departments, and members deal with uncertainty or attempt to rationalize or make predictable and controllable the results of their actions. It is primarily because of their implications for organizational design that it is important to recognize and understand the technological changes embedded in many planned organizational change programs.

Assessment of technological changes is also important because of the effect technology has on individual attitudes and behavior,[9,37] an impact often more substantial than that associated with structural characteristics of the work unit.[10] Changes in work-flow routineness, automation, availability of performance feedback, and control over the work pace, all reflect changes in technology's various phases and affect the psychological and behavioral responses of organization members. But technological changes may also occur as dependent variables in the study of organizational change. Structural changes, accomplished through the manipulation of organizational design and the introduction of management by objectives or other control systems may result in technological changes. Structures are the mechanisms for connecting individuals, roles, or work units with each other. These connections are accomplished through norms, influence and communication mechanisms, and authority structures. Changes in any of these may lead to the expansion or restriction of the skills and knowledge used to do work—the basis of technological change.

CONCLUSION

This review of research on technology suggests that past work has been fragmented and inconsistent. Twenty years after Woodward first suggested the importance of technology in organizational design, organizational scientists still sense that technology is important, yet they find its role difficult to articulate. This chapter suggests that it is necessary to specify more clearly the construct of technology before we are able to systematically assess its nature and organizational role. Focusing on the multiple phases of activity described before avoids the narrow, mechanistic view of technology in organizations as embodied in assembly lines or computers. Investigation of the interrelations among technological characteristics and phases may be the first step toward clarifying the role of technology in organizations. It may help us better describe how human knowledge and skill are channeled in organizations, which exist to apply knowledge in ways too complex for individuals to apply alone.

Assessment of planned interventions and their effects must address issues surrounding the phases of work flow affected by technological change. Change programs based on the behavioral sciences do not often formally attempt to alter the technology of a work unit. However, efforts to increase employee skills, discretion, or responsibility very often impact on support-technology activities, at minimum. This impact comes from increases in performance feedback or quality-control mechanisms or from giving employees greater discretion over the types of problems, clients, or materials they will process. These changes reflect alterations in input and output control activities, and they may enhance the effectiveness of core activities or even alter the nature of the technical core. Much of the payoff from organizational interventions may be realized through their impact on technology and the subsequent impact of the new technology on the organization's effectiveness and the well-being of its members.

REFERENCES

1. Huxley, A. Achieving a perspective on the technological order. *Technology and Culture,* 1963, **3,** 636–642.
2. Stanfield, G. G. Technology and organizational structure as theoretical categories. *Administrative Science Quarterly,* 1976, **21,** 489–493.
3. Layton, E. T. Technology as knowledge. *Technology and Culture,* 1974, **15,** 31–41.
4. Feibleman, J. K. Pure science, applied science, and technology: An attempt at definition. In C. Mitchum & R. Mackey (Eds.), *Philosophy and technology: Readings in the philosophical problems of technology.* New York: Free Press, 1972.
5. Woodward, J. *Management and technology.* London: Her Majesty's Stationery Office, 1958.
6. Woodward, J. *Industrial organization: Theory and practice.* London: Oxford University Press, 1965.
7. Dubin, R. *The world of work.* Englewood Cliffs: Prentice-Hall, 1958.
8. Form, W. H. Technology in social behavior of workers in four countries: A sociotechnical perspective. *American Sociological Review,* 1972, **37,** 727–738.
9. Rousseau, D. M. Measures of technology as predictors of employee attitude. *Journal of Applied Psychology,* 1978, **63,** 213–218.
10. Rousseau, D. M. Characteristics of departments, positions, and individuals: The relationship of context to attitudes and behavior. *Administrative Science Quarterly,* 1978, **23,** 521–540.
11. Hrebiniak, L. G. Job technology, supervision, and work-group structures. *Administrative Science Quarterly,* 1974, **19,** 395–410.
12. Lynch, B. P. An empirical assessment of Perrow's technology construct. *Administrative Science Quarterly,* 1974, **19,** 338–356.
13. Reimann, B. C. Dimensions of technology and structure: An exploratory study. *Human Relations,* 1977, **30,** 545–566.

14. Hage, J., & Aiken, M. Routine technology, social structure, and organizational goals. *Administrative Science Quarterly,* 1969, **14**, 366–376.
15. Rushing, W. A. Hardness of material as related to division of labor in manufacturing industries. *Administrative Science Quarterly,* 1968, **13**, 229–245.
16. Scott, W. R. Organizational structure. *Annual Review of Sociology,* 1975, **1**, 1–20.
17. Katz, D., & Kahn, R. L. *The social psychology of organizations,* 2nd ed. New York: Wiley, 1978.
18. Thompson, J. D. *Organizations in action.* New York: McGraw-Hill, 1967.
19. Perrow, C. A framework for the comparative analysis of organizations. *American Sociological Review,* 1967, **32**, 194–208.
20. Perrow, C. *Organizational analysis: A sociological view.* Belmont, CA: Brooks/Cole, 1970.
21. Hickson, D. J., Pugh, D. S., & Pheysey, D. C. Operations technology and organization structure: An empirical reappraisal. *Administrative Science Quarterly,* 1969, **14**, 378–397.
22. Peterson, R. B. The interaction of technological process and perceived organizational climate in Norwegian firms. *Academy of Management Journal,* 1975, **18**, 288–299.
23. Grimes, A. J., & Klein, S. M. The technological imperative: The relative impact of task unit, modal technology, and hierarchy on structure. *Academy of Management Journal,* 1973, **16**, 583–597.
24. Mahoney, T. A., & Frost, P. J. The role of technology in models of organizational effectiveness. *Organizational Behavior and Human Performance,* 1974, **11**, 122–138.
25. Morrissey, E., & Gillespie, D. F. Technology and the conflict of professionals in bureaucratic organizations. *The Sociological Quarterly,* 1975, **16**, 319–322.
26. Randolph, W. A., & Finch, F. E. The relationship between organization technology and the direction and frequency dimensions of task communications. *Human Relations,* 1977, **30**, 1131–1145.
27. Comstock, D. E., & Scott, W. S. Technology and the structure of subunits: Distinguishing individual and work group effects. *Administrative Science Quarterly,* 1977, **22**, 177–202.
28. Aldrich, H. E. Technology and organizational structure: A reexamination of the findings of the Aston group. *Administrative Science Quarterly,* 1972, **17**, 26–43.
29. Child, J., & Mansfield, R. Technology, size, and organization structure. *Sociology,* 1972, **6**, 369–393.
30. Mohr, L. B. Organizational technology and structure. *Administrative Science Quarterly,* 1971, **16**, 444–459.
31. Overton, P., Schneck, R., & Hazlett, C. B. An empirical study of the technology of nursing subunits. *Administrative Science Quarterly,* 1977, **22**, 203–219.
32. Van De Ven, A. H., & Delbecq, A. L. A task contingent model of work unit structure. *Administrative Science Quarterly,* 1974, **19**, 183–197.
33. Hannan, M. T. *Aggregation and disaggregation in sociology.* Lexington, MA: Heath, 1971.
34. Blalock, H. M. *Causal inferences in nonexperimental research.* Chapel Hill: University of North Carolina Press, 1964.
35. Bell, G. D. Determinants of span of control. *American Journal of Sociology,* 1967, **73**, 100–109.
36. Fullan, M. Industrial technology and worker integration in the organization. *American Sociological Review,* 1970, **25**, 1028–1039.

37. Rousseau, D. M. Technological differences in job characteristics, employee satisfaction, and motivation: A synthesis of job design research and sociotechnical systems theory. *Organizational Behavior and Human Performance,* 1977, **19,** 18–42.

38. Khandwalla, P. N. Mass output orientation of operations technology and organizational structure. *Administrative Science Quarterly* 1974, **19,** 74–97.

39. Freeman, J. H. Environment, technology, and the administrative interests of manufacturing organizations. *American Sociological Review,* 1973, **38,** 750–763.

40. Chase, R. B. The customer contact approach to services: Theoretical bases and practical extensions. *Operations Research,* 1981, **29,** 298–306.

41. Taylor, J. C. Some effects of technology in organizational change. *Human Relations,* 1971, **24,** 105–123.

42. Inkson, J. H. K., Hickson, D. J., & Pugh, D. S. Organizational context and structure: An abbreviated replication. *Administrative Science Quarterly,* 1970, **15,** 318–329.

The following sources are not referenced in the text but appear in Table 8-1:

Billings, R. S., Klimoski, R. J., & Breaugh, J. A. The impact of change in technology on job characteristics: A quasi-experiment. *Administrative Science Quarterly,* 1977, **22,** 318–339.

Blau, P. M., Falbe, C. M., McKinley, W., & Tracy, P. Technological organization in manufacturing. *Administrative Science Quarterly,* 1976, **21,** 20–40.

Zwerman, W. L. *New perspectives on organization theory.* Westport, CT: Greenwood, 1970.

Harvey, E. Technology and the structure of organizations. *American Sociological Review,* 1968, **33,** 247–259.

CHAPTER NINE

Assessment of Technologies and Their Utilization

WALTON M. HANCOCK, BARRY A. MACY, AND SUSAN PETERSON

This chapter reports the early stages of an effort to assess technologies in ways compatible with the objectives of comparison among organizations over time, and of joint sociotechnological system analysis. The first objective requires that multiple approaches to measurement are developed using methods that are comparable among differing technologies. The second objective requires that there are measurements not only of the gross features of an organization's dominant technology, but also of the variations that occur within an organization.

What follows is an introductory discussion of the implications of the fact that most organizations of interest have many technologies, not just one, even though, for the organization as a whole, there may be a dominant or core technology that gives rise to the others. Specific jobs and functional work groups possess distinctive technologies. Next, we present a proposed approach to the characterization of an organization as a whole, through the aggregation of technological data from the jobs and functional units within it. A third theme is then introduced: the assessment of the degree to which a given technology suits the work to be done and deviates from known and available preferred alternatives. The remainder of the chapter is an exposition of an approach to the assessment of the degree to which a given technology is fully utilized.

APPROACH AND CONCEPTUAL FRAMEWORK

The approach presented here involves description and assessment at three levels: (1) at the level of individual jobs, including their sociotechnical contexts; (2) at the level of the functional subunit (e.g., a department), that includes a number of related jobs; and (3) at the level of an entire organization or part of an organization that comprises interdependent functional subunits. In what follows, each level is illustrated with examples of aspects of interest and sources of assessment information.

1. *The Job.*   The technology of an individual's work role can have an important effect upon the job occupant and upon associated jobs.[1–7] In order to assess the technologies of the job and their impact on individuals, a number of aspects of jobs need to be assessed:

    a. Complexity (e.g., cycle time, number of different tasks)
    b. Resources used (e.g., machines, information, and people)
    c. Integration of tasks (e.g., the degree to which the job produces a coherent unit of product or service)
    d. Uncertainty (e.g., frequency of breakdowns, variability of materials)
    e. Interdependence (e.g., the degree to which an individual must depend on others and the nature of the interdependence)

    These assessments come largely from self-reports of people who perform the jobs and from the observations of trained observers.

2. *The Functional Unit.*   Much of the effectiveness of an organization depends on the way its work within a functional unit (e.g., department or work group) is linked into a work flow. A number of measures of the technology at this level are used. These include the following:

    a. Interdependence of jobs (e.g., measures of the existence of buffers [such as in-process inventories] and the amount of time it takes for a breakdown to cause production to stop)
    b. Effectiveness and efficiency of work-flow design
    c. Flexibility of the technology for major alterations or for variations in product or service demand.
    d. Complexity and sophistication of the control technology

    These properties are usually assessed through unit-performance (and failure, breakdown) records and through analysis by qualified work-system experts.

3. *Organizational System.*   It is important to measure the technologies within an organization as a whole system. Measures at this level include the following:

    a. Capital intensity of the technology
    b. Rigidity of the technology
    c. Complexity of the technology
    d. Integration of work flows

e. Modernity of the technology

f. Effectiveness of the utilization of the technology

g. Adequacy of maintenance schedules

Such measures are collected largely through interviews with experts in the organization and observation by outside engineering experts.

Table 9-1 displays in more elaborate form the kinds, qualities, and sources of information considered relevant for the assessment of technologies. In addition to distinguishing among three levels of technological systems—job, functional subsystem, and whole organization—the exhibit represents a scale of levels of abstraction and some variations in the theoretical or empirical resources to be employed.

Of particular importance is the scale of abstraction. Some measures are needed at a concrete and, therefore, a locally unique level. Others are needed at an intermediate level of abstraction, and yet others at a very high level of abstraction. The concrete measures allow for high-volume, objective, low-cost data for the detection of key performance variances and for detection of credible but relatively small changes over time. More abstract measures are intended to have the quality of generality so that comparison between organizations or between functional units becomes possible. For example, in comparing a welding shop with a hospital ward, counts of actual delay times are meaningless, while abstractions to the level of "schedule adaptivity" or "adequacy of coordination" allow comparisons as to approximate level against some common standard and as to directions of change. The paradigm proposed is that of a hierarchical pyramid of technological variables, with a small number of highly abstract but universally applicable descriptors at the top, and at the bottom, a very large number of concrete, unique, and precisely measured variables.

Not presented in Table 9-1 is an important distinction that arises from the aim of analyzing technology at different levels. A distinction is proposed between core technologies and support technologies. In most organizations, the distinction can readily be made between those technologies that directly add value to the product or service regarded as output and those technologies that aid the core but do not directly add to output value. An example is the parts supply and delivery unit that serves an assembly line. This distinction is useful in two respects:

1. It facilitates more realistic application of the "input–throughput–output" paradigm to different functional units of an organizaton as well as to the whole of the organization.

2. It provides a more certain guide to the identification of significant features of the technologies of a given organization, particularly when the focus of study is upon organizational subunits.

Table 9-1 Operationalization of the Technological Paradigm

Sociotechnical System "Level"	Illustrative Measures, Three Levels of Abstraction			Data Sources	Dominant Conceptual Orientation
	Concrete	First-Order Abstractions	Higher-Order Abstractions		
I. Job (individual or group)	Task cycle time Number of tasks Output Down time Errors Etc.	Repetitiveness Skill-level requirements Adequacy of tools, equipment, supplies Etc.	Automaticity Utilization of equipment capacity Adaptivity Etc.	Questionnaires Observation Records	Job design Human engineering/ergonomics
I. Functional subsystem (e.g., production department, service unit)	Output Delay time Buffer inventory and backlog Reject, rework Number of discrete operations, or transactions Etc.	Coordination requirements Schedule and material adaptivity Interdependence with other units Etc.	Modernity Automaticity Skill time requirements Adequacy of feedback Adequacy of coordination Etc.	Questionnaire Observation Records Interviews	Operations research Industrial engineering
III. Total system (subsuming I and II)	Output Unit cost System capacity Etc.	Output variety Adequacy of subsystem buffering Budgetary requirements Etc.	Modernity Automaticity Adaptivity Range Time System type (unit, batch, continuous flow, etc.) Etc.	Records Interviews	Management information systems Operations research Operational accounting Production Engineering

Finally, a given technological system needs to be assessed to determine (1) the alternative available technologies for accomplishing the same output; and (2) the degree of utilization of the full potential of the technology. Such assessments require intimate knowledge of the operations to be performed, and they may require methods of assessment that are quite different. The first requires expert opinions from professionals conversant with the range of technologies that could be employed; no measure except professional opinion currently exists. The availability of this information within a particular organization may be expected to vary with the size and quality of the technical staff. Multiple or external opinions may be desirable. The second, that is, assessment of the extent to which the present technological system is underutilized, does not require extensive knowledge of alternative technologies. It does require a comprehensive understanding of the functioning of the work place (i.e., work flow) and the means for estimating the potential increases in productivity that could be achieved by a fuller utilization of the potential of the existing technological system. Here too, experts are the best data sources.

CONCEPTIONS AND MEASUREMENT OF "BROAD" TECHNOLOGY

In the narrow sense, technologies can be thought of as the particular devices and materials that are used to produce a product or provide a service. Using this definition, technologies of different organizations or different parts of an organization are as different as apples and oranges. Comparisons are not only difficult, but no apparent need exists for making them.

Technology in a broader sense can be viewed not only to include the particular machines or other devices, but also the systems and procedures that support the machine. With this concept, one observes that different (narrow sense) technologies look more like different strains of apples or oranges because the support systems appear, in many instances, to have many similar characteristics. Materials, tools, and information have to be supplied to support the machine. Trained workers need to be available, machines need to be maintained, and the finished products have to be removed from the areas. The measurement of the broadly defined technology, therefore, seems to be desirable, at least for the following reasons:

1. *For Descriptive Purposes* If changes are occurring, we can evaluate the effect of efforts to change specified aspects. This is particularly important to the social scientist who is interested in evaluating the side effects in technological systems.

2. *For Prescriptive Purposes* If technologies share many common characteristics and one presumes a model of the proper role of the subsystem of the technology, then comparisons can be made and

change suggested to improve the technology on a cost-effective basis.

It is worthwhile to illustrate the significance of this by summarizing traditional and contemporary models of work. The traditional model employed by an industrial engineer has been the following.

$$\text{Get ready} \rightarrow \text{Do} \rightarrow \text{Put away}$$

This model was, and still is, sufficient for bench-type assembly operations. However, a more general model that appears to be applicable for all work is this one.

$$\text{Inputs} \rightarrow \text{Work place} \rightarrow \text{Outputs}$$

Amplification of the titles in the preceding model could be as follows.

Materials	Tools	Physical product
Information	Equipment	Information
Specifications	Training	Service
Instructions $\rightarrow$	Equipment maintenance $\rightarrow$	
Work sequences	Work to be done	
Supplies		

Some of the functions may not occur in certain work places, or they may be of little importance. The proposed view is that each of the functions of input, work-place activity, and output exist in order to enhance the productivity of the work place. Therefore, the *measure* of the need for the adequacy of the functions is whether or not they contribute to the work-place productivity. Examples of the differing relative importance of the various components are as follows:

1. On an assembly line, the timely provision of materials is very important to productivity of the aseembly-line work place, whereas information from the accounting system is usually of little immediate value to the worker.

2. An engineering-design unit requires effective methods for obtaining specifications and instructions concerning the design parameters; inputs of material have little or no consequence.

3. The outputs of the preceding two examples are substantially different. The assembly line produces a physical product that must be removed promptly or it will impede the work. In contrast, the engineering-design work produces a physical product (drawing) for which removal is of little importance.

Thus, a given work place can have a unique pattern of inputs, features of the work-place environment, and outputs that are essential to the objectives of the particular work place. Those factors of materials, information, and services that are deemed essential must be available, timely, and of acceptable quality in order for the system to achieve high productivity and ease of work performance.

CORE AND SUPPORT ASPECTS OF TECHNOLOGY

Since an individual work place (a "job") does not usually exist by itself, the output of one work place can become the input to another. The dependence of the output of one work place on the performance of the previous work place is part of the technology of the system, and it should be reflected in the attributes of the support system.

Core work is defined as work that directly adds value. Core situations are relatively easy to ascertain in an industrial organization because the words *value added* have long been associated with direct-labor work places. In service organizations, core work is harder to identify because value added is not a commonly used concept or measure. In these organizations, it is helpful to think of the "value-added" work as the work that constitutes the main services of an organization. Of course, if a service organization has no explicit definition of the services to be provided, core work is hard to identify.

Supportive work is defined as the work that enables the potential of the core work to be realized. Supportive work does not add value, but it enables the value to be added efficiently. Efficient core work may not be the only goal of an organization, but it is, at least, one of the more important goals.

A core or supportive work situation may have a number of work stations designed for work of a similar nature. Thus, an assembly line could be one core-work unit regardless of the number of people working, because all are performing analogous assembly tasks. Other examples of core units are an automatic screw machine group, the classroom in a public school, the kitchen in a restaurant, and the bed unit in an acute-care hospital. Examples of support units are the material handlers in an assembly plant, the duplication service in a university, and the laboratory in a hospital.

Another aspect concerns the work-place environment itself. It is assumed that the worker must have the following in order to maintain optimum productivity: (1) the equipment must be in good condition; (2) tools must be in good condition; (3) he or she must be able to sustain the work pace over periods normally expected; (4) he or she must have sufficient time to do the work and meet quality requirements; and (5) the work area must be free of controllable safety hazards.[8] Thus core work, worker environments, and support work can be viewed diagrammatically as in Figure 9-1.

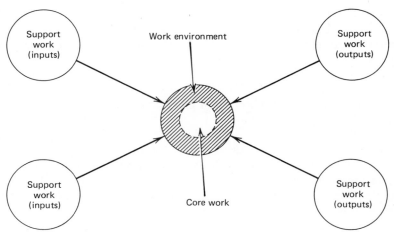

Figure 9-1.

The key features of the foregoing formulation of an approach to "broad" technology suggest a number of specific strategies for measurement, some of which are unprecedented or are weakly represented in past work. To illustrate the directions of our current measurement development, we next describe some specific operations that are being employed on a trial basis. These concern, respectively, (1) measurement of the overall technological complexity of a whole organization or of a functional subunit; (2) assessment of deviation from "most-appropriate" technology; and (3) assessment of the degree of utilization of a given technology.

ASSESSMENT OF TECHNOLOGICAL COMPLEXITY

Outlined in this section is an approach to the assessment of the overall technological complexity of a "whole" organization or of a functional subunit. The aim is to produce indicators that may be used to detect significant changes in complexity across a set of organizations engaged in unlike work. Applications have been made in several types of organizations, but the data shown here are contrived for illustrative purposes.

An organization may be thought of as the sum total of the core- and support-work activities. In order to obtain a unidimensional measure of the technological complexity of an organization, we may express core- and support-work situations mathematically as follows. Let

$$C_i = \text{a core-work situation}$$

$$S_j = \text{a support-work situation}$$

then the technology T of an organization is

$$T = \sum_{i=1}^{n} C_i + \sum_{j=1}^{m} S_j \tag{1}$$

where n are the number of core-work activities identified and m are the number of support-work activities identified. The particular values of n and m require an intimate knowledge of the work activities of an organization and why the organization exists. Thus identifying the magnitude of n and m may be difficult, but it is very instructive.

This expression helps to compare different organizations by the number of core and support units. Although an organization with a larger number of core and support units will be higher on the T-scale, the relative complexity of the support services is not considered. For example, an automotive assembly plant requires very complex production scheduling as compared to a plant producing auto parts. Yet each may have the same number of support activities. In addition, the core activities may be of the same number, but at different levels of technical complexity. Two mines may be engaged in removing coal, but one may use the most recent automated equipment and the other the pick and shovel. Such differences can be included in the equation as follows. Let

R_i = the rank of the core work on a technological complexity scale

R_j = the rank of the jth support work on a technological complexity scale of existing methods for doing the work.

Equation (1) then becomes

$$T = \sum_{i=1}^{n} R_i C_i + \sum_{j=1}^{m} R_j C_i \tag{2}$$

Expert opinion is necessary to obtain the most appropriate value of R_i and R_j. A complexity scale is suggested where the most highly developed technological state of a core or support system would be rated "1.0," and the most elementary would be given "0.1." All other technological states would become ordered by the expert opinion.

Most organizations have a low number of core-work situations regardless of the number of people they employ. For example, an automotive assembly plant has three core technologies: body framing, assembly, and painting. Most hospitals have at least four: medical service, surgical service, outpatient service, and intensive-care service. Most universities have three: teaching, research, and professional services. A restaurant has one: meal service; a hotel has two: bed facilities and meal service.

The same types of support services, but at different levels of complexity, are usually found in all organizations. For example, materials, supply, purchasing, scheduling, and equipment maintenance exist equally in number but in varying complexity.

Core Technologies and Complexity Estimates

Automobile Assembly Plant

Body framing	.7
Assembly	.7
Painting	.6
	$\Sigma R_i C_i = 2.0$

Hospital (secondary care)

Medical service	.5
Surgical service	.5
Outpatient service	.6
Intensive care	.8
	$\Sigma R_i C_i = 2.4$

University

Teaching	.3
Research	.9
Professional service	.4
	$\Sigma R_i C_i = 1.6$

Restaurant

Meal service	.4
	$\Sigma R_i C_i = .4$

Motel

Meal service	.4
Bed facilities	.5
	$\Sigma R_i C_i = .9$

These estimates illustrate—realistically, we think—some gross variations among common organizations in their estimated complexity of core technologies. Lest some saucier or surgeon be offended by the complexity ratings, the reader is reminded that what is represented is the complexity of the technology of the organization (or subunit), not that of an individual's job. The comparable estimates for the techological complexity of support technologies appears below:

Support Services C_j	Auto Plant	Hospital	University	Restaurant	Motel
Materials	.9	.5	.2	.3	.1
Purchasing	.8	.3	.2	.3	.1
Scheduling	.9	.4	.2	.1	.1
Equipment maintenance	.9	.2	.1	.1	.1

$R_{ij}*$

Applying Equation 2 to obtain an overall estimate of each organization's technological complexity, considering both core and support technological systems, the following results are obtained.

For the automobile assembly plant: $T = 2.0 + 3.5 = 5.5$
For the hospital: $T = 2.4 + 1.4 = 3.8$
For the university: $T = 1.6 + .7 = 2.3$
For the restaurant: $T = .4 + .8 = 1.2$
For the motel: $T = .9 + .4 = 1.3$

THE CHOICE OF THE MOST APPROPRIATE TECHNOLOGY

R_j of Equation 2 is an estimate of the technological complexity level of a particular support-work situation. Since the objective of support work is to aid in the achievement of the core-work potential, the question could be posed as follows: What is the most appropriate level of the support and core work in order for the full technological potential to be achieved? Substitution into Equation 2 of R_j' and R_i', which are estimates of the values of R_j and R_i where full potential can be achieved, would then give us an estimate of the T level that would be the most appropriate on a technological basis. If we call the revised level T', then the difference between T' and T is an indication of the total technological deficiency of the organization (assuming $T' \geq T$).

Perhaps a more interesting study for the researcher or practitioner is to obtain estimates of the more appropriate levels of R_j given that R_iC_i is unchanged. If we denote the value of T as T'' under these conditions, then

* The R_i and the R_j are the authors' estimates of typical situations for these organizations and are used for illustrative purposes only.

$T'' - T$ is an estimate of the potential improvement of the support activities. In many organizations, the capitalized equipment and/or most costly staff is concentrated in the core activities, rendering changes in core levels (R_iC_i) expensive. Changes in support activities are often relatively inexpensive because they commonly have a low requirement for capital investment. This suggests that effective changes will be feasible more often in the support activities than in core activities. Quantification of this concept can aid technical change agents in the determination of cost-effective technical changes. This approach should also be of interest to organizational theorists because the difference between T'' and T is a possible indicator of deficient organizational structure in the support organizations.

Methods of Obtaining Estimates of R_i and R_j

1. *Estimates of R_i.* The procedure suggested is for the observing expert to use a 10-point scale where 10 is assigned to the most advanced (usually the most complex) state of technology of C_i, and 1 to the most elementary. Also, it would be of great interest for the expert to put other commonly known technologies on the same scale in order to illustrate his relative rank ordering of the particular technologies in question.

2. *Estimates of R_j.* The procedures suggested in the preceding paragraph can be used also to obtain estimates of R_j when R_i is undergoing change. However, the sufficiency of R_j to supply the necessary support for the realization of the potential of existing R_iC_i can also be estimated more objectively using other methods, because all of the relevant information is resident within the organization. Some support systems are richly represented in existing management information systems, for example, delays due to maintenance, lack of parts, scheduling errors, and the like. Further, each worker within the system being studied can be viewed as an expert observer capable of reporting deficiencies in support received or in support provided. Techniques of time and motion study, work flow analysis, and the like may also be employed.

ASSESSING THE UTILIZATION OF A GIVEN TECHNOLOGY

An approach that appears to have promise for determining quickly the degree of attainment of the core work, and also for providing a partial basis for comparing the adequacy of the technology of organizations, is to obtain opinions from the workers themselves. Aside from substantial economies in professional time, this approach can produce low-cost information of high reliability and validity. The professional in his signal detection role frequently has to learn what the worker already knows; the worker, not the professional, is the resident expert. His expertise, however, needs to be tapped in a systematic manner in order to obtain a comprehensive view of the adequacy of the support technology and core work technology. Also, when one works within the suggested "broad" view of technology, significant factors are considered that are experienced and reportable by the workers but that are often not visible to the transient expert.

Workers in most cases can best supply information known as signal detectors. Signal detectors are those information items that provide knowledge as to whether or not there are aspects of the job (collectively, support, or core-work situations) that are not functioning as the existing technology should enable them to function. The quick and systematic detection of system deficiencies can enable changes in the operating system and/or the organization so that the potential can be more nearly achieved. After the change, the employees—through requestioning—can provide information to determine whether or not the changes have accomplished their intended result. Note that signal-detection questions do not ask the worker what corrections should be made, but only if the system (the part he or she personally observes) is functioning according to specified criteria (also readily observable).

Experience with this approach is still limited, although trials in several organizations of contrasting technologies suggest that it may have broad utility. The experience so far indicates that questionnaires are more cost effective and are probably more accurate than interviews; that questionnaires can be used with all types of workers one is likely to encounter; and that appropriate question formats can be devised for a variety of types of work systems. Appendix 9-1 illustrates, in general form, the kinds of questions that have been employed—obviously with adaptations to the characteristics of each situation.

In developing these questionnaire methods, several general guidelines have emerged. In the "input" questions, the criteria are stated first and the worker is asked to evaluate his or her experience against the stated criteria in order to minimize the tendency to confuse "ideal" and "normal" conditions. Where feasible, the worker is asked to state the frequency or the estimated economic consequence of deviation from the ideal. The questions are time constrained to obtain a reasonable time span of recollection and to avoid bias from unusual recent events; an effective set of questions may be as few in number as 15 to 25. It is essential to pretest the questionnaire for language clarity; and a half-dozen worker respondents from a given work group may be sufficient to provide stable response averages.

Appendix 9-2 presents a sample questionnaire that is similar to the one discussed in this chapter, but it is adapted for professional employees in a service organization.

Table 9-2 Examples of Technology Scales from Questionnaires

	Mean Level[a]	
Questions	Site 1 $t_1 : t_2$	Site 2 $t_1 : t_2$
1. Information When you are scheduled to start your assignments, do you have all the verbal and written information you need?	2.91 : 2.87	2.95 : 3.24
2. Professional Meetings Do you attend professional meetings having to do with your area of job assignment?	3.77 : 3.69	3.67 : 3.68
3. Job Feedback Do you know if the work you accomplished is of acceptable quality?	2.10 : 1.97	1.95 : 2.07
4. Time a. t_1: Do you have enough time to do your assignment well? b. t_2: Time limitations decrease the quality of my work (reversed scoring).	2.14 : 2.49	2.29 : 2.76
5. Training and Experience Do you have enough training and experience to accomplish your assignments?	1.72 : 1.56	1.82 : 1.67
6. Performance Improvement To what degree could your present job performance be improved by: a. More classroom instruction? b. More on-the-job training? c. Additional work association with an experienced person? d. Additional observation of other individuals? e. More contact with users of your work?	2.67 : 2.63	2.87 : 2.80
7. Communication with Supervisor a. How often do you discuss the details of your job assignment with your supervisor? b. How often do you get sufficient or clear guidance from your supervisor? c. How often do you provide recommendations to your supervisor concerning your assignments? d. How often do you discuss the quality of your work with your supervisor?	3.26 : 3.10	3.10 : 2.98
8. Discussion of Quality of Work How often do you discuss the quality of your work with: a. Those in relevant sites who use your work? b. Those in relevant groups who use your work? c. Those in relevant sections who use your work?	2.44 : 2.41	2.30 : 2.30

Table 9-2   (*Continued*)

	t_1 **Mean**[b]	
	Site 1	Site 2
When work has to be redone how often is it because of:		
a. Incomplete information?	2.43	2.63
b. Changing market or economic conditions?	3.83	3.45
c. Poor quality of work?	4.02	3.99
d. Schedules set by others?	2.92	3.02

[a] Responses range from 1 (always) to 5 (never) for all scales except Performance Improvement—here they range from 1 (not at all) to 5 (to a very great degree).
[b] Range of values: 1 (always) to 5 (never).

AN EXAMPLE OF APPLICATION

The following pages detail the results of an application of the approach to technology measurement outline in the preceding pages. The organization studied is a public utility engaged in the manufacture and delivery of electric power. The particular units reported here include a focal unit—called the experimental site—where a program of planned change was initiated, and a comparison unit from the same company, of similar size and type of function. Both are staffed largely by engineers and engineering technicians engaged in the design of physical facilities, one for power generation and the other for transmission. Over 200 individuals participated at each site. Site 1 comprised five functional subunits at the time of first measurement, T_1, to which a sixth was added before the second (T_2) measurement. Site 2 had four such subunits. Analogous groups, by function or by hierarchical rank, are identified in the following discussion.

Both sites were pretested to determine whether they are equivalent, as the design assumed. At Site 1 only, recommended changes were developed that were intended to alleviate problems brought to light by observation, interviews, and pretest responses. A posttest was carried out at both sites 18 months after the first to assess the actual effects of the changes.

Table 9-2 summarizes some of the data obtained by questionnaires at both sites. Mean responses are shown separately by site and for both T_1 and T_2 measurements. Inspection of the full data shows that few problems existed, arising from physical conditions. Supplies were readily obtained. There was "often" enough time to perform the work, and the workers "often" discussed the quality of their work with relevant others. However, communication with their supervisors about various matters was a "sometimes" matter. They did not strongly express a need for further training or for professional contacts. Disposal of finished work (drawings) was not a problem.

On the other hand, the data suggested major problems arising from deficient information flow prior to and during the performance of work. At both sites, the workers reported that they only "sometimes" had the necessary information when starting an assignment. They identified re-work as a common consequence. Incomplete information stood out as the attributed cause when rework did occur, as is shown in the responses to the questions in the table.

At Site 1, 22.4% of the jobs done had to be reworked (P). Rework took 27.0 hours on the average (R). It took 61.0 hours to do a normal job (N). The corresponding figures at Site 2 were 29.1%, 35.8 hours, and 163.1 hours. Using the formula

$$\frac{(.01P)R}{(.01)R + N}$$

gives 9.1% at Site 1 and 6.1% at Site 2 for the percentage of the time lost due to rework. The time spent idle (I) was 8.8% at Site 1 and 5.8% at Site 2. Adding this to the previous numbers gives values of 17.9 and 11.9 for the percentage of time spent unproductively at Sites 1 and 2, respectively, according to the aggregated reports of the employees. On-site observation confirmed that much of this loss could be attributed to the lack of proper information flow noted previously. In addition, lack of environmental-impact data and the necessity to involve higher administrative personnel in many decisions due to the deficiency of administrative guidelines were seen as major causes of inefficient core-work systems performance.

Company projections for Site 1 indicated that a substantial increase in work load would occur in the near future. As result, the Site 1 people concentrated their activities on reorganization of the environmental im-pact functions and on the establishment of administrative guidelines that would reduce delays and errors in communication and, thus, improve output. Note that these changes were all in support activities.

After the implementation of these planned changes, a second round of data was collected, 18 months after the first survey. Production time loss fell at Site 1 from 17.5% to 8.9%, a saving of 8.6 percentage points. In man-hours, this time saving by 290 workers is equivalent to a 26.1 person addition to the staff. Taking into account annual salary and fringe bene-fits costs per person, this is a savings of $638,406. During the same period, production time loss rose by .5% from 11.9% to 12.4% at Site 2, costing $33,266. These results suggest that Site 1 improvement was the result of the changes initiated within the organization, not the result of general environmental influences that worked on Site 2 as well.

The trends in the other four components of time loss are not shown here numerically. There was a moderate decrease in percentage of jobs needing rework at both sites and a small increase in the average hours to

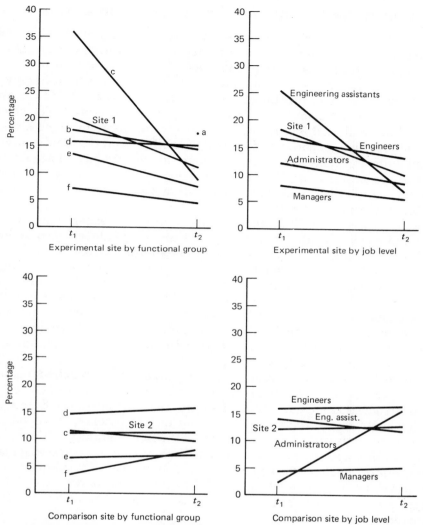

Figure 9-2   Change in production time loss t_1 to t_2—both sites by group and job level.

rework a job. Idle time did not change at Site 2 but decreased at Site 1. The most remarkable change occurred in the hours to complete a normal job; while decreasing slightly at Site 2, there was almost a threefold increase at Site 1. Probably this change reduced the production time loss. The increase in normal job time, due to having more and better information to start with, makes it possible to complete the job more efficiently before moving on to other work.

Analysis by Functional Groups and Job Levels

So far, the analysis of the data on time loss—the organization's major problem area with respect to the utilization of an existing work technology—has been reported only at the level of the two units that are compared. The measurement techniques used have shown where improvements in technology utilization were needed and what effects certain interventions had upon the achievement of system potential. The same data allow analysis by functional groups and by hierarchical job levels, thus offering two important additional possibilities: (a) the identification of subunits and classes of personnel where further change efforts might best be concentrated; and (2) the comparison of technology-related practices to identify those that appear to aid, or to impede, the achievement of system potential (Figure 9-2).

With respect to the allocation of changes within the experimental unit, the data show that all functional groups and all job levels display improvement in time loss following the interventions, but that the amount of gain was the greatest in one functional group and one job level (engineering assistants). In the comparison site, the changes were mixed in direction, thus offsetting for the unit as a whole, and none were as great as those found in the experimental site. In short, the analysis of time loss by job level and by functional groups confirms the relative change between Site 1 and Site 2, and shows that the improvements obtained at Site 1 occurred generally within that site.

The analysis of the technology-related practices by functional units and by job levels proved to be less informative in this case. The "practices" in question include attendance at professional meetings, fit-of-task assignments to the individual's training and experience, frequency of communications with the supervisor, and the like. Significant differences between sites appeared that follow distinctively different patterns for the several functional groups and job levels. The number of such differences increased between time 1 and time 2. The interpretation of these differences and their prescriptive implications is beyond the purpose of this chapter.

SUMMARY AND PROGRAMMATIC INTEGRATION

At both sites the overall assessment model served to provide a useful basis for quickly understanding, through the survey and observation processes, the utilization of the various technologies of the organizations involved. Testing the feasibility of comparing across many organizations with different technologies, using the model described in experiences to date, suggests that technology can be measured and compared by using such a concept.

This chapter reports early efforts to work out an approach and operational procedures for assessing the technological aspects of sociotechnical systems. The intent is to find ways to detect and evaluate changes in technological systems over time in order to make comparisons—among organizations with unlike technologies. In addition, the objective is to gain the ability to describe and assess technologies at the level of organizations as a whole and of the component subunits. The key ideas employed are the following:

Organizations have not one technology but several, of distinctively different characteristics; these are commonly segregated in different functional subunits.

Core technologies need to be distinguished from support technologies. A "broad" conception of technology is required, that is, a conception that allows inclusion of aspects of the work environment and work processes that are not, strictly speaking, inherent in the physical and informational factors alone.

Not only means for assigning technological systems to some gross generic types are needed, but also means to achieve (1) estimates of the appropriateness of a technology compared with available alternatives; (2) estimates of the fit of support technologies to core technologies; and (3) estimates of the degree of utilization of technologies.

There is need to employ, where feasible, information sources other than those dependent upon professional expertise—for reasons of cost and the known limitations of individual opinion.

The aim is not to supplant the existing available approaches to the assessment of technological systems, but to complement those approaches in ways that enlarge our capacities to evaluate sociotechnical systems and changes that are made in them. When treating technological systems, it is inevitable that there is a focus upon criteria of effectiveness and efficiency in work performance. The larger objective, however, is to understand the manner in which technological systems impact—for better or worse—upon nontechnological consequences and correlates, such as the experienced quality of working life and the adequacy of an organization in fulfilling its broader economic and societal roles. Such objectives require new methods for describing and assessing technologies—methods that do not now exist in forms of known scope, reliability, and validity.

The work has only started. The next stage involves extending the trial application of the suggested approaches to a wider variety of organizations, the establishment of the levels of reliability and validity in practical usage, and the examination of the fit of the approach proposed with other aspects of the task of sociotechnical analysis and system design.

The practical aspects of reliability and validity will be concerned with obtaining supporting data that can be compared to the responses of the employees. Here, the emphasis will be on the correctness of employee responses concerning the magnitude of problems. For example, employees' responses to the percentage of time an event takes may be subject to overestimation or under estimation. Fortunately, one can tolerate considerable errors in these responses and still have a very useful tool if the use of the tool is to determine quickly the major problems that exist. Considerable error can also be tolerated in the economic implications because, if our experience to date holds, the economic implications are so great that even if they are off by 50%, the same action should be taken.

REFERENCES

1. Aldrich, H. E. Technology and organizational structures: A re-examination of the findings of the Aston group. *Administrative Science Quarterly,* 1972, **17**, 26–43.
2. Pondy, L. Organizational conflict: Concepts and models. *Administrative Science Quarterly,* 1967, **12**, 296–320.
3. Pondy, L. Effects of size, complexity and ownership on administrative intensity. *Administrative Science Quarterly,* 1969, **41**, 47–60.
4. Woodward, J. *Management and technology.* London: Her Majesty's Stationery Office, 1958.
5. Woodward, J. *Industrial organization: Theory and practice.* London: Oxford University Press, 1965.
6. Woodward, J. *Industrial organization: Behavior and control.* London: Oxford University Press, 1970.
7. Pugh, D. S., Hickson, D. J., & Hinnings, C. R. An empirical taxonomy of work organization structures. *Administrative Science Quarterly,* 1969, **14**, 115–126.
8. Herrick, N. Q., & Quinn, R. P. The working conditions survey as a source of social indicators. *Monthly Labor Review,* 1971, **94**(4), 15–24.

APPENDIX 9-1   THE GENERAL WORK TECHNOLOGY SURVEY*

Ideally, when you do your work you should always have all the information, drawings, parts, tools, and materials you need. Consider the work you have done over the last three months with these questions in mind.

The Inputs to Your Work

1. How long does your average job take?
2. Do you have all the *information* you need to do your job? If you do not, what percentage of the time does this occur? How much longer does it take you to do the work?

* These questions may be put in interview or questionnaire form, and they can be accompanied by fixed response alternatives, if so desired.

3. Do you have all the *drawings* you need to do your job? If you do not, what percentage of the time does this occur? How much longer does it take you to do the work?

4. Do you have all the *parts* you need to do your job? If you do not, what percentage of the time does this occur?

5. Are the parts to specification? If not, what percentage of the time does this occur? How much longer does it take you to do the work?

6. Do you have all the *tools* you need to do your job? If you do not, what percentage of the time does this occur? How much longer does it take you to do the work?

7. Do you have all the *materials* you need to do your job? If you do not, what percentage of the time does this occur? How much longer does it take you to do the work?

8. Assuming you have all of the information, drawings, parts, tools, and materials you need, by what percentage would your output improve?

In order to be as productive as possible, you must know how to do your job. Your equipment and tools must be in good condition. Your area should be free of safety hazards, and you should be able to sustain your output over eight hours. Consider the work you have done over the last three months when answering the following questions.

The Work You Do

1. Are you adequately trained for the work you do? If not, for what percentage of your work do you feel that you are not adequately trained? How much longer does it take you to do the work than if you were properly trained?

2. Is your equipment maintained in good condition? If not, what percentage of the time does this occur? How much longer does it take you to do the work?

3. Are your tools in good condition? If not, what percentage of the time does this occur? How much longer does it take you to do the work?

4. Do you have all the tools you need? If not, what percentage of the time does this occur? How much longer does it take you to do the work?

5. Are there any safety hazards in your work place? What percentage of the time are you exposed to the safety hazards? You much longer does it take you to do the work?

6. Are you properly trained to produce work of acceptable quality? If not, what percentage of the time do you feel you are not properly trained? How much longer does it take you to do the work?

7. What percentage of the time do you have to do work over again? How much longer does it take you to do the work?

8. Assuming you are properly trained, have good equipment and tools, and have sufficient time and energy to do your work, how much would your present output increase (in %)?

When you finish with your work, you need a place to put it or you need to have it taken away so it will not interfere with the next job you do. Please keep this in mind when answering the following question.

The Output

1. Is your work removed or do you have some place to put it so that it does not interfere with your next job? If you do not, what percentage of the time does this occur? How much longer does it take you to do your work?

APPENDIX 9-2 GENERAL WORK TECHNOLOGY QUESTIONNAIRE*

APPENDIX 9-2

GENERAL WORK TECHNOLOGY QUESTIONNAIRE*

```
* * * * * * * * * * * * * * * * * * * * * * * * * * * * * * * * * * * * * * * * * * *
*                                                                                  *
*        This part of the questionnaire examines the technological environment in which you work,  *
*   focusing on the kinds of information and materials you need to do your assignments.  Two        *
*   stages of work are highlighted:  (1) the inputs to your assignments such as communications      *
*   and (2) the assignments you do including the pressures you experience.  This section of the     *
*   questionnaire begins by asking you to think of an ideal work environment and comparing          *
*   your own situation to that ideal.  Any questions that do not apply to your particular job       *
*   should be indicated under the category "Does Not Apply" and mark number 6.                      *
*                                                                                  *
*        Note that the scale descriptions may be different in different parts of the questionnaire. *
*   For example, they may ask how often you do something, what percentage of the time you           *
*   do it, or whether you think something is done to a great degree or not at all.                  *
*                                                                                  *
*        So, be sure to read the special instructions that appear in the boxes on each page.  Be    *
*   sure to read the scale descriptions before choosing your answers.                               *
*                                                                                  *
* * * * * * * * * * * * * * * * * * * * * * * * * * * * * * * * * * * * * * * * * * *
```

THE INPUTS TO YOUR WORK

IDEALLY, BEFORE STARTING A JOB, YOU SHOULD HAVE ALL THE INFORMATION, DRAWINGS, MATERIALS, AND INSTRUCTIONS YOU NEED TO DO THE JOB. IF YOU BEGIN AN ASSIGNMENT BEFORE YOU HAVE ALL THAT YOU NEED, YOU MAY NOT BE ABLE TO DO AS GOOD A JOB AS YOU CAN. CONSIDER YOUR PRESENT JOB WITH THIS IN MIND.

Scale: Always [1] Often [2] Sometimes [3] Seldom [4] Never [5] Does Not Apply [6]

1. When you are scheduled to start your assignments, do you have all the verbal and written information you need? .... [1] [2] [3] [4] [5] [6]   6:11

2. If you do not have all the information, is it readily available if you contact the appropriate person? (NOTE: Please check "Does Not Apply" if you answered question number 1 with a response of Always or Often) .... [1] [2] [3] [4] [5] [6]   6:12

3. When you do not have all the information needed to start your assignment, how often do you begin anyway? .... [1] [2] [3] [4] [5] [6]   6:13

4. When you do not have all the information needed to start your assignment, does it delay your work? .... [1] [2] [3] [4] [5] [6]   6:14

---

*Adapted for professional employees in a service organization.

5.   If you were to start your assignment without all
     the information you need:

     Always Often Sometimes Seldom Never Does Not Apply

     a.   Does the quality of work suffer? .... [1] [2] [3] [4] [5] [6]   6:15

     b.   What percent (%) of your work suffers? .... _____ % (NOTE: please fill in the   6:16-18
                                                                   percent - 0 - 100%)

     c.   How much does the quality of work suffer?   6:19

          [1]   To a very great degree
          [2]   To a large degree
          [3]   To some degree
          [4]   To a slight degree
          [5]   Not at all
          [6]   Does not Apply

THE WORK YOU DO

IN ORDER TO DO CONSISTENTLY GOOD WORK, YOU MUST HAVE SUFFICIENT TRAINING SO THAT
THAT YOU KNOW WHAT AND HOW TO DO YOUR JOB. THE TOOLS YOU NEED MUST BE AVAIL-
ABLE AND IN GOOD OPERATING CONDITION. IT IS IMPORTANT THAT YOUR WORK IS OF
ACCEPTABLE QUALITY. YOUR WORK AREA SHOULD BE CONDUCIVE TO WORK, AND YOU SHOULD
HAVE SUFFICIENT TIME IN WHICH TO COMPLETE YOUR ASSIGNMENTS. KEEP THIS IDEAL CON-
DITION IN MIND AS YOU ANSWER THE QUESTIONS BELOW.

---

6.   Do you have enough training and experience to accomplish your assignments?   6:20

     [1]   [2]   [3]   [4]   [5]

     Always   Often   Sometimes   Seldom   Never

7.   What percent (%) of the assignments you are asked to accomplish do you feel qualified for?
     (NOTE: please fill in the percent - 0 - 100%)   6:21-23

                         _____ %

8.   I am qualified for the assignments I am asked to perform.   6:24

     [1]   To a very great degree
     [2]   To a large degree
     [3]   To some degree
     [4]   To a slight degree
     [5]   Not at all

9. To what degree could your present job performance be improved by:

Scale headers: Not At All, To A Slight Degree, To Some Degree, To A Large Degree, To A Very Great Degree

a. More classroom instruction? .... [1] [2] [3] [4] [5]　6:25

b. More on-the-job training? .... [1] [2] [3] [4] [5]　6:26

c. Additional work association with an experienced person? .... [1] [2] [3] [4] [5]　6:27

d. Additional observation of other individuals? .... [1] [2] [3] [4] [5]　6:28

e. More contact with users of your work? .... [1] [2] [3] [4] [5]　6:29

f. More technical direction by your supervisor? .... [1] [2] [3] [4] [5]　6:30

g. More "face-to-face" communication by your supervisor? .... [1] [2] [3] [4] [5]　6:31

Scale headers: Always, Often, Sometimes, Seldom, Never, Does Not Apply

10. Do you attend professional meetings having to do with your area of job assignment? .... [1] [2] [3] [4] [5] | [6]　6:32

11. Do you know if the work you accomplish is of acceptable quality? .... [1] [2] [3] [4] [5] | [6]　6:33

12. How often do you discuss the details of your job assignment with your supervisor? .... [1] [2] [3] [4] [5] | [6]　6:34

13. How often do you get sufficient or clear cut guidance from your supervisor? .... [1] [2] [3] [4] [5] | [6]　6:35

14. How often do you provide recommendations to your supervisor concerning your assignments? .... [1] [2] [3] [4] [5] | [6]　6:36

Scale headers: Always, Often, Sometimes, Seldom, Never, Does Not Apply

15. How often do you discuss the quality of your work with:

a. Those outside .... [1] [2] [3] [4] [5] | [6]　6:37

b. Those in relevant divisions who use your work? ...... [1] [2] [3] [4] [5] | [6]　6:38

c. Those in relevant branches who use your work? ...... [1] [2] [3] [4] [5] | [6]　6:39

d. Those in relevant sections who use your work? .... [1] [2] [3] [4] [5] | [6]　6:40

e. Your supervisor? .... [1] [2] [3] [4] [5] | [6]　6:41

f. Your section co-workers? .... [1] [2] [3] [4] [5] | [6]　6:42

16. When you do your work over or modify it, is it because of:

Always Often Sometimes Seldom Never Have No Idea

a. Starting without all relevant information (i.e., drawings, specifications, design parameters, etc.)? .... [1] [2] [3] [4] [5] [6]   6:43

b. A change in information due to incorrect original information? .... [1] [2] [3] [4] [5] [6]   6:44

c. A change in information due to a change in the environment (i.e., customer demand shifts, customer specifications, etc.)? .... [1] [2] [3] [4] [5] [6]   6:45

d. Supervisory guidance not available? .... [1] [2] [3] [4] [5] [6]   6:46

e. A change in procedures, policies, practices, etc.? ...... [1] [2] [3] [4] [5] [6]   6:47

f. Establishment of new procedures, policies, practices, etc.? .... [1] [2] [3] [4] [5] [6]   6:48

g. Insufficient or incorrect materials? .... [1] [2] [3] [4] [5] [6]   6:49

h. Materials not available when needed? .... [1] [2] [3] [4] [5] [6]   6:50

i. Environmental specifications not completed? .... [1] [2] [3] [4] [5] [6]   6:51

j. Inadequate planning between branches? .... [1] [2] [3] [4] [5] [6]   6:52

k. Inadequate coordination between branches? .... [1] [2] [3] [4] [5] [6]   6:53

l. Delay in workflow between branches? .... [1] [2] [3] [4] [5] [6]   6:54

m. Inadequate scheduling between branches? .... [1] [2] [3] [4] [5] [6]   6:55

n. Poor quality of work by others? .... [1] [2] [3] [4] [5] [6]   6:56

o. Inadequate influence in setting schedules? .... [1] [2] [3] [4] [5] [6]   6:57

p. Arbitrary decisions by higher ups? .... [1] [2] [3] [4] [5] [6]   6:58

q. Don't know the reason .... [1] [2] [3] [4] [5] [6]   6:59

Always Often Sometimes Seldom Never Does Not Apply

17. Time limitations decrease the quality of my work. .... [1] [2] [3] [4] [5] [6]   6:60

18. Work schedules increase the quality of my work. .... [1] [2] [3] [4] [5] [6]   6:61

19. When you do not have enough time to do your work adequately is it because:

Always Often Sometimes Seldom Never Does Not Apply

a. You have been asked to meet an unreasonable deadline? .... [1] [2] [3] [4] [5] [6]   6:62

b. You do not have enough relevant information? .... [1] [2] [3] [4] [5] [6]   6:63

c. You do not have the necessary equipment? .... [1] [2] [3] [4] [5] [6]   6:64

d. You do not have the relevant drawings and specifications? .... [1] [2] [3] [4] [5] [6]   6:65

e. You do not have adequate training? .... [1] [2] [3] [4] [5] [6]   6:66

When you do not have enough time to do your work
adequately is it because:

		Always	Often	Sometimes	Seldom	Never	Does Not Apply	
f.	You have been asked to do too much work?	[1]	[2]	[3]	[4]	[5]	[6]	6:67
g.	The assignment's budget is too tight?	[1]	[2]	[3]	[4]	[5]	[6]	6:68
h.	The work is not adequately scheduled?	[1]	[2]	[3]	[4]	[5]	[6]	6:69
i.	The work flow is poorly coordinated?	[1]	[2]	[3]	[4]	[5]	[6]	6:70

INSTRUCTIONS: We realize that the following questions are difficult to answer. However, they are very important in order to obtain a measure of the impact of redoing or modifying assignments. This measure will help the economics portion of this meaningful area.

---

20. Thinking of your work over the past three months, what percentage (%) of your assignments had to be done over or modified? (Please fill in the percent - 0 to 100%)
    6:71-73

    _____ % of assignments

21. Thinking of these modifications or rework, did the quality of the finished work improve?
    6:74

[1]	[2]	[3]	[4]	[5]	[6]
To A Very Great Degree	To A Large Degree	To Some Degree	To a Slight Degree	Not At All	Have No Idea

22. Thinking of your work over the last three months, what percentage (%) of your time was spent on rework or modification? (Please fill in the percent - 0 to 100%)
    6:75-77

    _____ %

23. Thinking of your work over the past three months, what percentage (%) of your time was spent without a work assignment? (Please fill in the percent - 0 to 100%)
    6:78-80

    _____ % of time without assignments

24. Thinking of your work over the past three months, how many hours did your typical work assignment take to complete? (Please fill in the average number of hours per assignment, 0 to 999 hours; NOTE: If your typical assignemnts lasts longer than three months, report total hours needed for completion.)
    7:11-13

    _____ average hours per typical assignment

25. Thinking of your work over the past three months, how many hours did you spend redoing or modifying your typical work assignment? (Please fill in the average number of hours per assignment, 0 to 999 hours; NOTE: If your typical assignment lasts longer than three months, report total hours involved in redoing or modifying work.)   7:14-16

_____ average hours per typical assignment

26. On the average, what percentage (%) of time do you spend during an eight hour day being productive (i.e., a work day could be divided up into the following three components: (a) Meaningful work, (b) Less than meaningful work, and (c) No work at all. Please do not consider coffee breaks and lunch as "No work at all").

                 _____ %   7:17-19
                 Meaningful Work

   +   _____ %   7:19-21
                 Less Than Meaningful Work

   +   _____ %   7:22-24
                 No Work At All

                 _____

TOTAL =   100% of an eight hour day

CHAPTER TEN

Observer Ratings of Job Characteristics

DAVID A. NADLER AND
G. DOUGLAS JENKINS, JR.

This chapter presents an approach to the description and assessment of job characteristics through guided observations combined with a systematic reporting of the conditions observed. This basic methodology is familiar. There exist field-tested methods for describing jobs as to their time-and-motion properties,[1] their skill demand,[2] their health-related physical properties,[3] and the job elements that contribute to the wage value.[4] There does not exist, however, a standardized and field-tested procedure for measuring certain additional job characteristics that are thought important in the context of employee motivations, satisfaction, and personal development.

Such "psychological" aspects of jobs have not escaped attention, of course. Virtually all theory, research, and practice concerning the optimizing of jobs assume that the employee is responsive to the objective features of the job and the work environment. Many quality of work programs and other organization improvement programs include specific attention to job characteristics and to changes in jobs themselves. To test such theories, to conduct effective research, and to improve job redesign practices, we need to have a capability for measuring a wider range of job characteristics and for evaluating changes in them.

The convenience of interviews and questionnaires have led to a heavy reliance upon worker self-reports in appraising the job characteristics

Portions of this chapter appeared in G. D. Jenkins, Jr., D. A. Nadler, E. E. Lawler III, and C. Cammann, "Standardized Observations: An Approach to Measuring the Nature of Jobs," *Journal of Applied Psychology,* 1975, **60,** 171–181. Copyright 1975 by the American Psychological Association. Adapted by permission.

with which we are concerned. However, there is a risk in depending upon any one measurement method in the absence of corroborating alternative indicators. There is, further, the risk of bias because of two factors: (1) few job occupants have knowledge of a wide range of different job conditions to give perspective on their own jobs, and (2) no matter how objective he or she tries to be, the worker's perceptions are surely influenced in some degree by personal factors.

The use of the self-report by workers hardly needs defense, for job occupants also are singularly qualified observers and reporters. They have "observed" the job for some considerable time and under different conditions; they alone directly experience some features of the job that are not visible or inferable by an observer who is on the scene briefly. The data so produced, despite their limitations, are known to "work," in the sense of displaying useful validity in theoretical and experimental tests as well as in longitudinal predictive studies. An approach through structured observation by disinterested observers is no more "objective," but it does offer several advantages that, in principle, should result in enhanced validity of the descriptive and evaluative data.

1. Observers can report job behaviors and job conditions that are not contaminated by selective recall and retrospection.
2. Observers are independent, trainable, interchangeable, and replicable, and thus they allow control of personalistic bias.
3. Multiple observers and multiple periods of observation allow empirical verification of the data and degree of interrater agreement.
4. Trained observers can conduct their observations and prepare their summary reports in ways that fit the constructs to be used in the interpretation of the data; further, when job occupants are asked to report in a similar manner, the degree of job-occupant bias can be estimated.

This chapter describes the development and field testing of an observation procedure. The development includes the testing of an original instrument and procedures that were then improved by subsequent revision. The field testing includes the use of nonprofessional, briefly trained observers, on grounds that general use of the method would otherwise be precluded. The evaluation of the procedure includes the identification of certain conceptual variables that remain unmeasurable and the estimation of the reliabilities and validities of the measures obtained.

CONCEPTUAL FOUNDATIONS: WHAT TO MEASURE

While the method we describe is open ended as to information content, the work so far has been limited to a few aspects of jobs that are considered particularly relevant to the assessment of the quality of working life as experienced by the job occupant. All together, 28 job dimensions (aspects, variables, descriptors) and about 80 component ratings have been treated—some derived from explicit theoretical sources, others from prior research that suggested the importance of a certain dimension, and still others from internal analyses of the data collected.

The general nature of the dimensions measured is illustrated by Table 10-1. This table lists and defines, among others, the five job dimensions that together form the core variables in a particular theory concerning the motivation potential of jobs.[5] Additional variables were derived from the results of factorial analyses of national sample survey data concerning the importance given by workers to various attributes of their jobs and work environments.[6] All of the factorial dimensions that displayed both factorial generality for different subpopulations of workers and also some evidence of behavioral validity were included in the work here described. The content of the roster of variables changed during the course of the work. There were two stages of fieldwork and the results of the first stage showed that certain variables initially intended for inclu-

Table 10-1   Illustrative Job Dimensions

Variety: The extent to which the job provides the individual with the opportunity to do a number of different things, using different equipment, materials, or procedures, as opposed to doing the same things over and over again.

Autonomy: The extent to which the job allows the individual to feel personally responsible for a meaningful portion of the work by providing him/her with some say about how the work will be done, freedom to determine what will happen on the job, or discretion in the course of performing the job.

Internal feedback: The extent to which the job provides the individual with information about how he/she is doing; the degree to which just doing the job itself provides information about the quality and/or quantity of job performance.

Task impact: The extent to which the tasks performed as part of the individual's job make a visible change in relation to some ultimate product or service; the degree to which the worker makes a visible transformation and the degree to which that transformation is visible in the final product.

Task completeness: The extent to which the job enables the individual to produce an entire product or service; a job that involves a very clear cycle of perceived closure—a distinct sense of a beginning and an ending of a transformation process, with clearly visible and indentifiable outcomes.

Required skills: The extent to which adequate performance of the job requires specialized skills, training, or preparation, beyond what an average individual could obtain in under three months.

Certainty: The extent to which performing the job involves highly predictable events and behavior as opposed to events or demands that cannot be anticipated.

Conflicting demands: The extent to which the normal task performance puts the individual in situations where different people or tasks put demands on him/her at the same time.

---

sion had to be discarded on grounds of insufficient repeatability or insufficient differentiation from other variables. Some readers will find that their own favorite variables are omitted. If such variables can be defined in terms of observable conditions or behaviors, they can be accommodated in future revisions of the procedures described in this chapter.

Two previous studies have used standardized observation methods and variables similar to those employed here. Hackman and Lawler report results from the observation of 13 jobs in a utility firm.[7] Turner and Lawrence observed 47 jobs in 11 different companies.[8] Both studies were limited to a small number of descriptive variables; both used highly trained scientist-observers, and neither was designed to allow analysis of interobserver agreement. Nevertheless, both report evidence of validity, and their work helped us in choosing our preliminary variables for observation.

One additional conceptual issue needs comment in these introductory pages, namely, the identification of the entity that is observed. The two prior studies by Hackman and Lawler and by Turner and Lawrence both assumed that individuals holding positions with the same title were exposed to virtually identical tasks and environments. For many purposes this assumption is quite satisfactory, but if the data are to be used for analysis in relation to individual responses, then one must be less confident when attributing the generalized properties of "a job" to the particular version of that job held by a particular individual. Hackman has made the point that both workers and employers can and do modify jobs to suit a circumstance or a person.[9] The method we describe is for the measurement of specific units, each comprising a job and the person performing it, leaving it optional with the user to determine whether the cases observed are representative of their job class.

OVERVIEW OF THE METHOD: TRIAL 1

The components of the method include (1) an observers' guide that provides instructions on field procedure, what to observe, definitions of variables to be assessed, and scales for reporting the observers' judgments; (2) a training program for observers; (3) a system for sampling person–job units and time periods for observation; and (4) a means for summarizing the individual ratings and combining ratings into indexes representing key variables. Results will be presented later from two field trials, with some differences in methods used. We describe here the methods used in Trial 1; the modifications for Trial 2 will be mentioned in another context.

Observers' Guide

The guide has four parts that are to be used in sequence. The first merely reminds the observer of desirable steps in introducing himself/herself to the situation, establishing legitimacy, and gaining cooperation. The second provides for a brief period of "general observation" or acquaintance with the work situation. The third provides for "structured watching," that is, a period during which the observer is required to observe sequentially specified aspects of the job and work situation and to write down the key facts observed. In this part the observing is "structured" by the requirements of the observers' guide. The fourth part provides a set of rating scales on which the observer reports his or her estimates of the presence, frequency, degree, or intensity of various job characteristics. The key portion of the instrument, of course, is this part in which judgmental ratings are made. In the first version of the guide there were 59 rating scales presented in mixed order, but allocated on an a priori basis to 20 indexes.

On the cover of the guide is a suggested time allocation during on-site observation. It provides, for example, for 5 to 15 minutes for introductions, 15 to 45 minutes for "general observation," and the like, to a total of 50 to 90 minutes.

The format of the observers' guide is illustrated in the appendix to this chapter. Appendix 10-1 is the revised version of the guide and not the original one, but the two were similar as to rating and format characteristics.

Observer Selection and Training

The procedure is designed for use either by people already qualified as experts or by novices who participate in a process of special training. When used by experts, no special preparation is needed except a few trial runs to become familiar with the guide or, if possible, trial runs by pairs of observers so that points of divergent ratings can be discovered and resolved in discussion. In the case of novices, at least two days of special training appear to be necessary. The procedures used in the first field application (somewhat modified for the second) were as follows.

1.   Announcements were posted stating that observers were wanted for a research project. Applicants were told that they would have to attend a two-day training session before they were hired, but that they would be paid for attending the session. In the training session, the applicants worked on simulated observational tasks and obtained feedback on their performances. This method enabled the training activities to be used for selection purposes, since trainee performance on the simulated observation task could be used as an objective measure and predictor of observer performance at a research site.

2.   Four jobs similar to those performed by employees in the prospective sample were videotaped prior to the training. During the two-day training period each trainee rated the videotapes, using the observation instrument. Each rating was followed by sessions where the trainees

discussed their ratings. The training staff encouraged discussion when there were significant differences among the ratings of the trainees. Individuals talked about why they rated the tapes as they did, what cues they attended to, and how they reached a decision for each rating. The stated goal of these sessions was to move toward agreement among observers as each iteration of the cycle occurred.

3.   The ratings on the final observation of tapes were collected and used as the basis for selection decisions. Analysis of scores using three different measures of deviation and agreement were performed, and hiring decisions were made. Of a total of 51 trainees, 35 were hired. A refresher training session was held after observers had been in the field for three weeks. A shorter (half-day) version of the original training format was used. Based on the refresher training (and analysis of the data), two additional trainees were eliminated for marginal performance.

The observers were nonprofessionals. Almost all were college students; most of them were juniors, seniors, or first-year graduate students. The group included 19 men and 16 women. They were paid the current university minimum wage for clerks. All but a few worked as observers on a part-time basis.

The choice to use bright, educated novices rather than experts was deliberate, since an objective was to achieve a procedure suitable for application in situations where experts would be unavailable or too costly.

Sampling

Sampling involves both subjects and time. In the first application of the procedure, the populations studied were chosen from three work organizations: an auto parts manufacturer, a printing firm, and four departments of a large hospital. These units were chosen for diversity of jobs, not for representation. In some smaller units all members were included, while in large units a random sampling was used. Complete usable data were obtained from 448 person–jobs. Most of the jobs fell into six census occupational classifications: operative (19%), clerical (19%), professional/technical (18%), service (16%), craftsman/foreman (16%), and managers/officials (16%). Thirty-six percent earned over $10,000 annually, 75% had completed high school, 91% were white, and 62% were male.

The approach to these subjects was exceptionally careful, because they were being asked to participate in a larger study that involved not only the job-observation procedure but also interviews at home and a later follow-up study. Each received an explanatory and encouraging letter from the employer, from the union if appropriate, and from the Institute for Social Research. A representative of the institute then contacted each to answer questions and solicit consent; the declination rate was 10%. The job observations followed some days after the home interviews. The home interviews included a section providing the respondent's description of his or her job on 11 dimensions that would be assessed as well through job observations.

An approximation of time sampling was achieved by making a serial listing of blocks of time in the workweek (e.g., blocks of 1½ hours each), and then for each job, choosing observation periods from a random number table. Assignment of observers was opportunistic, to match the chosen observation times to the availability of the part-time observers. Each subject was observed twice, with at least two days intervening, and by two different observers. In addition, 48 observation periods were scheduled in which two observers worked independently but at the same time. The total number of observation periods accomplished was 941. In some instances an observation was rescheduled; these instances could arise, because, when asked, the person observed asserted plausibly that the scheduled period was not typical, or because of the intrusion of a disruptive event (e.g., employee called away from the job).

Data Analysis

The 59 ratings for each observation period, the associated identification and classification data, and the analogous data from the interviews were entered into a computing system. Transformations were made in the ratings to accommodate differences in scale length and reversals of "direction," and summative (mean-score) indexes were calculated for the a priori scales, with the component items equally weighted. The ratings of each job from two times and two observers were averaged. The data thus available allowed analysis for several purposes. The main purposes were to ascertain the repeatability of the ratings as between observers and between time periods, to ascertain the degree of homogeneity in multi-item indexes, and to test for convergence between the interview and the observation sources of data.[10] Additionally, it was possible to compare data quality as between different observers, classes of jobs, different times of work shift, and the like.

MODIFICATIONS OF THE METHOD: TRIAL 2

The results of the initial study, which are fully reported elsewhere, were moderately encouraging.[11] Three different types of analyses were used to assess the effectiveness of the job-observation instrument and process. It asked whether two trained observers using the same guide and observing the same work (either at the same or different time periods) would arrive at the same job ratings independently. Analyses using a chance-corrected measure of nominal scale agreement showed generally high agreement among observers. A second analysis tested the internal consistency of the multiple-item scales in the instruments. Analysis focused on whether items designed to tap the same job dimension did indeed correlate. Here the findings were encouraging—with moderate- to high-scale homogeneity for most of the major job dimensions. The final analysis assessed the convergent validity of the job-observation technology by determining the extent to which job observations converged with worker self-reports on the same job. A multitrait–multimethod matrix was constructed. Only moderate levels of convergence were attained, and the degree of discrimination among different job characteristics by observers was disappointingly low.

Two factors stood out as possible contributors to the somewhat disappointing results, and as factors that could be improved. First, the observers' guide, which some observers found onerously long and complex, contained elements now known to be unnecessary (e.g., counting of interaction events), and it contained elements that could be simplified. Second, the training for Trial 1 may have been deficient in that it provided no external norms or standards for "correct" performance, and it provided little exposition of the conceptual foundations of the variables to be rated.

Modification of the Observers' Guide

For Trial 2, several changes were made in the observers' guide. Most significantly, a number of observer tasks now determined to be unnecessary or ineffective were deleted. For example, schedules for counting interaction events, for reporting on certain safety conditions, and for reporting the presence or absence of certain physical conditions were removed. Certain briefer questions were added to the "general-observation" segment of the guide to help the observer focus upon the aspects of the job thought to be most critical in the rating judgements to follow. The net of these deletions and additions was to change a 30-page observers' booklet to a much simpler 16-page booklet, which is shown in the appendix.

Aside from simplification of the guide, two kinds of modifications were made as to the rating dimensions. Seven rating scales were added to represent the classes of interpersonal exchange that occurred during the period of observation; these were derived from the "people-related" activity list used for classification of jobs in the *Dictionary of Occupational Titles*.[12] Relatively minor changes were made in some scale descriptors to achieve a closer correspondence between the interview questions and the observers' rating scales. The revised guide included 38 job ratings grouped into 16 a priori scales.

Modification of the Training

In the training prior to Trial 1, the observers were given very little exposure to the conceptual framework into which their ratings would be fitted; the emphasis was on the mechanics of observation and rating. For Trial 2, some explanation was provided of what they were observing and why. Through lecture and discussion, the observers were introduced to basic concepts of job design and definitions of critical key concepts, in the hope that this orientation would help them to discriminate among different types of job characteristics.

To move beyond simple agreement between observers, an attempt was made to develop a standard against which the observers could test their own ratings. A panel of four expert raters, knowledgeable in job analysis and job design, provided the standard. Their ratings of the videotaped training jobs were discussed, modifications were made if necessary, and their explanations recorded. These were then summarized as the expert ratings. During training, to supplement intertrainee comparisons, the observer–trainees' ratings were compared to the expert ratings and their rationales.

New videotapes were developed encompassing a wider range of job types. In addition, the new training jobs were selected to be high on some job dimensions while low on others, providing an improved opportunity to train the observers to discriminate among the different dimensions.

Sampling and Field Procedures: Trial 2

The population of person–jobs for Trial 2 were drawn from two of the three organizations included in Trial 1, and included a number of individuals, a number of jobs, and some person–job units that were "the same" as those observed in Trial 1 about 20 months earlier. Data were collected from 147 individuals in 52 different jobs (DOT classifications) distributed among 6 job classes (census classifications). The procedures for the time sampling and observer assignment were similar to those in Trial 1. Each of the target jobs was observed on at least one occasion by a single observer. A randomly drawn sample of one third of these jobs was observed on a second occasion by a pair of observers who worked independently and who had not previously observed the target job. The observers were again drawn from the local student population. Of the 18 trainees, 10 were hired; they were paid at the then-current minimum hourly rate for clerks.

ANALYTIC PROCEDURES

Trials 1 and 2 both used the same analytic procedures, which will be described later. The analyses were aimed at testing repeatability, index homogeneity, and finally, convergent and discriminant validity. For each of these purposes we state the rationales for choice of method and enough identification of the procedures to allow their replication by others.

Repeatability

Several measures of interobserver agreement or repeatability for nominal and ordinal scales exist in the psychometric literature. The most common measure—percentage or proportion of agreement—suffers because it includes agreement that can be accounted for by chance; thus, it can be deceptively high if the number of categories is small or if only a few categories are used with any appreciable frequency. Cohen's weighted kappa, κ_w, provides a chance-corrected estimate of the proportion of agreement between raters.[13,14] In addition, the statistic allows for assessing partial as well as full agreement by assigning differential penalties to deviations from perfect agreement. Given the ordinal scales in the scoring system, it was decided that when there was perfect agreement between observers (i.e., Observers A and B both assigned ratings of, say 3), full agreement credit, or a weight of 1.0, would be given. When the ratings differed by only one category (i.e., Observer A scored 3 and Observer B scored 2 or 4), then one-half agreement credit would be given, or a weight of .5. Disagreement of more than one category between observers was given no agreement credit, or a weight of .0.

In general, κ_w is computed by subtracting the weighted proportion of agreement expected by chance (p_c, the sum of the weighted cross-products of the marginals) from the weighted observed proportion of agreement possible ($1 - p_c$). The formulas and computational procedures are described by Fleiss and associates.[14] Theoretically, κ_w may range in value from -1 to $+1$; however, maximum values require identical marginals. The extent to which the marginals differ lowers the practical maximum value of κ_w.

A κ_w value of 0 would indicate no increase in agreement above the "chance" level estimated from the cross-product of marginal proportions. Negative values of κ_w represent levels of agreement less than that to be expected by chance alone. Positive values represent levels of agreement between observers above that expected by chance.

Items on the job-observation instrument were placed a priori into one of the three repeatability and stability categories mentioned earlier, depending upon the characteristic being measured. They were then empirically placed, using the following criteria: category 1—κ_w (same time) < .33, κ_w (different) < .20; category 2—κ_w (same time) > .33, κ_w (different) > .20; category 3—κ_w (different) > .20. Any nonsignificant case, with $p > .01$, was assigned a κ_w value of less than .20.

The κ_w levels required for different categories are arbitrary and by usual conventions may appear low. It must be understood, however, that κ_w is a direct measure of the proportion of weighted agreement between observers *above* chance. It is not, except in special circumstances, equivalent to the familiar Pearson r. κ_w was set at a lower level for the overtime situation because characteristics of jobs often change from time to time. Given the behavior sampling technique employed in this study, it is very unlikely that the behavioral demands and characteristics of a job would be exactly the same at any two random points in time.

Homogeneity

The most common measure of the homogeneity or internal consistency of a set of items that comprise a scale designed to be homogeneous is Cronbach's coefficient alpha, which is the generalized equivalent of the Kuder–Richardson Formula 20. Because a major determinant of the value of this coefficient is the number of constituent items, the coefficient can be very high, even in cases where the intercorrelations among the items is very low. While the scales involved in the observation instrument are relatively short—none exceeding six items—it is still preferable to assess the homogeneity of the scales independent of scale length.[15] The Scott homogeneity ratio is such a measure.[16] The homogeneity ratio, which ranges from 0 to 1, expresses the ratio between two terms. The first term is the difference between the actual variance of the sum of the items and the variance expected if the items were uncorrelated. The second term is the difference between the variance expected if all items were perfectly correlated and the variance expected if all items were uncorrelated. This coefficient can also be interpreted as a weighted average of the scale's interitem correlation.

Convergence

Convergent and discriminant validity were assessed by calculating correlations between job dimensions rated by interview and observation and among job dimensions within each method. The multitrait–multimethod paradigm was used to examine the results.[10]

RESULTS FROM TRIAL 1

The results from Trial 1 are reported in detail elsewhere, and need only be summarized here.

Repeatability

A measure is considered to exhibit repeatability if it falls into categories 2 or 3 in the system presented earlier. Thirty two of the 59 measures showed empirical agreement between observers when ratings were made at the same time (i.e., the κ_w (s) values exceed .33). Of the 12 measures that were not expected to exhibit repeatability (e.g., operations of personality characteristics and resource adequacy), 9 failed to meet the .33 standard while 3 exceeded the standard. Of the 47 measures expected to be rated consistently by observers when ratings were made simultaneously, 30 exceeded the standard. The operations that failed were chiefly measures of external feedback, task feedback, work pressures, and effort.

When the ratings were made at different times, 19 of the measures showed acceptable agreement between observers. In two cases, this agreement was not predicted in advance. In the case of 12 items, this degree of agreement was predicted but not obtained. These failures primarily involved measures of feedback, worker pace control, and task identity.

Homogeneity

The scales designed to tap the concepts of variety, autonomy, rigidity, certainty, conflicting demands, cooperation, required skills and abilities, worker pace control, and effort were reasonably homogeneous; that is, they had homogeneity ratios greater than .60, that is, 60% of perfectly homogeneous operations. For the scales of external feedback, task feedback, task identity, comfort, work pressures, interruptions, and resources, homogeneity did not exist.

Convergence

Six of the scales could be meaningfully tested for convergence since they were also measured by the interview method, and the observation data demonstrated both repeatability and homogeneity. Table 10-2 presents the multitrait–multimethod matrix for these six scales. Entries on the main diagonal of the matrix are coefficient alpha values for the individual scales within a given method. The circled correlations in the lower left of the matrix are the convergence correlations between the same constructs measured by the two methods. Four of the six constructs assessed exhibit reasonable levels of convergence: variety, skills, autonomy, and pace control. Certainty and cooperation fail to show convergence between methods. It appears that what the observers assessed as certainty is related to what the respondents viewed as variety and skills and, to some extent, autonomy in their jobs. Cooperation, as measured by the observation instrument, did not correspond to any of the other five constructs measured by the interview.

The values in the upper-left and lower-right triangles (solid lines) are the monomethod triangles that contain the correlations between the constructs measured by a single method. The values in the heteromethod triangles (dashed lines) are correlations between the different constructs measured by different methods. A comparison between the data in the heteromethod triangles and the convergence correlations shows that both pace control and autonomy fail to exhibit discrimination. Both relate more highly to variety and skills, as measured by the interview method, than they do to the interview assessment of these constructs. On the other hand, the measures of variety and skills do show acceptable levels

Table 10-2 Multitrait–Multimethod Matrix for Study 1

Scale	Interview						Observation					
	1	2	3	4	5	6	1	2	3	4	5	6
Interview												
1. Variety	(.45)											
2. Skills	.41	(.79)										
3. Certainty	-.13	.04	(.58)									
4. Autonomy	.38	.44	.20	(.68)								
5. Worker pace control	.27	.11	.02	.25	(—)							
6. Cooperation	.21	.13	-.16	-.03	-.01	(—)						
Observation												
1. Variety	(43)	.43	-.12	.32	.21	.23	(.96)					
2. Skills	.42	(48)	-.10	.32	.22	.23	.83	(.98)				
3. Certainty	-.39	-.40	(14)	-.29	-.16	-.25	-.88	-.77	(.92)			
4. Autonomy	.39	.40	-.11	(35)	.27	.22	.87	.79	-.76	(.96)		
5. Worker pace control	.37	.36	-.08	.32	(30)	.18	.70	.64	-.55	.83	(.95)	
6. Cooperation	.22	.17	-.07	.12	.06	(16)	.42	.30	-.42	.33	.14	(.85)

Note. n = 448. Dashes indicate single-item scale.

297

of discrimination when the convergence correlations are compared with the correlations in the heteromethod triangles.

The correlations in the observation monomethod triangle are very high. It appears that observers have difficulty discriminating among the constructs of variety, skills, certainty, autonomy, and pace control, but they are able to discriminate between those dimensions and cooperation. A comparison between the convergence correlations and the monomethod triangles reveals that the criteria for discriminant validity are met for interviews but not for observations.

RESULTS FROM TRIAL 2

Repeatability

Table 10-3 includes a summary of the repeatability analysis for multi-item scales. For each scale, the means of both the same time ($\kappa_w(\text{s})$) and different time ($\kappa_w(\text{d})$) of the component items are averaged to obtain an estimate of scale repeatability. Detail, including the repeatability estimates of component items, is shown in Table 10-4.

In general, the measures of repeatability between two observers observing the same job at the same time tend to be lower than those found in Trial 1.[11] Most of the κ_w's for observation made at different times approximate the magnitude of those reported for the same items in Trial 1, although some are higher and some lower. If the categorization scheme already described is applied to these results, of the 31 items included in both instruments only 7 are categorized differently in this phase than they were in the first phase. The previous results are strongly replicated.

Of the new items and scales added for Trial 2, the operations of task impact, task completeness, interruption by others and unidentifiable individuals, and the DOT classification of mentoring, persuading, and serving were not repeatable. The remaining new operations were repeatable, *either* when observations were made at the same time *or both* when made at the same and different times.

Homogeneity

Tables 10-3 and 10-4 also contain, when appropriate and possible to compute, Scott's homogeneity ratio and the coefficient α for each a priori scale. Of the multi-item scales designed to be homogeneous, only conflicting demands, comfort, interruptions, and resources failed to meet the .60 criterion used in the first phase of this study.

Convergence

Eight of the scales can be reasonably examined for convergence, since they were measured in both the interview and by observations and exhib-

Table 10-3   Analysis of Observation Scales Study 2

Scale	Number of Items	Repeatability Estimates[a]		Scale Properties[b]	
		Mean of Item $\kappa_w(s)$	Mean of Item $\kappa_w(d)$	Scott H.R.	Coefficient α
Variety	3	.484	.298	.818	.925
Autonomy	5	.367	.351	.781	.946
Task feedback	2	.083	−.026	.733	.844
Task impact	2	.292	.017	.817	.899
Task completeness	2	.003	.003	.777	.871
Task uncertainty	4	.394	.125	.651	.875
Conflicting demands	2	.322	.024	.546	.783
Cooperation	2	.428	.233	.830	.907
Dependence	1	.033	.103	—[c]	—
Meaningfulness	1	.308	.211	—[c]	—
Required skills	3	.434	.501	.771	.905
Intellectual demands	2	.461	.469	.892	.939
Comfort	2	.380	.163	.576	.730
Interruptions	2	.318	.033	.569	.719
Resource adequacy	4	.325	−.046	.281	.592
Physical effort	1	.367	.139	—[c]	—
DOT people ratings	7	.336	.264	—[d]	—
Interaction ratings	5	.326	.143	—[d]	—

[a] $\kappa_w(s)$ is the weighted kappa statistic of agreement between two observers observing the same job/respondent at the same time. $\kappa_w(d)$ represents agreement between two observers observing the same job/respondent at different times.
[b] Scott's homogeneity ratio and Cronbach's alpha are based on the relationships of the coexistent items of the scales over the total sample of jobs/respondents observed ($n = 147$).
[c] One-item scale, no H.R. or α possible.
[d] Not a homogeneous scale; H.R. and α not appropriate.

ited repeatability in their constituent items. Table 10-5 presents the multitrait–multimethod matrix for the eight scales. Entries on the main diagonal of the matrix are internal consistency reliability estimates for scales within a given method. Entries marked by asterisks were single-item scales for which internal consistency reliabilities are impossible to compute. The correlations in parentheses in the lower left of the matrix represent the convergence between the same construct measured by the two methods. Five of the eight convergence correlations are significant at the .01 level: variety, autonomy, required cooperation, required skill, and intellectual demands. Two of these, autonomy and required cooperation, were significantly higher ($p < .05$) than in the previous study. None were

Table 10-4 Analysis of Observation Items: Study 2

Scale and Question	Repeatability Estimates[a]					Scale Properties[b]		
	$\kappa_{w(s)}$	$\kappa_{w(d)}$	$\kappa_{w(d)}$	Mean $\kappa_{w(d)}$	$\kappa_{w(d)}$ (combined)	Median r	Scott H.R.	Coefficient α
Variety						.815	.818	.925
1. How much *variety* is there in the job?	.421**	.289**	.266**	.278	.277**			
2. The job lets the individual do a variety of different things.	.449**	.363**	.211*	.287	.287**			
3. The job requires that the individual do the same things over and over.[c]	.584**	.324**	.338**	.331	.331**			
Autonomy						.782	.781	.946
4. How much *autonomy* is there in the job? That is, to what extent does the job permit the individual to decide by *himself/ herself* how to go about doing the work?	.337**	.345**	.262**	.304	.304**			
5. The individual has enough freedom as to how he/she does the work.	.515**	.303**	.373**	.338	.339**			
6. The individual has a lot to say over what happens on his/her job.	.345**	.521**	.530**	.526	.526**			
7. The job allows the individual to make a lot of decisions on his/her own.	.438**	.347**	.370**	.359	.359**			
8. The job denies the individual any chance to use his/her personal initiative or discretion of work.[c]	.204*	.203**	.248**	.226	.225**			

Task feedback			.733	.733	.844
9. To what extent does *doing the job itself* provide the individual with information about his/her work performance? That is, does the actual work itself provide clues about how well he/she is doing—aside from any "feedback" co-workers or supervisors may provide?	.065	.072	−.050	.011	.012
10. Just doing the work required by the job gives the individual many chances to figure out how well he/she is doing.	.100	−.034	−.090	−.062	−.062
Task impact			.817	.817	.899
11. How much does the work that the individual does on his/her job make a *visible impact* on the materials or objects being worked on or service being rendered?	.219**	−.058	.093	.018	.014
12. The job allows the individual to make a visible change in the materials worked with or service provided.	.364**	−.065	.097	.016	.016
Task completeness			.777	.777	.871
13. How much does the job involve the individual producing an *entire product or an entire service*?	.003	.058	−.028	.015	.015
14. On the job, the individual produces a whole product or performs a complete service.	.004	−.039	−.122	−.081	−.080
Task uncertainty			.642 (.820)[d]	.651 (.834)	.875 (.935)
15. How much *uncertainty* is there in the job?	.503**	.246**	.142	.194	.193**
16. The job requires the individual to be prepared to handle surprising or unpredictable situations.	.359**	.034	−.020	.007	.007

Table 10-4 (Continued)

Scale and Question	Repeatability Estimates[a]					Scale Properties[b]		
	$\kappa_{w(s)}$	$\kappa_{w(d)}$	$\kappa_{w(d)}$	Mean $\kappa_{w(d)}$	$\kappa_{w(d)}$ (combined)	Median r	Scott H.R.	Coefficient α
17. The job is one that is highly predictable and that rarely presents the individual with surprising or unpredictable situations.[c]	.443**	.216*	.098	.157	.156**			
18. The individual working on the job does tasks that are clearly defined.[c]	.269**	.169	.120	.145	.144*			
Conflicting demands						.538 (.670)[e]	.546 (.670)	.783 (.802)
19. On the job, other people make conflicting demands of the individual.	.296*	.116	−.050	.033	.034			
20. The individual working on this job is free from conflicting demands that others may make of him/her.[c]	.348**	.002	.027	.015	.015			
21. He/she is frequently interrupted for work-related reasons.	.305**	−.002	.031	.029	.014			
Cooperation						.830	.830	.907
22. To what extent does the job require the individual to *work closely with other people* (either "clients" or people in related jobs within the organization)?	.396**	.184*	.263**	.224	.223**			
23. The individual has to cooperate directly with other people in order to do his/her job.	.460**	.289**	.194	.242	.242**			

Dependence								
24. The individual has to depend on the work performed by others in order to get the materials or information he/she needs to do his/her work.	.033	.213*	-.007	.103	.099	—f	—	—
Meaningfulness								
25. The job is meaningful.	.308**	.270**	.151	.211	.210**	—f	—	—
Required skills								
26. To what extent does the job require the use of *sophisticated* or *complex* skills or knowledge?	.376**	.534**	.414**	.474	.474**	.722	.771	.905
27. The job requires a high level of skill.	.507**	.552**	.506**	.529	.529**			
28. The job is so simple that virtually anybody could handle it with little or no initial training.[c]	.420**	.506**	.498**	.562	.502**			
Intellectual demands								
29. How *intellectually demanding* is the job?	.411**	.626**	.309**	.468	.467**	.892	.892	.939
30. The job requires a high level of mental effort.	.512**	.580**	.361**	.471	.469**			
Comfort								
31. His/her work area is clean.	.471**	.289**	.373***	.331	.330**	.576	.576	.730
32. His/her job exposes him/her to dangerous or unhealthy conditions.[c]	.289**	.016	-.028	-.006	-.006			
Interruptions								
33. He/she is frequently interrupted for work-related reasons.	.305**	-.002	.031	.015	.014	.569	.569	.719
34. He/she is frequently interrupted for *non-work*-related reasons.	.330**	-.070	.172*	.051	.047			

Table 10-4 (Continued)

Scale and Question	Repeatability Estimates[a]					Scale Properties[b]		
	$\kappa_{w(s)}$	$\kappa_{w(d)}$	$\kappa_{w(d)}$	Mean $\kappa_{w(d)}$	$\kappa_{w(d)}$ (combined)	Median r	Scott H.R.	Coefficient α
Resource adequacy						.302	.281	.592
35. He/she is given enough space to do his/her job.	.125	−.156	−.033	−.095	−.092			
36. He/she is given adequate lighting for his/her particular job.	.516**	−.204	−.056	−.130	−.127			
37. He/she has adequate access to machinery, tools or other equipment.	.355**	−.031	.084	.027	.025			
38. The individual working on his/her job frequently had to stop to get things he/she needed and didn't have readily available.[c]	.304**	.126	−.105	.011	−.014			
Physical Effort						—[f]	—	—
39. The job requires the individual to exert a lot of physical effort.	.367**	.159	.118	.139	.139			
Dictionary of Occupational Titles						—[g]	—	—
40. Mentoring	−.091	.084	.047	.066	.064			
41. Negotiating	.445**	.200	.317*	.258	.261**			
42. Instructing	.636**	.203	.443**	.323	.330**			
43. Supervising	.455**	.504**	.416**	.460	.457**			
44. Persuading	.141	.261*	.283*	.272	.274**			
45. Speaking–signaling	.396**	.365**	.402**	.384	.382**			

	$\kappa_{w(s)}$[a]	$\kappa_{w(d)_1}$[a]	$\kappa_{w(d)_2}$[a]	$\kappa_{w(d)}$[a]	$\kappa_{w(d)}$[a]	[b]	[b]	[b]
46. Serving	.187	.164	.012	.088	.091	—	—[g]	—
Interactions								
How often does the individual interact verbally with:								
47. His/her supervisors.	.494**	.329**	.128	.229	.228**			
48. His/her co-workers (at the same level of the organization as the individual).	.355**	.220*	−.018	.101	.102			
49. His/her co-workers (at different levels of the organization from the individual).	.449**	.235**	.212*	.224	.224**			
50. Others (customers, clients, patients).	.184*	.261**	.016	.139	.137			
51. Unidentifiable individuals (can't tell who they are).	.148	.045	.000	.023	.023			

* $p < .05$ (two-tailed test); ** $p < .01$ (two-tailed test).

[a] $\kappa_{w(s)}$ is the weighted kappa statistic of agreement between two observers observing the same job/respondent at the same time. These values are based on a total N of 44 with exact Ns varying from 40 to 44. $\kappa_{w(d)_1}$ and $\kappa_{w(d)_2}$ represent agreement between two observers observing the same job/respondent at different times. Pairing of observers was arbitrary. Both statistics are based on a total N of 41 with exact Ns varying from 38 to 41. Mean $\kappa_{w(d)}$ is the average of $\kappa_{w(d)_1}$ and $\kappa_{w(d)_2}$. $\kappa_{w(d)}$ combined treats all observations of the same job/respondent at different times independently and is based on a total N of 82 with exact Ns varying from 76 to 82.

[b] Median r, Scott's homogeniety ratio and Cronbach's alpha are based on the relationships of the coexistent items of the scales over the total sample of jobs/respondents observed ($N = 147$).

[c] Reversed scoring

[d] Statistics when variable 16 is eliminated from the scale.

[e] Statistics when variable 21 is eliminated from the scale.

[f] Single item scale—statistics not possible to compute.

[g] Scale not constructed to be homogeneous—statistics not computed.

Table 10-5 Multitrait–multimethod Matrix of Convergence and Discriminant Correlations among Scales. Study 2 (N = 147)

Scale	Observation								Interview							
	1	2	3	4	5	6	7	8	1	2	3	4	5	6	7	8
Observation																
1. Variety	(.925)															
2. Autonomy	.691	(.946)														
3. Uncertainty	.623	.680	(.935)													
4. Conflicting demands	.336	.354	.525	(.802)												
5. Required cooperation	.559	.453	.646	.435	(.907)											
6. Required skill	.568	.693	.740	.360	.570	(.905)										
7. Intellectually demanding	.625	.763	.776	.447	.599	.896	(.939)									
8. Physically demanding	.052	−.072	.045	−.101	−.046	−.055	−.067	[a]								
Interview																
1. Variety	(.285)	.286	.305	.306	.344	.269	.322	−.092	(.609)							
2. Autonomy	.365	(.512)	.451	.419	.403	.333	.427	.004	.441	(.860)						
3. Uncertainty	.018	−.077	(−.070)	.161	−.043	−.005	−.018	−.185	.057	−.269	(.576)					
4. Conflicting demands	.030	.038	.181	(.055)	.214	.203	.185	−.051	.022	−.137	.267	(.333)				
5. Required cooperation	.276	.377	.334	.341	(.368)	.362	.413	.062	.260	.345	−.130	.041	[a]			
6. Required skill	.322	.410	.317	.248	.354	(.443)	.453	−.011	.413	.406	−.178	.050	.309	(.760)		
7. Intellectually demanding	.311	.460	.426	.315	.399	.439	(.433)	.002	.361	.522	−.122	.200	.356	.648	(.714)	
8. Physically demanding	−.118	−.243	−.232	−.151	−.120	−.251	−.318	(.149)	−.004	−.152	−.115	.183	−.147	−.100	−.015	[a]

[a] Single-item scales—internal consistency reliabilities are not possible to compute.

significantly lower. Uncertainty, conflicting demands, and physical demands failed to demonstrate adequate levels of convergence.

With respect to the discrimination among constructs, the median intercorrelation among constructs in the observation monomethod triangle decreased from .71 in Trial 1 to .53 in Trial 2.

Summary Comparison of Trial 1 and Trial 2

In the initial trial, the results indicated that the observation technique for assessing job characteristics was moderately successful. About two thirds of those operations expected to exhibit repeatability did so. With minor exceptions, scales intended to be homogeneous were, in fact, composed of homogeneous items. In four of the six instances where it was possible to test for convergence, the scales tended to exhibit convergence and some degree of discrimination.

The second trial was intended to replicate and refine the observation technology. The refinement of the method (the training and the instrument) was intended to increase the convergence of the constructs when measured by both interviews and observations, without sacrificing either the stability of homogeneity of the measures. The attempt was in large measure successful.

First, there was a substantial improvement (i.e., reduction) in the extent to which different constructs measured by observations were interrelated. The improvement in discrimination probably resulted from the concepts training provided the observers and the selection methods based on that training. This improved discrimination among constructs was achieved without any important loss with respect to the extent that the constructs were measured with repeatability and homogeneity.

The improvement with respect to convergent and discriminant validity was negligible. The three Campbell and Fiske criteria of discriminant validity were not met fully. First, convergence correlations failed to exceed elements in the same row or column of the monomethod triangles. Second, the convergence correlations failed to exceed elements in the same row or column of the heteromethod triangles. Thus, applying the strict standards of Campbell and Fiske, much still remains to be done with respect to discriminant validity.

With respect to repeatability and homogeneity, the modifications in training, selection, and instrument design did reduce somewhat the values of the κ_w's and the homogeneity ratios. For the most part, however, these decreases were not significant, and thus the findings of the first study as to data repeatability and homogeneity were substantially replicated.

In summary, this attempt to refine the observation methodology has been moderately successful, with certain distinct gains. The method is far from being fully satisfactory, however, and several problems remain to be resolved.

FUTURE STEPS

Given the continuing interest in optimizing work design, the search for improved means for measuring job characteristics needs to continue. While the approach described in this chapter clearly has severe limitations, it appears also to have some promise and some immediate utility. The immediate utility would be as an initial diagnostic aid, used by relatively experienced observers, to identify jobs that clearly are high potential targets for job redesign efforts. It could be used also after redesign to get an independent estimate of the extent to which desired job characteristics have been achieved or approached. For both diagnosis and assessment, the observers' ratings can be used in conjunction with complementary information from the job occupants, each providing some check on the other. In this context, as in others where person–environment relationships are in question, it appears to be essential to treat both observer and job occupant information jointly.

The second of the studies reported here, Trial 2, showed that some gains can be achieved by successive refinements in the observers' guide, in the rating-scale formats, and in the training of observers, but such future gains are likely to be modest until there is a better understanding of the sources of variance in job ratings—including the sources of undesirable variance. Four factors appear to invite consideration.

Correlational Agreement versus Metric Agreement

It appears to be quite easy on some job dimensions to achieve correlational agreement among observers and between observers and job occupants but to fail to achieve metric agreement. That is, they might agree that job **a** has more (or less) than job **b** of characteristic **z**, but still be quite far from agreement as to the absolute scale amount or degree of the dimension. This was displayed quite dramatically in our data, particularly when comparing observers and job occupants. Observers saw more safety hazard than did occupants; observers saw less task variety than did occupants. With respect to interobserver comparisons, some observers consistently across an array of jobs reported higher levels of a given dimension than did others. One can speculate that some of the descriptive concepts should be regarded not as inherent dimensions of a job, but rather as a product of complex interactions between other task characteristics and the characteristics of the job holder or observer. This is commonly called "bias," or "error," to be corrected by reference to some external, objective or consensus metric. The practice of observation and rating would be improved if distinctions could be made among the rated characteristics with respect to their vulnerability to scale displacement.

Differential Observability of Jobs

There is reason to suppose that some jobs are inherently more observable than others. One thinks, first, of a supposed high observability for jobs with a high content of physical activity and an environment dense with varied physical objects, and a supposed low observability for jobs with a high information-processing, decision-making content. The data in our Trial 1 allowed comparison among the jobs broadly classified by the census classification system. Some differences were found as to degree of interrater agreement, but these differences were small. No significant differences were found in Trial 2, with a smaller N of jobs. Nevertheless, it may well be possible to find a way to distinguish more observable from less observable jobs, and to do so would aid both theory and practice.

Implicit Theories of Job Structure

The discriminant validity data reported in this chapter are unimpressive. The high correlations among job dimensions that are conceptually different may arise from either valid or artifactual sources. A valid source would be observed if the dimensions treated did, in fact, tend to covary in the "real" world; the purposeful heterogeneity of the population of jobs studied would exaggerate the effects of such a valid source of low discriminability. A possible artifactual source would occur if the raters—either observers or job occupants—made their judgments within some shared "implicit theory" about the nature of jobs.[17,18] Such an implicit theory would be a set of presuppositions regarding the relationships among constructs—presuppositions that could be invoked by an observer either when deciding what to attend to or in making judgments in the absence of directly interpretable cues. In effect, the observer infers the presence of a characteristic not from direct observation but, instead, from the presence of other characteristics. If this intrusion of implicit theories should prove to be a significant source of low discriminability, implications follow with respect to the selection and training of observers.

Job redefinition

The degree of convergence between job ratings by observers and those by job occupants remained low, even though somewhat strengthened by the methods changes introduced for Trial 2. This result allows for several different interpretations and speculations. One view regards the rating discrepancies as error: The job occupants are merely untrained and biased, and they therefore are incompetent observers, or the observers are insufficiently trained and exposed to too small and unrepresentative a sample of on-job events and conditions. Viewed in this way, the matter invites empirical solution, for, in principle, the ratings with least error are those that can be shown to be most potent in hypothesis-testing systems of independently measured variables and in the prediction of future states and changes. An alternative view is that the ratings by occupants and by observers are discrepant, not mainly because of estimation error but because they have different referents. Hackman has suggested that jobs are always "redefined," within some limits, by the job holder, and the redefinition may be cognitive (e.g., a framework for viewing the objective features of the job) or objective (e.g., actually doing the job in a different way).[9] Alderfer suggests an affective redefinition in which the objective job is altered to provide more of those features that are more satisfying to the particular job occupant.[19] These job modifications may be highly significant, but may not be readily observable by others. The trained or expert observer may note repetitive, short-cycle tasks, but the occupant may note the absence of task distractions that impede revery. The variable *revery potential* does not appear on the observers' rating schedule; in rating repetitiveness, he or she may count the repetitions while the job occupant counts the interruptions in the task cycle. Both may be error free and "objective" but report about different aspects of the job. In addition, the concept of "a job" as an observable entity is called into question. As suggested earlier, it may be that this too is available for empirical inquiry. Do different persons performing "the same" job agree more with each other than they do with trained, independent observers? Does controlling for key personality or need characteristics of the job occupants yield higher correspondence between occupants' ratings and observers' ratings? The researcher is invited to use the instrument to provide the needed answers.

REFERENCES

1. Gilbreth, F. B. *Motion study.* New York: D. van Nostrand, 1911.
2. Fine, S. A., & Wiley, W. W. *An introduction to functional job analysis.* Kalamazoo: W. E. Upjohn Institute, 1971.
3. Guelaud, F., Beauchesne, M. N., Gautrat, J., & Roustang, G. *Pour une analyse des conditions du travail ouvier dans l'entreprise.* Aix-en-Provence: C.N.R.S., 1975.
4. Lytle, C. W. *Job evaluation methods.* New York: Ronald Press, 1954.
5. Hackman, J. R., & Oldham, G. R. Development of job diagnostic survey. *Journal of Applied Psychology,* 1975, **60,** 159–170.
6. Quinn, R. P., & Mangione, T. W. *The 1969–70 survey of working conditions.* Ann Arbor: Institute for Social Research, 1973.
7. Hackman, J. R., & Lawler, E. E. III. Employee reactions to job characteristics. *Journal of Applied Psychology,* 1971, **55,** 259–286.
8. Turner, A. N., & Lawrence, P. R. *Industrial jobs and the worker.* Boston: Harvard University, Graduate School of Business Administration, 1965.
9. Hackman, J. R. Toward understanding of the role of tasks in behavioral research. *Acta Psychológica,* 1969, **31,** 97–128.
10. Campbell, T. T., & Friske, D. W. Convergent and discriminant validation by the multitrait–multimethod matrix. *Psychological Bulletin,* 1959, **56,** 81–105.
11. Jenkins, G. D., Jr., Nadler, D. A., Lawler, E. E. III, & Cammann, C. Standardized observations: An approach to measuring the nature of jobs. *Journal of Applied Psychology,* 1975, **60,** 171–181.
12. U. S. Department of Labor. *Dictionary of occupational titles.* Washington, D.C.: U.S. Government Printing Office, 1965.
13. Cohen, J. Weighted kappa: Nominal scale agreement with provision for scale disagreement or partial credit. *Psychological Bulletin,* 1968, **70,** 213–220.

14. Fleiss, J. L., Cohen, J., & Everitt, B. S. Large sample standard errors of kappa and weighted kappa. *Psychological Bulletin,* 1969, **72,** 323–327.

15. Guilford, J. P. *Psychometric methods,* 2nd ed. New York: McGraw-Hill, 1954.

16. Scott, W. A. Measures of test homogeneity. *Educational and Psychological Measurement,* 1960, **20,** 751–757.

17. Staw, B. M. Attribution of the "causes" of performance: A general alternative interpretation of cross-sectional research on organizations. *Organizational Behavior and Human Performance,* 1975, **13,** 414–432.

18. Eden, D., & Leviatan, U. M. Implicit leadership theory as a determinant of the factor structure underlying supervisory behavior scales. *Journal of Applied Psychology,* 1975, **60,** 736–741.

19. Alderfer, C. P. *Existence, relatedness, and growth: Human needs in organizational settings.* New York: Free Press, 1972.

SURVEY RESEARCH CENTER
INSTITUTE FOR SOCIAL RESEARCH
THE UNIVERSITY OF MICHIGAN
ANN ARBOR, MICHIGAN 48106

ON-THE-JOB OBSERVATION GUIDE

Study Number:	☐☐☐	101:01-03
Observation Number:	☐	101:04
Deck Number:	☐☐☐	101:05-07
Respondent Number:	☐☐☐☐☐☐☐	101:08-14
Observer Number:	☐☐	101:15-16
Starting Time of Observation:	_____	101:17-20

(Use Military Time, e.g., 1 p.m. = 1300)

Introduction

This booklet is provided as a guide and data recording form for the standardized observation of job characteristics. It is designed to be used by observers who have been trained in its use. The guide is set up in the same order as the different timed phases of the observation. For each part of the observation guide, read the instructions and provide the appropriate information.

The major parts of the observation guide are as follows:

Part	Activity	Time Allotted for Each Part	
		Minimum	Maximum
I	Introducing yourself to the individual being observed and	5 minutes	15 minutes
II	General observation	15 minutes	45 minutes
III	Structured observation of the job	----	15 minutes
IV	Rating the job	----	15 minutes
V	Administrative information	----	----
VI	Editing (to be done away from the job)	----	----

USE THIS SPACE FOR NOTES

Part I.   Introducing yourself to the individual being observed and
orienting yourself to the job. (5 - 15 minutes)

OBSERVERS SHOULD BE WEARING THEIR SRC ID BADGES AS THEY
BEGIN OBSERVATIONS. THE INDIVIDUAL WILL NORMALLY HAVE
BEEN NOTIFIED AHEAD OF TIME THAT HE/SHE IS GOING TO BE
OBSERVED.

HAVING LOCATED THE EMPLOYEE, WAIT UNTIL A LOGICAL BREAK
POINT IN THE EMPLOYEE'S WORK AND INTRODUCE YOURSELF.
IN YOUR OWN WORDS, YOU SHOULD CONVEY THE FOLLOWING INFOR-
MATION.

---

1. Your name and SRC/UM affiliation.

2. What the study is.

3. Reminder of the previous interview.

4. Stressing of confidentiality and anonymity.

5. Brief explanation of what you will be doing.

6. Emphasizing that employee should continue with normal behavior.

7. Identify supervisor and co-workers.

8. Warning of possible interruption in 5-10 minutes.

AFTER HAVING ORIENTED YOURSELF TO THE JOB, YOU MAY ASK THE
EMPLOYEE ONE OR TWO QUESTIONS TO CLARIFY WHAT YOU ARE
OBSERVING. IN MOST CASES THERE SHOULD BE NO NEED TO ASK
ANY QUESTIONS. QUESTIONS SHOULD BE ASKED ONLY IN CASES
WHERE IT IS UNCLEAR WHAT THE EMPLOYEE IS DOING (FOR EXAMPLE,
IF EMPLOYEE IS WORKING ON A MATERIAL OR OBJECT OR WITH A
MACHINE THAT IS UNINTERPRETABLE BY THE OBSERVER). REMEMBER,
THIS IS NOT AN INTERVIEW. ONLY ASK THOSE QUESTIONS THAT ARE
ABSOLUTELY ESSENTIAL TO UNDERSTANDING WHAT THE EMPLOYEE IS
DOING.

Part II. General observation (15 - 45 minutes)

```
┌─────────────────────────────────────────────────────────────┐
│  THIS PERIOD SHOULD BE SPENT OBSERVING THE WORKER AND THE     │
│  JOB TO GET A FEEL FOR THE GENERAL CHARACTERISTICS OF THE     │
│  JOB AND THE SPECIFIC DEMANDS AND OPPORTUNITIES IT PROVIDES   │
│  FOR THE WORKER.  THE PURPOSE OF THIS PERIOD IS TO GET A      │
│  GENERAL ORIENTATION TO THE JOB BEFORE MOVING ON TO THE MORE  │
│  STRUCTURED OBSERVATION AND RATING TASKS.                     │
│                                                               │
│  THIS GENERAL OBSERVATION PERIOD WILL VARY IN LENGTH          │
│  DEPENDING ON THE TYPE OF JOB BEING OBSERVED.  THE PERIOD     │
│  SHOULD BE NO LESS THAN 15 MINUTES AND NO MORE THAN 45 MINUTES.│
└─────────────────────────────────────────────────────────────┘
```

Part III. Structured Watching

```
┌─────────────────────────────────────────────────────────────┐
│ A. AFTER OBSERVING THE JOB FOR WHAT YOU JUDGE TO BE AN ADEQUATE│
│    PERIOD (MINIMUM OF 15 MINUTES), ANSWER EACH OF THE FOLLOWING│
│    QUESTIONS, WRITING IN THE APPROPRIATE INFORMATION.          │
└─────────────────────────────────────────────────────────────┘
```

1. Does the employee repeat any activity or group of activities during the normal course of his/her work (are there any identifiable cycles)?

    [1] YES   [2] NO (if no, skip to next question and mark
                             a to d "NA")

    a. Describe the largest identifiable and repeated cycle.

    b. Describe the identifiable sub-parts of the largest cycle.

   c. What is the approximate length in time of the largest cycle?

     _____ Time

   d. How "regular" are the cycles? Describe to what extent they vary in length, type of activities done, sequence of activities, etc.

2. What tools, machinery, or pieces of equipment does the employee work with during the normal course of his/her work activities?

3. Does the employee's normal work involve working with automatic machines or equipment? (exclude hand tools or hand held power equipment, e.g., hand held drills, electric screwdrivers, etc.)

   [1] YES   [2] NO   (if no, skip to next question and mark a to d "NA")

   a. Does the pace of the employee's work activities appear to be controlled or constrained by the equipment he/she is working with? If so, how?

b. How much control does the employee seem to have over the activities of the machines or equipment he/she works with? Give examples.

4. Does the employee's normal work involve working with or on some type of material or object -- where a central part of the employee's job involves moving, working on, or is some way changing the material or object?

[1] YES   [2] NO (if no, skip to next question and mark
                         a to c "NA")

a. From where does the employee get his/her "raw materials" (materials or objects to be worked on)?

b. What does the employee actually do with the material or object (what is the transformation process)?

c. When the employee finishes working on the material or object, where does it go or where does he/she take it?

5. Does the employee's normal work involve dealing with other people for work related purposes?

[1] YES   [2] NO (if yes, how many in a specified time period
                         and in general what types of people)

6. What kinds of skills or learning appear to be necessary to perform the job adequately? (skills above and beyond what the average high school graduate could be expected to have coming in off the street)? List the skills

7. Does the employee relate to, refer to, depend on, or work from any oral or written instructions during the normal course of his/her work activities? (including such things as specification sheets, manuals, blueprints, etc.)?

    [1] YES   [2] NO (if yes, list)

8. Does the employee record any information (on paper, blackboard, etc.)?

    [1] YES   [2] NO (if yes, indicate what seems to be recorded, how, and where)

B. FOR EACH OF THE FOLLOWING STATEMENTS, CHECK THE NUMBER
INDICATING HOW MUCH YOU AGREE WITH THE STATEMENT AS A
DESCRIPTION OF THE EMPLOYEE'S JOB.

strongly disagree
disagree
slightly disagree
slightly agree
agree
strongly agree

1. His/Her work area is clean   [1] [2] [3] [4] [5] [6]

2. He/She is frequently interrupted   [1] [2] [3] [4] [5] [6]

3. He/She is frequently interrupted
   for non-work related reasons   [1] [2] [3] [4] [5] [6]

4. He/She is given enough space to
   do his/her job   [1] [2] [3] [4] [5] [6]

5. He/She is given adequate lighting
   for his/her particular job   [1] [2] [3] [4] [5] [6]

6. He/She has adequate access to
   machinery, tools or other
   equipment   [1] [2] [3] [4] [5] [6]

7. His/Her job exposes him/her to
   dangerous or unhealthy conditions   [1] [2] [3] [4] [5] [6]

C. DURING THE PERIOD OF OBSERVATION, HOW OFTEN WOULD YOU SAY
THE INDIVIDUAL ENGAGED IN EACH OF THE FOLLOWING ACTIVITIES?

Frequently   Occasionally   Never

                                        Mentoring: Dealing with individuals
                                        in terms of their total personality
                                        in order to advise, counsel, and/or
   [1]   [2]   [3]   guide them with regard to problems.

Frequently	Occasionally	Never	
[1]	[2]	[3]	**Negotiating:** Exchanging ideas, information, and opinions with others to formulate policies and programs and/or arrive jointly at decisions, conclusions, or solutions.
[1]	[2]	[3]	**Instructing:** Teaching subject matter to others, or training others (including animals) through explanation demonstration, and supervised practice.
[1]	[2]	[3]	**Supervising:** Determining or interpreting work procedures for a group of workers, assigning specific duties to them, maintaining harmonious relations among them, and promoting efficiency.
[1]	[2]	[3]	**Persuading:** Influencing others in favor of a product, service, or point of view.
[1]	[2]	[3]	**Speaking-Signaling:** Talking with and/or signaling people to convey or exchange information.
[1]	[2]	[3]	**Serving:** Attending to the needs or requests of people or the expressed or implicit wishes of people. Immediate response is involved.

Part IV. Rating the Job

WHILE STILL OBSERVING THE JOB, RATE THE JOB BY CHECKING
THE APPROPRIATE RESPONSE TO THE ITEMS IN THE FOLLOWING
SECTIONS OF THIS BOOKLET.

A. CHECK THE NUMBER ON EACH OF THE FOLLOWING SCALES WHICH
MOST APPROPRIATE DESCRIBES THE JOB YOU ARE WATCHING.

---

1. How much <u>variety</u> is there in the job?

    [1]   [2]   [3]   [4]   [5]   [6]   [7]

Very little; the individual does pretty much the same things over and over, using the same equipment and procedures almost all the time	Moderate variety	Very much; the individual does many different things, using a wide variety of equipment and/or procedures

2. How much <u>autonomy</u> is there in the job? That is, to what extent
    does the job permit the individual to decide by <u>himself/herself</u>
    how to go about doing the work?

    [1]   [2]   [3]   [4]   [5]   [6]   [7]

Very little, the job gives him/her almost no personal "say" about how and when the work is done	Moderate autonomy; many things are standardized and not under his/her control; but he/she can make some decisions about the work	Very much; the job gives him/her almost complete responsibility for deciding how and when the work is done

3. How much does the job involve the individual producing an <u>entire</u> <u>product or an entire service?</u>

     [1]   [2]   [3]   [4]   [5]   [6]   [7]

The job involves doing only a small part of the entire product or service; it is also worked on by others or by automatic equipment and he/she may not see or be aware of much of the work done on the product or service	The job involves doing a moderate sized "chunk" of the work; while others are involved as well, his/her contribution is significant	The job involves producing the entire product or service from start to finish; the final outcome of the work is clearly the results of his/ her work

4. How much does the work that the individual does on his/her job make a <u>visible impact</u> on the materials or objects being worked on or service being rendered?

     [1]   [2]   [3]   [4]   [5]   [6]   [7]

None at all; it is hard to tell what impact his/her work makes on the object or service	A moderate amount	A great amount; his/ her work is clearly visible, it makes a <u>noticeable</u> difference in the materials, objects, or service

5. To what extent does <u>doing the job itself</u> provide the individual with information about his/her work performance? That is, does the actual work itself provide clues about how well he/she is doing--aside from any "feedback" co-workers or supervisors may provide?

     [1]   [2]   [3]   [4]   [5]   [6]   [7]

Very little; the job itself is set up so he/she could work forever without finding out how well he/she is doing	Moderately; sometimes doing the job provides "feedback" to him/her; sometimes it does not	Very much; the job is set up so that he/she gets almost constant "feedback" as he/she works about how well he/she is doing

6. How <u>intellectually demanding</u> is the job?

    [1]   [2]   [3]   [4]   [5]   [6]   [7]

    Not at all, the   Moderately   Extremely, the
    job is very rou-   job is very
    tine and does   non-routine and
    not require any   involves a lot
    mental effort   of "thinking-
                                                              through" or pro-
                                                              blem solving

7. To what extent does the job require the use of <u>sophisticated</u> or
    <u>complex</u> skills or knowledge.

    [1]   [2]   [3]   [4]   [5]   [6]   [7]

    Very little; no   Moderate, some   Very much;
    skills are   skills are   highly complex
    required that the   required, but they   or sophisticated
    average person   would not be dif-   skills are needed
    would not already   ficult for the   to do the job
    have   average person to
                                obtain in a short
                                time (3 months)

8. To what extent does the job require the individual to <u>work closely</u>
    <u>with other people</u> (either "clients," or people in related jobs
    within the organizations)?

    [1]   [2]   [3]   [4]   [5]   [6]   [7]

    Very little;   Moderately;   Very much;
    dealing with   some dealing   dealing with
    other people is   with others   other people
    not at all nec-   is necessary   is an absolutely
    essary in doing   essential and
    the job   crucial part of
                                                              doing the job

9. How much <u>uncertainty</u> is there in the job?

[1]   [2]   [3]   [4]   [5]   [6]   [7]

Very little; the   Moderate   Very much; the
individual almost   uncertainty   individual is
always knows what   almost never sure
to expect and is   what is going to
never surprised by   happen; unexpected
something happening   things frequently
unexpectedly on the   happen
job

B. DURING THE NORMAL WORK ACTIVITIES
OF THE INDIVIDUAL, HOW OFTEN DOES
THE INDIVIDUAL INTERACT VERBALLY
WITH THE FOLLOWING INDIVIDUALS?

not at all   *constantly*

1. His/Her supervisors   [1] [2] [3] [4] [5] [6]

2. His/Her co-workers (at the same
   level of the organization as
   the individual)   [1] [2] [3] [4] [5] [6]

3. His/Her co-workers (at different
   levels of the organization from
   the individual)   [1] [2] [3] [4] [5] [6]

4. Others (customers, clients,
   patients)   [1] [2] [3] [4] [5] [6]

5. Unidentifiable individuals
   (can't tell who they are)   [1] [2] [3] [4] [5] [6]

C. PLEASE INDICATE HOW TRUE EACH OF
THE FOLLOWING STATEMENTS IS AS A
DESCRIPTION OF THE JOB YOU ARE
OBSERVING.

not at all true
a little true
somewhat true
very true

1. Just doing the work required by the job
gives the individual many chances to
figure out how well he/she is doing.   [1] [2] [3] [4]

2. The job lets the individual do a
variety of different things.   [1] [2] [3] [4]

3. The job requires a high level of
skill.   [1] [2] [3] [4]

4. The job allows the individual to make
a visible change in the materials
worked with or service provided.   [1] [2] [3] [4]

5. The job requires a high level of
mental effort.   [1] [2] [3] [4]

6. The job allows the individual to
determine his/her own work pace.   [1] [2] [3] [4]

7. The individual has enough freedom
as to how he/she does the work.   [1] [2] [3] [4]

8. The job requires the individual to
exert a lot of physical effort.   [1] [2] [3] [4]

9. The individual has to cooperate
directly with other people in order
to do his/her job.   [1] [2] [3] [4]

10. The job is so simple that virtually
anybody could handle it with little
or no initial training.   [1] [2] [3] [4]

11. The individual has to depend on the
work performed by others in order
to get the materials or information
he/she needs to do his/her work.   [1] [2] [3] [4]

12. The individual has a lot to say
over what happens on his/her job.   [1] [2] [3] [4]

13. The job requires that the individual
do the same things over and over.

not at all true   a little true   somewhat true   very true

[1] [2] [3] [4]

14. The job allows the individual to make
a lot of decisions on his/her own.

[1] [2] [3] [4]

15. On the job other people make conflicting
demands of the individual.

[1] [2] [3] [4]

D. PLEASE INDICATE HOW MUCH YOU AGREE
OR DISAGREE WITH EACH OF THE FOL-
LOWING STATEMENTS AS A DESCRIPTION
OF THE JOB YOU ARE WATCHING.

strongly disagree   disagree   slightly disagree   slightly agree   agree   strongly agree

1. The individual working on the
job does tasks which are clearly
defined.

[1] [2] [3] [4] [5] [6]

2. The individual working on this
job is free from conflicting
demands that others may make of
him/her.

[1] [2] [3] [4] [5] [6]

3. The job is meaningful.

[1] [2] [3] [4] [5] [6]

4. The individual working on his/
her job frequently had to stop
to get things he/she needed
and didn't have readily available.

[1] [2] [3] [4] [5] [6]

5. On the job, the individual
produces a whole product or performs a complete service.

[1] [2] [3] [4] [5] [6]

6. The job requires the individual
to be prepared to handle surprising or unpredictable
situations.

[1] [2] [3] [4] [5] [6]

7. The job denies the individual any chance to use his/her personal initiative or discretion at work.

strongly disagree *disagree* *slightly disagree* *slightly agree* *agree* *strongly agree*

[1] [2] [3] [4] [5] [6]

8. The job is one that is highly predictable, and that rarely presents the individual with surprising or unpredictable situations.

[1] [2] [3] [4] [5] [6]

Part VI. Administrative Information

ONCE YOU HAVE COMPLETED OBSERVING AND RATING THE JOB, BUT BEFORE LEAVING THE AREA WHERE THE INDIVIDUAL WORKS, FILL OUT THE FOLLOWING INFORMATION.

1. Was the observation completed?

   [1] YES   [2] NO

   Reason for incompleted observation: _____

   _____

   _____

   _____

2. How confident are you of the accuracy of your ratings of this job?

[1]	[2]	[3]	[4]
Not at all confident; I was not at all able to rate the job I observed accurately	Somewhat confident; my ratings are only partially descriptive of the job I observed	Moderately confident; my ratings provide a fairly accurate description of the job I observed	Very confident; my ratings accurately describe the job I observed

3. Ask the individual how typical the sequence you observed is of the work which is normally done?

    [1]   [2]   [3]

Not at all typical; he/she usually does a very different type of work

Somewhat typical; he/she often does similar work, but this observation period did not completely cover his/her job

Very typical; he/she usually does work of the type observed

4. Was this a validation observation, i.e., did another observer make this observation with you?

    [1] YES   [2] NO

5. Ending time of observation: _____

    (Use military time, e.g., 1 p.m. = 1300)

CHAPTER ELEVEN

The Observation of Organizational Behavior: A Structured Naturalistic Approach

DAVID A. NADLER, DENNIS N. T. PERKINS, AND MARTIN HANLON

A comprehensive approach to the description and assessment of organizational life requires the use of methods capable of capturing phenomena that are unanticipated or that are diffused in their form, time, or location. Significant events and changes can occur that are not well represented in documents, in personnel and performance records, in interviews or in data from questionnaires. Such elusive phenomena may occur over a considerable span of time, or in aspects of organizational activity not scheduled in advance for systematic assessment. They may be not fully anticipated during the formulation of concepts and hypotheses for the study. To discover these surprises the researcher needs to employ some process of observation that is open eyed, open minded, responsive to events, and flexibly adaptable to changing circumstances. The observer, himself or herself, must become the instrument for data collection.

The observer's task is to assemble information about complex and dynamic sequences of behavior that constitute a meaningful whole and to note the origins, conditions, and contextual factors that make the information interpretable. But, to be responsive and adaptable implies the risk of being undirected, atheoretical, biased, or responsive to interesting but trivial data. This chapter is addressed to the problem of balancing the risks and advantages attendant upon naturalistic observation of ongoing organizational behavior.

ADVANTAGES OF OBSERVATION AND ATTENDANT PROBLEMS

Observation has a number of distinct strengths as a data-collection method: Data gathering occurs in the actual presence of the behavior; the data lend themselves to the analysis of behavior over time—either continuously or at selected points in time; and the observer can interpret behavior within the context of collateral events and the climate and social structure of the organization. Furthermore, observation is adaptive. The focus of the observer's investigation can be shifted to take into account unexpected changes in the functioning of an organization, including unpredicted events and unanticipated consequences of organizational change.

While the scope and flexibility of observational methods constitute major strengths, these characteristics also underscore problems inherent in the method. The undefined scope and focuses of observation mean that the observer is faced with many choices. What events and action settings should be observed? What locations within an organization should be given most attention? What aspects of behavior and context should be recorded? The observer also must be continually aware of the fact that his or her presence in the organization, in subtle but important ways, may alter the situation being observed. Finally, observation is an active process. Since the observer is continually making choices about what to observe and how to integrate incoming data, no two observers will report exactly the same data or tentative interpretations about the functioning of an organization. Overcoming such sources of bias while preserving the unique advantages of observational methods is the topic addressed here.

This chapter presents one approach to observational research in complex organizations for assessment purposes. This approach is what we call "structured naturalistic observation." It is naturalistic because it does not predetermine what phenomena the observer will attend to. At the same time, the approach is structured, because specific procedures and guidelines are used to record observational data.

In the first section of this chapter, the rationale for structured observation will be developed. Following this, illustrative instruments and procedures of the method will be described and discussed. Third, some perspectives on how the technology might be implemented in the field will be presented.

THE RATIONALE FOR STRUCTURED NATURALISTIC OBSERVATION

The history of observation methods in the social sciences reflects a diversity of contexts, theoretical developments, and range of applications. Observation as a research method evolved more or less independently in different disciplines to address particular research problems. The absence of a common heritage contributes to some of the more intractable problems of observational research. Observation lacks a widely accepted and consistent terminology, and it lacks the degree of codification of procedures characteristic of some other research methods.

The observational methods used in the study of organizational behavior draw mostly from psychology, anthropology, and sociology.[1-3] Methods adapted from psychology have been used primarily for the observation of the behavior of individuals or small groups.[4,5] Typically, these approaches have focused on microbehavior, that is, specific, discrete instances of behavior that can be reliably observed, coded, and counted. Characteristic patterns of behavior for persons or groups are inferred from the analysis and aggregation of such data. Chapter 12 in this volume presents an application of this approach.

Another source of observational methodology has been anthropology. In organizational literature, work by Whyte and Sayles reflect this tradition.[6,7] The researcher immerses himself/herself in a situation and observes activity ranging from the microlevel to the macrolevel. The objective is to identify patterns of behavior and of contexts that aid in the development of explanatory frameworks for the case under study and for other similar cases.

Perhaps the most extensive contribution to the theory and methods of observational research in complex organizations has been from the discipline of sociology. The difficult issues of validity in observation-based research have received considerable attention.[8] The recent literature includes several useful attempts to provide how-to-do-it knowledge of observational methods.[9-10] The methodological and ethical dilemmas inherent in the role of the observer have also been extensively described.[11-14] Sociologists using observational methods clearly have demonstrated that the method can lead to important contributions to the understanding of complex organizations.

Bias and Structure in Observation Methods

Although organization researchers have used a wide range of observation strategies drawn from different disciplinary traditions, most of these strategies share one common characteristic, namely, that a single observer is the principal data-gathering instrument. Even with the use of some guides or procedures, it is ultimately the observer who sees the events and records them—or fails to do so.

The observer and the choices he/she makes while collecting data are key factors in insuring the validity of the findings, the richness of the data, and its generalizability. Gifted observers seem to identify the most significant aspects of behavior in organizations, interpret it with insight, and place it in an appropriate context for others' appreciation; less talented observers seem to miss or misinterpret it. Apart from such differences, human error in the selective perceptions and interpretations of data can confound observations of any kind. Hence the need for procedures that minimize error, guide the less-skilled observer, and do not limit the professional.

One means toward this end is to structure the actions of the observer, thereby reducing the number and scope of choices to be made. Two dimensions of observation lend themselves to structuring. First, the location and process of the observational activity itself can be structured. It is possible to specify the particular classes and types of events and particular places and times to be observed. An example reported in this volume is Goodman's scheme that defines and identifies specific types of interactions at meetings. Such structure reduces choices about whom to observe and what should be observed. Second, the method of recording, coding, and retrieving the observational data can be structured. The specific notational and coding schemes and the like can be specified, guiding the observer in recording data. An example of this approach is the standardized job-observation technique reported by Nadler and Jenkins in this volume, where fixed, closed-ended response categories are used for the rating of job characteristics. Structure, therefore, serves to reduce choices about how to record observations.

One can think of the range of observational methods and degrees of structuring in terms of a two-dimensional space, as is shown in Figure 11-1. One dimension represents the degree to which there is advance specification of the events, times, locations, persons, jobs, and the like that are to be observed—that is, the physical and temporal *process* of

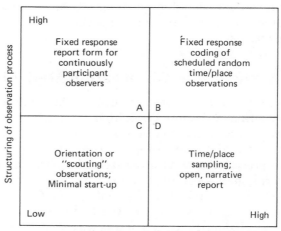

Structuring of observation content

Figure 11-1   Dimensions of observational structure.

observation. The second dimension represents the degree to which there is advance specification of the conceptual *content* of the observations, which may be specified in terms of what the observer should attend to or in terms of the forms of reporting. In the cells of the figure examples are given.

An observer entering an organization for the first time is likely to try to minimize structure and maximize flexible adaptivity on both dimensions (Cell C). If committed initially to a specific conceptual framework, such an observer may still engage in essentially unstructured observation processes, but record and report only, and in detail, those facts and judgments required by his or her analytic plan. Over time, an observer may systematically progress from minimally structured observation at the start, through a succession of increasingly structured (and more cost-effective) stages, to an ultimate stage in which both the observation processes and the content reporting are maximally specified. In such a progression, the early stages may emphasize open and responsive observations—perhaps with some tentative formulation of issues and hypotheses—and some tentative discoveries of optimal observation methods, which guide the later work. Alternatively, an observer may discipline himself/herself against any early judgments that constrain his or her later capacity to remain responsive and adaptive.

It should be noted in passing that there is also a third dimension of observation to be taken into account, namely, the number of observers. This dimension ranges from one—the single individual who depends wholly upon his/her own skills, intuitions, experience, and conceptual framework(s) to discern the significant features of the observed organization—to the extreme case in which very large numbers of resident participant–observers make reports of events, conditions, and changes. The latter case is, of course, the questionnaire or unstructured interview through which members of the organization are engaged *as observers,* not as subjects.

The fundamental trade-off is one of validity and reliability of data as opposed to flexibility, adaptiveness, and the possibility—however remote—for innovative insight. As the method becomes more structured, the choices available to the observer decrease, as do opportunities for bias or error. At the same time, reduction of choice mitigates the capacity of the method to be adaptive, to be integrative, and thus to adhere to the meaning of complex phenomena.

INSTRUMENTS FOR OBSERVATION

In view of the more structured character of some other components of the assessment plan reported in this volume, it was determined at an early stage that the naturalistic observations should be carried out with few constraints. Observers were to observe whatever they thought might be uniquely important or representative, intending especially to note events and conditions of kinds that might escape the more formalized data-gathering processes. They were to be constrained in reporting only to the extent necessary for their narrative observational reports to be usable. On the latter, three factors were thought important. First, the observers' reports had to be sufficiently organized, orderly, and complete so that they would be accessible to others for secondary or confirmatory analyses. Second, the reports had to be in a form that would allow joint use of data from multiple observers and assessment of the amount of agreement and complementarity among multiple observers. Third, since large volumes of information would be accumulated over extended periods of time, the reports would have to be amenable to some system for easy record search and information retrieval.

The question, then, was how to structure the communication of what was observed. Typically, if one was to observe activities involving people and to write down what was seen, the report would include various kinds of information. On one hand, the written account would probably include notation of specific activities or behaviors that occurred. These would be tangible and discrete occurrences, of kinds that could be verified objectively or by consensus if several observers were present or if the sequence was videotaped. On the other hand, the written record would probably include various attempts by the observer to "make some sense" of what was seen and heard, to identify patterns, and to determine cause and effect. These would be speculative, of course, since the observer could not know with certainty whether his or her attempt to make sense of the situation conformed with any reality. Finally, the observational record might reflect the kinds of feelings that the observer had while watching the activity or behavior. If the observer, for example, found one of the people being observed to be personally distasteful, that might influence how the observer paid attention to that person's behavior and how the observer "made sense" of that behavior.

The observer, therefore, upon observing a sequence of activities, communicates some perceptions of the tangible events, some interpretations of what those events mean, and some feelings that were experienced by her/him during this time period. The problem is that these aspects are frequently interwoven, and thus it is hard to use and evaluate the different types of information.

Those who have worked on the development of theory related to interpersonal communication and behavior have dealt with a similar problem in the observation of how individuals communicate information to each other.[15-16] One approach to improving the effectiveness of communication is to separate different types of data—that is, perceptions, interpretations, and affects—and to label them clearly. The naturalistic observation method presented here was based on this approach. The purpose of the instruments is to structure the recording (and thus communication) of data so as to distinguish and label the different kinds of information.

The General Observation Form

The core of the observation method is the general observation form (see Figure 11-2). The form includes provisions for recording observed information as well as spaces for various identifying and coding entries. Figure 11-3 is an example of a completed report.

Aside from the identification entries, the general observation form has five categories of information to be recorded. Table 11-1 provides a listing and descriptive summary of each of these categories. The first is the "overview of the event." This is a brief summary of the major activities, behaviors, and occurrences that happened during the observation period. This may be short—a few sentences—but it includes enough information so that someone reading through a series of observation reports could make a decision whether to read further or to go on to another report. It is, thus, a summary and overview that serves a purpose similar to a table of contents.

The second category—the "detailed observation" section—is the central component of the observation instrument and is intended to contain

Setting _____   Site _____
Event _____   Observer _____
Variables _____   Date/time _____

(title of observation)

Overview of event:

Detailed observations:

☐ more

Interpretations:

☐ more

Observer feelings:

☐ more

Attachments:

Figure 11-2   General observation form.

Setting	Top management	Site	Columbia National Bank
Event	Project committee meeting	Observer	Mary B.
Variables	Project evaluation; Project opposition	Date/time	1/16/76 11:30 A.M.–12:00 m.

Twenty-first Meeting of CNB Project Committee
(title of observation)

Overview of event:
Meeting was held to review progress of the project, to find out how initial meetings with the new consultants and branch staff had gone, to review evaluation procedures, and to meet with a representative of the consulting team. See attached agenda.

Detailed observations:
a. Meeting called to order at 11:30 by Cassis. Also in attendance are Norton, Flinton, Orlinoff, Burns, and Pote. Cassis reviews agenda.
b. Cassis calls upon Flinton to give progress report on the project to date. Flinton gives report, including the following: "We're making good progress although it may seem slow to you. We've finished the interviews in the different branches. Unfortunately, this took much longer than we expected because it was difficult to get cooperation in some branches. In other branches we got cooperation, but it was difficult to free people up during working hours, and many did not want to stay and be interviewed on their own time."
c. Norton replies: "What do you think all of this means? Do you feel that the problems you're having may be significant in terms of continuation of the project?"
d. Flinton: "No. I don't think it says anything about the project; I think it's just one of those things that we run into when doing something like this."
e. Others raise questions about the progress to date, including Pote and Burns.

Interpretations:
a. Why did the project run into so many problems in certain branches, not in others?
b. Flinton seems very defensive. Why? What does that mean?
c. Norton may be leading a group that is trying to "gun down" the project.

Observer feelings:
a. I was angry at Flinton for being defensive; she made me feel frustrated.

Attachments:
a. Meeting agenda.

Figure 11-3   General observation form.

the first-level perceptions of the objective events. It is a detailed, factual record of what occurred during the observational period, usually in chronological order. It is important to limit the information to the factual, that is, to tangible, discrete events and conditions that could be verified by other observers or from visual or sound records. It is important to avoid interpretation or causal attribution. The ultimate test of the

Table 11-1   General Observation Recording Format

1. *Overview of event:* A relatively brief summary of the major activities, behaviors, occurrences, etc. that happened during the observation. This is usually short (several sentences), but includes enough detail so that someone doing analysis can decide whether to read further. It is basically a descriptive summary of the entire observation.

2. *Detailed observation:* Serves as the core of the observational record. Includes detailed and chronologically ordered descriptive statements about the event that is being observed. The focus is on perceptions of the observer. This section is the basic "factual" record of the event being observed.

3. *Interpretations:* Statements by the observer proposing interpretations, attributions, or hypotheses explaining the specific activities and behaviors observed in the detailed observations. Interpretations might include attempts to identify patterns in the behavior, attribution of causes to behavior, speculation about the nature and meaning of events, etc. Usually these should be stated as propositions or questions.

4. *Observer feelings:* Descriptions by the observer of his/her own feelings while observing the behavior and activity that is recorded in the detailed observation section. Specifically, it is the positive or negative affective reactions that the observer experienced.

5. *Attachments:* A listing of any attached supportive material or documentation relevant to the behavior or activities included in the detailed observations. Items to be attached might be meeting agendas, membership lists, other observational instruments used during the event, handouts at meetings, diagrams, etc.

adequacy of the data in this section might be to ask if the observer is willing to show the entries to the individuals being observed for their verification. If the detailed observations are free of interpretation or observer affect, the information could, in principle, be shown to those involved without concern about misinterpretation.

The third section of the observation form is for "interpretations." The observer is to make statements that attempt to make sense of the activities and behaviors that have been observed. These are, in fact, propositions or hypotheses that cannot be immediately verified but that can guide future data collection by observation as well as data collection by other methods. Interpretations might include attempts to identify patterns of the behavior or activity that has been observed, attributions concerning the causes of behavior or the factors that motivated it, speculation about the nature and meaning of events, and the like. Ideally, interpretations should be propositions; that is, they should be tentative and testable in form. They might therefore be recorded as questions or hypotheses.

The fourth section concerns the reactions of the observer personally to the events that have been observed. The reactions are labeled "observer feelings." While the observer is present in the situation, he or she may experience different affective reactions to what is going on. These reactions develop over time, and they influence later choices about what behavior to observe and what interpretations to make. By making these feelings explicit, two purposes are achieved. First, the observer may become more aware of the feelings by writing them down, and thus be more able to correct for their potential bias. Second, others who use the observational record can take account of the observer feelings as a possible qualification on the data. In this section, therefore, the observer should attempt to write down very specifically the feelings that were experienced during the observation.

The final section is for "attachments." Frequently the observer is able to get access to supporting documents or other information relevant to the behavior or activity being observed. These might include, for example, meeting agendas, critical memos or correspondence, maps or floor plans, and sketches. The range of possible attachments is obviously large. These should be physically attached to the observation to which they are relevant, and they should be listed on the observation form itself.

In practice, an observation period of one or two hours might require the equivalent of 5 to 10 typewritten pages of report. The observer might write a tentative overview, and then make detailed notes during the period of observation, using a separate sheet for recording interpretations and observer feelings during the observation. In many cases, observers have found it useful to type their reports after the actual observation period; in these cases, the information can be noted serially and then, while typing, be put into the order specified in the form.

An alternative to this method involves a somewhat different version of the same observation form (see Figure 11-4). The same guides to categories and information are provided, but the form is set up so that detailed observation, interpretations, and feelings can be recorded concurrently and sequentially as they happen. This form does not have a section for an overview, but it does provide for variable coding for each of the different specifically detailed observations. Both forms include, basically, the same information; they are just formatted somewhat differently. The following material on coding and use of the instruments can be applied to either form.

Coding and Identification of Observations

A major problem in the use of observational data is that of accessing the data for analysis. If data are to be used for analytic purposes, they need to be identified so that they can be retrieved and so that specific observations can be related to variables in some conceptual or analytic framework. The general observation form provides space for labeling and coding of the information for purposes of retrieval or analysis. It is important to note that this approach is best used when some initial conceptual framework is employed to guide the observations. However, it also can be used in an inductive approach, with categories and variables for observation developed during the course of the study.

Setting _____   Site _____

Event _____   Observer _____

Page _____ of this observation   Date/time _____

(title of observation)

Time	Detailed observations	Interpretations	Feelings	Variable code

Figure 11-4   General observation form.

The general observation form calls for a variety of coding and identification data as is shown in Table 11-2. First, each observation is given a descriptive *title*. This title, while brief, should include enough information so that—together with the date—the observation might be entitled "Fourth Meeting of the Executive Committee" or "Project Staff Meeting," with the date indicated elsewhere. As will be seen later, the title is an important element of the data retrieval process.

The observation forms also include space for some other identifying information that is straightforward. The *site* refers to the organization or general location where all of a series of observations take place. *Observer* obviously refers to the name of the person doing the observation and recording, while *date/time* refers to the specific day and time period when the behavior or activities that are being observed occurred. These complete the identification.

Aside from such identification, each observation report provides three additional types of information that form the basis for the observation storage and retrieval system. That system rests upon three-level hierarchical coding, according to the *setting* in which the observation was made, the *type of event* reported, and the conceptual or descriptive *variables* of interest. In each case, codes need to be established before observation

Table 11-2   Information Needed to Identify and Code Observations

1. Title of observation: A short descriptive label for the event, activities, behavior being observed. Should be distinctive enough to enable this observation to be distinguished from others.

2. Site: Name of the project or organization where the observation is occurring.

3. Observer: Name of person doing the observation and recording the data.

4. Date/time: Date and time period when the behavior or activity was observed.

5. Setting: One of a number of predetermined categories specifying where the observed behaviors or activities occurred. Settings are generally geographically related, with the level of detail in determining settings as a function of the scope of the entire observational activity.

6. Event: One of a number of predetermined categories of behavior or activity likely to occur within the setting.

7. Variables: One or more of a number of predetermined descriptive or conceptual variables that will be helpful in locating observation reports pertinent to a given analytic or interpretive task.

begins, although there may be subsequent code changes and additions that necessitate recording of earlier observation reports.

The first level of coding is based on the fact that all observations occur within one of several unique *settings* within a research site. A setting may be defined as a physical location for the observations, and, indeed, most settings are geographically located. For example, while observing behavior in a manufacturing plant, different departments, such as plating, finishing, or packing, might be defined as "settings" for observation. These are obviously tied to physical locations. On the other hand, a setting in the same plant might be defined as the top management team of the plant. While that team may have a customary physical location, such as a conference room or suite of management offices, the members may also meet or interact frequently in other places. It may be more useful to define the setting by the personnel involved, rather than by place. Thus, settings may be defined by unlike criteria, necessitating a predetermined and mutually exclusive roster of settings for use in coding specific observations.

Within each setting, it is possible to observe a number of different *events* that may occur. Events are major classes of behavior or activity that take place repetitively over time. Thus, for example, when observing the management team of the plant, observations might be made of events, such as scheduled meetings, that occur weekly or monthly. Observations of events that do not fit into any pattern of recurrence are typically given the event label of "ongoing behavior." Table 11-3 shows a setting-event code from a current study.

The detailed observations and interpretations that are noted on the general observation form also can be described in a way other than by

Table 11-3 Examples of Setting-Event Codes[a]

Event Categories	Behavior
Setting: Surgical Unit 1	
1. Staff conferences	All formal staff meetings on the unit; with or without consultants.
2. Doctors' orientation	The monthly orientation meetings for physicians; also any other formal activities directly and primarily involving unit house, staff, and support physicians.
3. Scheduled observations	Limited to observations listed on the time/place random observation schedule.
4. Unscheduled observations	Unscheduled unit observations, brief visits to the unit.
5. Research events	Questionnaire administrations, formal interviews with unit staff, personnel roster reviews, etc.
6. Other	Residual category.
Setting: Surgical Unit 2	
1. Scheduled observations	As above
2. Unscheduled observations	As above
3. Research events	As above
4. Other	As above
Setting: Nursing Service Administration	
1. Surgery AD—Surgery 1 supervisors	All meetings involving the assistant director of nursing for Surgery and the SCN's, CS's of Surgery Unit 1.
2. Surgery AD leadership group	All meetings involving the Surgery AD and her supervisory staff under her direction, within and outside of Surgery Pavilion.
3. Surgery AD—consultants	All consultant work with Surgery AD where other hospital staff are not participants.
4. Director of nursing	All consultant activities involving the director of nursing, special projects within the nursing department initiated by consultants and the director of nursing.
5. Other	Residual category.
Setting: Project Steering Committee	
1. Steering Committee meetings	Includes meetings of SC subcommittee, working groups.
2. Interviews	Interviews with Steering Committee members, "one-on-one" meetings.
3. Other	Residual category.

[a] Taken from an observational study of a change project in a hospital. Names and other identifying information have been changed.

setting and event. Any research involves some variables or concepts of special interest to the researcher. The third level of coding involves labeling the observations in terms of the abstract variables to which the behavior or activities observed are relevant. The two general observation forms each provide a place for this labeling, although in different locations on each form. For example, a monthly staff meeting of top management in the plant might be labeled for its relevance to such variables as "leadership style," "conflict resolution," or "decision making." Variables for such coding can come from different sources. In some cases, a specific list of variables derived from a conceptual or theoretical framework might be used. In other cases, classes of variables might be developed as the observation proceeds. For example, specific themes (e.g., "quality improvement" or "executive succession") that repeat themselves in observations might be identified and then used to recode prior observations and to code subsequent observations as they occur.

When combined with the basic identifying information of title, site, observer, and date/time, this three-level coding scheme enables selective identification and retrieval of observation reports.

Storage and Retrieval of Observational Data

The three-level coding scheme forms the basis of a storage, retrieval, and analysis system. Completed observation forms and attachments are stored in notebooks. A notebook is reserved for each setting, and within settings, observations are inserted chronologically. Thus, knowing the setting and approximate date of an observation, the report is relatively easy to locate. Over time, however, numerous reports are accumulated. In a typical observation project extending over a year or so, several hundred observation forms may be filed, and it becomes more difficult to find the ones that are required. An aid for retrieval and analysis is needed.

One approach is to use an observation log sheet such as the one shown in Figure 11-5. Each time a report is placed in a setting notebook, it is also logged on this sheet. For each report, the key identifying information is provided, including the date of the observation, serial entry number, the title of the observation, the observer, and the codes for settings, events, and variables. The log form, which is stored in a master or control notebook that includes the codes and variable lists, is then the basic tool for retrieval of the records for analysis. Going back to the manufacturing-plant example, if one wanted to get a chronological record of all of the meetings of the management team, one could simply scan the event column in the logbook, noting all observations of that event (staff meetings) within the top management team setting. Similarly, if one wanted to identify events of conflict, the variable codes could be used to identify observations when conflict was observed. The date and the setting enable the observation to be located in the notebooks, once they have been identified as of interest to the analyst.

Site ______________________ Page number ________

Date	Entry no.	Brief description or title	Observer	Setting	Event	Variables

Figure 11-5 Observation log sheet.

The observation forms, categories of observation, coding schemes, and log sheets are the core of the naturalistic observation method described here. It is these elements that structure the observers' reporting so that the data are comparable, retrievable, and in a form that facilitates analysis. The structuring, however, is not intended to be constraining upon the observer, except as to the methods of reporting what is observed. The instrumentation does not preclude the use of, and integration of, other supplemental forms of observation and reporting. In practice, supplemental instruments are frequently used, including, for example, special standard rating forms, self-reports from individuals following a period of naturalistic observation, and the like. The range of feasible and useful supplements is limited only by the purposes of the research, the nature of the variables of special interest, and the ingenuity of the observer in devising ways to get additional information without risking disturbance of the natural flow of events.

OBSERVATION IN PRACTICE

Advice on observational methods tends to fall on a practicality continuum. At one end, the researcher is counseled to note key events or, perhaps, to be perceptive. Such sagacious advice is often linked with the suggestion that the adviser's theoretical orientation and research objectives should also be adopted, since these define what is "key" and what one should be perceptive about. At the other end of the continuum, the researcher is advised about the mechanics of note taking, filing, deportment at the observation site, and the like. The mid-range prescriptions appear to be those most difficult to generate and convey to others, perhaps because the means for effective practice of the observer's art are highly contingent upon features of the research setting and research objectives as well as upon the characteristics of the observer. Slavish imitation of previously successful observers is not necessarily the best course of action if the aim is to be responsive to a particular behavioral environment.

Characteristics of Observers

It seems inescapable that some individuals are more adept than others at conducting their observer roles in organizational environments. Although there are specific skills that can be taught—and experience itself is a good teacher—attention should be given to the prior demonstrated ability of individuals to establish rapport with a diversity of others, despite disparities in background, language, appearance, and role. This is not to say that observers must "be like" members of the organizations they study, or that they must adopt the norms of the research site. Tolerable differences may elicit data that would otherwise be missed, and variations in observer characteristics may produce concomitant variation in the phenomena actually observed. One study, for example, was conducted by two observers—one a Filipino female and the other a Caucasian male.[17] They found systematic variation in observed events: The Filipino found that her identity, perhaps because of novelty or assumed social distance, promoted respondent candor. On the other hand, she observed no instances of overt racial prejudice over a long span of time, although such were readily displayed to the Caucasian male observer.

Experience suggests that occasional observers should not attempt to "blend into" the organizational environment by extremes of local dress or changes in usual demeanor. Even if the role is to be one of "observer as participant," it will be obvious that the researcher is an outsider.[18,19] What is important, however, is that the observer maintain credibility as a representative of a respectable research enterprise. This implies that the observers would, ideally, have that appearance and manner that organization members expect an observer of given age and social status to have. The objective is, of course, to create as little disturbance as possible, and to minimize reactance to the observer as "instrument."

Reliability

It is entirely possible that individuals may be skilled at establishing rapport and may be able to enter the organization unobtrusively, but their ability to observe behavioral phenomena reliably is another matter. And this—along with valid interpretations—is the reason for their presence.

Observer reliability can be tested prior to entry by simultaneous dual observation of exemplary events. For example, it may be instructive for a pair of independent observers to report the "stream of behavior" that occurs in a research planning meeting or in a work setting of easy access. Divergences in recording can be used as discussion points, both to improve the reliability of observation and to identify potential sources of invalidity. Do the data recorded as "events" on the general observation form represent valid evidence for the inferences made in the "hypothesis" space? Do the naturalistic data logically relate to the key-word variables? Observer rating scales and such instruments as Likert's Profile of Organizational Characteristics[20] may be completed by two or more observers after a period of study, so that points of disagreement used to identify systematic biases in perception are discovered. Agreement on global rating scales does not, of course, confirm agreement on the component events used to form the overall judgment. Disagreement, however, does suggest the possibility of divergent reference frames or, possibly, misinterpretation of the meaning of research constructs.

An inherent dilemma in field observation is suggested by the foregoing comments. Reliability, in the sense of agreement between observers, while always reassuring, may not always be preferred over nonagreement. No single observer can observe and report everything of potential significance that goes on. No single observer can pursue a diversity of tentative lines of interpretation with equal diligence. A case can be made for strategies of dual observation in which there is agreement sought in "factual" event descriptions along with diversity, or knowing specialization of function, as to the development of interpretive schemata.

Sampling

In an organizational setting, conclusions reached by an observer may have diminished validity due to systematic bias in perception, or simply bias in sampling. But how does one know when to observe, whom to observe, and which settings are the most likely to yield valuable information.[7] The answer to this question must ultimately turn on local organizational properties and research objectives, but experience does suggest a few protective considerations and strategies.

The approach of sampling exhaustively—observing everything—is very rarely feasible, if ever; even in multiple participant-observation approaches, the observers, by becoming participants-in-role, deny themselves access to much of potential importance. The risk of "elite bias"[21] is considerable, as some individuals are more engaging, more articulate, or more accepting of the observer's role than are others. A small protection lies in keeping a tally of contacts with different classes of informants so that voids become evident. Similarly, a "setting bias" can occur in which certain locations are oversampled, not purposely, but for such irrelevant reasons as accessibility, predictability of schedules, comfort, habit, and the like. It is often feasible to moderate such a setting bias by including in the observation plan a distinguishable component that provides for a program of randomly assigned time–place observations (see Table 11-3) for an example. When personal observation periods must be rare or episodic, it may be possible to gain event coverage and continuity by creating a small set of semitrained, in-role, on-site informants who can be phoned on a daily, weekly, or monthly basis. In one field site, this was done openly to legitimate the informant's special role, and with a diversity of perspective among these informants. This allowed a kind of triangulation summary of key events based upon weekly telephone interviews about the same events with union, management, and consultant informants.

Intensity of Observation

It is useful to form, at an early stage, a realistic idea of the likely intensity and duration of the observation phase of an organization or change assessment project. The projected scale and duration substantially influence the early choices that need to be made with respect to such matters as the definition of the observer's role, the expectations and obligations that are implied for others, the form and detail of reporting, and the like.

At the most spartan level, the researcher may need only to serve two objectives: (1) to gain a sufficient orientation to the organization's technology and work flow, organizational structure, personnel composition, operating records, decision practices, and similar matters, so that he or she may proceed confidently with the introduction of nonobservational research procedures; (2) to compile an account of recent events that bear upon the projected study and arrange for getting reports from organization members or records on major episodes that occur during the course of the study period. At this level of effort, little consideration need be given to the format and detail of reporting, to the sampling of times and places, or to the clarification of an observer's role. The observer is after "public" information of kinds that are readily delivered by a small number of selected informants.

Perhaps the minimum level of effort deserving the label "structured naturalistic observation" would subsume the foregoing activities, and additionally, include the following:

1.   Observation of key scheduled organizational events of direct relevance to the research, such as meetings to discuss the progress of organizational change programs, the administration of research instruments, and so forth.

2.   Observation of other recurrent meetings that may identify issues for further exploration; provide a baseline for understanding the development of the setting; and generally help the observer to develop a picture of the organization.

3.   Observation of events of intervention, such as activities of change agents, which are designed to alter the structure and processes of the setting.

4.   Unstructured or semistructured interviews with key informants. Although there are dangers of bias in cultivating relationships with a limited sample of individuals, it will undoubtedly be true that some organization members can provide more, and more relevant, data than others. Moreover, it is likely that these individuals will be in a position to talk freely and be articulate in sharing their perceptions, so that the observer's cost/yield ratio will be great.

In such an intermediate level of observation, the time and event sampling becomes highly salient, although there are no hard and fast rules to apply. A key consideration is one of reactivity. To the extent possible, the observer should avoid disturbing the organizational ambience by his or her occasional visits. Some find a "handshake rule" to be a useful heuristic: After the initial-entry phase, the observer should enter the setting with sufficient frequency so that a handshake or other formal greeting is unnecessary. In essence, observers should strive to avoid making their arrival an "event" that calls attention to their presence, thereby altering the behavior setting of members.

In its most intensive form, the observers may assume a role of continuous living and working within the setting. This modality has the advantage of minimizing reactance, and it enables the observer to perform fine-grained analyses that otherwise would be impossible. These activities might include, for example, the following:

1. Structured interviews, which can be used to corroborate findings developed through other sources and which permit multitrait–multimethod checks on the research methodology.

2. Structured job observations, such as those described in Chapter 10. This would be particularly appropriate in studies designed to assess the impact of job-redesign or job-enrichment interventions.

3. Structured group observations (such as those described in Chapter 17), the results of which will be amenable to time-series analysis, thereby strengthening the design of studies involving single cases.

4. Combined questionnaire and interview formats in which respondents first complete survey instruments, then participate in open-ended discussions that provide an opportunity to clarify and elaborate on their questionnaire responses. This "internaire" strategy can inform later analyses of quantitative data. For example, critical misunderstandings that exist about the wording of questionnaire items may be uncovered by this process.

This level of effort enables the observer to seek out and develop rapport with individuals who would be reluctant to speak candidly with researchers engaged in more episodic data collection efforts. Such individuals may be suspicious of the research, or they may simply be intimidated by the presence of an academic or professional outsider. Yet, a balanced picture of the setting should include the views of these individuals, as well as more outspoken members. Intensive participant observation provides an opportunity to develop needed rapport, and thus it improves the likelihood of valid conclusions.

At the same time, the observer who becomes a part of the setting must be aware of the possibility of co-optation. Personal relationships may eclipse professional identity: One may "go native" and lose the capacity to be a critical onlooker.

Concluding Note

A persistent theme in this book, and especially in this measurement section, is the search for methods of information getting that are quantitative, replicable, and interpretable by others, and that are subject to tests for reliability and validity. The observational processes treated in this chapter defect from that theme, and for good reasons.

Along with the merits of careful measurement and quality control comes the defect that one must choose in advance what might be worth measuring. While wise choices can be made, it would be foolish or naive for a researcher to discount the likelihood of unanticipated and even unimaginable future events and states, or to foreclose the possibility of forming new images of familiar events. The prevalent paradigm of the social sciences assumes recurrence and regularity. On the other hand, a less prevalent but useful paradigm assumes that history never repeats itself exactly and that much of the recurrence and regularity we report arises from using fixed methods and fixed ideas that prevent the perception of novelty, that prevent the detection of important "facts," and that prevent the discovery of new ways to "explain" familiar facts.

Naturalistic observation, in our view, is an essential feature of a well-rounded, comprehensive approach to the assessment of an organization and of organizational change. At the most basic level, it can provide a chronological account of key events and circumstances that proves useful in the interpretation of quantitative information, and in the choice of analytic themes. In addition, the observers' reports, however impressionistic, should at least be compatible with the conclusions suggested by quantitative analyses, and thus provide an important facet of the triangulation strategy for arriving at confident conclusions from imperfect information. In addition, one can always hope that a perceptive, insightful, adaptive, open-minded observer will be able to see something not seen before but that is readily seen and confirmed by others or confirmed by measurement once the patterning and sequencing of events is suggested.

Unstructured naturalistic observation, however, is not immune to nor exempt from quality control. When two observers of "the same" setting do not agree and can not reach agreement in discussion, both reports are suspect. A summative account and interpretation of an extended sequence of events prepared by an observer should meet the minimal test of being—in the main—recognizable and plausible to the participants in the events, and it should ideally meet the test of illuminating the events for participants. In the end, the observations and conclusions, if in the form of generalizations or hypotheses, must be confirmable in other field situations.

REFERENCES

1. Hanlon, M. D. Observational methods in organizational assessment. In E. E. Lawler III, D. A. Nadler, & C. Cammann (Eds.), *Organizational assessment: Perspectives on the measurement of organizational behavior and the quality of working life.* New York: Wiley-Interscience, 1980.

2. Heyns, R. W., & Lippitt, R. Systematic observational techniques. In G. Lindzey (Ed.), *Handbook of social psychology.* Reading: Addison-Wesley, 1954.

3. Weick, K. E. Systematic observational methods. In G. Lindzey & E. Aronson (Eds.), *The handbook of social psychology* (*Vol. II*). Reading, MA: Addison-Wesley, 1968.

4. Argyris, C. *Interpersonal competence and organizational effectiveness.* Homewood, IL: Irwin-Dorsey, 1962.

5. Bales, R. F. *Interaction process analysis.* Cambridge: Addison-Wesley, 1950.

6. Whyte, W. F. (Ed.), *Money and motivation: An analysis of incentives in industry.* New York: Harper, 1955.

7. Sayles, L. R. *Managerial behavior: Administration in complex organizations.* New York: McGraw-Hill, 1964.

8. McCall, G., & Simmons, J. *Issues in participant observation.* Reading, MA: Addison-Wesley, 1969.

9. Bogdan, R., & Taylor, S. J. *Introduction to qualitative research methods.* New York: Wiley, 1975.

10. Schatzman, L., & Strauss, A. L. *Field research: Strategies for a natural sociology.* Englewood Cliffs: Prentice-Hall, 1973.

11. Erikson, K. T. A comment on disguised observation in sociology. *Social Problems,* 1967, **14**, 366–373.

12. Gold, R. L. Roles in sociological field observations. *Social Forces,* 1958, **36**, 217–223.

13. Miller, S. M. The participant observer and "over-rapport." *American Sociological Review,* 1952, **17**, 97–99.

14. Scott, W. R. Field work in a formal organization: Some dilemmas in the role of observer. *Human Organization,* 1963, **22**, 162–168.

15. Agryris, C. *Interpersonal competence and organizational effectiveness.* Homewood, IL: Irwin, 1962.

16. Argyris, C. *Intervention theory and method: A behavioral science view.* Reading, MA: Addison-Wesley, 1970.

17. Perkins, D. N. T., Nieva, V. F., & Lawler, E. E. III. *Managing Creation: The challange of building a new organization.* New York: Wiley-Interscience, 1983.

18. Junker, B. H. *Fieldwork.* Chicago: University of Chicago Press, 1960.

19. Palm, G. *The flight from work.* Cambridge: Cambridge University Press, 1977.

20. Likert, R. *The human organization: Its management and value.* New York: McGraw-Hill, 1967.

21. Sieber, S. D. The integration of fieldwork and survey methods. *American Journal of Sociology,* 1973, **78**, 1335–1359.

CHAPTER TWELVE

Observation of Meetings

PAUL S. GOODMAN AND EDWARD J. CONLON

The task of an observer-historian in organizational change experiments is made formidable by the fact that events seem to occur, for the most part, when the observer is not present. The meaning of episodic events may not become evident until later, when recollections are dim. Finally, significant "events" may display themselves as trends, gradually, over some span of time.

This chapter presents a structured observational system for capturing one important aspect of a quality of work intervention—the behavior of union and management representatives and the external consultants during scheduled meetings. In a standardized system, the observer-historian is able to systematically record, store, and analyze behavior over time among the major actors in the change effort.

A prominent feature of many organizational change efforts is the establishment of committees, task forces, and the like, or the engagement of previously existing formal groups into the change program. Such committees are responsible for the initiation, design, monitoring, and evaluation of all, or some aspect of, the program at the site. The principal actors in the change project are present at these meetings—often including union and management representatives, members of experimental work groups, the external consultants, and (occasionally) representatives of an external evaluation team. The meetings provide accessible, scheduled, and information-rich occasions for observation. The existence of a standardized procedure to measure behavior in these meetings is useful in that it provides a systematic way to record one aspect of the history of an experiment and to examine changes in relationships among the major actors. To some extent, the coded meetings are a verbal replay of important occurrences that may not otherwise be recorded. Additionally, the meetings can expose the orientation of the various constituencies toward important issues. They provide a barometer of changes in labor–management relationships, the problem-solving skills and abilities of the particular group being observed, and changes in role taking by constituencies over time. The major themes that may determine the success or failure of an intervention are generally exhibited as recurring issues in the discussions of these groups that are formally charged with directing planned change programs. To the extent the standard measurement procedures are used across sites, one can begin to build some generalization about factors that change the character of the relationship between the major actors and the consequences of these changes on the program's effectiveness.

In nearly all experimental sites mentioned in this book, an assessment team was expected to attend and observe such meetings as they could, to interview attendees about crucial events that occur or that are discussed in the meetings, and to review such documents as are available—agenda, minutes, work papers, and the like. These efforts comprise part of the naturalistic assessment of the change program, representing it in its holistic context, generating hypotheses, and guiding the collection of further data. The nature and purposes of this methodology are reviewed elsewhere in this volume, along with its strengths and limitations. In this chapter we move a step further by presenting a standardized coding scheme used to measure aspects of behavior in meetings.

STRUCTURED OBSERVATIONAL SYSTEM

The structured observational system can be divided into four sections. The first section concerns the process by which data are gathered. Here we refer not to the specific operational procedures, but rather, to the general process by which data are collected at a meeting. The second section concerns the coding system. The coding system indicates the specific operational rules for relating behaviors to specific nominal codes. The third section of the system is a set of computer programs. The purpose of these programs is to arrange the data for analysis and then—on instruction—to provide data about behaviors that occurred in a meeting or set of meetings. The programs are search programs that examine the data for specific behaviors that are displayed by identified individuals. The behaviors are specified by the coding system. The last section of the coding system concerns analysis issues. Basically, it identifies the kinds of questions and the forms of data that can be generated using the structured observation system.

Getting the Data

To collect data we need an observer to attend the designated meetings in an unobtrusive way. While his or her presence is understood, and he or she is a familiar face from other on-site activities, the role is defined as that of observer, not participant. When possible, a seat is chosen at the rear of the room that is well separated from the members of the meeting. The observer must become generally familiar with the identities and names of participants and with the technical terminology and local language that prevails in such meetings.

Under this structured observation system, the data are collected as an annotated transcript of the meeting. A transcript is a record of who said what to whom. There are alternative ways to develop such a transcript—by electronic means or by hand. It is often preferred to develop the transcript by hand, because any mechanical device may have a reactive quality, which is an effect to be avoided. Also, it is very difficult to tape a group of even modest size and attribute the interactions to particular individuals. The disadvantages of recording by hand are that the observer can miss some of the behaviors, and it is a tiring process.

In principle, it would be possible to code the events directly as the interactions occur, thus avoiding the preparation of voluminous pages of transcript. Experience indicates that direct, on-the-spot coding is too difficult for a single person unless the codes are greatly simplified. Also, it is common for the meaning of a single statement to be evident only in the context of what others say; in direct coding, some of the context is lost.

Developing a transcript by hand is not as difficult as it might appear. Notation conventions are established to ease the observer's task—for example, using initials for full names and abbreviations for recurrent technical terms. When interactions become very rapid or not sequential, the observer may use a summary code or select the aspect of the exchange that seems most significant. He or she may code, but otherwise omit, certain long exchanges that are not important as to content—for example, when someone tells a long, irrelevant but possibly entertaining story. Typically, the experienced observer can adequately record about 75% of the interactions on the spot. He or she may attempt to recall and reconstruct—after the meeting—some exchanges that were too complicated to record fully at the time of occurrence. Time notations can be kept so that the durations of periods or phases of the meeting may be estimated. Meetings may be recorded by two observers independently, to allow reliability checks.

Coding

The process of coding is very straightforward. The basic task is to assign numerical codes to points in the transcript. Codes may describe, for example, the type of meeting or a specific interaction. Training time to become proficient in the scheme is approximately four to six sessions, which are spread over several weeks. A training session might last two to three hours. Each meeting transcript should be coded independently by two coders, with the results compared and disagreement resolved by the original observer. In hiring coders, it is not necessary to look for any particular attributes other than facility in English and willingness to do coding work.

The Coding Scheme. The coding scheme is designed to operate at two levels of content and two levels of meeting and time-segment identification. The lowest content level is that of individual actions and interactions—that is, when Person A says something to Person B or to all others present, thus initiating an exchange or responding to another's action. The second level of content is the description of an episode—that is, a unified set of interactions that pertain to a particular problem, topic, or group function. The two identification levels refer, first, to naming the type of meeting, its date and location, and the names and identities of those present, and, second, to distinguish the sequential time segments of the meeting.

The coding scheme thus produces hierarchically arranged data of a particular identified *meeting,* with *interactions* partially clustered into *episodes,* and occurring in identified *time segments.* The computer programs, of course, are matched to this hierarchical structure to allow search for any desired combination of data (see Figure 12-1).

Coding of Meetings and Time Segments

In the case of the site where this system was first applied, the meeting identification codes were relatively simple. Four *types of meetings* were distinguished, defined, and observed—the types being distinguished by their sizes, the constituencies represented (e.g., union, management, consultants, experimental unit workers, etc.), and their purposes. For example, one such type of meeting had the name "steering committee"—a large group including both union and management representatives as well as members of the external consulting team, which was charged with the overall planning and conduct of the experimental changes. Further identification included the meeting date, the location (on or off the work site), and name of the recording observer. The coded names and formal roles of participants (e.g., John Jones, union officer) could also be entered as part of the identification data.

The time-segment code chosen for use at this site distinguished four equal-length quarters of each meeting.

Coding of Episodes

The coding of episodes—that is, a set of interactions pertaining to a distinguishable topic, problem, or group function—proceeds in two stages. First, the episode is coded as to type, and is given a name; second, if the episode is one in which some decision or action might be taken, the episode is further coded for its content and process characteristics.

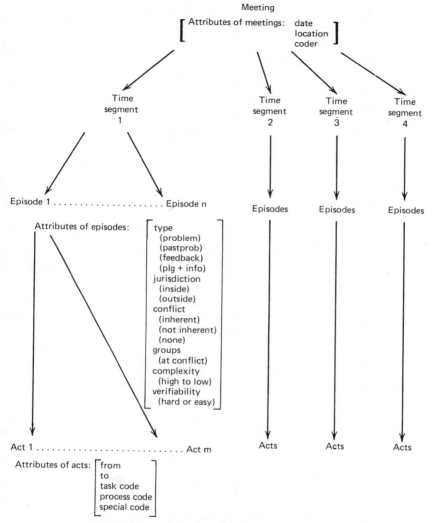

Figure 12-1   An outline of the coding scheme.

Four types of episodes are distinguished. *Feedback* is an episode of information exchange about past performance, incidents since the last meeting, comments about policy developments, and the like. *Planning and information* is an episode of content similar to that for feedback, but referring to the present or future, as in exchanges about upcoming events or planned actions. Episodes coded in the preceding categories are given a brief identifying name, but no further coding. *Problem* episodes center on identifying some uncertain, novel, or unsolved issue, and commonly they include the evaluation of the issue and the generation of possible resolutions or courses of action: They may include a resolution or agreed course of action. *Past problems* are episodes centering upon an issue that has been considered in the past but is not now considered a problem; such episodes commonly involve the clarification of the issue, review of actions taken, and the like, although if the issue is not considered fully solved, further (or modified) actions may be considered.

Episodes classed as *problem* or *past problem* are further coded with respect to the following matters: type of problem, jurisdiction of the group, conflict, groups that are parties to the conflict, problem complexity, and problem verifiability. The code categories are as follows:

1. *Type (of problem)*
   a. Task problem —pertaining to the production and service tasks of the organization.
   b. Organizational problem—pertaining to role conflicts or ambiguity, company policy, union contracts, and the like, but excluding problems that arise out of personal characteristics or differences.
   c. Interpersonal problem—problems arising from the personal characteristics or behavior of individuals, but excluding those better described as arising from organizational or role requirements.

2. *Jurisdiction (of the group)*
   a. Inside—the group has resources and authority to solve the problem.
   b. Outside—the group cannot alone solve the problem because of some outside contingency, such as law, union contract, other parties at interest, and the like.

3. *Conflict (source of)*
   a. Inherent—the conflict occurs because of an interaction between the type of problem and the discrepant values or goals that are present. For example, because of the goals of their respective constituencies, union and management representatives often differ on economic issues.
   b. Not inherent—the conflict arises from different preferences, viewpoints, or priorities that are not prescribed by the representational roles of those present.

4. *Groups (in conflict)*
   a. If there are two "sides" to the conflict and the parties split according to their constituencies, then one or two subgroups are coded for each side. (In the site of first application, five such subgroups were considered: workers from experimental

units, outside consultants, union representatives, management representatives, and "outsiders.")

5. *Complexity (of the problem)*

   a. The judgment of complexity rests upon three considerations weighed jointly: the number of subsidiary problems inherent in the main problem; the number of plausible alternative courses of action or decisions that are considered; the number of constraints and subgoals that must be satisfied or balanced. The coding categories (high, medium, and low) are defined by examples.

6. *Verifiability (of the solution)*

   a. This is coded either "easy" or "hard" on the basis of ease with which it can be determined, either now or later, whether the problem has been solved or substantially ameliorated. Coding is facilitated by reference to examples.

Coding of Interactions

An "act" here refers to an act taken by a participating member of the group being observed. Acts are usually verbal, although explicit gestures or facial expressions may be coded. Acts are coded in the sequence of their occurrence, according to five code sets. The first two of these are used to record the identity of the actor and the identity of the person (or the group) to whom the act is directed. The remaining three code sets are used to describe the nature of the act. Each act is allowed one entry from each of the three code sets, one of the options being "not applicable or not ascertained." The three code sets refer, respectively, to the *task* of the group, the internal work *processes* of the group, and to "*special*" properties of the act that have an affective, disruptive, integrating, or summarizing significance but that are not specifically task or process relevant. These three code sets appear, respectively, in Tables 12-1, 12-2, and 12-3. Knowledgeable readers will recognize these to be adaptations from Bales' interaction process analysis scheme.* The designation of whom a particular act is directed to is often difficult for a coder who was not actually present at a meeting. It is beneficial to have the observer, if he/she is not also the coder, review these designations.

Examples of Process Coding

Perhaps the most efficient way to demonstrate the use of the codes is by example. The following fictitious example is a segment of a record for one meeting. Since the example is taken from a study in a coal mine, the

---

* Bales, R. F. *Interaction process analysis.* Reading: Addison-Wesley, 1950.

Table 12-1   Task Codes[a]

Problem identification: (PI)
  S identifies, focuses, restructures, refocuses on problems, summarizes what's been said to focus on problems.

Orientation: gives (GO), asks (AO)
  S provides, repeats, clarifies information about problems, alternatives, search opportunities. Orientation is about solving problems, not the process of going about solving problems.

Substantive suggestions: gives (GS), asks (AS)
  S provides courses of action concerning where to look for solutions, about solutions themselves. The focus is on substantive problems (e.g., related to production or the experiment).

Procedural suggestions: gives (GSP), asks (ASP)
  S provides procedural suggestions about how to solve problems. S might say it should be done in a particular committee, or a particular individual should be asked. The suggestions are in the context of solving a problem. They are not general statements about how problems should be solved.

Opinions: gives (GOP), asks (AOP)
  S gives opinion, agrees, disagrees, expresses preference, evaluation, wish, analysis. Comment must be directed to task characteristic versus individual himself/herself. (An attack on an individual, his/her status, the group itself, would constitute a process comment.)

Evaluations: gives negative (GNE), gives positive (GPE), asks (AE)
  S agrees or disagrees with a statement made by another. Statement could be a suggestion, opinion orientation, definition of problem.

---

[a] "S" means actor.

conversation reflects the language of that industry. The men are discussing current problems in the work area. The code for each interaction is provided in the column at the right

Sample Discourse		Code
BURTON:	I would like to talk about the roof conditions. I understand they have been poor lately.	Problem identification
FLOYD:	Conditions have been poor since the last move.	Gives opinion
COX:	That's not true, for a while we were in sandstone.	Gives negative evaluation
BURTON:	We should deal with the roof problem first. That is more critical than the mine machinery. It is important to get some ideas about how to deal with the roof first.	Task performance strategy

Table 12-2 Process Codes[a]

Task performance strategies: (TPS)

S makes explicit statements about how the group operates or how it should operate. Statements about strategies for group effectiveness. Statements concern directions, strategies, suggestions.

Positive process statement: (PPS)

S provides reinforcements, approval, solidarity about the group or a member. Statements are independent of substantive aspects of the problem. Provides tension release (e.g., joke).

Negative process statement: (NPS)

S shows antagonism, criticism toward group functioning or individual. Attack may focus on other's status.

---

[a] "S" means actor.

Table 12-3 Special Codes[a]

Interruption (Int)

S substantially tries and/or does change course of conversation. The refocusing of attention is not a strategy intended to increase group effectiveness. Rather, it represents an attempt to treat an issue salient for S.

AW statement: positive (AWP)[b]

S makes positive statement indicating support of AW, commitment of AW, indicating inherent characteristics of AW, reason for a position.

AW statement: negative (AWN)

S makes statement indicating rejection of AW, low commitment.

Union statement: positive (UP)

S makes statement in support of union, commitment to union, inherent characteristics of union, reason for position.

Union statement: negative (UN)

S makes statements rejecting union. Attacks union.

Company statement: positive (CP)

S makes statements supporting company, indicating commitment.

Company statement: negative (CN)

S rejects company. Attacks company

Integrating role: (IR)

S connects data from past meetings to current meeting. Connects data from section to meeting. Purpose is to stimulate discussion problem solving, provide feedback.

Feedback, summarizing role: (SR)

S summarizes what has gone on in meeting, tries to clarify what has been said.

---

[a] "S" means actor.

[b] AW is a symbol for one of the experimental units in the site we studied. An AWP statement would be a positive statement directed toward that experimental group. Coding interactions toward the experimental group is not unique to any intervention—there always is some target group.

KING:	Easy for you to say . . . you don't run the miner (a machine).	Gives negative evaluation
FLOYD:	Burton is right. The miner won't do us any good with rock on it.	Gives positive evaluation
	Pause.	
BURTON:	O.K. Any other ideas?	Asks orientation
COX:	Dangerous for bolter . . . (tells of rock coming down).	Gives opinion
PRESCOTT:	Remember the last time we had roof problems, used more timber . . . water was the big problem then . . . slate roof . . . we also used different style bolts	Integrating role
COX:	More timber . . . good idea.	Gives positive evaluation
FISHER:	Agree.	Gives positive evaluation
FLOYD:	Up to the work group to make decision about this . . . that's part of an AW idea.	Gives opinion
JONES:	I think we should pull out of the current work area.	Gives opinion
KING:	You can't let the men make decisions. . . . This AW plan will never work.	Gives negative evaluation; AW negative

Data Entry and Programs

The data are initially entered to computer input cards (although other inputting procedures may be used). These cards for a particular meeting will be of four kinds. The first, a main/header card, identifies the meeting. There are four subsidiary header cards, each identifying one of the four time segments of the meeting. Each time-segment card is followed by episode cards (one per episode) and by interaction cards (one per four acts).

The function of the computer programs is to search through the set of coded interaction data and to perform a tabulation of these data according to a user search list. For example, it would be possible to tabulate all of the task interactions initiated by a specific group of individuals during discussions of issues characterized by potential labor–management conflict. The program is capable of generating five-way tables so that interactions may be tabulated, contingent on up to four conditions.

The general algorithm followed in the design of the analysis programs is a "tree-list" search structure. Within the structure, a master list describes the "tree" and provides the locations of all "tree dimensions" of any datum. The program is designed to search and tabulate data from any or all portions of the "tree."

Analysis Issues

The system as described was designed to permit analysis of quality-of-work labor–management groups. However, with adaptations, it can be applied to any kind of observable group. That is, there is nothing in the coding programs or analysis scheme that limits its use in a group context. The following examples illustrate the areas that can be analyzed.

1. *Labor–Management Conflict.* The interaction analysis permits analysis of the degree of conflict between labor and management.

2. *Labor and Management Problem-Solving Behaviors.* The interaction analysis permits analysis of types of problem-solving behaviors initiated by either group. For example, the frequencies of problem identification by various constituencies can be examined.

3. *Change Agent Problem-Solving Behavior.* The interaction analysis permits describing the character of change-agent (consultant) behavior.

4. *Pattern of Interactions among Labor, Management, and the Change Agent.* The interaction analysis permits one to examine relationships among these groups.

5. *Interaction Analysis over Time.* Time segments of meetings, or a series of meetings, can be analyzed to detect changes in the level of conflict or interaction pattern between labor and management.

6. *Predictors of Interaction Analysis.* All problems are coded as to whether they have been successfully resolved or ameliorated. Two analyses are possible: first, how problem characteristics relate to problem success; second, how interaction patterns vary with problem characteristics and problem success.

Example of an Analysis Product

To illustrate the analytic uses of data derived from meeting observations, we present an example taken from steering committee meetings at one experimental site. In this example, the investigators were interested in observing the dyadic behavior of the labor and management constituencies involved in a change program over time. In order to do this, dyadic interaction data were aggregated to three time periods (Period 1 omitted

Table 12-4   Profiles of Interaction Content within Dyads over Time

	Labor–management Dyads		Comparison Dyads		
	AW ↔ M	U ↔ M	AW ↔ RT	U ↔ RT	M ↔ RT
Period 2					
+ Evaluation	3%	5%	8%	4%	9%
− Evaluation	16%	12%	6%	10%	7%
Productive	11%	15%	16%	21%	11%
Informational	47%	51%	51%	38%	54%
Opinion	23%	17%	19%	27%	19%
Period 3					
+ Evaluation	2%	11%	7%	0%	8%
− Evaluation	6%	0%	3%	0%	1%
Productive	9%	0%	15%	6%	7%
Informational	68%	68%	64%	81%	73%
Opinion	15%	19%	11%	13%	11%
Period 4					
+ Evaluation	6%		14%		1%
− Evaluation	6%	—[a]	4%	—[a]	0%
Productive	5%		13%		2%
Informational	61%		50%		97%
Opinion	22%		19%		0%

[a] Union constituency not present at meetings.

from example) that were relevant to the entire experiment and further aggregated and tabulated according to five classes of interaction types: positive evaluation, negative evaluation, productive, informational, and opinion. Table 12-4* presents a tabulation of the data for the two labor–management dyads (AW ↔ M; U ↔ M) and three comparison dyads (AW ↔ RT; V ↔ RT; M ↔ RT). The cell entries correspond to percentages of interaction in the dyad, falling into the particular content category so that if 10 out of 100 interactions between the autonomous work group (AW) and management in Period 2 were productive, the "productive" entry in the AW ↔ column for Period 2 could be 10%.

Examining the trend in the AW ↔ M dyads over time, it is apparent that content patterns changed relatively little. There are, however, several small trends. The amount of positive evaluation changed from 3% in Period 2, to 2% in Period 3, to 6% in Period 4. In contrast, the amount of negative evaluation decreased from 16% in Period 2 to 6% in Periods 3 and 4. Similarly, productive interaction decreased while informational

* AW = experimental section; M = management; U = union; RT = research team.

content increased. Opinion exchange stayed about the same across all three time periods. These percentages can be compared with those between the research team (RT) and the labor and management constituencies. Table 12-4 could also be used to examine the dyadic behavior of the consultants.

Table 12-4 and other similar tabulations are useful for characterizing the roles played by various constituencies during programs of change. Table 12-4 illustrates several important trends. First, there was a slight improving trend in the evaluative interaction between labor and management. The productive category, however, does not provide evidence of increasing joint problem solving as might be hypothesized to result from a change program initiated jointly by labor and management. The increase in interaction that occurred between the AW and M constituencies was primarily informational, and although it might have provided for improved understanding between the groups, it is not synonymous with joint problem solving.

Reliability and Validity of Structured Observation System

Reliability.   A preliminary estimate of reliability was derived by examining the degree of agreement by two different coders in sample meetings. The overall agreement score was .65 (i.e., the number of agreements divided by total number of codes assigned). Since the coding system includes some 24 different cases, reliability indicators can be derived for codes for different subcategories. One major way we collapsed codes was into the task and process categories. (The respective reliabilities are .66 and .63, which are fairly close to the overall reliability.) An examination of individual codes shows much more variability. The greatest agreement (.91) appears in the "positive-process" code that deals with interactions indicating reinforcement and solidarity. The lowest reliability is, surprisingly, in the giving (.41) and asking-for (.44) opinion categories. It appears that coders had difficulty in separating opinion codes from evaluation codes. Although these data are preliminary in nature, they indicate some stability in the major codes.*

Validity.   Some indicators are available on the validity of the scale. One of the four hypotheses was that different groups would generate different types of problems. One labor–management committee was designed to resolve policy issues between labor and management, and another was to deal with the day-to-day operation of the experimental intervention. In analyzing the results from the coding system over a three-year period, we find, as expected, that technical problems were

---

* Note that these agreement rates are "worst case," as instances of disagreement are subject to review and to resolution by the original on-site observer.

more frequently identified in the day-to-day committee than in the policy committee (see Goodman, 1979). This seems to indicate that the coding system differentiates across groups.

Another hypothesis was that the actors in the experiment would modify their interaction pattern over time. Members of the experimental group would be expected to increase their interaction over time, while members of the consulting team would reduce their interactions. Data over a three-year period confirm these expected changes in interaction rates.

Some indication of convergent validity has been documented. Over time we find a decline in the number of codes relating to the elaboration of the experimental agreement. This is congruent with other measures that indicate a declining interest in the experimental activities as they moved into the third year of the experiment. The identification of similar trends with independent measures provides some additional evidence of the observation system's validity.

Concluding Comments

There have been few attempts to capture the processes of change during an organizational intervention systematically. The literature is characterized by many case studies, but there have been few replicable, quantified, and verifiable ways to assess the change process. The procedures described in this chapter attempt to collect a rich set of data on all the key, relevant actors in the change effort. Clearly, it is only representing a piece of the activity, namely, that unfolding in the meetings. However, the meetings are central to the change effort, and they provide an opportunity to measure what people do, rather than what they say they did or will do. The attractive features of this measurement device are the following.

1. It is comprehensive in capturing behavior from all the relevant actors.
2. It measures behavior.
3. It permits measuring trends over a period of time.
4. It permits measuring changes both within (e.g., union) and between groups.
5. It captures variables relevant for assessing the effectiveness of a change effort (e.g., communication, conflict, problem solving).

The disadvantages in this activity are the following.

1. It is limited to change programs where meetings are important. However, many projects have such a structure.
2. It is initially expensive to code and to analyze. This is true of the current method largely because of the high development costs of

doing the job. The development costs would not be found in subsequent applications since the recording system and program should be fairly generalizable.

3. The final disadvantage—that it narrows the observer's focus in the meetings to behavior observed in them—can become an advantage if the systematic observation is complemented by naturalistic assessment that places the meetings in the broader context of the participants' behavior in the change program. Just as naturalistic observation (see Chapter 11) prevents a fragmented analysis of the change effort, more structured data-gathering methods provide a check against the biases that may arise from exclusive reliance on less systematic observation.

REFERENCE

1. Goodman, P. S. Assessing organizational change: The Rushton quality of work experiment. New York: Wiley-Interscience, 1979.

CHAPTER THIRTEEN

Assessing Unions and Union—Management Collaboration in Organizational Change

R. J. BULLOCK, BARRY A. MACY, AND PHILIP H. MIRVIS

In organizations with employee unions, the unions are likely to have some significant role in the initiation, conduct, and outcomes of organizational change programs. At minimum, such a union may take a traditional role of nonparticipating watchdog that is responsive to members' interests and that reacts to initiatives taken by the management. In other instances, as in many quality of work life efforts, the union may have a role as equal partner with management in the planning and conduct of the activities. In some instances, the initiative comes from the union in a manner that is collateral to the established pattern of contractual relationships with the management. Whatever the role may be, it is likely to have a significant impact upon events, and therefore it comes within the purview of those aiming to describe and understand the processes of organizational change. The union itself may be impacted as to its structure, ways of working, and relationships with members. The management may be aided or constrained by the character of the union—management relationships. The change program may raise issues of value priority and strategy that are new to both parties.

Broadly speaking, three domains of inquiry are evident. The first concerns the union as an organization—its history, structure, relations with members, decision processes, and the like. The second treats the union—

management relationships, including the history of the relationships, procedures for mutual influence, modes of negotiation, accommodation, and conflict resolution. The third domain deals with the concurrent activities relating to an organizational change program, which may range from stolid perseverance in established patterns of relationships to the active creation of new forms of information exchange, influence, problem solving, decision making, and control.

Description and assessment in these three domains calls for a broad, inclusive stance on the part of the assessors, for it seldom can be known in advance what features of the situation will prove to be the most potent in determining events or which will be the most revealing for explanation. History, for example, is resident in records and in documents such as contracts, but also it is to be discerned by tapping recollections in interviews. Current events may be observed and be descriptively recorded, with complementary insights gained from interviews with the actors. Questionnaires may elicit attitudes, beliefs, and expectations of members regarding their unions and regarding changes that may occur over time.

Description and assessment require a range of methods and also attention to two critical matters. First, the inquiry must attend to both subjective and objective features of union–management relations, for the recorded and observable data are incomplete and often misleading. Second, the approach must be longitudinal in order to provide a changing historical context and to detect changes in the sequence of their occurrence. Further, the approach must include both descriptive purposes as well as purposes of causal imputation, influence, and the discovery of relationships among factors of context and causation.

One might think that a topic of such intrinsic interest to so many people might be well supplied with precedent, instruments, and procedures for study, but that is not the case. A review of the theoretical and methodological literatures shows there is little consensus about the key concepts concerning union organization, union–management relations, and collaboration. There is scant guidance on procedures for assessment. There are plenty of case studies about unions and union–management relations, of course, including anthropological and sociological inquiries and even diaries kept by organization and union members.[1-3] There are also some conceptual models of union organization, union–management relations, and even union–management cooperation in change programs.[4-7] The case studies tend to reflect the unique perspectives of the investigators, and the models—drawn primarily from laboratory studies and field observations—give few clues as to their operationalization in measurement. The few measurement procedures that are presented and evaluated tend to be of limited topical coverage and of intentionally restricted application.[8] Thus in conception and measurement we were left largely to our own imaginations and devices.

What follows is a report on progress. This chapter is organized around the three domains of interest in assessment of unions and union–management relations in organizational change. In each domain we describe the approach to conception and measurement and present the measures themselves in sufficient detail for use by other investigators. Preliminary results are reported on measurement quality whenever available. The analyses focus on data from the one organization for which the most complete data are available.

ASSESSMENT OF THE UNION AS AN ORGANIZATION

Unions purport to be, and usually are, democratic institutions. Previous conceptual and empirical work has been based on this fundamental perspective of union democracy.[6] Using this perspective of the union as a democratic organization, this section identifies some of the key concerns and characteristics of unions as organizations that must be considered in an assessment of unions and organizational change.

Conceptual Background

The first step to understanding a union is to understand its initial formation: precursors, processes, problems. Unions are formed when a significant number of eligible employees in an organization decide they prefer bargaining collectively with their employer. The union then may become the sole representative of the employees in bargaining wages, hours, and working conditions with the employer.

Students of organization theory could profit greatly by a careful investigation of the formation of a local union. There is an instructive contrast between the formation of a local union—normally called "organizing" and based on the premise that organizational power and influence are derived from members—and the formation of a plant or office where labels like "plant start-up" and "setting up an operation" describe primarily unidirectional influence processes. Those who form a local union are not "founders" but "organizers." The discrepancies between these labels dramatize significantly different organizational processes that are involved in the initial development of these two organizational forms—which have the same members.

To understand the initial formation of the union, one must begin with a study of union history. History is vital for understanding the current union situation, since it identifies critical events that have changed the organization and member roles and that have shaped current situational perspectives. In looking at the formation and history of the union, both the local organization and the international should be studied. Some locals function as independent, autonomous organizations, but many are part of a larger international union. In some industries, the collective bargaining agreements are centralized at the international level; in others, bargaining occurs at the local level with international assistance. Understanding of the international role, if any, is critical for understanding local union organization.

The role of the individual union member is similar to that of the citizens' role in a democratic government or any other democratic institution. Through the Labor–Management Reporting and Disclosure Act of 1959, union members are assured of certain democratic rights in their organization, including the right to nominate candidates, to support candidates openly and freely, and to run for office. The provision of these legal rights, however, does not imply that members will take active roles in the organization. The research indicates that, except for an active role in the initial formation of the union and in crisis situations (such as strikes), union members typically do not actively participate in the ongoing functioning of the union. Attendance at union meetings, where the business of the organization is transacted, is normally very low, with empirical attendance estimates at 5%, 10%, and 18%.[1,9,10] This low level of participation may be understood as instrumental behavior in which members see no need to participate so long as the union produces satisfactory outcomes.[11] It is also a result of the involuntary aspects of union membership, as dues payment and union membership are often required conditions for employment.[12] There are also member perceptions in many cases that their roles will have little impact on the collective-bargaining agreement.[13] The assessor of the union as an organization, therefore, should determine what the union-member role in the organization is, what the level and nature of participation in the ongoing affairs of the union is, and develop an attribution as to the reasons for the quantity and quality of participation.

In assessing the union as an organization, investigators can approach their studies with the same two basic theoretical perspectives used to study any organization: the goal-based perspective[14] and the system-theory perspective.[15,16] Both perspectives are useful for understanding unions. The assessor should know the varied goals of international officials, local officers, stewards, and members with respect to what each group sees as the purpose of the union, its strategy, and its effectiveness in accomplishing those purposes. Similarly, it is also useful to identify the repetitive cycles of events in daily affairs, to determine the nature of their inputs and outputs and transformation processes, and to understand the information feedback from the environment and from the union's members that generate adaptive changes.

Thus, to understand the union as an organization requires an investigator to understand several important aspects of the social system. Initial formation and history are vital for understanding the critical events that have shaped the organization and member roles over time. It is important to understand the local organization as well as the international, because of the variety of international–local relationships and the role that each plays in conducting the ongoing affairs of the union. Member behaviors and perceptions are equally important in understanding the implicit and explicit goals of the union, its strategies, and its effectiveness. The next two sections describe how these conceptual areas can be assessed by using both objective and subjective measurement methods.

Objective Characteristics

Once the assessor recognizes the union as an organization, he or she wants to answer the same basic questions that would be asked of any organization. What is its jurisdiction? What is its name? Is it associated with a larger, international union? What is its form of governance, and who are its leaders? In many cases, as occurred in our assessments of joint labor–management programs, multiple unions were present in an organization. In these cases, each union needs to be understood as a separate organization. What employee groups does each union represent? What proportion of the eligible members are in and active in each union?

Answers to such questions can be obtained in multiple ways. One is through interviews with union leaders, union members, and knowledgeable members of management. Another is through documentary data, such as the union constitution, bylaws, and local-governance papers. These basic documents provide a vast assortment of information. Local leadership functions and roles and how they relate to local governance should be described, along with those functions and roles of leaders in the regional and international unions. Included should be a description of such roles as business agents and district officers. It is necessary to understand the formal union arrangements with respect to boundaries, membership, key functions and roles, control and decision bodies, governance procedures, election practices, and the like. As with all organizations, interviews are needed to ascertain the ways in which the formal provisions are interpreted in practice, and the nature of informal deviation from, or additions to, the organizational "plan." A general listing of topics for assessment of the objective characteristics of unions is shown in Table 13-1.

Given a description of the union, the next questions are those of history. How long has the local union existed? The international union? Under what conditions did the local union form? What has been the definition of its purposes? What have been the key issues over its recent past? Are these international-union issues as well? Have there been political controversies within the union? What are the issues, if any, over which there is intraunion conflict—locally and internationally?

There are two main sources for answering such questions. Public documents can be helpful, since local newspapers provide vital information about local events, and national newspapers and journals provide compa-

Table 13-1   Assessment of Objective Union Characteristics

Assessment Area	Method
Unions involved	Introductory interview
1. Unionized segments of the work force.	
Employee group:	
Local union:	
International union:	
Number of members:	
Percentage of employees:	
Internal structure	Union documents
1. Leadership functions of the local union.	
Position:	
Function (duties):	
How chosen:	
Term of position:	
Pay:	
External structure	Union documents
1. Interface roles between the local and the regional or district union (e.g., business agent, district officer, organizer).	
Position:	
Function (duties):	
How chosen:	
Term:	
Pay:	
Locus of decision making	Union documents, interviews
1. What decisions are made where.	
Local decisions:	
Interface role decisions:	
District decisions:	
International decisions:	

rable data on the situation of the international union. If the history of the international union covers several decades, as it does for most, then condensed historical data are likely to be found in the documentary books on the labor movement. The most relevant historical data will be those of the immediate past, since they can suggest, or confirm, the presence of unresolved issues or of successful accomplishments that are not only history but that are also part of current and future events.

Such information can also be collected—particularly about the recent past—from union and management leaders of the period under review. If these persons are available, structured interviews can be used to reconstruct the important historical events and trends in a union's history.

Naturally, there is some bias in this subjective reporting of objective events, and multiple interviews about "the same" events are highly desirable.

Table 13-2 lists some key topics in the assessment of union history. It distinguishes between the early and recent histories of the local and international unions. Early history is most amenable to assessment through documentary data, since over time it takes on a "mythic" character and is subject to countless reinterpretations. Recent history, by contrast, may be more amenable to assessment by interviews. It is fresher and has more of an impact on the present. In both cases, documentary and interview data can be cross-checked for reliability and comprehensiveness. Reliability between the modes of data gathering gives objectivity to the data. Unreliability invites the assessor to investigate why history has been reinterpreted and how that colors the present. Appendix 12-1 presents a structured interview used in our assessments.

Table 13-2   Assessment of Union History

Assessment Area	Method
Early local history	Public records
1. What was the early situation?	
Year formed:	
Key historical events:	
Situation when formed:	
Statement of goals and purpose:	
Recent local history	Structured interviews
1. What are the recent situations?	
Election dates:	
Election results:	
Election issues:	
Current intraunion issues:	
Early international history	Public records
1. What was the early situation?	
Year formed:	
Key historical events:	
Situation when formed:	
Statement of goals and purpose:	
Recent international history	Structured interviews
1. What are the recent situations?	
Election dates:	
Election results:	
Election issues:	
Major convention issues:	
Current intraunion issues:	

Subjective Characteristics: Attitudes toward the Union

Typically, an informant's account of union-related events, conditions, and organizational processes will suggest the manner in which these factors are viewed by the membership generally. Such an inference, while informative, needs to be checked and supplemented through the direct assessment of the attitudes of the members. To this end, we have devised a questionnaire survey instrument for union leaders and one for members (Appendixes 13-2 and 13-3).

The relevant sections of the questionnaires focus upon three topics: (1) views of the labor movement generally; (2) assessments of the effectiveness and performance of the local union; and (3) assessments of the internal union organizational processes.

The first facet aims to assess the members' basic posture of approval or disapproval of the societal function of unions. The design of this segment of the questionnaire is derived from the work of Quinn and Staines in their study of a national sample of employed adults.[17] Their respondents tended to report unions to have either societally beneficial goals only or socially harmful or threatening goals only. There was much polarization of views about imputed union goals. In addition, the researchers ascertained that these views could be encompassed within two primary dimensions of attitudes, which they called service and power. "Service" referred primarily to the success and intention of unions to aid and protect their members; "power" referred primarily to union influences, intended or otherwise, upon external political and economic affairs. While the negative attitudes tended to center upon the power dimension and the positive attitudes upon the service dimension, the correspondence was far from perfect. Quinn and Staines found also that there are differences among population segments as to their union approval and their choice of reasons for their views. Our questionnaire, accordingly, provides for the measurement of respondents' degree of approval of unions generally, with respect to union power goals and union service goals. Such information can help clarify whether a given union local is dealing with a membership (or nonmembers) who are favorably disposed to unions in general and for what kinds of reasons. The information can also have potential use in determining whether, over the course of time or a change program, these attitudes have become modified (see Table 13-3).

A second focus of the questionnaire addresses leader and member attitudes toward the performance of their local union. Included are questions on global satisfaction and satisfaction with procedures, and extrinsic and task-related outcomes. Of relevance in assessing these latter two factors is the importance members attach to extrinsic versus task-related outcomes as well as satisfaction. Quinn and Staines, for example, found in their national sample that both union and nonunion members stressed

Table 13-3 Union Member Questionnaire Items and Scale Reliabilities

Measures	N	Internal Consistency Reliability*			Test–Retest Reliability*		
		a_1	a_2	a_3	r_{12}	r_{13}	r_{23}

I. Measures of Attitudes toward the Union Movement

Power   111   .80   .86   .85   .65   .58   .68[1]

  a. Union wage demands cause unemployment.
  b. Unions are becoming too strong.
  c. Union wage rates cause high prices.
  d. Unions impose too many restrictions on employees.
  e. We need more laws to limit the power of labor unions.

Service   243   .66   .66   .69   .51   .51   .62

  a. Unions protect against favoritism on the job.
  b. Unions improve wages and working conditions.
  c. Unions make sure that employees are treated fairly by supervisors.
  d. Unions interfere with good relations between employers and employees (reversed).

II. Measures of Attitudes toward the Local Union

Global satisfaction   248   .90   .92   .90   .67   .62   .66

  a. How satisfied are you with the success your union has in bargaining wage issues?
  b. How satisfied are you with the amount of communication between your union and its members?
  c. How satisfied are you with the success your union has in bargaining nonwage issues?
  d. How satisfied are you with the union's leadership?
  e. How satisfied are you with your ability to influence union decisions?
  f. All in all, I am very satisfied with the union.
  g. Participation in union activities is worthwhile.

Satisfaction with procedures   249   .72   .80   .76   .58   .57   .60

  a. How satisfied are you with the way your union handles grievances?
  b. How satisfied are you with the way union officers are chosen?
  c. How satisfied are you with the way issues are selected for collective bargaining?

Table 13-3 (*Continued*)

Measures	N	Internal Consistency Reliability			Test–Retest Reliability		
		a_1	a_2	a_3	r_{12}	r_{13}	r_{23}
Satisfaction with extrinsic outcomes	247	.84	.86	.85	.57	.54	.57
a. A better fringe-benefit package.							
b. Increased job security.							
c. Fairer promotion policies.							
d. Fairer pay raises.							
Satisfaction with task-related outcomes	247	.83	.86	.85	.54	.56	.60
a. Fairer job classifications.							
b. More participation in job-related decisions.							
c. More meaningful work for members.							

III. Perceptions of Internal-Union Governance Processes

Measures	N	a_1	a_2	a_3	r_{12}	r_{13}	r_{23}
Global evaluation	246	.75	.75	.79	.59	.61	.64
a. Members of my union are afraid to express their real views in union meetings (reversed).							
b. Decisions are made in the union without ever asking the people who have to live with them (reversed).							
c. In the union, everyone's opinion gets listened to.							
d. In general, I like the way the union handles things.							
Member influence	242	.88	.91	.94	.43	.43	.34
a. Deciding who will serve on a local committee.							
b. Deciding which issues will be brought up in bargaining.							
c. Deciding which issues to drop or compromise during bargaining.							
d. Spending local union funds.							
e. Resolving conflicts among union members.							
f. Deciding who to support if two union members conflict in a grievance.							
g. Deciding which strategy to use in bargaining with management.							
h. Deciding to raise dues.							
Group influence over way union is run	208	.58	.54	.65	.31	.42	.43
a. The membership.							
b. Local union leadership.							
c. International union leaders.							
d. Full-time professional union employees.							

Table 13-3 *(Continued)*

Measures	N	Internal Consistency Reliability			Test–Retest Reliability		
		a_1	a_2	a_3	r_{12}	r_{13}	r_{23}
Willingness to participate	250	.66	.73	.75	.60	.61	.66
a. Serve on union committee.							
b. Serve on a union–management committee as representative.							
c. Attend a regular union meeting or a union executive-committee meeting.							

* The alpha coefficients and test-retest reliabilities are for three questionnaire administrations at intervals of about one year.

the union's role in achieving extrinsic goals for members. Comparable data from a survey of local union leaders by Kochan, Lipsky, and Dyer confirmed this emphasis.[18] These last three authors found union leaders rank increased earnings (92%), benefits (79%), and security (68%) as more important union goals than interesting work (41%) and reduced work loads (22%). Nonetheless, since our instrument was designed for use in a variety of unions, ranging from professional associations to trade unions who might have unlike goals, it includes questions about both the importance of and satisfaction with these outcomes. The items that comprise the factors measuring attitudes toward the performance of the local union are shown in Table 13-3, along with their reliabilities.

A third focus of the questionnaire concentrates on leader and member perceptions of their union's internal governing processes. Once again, four factors emerged from the analyses, as is shown in Table 13-3. One factor is that of general satisfaction with the union's processes. Another refers to a member's influence on specific union activities. A third addresses the relative influence of members versus officials and professional union representatives on how the union is run. The fourth measures willingness to be active in union affairs. Within-measurement and across-time reliabilities are reported in the table.

Analysis of questionnaire data from one QWL site lends some empirical justification to this tripartite organization of attitudes toward unions. For example, the two factors on general attitudes toward unionism were highly correlated, but they were not significantly associated with attitudes toward the respondent's own local or its internal processes. The four factors of attitudes toward the local were also highly correlated, but much less so with ratings of the local's internal governance process. Finally, ratings of internal processes showed high intercorrelations. One exception was the measure of personal willingness to participate. These findings are similar to those reported by Glick, Harder, and Mirvis,[19] which showed a member's willingness to participate to be associated with both the degree of member influence and his/her overall assessment of the power of unions in society.

ASSESSMENT OF UNION–MANAGEMENT RELATIONS

Given an assessment of the union as an organization and given an assessment of a management organization by the means described in other chapters in this book, the investigator is now prepared to investigate union–management relations. The assessment of union–management relations treats the interface between two systems. It is an intersystem analysis. This section develops a conceptual background for approaching the assessment of union–management relations and then describes the assessment of both the objective and subjective characteristics of this intersystem interface.

Conceptual Background

Perhaps the best way to approach the study of union–management relations is to separate the relations into two parts: contract bargaining and contract administration. Contract bargaining, which is done through the collective bargaining procedure and is governed in part by federal and state regulations, involves the periodic negotiation of a union–management contract, which is usually done every two or three years. While the contract-bargaining process is critical for understanding union–management relations, it should be separated from the ongoing functioning of the relationship, which involves the administration of processes and procedures jointly determined in the collective-bargaining agreement.

The first step in understanding the contract-bargaining process is to understand the issues and dynamics of the regular negotiation. Before approaching the negotiation issues, the investigator should understand the principal goals of the union and management. The union has two primary goals: (1) acquiring benefits for its members (wages, fringes, working conditions, job security, availability of due process, etc.), and (2) the maintenance of its political power base (survival of the union, protection of its right to legally represent employees, role security for elected union officials, etc.). Management as an organization also has two fundamental objectives: (1) the achievement of productive, cost-effective operations, and (2) preservation of its political power base (survival of the organization, maintaining management's prerogatives, job security and advancement potential for supervisors and managers, etc.). The first task of the investigator, therefore, is to determine the more specific implicit and explicit goals that union and management bring to the interface. This task is assisted by isolating the issues involved in recent contracts.

There has been some significant thinking and research on the contractual bargaining process that serves as an important background for approaching the assessment of this aspect of union–management relations. Walton and McKersie[39] developed a behavior theory of labor negotiations conceived as four subprocesses: distributive bargaining, integrative bargaining, attitudinal structuring, and interorganizational bargaining. Kochan developed a more general model built on traditional bargaining perspectives: This model views the collective-bargaining process within the context of the external environment and looks at the impact of the collective-bargaining relationship on the goal attainments of the workers, unions, management, and the public.[20] An investigator of union–management relations can further develop some concept of the negotiation dynamics by reviewing field studies of the collective-bargaining processes,[21,22] and through laboratory research on the bargaining process.[23–25]

The second important aspect of the bargaining process to be assessed is a review of impasses encountered in the collective-bargaining process. Most but not all union–management relations have a history of strikes, arbitration, mediation, and other evidences of impasses reached in the bargaining process. The study of these impasses is important since it defines the major issues of disagreement in the interorganizational interface, and it uncovers the attitudinal and emotional processes that led to and followed from the impasses.

Research on strikes and other impasses may be helpful to the investigator in developing a picture of them. Economic research has demonstrated strike frequency to be directly related to declining real wages and lower levels of unemployment.[26,27] Sociological research has found strikes to be related to the nature of the industry, the structure of collective bargaining, and the size of the community.[28–31] Although there has been little organizational behavior research on impasses to date, there is clear evidence in the literature that the traditional variables should be supplemented with organizational, interpersonal, and personal characteristics. Kochan and Baberschneider found that probability of encountering an impasse was related to interpersonal hostility between the management and union, the amount of pressure on the union by its members, the presence of union pressure tactics, and the role of professional negotiators.[32]

Understanding these impasses is the basis of the third aspect of the collective bargaining relationship that is of interest to the union–management relationship assessor: conflict-resolution processes. There is currently much interest in the development of new and better conflict-resolution techniques, particularly in the public sector, and in the evaluation of multiple conflict-resolution techniques through comparative analysis of effectiveness.[33–35] Kochan identified three popular conflict-resolution procedures; these procedures are very useful in understanding union–

management relations.[20] Mediation is a relatively informal procedure where a neutral third party helps the management and union negotiators reach a voluntary agreement. In fact-finding, a neutral party holds a hearing and issues recommendations for resolving a dispute, although such neutral parties have no formal power. Arbitration adds to fact-finding a binding condition to the findings and recommendations of the neutral third party. In reviewing the history of arbitration between union and management, it is useful to distinguish voluntary arbitration (where the parties voluntarily agree to accept as binding the neutral's decision) from both compulsory arbitration (where the arbitration procedure was required by federal or state statute) and final arbitration (where the arbitrator is constrained to choose the final offer of either management or the union without the option to formulate a compromise solution).[32–35] Readers are referred to Kochan for a review of the empirical literature of these different techniques.

Once the investigator understands the history, antecedents, and results of critical events in the life of the contract-negotiation process between the management and the union, he or she is prepared to investigate the actual operation of these decisions on an ongoing basis. Apart from the dynamics of the negotiation process, the dynamics of the administration process may be cumbersome, conflict provoking, cooperative, and so on. The most important vehicle for understanding the ongoing administration of a contract is the grievance procedure, since invoking it is the clearest evidence of difference of opinion regarding contract terms and their implementation. In fact, the grievance machinery is sometimes viewed as the most important innovation of the collective-bargaining system in the United States. There are several areas to be investigated here, which include (1) the issues involved in grievances, (2) the frequency of grievances, (3) the levels at which the grievances are resolved (since contracts typically provide for a successive ordering of stages of appeal), (4) the amount of time required to resolve grievances, and (5) the extent to which arbitrators are used. Assessors also need to be aware of the extent to which key problems experienced by workers are introduced into the grievance procedure. In some cases, other formal or informal avenues are used to provide a system of industrial justice.[36]

A grievance procedure is a system for resolving disputes arising from the contract. The assessor of union–management relations should be cognizant of these processes. Most union contracts outline specific procedures for handling information transactions between the management and the union, for decisions in such areas as job bidding, accrual for vacation pay, the handling of overtime, weekend work and emergency pay, transfer wage policies, layoff and recall procedures, and the like. Lack of evidence regarding disputes in these decision areas during administration of the contract usually, but not always, indicates that the information and decision process is working to the satisfaction of both parties.

When these decision processes do not operate satisfactorily and the grievance procedure is ineffective, a third area of contract administration emerges—contract failure. Contract failure is a critical event that demonstrates that the collective-bargaining agreement is not governing the on-going relationship between the union and management. Past work in the area that is here called contract failure has looked at wildcat strikes, which are unauthorized, illegal strikes during the contract, work slowdowns, and work sabotage. To this list of contract failures, we would add evidence of contract disputes being resolved outside the grievance process.[37,38] It is important that the assessor of union–management relations be acutely aware of these contract failures, since they represent critical events in the day-to-day relationships between the union and management.

Objective Characteristics

The assessment of the objective characteristics of union–management relations is best accomplished through the analysis of pertinent documents, memoranda, and agreements as well as through interviews aimed toward the subjective reporting of objective events. There are several aspects of the relations between unions and management that are important in assessment, as is documented in Table 13-4. The history of union–management relations provides key contextual information that can be gathered through interviews of union and management leaders. Such interviews focus on such critical questions as the following: What has been the length, substance, and character of contract negotiations in recent years? Were there strikes in the recent past? On what matters? Have there been unauthorized work stoppages, wildcat strikes, slowdowns, or sabotage? Are there fundamental differences in philosophy between labor and management?

A second area for assessment is the nature of formal decision making as specified in contractual agreements. Most contracts will include information concerning pay and fringe benefits, grievance policies and discipline, but other policies and practices may not be codified. Thus, the assessor may have to look at not only contractual agreements but established practices in order to discern "understandings" regarding hiring regulations, layoff procedures, hours of work, training and promotion practices, and so forth.

Once the contractual issues have been identified and understood, the next area for assessment is that of grievance activity. While the contract should specify the formal procedures and steps and should define issues that may be grieved, company or union records must be examined to determine the level of grievance activity and the step at which grievances are settled. Of relevance in assessment are not only the numbers of grievances and stages of resolution, but also the length of time involved and

Table 13-4   Objective Characteristics of Union–Management Relations

Assessment Area	Method
Union–management history	Structured interviews
1. What has been the contract history for the preceding five years?	
Contract date:	
Contract issues:	
Strike over new contract:	
2. What have been the unauthorized work stoppages in the preceding five years?	
Wildcat strikes:	
Sabotage:	
Slowdowns:	
Formal decision procedures	Union–management contract
1. Are there guidelines for procedures in the following areas? What are they?	
Union shop:	
Dues check-off:	
No-strike clause:	
Hiring regulations:	
Promotion on seniority:	
Pay rates:	
Grievance procedures (steps, arbitration):	
Layoff procedures:	
Discipline process:	
Training:	
Benefits (vacation, sick time, etc.):	
Hours of work (overtime, shifts, etc.):	
Grievances	Company records
1. What is the grievance activity?	
Number of grievances:	
Types of grievance:	
Time required to settle grievances:	
Level at which settled:	
Informal union–management interaction	Structured interviews
1. What are the informal processes of interaction between union and management?	
Issues:	
Roles involved:	
Process of decision making:	

the substance of the grievances themselves. Categorization of the types of grievances and the time involved in their settlements should highlight the critical conflicts between unions and management and, by inference, the less important ones.

This assessment of contractual and grievance activity covers the periodic and episodic aspects of formal union–management relations; of equal interest are the informal relations. For example, contractual agreements focus only on the outcomes of bargaining. Walton and McKersie, however, note that bargaining includes many subprocesses.[39] Thus, the assessor may need to examine the roles that union members and international organizations play in the bargaining process and how they are responded to by union leadership. He or she may also need to consider how much of the bargaining is characterized by "horse trading" and how much by mutual problem solving. This will provide evidence as to the informal processes and politics that influence union and management relations. In addition, the assessor may also need to assess the character of union and management interactions from day to day in the workplace. Interviews with union officers, stewards, managers, and supervisors can identify the tone and content of these interactions. By comparing these informal processes with the formal ones, the assessor can come to understand how history shapes the present character of union–management relations.

Attitudes toward Union–Management Relations

The subjective perceptions of union–management relations by union members and managers can be assessed through a questionnaire survey (see Appendixes 2 and 3). Our questionnaires cover three aspects: (1) global satisfaction with the relations between union and management; (2) attitudes about the influence of the union on management policies and practices; (3) a measurement of dual loyalty of the individual employee toward the union and the company. Our measurement progress on these aspects of union–management relations has been limited. Some examples of representative questions are shown in Table 13-5. The data and reliability computations are taken from only one research site.

The table shows that at this site, global satisfaction was measured by a single question. A factor analysis showed there to be two dimensions of the influence of a union: the first covered issues of resources, including pay, benefits, and promotions; the second covered issues of work, including assignments, work procedures, and the like. The analysis showed no distinctive factor for dual loyalty. Although the concept is an integral part of role formation, particularly when organization members face conflicting expectations and pressures, the items used were unable to measure the phenomenon reliably.

Table 13-5 Measures of Attitudes toward Union–Management Relations

Measures	N	Internal Consistency Reliability*			Test–Retest Reliability*		
		a_1	a_2	a_3	r_{12}	r_{13}	r_{23}
Global satisfaction with union–management relations	101	.33	.31	.33	.40	.29	.52
a. How good is the relationship between the local union and the company's management?							
Union influence on resources	230	.83	.87	.84	.57	.54	.56
a. Pay raises associated with promotions.							
b. The way jobs are classified.							
c. Increasing fringe benefits.							
d. Who is promoted.							
Union influence on work	105	.88	.92	.94	.48	.43	.46
a. Deciding how work will be assigned.							
b. Making your work more meaningful.							
c. Determining work procedures in your area.							
d. Changing work procedures in your area.							
Dual loyalty	105	—(unacceptably low)—					
a. It is easy to be loyal to both the union and management.							
b. Basically, the union and management have similar goals.							
c. There is no reason why the union and management cannot work together.							
d. The union and management are generally opposed to each other.							
e. You can't be a union member and support management at the same time.							
f. The management here makes it easy to conduct union business.							
g. The management makes it difficult for me to talk to my group representatives or job steward.							
h. The union helps me deal effectively with management.							
i. Union members don't like it if you try to help management improve work effectiveness.							

* Alpha coefficients and test-retest reliabilities are from three questionnaire administrations at intervals of about one year.

Clearly this section of the questionnaire needs further development. The measures of union–management relations were highly intercorrelated with measures describing the union itself, and thus they failed to show adequate discriminant validity. The measure of global satisfaction needs additional questions, and the entire concept of dual loyalty must be reconsidered.

UNION–MANAGEMENT COLLABORATIVE CHANGE

Given an understanding of the union, the management organization, and the relationship between the union and the management, the investigators prepare to assess change in labor–management relations. This assessment involves the study of cooperative labor–management structures and processes.

Conceptual Background

Labor–management cooperative committees have existed in the United States since the early 1900s.[40,41] These cooperative committees have always been controversial because on the surface they seem to threaten the tradition of collective bargaining.[42,43] The success of union–management change involves the development of the collaborative relationship between the union and management that supplements rather than supplants collective bargaining. Samuel Gompers, who was president of the American Federation of Labor, wrote in the 1920s that "the union is just as necessary for the newer function—cooperation—as it is for defensive bargaining purposes . . . cooperation comes with maturity and development." Bill Murray, founder of the United Steelworkers, echoed those thoughts in the 1940s, suggesting that failure by the labor movement to develop a cooperative concern would lead to increasing tension and bitterness, thus reducing the opportunities for constructive accommodation and community of interests between managements and unions. The historical union position in the United States is to concentrate on the "business unionism philosophy," focusing on bread-and-butter issues of wages, hours, and working conditions.[44] The recent growth of interest in union–management collaborative change is based in part on the interest of union leaders and union members to collaborate on certain issues that supplement the traditional economic issues. Kochan, Lipsky, and Dyer reported that a majority of the union officers in their study felt that issues such as the content and control of work, the provision of adequate resources, and the maintenance of productivity were issues appropriate for a collaborative change program outside collective bargaining.[18]

Prior to the recent interest in union–management collaborative change, there were no conceptual models on which to base an understanding of joint union–management change or process. Recent work has begun to provide such a foundation, however, which the remainder of this section will briefly explore.

Kochan and Dyer developed a basic model of union–management change that consisted of 18 fundamental propositions.[45] The model was based on the assumption that union and management were separate organizations with distinct, often conflicting goals. The model assumed that the power and conflict characteristics of the relation were based on these structural differences. The first part of the model postulated that stimuli for union–management change would result from both internal and external pressures in the union and management organizations, coupled with the perception that the formal bargaining arrangements would be ineffective for dealing with these pressures. The second set of propositions predicted that the decision to participate in the joint ventures would be conditional upon both parties seeing the venture as an instrument for the achievement of their separate goals and that they would be more likely to arise if the parties could compromise and negotiate the goals of the venture. Participation would be more likely if the powerful individuals and coalitions in both groups did not oppose the effort. The final set of propositions speculated that continuing commitment to the cooperative venture would hinge on several conditions. The propositions, for example, suggested that continuing commitment was dependent on the achievement of some key goals in the early phases of the project, on the maintenance of the goals that were the basis of the project, and on the perception that the project was a successful vehicle for responding to the internal pressures that stimulated the project's original incursion. The propositions also suggested that the relationship with the collective-bargaining agreement was critical for commitment, including the proposition that long-term commitment was conditional on maintaining the security and the effectiveness of the traditional collective-bargaining agreement.

Brett presented two basic structural models that can be used to understand cooperative relationships.[5] In the single-channel cooperative model, the traditional union role is expanded into a cooperative system, with the union still representing employees. In the dual-channel cooperative model, the role of employees is expanded, with employee representatives, who may or may not be union members, participating in the cooperative structure. Brett presented eight propositions regarding these two models. Single-channel models were viewed as more effective for handling direct outcomes of traditional union–management relationships (such as strikes) and for issues with high priority for the union (such as wages and job security). Dual-channel models were proposed as being more effective for handling problems related to worker motivation. For the single-channel model to be effective in the system with successful bargaining, the structure would need to be composed of the same union and management representatives in both the collective-bargaining and

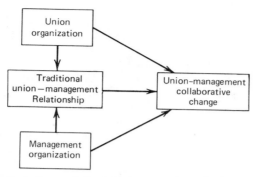

Figure 13-1 *A heuristic model of the key components of the assessment of unions and organizational change.*

cooperative structures; in an ineffective collective-bargaining system, the representatives would need to be different. For the dual-channel model to be effective, the labor representatives would need to be chosen by employees affected by the organizational change rather than by or from among union leaders. Two final ideas proposed that effective single-channel models would operate in an advisory capacity to collective bargaining, while effective dual-channel models should have the power to resolve issues and implement solutions.

The underlying model of the cooperative union–management quality of work life (QWL) projects can be understood through Figures 13-1, 13-2, and 13-3. Figure 13-1 describes traditional union–management relationships that are best seen as two parallel hierarchies interfacing in two primary processes. Both organizations are primarily vertically arranged

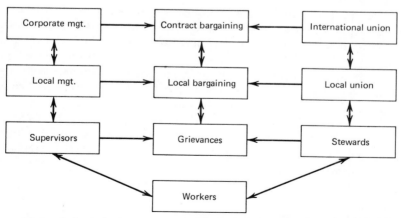

Figure 13-2 *A heuristic model of traditional union–management relations.*

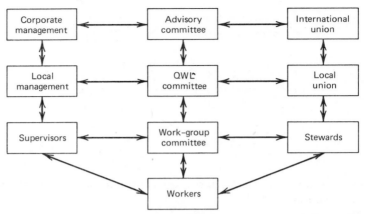

Figure 13-3 A heuristic model of QWL projects as union–management collaborative efforts.

groups with a clearly defined scope of responsibilities and authority. Workers, as members of both organizational structures, have responsibilities and allegiances to both. Primary processes that occur at the interfaces of two organizations are the periodic contractual-bargaining process and the ongoing contract-administration and grievance processes, as have been described in a earlier section of this chapter. The contract-negotiation process occurs primarily at the national or local levels, with the grievance process occurring at the local and department levels.

Figure 13-3 diagrams the supplemental structures and processes developed in a typical quality of work life change project. These structures should be conceived as being overlaid on Figure 13-2, with the management and union organizations remaining intact, yet adding another dimension to the relationship—that of cooperative problem solving. A high-level advisory committee is usually established between the international union and corporate management that provides commitment and overall direction to the QWL program. At the local level, a QWL committee is formed between the local union and local management. Both the advisory committee and QWL committee represent a forum for active collaboration, as do cooperative work-level committees formed as departmental groups or task forces and composed of supervisors, stewards, and workers. The formation of this supplemental cooperative structure is assisted by third-party consultants who work with the joint committees and task forces. The next two sections discuss objective and subjective approaches to the assessment of this supplemental cooperative relationship, its success and effectiveness, and its results.

Objective Characteristics

Union–management collaborative projects have a significant prior history. Events of significance may be revealed in interviews concerning the

Table 13-6   Objective Characteristics of Union–Management Project

Assessment Area	Method
Project history	Structured interviews
1. What conditions and forces gave rise to the effort to initiate a collaborative project?	
Project expectations and agreements	Union–management agreement
1. What are the expectations of both parties?	
Objectives:	
Procedural guidelines:	
Relation to contract:	
Termination procedures:	
Problem-solving structures	Structured interviews
1. What are the problem-solving structures that were created?	
Structures:	
Objectives:	
Representation:	
Operating guidelines:	
Informal decision-making processes	Direct observation
1. What are the informal processes for decision making?	
Roles:	
Decisions:	
Process:	

history of labor–management relations, but the assessor may also have to focus in detail on key events, attitudes, and expectations to understand the particular forces leading to the collaborative effort. In addition, there is a need to assess the expectations and contractual agreements of unions and management in the collaborative effort, their structure of collaboration, and the decision-making processes. Table 13-6 shows the several areas for assessment of union–management collaboration and some key questions about its objective character.

Subjective accounts of the objective factors leading to collaboration can be garnered through structured interviews of key managers and union leaders. Lawler and Drexler, for example, have identified a field of social forces that are favorable and unfavorable to the start-up of collaborative projects.[46] Among the favorable forces they list are the following:

1. Potential for improvement: complementary goals
2. Reduction of resistance to change
3. Likely permanence of changes

4. Avoidance of constraining legislation
5. Achieving noneconomic benefits for workers
6. Efficiency in reaching agreements

Among the opposing forces, they include these:

1. Differences in union and management goal priorities
2. Absence of precedent, experience, and example
3. Lack of knowledge of basic principles
4. Potential loss of power
5. Contractual protections and roles
6. Time frame (too long)
7. Ambiguity of goals and outcomes
8. Absence of qualified consultants

An assessor, through interviews and observations, can evaluate the strength of these favorable and opposing forces for collaboration at a research site. Drexler and Lawler, for example, have documented their impact on the start-up of one union–management venture.[47] An assessor can also assess the steps taken to manage these forces. In their work, Lawler and Drexler found that the key to effective start-up lay in reducing forces impeding cooperation rather than increasing the favorable forces.

A second area for assessment is the expectations and agreements of the union and management as embodied in their "shelter agreement" for the project. This agreement is typically outside the perspective of the contract and is supplemental to it; nevertheless, it contains important information about goals and expectations. One key element is the explication of roles and role arrangements. Gompers, for example, has asserted that it is incongruous for unions to generate policy jointly with management and then press employees' grievances.[48] Assessing the roles of union members in the collaborative effort therefore becomes a critical topic for investigation. Another key element in assessment concerns jurisdictional distinctions between collective-bargaining agreements, grievance procedures, and the joint union–management project. Kochan and Dyer suggest that a union–management project can be disengaged from some other aspects of the union–management relationship. Strauss and associates suggest it will interact and create cross-currents of consternation and confusion.[7,49] The assessor must therefore look at distinctions between these areas as detailed in the shelter agreement.

A third area for assessment concerns the problem-solving structures created in the joint project. Figure 13-2 depicts the "traditional" structures and processes in union–management relations. Formal interfaces are defined through bargaining and grievance activities. Figure 13-3 represents a collaborative model. Here four types of structures are present at the interface. These include a top-level advisory committee, composed of top management and the heads of the international union, as well as, on occasion, division managers, regional union representatives and a local quality of work life committee, composed of local managers and supervisors and union officials and stewards. The usual activities of such a quality of work life committee are to coordinate and direct the activities of the project, to consult with the advisory committee, and to work through departmental committees and ad hoc task forces in creating change. These latter two groups are composed primarily of supervisors, stewards, and nonmanagerial members of the work force.

A final area for assessment concerns the operations of these committees and their informal decision making. Several methods are appropriate here. Nadler, Hanlon, and Lawler, for example, surveyed union and management members of committees, as well as consultants, to measure the effectiveness of committee operations.[50] They found "ownership" of the project by key groups in the organization, clear and agreed goals of the committee, effective consultation, and mutual problem solving to be predictive of project success. They also found the organization's climate—trust, support for the project at all levels, and agreeable labor–management relations—to be an important influence. Another method of assessment is through on-site observations. Goodman's scheme for observing committee meetings and the naturalistic assessment methods described in this volume can be useful in documenting committee processes and decisions and in tracing the implementation of interventions into the organization. Finally, documentary data, including meeting notes, agendas, formal announcements, and the like can be reviewed in assessing union and management collaboration.

Attitudes toward the Union–Management Project

The subjective perceptions of managers and union members in the project can be measured by means of a survey (see Appendixes 13-2 and 13-3). Our survey instrument focuses on three aspects of union–management projects. The first addresses an overall assessment of the project. Two scales were verified, using factor analysis: satisfaction with the QWL program and member influence on QWL. Items comprising these scales and the scale reliabilities are reported in Table 13-7.

The second area for project assessment concerns the union's role in the change program. Two dimensions of the union's influence are identified. One focuses on union influence on resource decisions—pay, time schedules, and the like—and the other on work-activity decisions—procedures, assignments, and so forth. These scales are also reported in Table 13-7.

The final area of project assessment concerned perceptions of the labor–management committees. Factor analysis shows four dimensions to

Table 13-7   Attitudes toward Union–Management Program

Measures	N	Internal Consistency Reliability*			Test–retest Reliability*		
		a_1	a_2	a_3	r_{12}	r_{13}	r_{23}
Satisfaction with QWL program	222	NA	NA	.85	NA	NA	.69
a. The quality of work program has had a positive effect on labor–management relations at this company.							
b. The quality of work program has had a negative effect upon how I perform my work. (reversed)							
c. The quality of work program had improved my relationship with my supervisor.							
d. The quality of work program has brought more meaning to my life at this organization.							
e. A quality of work program should be introduced at other plants in this company.							
Employee influence on QWL	237	NA	NA	.79	NA	NA	NA
a. The quality of work committee listened to my point of view.							
b. I am not told what changes the quality of work program has been making. (reversed)							
c. I have a say in decisions the quality of work committee makes.							
d. I have a say in the decisions of the quality of work program.							
Union influence on QWL program work decisions	106	NA	.85	.93	NA	NA	.46
a. Making work more meaningful.							
b. Work procedures.							
c. Changing work procedures.							
d. Deciding work assignments.							
Union influence on QWL program resource decisions	82	NA	.90	.89	NA	NA	.47
a. Job classification.							
b. Management–union relations.							
c. Affirmative action program.							
d. Adjusted time schedule.							
e. Professional and career development.							
f. Employee profile.							
g. Management appraisal.							

Table 13-7   (*Continued*)

Measures	N	Internal Consistency Reliability*			Test–Retest Reliability*		
		a_1	a_2	a_3	r_{12}	r_{13}	r_{23}
h. Creating siting clearance staff.							
i. Fairer promotion policies.							
j. Division review.							
k. Per diem pay.							
Satisfaction with QWC	221	NA	NA	NA	NA	NA	.60
a. How satisfied are you with the progress of the quality of work committee in this company?							
b. All in all, I am satisfied with the quality of work committee.							
QWC power	210	.77	.84	.85	.30	.43	.73
a. Influencing important decisions in the organization.							
b. Dealing with important rather than trivial issues and problems.							
c. How much power does the quality of work committee have within the organization?							
QWC influence	87	.99	.93	.94	.36	.36	.61
a. Improving working conditions in the organization.							
b. Improving the effectiveness of the organization.							
QWC employee relations	140	.82	.82	.82	.31	.39	.73
a. Listening to the views of individuals.							
b. Gathering information about current conditions.							
c. Keeping employees informed about the activities of the quality of work committee.							
d. To what extent do you feel able to have your own concerns considered by the quality of work committee?							

* Alpha coefficients and test-retest reliabilities are from three questionnaire administrations at intervals of about one year.

committee evaluation: global satisfaction, power of the committee, impact on the organization, and the relations of the committee to the organization members. The measures can be found in the table.

Again, more measurement development is needed in this area. Analyses showed there were high intercorrelations among the measures of the program, the union's influence, and the union–management committee. As such, the measures show scant discriminant validity. It may be necessary to include a "don't know" category in this section of the questionnaire so that only knowledgeable members and therefore ones more able to discriminate between the concepts might venture an opinion about the project. Moreover, recording the numbers of members who "don't know" about the project would be useful data in their own right.

While this measurement was designed for assessment of collaborative projects, it may also be useful in assessing management-initiated ventures where union members are involved. Measures of project satisfaction and influence on the program are important indicators of project effectiveness in any situation. Moreover, measures of committee operations for a multilevel task force in a nonunionized organization would be useful. Only the nomenclature would need to be changed.

A Plan of Analysis

Once collected, data from these three domains—the union as an organization, union–management relations, and union–management collaboration in a joint project—must be arrayed in an analytic plan. At this point we have just begun such analyses. The plan is to use the baseline assessments of the union as an organization and of union–management relations as contextual variables for interpreting the process of collaboration. Later measurements, of course, can be outcome variables. Goodman, for example, used premeasurement and postmeasurement to assess the impact of a collaborative project on the union involved and on union–management relations.[51] In another project, the union and management established an early deadline for contract negotiations in order to minimize disruptions of the project and to insure its success. This outcome could be traced to the acceptance of the program itself.

Measures of the project itself are useful for descriptive purposes. When coupled with interview and observational data, they help to tell the project's "story." And there have been stories to tell. At one site, for example, the inability of the consultants to coordinate the roles of multiple unions led to their termination. Moreover, coordination problems severely hampered the program's effectiveness, even in the hands of a new consulting team.[19] At another site, a union election led to a discrediting of the program. At still another, the arrival of new senior managers, who were less favorably disposed to the project and the prospects of collaborating with the union, led to the project's cessation. In addition to description, these measures can also be used to assess project impact. At one site, correlations between members' assessment of the program and union–management committees were significantly related to changes in their attitudes and perceptions of their jobs and organization. Such measures could also be correlated with attitudes toward the union and toward union–management relations.

Summary and Tasks Ahead

One key assumption we have used is that multiple methods of gathering data are essential to understanding unions and union–management relations in general, and the operation of collaborative union–management structures in particular. The six methods described herein are summarized in Table 13-8. Documents such as the union contract, local agreements, constitutions, and bylaws are key sources of information for understanding the objective characteristics of the union and union management relations. Historical issues can be determined through interviews with the leaders of the period and through analysis of newspaper accounts of the events. The situation of the international union can be assessed through documentation of its history from books, periodicals, and from newspapers. Attitudinal assessments are best developed from questionnaire items administered to the union leadership and membership.

Table 13-8   Suggested Uses of Measurement Techniques

Method	Suggested Uses
Public documents (newspapers, periodicals, books)	History of the international union
	History of the local union
	History of local strikes and local conflicts
Union documents (constitution, bylaws, contract, agreements)	Leadership functions
	Interface roles with regional and international union
	Relevant decisions and locus of decision making
Company documents (personnel records, memoranda)	Grievance rates and grievance types
	Policy positions on key issues
	Arbitration history
Project documents (announcements, minutes)	Structures established
	Domain of problem-solving groups
	Key project events
Structured interviews (with union and management leaders)	Confirmation of information from written records
	Delineation of current issues
	Understanding of day-to-day interaction processes
Questionnaires (using fixed-response items)	Perceptions of union as an organization
	Perceptions of union–management relations
	Perceptions of union–management project

The results of one measurement strategy are reported in this chapter. Using as the primary example one of the ISR/NCQWL quality of work life projects, it was demonstrated that these basic conceptual areas were useful in documenting the backgrounds, activities, and effects of the project on relevant areas. Validity and reliability cannot be readily assessed for any of the conceptual areas except for those assessed through questionnaire techniques. In each area of perception, both internal-consistency reliability and test–retest reliability were reported.

As the survey questionnaire stands today in unpolished form, it can be used to answer or inform answers to many questions about collaborative labor–management projects. These include the following:

1. Do members' attitudes toward unionism influence their attitudes toward their union, union–management relations, and a joint project? Are they influenced by the project itself?

2. Do members' attitudes toward their union influence their attitudes toward labor–management relations and a joint project? Are they influenced by the project itself?

3. Do members' attitudes toward union–management relations influence a joint project? Are they influenced by the project itself?

4. Do members gain or lose influence as a result of a project? Does their union gain or lose influence? Does management?

5. Do union members view their leaders as more or less effective as a result of a collaborative project?

6. Does the membership of the collaborative committee affect its problem solving? Does it affect whether or not the project survives?

7. Does the committee segregate issues into areas for settlement by bargaining, grieving, and problem solving? Does this affect project success?

8. Do union representatives make a significant contribution to committees? Do members see it that way?

9. Do cooperative ventures create intraunion conflict?

10. Do cooperative ventures increase or decrease union member participation?

These questions and answers are multiplied in the case of multiple-union involvement in a project. Moreover, new questions are raised and answered when the measures presented here are used with data on productivity, grievances, cost-benefit comparisons, and management attitudes toward the project and its results.

Despite the promise of this aspect of assessment, more work is needed. Many of the measures in this chapter need further elaboration; some need reconceptualization; and a few may need to be discarded. Only the measures of the power and service dimensions of unionism have been shown to be valid indicators in national data. Others are congruent with measures developed by Biasatti and Martin for assessing union–management relations, but more normative and validity data are needed.[8] Finally, concepts and measures are needed for assessing those aspects of union politics, union–management relations, and union–management collaboration that are less amenable to survey measurement. Walton and McKersie have conceptualized the bargaining process, but no one has done a comparable job in the conceptualization of the process of union–management collaboration. We do not know how to think about or measure distinctions between bargainable versus collaboratively resolved issues in these ventures, the alternation between cooperative and adversarial postures by the parties, or the contrast between democratic and autocratic committee operation. Such issues may be central to project assessment and measurement will have to follow, not precede, concept development.

A final concern is access. At some sites, either the union, management, or the researchers vetoed the use of the instruments described herein, on grounds that no agreements could be reached on either administration procedures or joint sharing of the data. While we have been diligent in protecting the rights of all parties, including ourselves, to decline from participation voluntarily in an assessment, we have been less forward in identifying the advantages and disadvantages for the parties so that they might make informed choices. This work, plus concept and measurement development, constitute the tasks ahead.

REFERENCES

1. Tannenbaum, A. S., & Kahn, R. L. *Participation in union locals.* Evanston, IL: Row Peterson, 1948.
2. Bakke, E. W. *Mutual survival.* Hamden, CT: Archon, 1966.
3. Karsh, B. *Diary of a strike.* Urbana: University of Illinois Press, 1953.
4. Weinberg, E. Labor–management cooperation: A report on recent initiatives. *Monthly Labor Review,* April 1976, 13–22.
5. Brett, J. M. Behavioral research on unions and union management systems. In B. Staw & L. Cummings (Eds.), *Research in organizational behavior: Volume II.* Greenwich, CT: JAI Press, 1980.
6. Strauss, G. Managerial practices. In J. R. Hackman & J. L. Suttle (Eds.), *Improving life at work: Behavioral science approaches to organizational change.* Santa Monica, CA: Goodyear Publishing Co., 1977.
7. Kochan, T., & Dyer, L. A model for organizational change in the context of labor–management relations. *Journal of Applied Behavioral Science,* 1976, **12**, 56–78.
8. Biasatti, L. L., & Martin, J. E. A measure of the quality of union–management relations. *Journal of Applied Psychology,* 1979, **64**, 4.
9. Barbash, J. *American unions: Structure, government and politics.* New York: Random House, 1967.

10. Anderson, J. N. *Union effectiveness: An industrial relations systems approach.* Unpublished doctoral dissertation. Ithaca: Cornell University, 1977.

11. Tannenbaum, A. Unions. In J. G. March (Ed.), *Handbook of organizations.* Chicago: Rand-McNally, 1969.

12. Brett, J. M. Behavioral research on unions and management systems. In B. M. Staw & L. L. Cummings (Eds.), *Research in organizational behavior.* Greenwich, CT: JAI Press, 1980, **2**, 177–213.

13. Olsen, Mancur, Jr. *The logic of collective action.* Cambridge: Harvard University Press, 1965.

14. Derber, M., Chalmers, W. E., & Edelman, M. T. Assessing union–management relationships. *Quarterly Review of Economics and Business,* 1961, **1**, 27–28.

15. Yuchtman, E., & Seashore, S. E. A system resource approach to organizational effectiveness. *American Sociological Review,* 1967, **32**, 891–903.

16. Katz, D., & Kahn, R. L. *The social psychology of organization,* 2nd ed. New York: Wiley, 1978.

17. Quinn, R. P., & Staines, G. L. *The 1977 Quality of Employment Survey.* Ann Arbor, MI: Survey Research Center, Institute for Social Research, 1979.

18. Kochan, T., Lipsky, D. V., & Dyer, L. Collective bargaining and the quality of work: The views of local union activists. *Proceedings of the 27th Annual Winter Meeting, IRRA, December 28–29, 1974,* 150–162.

19. Glick, W., Mirvis, P., & Harder, D. Union satisfaction and participation. *Industrial Relations,* May 1977, **16**(2), 145–151.

20. Kochan, T. A. Collective bargaining and organizational behavior research. In B. M. Staw & L. L. Cummings (Eds.), *Research in organizational behavior.* Greenwich, CT: JAI Press, 1980, **2**, 129–176.

21. Hammermesh, D. S. Who wins in wage bargaining? *Industrial and Labor Relations Review,* 1973, **26**, 1146–1149.

22. Bowlby, R. L., & Schriber, W. R. Bluffing and the split-the-difference theory of wage bargaining. *Industrial and Labor Relations Review,* 1978, **31**, 161–171.

23. Rubin, J. Z., & Brown, B. R. *The social psychology of negotiations.* New York: Academic Press, 1975.

24. Hammer, T. H. The role of the union in organizational behavior: A study of relationships between local union characteristics and worker behavior and attitudes. *Academy of Management Journal,* 1978, **4**, 560–577.

25. Magenau, J. M., & Pruitt, D. C. The social psychology of bargaining and the quality of work: The views of local union activists. *Proceedings of the 27th Annual Winter Meeting, IRRA, December 28–29, 1974,* 150–162.

26. Ashenfelter, O., & Johnson, G. Bargaining theory, trade unions, and industrial strike activity. *American Economic Review,* 1969, **59**, 35–49.

27. Skeels, J. W. Measures of U.S. strike activity. *Industrial and Labor Relations Review,* 1971, **24**, 515–525.

28. Britt, D., & Galle, O. Industrial conflict and unionization. *American Sociological Review,* 1972, **37**, 46–57.

29. Shorter, E., & Tilly, C. *Strikes in France 1830 to 1968.* Cambridge: Cambridge University Press, 1974.

30. Snyder, D. Institutional setting and industrial conflict: Comparative analysis of France, Italy, and the United States. *American Sociological Review,* 1975, **40**, 259–278.

31. Stern, R. N. Intermetropolitan patterns of strike frequency. *Industrial and Labor Relations Review,* 1976, **29**, 218–235.

32. Kochan, T. A., & Baderschneider, A. Dependence on impasse procedures: The case of New York police and fire fighters. *Industrial and Labor Relations Review,* 1978, **31,** 431–449.

33. Stern, J. L., Rehmus, C., Loewenberg, J., Kasper, H., & Dennis, B. *Final offer arbitration.* Lexington, MA: Lexington Books, 1975.

34. Wheeler, H. N. How compulsory arbitration affects compromise activity. *Industrial Relations,* 1978, **17,** 80–84.

35. Kochan, T. A., & Jick, T. The public sector mediation process: A theory and empirical examination. *Journal of Conflict Resolutions,* 1978, **22,** 209–240.

36. Thompson, A. W., & Murray, V. V. *Grievance procedures.* Lexington, MA: Lexington Books, 1976.

37. Gouldner, A. W. *Wildcat strike.* Yellow Springs, OH: Antioch Press, 1954.

38. Brett, J. M., & Goldberg, S. B. Wildcat strikes in bituminous coal mining. *Industrial and Labor Relations Review,* 1979, **32,** 465–483.

39. Walton, R. E., & McKersie, R. B. *A behavioral theory of labor negotiations.* New York: McGraw-Hill, 1965.

40. Gold, C. *Employer–employee committees and worker participation.* Series No. 20. New York: School of Industrial and Labor Relations, 1976.

41. Weinberg, E. Labor–management cooperation: A report on recent initiatives. *Monthly Labor Review,* April 1976, 13–22.

42. Dubin, R. Union–management cooperation and productivity. *Industrial and Labor Relations Review,* January 1949, 195–209.

43. Strauss, G., & Rosenstein, E. Workers' participation: A critical view. *Industrial Relations,* 1970, **9,** 197–214.

44. Donahue, T. Speech before International Conference on Trends in Industrial and Labor Relations. Reported in *World of Work,* 1976, **1,** 6, 3–4.

45. Kochan, T., & Dyer, L. A model for organizational change in the context of labor–management relations. *Journal of Applied Behavioral Science,* 1976, **12,** 56–78.

46. Lawler, E. E. III, & Drexler, J. Dynamics of establishing cooperative quality-of-worklife projects. *Monthly Labor Review,* March 1978, 23–28.

47. Drexler, J., & Lawler, E. E. III. A union–management cooperative project to improve the quality of work life. *Journal of Applied Behavioral Science,* 1977, **13**(3), 373–387.

48. Gompers, S. *Labor and the employee.* New York: E. P. Dutton, 1920.

49. Strauss, G., Miles, R., & Snow, C. Implications for industrial relations. In G. Strauss, R. Miles, C. Snow, & A. Tannenbaum (Eds.), *Organizational behavior: research and issues.* Belmont, CA: Wadsworth, 1974.

50. Nadler, D. A., Hanlon, M., & Lawler, E. E. Factors influencing the success of labor–management quality of work life projects. *Journal of Occupational Behavior,* 1980, **1,** 53–68.

51. Goodman, P. S. *Assessing organizational change: The Rushton quality of work experiment.* New York: Wiley-Interscience, 1979.

APPENDIX 13-1 STRUCTURED INTERVIEW: UNION DESCRIPTION

1. List segments of the work force that are unionized or involved in an active organizing effort.

Employee Group	Local Union	International	No. of Members	% of Employee Group

2. Get copies of union constitution, bylaws, and local governance papers. Code, then feedback to check accuracy with union leadership.

   a. Structure of union in terms of where, what decisions are made.

Local	Organizer/ Business Agent	District	International

   b. Leadership functions, local

Position	Function [duties]	How Chosen	Term	Pay

   c. Other leaders, business agent–district officers who interface with local

Position	Function [duties]	How Chosen	Term	Pay

3. Describe the local union's history over the past five years.

Date	Leadership Election	Describe Opposition	Other Issues Over Which There Was Intraunion Conflict	Describe Opposition

4. Describe international union's history over the past five years.

Date	Leader-ship Election	De-scribe Oppo-sition	Int'l. Conven-tion Major Issues	De-scribe Oppo-sition	Other Issues	Describe Oppo-sition

5. Get copy of contract and any local agreements.

Code	Yes	No
Union shop		
Dues check-off		
No strike clause		
Hiring regulations		
Promotion on seniority		
Pay		
Grievance policy		
Layoff, procedures		
Discipline		
Training		
Benefits (vacation, sick, etc.)		
Hours of work (shift, overtime)		

6. Describe local labor-management history.
   a. When did union representation begin in the organization?
   b. Has there ever been a decertification election? Year?
   c. Describe contract history for preceding five years.

Date	Contract Negotiated	Strike over New Contract	Unauthorized Work Stoppage [specify wildcat, sabotage slowdown]	Major Grievances

7. Describe grievance policy (Xerox from agreement)
   a. Per-year grievance activity

Type	Percentage	Time to Settle	Level at Which Settled

8. What are the major areas of day to day union–management interaction?

Position of Source Informant	Issue	How Dealt with

9. Describe contract negotiation process at local level.

	Yes	No
Vote on contract		
Introduce local bargaining proposals		
Negotiates local wage agreement		
Negotiates local wage agreement, but follows guidelines of international agreement		
Negotiates local wage agreement, but has district or international representative for assistance		
Introduce international bargaining proposals		
Local representative participates in international bargaining		

10. How does union involve members for contract negotiation?
    Preparation
    Negotiation
    Ratification—understanding of contents

APPENDIX 13-2   SAMPLE QUESTIONNAIRE, BEGINS ON FOLLOWING PAGE

**SURVEY
RESEARCH
CENTER**

June, 1976

This questionnaire begins the second measure or "the during measurement phase" of the National Quality of Work Program being conducted in the Division of   During the past 18 months, your Quality of Work Committee (QOWC) has continued to seek ways to improve effectiveness, working conditions, and the quality of life in your organization as a place to work. You may already have participated in our research by answering questions on a series of questionnaires that were administered during the initial phases of the Quality of Work Program.

The purpose of these questionnaires is to help us understand the changes which may have occurred at   during the last year and one half. The questions in this survey deal with almost every aspect of organizational life -- for example, the nature of your job, your intergroup relationships, your supervisors, and the organization as a whole. The results of this survey will also be used by the QOWC and by the consultants. Again, we ask you to answer the questionnaire frankly and carefully. YOUR INDIVIDUAL RESPONSES ARE COMPLETELY CONFIDENTIAL. No one at   ., the Quality of Work Committee, or the consultants will be able to identify your responses in any way, since only averaged results will be included in our feedback reports. All questionnaires will be taken to ISR in Michigan for analysis and safekeeping.

To help insure your privacy, we prefer not to have your name on your questionnaire or any easily identifiable information. At the same time, we need to match this questionnaire with the last questionnaire you may have filled out in the past and with information obtained from other sources (such as personnel and payroll records). To meet these two conditions, we provide for each employee a special identification number assigned by our research staff. This will be used only for matching information from different sources and times, not for any other purpose. The codes and names will be only in our confidential files.

Your number is on a sticker attached to the following page. Although you can remove the identification sticker, we hope you will help us by leaving it there.

This questionnaire is partly designed especially for   and partly to include some standard questions allowing comparison among many different kinds of organizations. This is part of the National Quality of Work Program in which your Division is cooperating and which is paying for the cost of this survey. Therefore, some of the questions may seem a little unsuited to your own situation. Please answer them all as best you can taking them in order as they appear.

Thank you for your cooperation. We hope you find the questionnaire interesting and thought provoking.

Barry A. Macy
Assistant Research Scientist -

Aaron Nurick
Assistant Study Director

INSTITUTE FOR
SOCIAL RESEARCH

**THE UNIVERSITY
OF MICHIGAN**

ANN ARBOR,
MICHIGAN 48106

GENERAL INSTRUCTIONS

Most of the questions ask that you check one of several numbers that apper on a scale to the right of the item. You are to choose the <u>one</u> number that best matches the description of how <u>you</u> feel about the item. For example, if you were asked how much you agree with the statement, "I enjoy the weather in Chattanooga," and you feel that you do agree, you would check the number under "agree" like this:

I enjoy the weather in Chattanooga. .... [1] [2] [3] [4] [5] [6] [7]

Strongly Disagree / Disagree / Slightly Disagree / Neither Agree nor Disagree / Slightly Agree / Agree / Strongly Agree

Note that the scale descriptions may be different in different parts of the questionnaire. For example, they may ask not whether you <u>agree</u> or <u>disagree</u> but perhaps whether you are <u>satisfied</u> or <u>dissatisfied</u>, or whether you think something to be <u>likely</u> or <u>not likely</u> to happen, etc.

So, be sure to read the special instructions that appear in the boxes on each page. Be sure to read the scale descriptions before choosing your answers.

When you have finished, please place the questionnaire in the envelope, remove your name from the outside, and return the envelope to the designated place or person.

****

This is your Michigan Identification Number:

Label: 10:1-

These codes are for Michigan use only:

Deck: 10:9-

Project: 8

PART I

In this part we are interested in your impressions of the union membership. Please answer the following questions keeping in mind that we are interested in your ideas about the feelings of the membership.

All of your responses are strictly confidential; individual responses will not be seen by anyone in your union or in   We appreciate your help in collecting this important information.

1.	HOW MUCH TIME DO YOU FEEL THAT THE UNION MEMBERSHIP WANTS YOU TO SPEND ON EACH OF THE FOLLOWING ACTIVITIES?

		None At All		A Moderate Amount			A Great Amount	
a.	Improving their pay and benefits.	[1] [2] [3] [4] [5] [6] [7]						10:11
b.	Helping members solve day-to-day problems.	[1] [2] [3] [4] [5] [6] [7]						10:12
c.	Representing union member's grievances.	[1] [2] [3] [4] [5] [6] [7]						10:13
d.	Organizing union social activities.	[1] [2] [3] [4] [5] [6] [7]						10:14
e.	Improving job classifications and work procedures.	[1] [2] [3] [4] [5] [6] [7]						10:15
f.	Improving the way the union is run.	[1] [2] [3] [4] [5] [6] [7]						10:16
g.	Improving the utilization of employees on their jobs.	[1] [2] [3] [4] [5] [6] [7]						10:17
h.	Lowering the decision making power within	[1] [2] [3] [4] [5] [6] [7]						10:18

2.	HOW GOOD IS THE RELATIONSHIP BETWEEN THE LOCAL UNION AND . . .

		Very Poor		Fair		Good		Excellent	Have No Idea	
a.	. . . the union members.	[1] [2] [3] [4] [5] [6] [7]							[8]	10:19
b.	. . . . management.	[1] [2] [3] [4] [5] [6] [7]							[8]	10:20
c.	. . . the International Union or Valley-Wide Executive Committee.	[1] [2] [3] [4] [5] [6] [7]							[8]	10:21
d.	. . . the community.	[1] [2] [3] [4] [5] [6] [7]							[8]	10:22
e.	. . . the Quality of Work Committee.	[1] [2] [3] [4] [5] [6] [7]							[8]	10:23
f.	. . . the Cooperative Conference.	[1] [2] [3] [4] [5] [6] [7]							[8]	10:24

3. THE FOLLOWING STATEMENTS MIGHT DESCRIBE THE RELATIONSHIPS BETWEEN THE UNION AND MANAGEMENT. HOW MUCH DO YOU <u>AGREE</u> OR <u>DISAGREE</u> WITH EACH?

Response scale: Strongly Disagree / Disagree / Slightly Disagree / Neither Agree nor Disagree / Slightly Agree / Agree / Strongly Agree / Have No Idea

		Response							
a.	The union and management share most information.	[1] [2] [3] [4] [5] [6] [7]	[8]						10:2
b.	The union and management try to weaken each other's position any way they can.	[1] [2] [3] [4] [5] [6] [7]	[8]						10:2
c.	The union and management try to find creative solutions to problems.	[1] [2] [3] [4] [5] [6] [7]	[8]						10:2
d.	The union and management try to help each other whenever they can.	[1] [2] [3] [4] [5] [6] [7]	[8]						10:2
e.	The union won't listen to new ideas.	[1] [2] [3] [4] [5] [6] [7]	[8]						10:2
f.	Bargaining is tough but fair.	[1] [2] [3] [4] [5] [6] [7]	[8]						10:3
g.	Management tries to understand the union's problems.	[1] [2] [3] [4] [5] [6] [7]	[8]						10:3
h.	The union is only willing to negotiate about a few specific issues.	[1] [2] [3] [4] [5] [6] [7]	[8]						10:3
i.	The union and management are hostile toward each other.	[1] [2] [3] [4] [5] [6] [7]	[8]						10:3
j.	The union tries to understand management's problems.	[1] [2] [3] [4] [5] [6] [7]	[8]						10:3
k.	Management is only willing to negotiate about a few specific issues.	[1] [2] [3] [4] [5] [6] [7]	[8]						10:3
l.	Management won't listen to new ideas.	[1] [2] [3] [4] [5] [6] [7]	[8]						10:3
m.	Management and union are willing to try solutions which haven't been tried before.	[1] [2] [3] [4] [5] [6] [7]	[8]						10:3

4. IN GENERAL, HOW MUCH SAY OR INFLUENCE DOES EACH OF THE FOLLOWING GROUPS HAVE OVER THE WAY GRIEVANCES ARE HANDLED.

Response scale: Little or No Influence / Moderate Influence / A Great Deal of Influence / Have No Idea

		Response	
a.	The members	[1] [2] [3] [4] [5] [6] [7]	[8]	10:3
b.	Local union leaders	[1] [2] [3] [4] [5] [6] [7]	[8]	10:3
c.	Valley-Wide or Council union leaders	[1] [2] [3] [4] [5] [6] [7]	[8]	10:4
d.	Full time union professional employees	[1] [2] [3] [4] [5] [6] [7]	[8]	10:4

5. IN GENERAL, HOW MUCH SAY OR INFLUENCE DOES EACH OF THE FOLLOWING GROUPS HAVE OVER THE WAY THE UNION IS RUN.

Response scale: Little or No Influence / Moderate Influence / A Great Deal of Influence / Have No Idea

		Response	
a.	The members	[1] [2] [3] [4] [5] [6] [7]	[8]	10:4
b.	Local union leaders	[1] [2] [3] [4] [5] [6] [7]	[8]	10:4
c.	Valley-Wide or Council union leaders	[1] [2] [3] [4] [5] [6] [7]	[8]	10:4
d.	Full time union professional employees	[1] [2] [3] [4] [5] [6] [7]	[8]	10:4

6. AS A UNION LEADER, HOW MUCH TIME AND EFFORT DO YOU SPEND IN THE FOLLOWING ACTIVITIES?	None At All		A Moderate Amount			A Great Amount		

a. Improving pay and benefits .... [1] [2] [3] [4] [5] [6] [7]   10:46
b. Helping members solve day-to-day problems. .... [1] [2] [3] [4] [5] [6] [7]   10:47
c. Representing union member's grievances. .... [1] [2] [3] [4] [5] [6] [7]   10:48
d. Organizing union social activities. .... [1] [2] [3] [4] [5] [6] [7]   10:49
e. Improving job classifications and work procedures. .... [1] [2] [3] [4] [5] [6] [7]   10:50
f. Improving the way the union is run. .... [1] [2] [3] [4] [5] [6] [7]   10:51
g. Improving the utilization of employees on their jobs. ...... [1] [2] [3] [4] [5] [6] [7]   10:52
h. Lowering the decision making power within   .... [1] [2] [3] [4] [5] [6] [7]   10:53

PART VII

In this part we are interested in finding out how satisfied you are with your union and its activities. Follow the directions given in the boxes at the beginning of each set of questions.

All of your responses are <u>strictly confidential</u>; individual responses will not be seen by anyone in the division or in the union. We appreciate your help in providing this important information.

---

1. HOW SATISFIED ARE YOU WITH THE EFFORTS WHICH YOUR UNION HAS MADE TO GET EACH OF THE FOLLOWING OUTCOMES FOR ITS MEMBERS?

a.	A better fringe benefit package	[1] [2] [3] [4] [5] [6] [7]	8:11
b.	Increased job security	[1] [2] [3] [4] [5] [6] [7]	8:12
c.	Fairer job classifications	[1] [2] [3] [4] [5] [6] [7]	8:13
d.	More participation in job related decisions	[1] [2] [3] [4] [5] [6] [7]	8:14
e.	Fairer promotion policies	[1] [2] [3] [4] [5] [6] [7]	8:15
f.	Fairer policies for reductions in the work force	[1] [2] [3] [4] [5] [6] [7]	8:16
g.	More meaningful work for members	[1] [2] [3] [4] [5] [6] [7]	8:17
h.	Fairer pay raises	[1] [2] [3] [4] [5] [6] [7]	8:18
i.	Better utilization of employees	[1] [2] [3] [4] [5] [6] [7]	8:19
j.	More decision making power	[1] [2] [3] [4] [5] [6] [7]	8:20

(Scale: Very Dissatisfied, Dissatisfied, Slightly Dissatisfied, Neither Satisfied nor Dissatisfied, Slightly Satisfied, Satisfied, Very Satisfied)

---

2. HOW GOOD IS THE RELATIONSHIP BETWEEN THE <u>LOCAL</u> UNION AND . . .

a.	. . . the union members.	[1] [2] [3] [4] [5] [6] [7] [8]	8:21
b.	. . . management.	[1] [2] [3] [4] [5] [6] [7] [8]	8:22
c.	. . . the Quality of Work Committee.	[1] [2] [3] [4] [5] [6] [7] [8]	8:23
d.	. . . the Cooperative Conference.	[1] [2] [3] [4] [5] [6] [7] [8]	8:24

(Scale: Very Poor, Fair, Good, Excellent, Have No Idea)

---

3. HOW SATISFIED ARE YOU WITH THE . . .

a.	. . . way your union handles grievances.	[1] [2] [3] [4] [5] [6] [7]	8:25
b.	. . . way union officers are chosen.	[1] [2] [3] [4] [5] [6] [7]	8:26
c.	. . . way issues are selected for collective bargaining.	[1] [2] [3] [4] [5] [6] [7]	8:27

(Scale: Very Dissatisfied, Dissatisfied, Slightly Dissatisfied, Neither Satisfied nor Dissatisfied, Slightly Satisfied, Satisfied, Very Satisfied)

HOW SATISFIED ARE YOU WITH THE . . .

	Very Dissatisfied	Dissatisfied	Slightly Dissatisfied	Neither Satisfied nor Dissatisfied	Slightly Satisfied	Satisfied	Very Satisfied	Does Not Apply	
d. . . . success your union has in bargaining wage issues.	[1]	[2]	[3]	[4]	[5]	[6]	[7]		8:28
e. . . . union's leadership.	[1]	[2]	[3]	[4]	[5]	[6]	[7]		8:29
f. . . . your ability to influence union decisions.	[1]	[2]	[3]	[4]	[5]	[6]	[7]		8:30
g. . . . amount of communication between the union and its members.	[1]	[2]	[3]	[4]	[5]	[6]	[7]		8:31
h. . . . success your union has in bargaining non-wage issues.	[1]	[2]	[3]	[4]	[5]	[6]	[7]		8:32
i. . . . progress of the Quality of Work Committee.	[1]	[2]	[3]	[4]	[5]	[6]	[7]	[8]	8:33

This section asks you about your participation in union activities. For each section, follow the directions that are given in the boxes at the beginning of the list of questions.

---

4.   PLEASE ANSWER THE FOLLOWING QUESTIONS. ARE YOU CURRENTLY SERVING IN ANY OF THE FOLLOWING UNION OR ASSOCIATION OFFICES?

	Yes	No	
a. Are you currently serving as a section or local representative to a union-management committee such as the Cooperative Conference or Quality of Work Committee?	[1]	[2]	8:34
b. Are you currently serving as a Valley-Wide representative to a union-management committee?	[1]	[2]	8:35
c. Are you currently serving as a member of a task force created by the Quality of Work Committee?	[1]	[2]	8:36
d. Are you currently serving as a member of a union committee?	[1]	[2]	8:37
e. Are you currently serving on a Valley-Wide appointed committee?	[1]	[2]	8:38

---

5.   IF A UNION LEADER OR ANOTHER UNION MEMBER ASKED YOU TO, HOW LIKELY IS IT THAT YOU WOULD DO EACH OF THE FOLLOWING?

	Not At All Likely		Somewhat Likely		Quite Likely		Extremely Likely	
a. Serve on a union committee.	[1]	[2]	[3]	[4]	[5]	[6]	[7]	8:39
b. Serve on a union-management committee as a union representative.	[1]	[2]	[3]	[4]	[5]	[6]	[7]	8:40
c. Attend a regular union meeting or a union executive committee meeting.	[1]	[2]	[3]	[4]	[5]	[6]	[7]	8:41

HOW LIKELY IS IT THAT YOU WOULD DO EACH
OF THE FOLLOWING?

Not At All Likely / Somewhat Likely / Quite Likely / Extremely Likely / Does Not Apply

d. Serve on the Quality of Work Committee. .... [1] [2] [3] [4] [5] [6] [7] [8]   8:42

e. Serve as a task force member of a committee created
    by the Quality of Work Committee. .... [1] [2] [3] [4] [5] [6] [7] [8]   8:43

The next questions ask you to describe your union. Please do not try to show how much you like or dislike the union, just try to be as accurate and factual as possible.

6. HERE ARE STATEMENTS WHICH MAY (OR MAY NOT) DESCRIBE YOUR UNION. HOW MUCH DO YOU AGREE OR DISAGREE WITH EACH STATEMENT?

Strongly Disagree / Disagree / Slightly Disagree / Neither Agree nor Disagree / Slightly Agree / Agree / Strongly Agree / Does Not Apply

a. Members of my union are afraid to express their real
    views in union meetings. .... [1] [2] [3] [4] [5] [6] [7]   8:44

b. Decisions are made in the union without ever asking
    the people who have to live with them. .... [1] [2] [3] [4] [5] [6] [7]   8:45

c. All in all, I am very satisfied with the union. .... [1] [2] [3] [4] [5] [6] [7]   8:46

d. Participation in union activities is worthwhile. .... [1] [2] [3] [4] [5] [6] [7]   8:47

e. In the union, everyone's opinion gets listened to. .... [1] [2] [3] [4] [5] [6] [7]   8:48

f. In general, I like the way the union handles things. .... [1] [2] [3] [4] [5] [6] [7]   8:49

g. The Quality of Work Committee has given the union
    more influence with management. .... [1] [2] [3] [4] [5] [6] [7] [8]   8:50

7. HOW MUCH TIME AND EFFORT DO YOU THINK THE UNION LEADERSHIP SHOULD SPEND . . .

None At All / A Moderate Amount / A Great Amount

a. . . . improving your pay and benefits. .... [1] [2] [3] [4] [5] [6] [7]   8:51

b. . . . helping members solve day-to-day problems. .... [1] [2] [3] [4] [5] [6] [7]   8:52

c. . . . representing union member's grievances. .... [1] [2] [3] [4] [5] [6] [7]   8:53

d. . . . organizing union social activities. .... [1] [2] [3] [4] [5] [6] [7]   8:54

e. . . . improving job classifications and work procedures. .... [1] [2] [3] [4] [5] [6] [7]   8:55

f. . . . improving the way the union is run. .... [1] [2] [3] [4] [5] [6] [7]   8:56

This section is concerned with your impressions about how things are done in this union and how decisions are made.

As in the other parts, read the special directions in the boxes first.

---

8. IN GENERAL, HOW MUCH SAY OR INFLUENCE DOES EACH OF THE FOLLOWING GROUPS HAVE OVER THE <u>WAY GRIEVANCES</u> ARE HANDLED IN YOUR UNION?

Little or No Influence — Moderate Influence — A Great Deal of Influence — Have No Idea

a. The membership	[1] [2] [3] [4] [5] [6] [7] [8]	8:57
b. Local union leadership	[1] [2] [3] [4] [5] [6] [7] [8]	8:58
c. Valley-Wide or Council union leaders	[1] [2] [3] [4] [5] [6] [7] [8]	8:59
d. Full time union professional employees	[1] [2] [3] [4] [5] [6] [7] [8]	8:60

---

9. IN GENERAL, HOW MUCH SAY OR INFLUENCE DOES EACH OF THE FOLLOWING GROUPS HAVE OVER <u>THE WAY YOUR UNION IS RUN</u>?

Little or No Influence — Moderate Influence — A Great Deal of Influence — Have No Idea

a. The membership	[1] [2] [3] [4] [5] [6] [7] [8]	8:61
b. Local union leadership	[1] [2] [3] [4] [5] [6] [7] [8]	8:62
c. Valley-Wide or Council union leaders	[1] [2] [3] [4] [5] [6] [7] [8]	8:63
d. Full time union professional employees	[1] [2] [3] [4] [5] [6] [7] [8]	8:64

---

10. IN GENERAL, HOW MUCH SAY OR INFLUENCE DOES <u>YOUR UNION</u> HAVE WITH MANAGEMENT IN EACH OF THE FOLLOWING AREAS?

Little or No Influence — Moderate Influence — A Great Deal of Influence

a. Pay raises associated with promotions	[1] [2] [3] [4] [5] [6] [7]	8:65
b. The way jobs are classified	[1] [2] [3] [4] [5] [6] [7]	8:66
c. Increasing fringe benefits	[1] [2] [3] [4] [5] [6] [7]	8:67
d. The hours people work	[1] [2] [3] [4] [5] [6] [7]	8:68
e. Who is promoted	[1] [2] [3] [4] [5] [6] [7]	8:69
f. Reduction in work force	[1] [2] [3] [4] [5] [6] [7]	8:70
g. Deciding how work will be assigned	[1] [2] [3] [4] [5] [6] [7]	8:71
h. Employee discipline	[1] [2] [3] [4] [5] [6] [7]	8:72
i. Making your work more meaningful	[1] [2] [3] [4] [5] [6] [7]	8:73
j. Determining work procedures in your area	[1] [2] [3] [4] [5] [6] [7]	8:74
k. Changing work procedures in your area	[1] [2] [3] [4] [5] [6] [7]	8:75

PART THREE

EVALUATING PROGRAM PROGRESS AND OUTCOME

This section is concerned with the evaluation of outcomes of an organizational change program, including their valuation and relationship to the activities initiated under the program.

Chapter 14 presents observational criteria and questionnaire instruments for assessing the process and progress of change efforts. The chapter illustrates data-gathering steps taken by the author and other researchers in the Michigan program to measure progress at different phases of several change efforts in organizations. Instruments and observations are directed to the start-up of the programs, including knowledge about and attitudes toward them and the readiness to change. They are also directed to the implementation of interventions, including assessments of the work of consultants and participating organization members, and to adoption of interventions by units in the organizations and factors predicting adoption. A questionnaire on goal attainment is presented that can be used to estimate whether and how well an intervention "takes" in an organization. Finally, criteria for assessing factors amenable to the institutionalization and diffusion of change programs are reviewed. In addition, the chapter illustrates one means of distinguishing the shared and differential impacts of multiple interventions on an organization. All such measures reported in this chapter are used as needs and opportunities present themselves.

Chapter 15 focuses on means for evaluating the significance of changes in attitude measures over the course of a change program. The chapter reviews various approaches to change analysis and examines the merits of each through the example of data from one research site. The chapter also reports on statistical techniques for determining whether respondents' attitudes have changed in magnitude, or whether their understanding of the measured variable has changed. In the latter case, the authors note, change score analyses may produce misleading conclusions about the impact of a change program. The statistically unsophisticated reader may wish to read only the "discussion" section of this chapter.

The following chapter, Chapter 16, presents an econometric approach to analysis of the outcomes of organization change programs. Building an internal production function, the authors estimate the impact of nonprogrammatic versus programmatic variables on changes in the economic performance of a work organization. As in Chapter 15, the authors present various approaches to analysis, and they adjudge their merits through analyses of data from a research site. This chapter, taken together with the previous one, describes means for assessing the significance of changes in outcome variables and tracing them to the change program.

The final chapter in this section, Chapter 17, illustrates an approach to assessing the benefits versus costs of an organizational change program. The authors present a model of program inputs and outputs that expresses these factors in financial terms. A case study is used to illustrate a "synthesizing" model that compares program benefits and costs through different cost-benefit criteria. In addition, the authors report on "social" costs and benefits at the case site and discuss criteria for evaluating the overall "cost utility" of change programs.

CHAPTER FOURTEEN

Assessing the Process and Progress of Change in Organizational Change Programs

PHILIP H. MIRVIS

The assessor of an organization change program casts an envious eye upon those who can conduct social experiments under controlled conditions. Although the paradigm of the experimental evaluation may guide research planning, methodology, and measurement, the realities of project purposes (multiple), change interventions (often unknown in advance), and field conditions (seldom fully under control) make it plain that the classic canons for interpreting the outcomes will not apply. Thus, the assessor needs not only to conduct a broad evaluation of net outcomes—whether the intended and expected goals were achieved—but needs as well to reach some understanding of the conditions, processes, events, and action strategies that have aided or impeded goal achievement.

In the usual case of an organizational change program—say an effort to improve the quality of work life—there is no single independent variable that is manipulated and no single dependent variable that is changed, nor is there a single theory connecting the two that can be tested. Instead, there are likely to be many interventions, including some that none of the participants, least of all the assessors, identified at the start. There are also likely to be many goals achieved, and some outcomes of importance that no one intended may result. Finally, there may be several potential paths leading from the actions to the results.[1,2]

To fully appraise such change programs, it is therefore essential to monitor the introduction and implementation of the program, observe the work of change agents and program participants, assess the effect of the environment on the outcomes, and evaluate the program both as to intended and unintended results. The questions raised are innumerable. Which features were more and less effective? Was the program equally effective in all parts of the organization? Since lines of intended action may fail to be activated or, if activated, fail to be accepted or, if accepted, fail to have the desired effect, what are the conditions and causes that explain such results? Are they due to the change agent, members of the organization, incompatible elements in the program, or the theory underlying the program itself? Since programs sometimes never get started or, once started, are eventually discontinued, are there some initial conditions upon which the success of the program rests? Are there some ending conditions that influence its continuity? Taking steps, at the start of an evaluation, to gather the data needed to answer these questions enables the assessor to interpret the findings and to adjudge their generalizability as well as to formulate guidelines and cautions for the conduct of future change efforts.

The previous chapters have described various ways to assemble information that can later be employed in an interpretive fashion to deal with such basic questions. All are pertinent to the assessment of the process and progress of a change program. This chapter treats, by example, some of the additional steps that can be taken to help understand a change program in a particular organization.

CONCEPTUALIZING CHANGE: PROCESS AND PROGRESS

Organization change programs of the sort described in this volume have some obvious features that are susceptible to observation and translation into data. First, they involve people or groups of people with an organization. Second, these persons are assisted by an external consultant or consulting team. Third, these persons introduce changes into the organization that have particular characteristics. Fourth, these changes have both intended and unintended effects. Thus, it is possible to classify such programs as to the people or groups involved, the way change agents behave, the characteristics of interventions, and the aspect of the organization that is changed—much as theorists have so classified other organizational change programs.[3-6] In addition, it is possible to discern events in a change program and order them into a rough time sequence. The many three-, four-, five-, six-, and seven-step models of planned change provide ample evidence.[7,8] The result is a phase classification and time-ordered description of a change program. More problematic is the analysis and interpretation of the interrelation of these persons and groups, consultants, and activities in a particular stage of the change and of the forces moving the program through these stages. That requires an assessment of the dynamics—the processes and progress—of the change program.

There are many ways to model the processes of change. For example, Lewin's portrayal of driving and restraining forces or Watson's model of resistance to change can be used to highlight the dynamics of equilibria in an organization, while Schein's model of the mechanisms of change can be used to analyze ways these forces are "unfrozen" in the creation of change.[9–11] There are also many models of the progress of change. Lewin's model of unfreezing, change, and refreezing can be used to highlight the dynamics of progression in a change program, as can various models of innovation search and initiation.[12,13]

These and other models of the process and progress of change programs were used by assessors in their analysis and interpretation of change efforts evaluated in the Michigan program. This chapter illustrates some of these conceptualizations as they were developed in quality of work life experiments, such as those described earlier in this volume. The concepts and measurement methods, however, may well be more broadly applicable. In these experiments, we distinguish several program phases that present somewhat different tasks for the researcher who is interested in understanding the processes and outcomes that are involved.

The initial stage consists of the participants reaching agreement and commitment to *start-up* the program and form a representative committee. In quality of work life programs, this involves key union and management personnel in negotiations with each other—sometimes with a parent company and international union—and with others in the organization and union to establish the scope and boundaries of the project and to form a joint union–management committee. Once the committee is formed, it then identifies broad goals and principles for the change program and develops its working charter. During this start-up period a consultant or consultants are hired, and they begin working with the committee. Researchers are forming relationships with the committee and other interests in the organization, negotiating roles, and beginning their observations. They are also formulating agreements that provide for the protection of the participants' and researchers' rights in accordance with ethical standards governing organization research.[14]

This stage is followed by a period of diagnosis, problem identification, and planning in the committee, culminating in the *implementation* of specific interventions that have been agreed upon into the organization. Here, the researchers assess the work of the committee and consultants and identify the interventions that are being introduced into the organization. As Keidel illustrates, the range can be substantial, including changes having to do with administration, training, job design, work rules, and so on.[15] Interventions we have observed include such changes as well as those in management practices, pay and information systems, organization structures, basic technology, and the design of new plants and facilities.

These interventions, however, may be more or less effectively introduced. Similarly, they may be more or less enthusiastically received by experimental or "pilot" units in an organization. The next stage of the change program, therefore, involves the *adoption* of the program, or a specific intervention, by work units. Here the researchers assess the characteristics of the program or intervention, the readiness of work units to adopt and the potential adopter's attitudes toward the program, and environmental factors, such as time pressures and resource limitations, that may influence their receptivity and capacities to adopt. The actual assessment of the degree of adoption is equivalent to laboratory tests to determine whether a treatment "takes."[16] In the field, this is a measure of program activation, and it serves the important function of insuring against the negative appraisal of "nonevents"—interventions that were not fully carried out. Without such an assessment, it is possible to draw false conclusions about the effectiveness of a particular intervention or the model of change that underlies it.

Once adopted, it is expected that interventions will induce changes toward the achievement of desired goals or states, and that progress toward such states will be signaled by the achievement of *intermediate goals*. To assess such goal attainment, researchers operationalize a model of the internal processes of the organization that might link the intervention with its intended goals.[17] Then, these intervening variables are assessed to measure intermediate goal attainment. For example, some interventions, such as job enrichment, are directed toward the work environment and should have a measurable impact on job characteristics. Others, such as team building, are directed toward work relationships and should have a measurable impact on cooperation. Both should eventually improve the effectiveness of the organization and the quality of work life of its members. But tracing these sequential changes tests the theory behind the interventions and helps to determine how and why they succeeded or failed in inducing *changes* in the work environment and in organization members' attitudes and behaviors.

A final and distinguishable phase in change programs is that of making the successful and desirable interventions permanent and widely used. Here, an analysis of the *institutionalization* and *diffusion* of the program or specific interventions is needed. The former focuses on the durability of the program or intervention, while the latter focuses on the effectiveness of procedures undertaken to generalize it to other parts of the organization or to other organizations. As Walton has shown, many successful pilot programs have had little impact when management, unions, or consultants have been unable to effect their continuation and diffusion.[18] To assess institutionalization and diffusion, the researchers must look at the work of the committee and consultants, the impact of environmental factors, and the characteristics of units to which the program might be diffused.

As this progression suggests, merely introducing change into an organization does not automatically lead to changes in its effectiveness or in its quality of working life. A program may fail because of inadequate implementation or adoption; or it may fail because, despite effective introduction, the change does not lead to anticipated or desired outcomes.[19] The implication for a change program is clear: A valid model of change, an appropriate intervention, and an effective implementation and enthusiastic adoption are essential if successful results are to be achieved. The implication for evaluation is equally clear: Successful evaluation requires an assessment of both the theory and technology embedded in the intervention and its degree of "take" in the organization.

The following illustrations of concepts and approaches used in assessing the processes and progress of change programs treat, successively, assessments of characteristics of unions and management that influence program start-up, of factors influencing program implementation, of factors affecting the selective adoption of an intervention by units in an organization, of mid-program assessment of goal attainment, of the outcomes of distinct interventions, and of factors influencing program institutionalization and diffusion.

PROGRAM START-UP

Lawler and Drexler[20] have identified, by comparative analysis of several cases, a field of social forces favorable and unfavorable to the start-up of experimental programs involving union and management cooperation (see preceding chapter, page 391). Among the factors they cite are characteristics of each party, such as their dominant goals and internal political strains, the relationship between the parties, including their respective roles and bargaining history, and the start-up itself, including the formation of the joint committee and development of mutual commitment to the program. The key to effective start-ups, they contend, lies in reducing forces impeding cooperation (e.g., reducing threats) rather than increasing favorable forces (e.g., introducing incentives).

This conceptualization of program start-up lends itself to systematic appraisal through a "force-field" analysis. By this method, developed from Lewin's modeling of driving and restraining forces, the relative strength of forces favoring and opposing the initiation of a cooperative program can be assessed through informed judgment and confidential interviewing with union and management personnel. Then, as negotiations are undertaken between union and management, it can be ascertained whether steps were taken that lessened restraining forces or increased those favorable to cooperation.

Table 14-1 presents a summary of the dominant forces in a particular case. In the assessor's opinion, there were clear differences in readiness between top managers and supervisors, and in goals between management and the union. In addition, the pressure to "make something happen quickly" was adjudged to be both a bane and a boon for the program at the start-up point. This highlights points of scrutiny for the assessor, as steps are taken to reduce these opposing forces or to enhance the favorable ones. Does the labor–management shelter agreement identify compatible goals and provide a protective escape clause for the parties? Are seminars conducted for labor and management personnel to increase their knowledge about cooperative ventures and to make aims less ambiguous or more realistic? Does the joint committee include "new faces"? Does it develop a norm of consensus decision making? Are consultants carefully screened? Is provision made for training "in-house" facilitators? Answering such questions through an analysis of documents, through observations, and through interviews enables the assessor to evaluate the start-up process.

Using this general approach, though not specific instruments or observation guides, Drexler and Lawler found that third parties working with labor and management in an industrial plant significantly reduced the forces opposing a collaborative program.[21] These parties reaffirmed the status of collective-bargaining agreements, specified common goals, exposed the union and management personnel to successful programs in

Table 14-1   Forces Favoring and Opposing a Joint Union–Management Program

Forces Favoring L-M Cooperation	Forces Against L-M Cooperation
Knowledge and commitment of top union and management officials	Lack of knowledge in mid and bottom of management; "we vs. they" orientation
Interest in noneconomic benefits for employees	Conflicting goals: input versus democracy
Relatively harmonious labor–management relations history	Need to "shore up" union
Readiness to collaborate to improve company performance and job security	Concerns over profit sharing; U–M contract limitations
History of consultative management at top	Lack of models, experience, example for U–M Collaboration
Readiness to hire outside consultants	Absence of internal resources for training and consultation
	Fears of supervisors and stewards of losing power
Need for something to happen	Need for something to happen

other sites, established consensus decision making in the joint commit-tee, included an escape clause for each party in shelter agreements, and established mutual ownership of the program. All of this made the coop-erative venture, in Drexler's and Lawler's view, "less threatening, more understandable, and more practical."

Later, the consultants concentrated on cultivating cooperation be-tween the parties and in developing mutual working relationships on the joint committee, thereby increasing forces favorable to the success of the start-up. Once the consulting team was selected and the project was un-derway, however, management and the union could not agree on the relative emphasis to be given to economic and noneconomic objectives, and each began to see the consultants as favoring the interests of the other party. In the end, internal politics and power struggles within management and within the union led to the program's premature termi-nation. In essence, it did not "fail" since it never proceeded beyond start-up. Because Lawler and Drexler were present from the beginning and regularly observed the start-up process, however, they were able to trace the program's demise to the faulty start-up phase rather than to the theory underlying the program or its collaborative model. This kind of observation is essential, then, to drawing valid conclusions about the effects of a change program.

ASSESSING IMPLEMENTATION

The implementation of a change program follows the diagnosis of prob-lems and formulation of action plans. In union–management programs, as in most change efforts, the quality of the diagnosis and planning de-pends upon the effectiveness of the parties in gathering complete and valid information, fully digesting and openly evaluating its implications, and identifying appropriate and feasible solutions. A committee domi-nated by one party or another may be unable to gather unbiased data or to agree upon solutions to problems. Implementation, in turn, depends upon communicating ideas to experimental units and involving them in the activation of specific interventions. Even a harmonious committee may have difficulty implementing plans if it lacks acceptance and influ-ence in the organization.[22] The successful implementation of a change program also depends upon the quality of technical advice and facilita-tion offered by consultants, the clarity and desirability of the interven-tions, and the time and resources available and expended in the imple-mentation itself.[23]

At one experimental site, the ISR assessment team developed ques-tionnaire measures to assess organization members' views of the working committee, the consultants, and the overall change program (see Appen-dix 14-1). The organization, an automotive supplier plant, had started a quality of work life program three years prior to this measurement. The

Table 14-2   Questionnaire Indexes Used to Assess Member Views of the Implementation of a Change Program in an Auto Parts Supply Firm

Working Committee

1. *Working committee domination.*   A three-item index ($\alpha = .64$)[a] measuring the extent to which the working committee is dominated by management, the union, or the consultants. Sample item: "The working committee is dominated by management."

2. *Working committee effectiveness.*   A mean of three indexes: working processes, influence in the organization, and personal contact with employees. Working processes ($\alpha = .81$) was measured by four items, e.g., "The working committee is doing a good job"; personal contact ($\alpha = .71$) by two items, e.g., "I have a say in the decisions the working committee makes." Influence was a single item: "How much influence does the working committee have within the plant?" The reliability of the working-committee effectiveness index was .60.

3. *Working committee participation.*   A Guttman scale measuring employees' participation in the work committee. A score of 4 meant the respondent was currently a member of the committee; 3 indicated the respondent had been a member; 2, that the respondent had attended a working-committee meeting; 1, that the respondent had not participated in the committee in any way.

Project Staff

1. *Project staff effectiveness.*   A mean of two indexes: working processes and helpfulness to the employees. Working processes ($\alpha = .89$) was measured by four items, e.g., "The project staff listens to the employees' point of view"; helpfulness ($\alpha = .86$) by two items, e.g., "The project staff helps core groups with problems." The reliability of the project staff of effectiveness index was .83.

2. *Project staff role problems.*   A two-item index ($\alpha = .62$) measuring respondents' reactions to the staff role. Sample item: "The project staff pushes too hard for changes around here."

Work Improvement Program

1. *Clarity of the program.*   A two-item index ($\alpha = .53$) measuring the respondents' understanding of changes introduced by the program. Sample item: "I don't know what changes the work improvement program has made in the plant."

2. *Fairness of the program.*   A two-item index ($\alpha = .52$) measuring the fairness of the program. Sample item: "The work improvement program has been beneficial to only a few employees."

3. *Desirability of the program.*   A four-item index ($\alpha = .82$) measuring overall reactions to the program. Sample item: "The work improvement program has made a lot of good changes."

4. *Program overload.*   A two-item index ($\alpha = .53$) measuring the overload caused by the program. Sample item: "There are too many changes going on around here."

5. *Overall impact.*   A four-item index ($\alpha = .82$) measuring the impact of the program on such factors as trust and communication in the organization. Sample item: "The work improvement program has increased the amount of trust between employees and the company."

---

[a] α = coefficient alpha measure of reliability.

Table 14-3 Correlations between Measures of Working Committee and Staff Characteristics with Member Appraisals of a Change Program ($N = 190$)

Measure	Working Committee Dominance	Working Committee Effectiveness	Working Committee Participation	Project Staff Effectiveness	Project Staff Role Problems
Clarity of the program	-.42**	.29**	.21**	.22**	-.42**
Fairness of the program	-.28**	.41**	.07	.39**	-.36**
Desirability of the program	-.16	.52**	.14	.59**	-.33**
Program overload	.36**	-.32**	-.17*	-.40**	.47**
Overall program impact	-.23**	.53**	.19*	.61**	-.31**

* $p < .05$; ** $p < .01$.

program in the plant was directed by a committee composed of equal numbers of management and union members, and it was guided by a project staff of three consultants, two of whom worked daily in the plant and took up residence of the community.

Table 14-2 lists the indexes used and their reliability (coefficient alpha). Measures of the working committee included the respondents' appraisal of the committee's partisan domination and the committee's effectiveness. Measures of the project staff tapped the respondents' assessment of their effectiveness, including their working processes and helpfulness, and the problems engendered by the staff's role in the organization. Measures of the work-improvement program reflected its clarity to employees, its fairness, its desirability, the overload it caused, and its overall impact on trust and communication in the organization.

Table 14-3 reports the correlations between measures of characteristics of the work committee and project staff with measures assessing the implementation of the work-improvement program. It shows that the effectiveness of the committee and the consultants was positively related to appraisals of the fairness, clarity, and desirability of the change program and of its overall impact on trust and communication in the organization. Respondents who felt the committee to be dominated by labor, management, or the consultants or who saw the consultant's role as unnecessary and burdensome gave the program a negative appraisal. Respondent's direct participation in the working committee was only slightly related to its positive assessment. While there is a good amount of "halo" in these correlations, the results proved helpful, when used with other information sources, in forming conclusions about the process of change at this site. For example, Table 14-3 shows that characteristics of the project staff were as influential as characteristics of the committee itself in inducing supportive feelings and views—a finding that suggests consultants play important roles in introducing change when working with conflicting interests in an organization. Surprisingly, actual participation on the working committee was unrelated to ratings of the overall change program. Such analyses, when coupled with observation, can provide researchers with a clearer understanding of the influence of a working committee and consultants on program implementation.

CONDITIONS FOR TRIAL AND SUSTAINED ADOPTION OF CHANGES

In some situations, an organizational change program may involve the implementation of certain activities that depend for their adoption upon personal and environmental factors that are unique to each part of the organization. That is, the implementation is not, and perhaps cannot be, imposed on work units but is voluntary to some degree. Accordingly, one can expect that there will be some organizational units that reject the proposed intervention, while others give it a perfunctory try; still others will adopt the intervention and sustain it over some time.

Figure 14-1 presents a model of the key factors in the adoption of an innovation by work units. A first factor is the unit's need for change. Of relevance are its past and present performances and the presence of a "performance gap" between actual and desired levels. The unit leader's accountability for and dissatisfaction with performance is also a contributor to the need for change. The second factor is the unit's readiness for change. At issue here are the climate and working processes in the unit and their "fit" with the demands of the innovation. The third factor is the unit leaders' and staffs' views of the innovation. They will ask of a project change: What are our priority problems and is the proposed change likely to ameliorate them? What are the risks of not cooperating in a company-wide program? Do we have the resources of time, energy, and competence to carry out the activity? Is the proposed activity compatible with our values and purposes? The questions are many, but all are appraised as adoption decisions are made.[24]

The next factor is the unit's trial adoption of the innovation. Of relevance here are the unit's ability to "try" the project without committing itself to an irreversible course of action, the constraints facing the unit in early months of change, and the support given the undertaking itself. The final factor is the sustained adoption of the innovation as is reflected in its continued use, its ongoing support—in time and energy—by unit leaders and members, and its flexible adaptation to changing circumstances.

Each of these microstages in the implementation and adoption process is amenable to assessment through observation and survey measurement. At one research site, data were collected that showed there was great variation among work units in adoption of the proposed changes. Early on, efforts were made to gather systematic data on the reasons for this variation. The proposed new activity involved the adoption and use of an information feedback system by branches of a metropolitan bank.[25]

The feedback system itself was designed with a task force of bank employees from all levels for implementation in the branches. Managers and supervisors in the branches were expected to hold regular feedback meetings with their staffs to review the measures of branch performance and work attitudes, participatively solve problems, and set future goals. Table 14-4 lists the measures of degree of adoption and the measures of predictors of adoption gathered from branch leaders and personnel. The measures of adoption, first taken six months after implementation, and again, one year after implementation, asked branch employees to report the number of feedback meetings held in the branch that month and the quality of the meetings, including the interest shown in the program by branch leaders and their use of the data to solve problems participatively

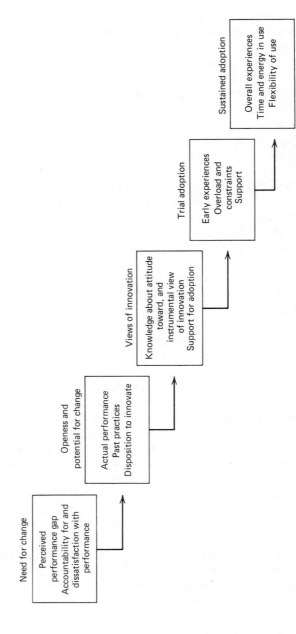

Figure 14-1 Stages in process of implementation and adoption of innovations.

Table 14-4   Measures of Program Adoption and Predictors of Adoption

Measures of Adoption

1. *Number of meetings.*   A three-item index ($r = .66$)[a] measuring the number of feedback meetings held in a branch in a given month. Sample item: "How many meetings are held each month for working with the feedback?"

2. *Quality of meetings.*   An eight-item index ($r = .90$) measuring the respondent's feelings that branch leaders were interested in the feedback system and used it for participative problem solving and goal setting. Sample item: "Employees are encouraged to participate in the discussion during feedback meetings."

Predictors of Adoption

1. *Perception of problem.*   Two separate two-item indexes measuring the *leaders'* ($r = .73$) and the *staffs'* ($r = .73$) appraisal of cooperation and teller effectiveness. Sample item: "In general, how would you rate cooperation among employees in this branch?"

2. *Leader's need for change.*   A single measure appraising the leaders' need for change; asked during interview: "Did you feel some changes needed to be made in the branch?" Scored positively when needed changes were consistent with changes offered by feedback system.

3. *Attitudes toward program.*   Two separate indexes: a six-item index measuring the *leaders'* ($r = .77$), and a three-item index measuring the *staffs'* ($r = .82$) attitude toward the feedback system. Sample item: "I looked forward to receiving the first few feedback reports."

4. *Expectations of benefits.*   Two separate indexes: a three-item index measuring the *leaders'* ($r = .62$), and a two-item index measuring the *staffs'* ($r = .89$) expectations of benefits from the feedback system. Sample item: "I thought the feedback system would help the branch work more effectively."

5. *Leader's knowledge of the program.*   A three-item index ($r = .60$) measuring the leaders' familiarity with the feedback system and their role in using it. Sample item: "I was unsure how I could most effectively use the feedback report."

6. *Leader's recognition of the program.*   A two-item index ($r = .62$) measuring the leaders' perception of the uniqueness of the program. Sample item: "It was just another project from Branch Administration."

7. *Leader's time pressures.*   A two-item index ($r = .62$) measuring time pressures facing branch leaders. Sample item: "I never seem to have enough time to get things done."

8. *Leader's problems in adoption.*   A two-item index ($r = .76$) measuring leaders' problems in adopting the feedback system. Sample item: "Sometimes I feel pressured into using the system."

9. *Leader's first experiences.*   A semantic differential scale measuring leader's reactions to his/her first use of the program ($r = .66$). A sample item asked leaders to rate the first reactions as *encouraged—discouraged.*

10. *Leader's time and energy given to the program.*   A four-item index ($r = .79$) measuring leaders' time and energy given to using the feedback system. Sample item: "How much time and effort did you put into planning for feedback meeting?"

---

[a] $r =$ Spearman-Brown corrections to Kuder-Richardson reliability estimates.

and to set goals. The predictors of adoption assessed the leaders' and staff members' perceptions of problems in the branches at the start of the program, their attitudes about the feedback system, and the benefits they anticipated from its use. Leaders were interviewed regarding their need to change, their knowledge of the philosophy and goals behind the intervention, and their recognition of the feedback system as not "just another program in the bank." Once they adopted the system, leaders were asked to report on time pressures and problems they encountered that hampered its use. They were also asked to appraise their first experiences in feedback meetings and the time and energy they devoted to the program.

Table 14-5 reports the correlations of these predictors with the trial (6 months) and sustained (12 months) adoption of the feedback system in

Table 14-5   Correlations between Measures of Program Adoption and Predictors of Adoption ($N = 26$ branches)

	Trial Adoption		Sustained Adoption	
Measure	Number of Meetings	Quality of Meetings	Number of Meetings	Quality of Meetings
Leaders' perception of problems	.52**	.22	.48**	.33*
Staffs' perception of problems	.43**	.14	.37*	.25
Leaders' need for change	.25	.00	.11	.24
Leaders' attitudes toward program	.20	−.13	.09	.23
Staffs' attitudes toward program	.62**	.31*	.52**	.50**
Leaders' expectation of benefits	.46**	.07	.28	.27
Staffs' expectation of benefits	.62**	.00	.60**	.40*
Leaders' knowledge of program	.11	.00	.13	.30
Leaders' recognition of program	.10	−.01	−.07	.23
Leaders' time pressures	−.31	−.14	−.24	−.26
Leaders' problems in adoption	−.38*	−.49**	−.40*	−.54**
Leaders' first experiences	.36*	−.09	.25	.28
Leaders' time and energy given to program	.48**	−.02	.46**	.44*

* $p < .05$; ** $p < .01$

the branches. Both the leaders' and staff members' perceptions of problems in their branches and their expectations of benefits from the program correlated positively with the number of meetings held in the branches. Staff attitudes toward and expectations for the feedback system correlated positively with the number and quality of meetings held, particularly in the second measurement. The leaders' reports of time pressures and problems in adoption correlated negatively with the quality and number of meetings. One leader commented upon the time pressures:

> The first priority is that we've got to be able to deal with the customer that's at the door . . . give them the service they're paying for . . . it was hard to find the time to take another hour on a Thursday evening, before a 12-hour Friday, and talk about a great new project we were going to learn something from.

Another reported a notable, but unavoidable, problem in the use of the system: "All of a sudden it seemed to kind of take the management of the branch a little bit out of our hands!"

In branches where the program was successfully adopted and sustained, teller performance improved, turnover decreased, and satisfaction and cooperation increased relative to a control group of branches. By contrast, in branches where the feedback system was not adopted, morale plummeted, turnover increased, and teller performance was unchanged.

Although such quantitative data obtained from the questionnaire were useful in understanding the dynamics of the adoption or nonadoption of the innovation in this case, their main utility in analysis and interpretation comes from their capacity to confirm or disconfirm ideas that were tentatively raised by collateral assessment information. At this site, for example, the researchers regularly visited branches to observe feedback meetings and interview key personnel. In addition, regular visits were scheduled with branch administration to assess the overall climate and conditions of work in the bank. These interviews and observations suggested that factors external to the implementation also influenced adoption of the innovation. For example, the bank's appraisal and reward system was oriented almost solely to branch profitability. By agreement, the feedback data were not reported to central branch administration, and performance gains not reflected in profitability could not be used in evaluations. Thus, as conditions at the site suggest and the findings in the table support, those managers in already profitable units did not adopt the change except in those instances where the program had evident intrinsic appeal to them and to their staff members. This finding highlights the importance in assessment of not only "tracking" implementation and adoption but also conditions in the larger organizations that may be affecting them.

ASSESSING INTERMEDIATE GOAL ATTAINMENT

If one is to reach a confirmation or disconfirmation of some theory about organizational functioning, it is necessary to examine cases in which the theory has been given a fair test. A "fair" test is, at minimum, one in which the program has been activated to the point where the theoretical conditions necessary for assessing its action implications are achieved. It is in this sense that one can speak of intermediate goals in an organizational change program—the goals of introducing the desired conditions— quite apart from the longer-range outcomes that are expected to flow from these desired experimental or demonstration conditions.

An illustration is provided from still another research site in which a team of organizational consultants set out to establish in a newly forming organization the properties of a "participative" system. The program assessors faced the usual problem of discerning a clear and concise set of intermediate program goals. Conferences with the consultants and the program participants, however, led to agreement on a list of 20 criteria that, if satisfied, would constitute evidence of a successful introduction of "participation."[26]

Intermediate goal attainment was assessed, in part, by a questionnaire survey administered to all nonmanagement members of the organization about nine months after the goals had been agreed upon and formalized. Other methods of assessment were used as well, but only the questionnaire results will be discussed here.

Figure 14-2 shows the survey results with respect to the 20 implementation criteria. In the questionnaire, the criteria were stated and defined, and the respondents indicated the extent to which these objectives had been achieved. The results are shown separately for each of two main units of the organization—production and quality assurance—as well as for the whole of the organization. The figure shows that, in general, the intermediate objectives were considered to be achieved only "moderately," that is, halfway between "not at all" and "to a very great extent." Except for certain "feedback" and "periodic review" items, the quality assurance department shows the greater goal attainment, a finding that confirmed the observers' reports that the initial and continuing acceptance of the program objectives was greater there.

The impact of the intervention on the achievement of participative management goals was assessed directly by questions to respondents regarding the extent to which the program activities (meetings, consultations, individual counseling, role-model demonstrations) contributed to the achievement of stated goals. Figure 14-3 indicates that the program made only a slight positive contribution to the specific goals of participation by employees. The contribution was greater in the quality assurance department than in the production department.

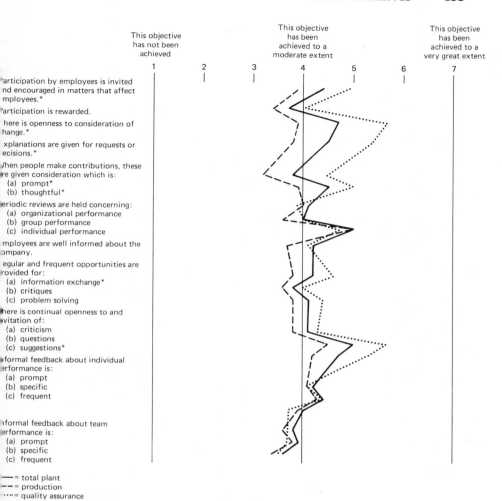

Figure 14-2   Attainment of goals related to participation.

Measures of goal attainment and program contribution, however, assess only the intended effects of the program. Of equal interest are the unintended consequences. In this site, as an example, the consultants had not prepared the organization sufficiently for the adoption of participation. Consequently, in the first months, countless hours were wasted making group decisions on technical matters, while legitimate sources of expertise were ignored in the spirit of full participation. The evaluators attributed this to the failure of the interventionists to introduce a contingency approach to decision making in the organization that specified when participative decisions were most appropriate.[27,28] In addition, the

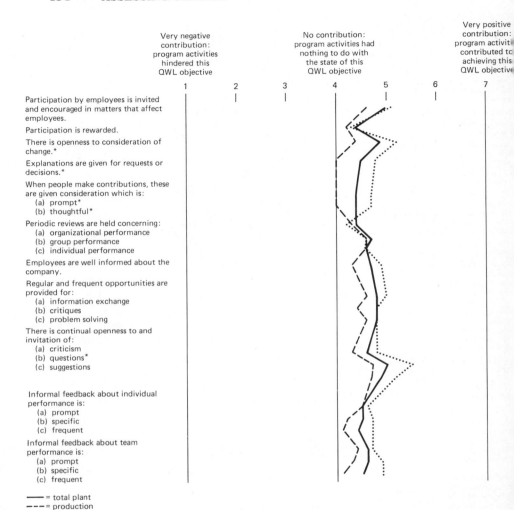

Figure 14-3 *Program contribution to the achievement of participative management goals.*

evaluators found that despite the partial achievement of participative management goals, employees reported that no increase occurred in personal influence, influence with their superiors, or influence over work decisions between the start and termination of the program. Measures of general work satisfaction and involvement in the organization actually declined. The evaluators attributed this to the shift from participative to consultative management in the organization over the course of the project and the accompanying feelings of guilt by leaders and betrayal by plant employees. They noted, moreover, that the technology in the plant and the time pressures facing employees during the first production runs both made the general use of participative decision making difficult.

With this assessment data, one can, with some confidence, conclude that the "participative" system of management was not, in this instance, given a trial at all—much less a "fair" trial. In the data shown, and in collateral information, it seems clear that because the consultants and firm members failed to activate the program fully, the theory of participation was not tested. However, this study does show how the failure to reach intermediate goals is linked with overall process failure.

EVALUATING SPECIFIC INTERVENTIONS AND THEIR EFFECTS

When an organizational change program is effectively implemented and reaches its objectives, general changes are expected in the work environment, in attitudes and behaviors, and, ultimately, in advantageous individual and organizational outcomes. Specific interventions in the program, however, are often expected to produce specific effects. A program for job enrichment should have a measurable impact on job attributes; a program of team building should have a measurable impact on autonomy and decision making in teams, and so forth. Tracing these expected effects tests the theory behind these change-program components and helps to determine why they succeeded or failed.

The assessment of specific expected outcomes from specific action components, as is suggested here, is complementary to the more general program evaluation. The advantage of the specific goal assessment is that it helps to determine which aspects of the program were or were not effectively implemented and adopted. As a result, the assessor can, in effect, test multiple theories and approaches to change within one setting. In this way, the overall program assessment approaches the condition of a "goal-free" evaluation.[29]

There are multiple approaches to assessment of specific interventions. The assessor can observe specific activities, obtain ratings of goal attainment, or ask employees to rate multiple interventions. In the automative supply plant mentioned previously, three specific interventions were distinguished. One was a "paid personal time" program in which employees, upon achieving early their production standard for a day, could earn paid personal time and leave the plant or remain and earn a performance bonus. The measures developed to assess the program were as follows: (1) *paid personal time*—whether or not an employee actually earned personal time; (2) *amount of paid time*—the minutes actually earned by a participating employee; and (3) *paid time evaluation*—a three-item scale ($\alpha = .66$) measuring employees' evaluation of the paid personal time program. The second intervention was an educational program consisting of voluntary courses in job skills, reading, language, and arts and crafts that was requested by, taught by, and attended by employees. The measures of this intervention were the following: (1) *educational attendance*—whether or not an employee attended a course; (2) *educational involvement*—whether or not an employee prepared or helped initiate a class or served on an education committee in the plant; and (3) *educational evaluation*—an index of two scales (α = .65) asking employees whether educational and training opportunities were better, the same, or worse than they were two years ago. The third intervention was the formation of "core groups", that is, voluntary small problem-solving groups in the plant, to analyze working conditions and introduce feasible changes of their own choosing. The measure of *core group membership* asked employees if they were currently or had ever been a member of a core group.

Table 14-6 reports correlations between measures of these specific interventions and participants' ratings of the overall change program and its impact. It shows, for example, that employees who participated in the paid personal time program saw the overall program as more fair, and that the more time off they earned, the more desirable they rated the program. Overall evaluations of the paid-time intervention were positively related to ratings of the overall change program. Interestingly, the table shows that neither attendance nor involvement in the education program was associated with a positive assessment of the overall program. It may have been that those attendees saw the educational effort as a less central feature of the overall program. Finally, the table shows that participation in a core group gave group members a clearer view of the overall program's goals.

Table 14-6 also shows some striking relationships between paid-time participation and ratings of program impact. It shows that those who participated in the paid-time activities felt the program enhanced their relations with their supervisors and the meaning of their work, but that it also decreased their job safety and increased their needs for health services. Collateral data on minor accidents and dispensary visits as well as self-reported data on incidents of back pain, headaches, and other somatic complaints experienced at work confirmed this trend. Such data suggest that employees were "pushing" themselves to produce more—making their work more challenging and bringing them closer to their supervisors but at some cost to their well-being.[30]

Other results in the table show there was a positive relationship between ratings of the paid-time program and of the overall program's impact. Given the lesser relationship between participation in the paid-time activities and program impact, this may be evidence of a "halo" effect around the program in the organization. Again, the table shows no relationship between participation in the educational program and rat-

Table 14-6 Correlations at $T2$ between the Major Interventions and the Impact of the Work Improvement Program

Ratings	Paid Personal Time	Amount of Paid Time	Paid Time Evaluation	Education Attendance	Education Involvement	Core Group Membership
Overall program						
1. Clarity of change	-.04	.02	.15*	.06	.11	.24**
2. Fairness of change	.16*	.02	.42**	.07	.07	.02
3. Desirability of change	.11	.21*	.59**	.14	.13	-.01
4. Negative reactions to change	.02	-.04	-.39**	-.07	-.10	-.12
5. Impact on climate	-.06	.07	.41**	.09	.11	.04
Program impact						
6. Impact on labor–management relations	.04	.17	.36**	.03	.05	-.09
7. Impact on management	-.02	.06	.35**	.12	.17*	.05
8. Impact on pay	-.01	-.01	.23**	.09	-.03	-.11
9. Impact on meaning of work	.19**	.27**	.55**	.08	.18*	-.06
10. Impact on meaning of life	.16*	.17	.46**	.14	.12	-.07
11. Impact on personal growth	.05	.24*	.32**	.02	.14	-.09
12. Impact on jobs	-.06	.04	.35**	.03	-.10	-.03
13. Impact on job security	-.07	.08	.26**	.12	-.09	-.11
14. Impact on safety	-.16*	.10	.15*	.04	.02	-.11
15. Impact on health services	-.20**	.14	.21**	-.07	-.04	-.14
16. Impact on participation	-.10	.20	.24*	.04	.11	.02
17. Impact on decision-making process	-.05	.02	.34**	.07	-.00	.11
18. Impact on supervisory relations	.19**	.27**	.55**	.08	.18*	-.06

$* p < .05; ** p < .01$

ings of the overall program's impact. Finally, no strong relationships are found between participation in core groups and ratings of program impact. On the surface, this seems counterintuitive since participation in problem-solving groups would be expected to increase ratings of program impact. Moreover, it casts the core group's effectiveness into doubt. Yet a closer look at collateral data showed that active core groups introduced substantive changes in their work areas and that both core-group members and work mates gave the program high impact ratings. By contrast, inactive core groups recorded few changes and gave the program lesser ratings. Thus, participation in active core groups, but not in an inactive core group, was associated with favorable ratings of program impact.

This approach to distinguishing specific interventions in an overall change program is but one means for evaluating their impact. At other sites, assessors tracked distinct interventions and their results through observation, interviewing, and examination of memoranda and performance records. Whatever means were chosen, the necessity of assessing the impact of distinct interventions was recognized in all program evaluations.

INSTITUTIONALIZATION AND DIFFUSION

Institutionalization of an experimental change program refers to the continuing reliance on the processes of making changes and to the durability of the beneficial effects achieved. Its continuity and durability depend, in large part, upon sustained support by management and the union, generally in the face of changing economic and social conditions, and upon legitimation by members of the organization at all levels.[31] At some point, the pilot program can mature into nonexperimental standard operating procedures. Diffusion refers to its spread throughout an organization.

In his appraisal of one experimental site, Goodman found that a regression occurred after early successes in the pilot units that first undertook the change program, and he found some resistance to the diffusion of the program to the rest of the organization.[32] Based upon observations and interview findings, Goodman attributed the lack of institutionalization to the absence of continuing support by all parties and to the failure to sustain in practice the alternative organizational structure developed in the program. Among the many factors contributing to the lack of diffusion, he found as significant the continuing mistrust by employees of management's intentions, the paucity of opinion leaders in employees' groups who could crystalize support for the program, and the uncertainty as to whether general principles or specific interventions would be diffused.

Guided by this theoretical orientation and system of observation, Macy undertook an analysis of factors that were favorable and unfavorable to the institutionalization and diffusion of programs at two quality of work life sites and arrayed them into a force field.[33] In one site, a service organization, the program is a regular fixture and is currently being diffused to other parts of the organization. In the other site, a factory, the program has been partly institutionalized, but its effects on management and employees seem to be waning. Nonetheless, the principles are being diffused to other units in the organization and to affiliated firms.

Table 14-7 lists some of the favorable and unfavorable forces at each

Table 14-7   A Comparative Analysis of Forces Favorable and Unfavorable to Institutionalization and Diffusion of Change Programs

Service Organization			Industrial Organization	
Favorable	Unfavorable		Favorable	Unfavorable
+		Institutionalization and sustained change at pilot site	+	−
+		Diffusion to other parts of the organization	+	
+	−	Goal attainment and positive results	+	−
+		Shared economic and noneconomic benefits	+	−
+	−	Top management commitment to project	+	
+		Union leadership commitment to project	+	
	−	Middle-management commitment to project		−
+		Rank-and-file union commitment to project	+	
+		Consultants' technical proficiency		−
	−	Consultants' relationship with participants	+	
+	−	Joint committees' effectiveness		−
+		Resources available for diffusion		−
	−	Transfer of relevant skills		−
+		Evaluation of the program by joint committee		−
	−	Bureaucratic barriers to diffusion	+	
	−	Loss of key opinion leaders and project personnel		−

site. In the service organization, the goals have not yet been fully realized, but limited benefits have been broadly shared with all personnel. In the industrial firm, significant goals have been achieved, and noneconomic benefits have been widely shared among employees. Top management, the union, and the hourly personnel in the industrial firm are strongly committed to the program, while commitment of top management in the service organization is not universal. Middle-management members in both sites resist the program; they have neither been integrated into it, nor fully oriented in its philosophy, nor trained with the needed interpersonal skills. The consultants at both sites have been effective in helping the working committee to analyze problems and introduce solutions. At the industrial site, the consultants are more an integral part of the organization and, although lacking formal authority, they have greater empathy with their clients, have values more consistent with the program, and have greater credibility. The consultants at the service site have more technical proficiency, but they devote less time and energy to the program. The joint labor–management committee at the service site is better organized, however, and it seems more adept at problem solving and decision making. It also has more actively evaluated the program. The service organization has more resources available for diffusing the program, but also has more internal bureaucratic barriers to face. Both organizations have lost some key program personnel.

It is premature to speculate about the sustained effect of the programs in these organizations or about their successful diffusion. But it can be said that there is a need for an assessment of these factors early on in a change program, for they may speed or slow progress and ultimately determine the program's fate. Sources of information range from early agreements, as are reflected in start-up documents, to opinions of leaders in the company and union about the desirability of the change. A sharp eye, guided by theory, is essential to this kind of judgmental assessment. Macy's analysis attests to the feasibility of assessing these forces; time will tell of its validity.

CONCLUDING NOTES

In this chapter we have described an assortment of ways to search out an understanding of the processes, events, and conditions that influence organizational change programs. The suggested methods pertained to the start-up conditions of such programs, their implementation into and adoption by the organization, the distinct effects of different interventions, and the appraisal of the potential for the continuity and diffusion of successful efforts.

The function of such methods in an overall assessment can be illustrated by a photographic analogy. At one extreme is the motion picture camera. Camera in hand, the skilled master can become immersed in the drama, confident that the camera will record events. There can be no assurance, however, that the recording will be objective, for by focusing on certain aspects of the setting, the master risks becoming fixated on certain themes and interpretations. The film *Roshomon* is the model: Several engaged observers produced dramatically different and incompatible pictures of the same events, with no possibility for discerning whose imagery was more or less "valid." There is a role for such observation—that is, for the trained observer's as opposed to the camera's eye—in assessing change programs. On-site observation provides a rich and passionate portrayal of an organization and its people in change—how better to assess a program to increase spirit in an organization.[34] But also assessing a program with the many methods described here provides a check against bias, fixation, and prejudice.

At the other extreme of the analogy is the still photograph. Taken after dramatic events, it can show vividly the effects of a stinging rebuke, a lost love, a murder—or when replaced by measurement—of an organization that has changed. When compared with earlier measures, it can also capture the drama, however singular, of changing events. But unless complemented by the assessment methods described here, not enough is shown of the intervening processes to explain the differences, and further, the chosen subject matter, preselected, may not reflect the crucial differences themselves.

The process assessments and measures described here can be likened to a photographic essay. They add depth to the film (observation) and breadth to the snapshot (premeasurement and postmeasurement); like a "stop-action" film, they provide a way in which significant events may be examined, reviewed, and evaluated. Students of photography study films, photos, and stop-action segments. When assessors of organizations use observations, experiments, and process measurements, they examine a change program more thoughtfully and evaluate its effects more thoroughly.

REFERENCES

1. Deutscher, I. Toward avoiding the goal trap in evaluation research. In F. G. Caro (Ed.), *Readings in evaluation resources.* New York: Russell Sage, 1977.
2. Angrist, S. S. Evaluation research: possibilities and limitations. *Journal of Applied Behavioral Science,* 1975, **11,** 75–91.
3. Burke, W. W., & Schmidt, W. H. Primary target for change: The manager or the organization? In W. H. Schmidt (Ed.), *Organizational frontiers and human values.* Belmont, CA: Wadsworth, 1970.
4. Sashkin, M., Morris, W., & Horst, L. A comparison of social and organizational change models. *Psychological Review,* 1973, **80,** 510–526.
5. Hornstein, H. A., Bunker, B. B., Burke, W. W., Gindes, M., & Lewicki, R. J. (Eds.), *Social intervention.* New York: Free Press, 1971.

6. Friedlander, F., & Brown, L. D. Organization development. *Annual Review of Psychology,* 1974, **25,** 313–341.

7. Lippitt, R., Watson, J., & Westley, B. *The dynamics of planned change.* New York: Harcourt Brace Jovanovich, 1958.

8. Bennis, W. *Changing organizations.* New York: McGraw-Hill, 1966.

9. Lewin, K. *Resolving social conflict.* New York: Harper, 1948.

10. Watson, G. Resistance to change. *American Behavioral Scientist,* 1971, **14,** 746–766.

11. Schein, E. The mechanisms of change. In W. Bennis, E. Schein, F. Steele, & W. Berlew (Eds.), *Interpersonal dynamics.* Homewood, IL: Dorsey Press, 1964.

12. Lewin, K. *Field theory in social science.* New York: Harper & Row, 1951.

13. Zaltman, G., Duncan, R., & Holbek, J. *Innovations and organizations.* New York: Wiley-Interscience, 1973.

14. Mirvis, P. H., & Seashore, S. E. Being ethical in organizational research. *American Psychologist,* 1979, **34,** 766–780.

15. Keidel, R. W. Theme appreciation as a construct for organizational change. *Management Science,* 1981, **27,** 1261–1278.

16. Charters, W. E., & Jones, J. E. On the risk of appraising non-events in program evaluation. *Evaluation Researcher,* 1973, **11,** 5–7.

17. Schulberg, H. C., & Baker, F. Program evaluation models and the implementation of research findings. In F. G. Caro (Ed.), *Readings in evaluation research.* New York: Russell Sage Foundation, 1971.

18. Walton, R. E. The diffusion of new work structures: Explaining why success didn't take. *Organizational Dynamics,* Winter 1975, 3–21.

19. Weiss, C. H. *Evaluation research: Methods for assessing program effectiveness.* Englewood Cliffs: Prentice-Hall, 1972.

20. Lawler, E. E., & Drexler, J. A. Dynamics of establishing cooperative quality of worklife projects. *Monthly Labor Review,* March 1978, 23–28.

21. Drexler, J. A., & Lawler, E. E. III. A union–management cooperative project to improve the quality of work life. *Journal of Applied Behavioral Science,* 1977, **13,** 373–387.

22. Nadler, D. A. Consulting with labor and management: Some learning from quality of work life projects. In W. Burke (Ed.), *The cutting edge.* La Jolla, CA: University Associates, 1979.

23. Nadler, D. A., Hanlon, M., & Lawler, E. E. III. Factors influencing the success of labor–management quality of work life projects. *Journal of Occupational Behavior,* 1980, 1, 53–67.

24. Zaltman, G., & Duncan, R. *Strategies for planned change.* New York: Wiley-Interscience, 1977.

25. Nadler, D. A., Mirvis, P. H., & Cammann, C. The ongoing feedback system: Experimenting with a new managerial tool. *Organizational Dynamics,* 1976, **4,** 63–80.

26. Perkins, D. N. T., Nieva, V. F., & Lawler, E. E. III. *Managing creation: The challenge of building a new organization.* New York: Wiley-Interscience, 1983.

27. Tannenbaum, R., & Schmidt, W. H. How to choose a leadership pattern. *Harvard Business Review,* 1958, **36,** 162–180.

28. Vroom, V., & Yetton, P. *Leadership and decision making.* Pittsburgh: University of Pittsburgh Press, 1973.

29. Scriven, M. Pros and cons about goal free evaluation. *The Journal of Educational Evaluation,* 1972, **3,** 1–5.

30. Ledford, G., Macy, B. M., & Lawler, E. E. III. *The Bolivar quality of work experiment.* Wiley-Interscience, forthcoming.

31. Seashore, S. E., & Bowers, D. G. Durability of organizational change. *American Psychologist,* 1970, **25,** 227–233.

32. Goodman, P. *Assessing organizational change: The Rushton mine experiment.* New York: Wiley-Interscience, forthcoming.

33. Macy, B. A. *Forces favoring and opposing organizational change: Two case studies.* Paper presented at the American Psychological Association annual convention, Toronto, Canada, 1978.

34. Duckles, M. M., Duckles, R., & Maccoby, M. The process of change at Bolivar. *Journal of Applied Behavioral Science,* 1977, **13,** 387–399.

APPENDIX 14-1

Illustrative Questionnaire Items:
Quality of Work Life Program Evaluation

6. HERE ARE SOME STATEMENTS ABOUT THE
   WORKING COMMITTEE AT   PLEASE
   INDICATE WHETHER YOU AGREE WITH EACH
   STATEMENT AS A DESCRIPTION OF THE
   WORKING COMMITTEE.

Strongly Disagree   Neither Agree nor Disagree   Strongly Agree   Don't Know

a. The Working Committee is dominated by management. ..... [1] [2] [3] [4] [5] [6] [7] [8] 3:28

b. The Working Committee is responsible for making
   changes here. .... [1] [2] [3] [4] [5] [6] [7] [8] 3:29

c. Core groups have a say in the decisions the Working
   Committee makes. .... [1] [2] [3] [4] [5] [6] [7] [8] 3:30

d. The Working Committee is dominated by the union. .... [1] [2] [3] [4] [5] [6] [7] [8] 3:31

e. The Working Committee is needed here. .... [1] [2] [3] [4] [5] [6] [7] [8] 3:32

f. The Working Committee listens to both labor and
   management views. .... [1] [2] [3] [4] [5] [6] [7] [8] 3:33

g. The Working Committee is doing a good job. .... [1] [2] [3] [4] [5] [6] [7] [8] 3:34

h. The Working Committee represents my interests. .... [1] [2] [3] [4] [5] [6] [7] [8] 3:35

i. I know what the Working Committee is doing. .... [1] [2] [3] [4] [5] [6] [7] [8] 3:36

j. I have a say in the decisions the Working
   Committee makes. .... [1] [2] [3] [4] [5] [6] [7] [8] 3:37

k. The Working Committee is dominated by the Work
   Improvement Project Staff. .... [1] [2] [3] [4] [5] [6] [7] [8] 3:38

8. HERE ARE SOME STATEMENTS ABOUT THE
   WORK IMPROVEMENT PROJECT STAFF AT
            PLEASE INDICATE WHETHER YOU
   AGREE WITH EACH STATEMENT AS A
   DESCRIPTION OF THE WORK IMPROVEMENT
   PROGRAM PROJECT STAFF.

They . . .

Strongly Disagree   Neither Agree nor Disagree   Strongly Agree   Don't Know

a. . . . listen to the employees' point of view. .... [1] [2] [3] [4] [5] [6] [7] [8] 3:4

b. . . . work well as a team. .... [1] [2] [3] [4] [5] [6] [7] [8] 3:4

c. . . . are doing a good job. .... [1] [2] [3] [4] [5] [6] [7] [8] 3:4

d. . . . are not needed at all. .... [1] [2] [3] [4] [5] [6] [7] [8] 3:4

e. . . . communicate well with the employees. .... [1] [2] [3] [4] [5] [6] [7] [8] 3:4

f. . . . push too hard for changes around here. .... [1] [2] [3] [4] [5] [6] [7] [8] 3:4

g. . . . help solve both management and labor problems. ..... [1] [2] [3] [4] [5] [6] [7] [8] 3:4

h. . . . help core groups with problems. .... [1] [2] [3] [4] [5] [6] [7] [8] 3:4

i. . . . have been a big help. .... [1] [2] [3] [4] [5] [6] [7] [8] 3:4

9. HERE ARE SOME GENERAL STATEMENTS ABOUT
    THE WORK IMPROVEMENT PROGRAM ITSELF AND
    THE CHANGES WHICH MAY HAVE OCCURRED HERE.
    PLEASE INDICATE WHETHER YOU AGREE WITH
    EACH STATEMENT AS A DESCRIPTION OF THE WORK
    IMPROVEMENT PROGRAM.

Column headers (angled): Strongly Disagree / Neither Agree nor Disagree / Strongly Agree / Don't Know

a. I can't tell who is responsible for the changes around
    here. .... [1] [2] [3] [4] [5] [6] [7] | [8]   3:49
b. There are too many changes going on around here. .... [1] [2] [3] [4] [5] [6] [7] | [8]   3:50
c. This is a better place to work than it was two years
    ago. .... [1] [2] [3] [4] [5] [6] [7] | [8]   3:51
d. I like things the way they used to be. .... [1] [2] [3] [4] [5] [6] [7] | [8]   3:52
e. I don't know what changes the Work Improvement
    Program has made in the plant. .... [1] [2] [3] [4] [5] [6] [7] | [8]   3:53

10. PLEASE INDICATE WHETHER YOU AGREE OR
    DISAGREE WITH THE FOLLOWING STATEMENTS.

The Work Improvement Program . . .

Column headers (angled): Strongly Disagree / Neither Agree nor Disagree / Strongly Agree / Don't Know

a. . . . has reduced the labor-management conflict in the
    plant. .... [1] [2] [3] [4] [5] [6] [7] | [8]   3:54
b. . . . has weakened the union. .... [1] [2] [3] [4] [5] [6] [7] | [8]   3:55
c. . . . has strengthened the authority of supervision. .... [1] [2] [3] [4] [5] [6] [7] | [8]   3:56
d. . . . has brought more meaning to my life. .... [1] [2] [3] [4] [5] [6] [7] | [8]   3:57
e. . . . will help the upcoming labor-management
    contract negotiations. .... [1] [2] [3] [4] [5] [6] [7] | [8]   3:58
f. . . . has increased the amount of trust between
    employees and the company. .... [1] [2] [3] [4] [5] [6] [7] | [8]   3:59
g. . . . has provided personal growth for me. .... [1] [2] [3] [4] [5] [6] [7] | [8]   3:60
h. . . . has increased decision making by lower level
    employees at .... [1] [2] [3] [4] [5] [6] [7] | [8]   3:61
i. . . . has made a lot of good changes. .... [1] [2] [3] [4] [5] [6] [7] | [8]   3:62
j. . . . has been beneficial to only a few employees. .... [1] [2] [3] [4] [5] [6] [7] | [8]   3:63
k. . . . has improved my working relationship with my
    supervisor. .... [1] [2] [3] [4] [5] [6] [7] | [8]   3:64
l. . . . has brought more meaning to my work at
    .... [1] [2] [3] [4] [5] [6] [7] | [8]   3:65
m. . . . threatens the traditional labor-management
    relationship. .... [1] [2] [3] [4] [5] [6] [7] | [8]   3:66

The first set of questions ask about the extent to which _____ has accomplished a number of specific QWL objectives. These objectives fall into three broad goal areas: Participative Management, Communication, and Meaningful Work. PLEASE CIRCLE THE NUMBER WHICH REPRESENTS THE EXTENT TO WHICH YOU BELIEVE EACH OBJECTIVE LISTED BELOW HAS BEEN ACHIEVED AT _____ .

		This objective has not been achieved.			This objective has been achieved to a moderate extent.			This objective has been achieved to a very great extent.	

1. Participative Management

    a. Participation by employees is invited and encouraged in matters that affect employees.   1   2   3   4   5   6   7   1:10

    b. Participation is rewarded.   1   2   3   4   5   6   7   1:11

    c. There is openness to consideration of change (i.e., honest listening).   1   2   3   4   5   6   7   1:12

    d. Explanations are given on reasons for requests or decisions (people are told "why").   1   2   3   4   5   6   7   1:13

    e. When people make contributions (such as suggestions), these are given consideration which is:

        (1) prompt.   1   2   3   4   5   6   7   1:14

        (2) thoughtful.   1   2   3   4   5   6   7   1:15

    f. Periodic reviews are held concerning:

        (1) organizational performance.   1   2   3   4   5   6   7   1:16

        (2) group performance.   1   2   3   4   5   6   7   1:17

        (3) individual performance.   1   2   3   4   5   6   7   1:18

2. Communication

    a. Employees are well informed about the company (procedures, events, policies, etc.).   1   2   3   4   5   6   7   1:19

COMMENTS

		This objective has not been achieved.			This objective has been achieved to a moderate extent.			This objective has been achieved to a very great extent.	

b. Regular and frequent opportunities are provided for:

(1) information exchange. .... 　1　2　3　4　5　6　7　　1:20

(2) critique. .... 　1　2　3　4　5　6　7　　1:21

(3) problem solving. .... 　1　2　3　4　5　6　7　　1:22

c. There is continual openness to and invitation of:

(1) criticism. .... 　1　2　3　4　5　6　7　　1:23

(2) questions. .... 　1　2　3　4　5　6　7　　1:24

(3) suggestions. .... 　1　2　3　4　5　6　7　　1:25

d. Informal feedback about <u>individual</u> performance is:

(1) prompt. .... 　1　2　3　4　5　6　7　　1:26

(2) specific. .... 　1　2　3　4　5　6　7　　1:27

(3) frequent. .... 　1　2　3　4　5　6　7　　1:28

e. Informal feedback about <u>team</u> performance is:

(1) prompt. .... 　1　2　3　4　5　6　7　　1:29

(2) specific. .... 　1　2　3　4　5　6　7　　1:30

(3) frequent. .... 　1　2　3　4　5　6　7　　1:31

f. Formal feedback is given by timely use of the performance review system. .... 　1　2　3　4　5　6　7　　1:32

g. A production feedback system has been developed and implemented to give people feedback about progress toward production goals. .. 　1　2　3　4　5　6　7　　1:33

h. When needed for common understanding, written documentation of goals and plans has been developed. .... 　1　2　3　4　5　6　7　　1:34

COMMENTS

3. Meaningful Jobs

		This objective has not been achieved.			This objective has been achieved to a moderate extent.			This objective has been achieved to a very great extent.	
a.	When practical, work is done by small teams.	1	2	3	4	5	6	7	1:35
b.	Jobs involve production of a "whole" or "substantial part" of the product.	1	2	3	4	5	6	7	1:36
c.	Jobs at are challenging.	1	2	3	4	5	6	7	1:37
d.	Jobs at have a great deal of variety.	1	2	3	4	5	6	7	1:38
e.	There are opportunities for autonomy at the:								
	(1) individual level.	1	2	3	4	5	6	7	1:39
	(2) team level.	1	2	3	4	5	6	7	1:40
f.	Responsibility is delegated to:								
	(1) individuals.	1	2	3	4	5	6	7	1:41
	(2) teams.	1	2	3	4	5	6	7	1:42
g.	Jobs at are designed so that you can tell from the task itself how well you are doing.	1	2	3	4	5	6	7	1:43
h.	There are opportunities for advancement.	1	2	3	4	5	6	7	1:44
i.	There are opportunites for learning.	1	2	3	4	5	6	7	1:45
j.	Employees have adequate technical training.	1	2	3	4	5	6	7	1:46
k.	Employees are given an appropriate amount of work.	1	2	3	4	5	6	7	1:47
l.	The work environment at is:								
	(1) clean.	1	2	3	4	5	6	7	1:48
	(2) safe.	1	2	3	4	5	6	7	1:49
m.	provides:								
	(1) fair pay.	1	2	3	4	5	6	7	1:50
	(2) fair benefits.	1	2	3	4	5	6	7	1:51

The previous questions asked about the extent to which   has achieved a number of Quality of Work objectives. Now we would like your perceptions about the extent to which the activities of the   consultants (Mary   , Ed   , and Cal   ) contributed to reaching these various goals. We feel it is important to ask these questions so that we are able to understand the alternative explanations behind various outcomes. For example, it is possible that: (1) objectives were accomplished only to a small extent, but the consultants made a major contribution in the progress that was made; or (2) objectives were reached, but   would have gotten there anyway—even without help from

FOR THE QUESTIONS BELOW PLEASE INDICATE THE EXTENT TO WHICH THE ACTIVITIES OF THE HIRI CONSULTANTS CONTRIBUTED TO REACHING THE FOLLOWING GOALS:

	Very negative contribution: HIRI activities hindered this QWL objective.		No contribution: HIRI activities had nothing to do with the state of this QWL objective.		Very positive contribution: HIRI activities contributed to achieving this QWL objective.		Don't know	

I. Participative Management

a. Participation is invited and encouraged in matters that affect the employees. ...

1	2	3	4	5	6	7	8	1:52

b. Participation is rewarded. ....

1	2	3	4	5	6	7	8	1:53

c. There is openness to consideration of change (i.e., honest listening). ....

1	2	3	4	5	6	7	8	1:54

d. Explanations are given on reasons for requests or decisions (people are told "why"). ....

1	2	3	4	5	6	7	8	1:55

e. When people make contributions (such as suggestions) these are given consideration which is:

(1) prompt. ....

1	2	3	4	5	6	7	8	1:56

(2) thoughtful. ....

1	2	3	4	5	6	7	8	1:57

f. Periodic reviews are held concerning:

(1) organizational performance. ....

1	2	3	4	5	6	7	8	1:58

(2) group performance. ....

1	2	3	4	5	6	7	8	1:59

(3) individual performance. ....

1	2	3	4	5	6	7	8	1:60

COMMENTS

The column headers (rotated) read:

- Very negative contribution: H, activities hindered this QWL objective.
- No contribution: HIRI activities nothing to do with the state of this QWL objective.
- Very positive contribution: h, activities contributed to achie... this QWL objective.
- Don't know.

2. Communication

a. Employees are well informed about the company (procedures, events, policies, etc.). ....

| | 1 | 2 | 3 | 4 | 5 | 6 | 7 | 8 | 1:61 |

b. Regular and frequent opportunities are provided for:

	1	2	3	4	5	6	7	8	
(1) information exchange.	1	2	3	4	5	6	7	8	1:62
(2) critique.	1	2	3	4	5	6	7	8	1:63
(3) problem solving.	1	2	3	4	5	6	7	8	1:64

c. There is continual openness to and invitation of:

(1) criticism.	1	2	3	4	5	6	7	8	1:65
(2) questions.	1	2	3	4	5	6	7	8	1:66
(3) suggestions.	1	2	3	4	5	6	7	8	1:67

d. Informal feedback about individual performance is:

(1) prompt.	1	2	3	4	5	6	7	8	1:68
(2) specific.	1	2	3	4	5	6	7	8	1:69
(3) frequent.	1	2	3	4	5	6	7	8	1:70

e. Informal feedback about team performance is:

(1) prompt.	1	2	3	4	5	6	7	8	1:71
(2) specific.	1	2	3	4	5	6	7	8	1:72
(3) frequent.	1	2	3	4	5	6	7	8	1:73

f. Formal feedback is given by timely use of the performance review system.

| | 1 | 2 | 3 | 4 | 5 | 6 | 7 | 8 | 1:74 |

g. A production feedback system has been developed and implemented to give people feedback about progress toward production goals. ....

| | 1 | 2 | 3 | 4 | 5 | 6 | 7 | 8 | 1:75 |

h. When needed for common understanding, written documentation of goals and plans has been developed. ....

| | 1 | 2 | 3 | 4 | 5 | 6 | 7 | 8 | 1:76 |

COMMENTS

The column headers (angled, left to right):

- Very negative contribution: HIRI activities hindered this QWL objective.
- No contribution: HIRI activities had nothing to do with the state of this QWL objective.
- Very positive contribution: HIRI activities contributed to achieving this QWL objective.
- Don't know.

3. Meaningful Jobs

a. When practical, work is done by small teams. ....

1	2	3	4	5	6	7	8	1:77

b. Jobs involve production of a "whole" or "substantial part" of the product. ....

1	2	3	4	5	6	7	8	1:78

c. Jobs at   are challenging.

1	2	3	4	5	6	7	8	1:79

d. Jobs at   have a great deal of variety. ....

1	2	3	4	5	6	7	8	1:80

e. There are opportunities for autonomy at the:

(1) individual level. ....

1	2	3	4	5	6	7	8	2:10

(2) team level. ....

1	2	3	4	5	6	7	8	2:11

f. Responsibility is delegated to:

(1) individuals. ....

1	2	3	4	5	6	7	8	2:12

(2) teams. ....

1	2	3	4	5	6	7	8	2:13

g. Jobs at   are designed so that you can tell from the task itself how well you are doing.

1	2	3	4	5	6	7	8	2:14

h. There are opportunities for advancement.

1	2	3	4	5	6	7	8	2:15

i. There are opportunites for learning. .....

1	2	3	4	5	6	7	8	2:16

j. Employees have adequate technical training. ....

1	2	3	4	5	6	7	8	2:17

k. Employees are given an appropriate amount of work. ....

1	2	3	4	5	6	7	8	2:18

l. The work environment at   is:

(1) clean. ....

1	2	3	4	5	6	7	8	2:19

(2) safe. ....

1	2	3	4	5	6	7	8	2:20

m.   provides:

(1) fair pay. ....

1	2	3	4	5	6	7	8	2:21

(2) fair benefits. ....

1	2	3	4	5	6	7	8	2:22

COMMENTS

Evaluating Attitudinal Change in a Longitudinal Quality of Work Life Intervention

BARRY A. MACY AND MARK F. PETERSON

Evaluation of change programs to improve organizational effectiveness and the quality of work life must counter several threats to the validity of conclusions drawn about their results. Anecdotal information, descriptive data, and graphic displays are simply not sufficient to test hypotheses about the impact of changes in the jobs, work environments, and interpersonal relations in an organization. What is needed are such factors as (1) longitudinal measurements of criteria of effectiveness and the quality of work life; (2) comparison of changes in treatment and comparison group conditions; (3) a research design that fits the demands of field situations but minimizes the central threats to validity; and (4) analysis of the significance of the changes with statistics that moderate the remaining threats and enable the researcher to test causal hypotheses. Other chapters in this volume describe our general approach to collecting attitude data, forming comparison groups, and implementing a research design. This chapter illustrates the approach in one site. It also compares various statistical methods for analyzing survey data gathered from the site at three points in time. The central questions addressed are: (1) What methods and statistics are appropriate for assessing changes in survey measurements in a field study? and (2) What are the strengths and weaknesses of the conclusions drawn from the use of these methods in evaluating the changes?

APPROACHES TO MEASUREMENT AND DESIGN

As noted in earlier chapters, field conditions—notably the duration of the change process, the multiplicity of interventions and the varying degrees of their implementation in organizational units, and the absence of randomly selected experimental and comparison groups—confound the evaluation of the impact of change programs on criteria of effectiveness and quality of work life. We rely on three strategies to address these threats to the validity of conclusions. One strategy is to undertake longitudinal measurements of the program. Such measurements increase the likelihood of identifying attitude changes that emerge from an intervention only at later points in time. Measurements over multiple periods also increase the likelihood of identifying spurious or transient changes— Hawthorne effects—that will not endure. Although such effects can never be fully ruled out as explanations for attitude changes, periodic longitudinal measurements can be helpful in identifying their onset and dissipation or, should the change endure, in discounting the Hawthorne hypothesis.

Another strategy is to compare changes in a group participating in an intervention with changes in a group that is not participating. Practical and ethical constraints make it difficult to select these so-called treatment and comparison groups randomly, and even without randomization, to distinguish these groups prior to the onset of the program. The use of a post hoc comparison group—a group that for whatever reason does not participate directly in an intervention—provides an alternative means for evaluating changes found in a participating group. Such comparison groups reduce threats to the internal validity of conclusions drawn about the program due to history and maturation.

The major remaining threats to the internal validity of conclusions have to do with *statistical regression,* the tendency for high- and low-scoring groups on initial measurements to move toward the mean in subsequent measurements, and the *initial differences* between participating and nonparticipating groups that interact with the intervention to influence later measurements.[1] The next section of this chapter explores statistical techniques for controlling or minimizing these effects.

A related threat to the validity of conclusions is that changes in survey measures may not reflect a change in respondents' statuses on the variable per se but rather in their responses to the measurement scale of the variable or in their reinterpretation of the meaning of the variable itself. An analytic technique comparing factor structures of questionnaire measures over time periods is presented as one means of assessing whether such changes are evident.

STATISTICAL TECHNIQUES FOR ANALYZING CHANGE

The most commonly used statistic for assessing change in survey measures of an organization is some form of t-test. In the case of pairwise t-tests, changes in one group over time are compared with changes in another group. For Student's t-tests, comparisons are made between the size of the difference between groups at one point in time and the size of the difference at a later point. With both statistics, confirmation of an hypothesis, say, that a treatment group changed more than a comparison group, depends partly on the assessor's judgment. Chance dictates that some change in the size of the differences will be recorded. Moreover, changes in some key variables affected by an intervention may also influence changes in other attitudes not directly affected (the "halo" effect). Thus it is important that the assessor use theory to guide the selection of the measures used in evaluating the change effort and to link observations of the change program with interpretations of recorded changes in attitude measurements.

In addition, both forms of t-test can be confounded by autoregressive effects. For pairwise t-tests, statistical regression implies that the subsequent score of a group that is above the mean for the entire population in initial measurements is likely to decline. Likewise, the mean value of a group that initially is below the population mean is likely to rise. Although some controversy exists as to whether or not autoregressive effects are a form of error or are "real" empirical phenomena, most theorists recommend that researchers distinguish between those changes that can be explained by the initial standing of treatment and comparison groups from changes that cannot be predicted from initial standing. Table 15-1, a review of statistical methods used in assessing change, shows that most researchers advise that more complex analytic procedures are preferable to t-tests and the simple comparison of change scores.

Suggestions in Table 15-1 about which analytical approach is optimal vary according to both the research design used and the qualities of the data collected. The greatest variability among the methods recommended occurs for research designs where there are random assignments to treatment conditions. In such cases, several distinct multiple regression or modified multiple regression approaches are suggested; they differ in their specific statistical operations for minimizing autoregressive effects. Kenny presents a persuasive argument that when random assignment is possible, the most appropriate procedure equates the variance in the premeasurements and postmeasurements (i.e., "standardized change score analysis").[9]

Differences among the recommendations vary less markedly for research designs in which random assignment to treatment group is not

Table 15-1 Selected Literature Concerning Change Analysis Methodology[a]

Author(s)	Research Designs Considered	Analytical Procedures Discussed	Criteria	Implications
Lord[2]	Single group pretest–posttest; experimental; quasi-experimental.	Correlation of treatment with change; analysis of covariance with prior score as covariate; analysis of observed gain.	Avoid regression effects; avoid measurement error; avoid assignment bias.	Use analysis of covariance rather than analysis of observed gain; results are open to suspicion.
Tucker, Damarin, & Messick[3]	Experimental; quasi-experimental (not explicitly discussed).	Analysis of observed gain; correlation of treatment and independent, reliable gain; correlation of treatment and other gain estimates.	Avoid measurement error in prior score; distinguish between gain predictable from prior score and gain independent of prior score.	Correlate treatment with estimated independent, reliable gain.
Bohrnstedt[4]	Comments primarily directed toward nonexperimental designs seeking causal relationships between two variables at two points in time; occasional notes applicable to assessing treatment effects in previously noted designs.	Analysis of observed gain; partial correlation of treatment and dependent variable controlling for prior score; standardized and unstandardized regression coefficients controlling for prior score.	Avoid measurement error in prior score; avoid confounding without outside variables; avoid regression effects.	Use partial correlations controlling for prior score and correcting for measurement error.
Cronbach & Furby[5]	Experimental; quasi-experimental; single group pretest–posttest; experimental and quasi-experimental considering variables interacting with treatment.	Analysis of observed gain with and without correction for measurement error in both prior score and later score; correlation of treatment with residual gain correcting for measurement er-	Avoid measurement errors; distinguish between treatment's association with gain predictable from prior score and gain independent of prior score.	Use analysis of covariance correcting the covariate for various other variables; results are open to suspicion.

...ror in prior score and later score; "a logarithm for correlation treatment with the independent gain."

	Design	Analysis	Problem to avoid	Recommendation
Golembiewski, Billingsley, & Yeager[6]	Experimental, quasi-experimental and quasi-experimental with multiple posttests or multiple pretests; single group pretest–posttest.	Confirmatory factor analysis; mention nonmetric data structure comparisons.	Distinguish among real change, instrument calibration change, and factor structure change.	Use confirmatory factor analysis to identify factor structure change.
Bryk & Weisberg[7]	Experimental and quasi-experimental; nonequivalent control group design with pretest and posttest.	Linear growth system with independent parameters; standardized gain scores; Belson approach to ANCOVA.	Use more randomized experiments; develop mathematical models consistent with the processes (growth) generating the data such as the "value-added analysis."	Generally concluded that statistical adjustments are inadequate without equivalent other growth systems across traditional groups.
Werts & Linn[8]	Experimental.	Regression of later score on treatment and prior score; regression of observed gain on treatment and prior score; regression of observed gain on treatment; regression of residual gain on treatment and prior score; and regression of residual gain on treatment.	Avoid "specification error" (i.e., misleading regression coefficients due to including variables in the regression model in inappropriate ways).	Use a regression model with the later score as the dependent variable and all its hypothesized determinants including the prior score and the treatment as predictors; correct the regression for measurement error in all predictors.
Kenny[9]	Experimental; quasi-experimental.	Analysis of covariance with and without correction for measurement error in prior score; analysis of observed gain; "standardized change score analysis."	Avoid group assignment biases (e.g., selection based on observed pretest score, selection based on true pretest score, selection based on group differences).	Use analysis of covariance correcting for measurement error in prior score.

Table 15-1 (Continued)

Author(s)	Research Designs Considered	Analytical Procedures Discussed	Criteria	Implications
Linn & Slinde[10]	Single group pretest–posttest; experimental (posttest only and pretest–posttest); quasi-experimental.	Analysis of observed gain, residual gain, and estimated true gain; part and partial correlation of treatment with later score controlling for prior score with and without correction for measurement errors; partial regression weights of later score or gain score on treatment, other variables and prior score with and without correction for measurement error; pairwise T-tests.	Avoid attributing gain predictable from prior score to a treatment; avoid measurement error; avoid interpretation problems due to instrument calibration changes.	Use regression analysis where the treatment, other variables, and the prior score are predictors; correct for measurement error on all predictors; results are open to suspicion.
Zmud & Armenakis[11]	Single group pretest–posttest; single group "abbreviated time series"; experimental; quasi-experimental.	Confirmatory factor analysis; analysis of simple difference scores; pairwise T-tests and analysis of variance; real change is distinguished from instrument calibration change by comparing change in "actual" and "ideal" items.	Distinguish among real change, instrument calibration change and factor structure change; minimize threats to internal validity (especially) and external validity.	Use confirmatory factor analysis to identify factor structure change; if no change of this kind appears, compare changes in parallel "actual" and "ideal" items to distinguish real changes from instrument calibration changes; use pairwise t-tests or analysis of variance to assess treatment-induced change.

[a] Notes 2–11 in table text refer to chapter references.

possible. The usual recommendation is to use analysis of covariance with initial standing on attitude measures as covariates,[2,5] or multiple regression using both initial standing on the dependent attitude measure and a variable representing treatment conditions as predictors,[12] or one of these methods together with a correction for unreliability (attenuation) in the predictors.[4,8–10] The analysis of covariance and modified regression procedures that have been recommended are basically the same and are subject to the same assumptions when the independent variable in the analysis of covariance is "dummy" coded for use in the regression model.[13] In addition to reducing autoregressive effects, analysis of covariance encourages the researcher to consider whether or not the relationship between initial standing and later standing is similar for the treatment and comparison groups (i.e., by testing equality of slopes). Linn and Slinde[10] emphasize that correction for attentuation is especially important because measurement error can change the sign as well as the magnitude of predictor coefficients (e.g., partial correlations or regression coefficients) where more than one predictor is involved.

Several theorists recommend that, in addition to initial standing, other variables, such as job level, that are associated with a particular treatment or dependent variable should be statistically controlled.[5,8] When such extraneous factors interact with the intervention, attitude changes that would otherwise be attributed solely to the intervention effects on the treatment group can be attributed more appropriately to the intervention affecting employees at different levels of the organization.

Rather than making a general recommendation about how to analyze change when random assignment is not possible, Kenny[9] suggests different procedures for data analysis in research designs with different kinds of nonrandom assignment. He suggests that in some cases, the usual selection biases limiting nonrandom assignment are minimal. For example, random assignment can be assumed when changes in two organizations receiving different treatments are compared. In such situations, analytic procedures assuming random assignment are still appropriate.[2] Several authors note, further, that no analytic procedure can completely compensate for the kind of assignment biases that usually result from the lack of random assignment. Interactions between group assignment and treatment effects often remain legitimate alternate hypotheses in such designs when analyses appear to indicate "treatment effects."[2,5,10]

To determine whether an observed change in survey measures represents a change in the respondents' attitudes toward the concept, as opposed to an effect of the interval of measurement or the meaning of the concept itself, a procedure for comparing factor structures has been developed by Ahmavarra.[14] Using this and other procedures, Golembiewski, Billingsley, and Yeager note that "change" is not a unitary concept and find that at least three possible types of change might occur.[6]

1. *Alpha Change.*   Involving a variation in the level of some existential state, given a constantly calibrated measuring instrument related to a constant conceptual domain.

2. *Beta Change.*   Involving a variation in the level of some existential state, complicated by the fact that some intervals of the measurement continuum associated with a constant conceptual domain have been recalibrated.

3. *Gamma Change.*   Involving a redefinition or reconceptualization of some domains, a major change in the perspective or frame of reference within which the phenomena are perceived and classified, or in what is taken to be relevant in some slice of reality.

This third type of change, gamma change, implies a "redefinition of the relevant psychological space" as a result of some intervention.[6] By contrast, alpha change is a change in the degree of a given conceptually stable psychological state. For change analysis, alpha change indicates that employees are interpreting the variables in a survey instrument in the same way over time. To assess this type of change, according to Golembiewski and colleagues, requires that the researcher determine the coefficient of congruence between factor structures across time. If these coefficients are greater than .85, it can be concluded that any measured changes are not gamma changes.

The Ahmavaara method tests for the congruence of two factor structures, for example, Time 2 versus Time 1 or Time 3 versus Time 2. Briefly, this procedure rotates the T_2 factor matrix into the space of the T_1 factors, forming a check or comparison factor matrix. An intraclass correlation coefficient and a product-moment correlation are computed between the check matrix "C" and the T_2 target factor matrix. If factor structures remain stable over time, the recorded changes in survey data reflect a change in the respondent's rating of the "same" concept over the time period rather than a change in the meaning of the variable. This procedure can help researchers to conclude whether and how attitudes toward a particular concept have changed over time.

Used in concert, these various change analyses can help to control for or minimize many of the factors that confound the assessor's conclusions about the impact of a change program. Although there are some differences among these techniques, the most notable theme in Table 15-1 is the similarity among the various approaches and recommendations.

AN ILLUSTRATIVE EXAMPLE OF DESIGN, MEASUREMENT, AND CHANGE ANALYSIS

The cooperative quality of work life experiment to be evaluated here occurred within one division of a public utility.[15,16] The focal point of the experiment was known as the power company division (PCD), which had the responsibility for planning and designing power transmission facilities. The division consisted of 380 employees including 50 management personnel, 145 engineers and associated professionals, 145 technical support people, and 40 clerical and administrative employees. The project involved the total division in a change effort in which management and two unions, an engineer's association and an office worker's union, formed a Quality of Work Committee (QOWC) and, together with consultants, jointly tried to improve the quality of work life and effectiveness of the organization. The central evaluative question addressed is whether employee participation in the interventions in PCD, brought about by participation on various committees or in particular interventions, influenced changes in selected attitude measures.

The Program of Change

Approval for the project was obtained from management and the two unions in mid-1974, and soon thereafter the QOWC was formed. That committee then hired a team of social-science consultants to aid in implementing the program. The consultants began by interviewing—individually and in groups—some 228 organization members and reporting their findings in a week-long workshop. During this session, an agenda for change was developed.

As change opportunities were identified, the committee appointed a task force of division employees to address each particular problem area. Each task force was given a mandate and was charged with periodically reporting to the committee. Throughout 1975 into 1976, nine task forces were formed with assignments to develop, for example, new programs of performance evaluation, merit rewards, and flexitime work scheduling. In March 1976, the initial team of consultants left the project. In addition, several key members of the committee were replaced, and the top management representative was promoted to another post in the firm. This slowed project activity.

In 1977, a new team of consultants was hired and four new task forces were formed, including those focusing on work flows and work experiments. During this time, steps were taken toward institutionalizing the project by linking it with an existing cooperative labor and management structure. By January 1978, the experimental program was ended, its new work structures and processes having been transferred to the control of a permanent labor and management body known as the "new cooperative conference."

Identifying Treatment and Comparison Groups

In all, 13 separate task forces operated in PCD during the experimental period. They included over 100 employees, or roughly one third of the work force. Each of these task forces, along with the QOWC, introduced change into the organization.

It was impossible, prior to the formation of these committees, to identify which employees would and would not participate on task forces. Afterwards, however, it was possible to identify three levels of participation: (1) membership in the central QOWC; (2) membership on a task force; and (3) participation as an organization member. The first two represent *direct participation* in the intervention. The latter represents *indirect participation*.

There is reason to believe that the level of participation in an intervention influences members' reception of the changes and their subsequent work attitudes and behaviors.[17,18] QOWC and task force members had the opportunity to provide direct input into the decision making in the division and receive almost immediate feedback on their ideas. Such direct participation not only increases those employees' authority, it may also lessen their resistance to change.[19,20] By contrast, the other employees were "constituents" of the task forces and committee. Although they were knowledgeable about the project, they did not directly experience an increase in authority or responsibility, not did they earn any formal "ownership" of the change processes. They served as reactors to, rather than initiators of, change in PCD.

Thus it can be hypothesized that the reactions of the direct and indirect participators toward the program will differ and that this will be reflected in different changes in their work attitudes. To test this hypothesis, the assessors developed a post hoc research design comparing changes in attitudes between those who had direct and indirect participation in the experiment.

Selecting Variables to Test the Impact of the Program

The method of participation represented by the QOWC and task forces is structural: It refers to a system in which rules, procedures, and processes formally establish the decision-making avenues.[21] This pattern is commonplace in European work experiments and not uncommon in United States experiments.[22,23] Seashore suggests that this form of participation is likely to have an impact on organizational behavior that is distinct from the more informal aspects of influence.[24] Katz and Georgopoulos go further and suggest that it may be only those who participate directly in an intervention of this sort that derive any psychological benefit.[18]

To examine this proposition, five variables were identified for analysis: job satisfaction, job involvement, internal work motivation, intention to leave the organization, and acceptance of lower-level decision making. It was expected that job satisfaction would increase among the directly participating members since they were likely to find involvement on the committee and task forces challenging and rewarding, develop new skills and a broader organizational perspective, and see the fruits of their own influence. Job involvement was expected to increase since participation would engender more commitment to the organization. For the same reason, employees' intentions to leave the organization were expected to decline and their internal work motivation to increase. Members' acceptance of lower-level decision making was expected to increase for both direct and indirect participants since both groups would attribute changes introduced in the organization to their influence as members and constituents of the committee and task forces.[25]

Measures of these variables were taken prior to (T_1), during (T_2), and following (T_3) the change program. These measurement occasions accommodate the fact that the committee and task forces were formed between T_1 and T_2 and continued through T_3. In this light, two sets of hypotheses were employed to guide analysis. The first set pertains to changes over time, for each variable and each group. The second set pertains to *relative* change between groups, with controls for each individual's initial job level and initial scores on the variables.

Hypotheses 1-a to 1-d.   Between T_1 and T_2, and again between T_2 and T_3, those directly participating in the PCD intervention will display increases in job satisfaction (1-a), job involvement (1-b), internal work motivation (1-c), and intention to turnover (scale reversed, 1-d). Those indirectly participating will display no change.

Hypothesis 1-e.   Acceptance of lower-level decision making will increase across both time periods for both groups.

Hypotheses 2-a to 2-e.   Controlling for individuals' initial job level and initial variable scores, those directly participating will be higher than those indirectly participating at both T_2 and also T_3 in job satisfaction (2-a), job involvement (2-b), internal work motivation (2-c), intention to turnover (scale reversed, 2-d), and acceptance of lower-level decision making (2-e).

Sample

The sample for analysis consisted of 243 members of the PCD staff who were continuously employed throughout the period of study and who had completed survey questionnaires on all three occasions of survey administration. These "veterans" were 64% of the average work force during the period. While the total response rate was in excess of 85% on each survey occasion, staff turnover and other factors reduced the proportion of persons with sufficiently complete data to 64%. The sample included managers (11%), professional engineers (46%), semiprofessional engineers (32%), and clerical support staff (11%). Seventy-nine individuals were designated as direct participators, that is, serving as members of the QOWC or of a task force, and the others as indirect participators.

The demography of the sample should be noted. Seventy-five percent were voluntary members of one or the other of two unions, and 15% were not eligible for union membership because of their positions. Eighty-five percent were male. Fifty-eight percent had a college degree, and another 30% had some college-level education. The direct participation group included all demographic categories, but with some overrepresentation of managers and an underrepresentation of clericals and ethnic minorities.

Procedures

The Michigan Organizational Assessment Questionnaire, described elsewhere in this volume, was administered at three points in time: September 1974, June 1976, and January 1978. These dates signal the *before* measures (T_1), *during* measures (T_2) and *after* measures (T_3). The change program began concurrently with the T_1 survey.

Table 15-2 lists the indexes to be considered in this illustrative ana-

Table 15-2   Survey Indexes Used To Assess Longitudinal Change at the PCD Quality of Work Site[a]

Job satisfaction.   A two-item index (α: $T_1 = .69$; $T_2 = .77$; and $T_3 = .76$) measuring the extent of job satisfaction. Items: (1) All in all, I am satisfied with my job; and (2) In general, I like working here. Index intercorrelations across times are: $r_{12} = .56$; $r_{13} = .56$; and $r_{23} = .58$.

Job involvement.   A three-item index (α: $T_1 = .63$; $T_2 = .70$; and $T_3 = .69$) measuring the commitment and involvement in one's job. Items: (1) I am very much personally involved in my job: (2) I live, eat, and breathe my job; and (3) The most important things that happen to me involve my job. Index intercorrelations across times are: $r_{12} = .64$; $r_{13} = .65$; and $r_{23} = .73$.

Intention to turnover.   A two-item index (α: $T_1 = .80$; $T_2 = .72$; and $T_3 = .76$) measuring intention to leave the organization. Items: (1) How likely is it that you will actively look for a new job in the next year? and (2) I often think about quitting. Index intercorrelations across times are: $r_{12} = .65$; $r_{13} = .51$; and $r_{23} = .60$.

Internal work motivation.   A three-item index (α: $T_1 = .60$; $T_2 = .65$; and $T_3 = .76$) measuring one's work motivation. Items: (1) I feel bad when I do a poor job; (2) I get a feeling of personal satisfaction from doing my job well; and (3) When I do my job well, I feel I've done something worthwhile. Index intercorrelations across times are: $r_{12} = .60$; $r_{13} = .42$; and $r_{23} = .56$.

Acceptance of lower-level decision making.   A three-item index (α: $T_1 = .77$; $T_2 = .77$; and $T_3 = .82$) measuring management's acceptance of lower-level input into decision making. Items: (1) I feel free to tell people higher up what I really think; (2) Decisions are made around here without ever asking the people who have to live with them; and (3) It is hard to get people higher up in the organization to listen to people at my level. Index intercorrelations across times are: $r_{12} = .67$; $r_{13} = .63$; and $r_{23} = .70$.

---

[a] The alpha coefficients of internal consistency are based on the total analysis population, $N = 243$.

lytic procedure, the items within each index, and the reliability (coefficient alpha) of each index.

Four analytical techniques are selected to analyze these variables. These methods were: (1) pairwise t-tests; (2) Cronbach and Furby's variance–covariance algorithm; (3) analysis of covariance with initial Time 1 status as a covariate and subsequent scores as the dependent variable; and (4) analysis of covariance with initial scores as a covariate as well as other variables including job title and salary classification.

Pairwise t-tests were undertaken because mean comparisons between one group at several time periods is one of the most common methods of measuring the effects of an intervention. This technique answers this question: Is there a difference in attitudes between two points of time? The Cronbach and Furby[5] algorithm (adopting Tucker, Damarin, and Messick's[3] base-free change measure) was included as probably the most precise technique to measure independent change. This technique answers this question: Is the change related to direct participation? To answer this question a dichotomous "dummy" variable representing direct and indirect participation was employed. However, no attempt was made to control for additional confounding variables.

The two analyses of covariance were included because they have generally been recommended as the most appropriate method, given the post hoc research design. One analysis included only the prior score at the beginning of the period for which change was to be assessed. However, in many studies, as in the present one, it has been observed that other variables covary with the dependent variables of interest. Thus, the second covariance analysis method included each individual's job level (in the form of a four-category "dummy" variable) as a covariate along with the prior score.*

Analysis Plan

The research design forms what Campbell and Stanley[1] call a nonequivalent control design as is depicted here.

$$ODP_1 \quad X_1 \quad ODP_2 \quad X_2 \quad ODP_3$$
$$OIDP_1 \quad \quad OIDP_2 \quad \quad OIDP_3$$
$$DP = \text{directly participating group}$$
$$IDP = \text{indirectly participating group}$$
$$X_1 = \text{intervention}$$
$$X_2 = \text{intervention continues}$$

---

* It should be noted that some theorists question the use of these techniques. First, some contend, they depend on an error-free covariate and second, on the random assignment of groups to treatment and comparison conditions. Other theorists, as noted before, recommend these techniques also for nonrandom experimental research designs.[2]

This design indicates that O_1 is the Time 1 administration of the baseline or initial questionnaire. O_2 and O_3 represent the Times 2 and 3 questionnaire administrations. X_1 represents the beginning of the formal quality of work life intervention and the formal participation of the directly participating individuals by the formation of the QOWC and task forces. X_2 represents a continuation of this formal participation and representation of these committees from T_2 and T_3. The significance levels of the aforementioned hypothesized changes are assessed by different methods. The "treatment" group (directly participating) is compared to the nonequivalent "comparison" group (indirectly participating) at PCD, taking into account initial differences between the two groups at T_1. In this analysis, "treatment" is assumed to result from formal membership on the QOWC and/or the 13 task forces, and the "absence of treatment" is equated to nonmembership on the committee or task forces.

Index Properties

Table 15-3 provides descriptive statistics about the five indexes, including the number of matched veterans providing data across time for each

Table 15-3   Index Means, Standard Deviations, and Number of Respondents for Directly and Indirectly Participating Groups at the PCD Quality of Work Site[a]

Index		Directly Participating Group			Indirectly Participating Group		
		N	$\bar{X}$	S.D.	N	$\bar{X}$	S.D.
Job satisfaction	T_1	81	5.17	1.31	149	5.00	1.23
	T_2	82	5.52	1.04	159	4.99	1.23
	T_3	84	5.53	1.17	159	5.07	1.14
Job involvement	T_1	81	3.69	1.11	149	3.59	1.07
	T_2	82	3.93	1.07	158	3.48	1.07
	T_3	84	3.89	1.07	159	3.55	1.00
Intention to turnover[b]	T_1	81	2.16	1.39	149	2.51	1.42
	T_2	82	2.06	1.11	161	2.56	1.33
	T_3	84	2.07	1.26	159	2.46	1.38
Internal work motivation	T_1	81	6.07	.50	149	5.79	.77
	T_2	82	5.95	.58	159	5.70	.78
	T_3	84	6.00	.79	159	5.73	.79
Acceptance of lower-level decision making	T_1	80	3.85	1.42	147	3.22	1.38
	T_2	82	4.50	1.25	159	3.49	1.18
	T_3	84	4.53	1.25	157	3.56	1.26

[a] All indexes are 7-point response scales.
[b] Reversed index.

Table 15-4   Intercorrelations between Measurement Times of Indexes for Directly and Indirectly Participating Groups at the PCD Quality of Work Site[a]

Index	Directly Participating Group			Indirectly Participating Group		
	r_{12}	r_{23}	r_{13}	r_{12}	r_{23}	r_{13}
Job satisfaction	.53	.53	.58	.58	.59	.56
	(80)	(82)	(81)	(147)	(158)	(147)
Job involvement	.75	.78	.69	.58	.68	.62
	(80)	(82)	(81)	(146)	(157)	(147)
Intention to turnover	.65	.57	.53	.65	.59	.49
	(80)	(82)	(81)	(149)	(159)	(147)
Internal work motivation	.39	.57	.33	.56	.45	.58
	(80)	(82)	(81)	(147)	(158)	(147)
Acceptance of lower-level decision making	.64	.71	.66	.65	.63	.58
	(79)	(82)	(80)	(145)	(156)	(143)

[a] N's in parentheses; for $N = 80$, $P \leq .01$ for $r \geq .28$; for $N = 145$, $p \leq .01$ for $r \geq .21$

index, index means, and standard deviations. The information appears separately for the directly and indirectly participating groups. The standard deviations for all variables except internal work motivation are above 1.0. The standard deviations do not vary between groups or across time in any systematic way. Mean differences exist both between groups and across time; these will be considered as the results of the analytical change methods are presented.

Intercorrelations for each group among the T_1, T_2, T_3 indexes are presented separately in Table 15-4. The generally high correlations indicate considerable similarity in the differences among the responses of individuals within each group over time. Such similarity of correlations is not inconsistent with either large or small changes in index means. The correlation of a variable at one time with the same variable at another time reflects the relative standing on the variable of different individuals at different times. Low correlations indicate a large change in relative standing over time, while high correlations show a small change. The pattern of correlations indicates that greater changes occurred for an individual's relative standing in internal work motivation than for the attitudes reflected in the other indexes. The change in internal work motivation is especially evident in the low correlations of this index between T_1 and the other two measurement periods for the directly participating group.

Table 15-5 presents the T_1, T_2, and T_3 intercorrelations among the five indexes separately for both groups. In general, the correlations among

Table 15-5   Intercorrelations among Indexes and across Time for Directly and Indirectly Participating Groups at the PCD Quality of Work Site[a]

	Time 1				
Job satisfaction (JS)	1.0				
Job involvement (JI)	.51(.50)	1.0			
Intention to turnover (T)	−.76(−.58)	−.42(−.33)	1.0		
Internal work motivation (WM)	.22(.39)	.31(.26)	−.15(−.27)	1.0	
Acceptance of lower-level decision making (DM)	.47(.48)	.46(.20)	−.33(−.39)	.11(.15)	1.0
	JS	JI	T	WM	DM

	Time 2				
Job satisfaction (JS)	1.0				
Job involvement (JI)	.46(.41)	1.0			
Intention to turnover (T)	−.58(−.57)	−.23(−.25)	1.0		
Internal work motivation (WM)	.58(.40)	.35(.40)	−.36(−.27)	1.0	
Acceptance of lower-level decision making (DM)	.50(.53)	.28(.24)	−.41(−.32)	.39(.21)	1.0
	JS	JI	T	WM	DM

	Time 3				
Job satisfaction (JS)	1.0				
Job involvement (JI)	.47(.45)	1.0			
Intention to turnover (T)	−.72(−.61)	−.32(−.28)	1.0		
Internal work motivation (WM)	.66(.31)	.46(.37)	−.62(−.12)	1.0	
Acceptance of lower-level decision making (DM)	.52(.40)	.47(.21)	−.50(−.39)	.43(.17)	1.0
	JS	JI	T	WM	DM

[a] (a) *Indirectly* participating group correlations in parentheses; *directly* participating group correlations without parentheses; (b) Time 1 N for directly participating groups was 80–81, Time 1 N for indirectly participating groups was between 147–149; (c) $T_2 N$ for directly participating groups was 82, $T_2 N$ for indirectly participating groups was between 158–159; (d) $T_3 N$ for directly participating groups was 84, $T_3 N$ for indirectly participating groups was between 156–159; (e) For $N = 80$, $p \leq .01$ for $r \geq .28$; for $N = 145$, $p \leq .01$ for $r \geq .21$.

the indexes are moderate to strong, and they do not differ greatly either between the two groups or across time. The relationships that are the strongest in magnitude are between job satisfaction and intention to turnover (r's between −.57 and −.76). The weakest correlations are those between work motivation and acceptance of lower-level decision making (r's between .11 and .43). The correlations that differ the most between the two groups occur at T_3. These differences may be a result of a change in level or causal association among the variables due to the change effort. Differences among the correlations at T_1, T_2, and T_3 primarily involve internal work motivation for the directly participating group. The differences may indicate questionable reliability in the internal work motivation index or a real change over time in the causal association of other variables with work motivation.

Change Analysis

The comparisons between factor matrix structures[14] of the set of items for each index at the three time periods show virtually no "gamma" change in the "conceptual space" or the construct measured by the indexes. The coefficient of congruence[6] indicates 98% consistency in factor structures both between T_1 and T_2 and between T_2 and T_3.* Thus any difference in an index over time is attributed to real (alpha) change or index calibration (beta) changes.

The other analytic procedures and methods, therefore, assess whether or not alpha or beta change occurred. As previously described, the pairwise t-tests evaluate the hypothesis that a variable changes over time.

The results of the pairwise t-tests are shown in Table 15-6. For the directly participating group, there are significant changes in the hypothesized direction for job satisfaction, job involvement, and acceptance of lower-level decision making between T_1 and T_2. As predicted, the only significant difference between T_1 and T_2 is for acceptance of lower-level decision making in the indirectly participating group. The t-value for this variable is smaller in the indirectly participating group (3.37) than in the directly participating group (5.06). There are no significant differences in any index between T_2 and T_3 for either group. Thus Hypotheses 1a, 1b, and 1e are supported for the comparisons between T_1 and T_2 but not for those between T_2 and T_3. With the present pattern of results, the conclusion would be reached that the direct group changed more between T_1 and T_2 than did the indirect group.

The results of the other methods used to assess change at PCD appear in Table 15-7. Two of these techniques, the Cronbach and Furby algorithm and the analysis of covariance using only prior score as a covariate, provide very similar findings. The significance levels obtained differ only slightly between the two different methods. Using both procedures, significant differences in the directions predicted are obtained between

---

* As a result of the varimax rotation of the OSIRIS factor analysis, four factors were identified on which the five indexes loaded more heavily. Two indexes, job satisfaction and intention to turnover, both loaded heavily on the same factor but in opposite directions when four, five, and six varimax factor rotations were used. The final between-time comparisons were made using the four-factor solution.

Table 15-6   Pairwise T-tests between Times for Direct and Indirect Participation at the PCD Quality of Work Site

Variable	Times Compared	
	T_2-T_1	T_3-T_2
	Directly Participating Group	
Job satisfaction	2.66*	.20
Job involvement	2.71*	.52
Intention to turnover	−.52	.10
Internal work motivation	−1.81	.90
Acceptance of lower-level decision making	5.06*	.27
	Indirectly Participating Group	
Job satisfaction	−.11	.92
Job involvement	−1.00	.61
Intention to turnover	.50	−1.10
Internal work motivation	−1.59	.52
Acceptance of lower-level decision making	3.37**	1.13

$* p \leq .01; ** p \leq .001$

the groups at T_2 (controlling for T_1 score) for job satisfaction, job involvement, intention to turnover, and acceptance of lower-level decision making. In each case the differences, consistently in the direction predicted, reflect a more desirable consequence of the intervention for the directly participating group than for the indirectly participating group. When the significance of differences between the groups at T_3, taking the T_2 scores into account, are compared with these two techniques, one would infer from the Cronbach and Furby algorithm that a significant difference for acceptance of lower-level decision making occurred. The difference obtained when analysis of covariance is used falls short of usual significance levels ($p = .09$). This is the only comparison between T_2 and T_3 reaching significance for any variable, using either technique. Thus, Hypotheses 2a, 2b, 2c, and 2e are supported for the changes between T_1 and T_2, using both techniques. Only the Cronbach and Furby algorithm shows a significant change consistent with Hypothesis 2a between T_2 and T_3 for acceptance of lower-level decision making.

Several suggestions have been made about circumstances in which the results obtained using t-tests should diverge from those obtained using procedures that correct for initial standing and other variables. Lord suggests that statistics based on raw gain are biased when the mean score for one of the treatment groups is initially low.[2] It is also implicit in

Table 15-7   Different Change Analysis Methods of Assessing Consequences of Direct and Indirect Participation at the PCD Quality of Work Site[a]

Variable	Time Periods Compared	
	T_2-T_1	T_3-T_2
	Cronbach and Furby Matrix Controlling for Prior Score (Gamma)	
Job satisfaction	−.17**	−.11
Job involvement	−.19**	−.04
Intention to turnover	.13*	.05
Internal work motivation	−.05	−.11
Acceptance of lower-level decision making	−.28***	−.13*
	Analysis of Covariance Using Prior Score as a Covariate (partial F)	
Job satisfaction	11.0**	1.7
Job involvement	9.3**	.3
Intention to turnover	3.9*	.2
Internal work motivation	1.1	1.9
Acceptance of lower-level decision making	22.1***	2.9
	Analysis of Covariance Using Prior Score and Job Level as Covariates (partial F)	
Job satisfaction	5.4*	.4
Job involvement	3.3	.2
Intention to turnover	.9	.1
Internal work motivation	.2	1.2
Acceptance of lower-level decision making	13.6***	1.9

* $p \leq .05$; ** $p \leq .01$; *** $p \leq .001$

[a] Negative gamma indicates that the directly participating group increased more than the indirectly participating group.

many discussions of residual gain analysis and the analysis of covariance that t-tests should approximate much more complex procedures to the extent that there is no correlation between initial standing and the final standing on the dependent variable. This should also be the case for other covariates like job level.

Given these viewpoints, it is somewhat surprising how similar the conclusions reached with these more complex methods would be with the present data using comparisons of t-tests. Three of the same indexes, job satisfaction, job involvement, and acceptance of lower-level decision making, would be concluded to have changed betwen T_1 and T_2, whichever technique was used. Using analysis of covariance and the Cronbach and Furby algorithm, intention to turnover would also be concluded to have changed. From the Cronbach and Furby procedure, but not the other two techniques, it would also be concluded that acceptance of lower-level decision making changed between T_2 and T_3. The similarity in the conclusions reached when using these three techniques is not due to an unusually low relationship among the T_1, T_2, and T_3 values of each of the five indexes. These correlations range from .43 to .73 with a median of .60. Taking the prior score into account, through either analysis of covariance of the Cronbach and Furby algorithm, appears, however, to provide a slightly more sensitive test of the hypotheses about the comparative change in the two groups than would t-tests. This difference in sensitivity is an additional advantage over the comparison of t-tests.

The results obtained when analysis of covariance is performed, using both initial standing and job level as covariates, diverge in important ways from those obtained using the other techniques (see Table 15-7). Generally, the significance levels obtained using analysis of covariance in this way are lower than is the case for the other techniques. In particular, when job level as well as initial standing is used as a covariate, job involvement and intention to turnover do not appear to change more between T_1 and T_2 for the direct group than for the indirect group. When the Cronbach and Furby algorithm and the analysis of covariance are used, controlling only for initial standing, both variables do appear to have changed. Additional analysis (data not shown) indicate that job level is significantly related ($p < .01$) to four of the dependent variables (all except internal work motivation) at both T_1 and T_2 (the corresponding eta's range from .04 to .07). Also, as already described, the ratio of managers directly participating in a committee to managers not participating in a committee is higher than is the ratio of directly participating to indirectly participating professional, semiprofessional, or clerical employees. Thus when a variable such as job level is related both to the treatment condition and to the dependent variables of interest, the decision about whether to include that variable as a covariate may have an important impact on the conclusions drawn from the analyses.

In summary, the pattern of results that appears when these four approaches to analyzing change are compared shows considerable consistency among them with a few important differences. Pairwise t-tests appear to provide a slightly less sensitive test than do the more complex inferential tests that take initial standing into account, on the hypothesis that an intervention affected the direct group more positively than it affected the indirect group. This result is consistent with the statement of Lord: "In general, the analysis of observed gains (as opposed to covariance analysis) results in a built-in bias in favor of whatever treatments happen to be assigned to initially low-scoring groups. This bias is not likely to be large unless the number of individuals per group is small; thus analysis of observed gains will often not be seriously misleading" (p. 37).[2] The major difference among the change analysis techniques appears with the adjustment for job level—a variable associated with both group assignment (direct versus indirect) and with many of the dependent variables. Taking job level into account prevents the misattribution of changes in job involvement and intention to turnover to the intervention instead of job level. Under some circumstances, it appears that an inappropriately small number of significant changes may be inferred if some variables are not taken into account, while an inappropriately large number may be inferred unless others are considered.

Discussion

It is quite clear that some changes in attitudes associated solely with the levels of participation in PCD occurred in this example. A link between direct participation in the change experiment and greater positive psychological effects is found for employees directly participating as compared to indirectly participating in the quality of work life experiment. This longitudinal field study and the empirical results support the prior results of a body of research on the impact of representative labor–management groups upon organizational members,[25–29] and on the impact upon persons, particularly, of direct participation in such activity.[30,31]

Important differences appear when several techniques for analyzing change data are used to assess some of the effects of a quality of work life intervention. Such differences imply that the conclusions drawn in at least some previous empirical studies of organizational change using simpler inferential change methods may be inappropriate. Autoregressive effects and biases due to nonrandom assignment to treatment groups may result in t-tests or the analysis of raw gain scores yielding ambiguous and misleading conclusions. In the typical analysis of a change effort where t-tests or raw gain scores indicate change to be only marginally significant or insignificant, other, more complex inferential change techniques might indicate different results. Empirical studies using t-tests must be interpreted cautiously if initial differences exist between the treatment and comparison groups either on the dependent variable or on other variables that could explain why the groups would respond differently to the same intervention.

One of the especially useful analytical procedures takes into account differences between treatment and comparison groups that may be confounded with the intervention (e.g., job level in the PCD example). Our results show that, when random assignment to treatment and comparison groups is not practical, it is advantageous to measure variables likely to be associated with group assignments.

When valid measures and longitudinal data exist in conjunction with comparison groups, they should be fully exploited in change analysis. Changes in factor matrix structures (e.g., gamma changes) should generally be considered first. Since such changes are rarely assessed, it is not yet possible to determine either how often or in what kinds of interventions they are likely to occur. It may be that gamma changes will appear primarily in experiments designed to change attitudes or perceptions or organizational members (e.g., developmental programs), rather than in intervention experiments designed to change the participation level and providing structures to increase lower-level input in the decision-making process (e.g., such as the intervention at PCD).

Different procedures for assessing mean changes (e.g., alpha or beta change) should be appropriate for the concerns of the various audiences to which the results of the experiment will be presented. People at the experimental site and many practitioners, for example, will be interested in attitude change occurring at the site. Pretest and posttest means, raw gain scores, and t-tests for both treatment and comparison groups are likely to be of some interest. For others who are interested in knowing whether the same changes can be expected elsewhere for similarly composed groups, the results of analysis of covariance, using initial standing as a covariate, will be useful. Those whose interests are in refining a theory about a particular set of dimensions or in generalizing to groups composed in a different way will require additional analysis. For such an audience, analysis of covariance and the Cronbach and Furby "independent" gain score procedure (if random assignment can be assumed), including covariates measuring potential confounding variables in addition to initial standing on the dependent variable, is required.

The long-term scientific consequences of a change program are likely to be greatest when the results of the program are assessed by procedures that promote generalization to other settings. While t-tests may be useful for some audiences, more complex and multivariate procedures that account for initial standing on the dependent variable as well as additional key variables that are associated with group assignment yield greater knowledge and broader generalization. Adaptive field experiments should be designed, and relevant variables should be measured, to take advantage of such multivariate analytical procedures in the analysis of change data.

REFERENCES

1. Campbell, D. T., & Stanley, J. *Experimental and quasi-experimental designs for research.* Chicago: Rand-McNally, 1963.

2. Lord, F. M. Elementary models for measuring change. In Chester W. Harris (Ed.), *Problems in measuring change.* Madison: University of Wisconsin Press, 1963, 21–38; see also Lord, F. M. Significance test for a partial correlation corrected for attentuation. *Educational and Psychological Measurement,* 1974, **34,** 211–220.

3. Tucker, L. R., Damarin, F., & Messick, S. A base-free measure of change. *Psychometrika,* 1966, **31,** 457–473.

4. Bohrnstedt, G. W. Observations on the measurement of change. In F. Borgatta (Ed.), *Sociological methodology.* San Francisco: Jossey-Bass, 1969, 113–133.

5. Cronbach, L. J., & Furby, L. How should we measure "change"—or should we? *Psychological Bulletin,* 1970, **74,** 68–80.

6. Golembiewski, R. T., Billingsley, K., & Yeager, S. Measuring change and persistence in human affairs: Types of change generated by OD designs. *Journal of Applied Behavioral Science,* 1976, **12,** 133–157.

7. Bryk, A. S., & Weisberg, H. I. Use of the nonequivalent control group design when subjects are growing. *Psychological Bulletin,* 1977, **84,** 950–962.

8. Werts, C. E., & Linn, R. L. A general linear model for studying growth. *Psychological Bulletin,* 1970, **73,** 17–22.

9. Kenny, D. A. A quasi-experimental approach to assessing treatment effects in the nonequivalent control group design. *Psychological Bulletin,* 1973, **82,** 345–362.

10. Linn, R. L., & Slinde, J. A. The determination of the significance of change between pre- and posttesting periods. *Review of Educational Research,* 1977, **47,** 121–150.

11. Zmud, R. M., & Armenakis, A. A. Understanding the measurement of change. *Academy of Management Review,* 1978, **3,** 661–669.

12. Goodman, P. *Assessing organizatinal change: The Rushton quality of work experiment.* New York: Wiley-Interscience, 1979.

13. Kerlinger, F. N., & Pedhazure, E. J. *Multiple regression in behavioral research.* New York: Holt, Rinehart and Winston, 1973.

14. Ahmavaara, Y. Transformation analysis of factorial data. *Annals of the Academy of Science Fennicae,* Series B, 1954, **881,** 54–59.

15. Macy, B. A., & Nurick, A. J. *Assessing organizational change and participation: The TVA quality of work experiment.* New York: Wiley-Interscience, forthcoming.

16. Nurick, A. J. *The effects of formal participation in organizational change on individual perceptions and attitudes: A longitudinal study.* Unpublished doctoral dissertation, University of Tennessee, Knoxville, 1978.

17. Lammers, C. J. Power and participation in decision-making in formal organizations. *American Journal of Sociology,* 1967, **73,** 201–216.

18. Katz, D., & Georgopoulos, B. S. Organizations in a changing world. *Journal of Applied Behavioral Science,* 1971, **7,** 342–370.

19. Drought, N. E. The operations committee: An experience in group dynamics. *Personnel Psychology,* 1967, **20,** 153–163.

20. Coch, L., & French, J. Overcoming resistance to change. *Human Relations,* 1948, **1,** 512–532.

21. Walker, K. F. Workers' participation in management problems: practice and prospects. *International Institute for Labor Studies Bulletin,* 1973, **12,** 3–35.

22. Davis, L. E., & Cherns, A. B. (Eds.). *The quality of working life: Volumes I and II.* New York: Free Press, 1975.

23. Cummings, T. G., & Molloy, E. S. *Improving productivity and the quality of work life.* New York: Praeger, 1977.

24. Seashore, S. E. *Participation in decision-making: Some issues of conception, measurement and interaction.* Paper presented for the Thirty-Seventh Annual Meeting, The Academy of Management, 1977.

25. French, J. R. P., Israel, J., & As, D. An experiment on participation in a Norwegian factory. *Human Relations,* 1960, **13,** 3–20.

26. Walton, R. E., & McKersie, R. B. *A behavioral theory of labor negotiations.* New York: McGraw-Hill, 1965.

27. Kochan, T., & Dyer, L. A model for organizational change in the context of labor-management relations. *Journal of Applied Behavioral Science,* 1976, **12,** 56–78.

28. Peterson, R. B., & Tracey, L. Testing a behavioral theory model of labor negotiations. *Industrial Relations,* 1977, **16,** 35–50.

29. Ledford, G., Macy, B. M. & Lawler, E. E. III. *The Bolivar quality of work experiment: 1972–1978.* New York: Wiley-Interscience, forthcoming.

30. Lowin, A. Participative decision making: A model, literature critique and prescriptions for research. *Organizational Behavior and Human Performance,* 1968, **8,** 68–106.

31. Seigel, A. L., & Ruh, R. A. Job involvement, participation in decision making, personal background, and job behavior. *Organizational Behavior and Human Performance,* 1973, **9,** 318–327.

CHAPTER SIXTEEN

Assessing the Economic Consequences of Organizational Change

DENNIS EPPLE, PAUL S. GOODMAN, AND EDUARD FIDLER

A major problem in assessing organizational change is estimating the economic effects of organizational change efforts. While organizational interventions differ in their emphasis on economic goals, it is clearly a major effectiveness criterion.

A cursory review of the literature on assessing organizational change, e.g. Glaser, will show there is little substantial evidence to document changes in economic indicators such as productivity. Most studies simply assert that productivity is improved or increased by some percentage, without detailing the source of data or identifying the cause of the change. The basic problem with these reports is that production is a function of a number of controllable and uncontrollable variables. An organizational intervention simply adds another variable to the complex production function. Separating out its effect is a difficult analytical task. Unfortunately, many of the reported assessments of economic effects of organizational change have not incorporated the appropriate control groups or statistical techniques.

Why have we not made more progress in estimating economic effects? One reason is that much of the research in this area has been done by social scientists who are more interested in psychological than economic outcomes of work. These individuals also tend to be less familiar with econometric techniques. Another reason is that many people involved in introducing organizational change have been more concerned with the process of change than with the outcome. In other cases, companies have not been willing to make economic data available, or the resources have not been available to analyze economic data. Finally, there have not been good analytic models available to assess productivity changes in organizational experiments.

This chapter focuses on assessing one type of economic indicator—productivity. We will first examine three methods for estimating productivity changes as a function of organizational experiments. Second, we will identify some of the critical issues in this type of estimation. Our discussion will be built around a specific organizational intervention, although our general analytic strategy is not limited to this case (see Goodman[2] for more detail.)

THE SETTING

The three models used to estimate productivity differences are examined in the context of an experimental intervention in a coal mine. However, the forms of the models are presented at a general level to enable the models to be generalized to other settings. Clearly, some of the variables in the models need to change in different settings, but the form of each model and the testing procedures do not.

The Rushton Mining Company entered into a quality of work (QOW) experiment in 1973.[2] One of the three sections (mining departments) became an experimental section. Autonomous work-group teams were created in that section with the aid of outside consultants. While it is not possible to detail the experimental intervention, the communication, decision making, authority, and reward systems of that section were substantially modified. The basic hypothesis was that these changes would increase productivity levels and the quality of working life.

The design of this study permits comparing productivity of the experimental section against two other mining sections. In a sense, these sections can serve as control groups to assist in isolating the effect of the experimental intervention on productivity. However, since these three sections are not perfectly matched as to men, machinery, and physical conditions, nor were the sections randomly assigned to conditions, the design is not truly an experimental design. At best, this study can be classified as a quasi-experimental design; contrasts within the experimental section over time or between experimental and control sections cannot definitely isolate the experimental effect on productivity.

Coal-mine production is generally stated in terms of tons produced (per section). The set of variables affecting production is complex. Some variables are controllable, such as the number of men working or the type of equipment. Other variables are uncontrollable, such as the character of roof and runway conditions. In comparing differences in tons produced per section it is important to understand which variables contribute to production. For example, if the experimental section outproduces the control sections but the latter have very poor roof conditions, then the difference in productivity may be caused by uncontrollable physical conditions rather than the experiment. To analyze productivity differences, we need to estimate a production function that includes the major predictor variables, and then to identify whether there are shifts in the coefficients of these variables that can be attributed to the experimental intervention.

EVALUATION PROCEDURES

Since it is not possible to control nonexperimental variables (e.g., roof conditions) that differentially affect the experimental and control groups, it is necessary to statistically control for these differences. We adopted three alternative methods for estimating productivity changes after correcting for changes in uncontrollable variables across the experimental and control sections. (Where not indicated otherwise, the experimental section prior to the experiment and the nonexperimental sections are referred to as the control sections.)

All three methods seek to identify differences in the structure of the production function (i.e., the relationship between resources used and quantities produced) between the experimental section and the control sections. Thus, we began by estimating a separate production function for each section for each year. The appropriate positive or negative signs can be specified a priori for almost all variables in the production function equation. For example, output should be positively related to working time and to the roof-and runway-condition variables. Before accepting the estimated equation for an individual section, we examined the estimated production functions to determine if all coefficients that were significantly different from zero had the predicted sign. In the few instances in which initial estimates did not conform to our expectations, we determined whether exceptional circumstances (e.g., unusual physical conditions) in a particular section might have given rise to an unreasonable coefficient estimate. In some cases, dummy variables were introduced to account for such special circumstances.

In principle, the production functions in all the control sections should be identical, since the production function is intended to capture the technological relationship between input and output under nonexperimental conditions. If the production functions are different prior to the experiment, then the notion of a well-defined control group is subject to question. In practice, it may not be feasible to measure all variables that affect production, and, by conventional testing procedures, the hypothesis of homogeneity of the control sections may be rejected. If differences among the control sections are significant, an effort should be made to determine the reasons for the differences. For example, important variables may have been omitted, or the chosen functional form may be too restrictive. If differences among the control sections cannot be reconciled, then one may wish to select one or more control sections as being more appropriate than others or one may wish to examine the experimental section against various control sections or combinations of control sections. We will discuss these and related issues later in this chapter.

The first and simplest procedure is to test for differences in the constant term in the production function across sections. With this test, differences among the sections, if any, including differences caused by the experiment, are assumed to affect only the constant term. Given this assumption, the homogeneity of the sections in the control group or a subset of the control group can be tested by an analysis of variance, that is, by testing whether a significantly higher proportion of variance is explained by allowing a different constant term for each section than by imposing the same constant term across all sections. If the experiment enhanced productivity, this would be reflected by a higher constant term in the production function for the experimental section than in the production functions for the control sections. The F-test can be applied to determine whether the difference in the constant term between the experimental and control groups is significant. If there is only one control section, then this reduces to a t-test of the difference between the intercepts of the production functions for the experimental and control sections.

As a simple illustration of this test, suppose that the production function has only a single input—man-hours—that no other variables influence production, and that the function is linear in the relevant range. Then the production function is of the form

$$Q = a + bH$$

where Q is production, H is hours, and a and b are coefficients to be estimated. The first method of testing assumes that b is the same before and after the experiment, and that the effect of the experiment, if any, will be to increase a (Figure 16-1). The preceding approach has the advantage of being both simple to apply and easy to interpret. The disadvantage of the procedure is the assumption that the coefficients on both the controllable and uncontrollable variables are the same across the experimental and control sections. It is not obvious, a priori, that this should be the case. For example, if the result of the experiment is that the men work more efficiently in the presence of adverse conditions, this would be reflected on the coefficients of the conditions variables rather than the intercept. The two additional tests to be described do not require such restrictive assumptions.

The second method is to test for differences in any of the estimated coefficients of the production function across the sections. The maintained (null) hypothesis is that all the coefficients in the production function are the same in all sections. The alternative hypothesis is that one or

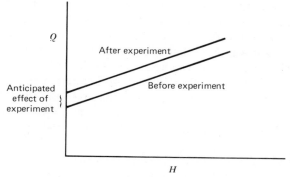

Figure 16-1.

more of the coefficients differ across sections. Thus, if the experiment resulted in a significant change in the production function in the experimental section, the maintained hypothesis should be rejected when the experimental section is compared to the control sections.

The maintained hypothesis in the first step of the test is that the coefficients in all sections are the same. The alternative is that the coefficients in all are different. Since the tests are sequential, the form of each subsequent test will depend on the outcome of the one preceding.* One simple sequence is as follows: If the null hypothesis of the first test is rejected, the production functions of the sections are not all alike. The second step would then be to test whether the production function is the same for all control sections. If so, the control groups would be combined to yield a single production function, and this function would then be compared to the experimental section. Selective testing of subsets of the coefficients would determine more precisely which of the coefficients differ between the experimental and control-section production functions.

A great many other outcomes are possible. As we have already indicated, the control sections might be found to differ among themselves. The sections might be the same in each year and different across years. The control and experimental sections might be found to be all alike. Rather than enumerate all possible sequences, we will defer further discussion until the results section where our actual test sequence is presented.

The second testing procedure described previously also has several limitations. The power of the analysis of variance test is much greater

---

* The probability of obtaining a given conclusion is not independent of the test sequence. Ideally, we would like to compute the probability of obtaining a particular conclusion taking account of the test sequence. However, in the absence of knowledge of the true values of the parameters of the model, such a calculation is not possible. Thus, confidence regions for a given level of significance are determined by treating each step of the sequence as independent of the outcomes of previus steps in the sequence.

when one uses a single production function for the control sections in a test against the experimental section than when one tests the control sections—each with a different production function—against the experimental section. For a given level of significance, one may get ambiguous results from the analysis of variance test because the power of the test changes when different combinations of coefficients or sections are tested. A second problem is that individual coefficients may be different in the experimental section relative to the control sections, but some may be higher and others lower so that the net effect on productivity is not clear cut.

The nature of this test can be illustrated by use of the simple production function introduced before. In Figure 16-2 we illustrate one possible effect of introducing an experiment. Both the intercept and the slope of the production function are changed. If the experiment has this type of effect, then it is clear that the first method of testing already discussed will be inappropriate. While the second method will indicate that a change has occurred, it will not necessarily indicate the desirability of the change. If the range of H normally employed is to the right of the intersection of the production functions in Figure 16-2, then the change will be desirable, whereas the change will be undesirable if the range of H normally employed is to the left of the intersection. Our third method of testing is designed to resolve this ambiguity.

The third method used to test the experimental section against the control sections provides an alternative that may be conclusive even if the analysis of variance tests are ambiguous for either of the reasons identified previously. This procedure requires only the production functions for the control sections. The values of the variables observed in the

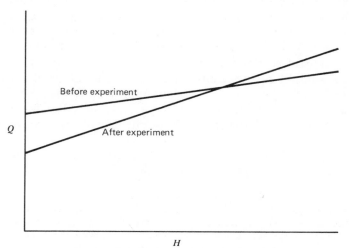

Figure 16-2.

experimental section are substituted into the estimated production functions for the control sections. This provides a prediction of the amount that would have been produced had the resources from the experimental section been used in the control sections under similar physical conditions. The actual average weekly production from the experimental section can then be compared to the predicted average from the equations for the control sections. If the predicted amount from the control sections was significantly lower (higher) than actual production from the experimental section, one would conclude that under similar physical conditions the experimental section was more (less) productive than the control sections. The relevant test statistic has the t-distribution. The derivation of the test statistic can be found in Goodman.[2]

Relative to the second method, the third method of comparison has the advantage of simplicity. The information on productivity is summarized in a single statistic comparing mean actual output of the experimental section with mean predicted output from using the same resources in the control section. The second advantage relative to both of the alternative tests is that one need not estimate a production function for the experimental section. For purposes of this test, any shifting of the production function of the experimental section will be reflected in the production of that section. Finally, the power of the test is greater than that of the analysis of variance test because the latter test compares the sections along several dimensions (as many dimensions as there are estimated coefficients), while the former test is based on a single dimension (production).

Using the simple example introduced previously, we illustrate our third procedure in Figure 16-3. Only the production function for the experimental section is estimated. Now, suppose that $\bar{H}$ man-hours per period are used in the experimental section during the experimental period. Using the production function for the control section, we obtain a predic-

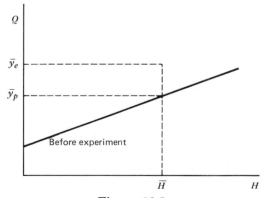

Figure 16-3.

tion of the amount that would have been produced in the control section with $\bar{H}$ man-hours per week. This is denoted $\bar{y}_p$ in Figure 16-3. Actual average production in the experimental section will be measured. Suppose that average production in the experiment is $\bar{y}_e$ in Figure 16-3. Our third method is designed to test whether the vertical distance $d = \bar{y}_e - \bar{y}_p$ is significant. Note that since measured production, $\bar{y}_e$, for the experimental section is used, it is not necessary to estimate the production function for the experimental section.

The evaluation results are not based exclusively on any one of the preceding tests. The multidimensional nature of the analysis of variance test enables one to identify differences among the sections that may not be reflected in the production figures. These differences are of interest in themselves as a supplement to the simpler test of differences in productivity.

METHODOLOGY

Sample

The analyzed data set consists of 92 weeks of production data in 1973 and 1974 for the three mining sections—experimental (South), North, and East. (More detailed and extensive analyses appear in Goodman.[2]) The sample year 1973 starts at January 2, 1973, and ends at December 1, 1973. From these 48 weeks, two were deleted, which represents the miners' vacation period in July. Therefore, the 1973 data are based on 46 weeks.

The experimental year begins in the first week of December 1973 and runs through November 9, 1974. From these 49 weeks, the two-week vacation plus another week lost from the memorial week strike (August 17, 1974 to August 24, 1974) were deleted, leaving 46 weeks for analysis. In the remaining period in November and in the first week of December, there was no production because of the national coal strike. Since there were only a few remaining actual production weeks in December and since the work in that period was under a new contract, we decided to include those weeks in the 1975 data.

Variables

Table 16-1 describes the major variables used in the analysis. The label or acronym, variable name, and description are given; then the operational form and source of the data are identified. The means and standard deviations are for all three sections for the 1973 and 1974 time periods.

Our prior expectations about the coefficients are indicated in Table 16-2. Since we are using a linear approximation to the production function, and the conditions variables may shift the function up or down, we do not

Table 16-1 Variable Descriptions

Acronym	Variable Name	Meaning of Variable	Operational Form	Source	Mean	Standard Deviation
COALBO	Coal and bony height added together	Height from ceiling to the floor	Inches	Company records	64.0	4.8
ROOF	Roof conditions	Quality of roof	1 to 5 scale 1 very bad—5 very good	Rating from superintendent	3.9	1.3
RUNWAY	Runway conditions	Quality of runway	1 to 5 scale 1 very bad—5 very good	Rating from superintendent	3.5	1.7
PILLARING	Pillaring	(See Baseline Report, 1975)	Number of shifts pillaring per week	Company records	1.13	3.4
ABSEN	Number of total absences	Number of total absences	Total absences per week	Company records	4.8	4.0
MOVES	Major moves	Measure of the distance between face and feeder	Assumes the value zero for the weeks with a major move (i.e., a move of more than 299 minutes) and increases by one for each week without a major move.	Created by analysts based on moves delay	1.7	1.8

Table 16-1 (*Continued*)

Acronym	Variable Name	Meaning of Variable	Operational Form	Source	Mean	Standard Deviation
AVMAN	Average man days	Average man days worked per days of the week	Total man days worked per week/days per week worked	Created by analysts based on company records	18.4	2.6
MOMINDEL	Moves and minor delays	Moves and minor delays	Moves and minor delays—minutes	Created by analysts based on company records	452.9	428.0
COMDEL	Combined delays	Combined delays	Car, machinery, bolter physical, and miscellaneous delays—minutes	Created by analysts based on company records	782.2	650.6
EXOUTDEL	Autonomous work-group obligation and outside delays	Autonomous work group and outside delays	Autonomous work group obligation and outside delays—minutes	Created by analysts based on company records	79.3	275.9
ACWOT	Actual crew working time	Actual crew working time	Maximum possible crew working time minus total delays in minutes	Created by analysts based on company records	4231.0	894.0
DU__	Denotes dummy variable	Introduced for periods of abnormal conditions	One during weeks when abnormal conditions prevail	Created by analysts based on company records	—	—
(Dependent Variable)	Average weekly production	Average weekly production	Average raw coal tons produced per shift	Company records	—	—

Table 16-2   Variables
Included in Production
Function

Independent Variables	Anticipated Sign
CONSTANT	?
COALBO	+
ROOF	+
RUNWAY	+
ABSEN	−
MOVES	−
PILLARING	+
AVMAN	+
MOMINDEL	0
COMDEL	0
ACWOT	+

have a priori expectations concerning the sign of the constant term. Improvements in conditions should increase production as indicated by the positive signs on the physical conditions variables in the table. The moves variable is designed to measure the distance of the miner from the feeder (conveyer belt) and should therefore be negative. Since pillaring is more productive than developmental mining, we expected a positive effect on the pillaring variable. Increases in crew size should enhance production, giving a positive sign to the man-days variable. Delays were expected to have no effect beyond the reduction in working time. Since delays have been deducted from potential crew time in constructing ACWOT, we expect zero coefficients on the delay variables when delays are entered separately. Crew time should have a positive effect on production.

RESULTS

The production function estimates are presented in Table 16-3. A comparison of the coefficient estimates across the various sections reveals that, where coefficients are statistically significant, they do have the anticipated sign.

We now turn to the results derived from our tests. The first method of testing serves to indicate whether there were differences in any of the intercepts of the model across the sections.

In row 1 of Table 16-4 we require the intercept for the five control sections to be the same and test to determine whether the intercept for South 74 (experimental) is significantly different. The estimated difference of −48.9 is small, relative to average weekly production, and is not

Table 16-3 Production Model II, Medium Aggregated Delays

East 73 — $R^2 = 0.9125$; $Dw = 1.05$

Variable	Coefficient	T-Value
CONSTANT	1845.	0.8051
COALBO	-49.33	-1.514
ROOF	-71.30	-0.9155
RUNWAY	178.7	3.268
ABSEN	-12.47	-0.5925
MOVES	-194.7	-2.404
AVMAN	45.21	1.472
DU I N73	-1294.	-1.168
EXOUTDEL	-0.1949	-0.7866
MOMINDEL	-0.05737	-0.3810
COMDEL		
ACWOT	1.239	11.35

North 73 — $R^2 = 0.9098$; $Dw = 1.917$

Variable	Coefficient	T-Value
CONSTANT	-2800.	-1.021
COALBO	-11.06	-0.2450
ROOF	149.7	1.194
RUNWAY	458.5	6.240
PILLARING	15.30	0.3376
ABSEN	40.05	0.4176
MOVES	108.9	1.274
AVMAN		
DU 1-5 873	-1619.	-2.103
EXOUTDEL	-2.987	-1.549
MOMINDEL	-0.1291	-0.3559
COMDEL	-0.08661	-0.4794
ACWOT	1.090	6.984

South 73 — $R^2 = 0.8088$; $Dw = 1.5$

Variable	Coefficient	T-Value
CONSTANT	-1392.	-0.6773
COALBO	12.76	0.4857
ROOF	68.41	0.7221
RUNWAY	-51.53	-0.4656
PILLARING	29.97	0.4976
ABSEN	-6.050	-0.1500
MOVES	-20.28	-0.3184
AVMAN	46.97	0.5458
DU 1-5 873	-2644.	-4.719
EXOUTDEL	-2.357	-0.9867
MOMINDEL	-0.0604	-0.2107
COMDEL	0.0569	0.2032
ACWOT	1.011	6.794

Total — $R^2 = 0.8537$; $Dw = 1.400$

Variable	Coefficient	T-Value
CONSTANT	-2287.	-3.448
COALBO	-4.247	-0.4983
ROOF	75.29	2.244
RUNWAY	155.9	5.952
PILLARING	45.27	4.162
ABSEN	17.01	1.783
MOVES	-82.45	-2.970
AVMAN	83.15	5.475
DU I N73	-1638.	-2.705
DU RUMW 5 N73	1079.	6.334
DU 1-5 873	-1729.	-6.016
DU 23,39-43 N74	-1341.	-5.133
COMDEL	-0.0218	-0.3006
MOMINDEL	-0.1663	-1.684
EXOUTDEL	-0.3037	-2.160
MBCDEL	0.1307	0.4083
ACWOT	1.143	20.39

	East 74		North 74		South 74	
	Coefficient	T-Value	Coefficient	T-Value	Coefficient	T-Value
CONSTANT	-3238.	-1.660	-3896.	-1.385	-7947.	-1.642
COALBO	-22.32	-0.8761	-14.73	-0.5448	44.62	0.7431
ROOF	389.5	2.987	102.4	0.9332	441.1	3.312
RUNWAY	11.40	0.1750	127.6	1.484	-103.6	-0.9025
PILLARING	22.11	2.167			110.1	4.388
ABSEN	30.73	1.888	29.71	1.208	30.63	0.628
MOVES	-32.47	-1.198	17.32	0.2421	-115.0	-1.97
AVMAN	196.6	3.008	148.4	1.629	128.6	1.539
DU 23,39-43 N74			-1168.	-2.858		
EXOUTDEL	-0.3979	-0.6405	-0.8868	-0.4237	-0.1092	-0.4884
MOMINDEL	-0.2954	-1.667	0.1521	0.6654	0.01382	0.05075
MBCDEL			0.6526	1.639		
COMDEL	-0.0186	-0.1123	0.2175	0.9918	0.1283	0.4777
ACWOT	1.000	10.41	1.238	7.330	1.269	6.492

East 74: $R^2 = 0.8964$; $Dw = 2.0$

North 74: $R^2 = 0.8621$; $Dw = 1.597$

South 74: $R^2 = 0.8322$; $Dw = 1.57$

Table 16-4   Tests for Differences in Intercepts across Sections—Method 1

Sections included in regression	Section Coefficients[a]					
	E73	N73	S73	E74	N74	S74
ENSEN, S74	B[b]	B	B	B	B	−48.9
E73,N73,S73,E74,N74,S74	−60.6 (.35)	−597.5 (2.4)	B	−308.1 (1.8)	−321.3 (2.0)	−190.6 (.99)
E73,N73,S73,E74,N74	9.1 (.05)	−535.7 (2.4)	B	−103.4 (.65)	−289.9 (1.98)	
E73,E74	B			−115.4 (.94)		
N73,N74		B			372.2 (1.91)	
S73,S74			B			−163.9 (.44)

[a] t-ratios are shown in parentheses.
[b] Sections denoted with a "B" in a given run were used as a base against which the remaining section intercepts were compared.

significant. In row 2, all of the section intercepts are allowed to be different with South 73 used as a reference. The coefficients for North 73 and North 74 are significantly lower than the coefficients for South 73 at the 5% level, and the coefficient for East 74 is significantly lower at the 10% level. This result indicates that the intercepts for the control group are different, and this is confirmed by row 3 of Table 16-4, which includes only the five control sections. North has a significantly lower intercept than the remaining control sections in both years. In the remaining three rows, the intercept of each section in 1974 is compared to the 1973 intercept. The difference is significant only in North.

The results in Table 16-4 provide no evidence that the intercept has been shifted upward by the experiment. This conclusion emerges in the first, second, and sixth rows when South 74 (experimental) is compared to various control groups. The results in Table 16-4 do, however, suggest that there are significant differences among the intercepts of the sections in the control group. The results of method 2 (see the later discussion) provide a more general test for differences in any of the coefficients across the sections.

In row 1 of Table 16-5, we test whether individual production functions for the six sections fit the data significantly better than a single function applied to all six. At the 5% significance level, the sections are not significantly different. Since the power of the F-test varies considerably when various sections are combined, we present the results of several alternative tests. The results in the second row indicate that the control sections are not significantly different. When a single function for the five control sections is tested against the experimental section in row 3, the difference proves to be significant at the 1% level.

Further evidence of the similarity of the control sections is provided in rows 4 and 5. In row 4, a single function for the three sections in 1973 is tested against separate functions for each section, and no significant difference is found. In row 5, the combined control group in 1973 is compared to the combined control group in 1974, and again no difference is found.

Row 6 indicates no significant difference across experimental and control groups in 1974. However, when the experimental and control groups are combined in 1974 and tested against the combined control group in 1973, a significant difference is found as is indicated in row 7. This should be contrasted to the results in 5 where no significant differences were found when the experimental section was not included in 1974. Finally, the models for each of the sections are compared across years in rows 8, 9, and 10. Here it is found that one of the control sections differs between 1973 and 1974, but the production function for the experimental section in 1974 is not significantly different from the production function in 1973.

The results in Table 16-5 indicate difficulties one may typically expect to encounter in applying method 2. The outcome of the tests is dependent on the way in which sections are combined to perform the test. If one is confident that all experimental sections are alike, they can be combined as a single group and tested against the experimental section, as we have shown in row 3 of Table 16-5. If one is less confident of the homogeneity of the control sections, then one might prefer not to impose the a priori restriction that all control sections have identical production functions.

Table 16-5   Analysis of Variance Results—Method 2

Sections	Production Model	
	DF	F
E73,N73,S73,E74,N74,S74 vs. TOTAL	56/203	1.39
E73,N73,S73,E74,N74 vs. ENSEN	44/169	1.10
ENSEN, S74 vs. TOTAL	12/247	3.28[a]
E73,N73,S73 vs. ENS 73	21/102	.99
ENS 73, ENS 74 vs. ENSEN	12/201	1.29
E74,N74,S74 vs. ENS 74	24/100	1.43
ENS 73, ENS 74 vs. TOTAL	12/247	1.86[b]
E73,E74 vs. East 73 + 74	11/ 69	1.96[b]
N73,N74 vs. North 73 + 74	10/ 67	.85
S73,S74 vs. South 73 + 74	12/ 67	.93

[a] Significant at the 1% level.
[b] Significant at the 5% level.

In this case, a test, such as that in row 1, is more appropriate. The contrast between the results of rows 1 and 3 indicate that the stand one is willing to take about the homogeneity of the control sections affects the power of the test and, hence, the likelihood of the test yielding a finding of statistical significance. Nonetheless, tests of the form in Table 16-5 are informative about the relative homogeneity of different sections. However, tests of this type should be supplemented by a more detailed comparison of individual coefficients in production functions of various sections.

Additional tests were conducted to explore possible differences between South 74 and the control group. In these tests, additional dummy variables were included to allow the "roof," "runway," and "pillaring" coefficients to differ for South 74 when it was included in estimating a single production function for the experimental and control groups combined. When differences are allowed in the coefficients of the three variables previously identified, the production functions for the experimental and control sections are not otherwise significantly different.

The conclusion of the F-tests is that weak evidence exists that the experimental and control sections are different. The differences appear to be attributable to the roof, runway, and pillaring coefficients. These differences in the coefficients of the conditions variables may be attributable to the experiment, though such differences would not have been predicted a priori. For example, it may be that the experiment caused the crew to work at the same productivity level independent of runway conditions, giving rise to the insignificant coefficient on runway in Table 16-3 for South 74. The higher coefficient on pillaring indicated greater productivity in pillaring in the experimental section. If the higher coefficient on roof is to be attributed to the experiment, one would have to conclude that the experiment made productivity more sensitive to changes in roof conditions. Since the coefficients on roof and runway in South 74 differ in opposite directions from those of the control group, sampling errors rather than experimental effects may be the causes of these differences.

The results of the test of intercepts appear in some respects inconsistent with the results of the analysis of variance test. The intercept tests indicated no significant effect of the experiment, while the analysis of variance tests indicate a significant difference between the experimental and control groups. Also, the intercept tests indicated that North differed significantly from the other control sections, while the analysis of variance tests suggests that what differences exist are attributable to East.

The explanation of these seemingly inconsistent results is traceable to the underlying assumptions and the relative power of the tests. The intercept test is predicated on the assumption that differences, if any, will be reflected in the intercepts. Offsetting differences in the other coefficients may not be picked up by the intercept test. In contrast, the analysis of the variance test allows for quite general differences, but the discriminatory power of the test is lower than that of the intercept test. Clearly, it is desirable to have a single summary measure of the effects of the experiment. The intercept test is unsatisfactory because there is no a priori reason to expect only the intercept to be affected. The analysis of variance test identifies differences but does not indicate the net effect of those differences on productivity. It is for these reasons that we developed the third method of testing for differences in productivity.

Both the intercept test and the analysis of variance test cast doubt on the hypothesis that all sections in the control group have the same production function. Therefore, we conducted the means test not only with the combined control group, but also using only South 73 as the control group. If unobserved variables are responsible for differences among the control sections. South 73 may be a more reliable control, since such unobserved variables may differ less over time for a given section than they vary across sections.

The results of means tests are presented in Table 16-6. For the results in the upper half of the table, the production function for South 73 was used to obtain predicted average weekly production. This prediction is obtained by substituting the independent variables observed in each week in South 74 into the estimated production function for South 73. The average of these predictions, denoted y_p, was then subtracted from actual average production in South 74 to obtain the estimated difference, d. The difference is an estimate of the amount by which average weekly production in South 74 exceeded the amount that would have been produced had the same resources been used under similar physical conditions in South 73. The results in the bottom half of the table were obtained by applying the same procedure using the production function estimated when the data from all the control sections were combined.

The results indicate that average tonnage produced per week in South 74 was not significantly different from the amount that would have been

Table 16-6 Tests for Differences
between Predicted and Actual
Means—Method 3

Control: South 73	
$\bar{y}_p$	4619
$d = \bar{y}_e - \bar{y}_p$	97
t	.17
Control: Combined Nonexperimental Sections	
$\bar{y}_p$	4708
$d = \bar{y}_e - \bar{y}_p$	8
t	.03

produced had the same resources been used in the nonexperimental sections under similar physical conditions. This conclusion is obtained, using either South 73 or the combined nonexperimental sections as the control.

The basic results across the three methods indicate there are no significant productivity changes. In a more comprehensive analysis over a larger data set, similar results are reported (Goodman, 1979). Since the purpose of this chapter is to examine alternative procedures, we will not explore the substantive reasons for these results,[2] but, rather, some critical issues underlying the proposed estimation procedures.

CRITICAL ISSUES

The evaluation methods we have discussed involve estimation and testing of coefficients or sets of coefficients of a regression model. The use of ordinary least squares for estimation and t- and F-statistics for testing will be appropriate only if the model satisfies certain assumptions. Later, we identify those assumptions and discuss ways in which the appropriateness of those assumptions can be checked. While there is no foolproof procedure for determining that the assumptions are satisfied, it is often possible to identify departures from the assumed condition. Where departures are identified, modification of the model or choice of a different estimation procedure will often overcome or mitigate the problem.

Issues that should be considered in specification of a model are selection of variables, choice of functional form, specification of the properties of the error term, measurement of variables, and choice of an appropriate level of aggregation.

Selection of Variables

It is possible to misspecify a model by including irrelevant variables or by failing to include relevant variables.

Inclusion of extraneous variables does not cause a bias in estimation of coefficients or standard errors. Consequently, statistical tests involving the estimated parameters are valid. However, the inclusion of extraneous variables does reduce the efficiency of the estimators. As a result, less-precise estimates of the parameters are obtained, and tests of hypotheses are more likely to be ambiguous.

Exclusion of relevant variables is generally a more serious problem. If a variable that actually influences production is excluded from the model, and the excluded variable is correlated with any variable included in the model, the estimated coefficients on the included variables will be biased. Thus, exclusion of relevant variables can be expected to result in incorrect signs and magnitudes of estimated coefficients of included variables.

Coefficient estimates that depart in sign or magnitude from prior expectations may be an indication that important variables are omitted.

Choice of Functional Form

Theory generally provides little guidance concerning the appropriate choice of functional form. However, a linear equation will often provide a good approximation to the true function within the range of observed values of the variables. The validity of the linear specification can be tested if the linearity assumption is in doubt. One simple procedure is to adopt a functional form that contains the linear function as a special case and to test whether the nonlinear terms are significantly different from zero. For example, in our evaluation of the coal-mine experiment, we recognized that the production function could not be linear throughout its range. Beyond some point, extra workers added in a given mine will make a relatively small contribution to productivity because there is simply very little that the extra workers can do to enhance production. Therefore, we estimated a quadratic fraction of crew working time and included interaction terms between working time and other variables. We found that these additional variables did not significantly contribute to the fit of the production function. Therefore, we adopted the linear specification as an adequate approximation within the observed range of values of the variables.

Properties of Error Terms

For ordinary least squares to give unbiased estimates of the coefficients of the production function, it is necessary that the residuals be uncorrelated with explanatory variables in the model. There are several ways that a correlation between residuals and explanatory variables can arise. We indicated before that exclusion of relevant variables can result in biased parameter estimates. The reason is that the error term in the misspecified model includes the effects of the excluded variables. Hence the error term in the misspecified model will be correlated with the included variables if the excluded variables are correlated with the included variables.

A more subtle way that correlation between residuals and explanatory variables can occur is illustrated by the following example. Suppose that a mine has some workers who are assigned to a particular section on a discretionary basis. Suppose further that a section receives additional men if its production is found to be falling short of some normal level of output. Such an assignment policy essentially involves assigning extra men to a section when the error term in the section's production function is negative. Hence the true error term will be negatively correlated with the explanatory variable *working time*. As a result, the estimated coefficient on working time will be biased downward. It will appear the extra workers contribute little to production, not because they in fact contribute little but because they are only assigned when production is falling short of the level normally expected. If the extra workers bring production back to the normal level, they will appear, statistically, to have contributed little or nothing at all because their presence simply offsets a negative realization for the unobserved error term.

As the second example indicates, relatively subtle forces can cause a correlation between the error term and the explanatory variables. Since the errors are unobserved, it is difficult to statistically detect the presence of such a correlation. Thus only a careful specification of the production function based on knowledge of actual policies for allocating workers, machines, materials, and the like can guard against this very important type of misspecification.

The three evaluation methods that we have discussed involve making statistical inferences about the effects of the experimental intervention. For these inferences to be valid, it is not only necessary that coefficient estimates are unbiased but that standard-error estimates are unbiased as well. The latter condition requires that the errors are mutually uncorrelated and that they have constant variance.

Correlation among residuals for different observations can arise for several reasons. A circumstance in which such a correlation is frequently encountered is when a production function is being estimated, using a time series of observations for a given producing section. The presence of an unobserved variable that changes through time can induce serial correlation in the error terms even if the unobserved variable is uncorrelated with the explanatory variables. For example, working conditions in a mine section can gradually change over time. Some physical conditions that affect production (e.g., roof and runway conditions) can be measured, but others will be difficult to quantify systematically. Changes in these unmeasured conditions may manifest themselves by a positive correlation between the error term in a given period and the error term in the immediately preceding period. Standard tests for autocorrelation are available.[3] Where autocorrelation is found, as it was in our evaluation of the mine intervention, estimation procedures are available that correct for the problem.

For cross-sectional analysis (e.g., comparison of different experimental and control groups), correlation among disturbances can occur if all groups are affected by similar random shocks. For example, company-wide policy changes or technological changes can cause such cross-sectional correlation. A simple procedure for detecting the presence of such effects is to estimate the production function separately for each group and then examine whether the estimated residuals are correlated across sections. If the residuals are correlated, estimation procedures are available to take account of this correlation.

When the assumption that the disturbances have a constant variance is violated, the disturbances are said to be "heteroskedastic." For example, if an organizational intervention leads to less erratic work behavior, the variance in production in the experimental section may be less than in the control section. Where heteroskedasticity occurs, it is normally possible to weight the observations in a way that mitigates the problem.

Many of the specification problems that occur in practice can be detected by a careful study of the residuals. Thus, it is generally fruitful to plot the residuals against time and against the explanatory variables. Where more than one section is involved, the residuals from one section can be plotted against the residuals from another. If systematic patterns are detected in these plots, the reason can normally be traced to one or more of the specification problems discussed previously.

Measurement Problems

Another implicit assumption of regression analysis, which is less frequently discussed, especially in behavioral-science applications, is that both dependent and explanatory variables have to be intervally scaled, except for dummy (0–1) explanatory variables. If, however, some variables are only ordinally scaled and they are treated as interval variables, the parameter estimates may be biased. Since the researcher usually knows which variables do not conform to the interval scale assumption, alternative estimation techniques can be used that do not make stringent scaling assumptions. For example, an ordinally scaled explanatory variable can be decomposed into several dummy (0–1) variables, and the assumption that the ordinal scale has interval scale characteristics can be tested easily. In our study, we had two rating scales reflecting physical working conditions as independent variables. We tested the hypothesis that the ordinal rating scale (from 1 to 5) actually has interval scale properties by introducing a dummy variable for each scale value, and we found that the rating scale did not significantly depart from an interval scale.

Testing whether an ordinally scaled dependent variable has interval scale properties is more complicated and can be achieved by means of a maximum likelihood procedure.[5] The dependent variable will not be ordinal if output is measured directly, and this problem will not arise.

Measurement errors in the independent variables can lead to biased parameter estimates. To some extent, this problem will often be beyond the control of the experimenter since resources will not normally be available to set up a separate measurement system for the economic variables. In our evaluation, we tried where possible to evaluate the degree of convergence among common ratings of the same phenomena.

Questions of validity also affect the researcher's ability to estimate productivity effects. The major problem in our evaluation arose in connection with our measure of productivity that came from the foremen's estimates. Bosses in the experimental section might have wanted to make their sections look better, while bosses in the control sections might have overstated production to make their sections look comparable to the experimental section. We attacked this problem, first, by comparing the bosses' production estimates with alternative measures of productivity (i.e., surveyor's estimates). Second, we examined the social context of the evaluation system and found that pressure to overstate production appeared to be constant across all mining sections and between the baseline and experimental periods.

Where production data are available for time intervals of varying length (e.g., day, week, month), a question arises as to the appropriate interval to use. Strictly speaking, if the function is linear, unbiased parameter estimates should be obtained regardless of the time interval used. The precision of the parameter estimates should increase by using the larger number of observations available when a shorter interval is used. In practice, there are limits to the gains from shortening the time interval. The costs of measurement increase as the interval is shortened, and measurement errors may become more severe as it is shortened.

For our evaluation of the mine intervention, we estimated the production functions using both daily and weekly data and found comparable results. We felt that measurements based on weekly observations were more accurate, and we conducted the bulk of our evaluation using weekly data.

Control Groups

Another assessment issue concerns control groups. The lack of improvement in productivity might be explained by the fact that the other sections are not equivalent to the experimental section and the comparison with these groups is inappropriate. We tried to respond to this question by developing a model that would be generalizable across sections. Indeed, the analysis examining the production functions across the different sections showed a great deal of similarity. The other analytic approach was to treat each section as its own control group. That is, we compared the performance of the experimental section in the baseline with its performance in the experimental year. Our overall strategy was to acknowledge that there was a potential problem of equivalence, and to use our analytical procedures with alternative control groups. We obtained a relatively consistent picture across these different strategies, and hence felt more certain about the validity of our results.

CONCLUSION

Assessing the economic consequences of organizational interventions is an important task. The long-run viability of organizational interventions will depend in part on their economic viability. In the past, researchers have made claims about productivity changes, but, in our judgment, their estimating procedures have been too primitive to tease out intervention effects from competing explanations.

To estimate economic consequences, the researcher must do the following:

1.   Theoretically determine the relevant production model or production function. This can be derived from prior research, interviewing key personnel and/or observing the production process. It is *the* first critical step.

2.   Generate a set of reliable and valid measures of the key variables. In most cases one will have to use the existing company measures because of the high cost of setting up a new information system. However, care should be given to estimating the reliability and validity of these measures.

3.   Estimate the production functions and examine their validity relevant to a priori expectations and revise the model, if necessary.

4.   Adopt one of the three methods we proposed for separating out intervention effects from alternative explanations for productivity changes. Our preference is to use the means test (method 3). Information on productivity is summarized in a single interpretable statistic. One need not make any assumptions about changes in the production function in the experimental work area. Also, the power of the test is greater for this method as compared with the analysis of variance approach (method 2).

5.   Pay close attention to the critical issues identified in the last section of this chapter. Problems in misspecifying the input variables, their functional form, and autocorrelation of the residuals seriously confound estimating productivity effects. The statistical technology is available to deal with these issues. The task is for the researcher to be sensitive to these issues and apply the appropriate statistical techniques.

After the economic effects have been estimated, the next step is to incorporate these results in a traditional cost-benefit analysis. A procedure for doing a cost-benefit analysis of an organizational intervention has been proposed by Goodman.[2]

REFERENCES

1.   Glaser, E. M. *Productivity gains through worklife improvement.* New York: Harcourt Brace Jovanovich, 1975.

2.   Goodman, P. S. *Assessing organizational change: The Rushton quality of work experiment.* New York: Wiley, 1979.

3.   Johnston, J. *Econometric methods,* 2nd ed. New York: McGraw-Hill, 1972.

4.   Kmenta, J. *Elements of econometrics.* New York: Macmillan, 1971.

5.   McKelvey, R., & Zavoina, W. A. Statistical model for the analysis of ordinal level dependent variables. *Journal of Mathematical Sociology,* 1975.

CHAPTER SEVENTEEN

Evaluating Program Costs and Benefits

PHILIP H. MIRVIS AND BARRY A. MACY

Consider the most fundamental question in the evaluation of change programs: Do the ends justify the means? In earlier conceptions of quality of working life, the question was more readily answered, for people were regarded as economic resources (means) to be used for economic benefits (ends).[1] Thus it was wholly rational to implement changes to train employees, enrich their jobs, provide them with better equipment, improve their physical working conditions, or find ways to reduce accident rates— to the extent that these improved the economy of the firm or of the society. The ends of first concern in assessment were financial and quite readily accountable, as were the costs involved.

The intrusion of intangibles into the cost-benefit equation considerably "enriches" the assessor's own job, but it does not remove the obligation to "cost-out" programs. Today, most people acknowledge intangible costs (e.g., loss of goodwill or self-esteem) and intangible benefits (e.g., employee well-being and cooperation). Thus an array of factors once thought unmeasurable are being brought into the domain of assessment, both in terms of theory, as in human-resource accounting, and in terms of economic valuation, as in the case of estimating the delayed dollar costs of worker exposure to toxic chemicals.

This chapter describes efforts to estimate the costs and benefits of change programs in monetary terms and, when such valuation proves possible, also in terms of their social utility. Both valuations are needed, for even as evaluators give increased weight to the benefits of these programs to society—the welfare of workers' families, or the next generation of citizens—they cannot overlook the immediacies of the worker's employment and income, and of the employer's fiscal health and efficiency.

Regarding the economics of change programs in organizations, the existing evidence is scanty.[2-4] Even for such well-researched topics as work-place safety programs, for example, an uninformed debate continues about costs and benefits. With regard to the costs and benefits of programs such as job enrichment, sensitivity training, participative management, work-group autonomy, and the like, the situation is worse. Employers, labor leaders, public policy makers, and professional change specialists themselves draw their views largely from theory, ideology, experience, or hope. This can and must be changed for two reasons: (1) The choices made about the alternative approaches to improving working life require knowledge about and consideration for their economic consequences, and (2) The chief, but by no means only, impediment to undertaking work-place improvements is the belief that they are usually costly and uneconomical. A major impetus to the improvement of the quality of work life would be the accumulation of credible evidence that such improvements need not threaten and may, indeed, benefit the economic standing of the employer, the worker, and society.

A FRAMEWORK FOR EVALUATION

Organization change programs produce multiple effects: The work environment may be altered, attitudes and behavior may be changed, and financial and social benefits may accrue. Assessment research is designed to measure and interpret these effects. Assessment research is also intended to test the theory and principles that underlie the change program. These dual objectives require

1. Specification of a theory of organization behavior and change.
2. Measurement of the program implementation and its effects within a research design suited for drawing causal inferences.
3. Assessment of the costs and benefits of the program.

Theory, Measurement, and Research Design

Previous chapters in this volume have described our theories of organization behavior and change. They posit that a change program results in changes in the work environment that affect organization members' attitudes and behaviors. Such attitudinal and behavioral effects, in conjunction with changes in an organization's structures, technology, and markets, in turn affect program results. To assess the significance of these results requires as assessor to measure an inclusive range of variables likely to be influenced by a change program and statistically test the significance of changes in these measures over time. In addition, the assessor must monitor the implementation of the program to formulate hypotheses about the intervening processes that produce those results and to account for nonprogrammatic factors that may influence them.

To demonstrate that changes in intervening processes and outcomes are due to a change program requires the use of two assessment strategies. First, such changes can be evaluated by means of an experimental research design. As the previous chapters noted, however, random selection of experimental and control units in organizations is often impossible, and finding units with comparable structures, technologies, and markets is equally impractical. Thus, our strategy has been to use "quasi-experimental" designs that include comparison units that do not participate in a change effort.[5] This eliminates some, but by no means all, threats to the validity of conclusions drawn about the relative impact of a change program.

Another strategy is to specify and test a model of the change dynamics.[6] The case of Goodman's modeling of the production function of a coal mine in the previous chapter is an example. By measuring nonprogrammatic variables, such as mining conditions, roof heights, and the like, and statistically testing their impacts on mining output, Goodman was able to assess the relative impacts of these factors versus programmatic variables on program results. Unfortunately, it is not always feasible to specify such a production function nor to gather the necessary data. Thus, our strategy has been to gather and analyze these data where available and, where unavailable, to estimate the relative impacts of nonprogrammatic changes in structure, technology, and markets.[7] These estimates have been made by knowledgeable experts on assessment teams and, of course, by site personnel. As previous chapters have described such evaluations of attitudinal, behavioral, and performance data, this chapter will present a summary for evaluating changes in financial terms.

Financial Assessment

Although specific practices differ, financial assessment generally involves an accounting of the costs and benefits of altered resource allocations—in our case, resources expended in or diverted from other uses and applied to a change program. In assessments, these resources are treated as inputs and the benefits that accrue are treated as effects. The cost of inputs into the program include the direct financial expenditures (variable costs), the indirect expenditures (fixed costs) that are diverted from normal use and applied to the program, and the opportunities that are "sacrificed" (opportunity costs) by the allocation of resources to the change program rather than to other productive ends. The benefits, then, represent the net beneficial effects or losses that result from the change program.

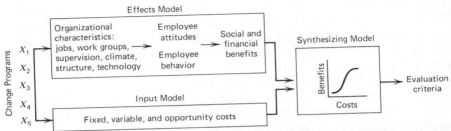

Figure 17-1 Framework for assessing costs and benefits of change programs.

Figure 17-1 presents a simple model for the financial assessment of change programs in organizations. It depicts five change programs, x_1-x_5, and three distinct analytic components: (1) an *input model* for identifying the fixed, variable, and opportunity costs of the change programs; (2) An *effects model* for measuring and tracing the impact of the programs on the work environment, employees' attitudes and behavior, and, ultimately, on social and financial benefits; and (3) a *synthesizing model* for comparing the costs and benefits and for determining the relative effectiveness of the programs.

With a theory of organizational change, measurement of relevant variables, and a sound research strategy, the assessor is prepared to conduct a financial assessment of a change program. The next section of this chapter describes the distinct analytic functions of financial assessment; later sections present illustrative examples of these analyses and the criteria that may be used in evaluating the costs and benefits of change programs.

THE ANALYTIC FUNCTIONS: INPUTS, EFFECTS, AND SYNTHESES

The Input Model

Following the early proposals for human-resource accounting, guidelines have been developed for identifying the cost of human-resource allocations and computing an organization's investment in personnel.[8] These guidelines and the investment theory that underlies them can also be applied to the assessment of inputs into any program directed toward human resources, since the theory provides the basis for equating resource inputs and outputs over time and for representing them in the common metric of dollars.[9] It should be emphasized, however, that the researcher is not interested in assessing the *investment value* of these inputs and their depreciation over time. First, it has not been established that human beings legally or morally can be valued as assets, although surely their actual and expected services can be. Second, there are analytic problems in reporting these expenditures at their gross, book, or net current economic value.[10] Given these troubling theoretical and methodological concerns, Mirvis and Macy argue that expenditures on human resources should be treated as *costs* and then discounted over time.[11] These costs can be compared with the present value of future benefits in the common metric of the cost-benefit calculus.

These quandaries notwithstanding, human-resource accounting guidelines can be used in assessing the variable, fixed, and opportunity costs of quality of work life programs. Variable costs in these programs include the fees paid to consultants and any expenses associated with their activities. These costs vary, of course, depending on the type of program and the intensity and duration of consultant involvement. The host organization also incurs variable costs including, for example, direct program expenditures such as supplements to employees' overtime pay. All such variable costs can be assigned to the change program. The fixed costs of a program include salaries, wages, and benefits associated with the employee's time diverted from normal work and also the overhead burden assigned to that time; these are fixed costs since they would be incurred with or without the change program. Opportunity costs include the profit contribution of an employee's "lost" time. They represent the value of opportunities foregone by investing resources in the change program.[12]

The assessment of these program inputs involves more than gathering the necessary data and grouping them into appropriate cost categories. Before completing the cost analysis, the researcher also has to determine the *economic value* rather than only the *measured cost* of the inputs. This involves (1) discounting the effect of inflation on direct costs, (2) determining whether fixed costs are simply transferred, without loss, from the organization to the program and, therefore, cannot be valued as program costs, and (3) assessing the opportunity value of time, supplies, and facilities that are contributed to the change effort.

The adjustment for inflation often is significant. It is accomplished by converting direct expenditures to the program in the later years to their equivalent in base-year dollars. This is necessary because inflation rates vary from year to year, and the same expenditures in high and low inflation years have a different economic value. Moreover, because some programs incur their heaviest costs in an early year and no others in a later year, two compared programs might have identical measured costs, but their economic values might be substantially different.[13]

To determine whether any fixed costs should be allocated to the program, the analyst considers whether salaries, benefits, and the overhead costs of employees are, in effect, transferred from the organization to the program. When it can be assumed that these costs would be incurred by the organization regardless of the change program, they represent no real cost to the program.[14] However, when it can be determined that the unit from which resources were diverted was less productive, incurred additional costs as a result of the transfer, or was unable to save expenses through staff reductions or attritions, such costs can be transferred to the program. By focusing on these costs, the assessor is, in effect, determining the transfer price of the resource reallocation and treating it as a program expenditure.

In order to value the opportunities foregone by expending resources in a change program, rather than to another productive end, the assessor must estimate the "market value" of such an expenditure. One measureable opportunity cost, for example, if the profit contribution of employees' labor that is lost when they interrupt their normal work to participate in program activities. Should the firm not be making a profit, however, the measured cost of this time would be understated, and the analyst would have to determine the market value of lost products or services. This principle applies as well to time, supplies, and facilities volunteered or contributed to the program. There are instances, however, when market value does not reflect the economic value of a resource, as in the case of volunteered leisure time, where the market value may be too high.[14] In such cases, the researcher needs to use a corrective factor to reflect the marginal contribution of the resource to the program.

These three analytic adjustments may prove to be trivial, or they may significantly affect the valuation of inputs and, as a result, the cost-benefit comparison. For this reason, analysts often prepare several cost estimates and group expenditures into categories of actual and discounted direct costs, fixed costs, and opportunity costs.

The Effects Model

According to the theory of organization behavior and change that underlies quality of work life programs, change should be observed in the work environment and in the attitudes and behaviors of working people before change in the operating effectiveness of the organization and the quality of working life of its employees is observed. These constitute the intervening variables in the effects model, and they can be assessed using observational, interview, and questionnaire instruments presented elsewhere in this volume. The task of the assessor is to array these into a model of change dynamics and trace the impact of changes in these variables on financial results.

In an earlier chapter we described the means for identifying financial variables likely to be affected by a change program and for disaggregating them from gross financial measures for purposes of program assessment. Specifically, we presented methods and procedures for assessing the rates of participation—membership behaviors, including absenteeism, turnover, and the like, and of performance-on-the-job behaviors, including accidents, productivity, and so forth, and for "costing out" the monetary savings associated with changes in these behaviors. Using this methodology, a researcher can identify the financial effects of an organizational change program.[15] Variable savings might include increased marginal productivity achieved by increased product or service quantity or quality, by reduced overtime or supply and material consumption, and by less unscheduled downtime. Wages and the expense of maintaining a replacement work force to cover time lost to absenteeism, accidents, and grievances could also decrease. Fixed cost savings could potentially be realized if some of the service demands placed upon the personnel, industrial relations, safety, and quality-control departments were reduced. Opportunity savings might be realized if time formerly spent in replacing absent workers or training replacements could be put to more productive use. By measuring behaviors and estimating their financial impact, the research can report the total savings. In addition, to correct for fluctuations in the size of the work force, the savings can be reported on a per-employee basis.

The validity of these cost-savings estimates rests upon the explanatory power of the theory used in the effects model and upon the qualities of the experimental design used in their interpretation. Theory identifies the program effects that are to be measured and specifies the time lag between measurements; design and statistical analyses are used to distinguish which cost savings are attributable to the change program. In order to validate the model of program effects, the researcher traces the impact of the program on the work environment, the attitudes, and the behaviors of organization members and, if possible, observes concomitant changes in these variables over time in experimental, as opposed to, comparison units. Statistical tests may be used to insure the changes are not trivial or random.

As in the assessment of program inputs, program benefits can be misestimated as result of inflation. Benefits earned later in the program, as an example, have less value than the same dollar benefits earned earlier. Thus, the program benefits also have to be discounted to their base or present value. Benefits also have to be considered in relation to fluctuations in the personnel roster of the organization. In reporting program benefits, analysts may choose to prepare several estimates that report total measured benefits, the economic value of benefits, and benefits per person during the different measurement periods.

Additional Features of the Effects Model

The foregoing discussion indicates how change-program effects can be dollar valued to a substantial degree. Nevertheless, some effects implied by the model are excluded from such an analysis unless inserted and dollar valued by some judgmental process among the beneficiaries or observers of the program. There are three such considerations: consumption values, externalities, and benefit composition.

Consumption Values. Organizational change programs are commonly assumed to produce some gains or losses that can not be readily valued because their values (utilities) arise in direct consumption. For example, if a change program led to more challenging jobs, increased satisfaction and self-esteem among employees might follow; satisfaction and self-esteem have value in themselves, beyond their measurable market and economic values captured through behavioral assessment. These values must be considered, along with accounted values, even though they are not ordinarily assigned a value in dollar terms.

There are, however, some means of estimating these values—for both employees and for an organization. In *The 1977 Quality of Employment Survey,* for example, a national sample of employees was asked whether they would trade a 10% pay increase for alternative employment arrangements.[16] Some 48% of employees said they would trade the increase for more paid vacation, 25%, for more job security, and 25%, for more challenging work. With respect to the value of alternative work arrangements to an organization, Goodman attempted in his assessment of a joint labor-management project to estimate the value added to the firm as a result of the program.[17] To assign a value to this "intangible," Goodman obtained from professional appraisers their hypothetical bids for the purchase of two firms. The firms were identically described except for certain human and organizational characteristics whose differences reflected prechange and postchange program conditions. Significantly higher bids were made for the organization described as having the conditions following the change effort.

Externalities. In some organizational change programs, certain spillover effects are observed—secondary and tertiary effects that have values, either positive or negative, but that are not experienced or accountable within the work place. Such factors are not represented directly in the assessment model, they are often not anticipated and measured, and they can take widely differing forms. Examples are a park contributed for community use whose benefits are diffused outside of the work place; a job-satisfaction increase translated into general life satisfaction, or into increased community participation; and happier and healthier children because of their parents' work-place changes. Some side effects are less desirable as when a prospering and growing firm strains the community's road and sewerage systems. In principle, such benefits and losses can be internalized into the assessment scheme, but in practice they are likely to be taken into account in less systematic ways.

Benefit Composition and Distribution. The final step in assessing the benefits of a change program is determining their composition and distribution to beneficiaries. Of interest to the assessor, then, is not only the amount of social and financial benefits, but their composition. As an example, a program that yields dollar savings from reduced absenteeism, illness, and accidents might be adjudged differently from one that produces increased work output, even though both might show comparable financial benefits. Of interest, too, is the distribution of the benefits. A program where the satisfaction or turnover of supervisors increased markedly and of employees only slightly might be evaluated differently than one where such effects occurred uniformly throughout the organization. Similarly, overall financial return might be differently valued if the gain accrues only to owners and is not shared in some appropriate degree with the employees.

There are, of course, means for assessing the "value" of various benefit compositions and distributions in financial terms. For example, a program that increases satisfaction and reduces accidents and turnover would be expected to return benefits over a longer period than one that increases pressures on employees and produces short-term increases in productivity. Extending the assessment period would account for this effect. A program that profits owners more than employees, as another example, represents a transfer payment from one group to the other that might have differing marginal values to each. Assessing the subsequent use of these resources—as to whether they increase or decrease wages, prices, and employment—is one means of estimating the value of the transfer payment and evaluating its marginal value to owners versus employees.

Synthesizing Model

In comparing the costs and benefits of change programs in organizations, the researcher is concerned with the relationship of program inputs and effects. The evaluative questions are whether resources (means) have been used beneficially, effectively, and usefully to improve the quality of life at work (ends).

The evaluation of the costs and benefits of an organizational change program is premised on the belief that resources are scarce in any organization. Thus, management, unions, or a funding agency may seek to have a *cost-beneficial* program. These can be of two kinds: (1) a program that maximizes the net present value of benefits minus costs, or (2) a program that maximizes the ratio of benefits to costs.[18] Both computations can be reported in base-year dollars and on a year-to-year or overall program basis. The former indicates the magnitude of net program benefits and the latter their relationship to costs—irrespective of magnitude. While both represent important evaluation criteria, sole reliance on the benefits/costs ratio may cause decision makers to cease support of a program, short of the point of optimal net return.[19,20]

Another aim of decision makers may be to have a *cost-effective* program. These can be of two kinds: (1) a program that maximizes benefits while keeping expenditures within a predefined range, or (2) a program that returns a predefined range of benefits while keeping expenditures to a minimum.[18] The former constrains resource allocations and preserves moneys for expenditure toward other ends, while the latter targets moneys towards ends that have, explicitly or implicitly, been ordered against other organizational goals.

A third strategy may have decision makers seeking *cost utility* with their programs. With this strategy, it is acknowledged that managers, unions, or funding sources have distinct preferences for the outcomes of an organizational change program.[21] There may be two kinds of preference orderings for change efforts: (1) A program that maximizes an overall utility function that incorporates the preferences of all parties, or (2) A program that maximizes the utility function for any one party or set of parties. The former represents the optimal composition of benefits for the parties involved, while the latter provides an indicator of the utility of the benefit distribution for each affected party. The criteria of cost utility is whether the costs overall, or to each party, have been worth the value received.

These three approaches to assessing the costs and benefits of a change program represent them in complementary ways. Cost-benefit and cost-effectiveness criteria focus on various optimal relationships of benefits to costs, while cost-utility criteria focus on benefit composition and distribution as well. This third evaluation criteria can be used with either the first or second in providing a full accounting of program results.

The remaining sections of this chapter illustrate the analytic functions for assessing program inputs, effects, and their relationships. Three examples are presented. In the first case, program inputs—the number and costs of meetings by engineers in a public utility—are measured and related to changes in their work environment and attitudes following a change program. In the second case, program effects—changes in the performance of bank employees—are measured and the relationship between attitudes, behaviors, and their costs are analyzed to validate the effects model. The final case presents an analysis of the costs and benefits of a change effort in an automotive supplier plant. These cases are chosen to illustrate the assessment problems that can be encountered as well as modes of solution.

EXAMPLE 1: ASSESSING PROGRAM INPUTS

In this case, the costs of a quality of work life program have been computed for an engineering design division of a major utility. Over 380 unionized employees, mostly professional engineers and draftsmen responsible for preparing designs and technical drawings, were involved in

Table 17-1   Interrelationships of Program Costs and Hours, U.S. Utility (N = 10)

	Consultant costs	Participant costs	Participant hours	Total costs
Consultant costs	1.0			
Participant costs	.97**	1.0		
Participant hours	.99**	.97**	1.0	
Total costs	.90**	.89**	.92**	1.0

an 18-month change effort. The major variable costs of the program included the fees and expenses of several consultants totaling $124,346, and the employees' time spent in meetings and training activities totaling 8275 hours at a cost of $95,898. This latter figure includes fixed costs and lost-profit contributions transferred from design units to the program. As a result, total project costs during this period were $220,244.

Table 17-1 reports the intercorrelations between the consulting expenses, participant hours and costs, and total costs, for 10 participating departments. It indicates significant relationships between the two cost components and shows that both are related to project hours and, of course, total costs.

Table 17-2 shows the relationships of these cost components and hours with changes in the work environment, employees' attitudes, and self-

Table 17-2   Relationship of Program Costs to Individual and Work Environment Changes[a] U.S. Utility (N = 10)

	Intrinsic motivation	Absenteeism	Supervisory support and work facilitation	Effort-to-performance beliefs
Consultant costs	−.53	−.20	.02	.75**
Participant costs	−.58*	−.22	.07	.72**
Participant hours	−.52	−.19	.00	.77**
Total costs	−.31	−.16	−.20	.90**

[a] Reported as residual gain scores.

* $p < .05$; ** $p < .01$.

reported attendance. The changes are reported as residualized gain scores, calculated by partialling out—through regression—that portion of change that would be predicted simply from the initial measurement. Interestingly, the table shows that project costs and hours are negatively related to changes in intrinsic motivation, and they are positively related to change in employees' beliefs that work effort leads to good performance. In the early stages of the program, the consultants and participating units met to examine work flows in the division and to identify the reasons for delays in the preparation of designs and drawings. The table suggests that the amount of time spent in these meetings was positively associated with improvements in the work flow. Figures 17-2 and 3 show this effect on the unit members' beliefs that their efforts would lead to good performances. At the same time, Table 17-2 also shows that the amount of time in meetings and the consultants' involvement was negatively associated with unit members' beliefs that they were personally responsible for their work (a major component in this organization of the intrinsic motivation measure). Given that the amount of supervisory support and work facilitation was unrelated to program activities, it appears that either the consultants' involvement, the changes in the work flow that resulted from program meetings, or both, deprived employees of some of the intrinsic motivation they derived from the work itself.

This instance illustrates the advantages of assessing the initial impact of program inputs in a quality of work life program. When researchers assess not only the costs of the program, but also the relationship be-

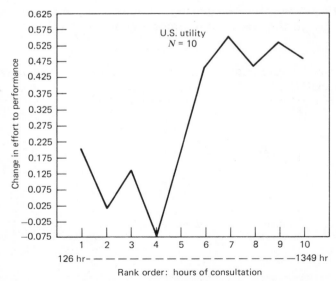

Figure 17-2   Hours of consultation and changes in effort-to-performance beliefs.

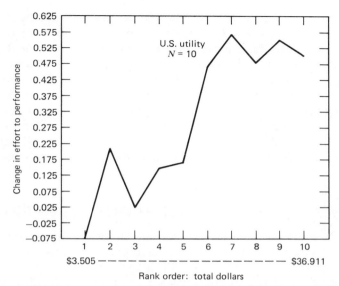

Figure 17-3 Total project costs and changes in effort-to-performance beliefs.

tween costs and initial effects, they can trace changes in the work environment and employee attitudes to particular program activities and, by noting areas of attitude change and the intervening time lag, they can test and validate the theory behind the intervention. Such information can also be useful to the consultants since it can stimulate and guide changes in the direction and intensity of their activities. Finally, it can highlight the initial impact of the program for program decision makers, including both its positive and negative effects.

Nevertheless, the results of such analyses must be closely scrutinized. An analysis of variance of the gain scores reported in Table 17-2 showed that none of the measured changes were statistically significant. Thus, although the relationships were significant between program costs and hours and the measured changes, the fact that the changes themselves were not significant lessens the importance of both the positive and negative trends. Second, there are only 10 units in these analyses, which can raise questions about the stability of the relationships. In such instances, stability coefficients could be computed over several measurement periods to assess changes in the relationships. Third, these analyses assume there is a linear relationship between costs, hours, and the measured changes and a specifiable time lag between their optimal relationship. The relationships could be curvilinear, and the optimal time lag varied, but these too can be statistically estimated. Finally, the cost and hour computations are only estimates. To correct for misestimates, confidence intervals could be assigned to them, specifying high and low estimations.

This financial analysis of program inputs does not address the quality of the program inputs or their implementation. Survey instruments can be used to evaluate these aspects of the program, including the consultants' effectiveness, the character of program meetings, and so on. These measures of implementation can also be correlated with changes in the work environment and job attitudes. Used in conjunction with cost estimates, they provide for an assessment of both the quality and quantity of inputs into the change effort. Organization theory predicts that such inputs will affect the work environment, job attitudes, and behavior of employees. The next example explicates such an analysis of program effects.

EXAMPLE 2: ASSESSING PROGRAM EFFECTS

In this case, a model predictive of changes in an organization's financial results is provided. The organization—a full service bank—consisted of a home office and 20 retail branches. Prior to a change program, measures were taken of the attitudes and satisfaction of tellers. Baseline measures of attendance, turnover, work performance, and their costs were also gathered for a one-year period before the study. Table 17-3 shows the average cost per incident of absenteeism and turnover. The key measure of teller performance—shortages in balancing—was estimated to be $8.23 per incident.

The costs of behavior at the bank are somewhat different than those typical of industrial organizations. The cost of lost productivity of absentee tellers was impossible to compute directly, for example, as all customers were served, though some possibly in substandard fashion. Thus a surrogate measure was computed: the overhead burden normally absorbed by employees plus the lost contribution to profit. Other fixed costs of absenteeism and turnover were a supervisor's time in acclimating replacement personnel and organizational costs in selecting and training new employees.

The problem associated with the use of performance indicators is their degree of independence from employee control. In manufacturing organizations operating at full capacity, with engineered standards, much of the variance in performance is attributable to employees. A bank has no full-capacity counterpart, and lending and deposit activities are largely dependent upon economic conditions. This dependence can be reflected in budgets, but oftentimes economic shifts are too abrupt for budgetary adjustment. As a result, many performance measures at a bank, unlike those in many industrial organizations, were not adjudged to be significantly related to factors in the human organization. There was, nevertheless, one performance measure that related to human factors: teller balancing (overages and shortages). Thus to test a model of program effects a relationship was specified linking (1) tellers' attitudes toward their jobs

Table 17-3   Cost per Incident of Absenteeism and
Turnover

Variable	Cost (in dollars)
Absenteeism	
Absent employee	
Salary	23.04
Benefits	6.40
Replacement employee: training and staff time	2.13
Unabsorbed burden	15.71
Lost profit contribution	19.17
Total variable cost	23.04
Total cost	66.45
Turnover	
Replacement acquisition	
Direct hiring costs	293.95
Other hiring costs	185.55
Replacement training	
Preassignment	758.84
Learning curve	212.98
Unabsorbed burden	682.44
Lost profit contribution	388.27
Total variable cost	293.95
Total cost	2,522.03

and (2) their number of transactions with (3) their balancing rate. However, since staffing levels at the bank were adjusted to equalize transactions, that variable was treated as a constant, and attitudes were posited
to be predictors of balancing rates.

Mirvis and Lawler developed a methodology for assessing such relationships and tracing the effect of changes in attitudes on behavior and
its financial consequences.[22] Building on the work of Likert and Bowers,
they correlated relevant job attitudes with an employee's behavior, and,
using the cost calculations presented previously, determined the cost per
employee associated with existing levels of satisfaction, motivation, and
other work attitudes measured in the organization.[23]

In applying this methodology to the bank data, they found the correlation between bank tellers' intrinsic motivation and time required for
balancing shortages to be $-.23$. Since the average number of shortages
per teller per month was 3.07 incidents (valued at a cost of $8.23 per
incident, or $25.23), it was estimated that an increase in intrinsic motiva-
tion of .5 standard deviation unit would reduce shortages per teller to
2.87 incidents, or $23.62 per month (see Figure 17-4). Using this method-

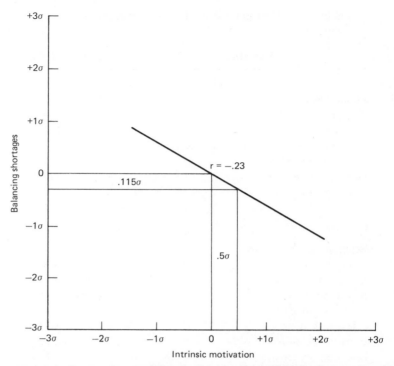

Figure 17-4   A change in an attitude (intrinsic motivation) associated with a change in behavior (fewer shortages) among bank tellers.

ology, gains in intrinsic motivation were predicted to yield cost savings estimated on the basis of the amount of behavioral variance accounted for in the attitude-balancing rate relationship.

Following the implementation of a change program in the bank, intrinsic motivation scores increased .145 σ and shortages per teller decreased to $21.71 per month—somewhat greater than anticipated but in the predicted direction. The actual cost savings exceeded the prediction. This methodology assumes a constant attitude–behavior relationship, however, and over the course of a change project, this relationship can change, thus invalidating previous estimates. Further, it assumes a linear relationship, but, again, this relationship may become curvilinear. While these factors complicate the analysis of program effects, they can be accomodated statistically. Either or both could have accounted for the difference between predicted and actual cost savings in the bank. Finally, this assessment of benefits, like that of costs, incorporates estimations. While the accuracy of these estimates can be verified through time-sampling observation, some estimation is always present.

This example illustrates the advantages of validating the model of program effects. Merely reporting financial gains over time does not guarantee that the improvements resulted from the quality of work life program. Changes in a firm's technology, in its product or labor market, or simply in economies of scale may account for financial losses or savings. It is therefore important for an assessor to validate the theory of change dynamics by tracing the effect of the program on the work environment, attitudes, and behavior and by statistically controlling, where feasible, for the impact of nonprogrammatic variables. This enables the assessor to relate gains to the change program itself.

EXAMPLE 3: COSTS AND BENEFITS

In this case, the costs and benefits of the first 56 months of a quality of work life program were assessed in a manufacturing plant. The average number of hourly employees ranged from 537 to 893 over the course of the study; average hourly wages ranged from $2.67 to $3.78; and average fringe-benefit costs ranged from 24% to 40% of hourly wages.

The change program was directed by a joint committee, composed of union and management representatives, who worked with a three-person consulting team to analyze problems, review opportunities for change, and introduce new programs. Several pilot actions were begun in the plant, including a job-rotation effort in one area and production planning meetings in another. An education program offering courses in language, reading and literature, and the arts was begun, as was a community day-care center. A major feature of the change effort was a "paid personnel time" program in which employees, upon reaching their production standard for the day, would have the remainder paid for use as personal time. The employees could leave the plant during this time, attend classes, or remain working and earn a performance bonus. This intervention was suggested by the employees, and it was endorsed by the joint committee and the consultants.

The major direct cost of the program was for the consultants' fees and expenses, totaling $389,746 in the 56 months. The employees' time spent in meetings, interviews, and training was treated as a nontransferable fixed cost, but the profit contribution associated with this time was valued at an opportunity cost of $66,659. Total costs of the project were $455,405. This figure does not include the "paid personal time" of $662,680 since that expense would have been incurred regardless of the change program. It also does not include the value of unpaid time contributed by the consultants, hourly workers, and salaried personnel, nor the costs of facilities used for program activities since they were not measured. The cost estimates were not discounted to base-year dollars, however, since the value of this contributed time and the facilities more than offset the value of such a discount.

Behavioral and financial data were collected prior to and throughout the program, which covered 56 months. Based on the change program, these behavioral and financial data were divided into five groupings:

Phase 1—May 1972–March 1973 (baseline period)

Phase 2—April 1973–February 1974 (study period)

Phase 3—March 1974–January 1975 (experimental period)

Phase 4—February 1975–December 1975 (plant-wide change)

Phase 5—January 1976–December 1976 (continuation)

An earlier chapter on assessing the rates and costs of employee behavior reported the frequency and rates of turnover, absenteeism, accidents, and grievances as a percentage of total incidents for the first five phases of program assessment, the rates of productivity as a percentage of standard, and the rates of product rejects, downtime, and supply-use variation as a percentage of manufacturing costs (standard labor dollars). It reported decreases in rates of absenteeism, turnover, OSHA accidents, grievances, and product rejects over the course of the program. Rates of understandard production, downtime, supply use, and minor accidents varied somewhat over the phases, but generally declined. Minor illnesses increased, and grievances fluctuated considerably.

The assessor is interested in not only reporting these trends but also in assessing their significance. An analysis of variance of the monthly rates showed changes in absenteeism, turnover, OSHA accidents, and all of the performance measures to be statistically significant ($p < .01$). However, as in any time-series analysis, such findings may be due to seasonal trends or to autoregressive (i.e., nonindependent) errors in the measures of monthly data. Accordingly, a statistical test was applied to the monthly data that corrected for the simple linear autoregressive effect, but, again, the changes were found to be statistically significant.[24] Other analytic procedures, such as the interrupted time series or moving average analysis, would have to be applied to the data to correct for nonlinear autoregressive effects and fully assess the significance of the monthly trends.[25]

The assessor is also interested in tracing the measured changes to the quality of work life program. In this case, when comparisons were made between a unit whose members were participating in the paid personal time program and one where there was no participation, changes in rates of understandard production and machine downtime were significantly greater in the experimental unit. This attests to the effect of this intervention. However, as in any organizational change effort, there were nonprogrammatic factors that influenced the measured results. Five such variables were noted at the site: increased managerial effectiveness, technological changes and capital investments, changes in the labor-relations climate in the auto industry, changes in the product market, and shifts in the organization's product mix. Of these five factors, the first three were clearly influenced by the change program since training and joint problem solving at the site enhanced managerial effectiveness, innovations and capital investments were initiated by program participants, and the change in labor relations in the industry was coincident with the change in labor relations at the plant. Ideally, a production function could be created to account for the impact of these and the other two factors on program results. Unfortunately, the data were not available to test such a model of change dynamics fully. In the assessors' opinion, however, the program and the nonprogrammatic factors influenced by it accounted for the bulk of the changes in absenteeism, turnover, grievances, and accidents, while between 50–75% of the changes in performance could be traced to program activities. The lack of an experimental design or a production function that traces the impact of programmatic and nonprogrammatic variables makes this an "educated judgment" at best.

Finally, the assessor wants to evaluate the effects of the change program in financial terms. Table 17-4 shows the actual (i.e., concurrent) value of the several outcome variables, as reported in the earlier chapter, while Table 17-5 shows the same variables expressed in discounted dollars (i.e., deflated to base year). As might be expected, the actual cost of an incident—say an absence—increased over the periods and, thus, so did the total costs of absenteeism over the course of the program. The inflation-adjusted figures, however, tell quite a different story. By reporting the variables in base-year dollars, Table 17-5 shows that the total value of nonproductive behaviors and performance measures rose initially and then decreased substantially. The discounted value per employee, computed by dividing the period costs by the average number of employees in the plant for the period, decreased continuously from the base year.

Using the cost data presented earlier and the discounted benefit data reported here, Table 17-6 compares the costs and benefits of the program. It can be seen that during Phase 2, the greatest costs were incurred in the program and the "benefits" were actually a loss when compared with the base year. In Phase 3, benefits accrued as a result of reduced rates of costly behavior and better performance, but they were more than offset by program costs. Favorable differences between the costs and benefits in Phases 4 and 5 were sufficient to produce a balance of net benefits in discounted dollars compared to program costs.

The costs and benefits of this program can be arrayed in several ways for evaluation purposes. To assess total costs and benefits, two calculations can be used. One subtracts costs from benefits to arrive at a net benefit figure. The other divides benefits by costs to arrive at a benefit/

Table 17-4 Actual Dollar Value[a] of Behavior and Performance at Quality of Work Life Site: 1972–1976

Behaviors and Performance	Phase 1 5/72–3/73		Phase 2 4/73–2/74		Phase 3 3/74–1/75		Phase 4 2/75–12/75		Phase 5 1/76–12/76[b]	
	Estimated Cost per Incident ($)	Estimated Total Cost ($)	Estimated Cost per Incident ($)	Estimated Total Cost ($)	Estimated Cost per Incident ($)	Estimated Total Cost ($)	Estimated Cost per Incident ($)	Estimated Total Cost ($)	Estimated Cost per Incident ($)	Estimated Total Cost ($)
Absenteeism										
Total absences	$ 50.24	$ 280,339	$ 53.15	$ 394,533	$ 62.49	$ 417,683	$ 73.63	$ 364,469	$ 80.06	$ 462,126
Turnover										
Voluntary	109.63	11,840	131.68	30,741	150.69	15,370	157.59	4,255	160.65	7,805
Involuntary	109.63	9,976	131.68	22,302	150.69	12,357	157.59	946	160.65	10,014
Accidents and illnesses										
Minor accidents	6.04	15,716	5.71	28,247	6.45	29,934	8.67	28,689	9.15	30,237
Minor illnesses	6.04	11,416	5.71	27,254	6.45	34,264	8.67	32,374	9.15	39,496
Minor revisits	6.04	9,006	5.71	11,740	6.45	12,468	8.67	13,378	9.15	13,948
OSHA accidents	661.26	152,751	690.31	182,259	1,106.52	204,706	1,855.15	283,038	1,256.86	191,252
Grievances	29.53	1,536	34.44	654	56.10	1,851	61.90	4,463	54.52	2,299
Product rejects		563,619		661,668		525,758		461,226		619,974
Production under standard		208,222		339,442		631,268		218,360		433,683
Manufacturing costs										
Supply variance		27,493		37,329		45,800		65,050		16,308
Machine downtime		75,347		101,301		82,619		89,939		141,459
Total costs		$1,367,261		$1,837,470		$2,014,078		$1,566,987		$1,968,601
Costs per hourly employee		$ 2,546		$ 2,377		$ 2,678		$ 2,261		$ 2,346

[a] Actual dollar values are estimated costs of the behaviors in each phase.
[b] Phase 5 costs have been multiplied by 11/4 to make them comparable to other phases.

Table 17-5   Discounted Dollar Value[a] of Behavior and Performance at Quality of Work Life Site: 1972–1976

Behaviors and Performance	Estimated Base Costs ($)	Phase 1 5/72–3/73 Estimated Total Cost ($)	Phase 2 4/73–2/74 Estimated Total Cost ($)	Phase 3 3/74–1/75 Estimated Total Cost ($)	Phase 4 2/75–12/75 Estimated Total Cost ($)	Phase 5 1/76–12/76[b] Estimated Total Cost ($)
Absenteeism						
Total absences	$ 50.24	$ 280,339	$ 372,932	$ 335,804	$ 248,688	$ 289,998
Turnover						
Voluntary	109.63	11,840	22,365	11,182	2,960	5,326
Involuntary	109.63	9,976	16,225	8,990	658	6,834
Accidents and illnesses						
Minor accidents	6.04	15,716	29,880	28,032	19,986	19,960
Minor illnesses	6.04	11,416	28,829	32,085	22,553	26,072
Minor revisits	6.04	9,006	12,418	11,675	9,320	9,208
OSHA accidents	661.26	152,751	172,589	122,333	101,173	100,622
Grievances	29.53	1,536	561	974	2,126	1,245
Product rejects		563,619	485,262	391,784	350,544	343,671
Understandard production		208,222	272,964	208,222	173,227	199,472
Manufacturing cost						
Supply variance		27,493	27,493	34,367	49,489	9,622
Machine downtime		75,347	74,232	61,860	68,734	78,356
Total costs		$1,367,261	$1,515,750	$1,247,308	$1,049,458	$1,090,386
Costs per hourly employee		$2,546	$1,961	$1,659	$1,514	$1,300

[a] Discounted dollar values are estimated costs of the behaviors in Phase 1 (baseline) applied to Phases 2, 3, 4, and 5.
[b] Phase 5 costs have been multiplied by 11/12 to make them comparable to other phases.

Table 17-6 Costs versus Discounted Benefits[a] at Quality of Work Life Site: 1972–1976

	Phase 2 April 1973–February 1974	Phase 3 March 1974–January 1975	Phase 4 February 1975–December 1973	Phase 5 January 1976–December 1976[b]	Grand Totals
	Costs				
Social science consultant fees, expenses, etc.	$145,500	$129,746	$ 43,800	$ 69,700	$389,746
Site employee time,[c] training activities, intervention meetings, interviews, etc.	4,841	7,326	20,724	33,768	66,659
Total	$150,341	$137,072	$ 64,524	$103,468	$455,405
	Benefits				
	(Difference from Base Year)	(Difference from Base Year)	(Difference from Base Year)	(Difference from Base Year)	
Absenteeism	($ 92,593)	($ 55,465)	$ 31,651	($ 9,659)	
Turnover					
Voluntary	(10,525)	658	8,080	6,514	
Involuntary	(6,249)	986	9,318	3,142	
Accidents and Illnesses					
Minor accidents	(14,164)	(12,316)	(4,270)	(4,244)	
Minor illnesses	(17,413)	(20,669)	(11,137)	(14,656)	
Minor revisits	(3,412)	(2,669)	(314)	(202)	
OSHA accidents	(19,938)	30,418	51,578	52,129	
Grievances	975	562	(590)	291	
Product rejects	78,357	171,835	213,075	219,940	
Understandard productivity	(64,742)	0	34,995	8,750	
Manufacturing Costs					
Supplies	0	(6,874)	(21,996)	17,871	
Downtime	1,115	13,407	6,613	(3,009)	
Total	($148,149)	$119,953	$317,803	$276,875	$566,482

[a] Discounted value of benefits are estimated costs of the behaviors and performance in Phase 1 (baseline) applied to Phase 2, 3, 4, and 5.
[b] Phase 5 costs have been multiplied by 11/12 to make them comparable to others.

cost ratio. To assess costs and benefits per employee, these same calculations can be made. The results of these calculations are as follows:

Total Costs

	Phase 2 150,341 Diff/Base	Phase 3 137,072 Diff/Base	Phase 4 64,524 Diff/Base	Phase 5 103,468 Diff/Base	Phases 2–5 455,405
Total dis-counted benefits	(148,149)	199,953	317,803	276,875	566,482
Net benefits	(298,490)	(17,119)	253,279	173,407	111,077
B/C ratio	−.98	.88	4.93	2.67	1.24

Cost/employee

	Phase 2 195 Diff/Base	Phase 3 182 Diff/Base	Phase 4 93 Diff/Base	Phase 5 123 Diff/Base	Phases 2–5 593
Discounted benefits/ employee	585	887	1032	1246	3750
Net benefits/employee	390	705	939	1123	3157
B/C ratio per employee	3.00	4.87	11.09	10.13	6.32

These calculations show the net benefit of the program to be $111,077. When expressed as a benefit/cost ratio, the estimate is $1.24 return for each dollar spent. The calculations also reflect the impact of changes in the size of the work force over the periods of assessment. The net benefit per employee is estimated to be $3157 and the benefit/cost ratio to be $6.32 return for each dollar spent per employee. These latter figures attest to the magnitude of the benefits of the program as the costs of absenteeism, turnover, grievances, understandard production, and product rejects declined during the program despite increases in the size of the work force.

Each of these statistics is important in determining whether the program was cost beneficial. Expressed in terms of total costs and benefits, they show a favorable return to the organization. Expressed in per-employee terms, they show a substantial net return per employee. As noted, of course, not all of the benefits reported can be traced directly to the change program and not all benefits are accounted. It remains for decision makers to use these data in evaluating the program's benefits from their particular perspectives.

In addition, other criteria can be presented to inform their evaluations. Since no explicit limits were placed on expenditures and no targets set on objectives, no cost-effectiveness calculations could be made. Nevertheless, evidence was gathered evaluating nonfinancial outcomes that can be used in assessing the social utility of the program. Interviews and questionnaires showed that employees participated in more group and supervisory decisions over the course of the project and that work resources became more accessible to them. In addition, they felt that their job security increased. At the same time, employees felt, at the end of the program, that their pay was less likely to be contingent upon their performance, and their pay satisfaction decreased significantly. In the final interviews, employees reported less alienation from their work, but their overall job satisfaction was unchanged.

These complementary data illustrate the importance of assessing *both* the financial and social effects of the program and integrating the findings for overall utility evaluation of benefit composition and distribution. Consider, for example, the "paid personal time" program. All told, 87% of the hourly employees ultimately participated in the program, earning an average of 70 minutes of paid personal time per day. Of these employees, the great majority (80%) left the plant; they reported they spent their time enjoyably (78%) and doing something interesting to them (70%). There was no evidence that they were more likely than those who did not receive paid personal time to attend classes in the education program ($r = .06$) or earn income from an extra job ($r = -.06$). Instead, they spent their time relaxing (34%) or working around the house or on the land (46%).

In evaluating the effects of initiatives like the paid personal time program, the analyst is interested in not only how much time was received or how it was used, but also in who participated in the program, its effect on the organization, and its effect on the participants themselves. Although the great majority of hourly employees received paid personal time, only 6% of the salaried employees participated. Moreover, they received an average of only 18 minutes of paid personal time per day. Women were more likely than men to participate ($r = .28$), and low-income groups more likely than high-income groups ($r = .39$). Consequently, 33% of the employees felt that the program was unfair to some employees in the organization.

The program also had an effect on the work environment and on work relations in the organization. Employee participation in work decisions increased in the plant over the course of the project. This may have improved planning and the availability of work resources, thus enabling the employees to achieve their production standards and earn personal time. At the same time, relations suffered between employees (who received personal time) and supervisors (who did not), and employees reported significantly less support and assistance from their supervisors at the end of the period of study. Moreover, their integration and satisfaction with work groups also declined. Thus it is not surprising that 56% of the employees reported that the paid personal time program—although highly valued—created problems in the plant.

The program also had other effects on the participants. As noted, most spent their paid personal time enjoyably. However, in order to reach their production standard and receive paid time, employees had to work more quickly, alertly, or strenuously. Data on incidents and rates of behavior show that minor illnesses in the plant increased over the course of the study and, at its end, more employees reported having headaches (increased from 62 to 72%), back pain (from 25 to 46%), being worn out at the end of the workday (from 33 to 52%), and having trouble sleeping at night (from 56 to 77%). Thus the benefits of the paid personal time program appeared to come at considerable cost to the employees' personal welfare.

These comments illustrate the complexity of assessing the costs and benefits of quality of work life programs. From a financial vantage alone, the discounted value of the program's benefits exceeded its costs. The net discounted benefit per hourly employee was $3157 from the base period. During this time, the benefits were returned to employees in the form of salary increases from the base year of $.16, $.57, $.89, $1.11 per hour in Phases 2, 3, 4, and 5, respectively. Totaling this salary increase for each 11-month phase, minus the unpaid absence, leave, and plant shutdown time, yields a total salary increase per employee of $4304 over the course of the study. However, when adjusted for inflation by the consumer price index, the increase from the base year is $−.05, $.11, $.27, and $.35 per hour, yielding a total benefit per employee of $1074, which is substantially below the discounted benefit to the organization.

No data were collected on the outcome preferences of the firm's management, union, the funding agency, or employees. Consequently, it is impossible to assess the utility of the net social and financial benefits overall to each group. One key question is whether the marginal utility of the benefits returned to employees in the form of salary increases, paid personal time, increased influence and satisfaction, and so forth were offset by increases in minor accidents and illnesses and decreases in self-reports of health and well-being. Another key question is whether they viewed their contribution to the firm's profits to be a "just" transfer payment.

There was more tangible evidence that the program had utility in the eyes of the marketplace. After completion of the study, the firm was acquired by another firm at a purchase price significantly greater than its estimated market value. The purchaser wanted to acquire the firm partly for its quality of work life program, as it also was undertaking programs of that sort in its own operations and wanted to learn from its acquisition's experiences. These examples attest to the utility of the intangible benefits of quality of work life programs, relative to the costs of starting and maintaining them. They also emphasize the importance of fully appraising the effects of such programs. Otherwise, key value decisions that are rightly the province of decision makers are made by the evaluator.

CONCLUSION

That evaluations of programs to improve organizations and the quality of work life of their members are based upon criteria of cost benefit, effectiveness, and utility raises broad questions of public purpose and private interest. If the results of such programs are deemed public goods, then public support in the form of enabling legislation, money, and, if necessary, sanctions might be warranted. If, by contrast, there are deemed to be private benefits to the organization, then the marketplace will govern program development.

The critical task for evaluators in the next decades will be to document the public goods and private benefits that follow from organizational change programs. The evidence presented here suggests that both can result from such experimentation; organizations and society can benefit from increased employee skills, teamwork, and commitment as well as improved labor–management relations. But this brings us full circle to the problem mentioned at the beginning of this chapter: The evidence is scanty and unreliable that organizational change programs can indeed improve organizational effectiveness and the quality of work life. As of this point, however, it can be stated that there is some utility in experimenting with such programs. Using these criteria, the valued end is as much the knowledge gained about the conduct and effects of a change program as the effects themselves. Knowledge gained can serve as a private benefit to the organization, shareholders, and unions; it is also a public benefit to society when it is gathered by reliable analysts and made public. This explains the interest in and support of these programs by organizations and research agencies. It also justifies the support and conduct of assessment research.

REFERENCES

1. Seashore, S. E. Assessing the quality of working life: The U.S. experience. *Labour and Society,* 1976, **1**, 69–79.
2. Katzell, R. A., & Yankelovich, D. *Work, productivity, and job satisfaction: An evaluation of policy-related research.* New York: Psychological Corporation, 1975.
3. Srivastva, S., Salipante, P. F., Jr., Cummings, T. G., Notz, W. W., Bigelow, J. D., & Waters, J. A. *Job satisfaction and productivity.* Cleveland: Department of Organizational Behavior, Case Western Reserve University, 1975.

4. Kahn, R. L. Organizational development: Some problems and proposals. *Journal of Applied Behavioral Science,* 1974, **10,** 485–502.

5. Weiss, R. S., & Rein, M. The evaluation of broad-aim programs: Experimental design, its difficulties, and an alternative. *Administrative Science Quarterly,* 1970, **15,** 97–109.

6. Campbell, D. T. Keeping the data honest in the experimenting society. In H. Melton & D. Watson (Eds.), *Interdisciplinary dimensions of accounting for social goals and social organizations.* Columbus, OH: Grid, 1972.

7. Lawler, E. E. III. Adaptive experiments: An approach to organizational behavior research. *Academy of Management Review,* 1977, **2,** 576–585.

8. Brummet, R., Flamholtz, E., & Pyle, W. Human resource measurement—A challenge for accountants. *The Accounting Review,* 1968, **43,** 217–224.

9. Flamholtz, E. G. *Human resource accounting.* Encino, CA: Dickenson, 1974.

10. Rhode, J., & Lawler, E. E. III. Auditing change: Human resource accounting. In M. D. Dunnette (Ed.), *Work and nonwork in the year 2001.* Monterey, CA: Brooks/Cole, 1973, 154–178.

11. Mirvis, P. H., & Macy, B. A. Human resource accounting: A measurement perspective. *Academy of Management Review,* 1976, **1,** 74–83.

12. Rothenberg, J. Cost-benefit analysis: A methodological exposition. In M. Guttentag & E. Struening (Eds.), *Handbook of evaluation research, Vol. 2.* Beverly Hills: Sage Publications, 1975.

13. Levin, H. M. Cost-effectiveness analysis in evaluation research. In M. Guttentag & E. L. Struening (Eds.), *Handbook of evaluation research, Vol. 2.* Beverly Hills: Sage, 1975.

14. Klein, T. A. *Social costs and benefits of business.* Englewood Cliffs: Prentice-Hall, 1977.

15. Macy, B. A., & Mirvis, P. H. Measuring quality of work and organizational effectiveness in behavioral-economic terms. *Administrative Science Quarterly,* 1976, **21,** 212–226.

16. Quinn, R. P., & Staines, G. L. *The 1977 Quality of Employment Survey.* Ann Arbor: Institute for Social Research, 1979.

17. Goodman, P. *Assessing organizational change.* New York: Wiley-Interscience, 1979.

18. Merewitz, L., & Sosnick, S. H. *The budget's new clothes.* Chicago: Markham Publishing Co., 1971.

19. Musgrave, R. A. *The theory of public finance.* New York: McGraw-Hill, 1959.

20. Quirin, D. *The capital expenditure decision.* Homewood, IL: Irwin, 1967.

21. Monsen, R. J., & Downs, A. A theory of large managerial firms. In P. Lebreton (Ed.), *Comparative administrative theory.* Seattle: University of Washington Press, 1968, 56–57.

22. Mirvis, P. H., & Lawler, E. E. III. Measuring the financial impact of employee attitudes. *Journal of Applied Psychology,* 1977, **62,** 1–8.

23. Likert, R., & Bowers, D. G. Improving the accuracy of P/L reports by estimating the change in dollar value of the human organization. *Michigan Business Review,* 1973, **25,** 15–24.

24. Durbin, J. Testing for serial correlation in least-squares regression when some of the regressions are lagged dependent variables. *Econometrica,* 1970, **38,** 410.

25. Glass, G., Willson, V., & Gottman, J. *Design and analysis of time-series experiments.* Boulder, Colorado: Associated University Press, 1975.

PART FOUR

ISSUES IN ASSESSING CHANGE

This section concerns some issues that are raised by the foregoing approach to assessing organizational change. The focus is more on questions than on answers, more on what needs to be done than on what has been done, and more on unresolved problems than on successful solutions. The intention is to leave the reader with a sense of an unfinished journey. Much has been learned and done, useful measures have been developed, but at the end of Chapter 18 the reader will probably feel that a large research agenda remains for the person who wants to measure organizational change.

CHAPTER EIGHTEEN

Measuring Change: Progress, Problems, and Prospects

EDWARD E. LAWLER III, STANLEY E. SEASHORE, AND PHILIP H. MIRVIS

Concluding chapters are often used to summarize and integrate the earlier ones. In this case, we question whether it is possible or desirable to do that, for the material is complex, the parts lend themselves to independent examination and evaluation, and the potential forms of integration are numerous. Further, the measurement development program described in this volume is better viewed as an unfinished venture, and this book as a progress report, rather than a final one. We choose, therefore, to comment on some areas in which progress has been made, on some voids and inadequacies that invite attention, and on some strategic issues that might guide future work.

SCOPE OF TOPICAL COVERAGE

The first 17 chapters of this book demonstrate that the measurement program has done rather well in fulfilling the important objective of being broad in scope. It covers a wide variety of topical measurement areas with a variety of research methods. In some cases, but not all, there are alternative ways to measure key variables. Most of the measures lend themselves to consistent use in multiple sites, and thus to comparative analysis. In important respects, the measures fit the tasks that they were designed to do. However, along with this positive judgment, it is important to point out that not all measures are equally well developed and some important areas remain unmeasured.

The domain of employee attitudes, perceptions, and preferences, not surprisingly, is relatively well treated in the MOAQ instrument described in Chapter 4. This instrument derived from a long history of prior work on the relevant conceptual, methodological, and interpretive issues. Although already rather long, this instrument still needs further expansion and further validation. The modular structure of the questionnaire allows addition of new topics and selective use of the modules pertinent to a particular case. Among the areas for expanded coverage are the problem-solving process of organizations, communications, intergroup relationships, and the degree of integration between the employee's work and nonwork roles. The validation of the resulting data in the context of prediction of outcomes and evaluation of outcomes remains only partially explored.

Chapter 5 describes a relatively new thrust in the assessment of organizations and of organizational change, namely, the measurement and costing of nonproductive behaviors by organizational members. Pioneering work on human-resource accounting—based at ISR—provided a starting point for concepts, definitions, measures of individual behaviors in organizations, and the means for representing those behaviors in financial terms. It is indeed possible to track economic outcomes of organizational change programs and to trace them to changes in attitudes and in the work environment. The findings in Chapter 5 show that nonproductive behaviors in organizations have significant costs and that cost savings can be realized by introducing changes into the work environment that increase the employee's satisfaction and motivation. The methodology reported, however, requires a considerable amount of effort on the part of assessors and some familiarity with organizational record-keeping and cost-accounting practices. In addition, the measures must be adapted to fit the performance criteria and productive outputs of different organizations. It would be very convenient if simple approaches could be developed; wide use of such indicators might depend upon the incorporation of these variables into existing, efficient management information systems.

The treatment of organizational structure in Chapters 6 and 7 represents an effort to expand the description and assessment beyond the traditional scope. Provisions are made for obtaining information concerning hierarchy, division of work, allocation of responsibilities, and other formal features of organizations, but a focus upon relational structures and on the distribution of influence is added. These aspects of structure are often divergent from the formal plan of an organization, and they may well be more sensitive indicators of organizational changes and of potential organizational problems than are the more traditional measures. They have, also, the property of being measurable and comparable during periods of change in formal structures. The validation of these measures in diagnosis and assessment remains limited, and the future value of these procedures is speculative.

In the topical area of technology, our effort has been directed away from the global, static characterizations that have prevailed in organizational studies toward an approach that will allow distinctions between core and support technologies, and distinctions between the technological environments experienced differentially by individuals and subgroups in an organization. This developmental work—reported in Chapters 8 and 9—consists primarily in the formulation of conceptual guides that can form the basis for future development of operational instruments and procedures. An example is provided of one successful effort to estimate deficient utilization of a technological system and to suggest corrective steps. We feel that this important domain for assessment is of prime importance in organizational studies and is one that should have priority for future development.

The study of jobs and work environments is typically conducted with observational methods or questionnaire methods, but seldom with both. Chapter 10 reports our effort to ascertain whether the two methods are interchangeable, or perhaps mutually translatable. The job observation procedures described in that chapter are well developed and field tested, and they have produced data known to have utility in analytic and predictive schemes. Nevertheless, when compared with questionnaire data from job occupants, it is clear that the two methods can produce discrepant data. It is not clear whether we are dealing with error of measurement or with errors of conception and meaning. Perhaps the implicit theories built into the observational scheme do not match the job holders' own theories about the nature of their social and physical environments. Improvements are needed in the ways we interpret and evaluate such information.

Chapters 11 and 12 represent our effort to guide, to systematize, and to quantify the information obtained by on-site observers who may be present continuously or episodically during a period of organizational activity and change. Chapter 11 provides procedures and aids for a "structured, naturalistic" assessment of organizational behavior; Chapter 12 provides a means for observing and coding events at meetings. These procedures lie between those that prescribe in advance the conceptual dimensions that are to be measured and quantified, on the one hand, and those that provide maximally for the intuitive or integrative interpretation of events by an unconstrained observer. The intended advantages are to obtain immediate observational data, which is open as to scope and focus, in forms that allow interpretation by colleagues, by the observer after time has passed, or by others who approach the interpretation task from different perspectives.

In the domains of union–management relations and union organizational structures, we offer nothing novel as to method of approach; the main task and aim has been to formulate a conceptual framework that may guide the researcher's attention to factors that are commonly overlooked. The methods described remain rudimentary, although promising, and they are insufficiently field tested.

Chapters 14 through 17 refer less to construct identification and variable measurement, and more to the procedures of analysis that are pertinent to the assessment of change and of the economic consequences of change. They deal, respectively, with the perceptions and attitudes of program participants regarding an organizational change program, with the confirmation that attitude change has actually occurred, with the linkage of organizational change to economic outcomes, and with the overall cost-benefit evaluation of an organizational change program. These chapters attempt to move from measurement of descriptive variables to the evaluation of their psychological and economic correlates.

STRENGTHS AND LIMITATIONS

The preceding remarks remind the reader of the scope of topical coverage that has been attempted, the variety of methods employed, and some of the analytic methods that can help to bring order and confident conclusions out of unavoidably complex data. We turn now to mention some of the strengths and limitations of the assessment program.

Scope of Measurement

The potential number of variables measured in the assessment program is staggering. Moreover, the measures available are not bounded by single disciplines or theories; instead, they are drawn from multiple disciplines and incorporate a number of theoretical streams. We regard this as a strength of the measurement program because change programs and the measurement problems they pose rarely honor disciplinary and theoretical boundaries. In addition, it is our view that assessors should make selective use of the instruments with an eye to needs, resources, and opportunities.

From our experiences to date, we can conclude that under near-ideal conditions, the scale of the fieldwork, the intrusion into work settings and time schedules, absorbed and unaccounted costs, and the risk of unauthorized revelations do not prohibit the application of the full range of methods and procedures. Nevertheless, we have found that the full array of field activities is likely to be used only rarely—for at least three reasons. First, the measurement program is plainly one of "overkill," which is justified on grounds of development and validation of measurement components but which at times exceeds the assessment requirements and the participants' patience and goodwill. Second, some components may be inapplicable in certain organizations. For example, meetings cannot be observed in cases in which meetings do not occur; the properties of work groups cannot be assessed where stable work groups do not exist; the organizational structure of a union cannot be described if there is no union. Third, there are economic, political, and ethical reasons for omitting some aspect of assessment in a given case; the costs and risks must be compared with expected benefits.

A limitation of the program is that we provide scant guidance for the would-be assessor in choosing the most appropriate measures and in developing an overarching assessment package for his or her needs. Our preferences, as were articulated in Chapter 1, are for measures of concepts that represent valued ends to parties at the research site, that are useful in understanding factors contributing to the achievement of those ends, that exploit contemporary theories and empirical resources, and that might be useful for comparative purposes either within an organization over time or across organizations. Others, with their own theoretical preferences, client or constituency base, and resources might choose differently. In our view, the choice of variables and methods for any assessment effort must be based upon a good understanding of the intended change program in a site and upon a facility with the theory and operations embedded in the measures to be used. Of necessity, then, some scouting and self-assessment must precede the design of a measurement system in any organization.

Voids

Extensive though the described measures are, they are still not sufficient. Some important areas are simply not accounted for very well, or at all, by the measures presented in this volume. Notably absent is significant measurement of aspects of an organization's environment. This is potentially a serious ommission since we have found that a wide range of environmental conditions can affect the course of change projects. Organizations vary greatly in their vulnerability to market and supply fluctuations, to intrusions from corporate headquarters, general economic conditions, new legislation, and the like. Part of the problem in representing the environment, of course, is that such a wide range of factors can be potentially relevant to the process and outcome of a change program. In our studies of change efforts, we have relied on observers' accounts of the import of environmental factors on program results. Still, this does not excuse the relative neglect of quantitative and systematic measurement of the environment. Such measures clearly need to be added.[1]

Also missing from the measurement areas directly covered by existing instruments is the culture of the organization under study. Admittedly, much of the data collected on organizational practices, norms, and policies as well as supervisory and work-group behaviors can be used to identify and represent key facets of organizational culture. Observers can also draw inferences about cultural norms from their data. But no systematic measures have yet been developed to represent key cultural variables in an integrative theoretical framework. This is an important weakness, since a firm's culture and change in that culture are inextricably linked to change efforts.[2]

Considerable progress has been made in the area of evaluation—and more needs to be made. Work on modeling and measuring the process and progress of change, as is reported in Chapter 14, has been opportunistic. Guidelines for assessing the start-up, institutionalization, and diffusion of change efforts are crude. They arose from our needs to systematize observers' unsystematic reports of the role of those factors in the change effort. They need theoretical bolstering and stronger linkage to theories of planned change. Measures of program adoption, goal attainment, and the contribution of consultants to project success need further refinement as well.

Finally, measures of program implementation in general and in the context of joint labor–management efforts in particular need refinement. We do not yet know how to measure "political" factors in the change process, including the definition of bargainable topics that are for various reasons excluded from joint committees' agendas, the reasons the parties adopt collaborative and contrient postures, and the reasons that some changes are democratically presented to the organization while others are seemingly imposed. Such factors may be central to successful implementation of new initiatives in an organization. Further development of measures of these factors will have to follow—not precede—the formulation of improved models of the process of change.

Combined Use of Objective, Subjective, and Phenomenological Data

The assessment program spans the scale of objectivity from readily confirmable "hard" data, through participants' somewhat discrepant reports about objective conditions and events, to data intended to capture the unique reality experienced by each participant or class of participants. These various kinds of information serve different analytic and interpretive purposes; we are confirmed in the belief that all are important, that all can be employed constructively, and that all can be used to advantage jointly. Some evaluators rely exclusively upon objective information, whereas others choose to focus upon the phenomenology of experienced quality of working life. They are entitled to their preferences. However, some "hard" results are best understood analytically and theoretically by reference to the phenomenology of individual members of the organization. In some diagnostic and change planning tasks, it becomes important to be able to estimate whether a problem arises from objective factors or from phenomenological factors, and, thus, what sort of change activity might best suit the case. Given the interests of different constituencies with a stake in the organization and given the interests of different researchers with dissimilar theoretical or professional interests, the diversity of types of information collected is not only justified but it is required.

Such diversity of classes of data, however, can complicate assessment. First, some assessors are more experienced and more adept at using one or another of the measurement approaches. Assessment teams can be formed in ways to insure complementarity. For assessors without partners, however, this can be a real problem. Second, some sites prove more amenable to one class of data or another. Not surprisingly, elements of the assessment package prove to be more compatible with some organizational forms than with others. In general, the more "structured" components and those reliant on organizational record systems are usable with organizations that are relatively highly bounded, have relatively stable membership over time, are relatively free from massive environmental disruptions over the period of study, and have technologies that induce or require sophisticated information management systems. All but two of the many organizations studied have had these properties in sufficient degree to sustain the use of attitude questionnaires, record abstraction procedures, and semistandardized interview schedules. In the two other cases, the researchers had to rely on observation and unstructured interviewing, with very little access to "objective" data.

The merit of the assessment program in providing diverse kinds of data is also a source of difficulty for those who analyze and interpret these data. This volume does not offer guidelines for integrating objective, subjective, and phenomenological data into a gestalt—a unified image of the key features of organizational state and change process. It is particularly telling that many authors of change-program case reports have had considerable difficulty in formulating broadly coherent interpretations. They complain of data overload, of the lack of guiding norms or rules for dealing with apparently discrepant information, of an inability to separate figure from ground in searching for some overarching view that is in harmony with their information base. The least productive response is to ignore much of the collateral or discrepant information, although this is often appropriate for hypothesis testing or theory spinning. A more productive approach, at this stage in the art of organizational assessment, is to adopt a team approach, assuming that persons of unlike theoretical preferences can, in interpretive collaboration or combat, arrive at a view that appears plausible to themselves and to readers.

Confirming Evidence

One of our intentions was to provide means for obtaining confirmatory information on topics that are either critical to interpreters of the assessment data or else of uncertain significance in the absence of confirmatory data. On this point we can conclude, without any hesitation, that multiple measures and alternative information sources have proven their worth by allowing strong interpretation of the data—and occasionally, by adding credibility to findings for diverse users who have unlike preferences and prejudices regarding "hard" data, observers' reports, and questionnaires.

Nonetheless, the inclusion of confirming evidence in the measurement program presents some problems. First, data collection requires time and money. The redundancy built into confirmatory evidence makes its collection costly. Second, the reasons for redundancy, while agreeable to researchers, may seem less so to others. We can provide no firm guidelines on which variables need confirmatory measurement and which do not need it. To some extent, that will depend upon the estimated significance of the data and the opportunities to collect it at any research site. Suffice it to say that an assessor often will have to choose between redundancy and breadth in the use of the instruments presented here.

Case Histories

It is essential in any longtitudinal study of organizational change to generate a historical account of key events, of environmental intrusions, and of phases of change as they occur. It is essential, also, to have some way to impute meaning to such observations. This facet of the assessor's task remains more of an art and a mystery than a domain of prescribed method. As our research proceeded, we became increasingly convinced of the importance of having a historical account based on current observations, and increasingly dissatisfied with our means for acquiring appropriate information and our means for using it.

Advice from a noted historian and a social anthropologist was not of much help. In essence, their common view was that one should find bright people to do the observing and depend upon their intuitive or integrative capacities to make sense of the events and to report them in such a way that others would find the interpretations accurate, insightful, and persuasive. Often as not, however, we have found that multiple observers arrive at different conclusions and occasionally offer discrepant interpretations. Being partial to procedures that make data public and expose interpretations to challenge or difference of opinion, we undertook to develop the procedures described in Chapters 11 and 12; the former describes a way of concurrent recording of observations of events, and the latter, a way of recording the proceedings of meetings. Both produce information accessible to tests of reliability and to use in independent or collaborative interpretational processes. We think this is a move in the right direction, but one that involves high costs in data getting and some risk as well of losing the coherence and insights that can be produced by a single observer who is selective in attention and who forms an interpretive schema as the events unfold.

We are left with an unfinished task and an unanswered query. In the assessment of organizations and of organizational change, should the task of description be methodologically prescribed as to substance and recording, or should it be left to an astute observer who is encouraged to be flexible, responsive, selective, and economical in sifting out the observations worth recording and reporting? The choice of method rests partly upon whether one assumes there is only one history to be reported as accurately as possible, or whether, instead, one assumes that there are many histories—all valid, all different, and some not discernable until long after the events that are directly observed have occurred.

The approach we suggest is to arrange for some systematic, concurrent reporting of events and to complement that with the reports of one or more self-directed and unconstrained observer-interpreters. Further enriching and protective steps have been tried with some success. One can invite independent reports from on-site participants or change agents. One can undertake the exercise (analogous to that prevalent among historians and biographers) of having the same set of documents and field notes examined by interpreters of unlike and complementary theoretical persuasions.

SOME STRATEGIC ISSUES

The Michigan Organizational Assessment Program was undertaken with multiple purposes—too many, some would say. Two of these had priority as to immediacy of attention. The task of developing improved means for assessing organizations and organizational change has been advanced, and this book is the product. The application of these methods in a limited number of demonstration cases has been completed, and case reports are in print or approaching conclusion. But there also have been purposes of a broader sort that are strategic, rather than tactical, in the sense that they pertain to the long-range development of the arts of management, of improved societal functioning, and of the development of a science of organizations. We shall discuss several of these issues.

Assessing, Learning, and Changing

Approaches to the assessment of organizations and of organizational change can be narrowly focused upon academic or scientific ends or upon the provision of immediate aid to a particular organization. But there is a further purpose that, in the long run, may be the more important. That purpose is to generate information that can stimulate and guide the improvement of management practices. This involves learning of a different kind. It rests upon the pooling of the experiences of many organizations, their failures as well as their successes, and making this information available to others who may be thinking of undertaking some change in their own practices.

All too often the adoption of new policies and practices to govern organizational life has been based upon fad or fashion, or on the chance encounter with an advocate of one change or another. Organizations typically lack good information on the merits and hazards of new practices and their appropriateness to a given case. Public reports of success and failure are rarely complete, and are rarely in a context that allows thoughtful analysis, comparison, and interpretation.

Several features of the Michigan assessment program were emphasized because they might serve the end of societal learning.

1. *Comparative Data.* This feature is important since it is needed if judgments are to be made about the relative effectiveness of different approaches to organization design and management.

2. *Broad Measurement Net.* Different adopters, evaluators, and constituents look for different kinds of information. The assessment program includes a wide range of data. The hope is that with a broadly applied measurement package, most individuals can find the data they need to reach or to test their own conclusions about the likely effectiveness of any approach.

3. *Outcome and Process Data.* Outcome data, particularly financial outcome data, are very important in the minds of most adopters and as a result they are stressed, but they are not enough. Successful transfer of a change strategy from one site to another requires knowledge about how it was installed and what it took to make it work. Hence, the program includes process observations designed to provide such data.

Although these features of the program are intended to aid the pooling and public use of the results of change-program assessments, it remains to be seen whether that will occur and whether a significant impact will follow. Much depends upon the extent to which common assessment practices are adopted widely, upon the acceptance of norms of full reporting, and upon the accumulation of data across a diverse number of assessment sites and change programs. The latter factor is particularly important, for without such comparative data and confirmation of results in different circumstances, the interpretations drawn about the efficacy of interventions and change processes may be idiosyncratic. Examples and their lessons can be valuable, but the greater need is for information about the effectiveness of particular approaches to change as they are applied in a broad range of organizational settings.

Cross-Site Comparisons

One strategic feature of our approach to this work needs further comment—namely the use of cross-site comparative analyses. Comparisons of two kinds were planned with quite different functions. First, it was intended that an effort would be made to use the experimental control principle as an aid in detecting valid changes in the target site and as an aid in tracing causal factors. This feature of experimental design requires a comparison organization as alike as possible to the focal organization, but one that is insulated from change interventions. The control organization, ideally, would display only those changes that arise from background or environmental factors shared with the focal organization and none of the changes attributable to the purposeful intervention program. Protection would be provided against false attribution of program effects. The second kind of comparison involves organizations that are purposefully different from one another—to allow detection of change-program features that seem to "work" across a variety of situations and to guard against overinterpretation of instances of unique and nonreplicable program successes.

However, our experience has confirmed there are severe limits to these aspirations. In many sites, because of the characteristics of the organization and change program, assessors' preferences, and clients' interests, measurements were tailored more to local circumstances and less to our comparative aims. Still, a core of potentially comparable questionnaire, record, and observational data was gathered at most sites. In 4 out of approximately 12 attempts, we have been able to make effective use of the principle of interorganizational comparison in the quasi-experimental design for assessing change. In three of these instances, the "controls" provided information of some significance for the interpretation of change processes or results, even though the controls were part of the same parent organization. In some promising instances, the comparison units proved to be contaminated by exposure to the change program or were easily shown to be noncomparable in ways that preclude confident comparison. Thus, while the principle remains sound, the practice is dubious, except in those unusual instances in which comparable organizations exist, provide access for assessment, and can be assessed at moderate cost. A modified form of the application of the principle proved possible in two sites—both relatively large—in which a change program "took" in some subunits but left others relatively untouched by the intervention.

The second form of comparison has also been, so far, of limited success, although, we think it is of great promise. Our host organizations have had a most satisfactory diversity as to size, technology, member composition, and other features, but it is questionable whether any two have been exposed to "the same" intervention treatment. Eight of these organizations have in common certain program start-up features (e.g., formation of a joint labor–management steering committee and an initial charter for the committee's functioning). A comparison of these cases is in preparation to examine similarities in activities, processes, and outcomes, and to examine the reasons for their divergence. The accumulation of a sufficient number of comparable cases may take some time, and it will surely rest upon the adoption of comparable intervention strategies and assessment methods in many otherwise independent enterprises.

Summary Outcomes

This book is largely silent on the issue of combining outcomes from different domains in order to reach an overall conclusion about the effectiveness of a change effort. This is by design. The decision was made early on simply to report how the organization had changed on a wide array of outcome measures. No common metric was developed so that measures could be combined, nor was a weighting system developed that argued that gains in some measures are more important than gains in others. The rationale for not doing this is simple and to us persuasive. It is that different constituents value outcomes differently, and thus it is best to let interested parties reach their own overall conclusions. There also are practical problems in trying to translate diverse outcomes to a common metric. Turnover, job satisfaction, and product quality, for example, are not easily placed on a common scale as Chapter 16 suggests. This leads us to the position that, at this point, it is best not to try to develop a single overall measure of the effectiveness of an organizational change program. This conclusion certainly will not satisfy all, nor will it put this issue to rest. The resolution is likely to come about as constituents learn to employ a more richly complex array of considerations when forming an outcome evaluation for a particular purpose. There is a parallel in the relatively simple domain of the fiscal performance of organizations. Investors, bankers, and suppliers are not satisfied with only the "bottom line"—net worth or net profit—they want also the data on rates of change in growth, capital investment, market share, reserves, and other outcome variables. No single indicator is sufficient.

Monitoring and Directing Change Programs

Most of the work described in this book has been conducted in circumstances designed to separate observation and measurement from the design and conduct of change programs. The reasons for this are described in Chapters 1 and 2. We are, nevertheless, left with the strategic issue of linking assessment activity to concurrent program management and adaptive response to change processes and situational changes as they occur. To serve this function well, the assessment methods must have certain properties in greater degree—properties that for our short-run purposes we have tried to minimize. For optimum use in program guidance, the assessment methods described in this book need to be used selectively or adapted to insure (1) continuous or frequent measurement; (2) quick analysis and interpretation; (3) simplicity and low cost; and (4) emphasis upon the language and concepts of on-site users.

The requirements for optimizing methods development and theoretical utility are somewhat at odds with the requirements for immediate program utility. Most of the procedures described in this book lend themselves to this kind of adaptation and have been so used. Some of them, however, appear not to be adaptable. Examples of the latter are the procedures for assessing the structures of interpersonal relationships and of influence, and the procedures for cost-benefit estimation—these require a large data base and complex analytical procedures. Some other procedures are readily adaptable, as in the case of abbreviated standard interviews and short-form questionnaires, which can in fact be administered and analyzed locally by nonprofessionals for their own use after some period of orientation and experience. At some of the host organizations, the procedures for collecting and summarizing concurrent behavioral data have been made a permanent part of the ongoing organizational monitoring system.

Theory Building, Theory Testing

A subsidiary, although important, purpose of the Michigan organizational assessment program has been to provide a data base that can advance the development of theories about organizational functioning. Certain features of the program appear to serve this purpose. We draw attention particularly to the provisions for (1) a broad scope of measures, many with established statistical and conceptual properties; (2) linked data pertaining to individuals, groups, and organizational systems; (3) comparable data from multiple organizations; (4) multiple methods of measurement; (5) representation of both objective and phenomenological characteristics; and (6) longitudinal data, both measurements and observations, over periods of intended organizational change.

A further intention is important, namely, that the data should be accessible for diverse theoretical purposes to people of diverse theoretical interests. Accessibility has two aspects. First, as any researcher experienced in secondary analysis knows, data are not accessible, practically, unless they are archived in a manner that allows efficient, low-cost access and quality control. To this end we have invested considerable effort in developing a data management system that allows computer-aided selective access to whatever combinations of data a researcher may want. The second aspect of accessibility concerns the ethics of organizational research and the respect for participants' privacy and confidentiality. The data are not "public" except under conditions that protect the participants. So far, a dozen researchers of diverse theoretical orientations and in different institutions have made effective use of the archived data.

Empirical research on organizations commonly takes one of a few design strategies: (1) hypothesis testing or replication; (2) context explication in which the aim is to ascertain the conditions under which a phenomenon occurs; (3) cross-theory integration or linkage; or (4) invention of new or modified speculations and interpretations. The assessment program can produce data that support all of these methods of inquiry. Examples are as follows:

1. The data have allowed, as a by-product of the main purposes, the testing of a notion that some forms of employee reward are mutually compatible (additive or multiplicative in effect), while others are incompatible.

2. The multiple-site feature of the data allowed the examination of the effectiveness of certain properties of pay systems in a variety of organizational contexts.

3. The multiple-level feature of the data allowed the assessment of the relative impact of individual differences among managers and of organizational unit differences upon the decision to adopt a change activity.

4. The observation of a number of cases in which joint labor—management committees were formed allowed the development of an initial, grounded theory concerning the forces that promote and restrain successful initiation of such committees.

In planning the development of the assessment program, we chose pluralism as to theoretical orientation, in recognition of the phenomena under study. Organizations are complex social systems, and organizations are multilevel and multivariate. The understanding of organizations requires contributions from psychological, sociological, economic, and other disciplinary bases, and further, it requires that these different orientations be brought to bear jointly in understanding a complex process of organizational change or maintenance of equilibrium. Joyce has noted that our diversity of theoretical inclusions may—by diffusion of attention—militate against the development of truly innovative theories.[3] Others have noted that the same "defect" of our approach may press toward a theory that is eclectic, comprehensive, and fully exploitative of established but presently unconnected variables. Our expectation, therefore, is that developments in theory that derive from such data may be more integrative than revolutionary. In other respects, the flexibility of the assessment program, the autonomy given to project investigators and secondary analysts, and the longitudinal features of the data may well encourage new insights and flights of theoretical fancy. Grounding may be the key here. The more we study organizations that are experimenting with self-directed change and the more open we are to varieties of information about the events, the greater are the chances for an innovative explanatory view of the processes that are involved.

REFERENCES

1. Lawler, E. E. III, Nadler, D. A., & Camman, C. *Organizational assessment: Perspectives on the measurement of organizational behavior and the quality of work life.* New York: Wiley-Interscience, 1980.

2. Tichy, N. *Managing strategic change: Technical, political, and cultural dynamics.* New York: Wiley-Interscience, 1983.

3. Joyce, W. F. The Michigan quality of work life program: An analysis of assumptions and method. In Van de Ven, A., & Joyce, W. A. (Eds.), *Perspectives on organization design and behavior.* New York: Wiley-Interscience, 1981.

Author Index

Numbers in parentheses are reference numbers and indicate that the author's work is referred to although his name is not mentioned in the text. Numbers in *italics* show the pages on which the complete references are listed.

Subject Index